# The Anthropology of Taiwanese Society

Contributors

Emily Martin Ahern
Chung-min Chen
Lawrence W. Crissman
Hill Gates
Stevan Harrell
Lydia Kung
Harry J. Lamley
Sidney W. Mintz
Burton Pasternak
Gary Seaman
Lung-sheng Sung
Edgar Wickberg
Edwin A. Winckler
Arthur P. Wolf
Alexander Chien-chung Yin

Sponsored by the Joint Committee on Contemporary China
of the American Council of Learned Societies
and the Social Science Research Council

# The Anthropology of Taiwanese Society

Edited by

Emily Martin Ahern and Hill Gates

Stanford University Press, Stanford, California

1981

Stanford University Press
Stanford, California

Printed in the United States of America
ISBN 0-8047-1043-0
LC 79-64212

# Preface

In August 1976, thanks to the gentle prodding of Arthur Wolf, the enthusiastic guidance of Myron Cohen, and the generous support of the Joint Committee on Contemporary China of the Social Science Research Council, thirty social scientists, mostly anthropologists, met for a week at Wentworth-by-the-Sea, Portsmouth, New Hampshire, to explore the state of Taiwan anthropology and to criticize its products. Papers that had, for the most part, been previously circulated to all conference participants were presented by Emily Ahern, Göran Aijmer, Chung-min Chen, Myron Cohen, Lawrence Crissman, Donald DeGlopper, Stephan Feuchtwang, Morton Fried, Hill Gates, Katherine Gould-Martin, Stevan Harrell, Hsu Chia-ming, Lydia Kung, Harry Lamley, John McCreery, Michael Moser, Burton Pasternak, Barbara Pillsbury, Gary Seaman, Lung-sheng Sung, Wang Sung-hsing, Edgar Wickberg, Edwin Winckler, Arthur Wolf, and Alexander Chien-chung Yin.

A number of scholars who did not write papers also attended the conference in the capacity of discussants, commentators, and sources of inspiration. Professors Norma Diamond, Bernard Gallin, G. William Skinner, and T'ang Mei-chun assisted in this way, though we regretted the absence of Professor Li Yih-yuan, whose busy schedule prevented his attendance. Professor Sidney Mintz represented the nonsinic branches of anthropology, a task he performed with insight and charm. His helpful Afterword completes this volume. Susan Greenhalgh, a Columbia University graduate student, and Robert Weller, a Johns Hopkins University graduate student, took on the substantial labor of preparing a lengthy and valuable summary of the proceedings from tape recordings and notes. Dr. Patrick Maddox, then of SSRC, carried his earlier administrative role over into the conference itself, where his presence smoothed many practical problems during the week-long gathering.

Participants shared the responsibility for formal discussions of papers with the discussants, and the sometimes demanding job of chairing each session rotated within the group. Discussion of the papers and of the prepared critiques by formal discussants spilled over from the six-or-more-hour daily sessions into a nonstop seminar laced with field-workers' "war stories" and references to a mystifying menagerie of champion pigs, cans of worms, and black dogs. As anthropological argument filled up the days, various themes isolated themselves, some apparently irreconcilable positions were clarified to the point of discussability, and a number of theoretical alliances were forged.

The conference on Taiwan anthropology was a genuinely collective effort, and the effects of this approach are well demonstrated in the final versions of the papers presented here. For the work they did at Wentworth, participants deserve not thanks but mutual congratulations for a job well done. The varied contributions so enlivened that week and, we believe, the future of Taiwan anthropology, that we can only regret even more voices were not there to be heard.

We owe thanks to several people for help in preparing this volume for publication. Chung-min Chen did the calligraphy for the Character List; Wang Sung-hsing assisted in checking the Character List's accuracy; and Sergio Chavez prepared the map. Finally, we owe special thanks to Stanford University Press. J. G. Bell's encouragement and guidance were indispensable; and Norris Pope's energetic editing did much to make the collection a book, and to make the book readable.

E.M.A.
H.G.

# Contents

# Contributors

EMILY MARTIN AHERN received her Ph.D. from Cornell University in 1971. She has taught at the University of California, Irvine, and at Yale University, and is now Professor of Anthropology at the Johns Hopkins University. She is the author of *The Cult of the Dead in a Chinese Village* (1973) and *Chinese Ritual and Politics* (forthcoming).

CHUNG-MIN CHEN studied anthropology at the National Taiwan University and then at Michigan State University, where he received his Ph.D. in 1975. He has done fieldwork in Taiwan and Malaysia, his research focusing on rural Chinese society and overseas Chinese communities. He is currently Associate Professor of Anthropology at Ohio State University and an Adjunct Research Associate at the Institute of Ethnology, Academia Sinica. He is the author of *Upper Camp: A Study of a Chinese Mixed-Cropping Village in Taiwan* (1977).

LAWRENCE W. CRISSMAN is a Lecturer in the School of Modern Asian Studies at Griffith University, Australia. He was a London-Cornell Project exchange student at the London School of Economics and Political Science before undertaking field research in Taiwan in 1967–68. He received his Ph.D. from Cornell University in 1973 while teaching at the University of Illinois, Urbana-Champaign. In addition to articles on marketing systems and central-place theory derived from his dissertation, he has published on social networks, overseas Chinese, and Southeast Asian ethnicity.

HILL GATES received her Ph.D. from the University of Michigan in 1973 and is now Associate Professor of Anthropology at Central Michigan University. Working largely in urban anthropology, she has done field research in Taiwan in 1968–70, 1974–75, and 1980, where she has focused on political and social change in Taiwan's rapidly evolving economy.

STEVAN HARRELL is Assistant Professor of Anthropology at the University of Washington, where he teaches both anthropology and Chinese studies. He received his Ph.D. from Stanford University in 1974, and has carried out field research in Taiwan in 1970, 1972–73, and 1978. He is the co-editor of *Other Ways of Growing Old: Anthropological Perspectives* (1981).

LYDIA KUNG is Assistant Professor of Anthropology at Yale University, where she received her Ph.D. in 1978. She spent 1974 in Taiwan collecting data for her doctoral dissertation on factory women, and she has published on this topic. Her research continues to focus on Chinese industrial organizations.

HARRY J. LAMLEY, Professor of History at the University of Hawaii, received his Ph.D. from the University of Washington in 1964. A specialist in Chinese local history of the Ch'ing and Republican periods, he has had a strong interest in Taiwan ever since his first stay on the island in 1956–59. He has published on Taiwanese walled cities, the Taiwanese gentry, and early Japanese rule in Taiwan, as well as on violence in Southeastern China. He is currently working on Chinese communal feuding.

SIDNEY W. MINTZ was educated at Brooklyn College and at Columbia University, where he received his Ph.D. in 1951. A specialist in the Caribbean region, he has taught at Yale, Princeton, and elsewhere, and is now Professor of Anthropology at the Johns Hopkins University. He has carried out fieldwork in Puerto Rico, Jamaica, Haiti, and Iran, and his publications include *The People of Puerto Rico* (1956), written with Julian H. Steward and others, *Worker in the Cane* (1960), *Caribbean Transformations* (1974), and several edited volumes. In 1972 he was Lewis Henry Morgan Lecturer at the University of Rochester, and in 1979 Christian Gauss Lecturer at Princeton.

BURTON PASTERNAK, Associate Professor of Anthropology at Hunter College, City University of New York, received his Ph.D. from Columbia University in 1967. He has done extensive field research in Taiwan, where he has focused primarily on rural social and economic organization. He is the author of a number of articles and of *Kinship and Community in Two Chinese Villages* (1972).

GARY SEAMAN received his Ph.D. from Cornell University in 1974 and is the author of *Temple Organization in a Chinese Village* (1978). Noted for his ethnographic films on China, he has been invited to show his films and speak at a number of American universities, and his films have been shown at meetings of the Association for Asian Studies, the American Anthropological Association, and the Conference on Visual Anthropology. He is currently at Austin Community College, in Austin, Texas.

LUNG-SHENG SUNG received his Ph.D. in anthropology from Stanford University in 1975. He has taught at the City College of San Francisco and at Indiana University, where he is now an Adjunct Assistant Professor in the

Department of East Asian Languages and Cultures. His research interests are in Chinese kinship systems and inheritance.

EDGAR WICKBERG, Professor of History at the University of British Columbia, received his Ph.D. from the University of California, Berkeley, in 1961. A specialist in the late Ch'ing period, he has published articles on Chinese land tenure and on Chinese influence in the Philippines, and he is the author of *The Chinese in Philippine Life, 1850–1898* (1965). His research interests currently focus on Chinese land tenure.

EDWIN A. WINCKLER holds a Ph.D. in political science from Harvard University and teaches sociology at Columbia University. He studied political anthropology at the London School of Economics and Political Science under Maurice Freedman and at Cornell University under G. William Skinner. During the 1970's, he spent three years in Taiwan doing fieldwork. In addition to continuing research on the PRC, he is completing two books about Taiwan, one on dependent modernization and authoritarian participation, the other on dependent urban development.

ARTHUR P. WOLF, Associate Professor of Anthropology at Stanford University, received his Ph.D. from Cornell University in 1964. He is known for his work on incest and on Chinese religion, and more recently for his book *Marriage and Adoption in China, 1845–1945* (1980), written with Chieh-shan Huang. He spent the academic year 1980–81 in China doing a follow-up study of the classic demographic surveys of John Lossing Buck.

ALEXANDER CHIEN-CHUNG YIN, a native of Shensi, is Chairman of the Department of Archaeology and Anthropology at the National Taiwan University. He received his training in anthropology first at the National Taiwan University, where he was awarded an M.A. in 1969, and then at the University of Hawaii, where he was awarded a Ph.D. in 1975. His research interests range from internal migration and common interest groups to urban studies and religion. He has published a number of articles based on his extensive fieldwork in Taipei, Kaohsiung, and Peng-hu.

# The Anthropology of Taiwanese Society

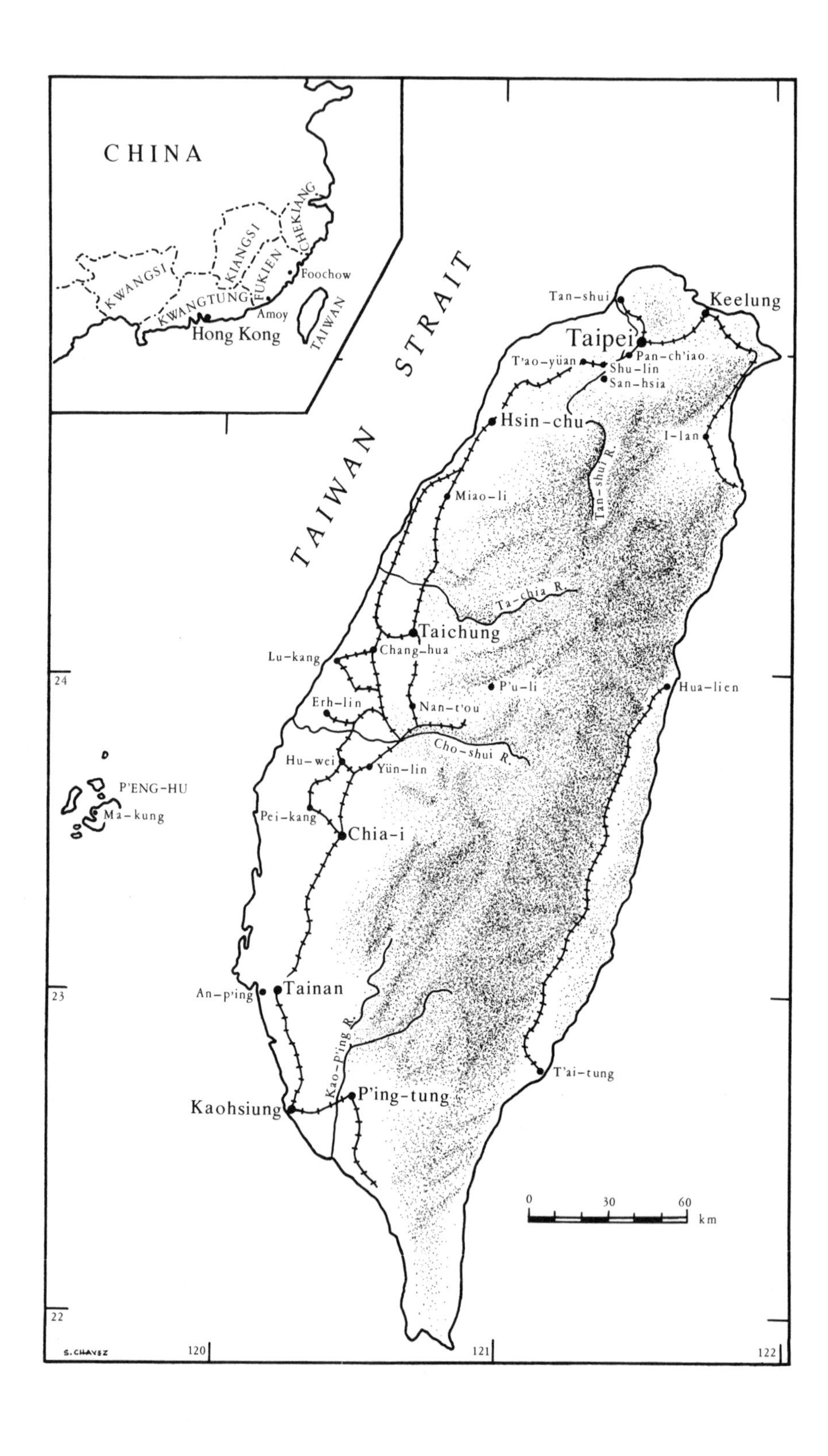

CHINA
KWANGSI
KIANGSI
CHEKIANG
FUKIEN
KWANGTUNG
Foochow
Amoy
Hong Kong
TAIWAN
TAIWAN STRAIT
Tan-shui
Keelung
Taipei
Pan-ch'iao
T'ao-yüan
Shu-lin
San-hsia
Hsin-chu
I-lan
Tan-shui R.
Miao-li
Ta-chia R.
Taichung
Chang-hua
Lu-kang
P'u-li
Hua-lien
Erh-lin
Nan-t'ou
Cho-shui R.
Hu-wei
Yün-lin
P'ENG-HU
Ma-kung
Pei-kang
Chia-i
An-p'ing
Tainan
Kao-p'ing R.
T'ai-tung
Kaohsiung
P'ing-tung
0
30
60
km
24
23
22
120
121
122
S. CHAVEZ

# Introduction

Hill Gates
Emily Martin Ahern

Anthropology emerged in Taiwan in the 1950's, a surprisingly vigorous transplant whose European, American, and Chinese rootstocks quickly crowded out the earlier luxuriant Japanese ethnography. Particularly since the publication of Bernard Gallin's *Hsin Hsing, Taiwan: A Chinese Village in Change* (1966), Taiwan has been the site and subject of an extraordinary amount of research. Initial interest was due, no doubt, to the island's peculiarity as the only part of China accessible to Western social scientists. But having come to find China, anthropologists stayed to study Taiwan. By the early 1970's, a torrent of monographs and papers produced in the course of this research began to demand interpretation, analysis, and assessment.

Participants in the Conference on Anthropology in Taiwan, held in Wentworth-by-the-Sea, Portsmouth, New Hampshire, in August 1976, were originally asked to direct their efforts toward three goals: to make progress in formulating an integrated model of Taiwan's social organization useful to non-Taiwan and non-China anthropologists as well as to Taiwan specialists; to expose weaknesses and gaps in recent Taiwan anthropology and so guide future research in the most fruitful directions; and to establish research priorities, taking into account the fact that Taiwan's unique traditions and experience of industrialization may not always remain open to non-Chinese investigators.

The three papers that together sketch the framework of Taiwan's society and thereby bring us closer to reaching the first conference goal are Edwin Winckler's "National, Regional, and Local Politics," Lawrence Crissman's "The Structure of Local and Regional Systems," and Hill Gates's "Ethnicity and Social Class." Readers interested in Taiwan's politics and economics, in dependency theory, or in the anthropology of complex societies might do well to begin with these papers. Winckler's review of political studies in Taiwan emphasizes the importance of events at the national level within a society characterized by a very high degree of political centralization and power, of whose workings we—and perhaps most participants in the system—are largely ignorant. Although people involved in provincial and regional politics are concerned about the local allocation of resources, they are more concerned about gaining access to the central sources of power and funds through upward mobility.

Crissman's examination of the politics of local systems fits neatly into this setting. Crissman shows how the "moral community" based on shared norms is connected to the administrative divisions of the Chang-hua countryside through the efforts of local factions to elect officials. These factions mobilize around local personalities and issues or around the possibility of tapping the central sources of power more directly. Crissman contends that a variety of organizational patterns affect political interaction. Indeed, marketing systems, kinship ties (often shaped by marketing systems), and various voluntary associations all support the local political factions that operate in the political world Winckler describes. Finally, Crissman compares contemporary political behavior with patterns of gentry control in prerevolutionary mainland China, concluding that factional organization may be more decisive in shaping rural social organization than the economic and the ecological factors commonly associated with central-place theory.

Hill Gates's study of social class and ethnicity complements these descriptions of the political continuum by linking social stratification and Chinese subcultural "ethnicity" with national political and economic patterns and with Taiwan's international position. Showing how present class relations are a legacy of Japanese colonialism, the early refugee monopoly of power, and the impact of foreign investment, Gates explores some social consequences of the tension between political organization and economic expansion in Taipei.

In their broad approaches, Winckler's, Crissman's, and Gates's papers supply the beginnings of an integrated model of Taiwan's social organization and make clear how many gaps must be filled to complete such a model. In general, other papers in this collection are more narrowly focused. Yet the ease with which many of these fit into the wider framework is an indication—we trust—of both the validity of the framework and the quality of the ethnography. Emily Ahern's study linking village rituals to national politics and Chung-min Chen's analysis of monopoly agribusiness influences on village politics are especially striking examples.

The papers in this book, like the conference discussions, are grouped under six headings: political organization, local organization, economic organization, ethnicity, the family, and religion. One paper in each section (with the exception of the section on religion) aims at summary and synthesis, and the one or two others in the same section offer more detailed studies of particular problems. After briefly reviewing the remaining papers, we shall return to an overview of the issues that sparked the energetic conference sessions and to the contribution that we hope this book will make to Taiwan anthropology.

In the first section, on political organization, Winckler's initial paper is followed by Chung-min Chen's "Government Enterprise and Village Politics." This paper examines the state sugar monopoly's political significance in a village in the southern part of the Chia-nan Plain. Chen's discovery that elected local officials are often commissioners for the Taiwan Sugar Corporation illustrates how extensive a major corporation's influence in the countryside can be. The fact that rural sugar growers own and operate their own farms tends to obscure the nature of the sugar economy—a highly centralized economy that is controlled through price setting, fertilizer supply, production loans, and irrigation procedures.

Edwin Winckler next responds to his own earlier plea for more macro-level studies with a second paper, "Roles Linking State and Society," a case study of regional elites in northern Taiwan. Winckler's discussion of the interaction of "managers, contenders, and publics" in electoral and party contests provides important insights into the complexities engendered by an authoritarian regime that espouses democratic methods of selecting leaders. This paper also contributes to our understanding of grass roots politics by showing how effectively middle-level participants filter power out of the highly centralized system, leaving little independent authority for those below them in the political hierarchy.

In the section on local organization, Stevan Harrell's "Social Organization in Hai-shan" adopts a materialist approach to explain variations in the pattern of village integration and lineage structure. Harrell compares three nearby communities that differ markedly in their physical arrangement and in their social organization. He attributes the differences in social organization to differences in the villages' environments and to differences in the outside social pressure that they had to contend with—matters that produced local variation over the relatively short period of a century.

Burton Pasternak's "Economics and Ecology" provides an extensive survey and critique of the literature relevant to these two subjects. Pasternak shows that important contributions have been made by Taiwan anthropologists in the areas of frontier social and economic organization, central-place theory, and family economy. Pasternak's central concern with finding explanations of intracultural variation leads him to examine Taiwan in historical terms and to compare the island with pre- and post-1949 mainland China. Pasternak also makes a number of pointed suggestions for future research and reminds us how extensively anthropologists of Taiwan have relied on explanations that are ultimately ecological or economic in nature.

Lydia Kung's "Perceptions of Work among Factory Women" describes how factory women experience work and how their experiences change their views of work and, ultimately, of themselves. Kung's premise that the work experience itself is worthy of study is a fresh one for Taiwan; as a result, her research begins to document the social perceptions and self-perceptions from which class consciousness among Taiwan's women factory workers develops. The conclusion that the work experience is as important as income in shaping women's attitudes does not come as a surprise in view of how small factory women's income is and how little they retain after sending home remittances for a parent's comfort or a brother's education.

Edgar Wickberg, addressing himself to "Continuities in Land Tenure, 1900–1940," supplies valuable insights about the stability of land tenure throughout the Ch'ing, Japanese, and early Kuomintang periods. Wickberg's research on Ch'ing land tenure shows how this system was able to absorb the effects of Japanese colonialism, including an early Green Revolution, without major institutional change. A case study based on data from both land records and household registers (P'eng-fu village in the period 1900–1905) reveals a farming community in which 74 percent of the land was owned by absentee landlords and investors, 6 percent by temples and surname corporations, and only 1 percent by the public. This was clearly an economic environment in which capitalist, externally controlled agriculture was the norm. Wickberg's essay strongly supports the view that the special characteristics of Taiwan's economy have deep roots in the past.

In the section on ethnicity, Harry Lamley examines "Subethnic Rivalry in the Ch'ing Period," linking ethnic relations to local ecology, to the effectiveness of Ch'ing government, and to a continued flow of people and prejudices from Fukien and Kwangtung. Economic changes also affected Chang-chou, Ch'üan-chou, and Hakka solidarity: the eight decades following 1782 were outstanding for both economic development and an intense reassertion of ethnic hostility (which took the form of massive feuds as well as sharp economic and scholarly competition).

In "Voluntary Associations and Rural-Urban Migration," a paper that spans the important transition from Japanese to Kuomintang rule, Alexander Chien-chung Yin emphasizes the adaptive functions of voluntary associations set up by P'eng-hu migrants in Kaohsiung. From 1908, migrants from the P'eng-hu islands (the Pescadores) came to Kaohsiung in large numbers in response to the demand for construction laborers at the Kaohsiung harbor. Yin documents the development of several of the powerful voluntary associations that helped these migrants make a significant place for themselves in Kaohsiung society and politics. Though Yin does not focus on this point, his work also provides a rare case study of contemporary ethnic group formation.

Arthur Wolf synthesizes two decades of kinship studies in "Domestic Organization." Wolf begins by reviewing the major landmarks in the field (though he modestly ignores his own important contributions), then discusses the common characteristics of this work. Topics touched upon include property rights (especially important because of the frequency of land transactions), the relationship between property rights and the size of the domestic labor force, social class and domestic organization, regional differences (which Wolf suggests were more profound than class differences before 1935), and the underlying uniformity of Chinese domestic institutions. Wolf also presents new data and conclusions about his own specialty, Taiwanese forms of marriage.

Lung-sheng Sung takes up a topic of central concern in kinship studies in "Property and Family Division." Sung contends that many of our difficulties in understanding Chinese inheritance patterns and family form result from our failure to understand that very different rules govern the distribution of inherited and acquired property. Inherited property belongs to the descent line and is distributed equally among living line members (sons). Acquired property, by contrast, belongs to the family and is distributed among all family members—either on a per capita basis or according to a formula that recognizes individual effort. Sung concludes that wealth and poverty per se are less significant in determining the form of the Chinese family than the conditions under which family property is obtained and worked.

The final papers in this volume deal with Taiwanese religion and ritual. The Taiwan anthropologist who has not contributed to this topic is a rarity; thus, the material accumulated is substantial and as yet difficult to analyze or even summarize. We include here two papers that illustrate, without beginning to exhaust, problems currently being explored in this critical area.

In "The Sexual Politics of Karmic Retribution," Gary Seaman concentrates on the interface between popular liturgical texts and customary kinship ritual. The ceremony of "breaking the blood bowl," where a son symbolically drinks the polluting blood of his birth as an act of filial piety for his deceased mother, is intended to sever the supernatural links between mother and son and thus free both for spiritual transformation. Seaman goes beyond the native interpretation to suggest that the ritual maintains female political inferiority.

In the final paper of this collection, "The Thai Ti Kong Festival," Emily Ahern examines the pigs, people, and politics of competitive sacrifices held annually in a township in northern Taiwan. This ritual draws the attention and cooperation of large numbers of people and serves multiple social and political functions. The pigs raised specially for the sacrifice are transformed from despised animals to the highest offerings that can be made to the gods, and thereby become vivid symbols of the possibility of moral redemption and social mobility. Other aspects of the ritual reveal to participants the true nature of political power in Taiwan, emphasizing local concerns and Taiwanese identity vis-à-vis the interests of the predominantly mainlander national government.

These papers along with other conference papers and conference discussions raise a number of issues of more general interest that—put before the reader here—may serve to encourage new research in profitable directions and thereby fulfill a major conference goal. One of these issues is so pervasive that it cannot be avoided by anyone interested in Taiwan. The anthropology of Taiwan has often been strongest where it has focused on the local, the particular, the ethnographic. In the field and in the armchair, we have come to know Taiwan as perhaps no other part of China. But in what sense is Taiwan really a part of China?

Obviously, this question cannot be answered by the Shanghai Communiqué. That the authorities in both parts of a politically divided China claim an essential unity for the nation is well known and need not divert us from the quite independent question of Taiwan's cultural connection with the present-day mainland and with China's past. Anthropologists live with this question in every step of their training—learning the language, becoming acquainted with the classics, reading 1940's ethnographies of Yunnan and Shantung, developing the instinct for telling if a book with "China" in its title deals with Taiwan, Hong Kong, the PRC, or the T'ang dynasty. We learn to assume that Taiwan is a part of China, a natural offshoot, a present incarnation of a marvelously complex tradition. And so it is; but also, it is not.

As well as being a Chinese province, Taiwan is a small, rapidly changing society with the densest population in the world, a quarter of its labor force employed in industry, and unique relationships with Japan and the United States. These factors shape the social life and culture of the island's inhabitants, as do the island's Chinese heritage and its intense though peculiar relationship with the enormous mainland beyond the strait.

Taiwan anthropologists disagree profoundly on the relative significance of cultural traditions and material circumstances in influencing contemporary behavior and beliefs. In this, they mirror the vigorous debates over the role of culture and economics that, though not new to anthropology, have found strong contemporary restatement in the works of scholars such as Marvin Harris and Marshall Sahlins. Materialists, idealists, eclectics, and exponents of dialectical modes of analysis all test their theories in Taiwan. The framework that they consciously or unconsciously bring to their choice of problems, formulation of hypotheses, and selection of data powerfully affects the studies they produce.

It is true, sometimes, that the relentless empiricism of fieldwork pays off in adventure when an accumulation of carefully collected data explodes a previously cherished theory. Arthur Wolf gives us an example here of honorable retreat from an initial assumption: his most recent demographic data reveal that the proportion of major and minor marriages in a region of northern Taiwan was due not to people's preferences, family choices, or cultural ideals (as he originally assumed), but to the supply of female children available for adoption. Many if not most anthropologists' hypotheses about behavior are not formulated clearly enough, however, to allow for their falsifiability. Conclusions drawn from data in such cases are more directly influenced by the theoretical framework within which problems have been conceived, explored, and tested.

The assumptions about Taiwan's relationship to China that anthropologists bring to their work do much to shape the future of the field. The papers by Chen, Harrell, Kung, and Gates, to cite only the more obvious examples, take as their main subject the shaping of social relations by forces that are external to the actors and have no necessary connection with tradition. Others, such as those by Wolf, Sung, Seaman, and Ahern, concern behavior associated with attempts to conform to cultural principles that are linked or can easily be linked to the Chinese past.

It should not surprise us that the second perspective has been more characteristic of Taiwan anthropology than the first. Taiwan is the only province of China that has not undergone the sweeping changes of a socialist revolution: Chinese life has greater continuity with the past there, it can be argued, than anywhere else. During fifty years of rule, the Japanese did not intentionally alter Chinese customs and social relations; subsequently, the Kuomintang government actively promoted adherence to Confucian ideals of social order. Anthropologists have therefore gone to Taiwan to study what they could no longer study in other provinces. It was Taiwan's representativeness, not its special qualities, that first attracted their interest and inspired such splendid contributions to our understanding of Chinese life as Margery Wolf's *The House of Lim.*

Interest developed somewhat later in Taiwan's historical particularity and hence in what Stephan Feuchtwang described at a conference session as discovering "at what level Taiwan exists in a worldwide economic system whose highest level is the international system of commerce and investment, and whose lowest level is the smallest unit of production." (It should be noted, however, that the first English-language ethnography, Bernard Gallin's *Hsin Hsing*, was able to treat Taiwan as representative as well as particular, as have many since.) In general, anthropologists who approach Taiwan as a unique setting, as Burton Pasternak did in *Kinship and Community in Two Chinese Villages*, have been either less numerous or less outspoken. Their voices are only beginning to be heard.

It may be that a different approach—a dialectical one is an obvious possibility—will end this division by enabling researchers to integrate both viewpoints. Such a trend has been slower to emerge in the Taiwan field than in anthropology in general, where French Marxists like Maurice Godelier have presented powerful challenges to traditional theories. At present, perhaps only Stephan Feuchtwang brings a dialectical approach to the study of Taiwan. In the meantime, Taiwan anthropologists of both traditional persuasions might do well to look for more specific tests of the adequacy of their positions by formulating their hypotheses more precisely and by giving greater attention to the critical Japanese period. To those who stress cultural continuity, the Japanese period is the bridge to the past; to those who suspect that the Japanese period changed Taiwan significantly, these decades must be shown to have produced major transformations. One paper in this volume, by the historian Edgar Wickberg, suggests that there were significant continuities throughout this period in land tenure, surely among the most important factors in economic and social relations. Such issues deserve more exploration by anthropologists.

It may be that this task awaits yet another generation of scholars. Among Westerners at least, these scholars must be paragons willing to learn not only Mandarin and a local language but Japanese as well. We may predict, however, that anthropologists whose native language is Chinese will continue to produce the bulk of historical studies of Taiwan after the models furnished by Wang Sung-hsing and others.

A second major issue pervaded conference discussions and reverberates in these pages. Whereas the first issue may someday be settled, this second one may never be. We refer here to the quarrel between those who regard anthropology primarily as a nomothetic enterprise and those who value its idiographic qualities—between those who see anthropology as science and those who see it as art. We hold that though physicists may speak of "charm" and astronomers of the mind-like operation of the universe, thus uniting art and science, in the workaday world of spirit mediums and caloric intakes, a crude distinction still obtains between studying an event as a thing in itself and studying it as a specific example of a more general phenomenon from which law-like conclusions may be drawn. This dichotomy is not congruent with the earlier one, for those who focus primarily on cultural factors and those who focus primarily on economic factors are equally concerned with explanations and causality. The nomothetic tradition is strong in anthropological training, as is (even if we do not always handle it very convincingly) a fascination for the wholeness and essence of the object of study. Fieldwork inculcates a feeling that having tasted *our* pear, we prefer it to those we cannot sample. China anthropologists seem particularly prone to this gentle vice, as demonstrated by the relative weakness of this field's links with the rest of anthropology. Indeed, China might almost not exist—if one judges by the tables of contents and indexes of major textbooks and anthropological journals—though Mexican, Indian, and European peasants have shown the way to insights worthy of general notice.

In these essays the work of defining Taiwan's significance with respect to more general phenomena and hypotheses certainly goes forward: scholarly generalists, we hope, will have fewer reasons to slight the Chinese world. It may be, however, that the special "feel" for a culture—if well expressed—is what allows anthropology to transcend the bounds of discipline and enter into educated discourse, influencing the culture of our time. Like it or not, Mead's *Coming of Age in Samoa* has affected the English-speaking world far more deeply than Murdock's *Social Structure*. The intense focus on one small segment of humanity, the act of one person trying to understand and appreciate others in their complex totality, is one that many find a worthy end in itself.

If anthropology is defined not by its subject matter or methods but by the tensions created by these two dichotomies—often all present within a single practitioner—Taiwan anthropology can certainly claim to travel in the mainstream. And if the Wentworth group and these papers are representative, we can indeed expect interesting new syntheses from people who so passionately disagree with one another.

# Part One

# Political Organization

# National, Regional, and Local Politics

Edwin A. Winckler

Authoritarian political systems are the most common type in the world today, particularly in societies still struggling for political integration, economic development, and sociocultural modernization (Linz 1964, 1973, 1975). Despite this widely recognized fact, authoritarian regimes remain a relatively underconceptualized, under-researched, and underdebated subject within comparative political sociology. Examinations of the relationship between the organization of state power on the one hand, and the internal social structure and external environment of particular societies on the other, are few and preliminary. Explorations of the subnational levels of such systems are even fewer. Systematic confrontations of alternative models of their dynamics—Marxist or pluralist, institutional or cultural, national-modernization or world-system—are almost nonexistent. In the further development of this literature, Taiwan should occupy a significant and provocative place.

### *Historical Change and Political Identity*

More than most places in a world of accelerating change, Taiwan has undergone in the past century repeated political redefinition. (For telling symbolism, see Crozier 1977.) Located at the intersection of successive spheres of influence—Ming, Portuguese, Spanish, Dutch, Ch'ing, British, French, Japanese, American, Republican Chinese, Communist Chinese, and even Soviet—the island has repeatedly been buffeted by political typhoons originating far from its shores and vastly exceeding the power of the island's own inhabitants. In its Chinese imperial, Japanese colonial, and Chinese Nationalist eras, Taiwan has displayed at least three different types of authoritarian regime. Moreover, scholars have emphasized different aspects of each of these eras, creating still more varied images of authoritarianism. Despite these differences, however, one thing has remained the same: the island has remained subject to exogenous political elites with exogenous policy objectives.

In the nineteenth century, Taiwan was a frontier area on the periphery of the empire and among the last parts of China to receive Han colonization and imperial administration. Nevertheless, because of its interaction with foreign powers, Taiwan was among the first parts of China to begin administrative modernization. The appearance of foreigners off Taiwan in the 1870's first hastened the completion of Taiwan's traditional administrative system of walled capitals, then precipitated Governor Liu Ming-ch'uan's experiments with such modern innovations as railroads, the telegraph, and electric lights. Even within the parameters of late Ch'ing Taiwan—foreign threat, imperial administration, frontier society—there was significant variation as new problems arose or different factions within the imperial government tried new solutions. For example, the court—after having instructed Liu Ming-ch'uan to replace his predecessor's approach with an all-out attempt at modernization—accepted the recommendation of Liu's successor to abandon modernization and return to fiscal and cultural conservatism. Nineteenth-century Taiwan has accordingly been studied as a frontier area (Pasternak 1969; Lamley this volume); as an example of the formation of an imperial scholar-elite (Lamley 1964; Meskill 1970); as an example of late Ch'ing administrative development (Myers 1971, 1972a, 1972b; Lamley 1977); and as an example of the politics of early Chinese modernization (Chu 1964; Speidel 1968; Lamley 1969).

In 1895 Japan preempted Chinese experiments by occupying Taiwan after a brief war. Taiwan's subsequent development was largely determined by the Japanese navy, who saw the island as a potential platform for launching invasions of the Philippines and Southeast Asia. (The Japanese army, preoccupied with expansion in Korea, Manchuria, and China, showed less interest.) Accordingly, pacification, attention to logistics, the development of resources, the modernization of agriculture, and the beginnings of industrialization all followed in relentlessly logical order, under a relentlessly authoritarian administration. Again, however, Taiwan's development was not uniform. In the period between 1910 and 1930, for example, Japan de-emphasized its maritime strategy, allowing economic development to serve private more than military interests. The exposure of a few overseas Taiwanese students to higher education and liberal politics in Japan catalyzed a new nationalistic political consciousness that could not have emerged indigenously. The Japanese period has thus been studied as an example of the factional politics of military imperialism (Kerr 1974); as an example of colonial administration of economic development (Barclay 1954; Chang & Myers 1963; Ho 1971, 1978; Myers & Ching 1964; Myers 1973); and as an example of colonial domination and nationalistic response (Ching-chih Chen 1967, 1973; Edward Chen 1972; Lamley 1970–71; Kerr 1974; Tsurumi 1967, 1977).

Reversion to China in 1945 plunged Taiwan into the brutal dangers of the Chinese civil war. Between 1945 and 1949 Taiwan fell largely under the sway of the "coastal" orientation within the arriving Nationalist elite and the returning pro-Nationalist Taiwanese. Taiwan was treated as though it were Fukien, i.e., a potentially wealth-generating but relatively peripheral frontier province dangerously exposed to Japanese influence and dangerously populated by what was perceived as a dissident intelligentsia (Kerr 1965, 1974). Then in 1949 the remnants of the Nationalist elite arrived from all parts of the mainland, replacing many of the earlier carpetbaggers, both mainlander and Taiwanese. To enhance its control, the new Nationalist government made some effort to balance "returnee" Taiwanese with those who had retained stronger ties to Taiwan during the Japanese period. For much of the 1950's, many Nationalists regarded Taiwan as a wartime Szechwan, a temporary headquarters from which to recapture the heartland of China. Since the early 1960's, Taiwan has resembled early twentieth-century Shanghai, open to international investment and trade for development as a long-term political base in its own right. This liberalization of economic policy, however, coexisted with periodic crackdowns on independent journalists and opposition parties (Mancall 1964; Peng 1971; Huang 1976). Taiwan's situation in the 1970's has little precedent in history and few analogies in the contemporary world—it is embattled and dependent like Israel; divided like Korea and Germany; increasingly isolated but, like South Africa, still in economic demand. Meanwhile, nonparty Taiwanese politicians have advanced from cautious withdrawal in the 1950's to tentative participation in the 1960's, and then to active challenge of the Kuomintang in local elections in the 1970's. A key question for the 1980's is whether the basic rules of politics, essentially the same for a quarter of a century, are now being changed irreversibly by the normalization of U.S.-PRC diplomatic relations, by the succession of generations within the Nationalist elite, and by the assertion of political power by the native Taiwanese.

This complex and changing situation has been viewed from many angles, ranging from the global perspective of international relations to the village perspective of traditional anthropologists, and from the laudatory response of visiting foreigners to the bitter memories of political exiles (Peng 1972). Nevertheless, we still lack descriptive overviews of the top, middle, and to a lesser extent, bottom levels of Taiwan's political system. Such overviews would help to identify each level's participants, conflicts, institutions, resources, issues, and outcomes. They would illuminate the linkages and boundaries between the many networks and organizations at different levels of the system. They would highlight political change and continuity through the Ch'ing, Japanese, Republican, Nationalist, and post-Chiang eras in Taiwan, and through the Republican era on the mainland. Finally, they would relate politics on Taiwan to general theories of political development in authoritarian, one-party states heavily involved in the world economy.

By these admittedly high standards we do not know much about politics on Taiwan. The most penetrating introduction remains the special *China Quarterly* issue entitled *Formosa Today* (Mancall 1964); and the best recent overview is Ralph Clough's *Island China* (1978). But with few exceptions, the questions raised by the essays in the Mancall volume have not been answered by detailed studies or even by critical journalism. Fieldworkers have avoided political questions since details about politics are hard to obtain and the risks to informants are great. Also, however, scholars have lacked adequate models of authoritarian political systems and therefore do not know what information to gather. What kind of political system has existed on Taiwan over the past hundred years is itself a controversial question as a result of the complexity of Taiwan's history, the political implications of the subject, and the differing preoccupations of different scholarly disciplines.

### *External Involvements and National Institutions*

For the top level of Taiwan's political system—where the international environment, the national government, and the highest levels of the provincial government interact—we find very little systematic description or theory. The Republic of China's own *China Yearbook* provides perhaps the best formal and legal description of the distinctive five-branch organization of the central government and of the unusual institutional arrangement in which a central and a provincial government administer essentially the same territory. Although it does not delve into the workings of the political system or into the behavior of participants, the *China Yearbook* provides elementary biographic information on an unsystematic selection of political, economic, and sociocultural leaders, and gives chronologies of important political events. Publications from Taiwan seldom bring together information on people and policies to illuminate who did what and how. Excellent survey articles (Jacobs 1971; Tai 1970; Walker 1974; Wei 1973, 1974, 1976a, 1976b; Tien 1975) and annual status reports in *Asian Survey* (by Appleton, Kallgren, Gurtov, Plummer, Cheng, Jacobs, McBeath, and others) have provided periodic updates of political trends and events. Aside from the outdated Mancall volume, however, no book-length political history or institutional analysis establishes a theoretical framework for assessing Taiwan's domestic political development.

The basic nature of the political system remains undefined. If the island has been a military and political client of the United States, we know little about the international and interbureaucratic workings of the relationship (but see Montgomery 1962, 1964). If the island has been a dictatorship ruled by Chiang Kai-shek and his son Chiang Ching-kuo, we do not have political biographies of either for their Taiwanese periods (but see Durdin 1975). If the island has been a police state dominated by military interests, we lack institutional descriptions and political histories of its internal and external security agencies (but for an early sketch, see Riggs 1952). If the island has been successful in managing its economic development, we do not have a political account of the persons, agencies, and interests involved. If the island has been ruled by the Kuomintang, we know little more about the party's politics and administration than its own glossy brochures tell us (but see Tai 1970; Shieh 1970; Jacobs 1971).

Finally, we need to know the relative weights of setting, personality, security, economics, and ideology, and how these elements fit together.

To be sure, Taiwan's numerous external involvements have not escaped attention, particularly insofar as they involve the PRC and affect the United States. Books and articles have dealt with the Taiwan Strait crises of 1954 and 1958, Nationalist defense policy, U.S. military aid, and the military viability of the island (for an excellent summary and bibliography, see Clough 1978). In the 1950's and 1960's, the U.S. Seventh Fleet simultaneously protected Taiwan from the PRC and restrained it from attacking the PRC. In the 1970's, the most important guarantee of Taiwan's security has been the PRC's unwillingness to increase its vulnerability to the USSR by expending large amounts of scarce military resources against Taiwan's well-trained and well-equipped defenses.

The role of foreign aid and trade in Taiwan's economic development has also received attention (Jacoby 1966; Hsing 1970; Lin 1973). The high growth rates of the 1960's were based on exports; by the late 1970's total annual foreign trade (imports plus exports) equaled the entire Gross National Product. Furthermore, although most of the capital financing Taiwan's economic development has been formed internally (Fei & Ranis 1975), U.S. aid, overseas Chinese investment, and international loans provided catalyzing supplements at critical moments. Taiwan's complex economic relationships with the United States, Japan, Europe, the Middle East, and many developing countries have been and still are constant subjects of discussion in Far Eastern business periodicals.

Nevertheless, in light of the current interest of social scientists in "world-system" models that relate a nation's development to its international environment, a striking deficiency in the literature about the top of Taiwan's political system is its failure to explore the internal implications of the island's external connections. Journalistic reporting of international events and fieldwork on local development have remained separate, and neither journalists nor social scientists have assessed theoretically the links between the international, national, and local levels of Taiwanese politics (though see, for example, Tozzer 1970; Uhalley 1967). Exceptions among anthropological writings include Barbara Pillsbury's study of the two factions within the Moslem community in Taipei (1978) and the papers by Gates and Kung in this volume. Pillsbury demonstrates a link between Taiwan's relations with Arab states, the role of Moslems in national Chinese politics, and the local issues within the Moslem community itself. Although Taiwan's Moslems might seem an exceptional case, the extensive involvement of overseas Chinese with Taiwan must generate similar complications, not to mention the involvements of Japanese, Americans, and other foreign nationals.

Another fruitful but underexplored topic is the relationship of the post-1949 Republic of China with political developments in the preceding Republican period on the mainland. There are distinct continuities from the earlier period at the national, provincial, and local levels. Indeed, the Republic of China's national institutions were forged on the mainland in the course of a struggle for sovereignty against warlords, communists, and Japanese. Robert Bedeski (1975) has argued that the parameters of the modern party-state created in Nanking around 1927—and later accepted by the Chinese communists for their regime—included in theory a multiclass coalition party, a professional but highly politicized army, and a party dictatorship that would dismantle itself when full sovereignty was achieved and the masses were qualified to take over democratic government. Thus, the evolution of political institutions in postwar Taiwan must be viewed against their Republican origins and initial aims as well as against contemporary demands and expectations. In particular, the Kuomintang's own position is paradoxical. On the one hand, it claims to be the ultimate source of political legitimacy and governmental performance in the Republic of China. On the other hand, its original program calls for its disestablishment under conditions very like those now prevailing on Taiwan. In any case, contemporary Taiwan requires something closer to the social welfare organization that the party is rapidly becoming than the vanguard of national mobilization that the party was originally conceived to be. In the range of possible authoritarian regimes, the Republic of China may well be in transition from one that combines party and military institutions to one that relies primarily on government and security institutions with little role for the party at all.

Historical continuity with Republican China is also important at the provincial and local levels. One can hardly understand the treatment of Taiwan between 1945 and 1949 apart from the difficulty that the central government had experienced in bringing other provinces under its control, and the role as a frontier resource area that leaders assumed the island would play in the nation as a whole. In the late

1940's adventurous young men accepted assignments in Taiwan's provincial government the way a bright young New Yorker might for career reasons have accepted a company assignment to Oregon in the same period, little thinking that his decision would lead to permanent settlement. Many such young men were first-rate technocrats who came to the attention of national leaders in the early 1950's when the provincial government had a large role in administering the island because the central government was still disorganized after its hasty retreat from the mainland. The Nationalist regime's move to Taiwan and the dividing of responsibilities between the provincial and central governments deserve more study than they have received. Finally, experiments with local management of development projects and with local self-government were not devised to pacify the Taiwanese: they had been an intrinsic if intractable part of the Kuomintang's program on the mainland as well. Consequently, there could be no better preface to local politics in Taiwan than Philip Kuhn's sensitive evocation of the dilemmas of "control, autonomy, and mobilization" faced by the Kuomintang in dealing with local, "bad" gentry on the mainland before 1949 (Kuhn 1975, 1977).

Let us turn to central political institutions and groupings after 1949. In the 1964 Mancall volume John Israel noted the disintegration of all the Nationalist cliques of the 1940's except for the Whampoa military cadets, who still remained personally loyal to Chiang Kai-shek. Israel identified the two major groupings of the early 1960's, one centering around the development-oriented Vice-President, Ch'en Ch'eng, and the other around the then security administrator, Chiang Ching-kuo. In 1971 Bruce Jacobs summarized central political institutions and staffing at the end of the 1960's. He analyzed the continuing dominance of mainlanders, particularly those from the lower Yangtze, despite the gradual infusion of younger and better-educated leaders, including some Taiwanese. He described Chiang Ching-kuo's then new role in economic affairs, noting the continuing debate between younger technical-economic experts and older military-security advisers. He predicted that "if the experts succeed in converting Chiang to their way of thinking, a government with a large number of economic and scientific experts led by Chiang and Yen would probably control the military and begin some democratization" (Jacobs 1971: 154).

One can argue that this is approximately what has since occurred, if one interprets democratization as "Taiwanization" and allows for the possibility that political rather than economic advisers advocated the policy. However, one can also argue that the implicit association of economic development with democratization, the interpretation of democratization as "Taiwanization," and the opposition between older military advisers and younger technocrats are all at least partially misleading. In Taiwan, as in other rapidly developing authoritarian states, economic expansion and political control can be mutually reinforcing rather than functionally incompatible (O'Donnell 1973). The substitution of Taiwanese for mainlander cadres in a Leninist party and authoritarian government—a substitution that has not gone very far or very fast in any case—is not necessarily equivalent to the concession of power to popular sovereignty. Nor need it lead to such a concession. There are young and progressive military officers as well as old and reactionary ones; and the role of the military may become more decisive, regardless of economic development. In any case, the principal obstacles to both "Taiwanization" and democratization have been those mainlanders in the party headquarters who have a vested interest in the status quo and genuinely fear letting popular sovereignty outgrow party control (Winckler this volume).

In view of Taiwan's exceptional economic success, our lack of detailed analyses of the politics of development is also striking. The few accounts we have of national politics abstract the political system almost completely from its impressive accomplishment. There are no studies of the ROC's ministries of economics, finance, or trade, or of its central planning agency, budget office, or central bank (though see Caldwell 1976). Nor are there studies of how these institutions interact in the policy-making process, let alone attempts to relate variation in that process to variation in the political stakes or economic problems involved. Neil Jacoby's informative evaluation of the economic effectiveness of American aid remains innocent of Chinese politics (Jacoby 1966).

## *Provincial Government and Regional Elites*

For the middle level of Taiwan's political system—the territorial, functional, and representative agencies of the provincial government and their extensions at the county and municipal level—we are only slightly better off. Let us consider territorial agencies first. To date no one has studied the routine administration of a county or municipality, the electoral politics of selecting local executives, or the impact of electoral politics on local administration. Until the 1980's the basic fact about such governments has been that they command few allocable revenues and have few productive employees. Local governments share the taxes they collect with the provincial and central governments, leaving funds sufficient to cover only the salaries of local administrators and the costs of Taiwan's generous nine-year education system. Since each of these expenditures occupies nearly half of the local government's budget, little money is left over for discretionary local projects. Such projects would in any case be designed and supervised by the technical, accounting, personnel, administrative, and security agencies of the provincial government. Local representatives of these "systems" report to their provincial superiors rather than to local executives; often little motivated to serve the locality, they look forward instead to assignments at the provincial level. Local executives have little control over the appointment of these nominal subordinates and little power to coordinate their activities. Accordingly, one theme of local politics is the attempt of both party and nonparty local executives to make local government more responsive to the needs of the locality. A second theme is the attempt of local executives to achieve local development by mobilizing extrabudgetary sources of revenue—i.e., special projects financed by the provincial or central government, by private investment, or even by philanthropic contributions. More often than not, however, a third theme emerges—the attempt of local executives to repay campaign debts or enrich themselves by allocating public resources to private interests. Local projects can be used to enhance selected property values and to grant contracts to favored firms. Studies of field administration in Taiwan might thus concern the relationship of locality to province, the process of coordinating local agencies, or the relationship of local government to its environment.

Analysis of the functional agencies of the central and provincial government provides a second approach to the middle levels of government and to regional politics and development. In general, the more closely such agencies are related to the military and economic needs of the island, the greater their budgets and proficiency. Some—such as the provincial water conservancy, land administration, and highway bureaus—have had to rely on other agencies, consultants, and contractors to carry out large-scale projects. Others—such as the central electric power and provincial public works and railway agencies—have done remarkably good jobs on their own. My own dissertation (1974) deals with the interaction of territorial, functional, and representative agencies at the central, provincial, and local levels in the course of several regional development projects. It includes descriptions of the six functional agencies just listed; though the physical facilities they manage were begun by the Japanese, their organization and personnel networks were derived largely from Republican China. The dissertation examines the implementation of regional flood control, new town, and transportation projects. In general, the greater the political and technical uncertainty surrounding such projects, the longer and more tortuous their implementation, and the less predictable the nature of their contribution. The involvement of many levels of participants in these projects—ranging from international agencies through all levels of government to regional elites and, finally, to ordinary local citizens—underlines the inadvisability of treating one level while ignoring the others.

Representative institutions and electoral processes provide a third object of study at the middle levels. Arthur Lerman has written a dissertation (1972) about the provincial assembly—a weak branch of a weak level of government, but a branch that nevertheless allows him to see how some influential members of Taiwan's regional elites pursue their interests above the local level. Lerman asks whether coalitions of regional leaders within the assembly are based on prior personal, local, and business affiliations, and concludes that in general they are not. Lerman also provides a careful statement of the cultural discrepancies between the national elite's ideals of local democracy and the actual functioning of local democracy (1977). The national elite would like democracy to liberate the energies of the people, channel them into public affairs, and discipline them into the orderly pursuit of a unified general will. These ideals include traditional Chinese political values rephrased in the language of Western democracy. However, as a result of experience with Leninist party organization and Western science during the Republican period, the national elite also believes that the masses should defer to its broader political vision (the cadre ethic) and that democracy should yield results convergent with technocratic analysis (the expert ethic). In contrast to these ideals, the exigencies of recruiting votes in competitive elections have resulted in unprincipled, particularistic, divisive, and corrupt behavior on the part of both elite political managers and local politicians.

Faced with such contradictions, elites in many developing countries have suppressed local democracy. The response of the national elite on Taiwan has been to restrict the scope and frequency of elections along with the duration and issues of campaign activities. Democracy must remain restricted in this way until local behavior meets the elite's ideals. Local politicians, less repelled by such imperfections, rationalize them as serving the needs felt by their constituents. Lerman argues that the national elite has refrained from abolishing local elections altogether primarily to maintain the appearance of popular support. With the loss of the mainland and the withdrawal of international recognition, the diplomatic support of the United States for "Free China" was among the few remaining reasons why the national elite remained in power.

Although many commentators in the 1950's and 1960's understood that the Nationalist government instituted local elections partly to please the United States, Lerman provides an account distinctive for its sensitivity to the dilemmas posed for the Nationalist elite by its particular formulation of democratic political development. In addition, Lerman provides a helpful synthesis of the political observations of fieldworkers (such as Gallin and Crissman) and the theoretical writings of comparative political scientists (such as Weiner and Scott). However, Lerman's formulation loses in political realism what it gains in theoretical elegance. It needs to be stated more baldly that if local politics in Taiwan is divisive and corrupt, this is largely the result of the manipulated form of participation that the Nationalist elite has institutionalized. There has been no lack of Taiwanese politicians eager to raise fundamental issues of principle, not only during election campaigns but also in legislative debates and through political journalism. Particularly since the rise in prosperity and education during the 1960's, the real impediments to local democracy in Taiwan have had less to do with cultural contradictions than with political objectives and political power. Simply put, the Nationalist elite maintains the intention and capacity to retain power, and the United States has remained willing and able to assist it in doing so.

Understanding the relationships among central, provincial, and local politics requires, in addition to studies of government, detailed, longitudinal studies of regional elites. A dozen or so great Taiwanese families survived the transition from the Ch'ing to the Japanese periods, adapting to the agricultural and professional opportunities open to them under Japanese rule (Lamley 1964). Surprisingly, the extent to which these and other less prominent but wealthy families survived the transition from the Japanese to the Nationalist period has not been the subject of much research (though see Mendel 1970, 1974). One wonders how these families have adapted to the commercial and industrial opportunities open to them under Nationalist rule and to what extent they continue to pursue—however obliquely—distinctly Taiwanese social and political aspirations.

From interviews one glimpses a struggle between the indigenous, nonparty Taiwanese who had collaborated with the Japanese, and the returnee, Kuomintang-affiliated Taiwanese who had become committed to Nationalist policies. An early example of this struggle was the defeat of the Taichung landlord Lin Hsien-t'ang by returnee financier Huang Shao-ch'ing for the speakership of the provincial assembly in 1946. After land reform, the larger landlords either withdrew from politics or joined the returnee economic establishment. A new struggle arose in the early 1950's. On the one hand were the largely party-affiliated Taiwanese "ins" who, in competition with mainlander businessmen, dominated the economy. On the other hand were the formerly anti-Japanese local "outs" who were confined to smaller-scale enterprises and who attempted to assemble an antiestablishment political base from smaller businessmen, local nonparty politicians, and the masses. The defeat of the petite bourgeoisie by the grande bourgeoisie is perhaps symbolized by the purge of Lin Ting-li, the deputy speaker of the provincial assembly in 1956, by the repression of a movement to form an opposition party around 1960, and by the containment and eventual co-optation of the independent politician Kao Yü-shu between the mid-1950's and the mid-1960's. When export-oriented economic development was beginning, the central government's control of foreign exchange and other external transactions gave it increased leverage over domestic businessmen. In the 1970's, however, both the international reputation and the domestic legitimacy of the central government have come to rely so heavily on economic performance that the central government has become dependent on Taiwanese and mainlander businessmen as a class. Moreover, the new wealth generated by economic development and the new political sophistication generated by contact with other countries have begun to flood the political marketplace. The issues and price of politics have risen to the point that they can no longer easily be controlled by the Kuomintang. Despite all the socioeconomic change that has occurred, however, there is still significant political continuity between the older generation of indigenous anti-Japanese, local Taiwanese leaders who never joined the Kuomintang, and the younger generation of independent, nonparty politicians now challenging the Kuomintang's near monopoly of local political leadership. Yet exactly how the changing political and economic base of regional elites may have generated successive political cleavages largely remains to be explored.

Some of these issues were raised in a prescient and informative article by Allan Cole entitled "The Political Roles of Taiwanese Enterprisers" (1967). Cole's basic finding was that, at least in the 1960's, most Taiwanese businessmen cared little about politics and participated only to the extent necessary to protect or promote their business interests. The larger, the more capital-intensive, and the more export-oriented the business, the greater the necessity of government contacts to minimize competition and to maximize allocations of foreign exchange and other scarce resources. Cole might have added that in many cases political involvement was not only the result of business interests but also the foundation for economic success. Cole reported that big businessmen whose large holdings and complex operations were subject to government intervention were extremely reluctant to finance antiparty politicians—though a few may have done so secretly through affiliated small-scale companies. Though businessmen were often influential in selecting candidates for local offices, relatively few of them became candidates for office themselves. By the end of the 1970's, however, Cole's description was becoming increasingly outdated: younger businessmen have become more able and willing not only to finance other independent candidates, but also to run for local office themselves.

## *Local Government and Community Politics*

For the bottom level of Taiwan's political system—politics in boroughs or townships and their component villages, or in urban districts and their component wards—we have many short descriptions and some short analyses, usually parts of field studies devoted principally to other topics (but see Gallin 1963, 1964; Ku 1966; Walker

1968; Kuo-chang Wang 1968; Long 1968, 1969; Yang 1970; Cohen 1976; Chen this volume). Probably the best, brief, overall sketch of local politics is Larry Crissman's paper "Each for His Own: Taiwanese Political Response to KMT Local Administration" (1969), which regrettably remains unpublished. Crissman stresses the opportunistic rather than the social and structural basis of political initiatives and alignments, particularly in politics above the village and township level. He indicates the overriding role of the Kuomintang's electoral strategies and nominating procedures in local politics, and raises the issue of possible links between local political factions and political conflicts at higher levels.

Despite Taiwan's frequent elections, we do not have many systematic accounts of the candidates, campaigns, publics, and voting standards that these elections involve. A recent exception is Bruce Jacobs's dissertation (1975) on a rural township in Chia-i county. In this township voters are allowed considerable freedom in selecting local officials, largely because those officials have little political or economic power. Local politics is accordingly a competition between two local factions, each organized through personal relationships. Relationships based on locality are the most important ones among leaders and between leaders and voters. Agnatic kinship remains the most important relationship within villages, though affinal kinship provides the most important relationship across villages. The experience of having worked together in a formal organization is particularly crucial to the establishment of ties among leaders. Finally, the informal line dividing the township into two rival political territories coincides with current boundaries between rival marketing and marriage network areas, and with historical boundaries between police, tax, and school districts during the Japanese period.

In contrast to Jacobs's portrait of a do-nothing township politics preoccupied with allocating prestige is Benedict Stavis's sketch (1974) of the active contribution of township government to agricultural development (see also Wang & Apthorpe 1974; Chen this volume). Describing Pu-yen, the Chang-hua township containing the village studied by Bernard Gallin, Stavis concludes that although closely supervised by higher levels of government, the township and quasi-governmental bodies such as the farmers' association and irrigation association do provide the national government with a crucial link to rural villages, both for implementing policies and for collecting information. As a result, the township government can influence the distribution of roads, schools, and community development programs among villages and affect the fortunes of the several dozen families having jobs, contracts, or contacts with the township office. Farmers have little influence over the rural policies of the central government; but, since government policy "has been to assure political stability and modest growth in rural incomes, there has been no fundamental conflict" (1974: 122).

For the lowest level of the state-sponsored political system, we have Gallin's detailed description of how electoral participation penetrated to ordinary citizens, altering the relationship between kinship and politics (1968). In the 1950's, the division of village offices and the support of township candidates were matters negotiated by the leaders of the two major lineages within the village. Elections merely ratified the consensual selection by the village elite of leaders with the traditional credentials of relatively high statesmanship, education, and prestige. Gradually, however, new contestants for township office began to use local politics not to display established wealth and status, but to acquire them. Vote buying and other competitive tactics led to the withdrawal of some traditional leaders and to the election of less respectable, less qualified, and less disinterested officials. In 1959, for the first time, ordinary voters rather than members of the township council elected the township executive; and in 1961, again for the first time, members of the township council were elected from new multivillage electoral districts rather than from individual villages. These changes weakened the relevance of the lineage and village as units of political allegiance and replaced them with township-wide factions, forcing villagers to choose sides in terms of their own changing extravillage political and economic interests. Thus neither intravillage agnatic ties nor crossvillage affinal relationships any longer provided automatic guides to political affiliation. Interestingly, although the majority of village families sided with one of the two township-level factions, the poorer and less secure families tended to remain neutral, at least in public. Evidently, they could not afford to offend the now highly partisan township officials, who rewarded their public supporters and penalized their public opponents. At the same time, the willingness of aspiring politicians to pay even token amounts for the votes of ordinary villagers showed villagers that they had some real political power, however limited. Finally, since township officials controlled access to modern agricultural technology, local factions became a new channel for integrating even the poorest villagers into a wider and changing world (see also Yang 1970).

However local the scale, elections such as those described by Gallin still involve politics oriented to positions and procedures defined by the state. Some political scientists would draw the line here between institutional politics and the political aspects of other social relations. However, other political scientists would join most anthropologists in defining politics more broadly to include making decisions and resolving conflicts within local communities, private organizations, and personal relationships. These parapolitical contexts may be studied not only for their intrinsic significance but also for the light such study can shed on the relationship between parapolitical and conventionally political behavior. For Taiwan, this broad definition of politics opens a large literature of which we may briefly note only a few illustrative examples.

Nongovernmental settings for politics in Taiwan differ in many ways—for example, in terms of the number of participants involved, the spatial scale of operations, and the balance between impersonal and particularistic bases of organization. At one extreme are large-scale corporations involved in international and national trade and requiring capital and labor far in excess of what family and friends can provide. In the middle are regional and local economic firms and voluntary associations placing approximately equal reliance on personal networks and formal organization. And at the other extreme are natural communities, primary groups, and friendship networks based almost exclusively on personal relationships. The available literature does not really even begin to suggest the many possible combinations of political settings along these dimensions, let alone to exhaust them.

The import of technology and materials, the export of both agricultural and industrial products, and the modernization and enlargement of corporate enterprises have been central features of Taiwan's economic and political development for half a century. Nevertheless, little fieldwork has been done on modern socioeconomic organizations on Taiwan, let alone on the politics within and between them. The principal exception is Robert Silin's pioneering study of the leadership style within one of Taiwan's largest manufacturing firms. (Since Silin's analysis focuses on the cultural principles structuring interactions between the corporate leader and his managerial assistants, it will be discussed in the next section.) Important fieldwork in the late 1970's by Denis Simon on the political economy of technology transfer and by Thomas Gold on the social organization of the textile, electronics, and petrochemical industries promises to cast some light on the politics of large-scale industry in Taiwan. Smaller-scale businesses have been treated in Donald DeGlopper's work on artisans in the historic commercial city of Lu-kang. Although the fluid relations among Lu-kang's family firms remain contingent upon mutually satisfactory performance, transactions are facilitated by the solidarity of Lu-kang's citizens vis-à-vis the outside world. (See Silin 1976; DeGlopper 1973, 1974, 1977.)

For a still smaller organizational and spatial scale, Burton Pasternak contrasts village organization in Ta-tieh, a prosperous Hakka farming village in southern P'ing-tung county, and Chung-she, a modest Hokkien farming village in northern Tainan county (1972). Ta-tieh is highly integrated; villagers take an active interest in local affairs; a strong feeling of solidarity prevails; and village headmen play a major role in settling village disputes. Chung-she, by contrast, is riven by antagonisms; community activities are minimal; and headmen are effective mediators only when they come from the lineage group dominant before Taiwan's retrocession and land reform. Pasternak suggests two basic hypotheses that explain differences in contemporary community organization as the result of differences in historical political environments. The first hypothesis is that "small agnatic groups were most likely to develop into single-lineage communities on open frontiers where competition for strategic resources was minimal, whereas the need for cooperation across agnatic lines for purposes of exploiting the environment or for defense tended to generate or reinforce the development of multi-lineage communities." The second hypothesis is that "higher-order (i.e. nonlocalized) descent groups resulting from an aggregative process seem to be associated with situations where territorially discrete and numerically weak agnatic groups have been confronted by a large and persistent common enemy." (1972: 18–19.) Pasternak thus dismisses ethnicity, Japanese influence, and current urbanization as causes for the differences between his two villages, and emphasizes instead initial settlement patterns, the distribution of wealth, and need for cooperation across agnatic lines for economic and defense purposes. (See Chung-min Chen 1977: 188–91.)

Also for the community level, anthropologists have begun to examine the political significance of religious organizations. Stephan

Feuchtwang describes the partial success of the Ch'ing, Japanese, and Nationalist governments in reducing the scale and significance of community religious festivals. The continuing role of such festivals as a symbol of community solidarity against outsiders is a theme recently taken up in greater depth by Emily Ahern, Hill Gates, and others. Wang, Feuchtwang, Schipper, and Gates describe the role of temples in internal community politics and governance. In addition to symbolizing community identity and displaying family prestige, the pooling of resources across family lines to build temples and their courtyards provides public space needed for both work and leisure. (Feuchtwang 1976, 1977; Rohsenow 1973; Ahern this volume; Shih-ch'ing Wang 1974; Schipper 1977.)

Rohsenow (1973) and Ahern (1978) have explored the practical significance of religious practices to individuals in both rural and urban areas for modeling their bureaucratic political environment, codifying political strategies, and learning political skills. The hierarchy of gods mirrors the hierarchy of state officials, and the procedures for petitioning the two are analogous. Powerful gods, like powerful officials, may be indispensable in crises but should stay in their offices and mind their own business until, through appropriately deferential formulas, people request their services. Rohsenow describes (1973: 167–69) the "mandarin strategy" that communities and individuals employ to keep both gods and officials at a safe distance.

> The best defense against interference is to encourage the official's natural desire for the privilege and deference he considers his due. Not only exaggerated politeness, but a constant pressure against the official's lowering himself to personal involvement with trivial facts and tedious tasks, place him on a pedestal of considerable height. His position and prestige come to require that he remain aloof, shut up in his special office or building, approachable only through intermediaries and with special ceremonies, all of which insulate him against knowledge and control of the actual situation. The "mandarin strategy" is applied with subtle but constant pressure from below on everyone in authority, from head of a household to Chiang Kai-shek. . . . To be seen in its fullest flower, the mandarin strategy should be observed among high-ranking officials, where its continued use over decades of Nationalist rule has resulted in a high degree of alienation of some officials from political reality.

Although some parapolitical objectives involve relationships with coreligionists, economic partners, and political allies who are not kinsmen, the most fundamental parapolitical objectives for most Taiwanese remain within the family. The relative power of husbands and wives, fathers and sons, and brothers and sisters—over decisions of marriage, adoption, investment, consumption, and inheritance—accordingly defines a minute but intense parapolitical system. In the literature on Taiwan, perhaps the best documented and most controversial such issue concerns the division of a family's property among the sons following the death of their father. Margery Wolf provides a classic description of the pressures on an extended family once held together by the leadership of a highly respected father. In Wolf's view, family pride supplements economic rewards as a cohesive influence, whereas the perceived interests and political role of women supplement rivalry between brothers as a divisive influence (1968). In contrast, Myron Cohen emphasizes exclusively the economic interests of males as the basic source of both family cohesion and family conflict (1976). In his paper in this volume, Arthur Wolf provides demographic data supporting an emphasis on rivalry between uterine families (a woman and her children versus her mother-in-law and the mother-in-law's children) rather than on rivalry between conjugal units (a woman and her husband versus her sisters-in-law and their husbands) as the most significant factors in family conflicts.

Finally, friendships, sworn brotherhoods, patron-client ties, and other similar relationships constitute a still smaller scale of parapolitical organization. For example, Bernard and Rita Gallin (1977) have distinguished between affective, horizontal sworn brotherhoods (usually formed by young men to formalize personal friendships) and instrumental, vertical sworn brotherhoods (usually organized by men over 30 to facilitate their upward mobility). The Gallins explain that Taiwan is run by a strong bureaucracy that uses its extensive patronage network to exchange material incentives for political obedience and electoral support. Modern, private, formal organizations often lack the broad range of personal ties and mechanisms for strengthening personal relationships that are required for dealing with bureaucrats inclined to favoritism. The small scale, multiple bases, flexible mechanisms, diverse membership, and frank emphasis on patronage of the sworn brotherhood provide an apt solution.

A classic summary of the delicate balance between instrumental and expressive themes in Chinese personal relationships is Margery Wolf's characterization (1968: 53) of a Taiwanese dinner party.

> A Taiwanese dinner party is a seemingly informal affair that operates under very formal rules. Even in the village, feasts are rarely simple expressions of hospitality. The guests are poor relatives, wealthy relatives to whom the host is indebted, friends, business associates, and men to whom he owes social or monetary debts. [At more select parties] each guest is invited for a definite if unspecified purpose: The man who is pressed by his host into the most honored position at the table knows he is being thanked for a favor, or about to be asked for one; the guest who finds himself sitting in an undesirable spot is silently informed that the favor he requested will not be granted; another guest is made to understand that his friendship is valued but should not be pressed by a special request.

Finally, Wolf provides a sensitive description of the informal political influence of women within small communities. Solidarity among women is not based on their relationships to men; instead, women's relationships are based on interaction in a common workplace outside the home such as a laundering spot or in a convenient leisure gathering place such as a cigarette and candy stall. Their influence is based on their ability to make men lose face by gossiping about behavior that does not meet community standards. However, in their informal roles within the family and neighborhood, women can develop considerable skills at mediation and leadership that can be transferred to a larger political arena when the national system declares it legitimate (M. Wolf 1972, 1974).

### *Political Culture and Political Socialization*

Taiwan's kaleidoscopic history has left its citizens with major conflicts of political identity. High Confucianism, local Taoism, Chinese patriotism, Taiwanese nationalism, mainlander solidarity, Nationalist ideology, and Western ideals blend with shifting emphases. The ultimate resolution of these conflicts of identity, like their generation, depends in large part on the changing international balance of power in East Asia. Nevertheless, as of the late 1970's the fragile possibility of a merged Taiwanese and mainlander political identity has arrived.

To the study of this delicate process, analysis of political culture and political socialization will no doubt contribute. Several authors have attempted to formulate what is enduringly Chinese about political culture on Taiwan (Wilson 1970; Winckler 1974; Silin 1976; Wei 1976a; Lerman 1977; Pillsbury 1978). The psychocultural diagnosis—the idea that the Chinese depend on authoritarian leadership and suffer from a schizophrenic separation between their ideals of high propriety and their acceptance of the practical exigencies of politics—has become so familiar that it is beginning to be superseded by more political hypotheses assuming strategic rationality (Ahern this volume, 1978; Wei 1976). Anthropologists have explored the use of local popular religion as both a source and an emblem of the solidarity of local communities vis-à-vis the state—Ch'ing, Japanese, and Nationalist (Saso 1970; Rohsenow 1973; Feuchtwang 1974; Shih-ch'ing Wang 1974; Cohen 1976; Schipper 1977; Ahern this volume). Periodic local festivals do not merely commemorate past communal successes in self-defense or economic enterprises, but also serve as a matrix for many current forms of practical community cooperation.

Surveys of student attitudes (Appleton 1970) and student voting behavior (Wei n.d.) and discussions of the political socialization of Taiwanese schoolchildren (Wilson 1970; Martin 1975) explore the impact of contemporary political ideologies. Appleton finds that mainlanders and Taiwanese largely share a common political culture that supports many democratic values, though this support is not as strong as that found among, for example, American students. Appleton attributes political differences among students in Taiwan to the current domination of the political system by mainlanders rather than to the effects of the Japanese occupation. Students from mainland families tend to be slightly more accepting of authority and slightly more inclined toward civic involvement than students from Taiwanese families. Taiwanese students become less political, more private, and more conservative as their years of schooling increase, and those who appeared disaffected with their government and society expressed their feelings more by withdrawal than by dissent.

Of the literature on Taiwan's political culture and political socialization, I shall discuss only monographs by Wilson, Silin, and Ahern. Richard Wilson combines a psychocultural model of group processes in Chinese society derived from the work of Richard Solomon with a research design derived from studies of the political socialization of American schoolchildren to produce a pioneering study of the political socialization of primary schoolchildren in Taiwan (1970). Wilson argues that the intense involvement of individuals with groups is created in Chinese society through the mechanism of face and regulated through the threat of shame. Pressure for conformity creates the need for a clear definition of group values, which is provided by the leader, who articulates these values and epitomizes the "face" of the group. Hostility felt by followers arising from the immunity of the leader from criticism and from the followers' lack of protection against the leader's power to humiliate them may result in hostility directed against out-groups, in in-group conflict, or in overt conformity combined with covert cynicism. As Wilson thinks should be the case for a successfully modernizing society on Taiwan, the style of authority in family, school, and polity are congruent, with the individual finding some relief in the family from secondary group pressures.

Wilson's systematic data illustrate the strength of formal survey methods. Nevertheless, to what extent do the responses of Chinese children to questionnaires administered at school by a foreigner count as evidence for what they really think and actually do in other social contexts? It is regrettable that Wilson did not have the resources to explore in greater detail children's responses to school as an arena of formal and informal political interaction with peers, teachers, administrators, and parents. Moreover, the playground, neighborhood, and village or urban ward are also relevant to the development of political attitudes. Wilson attempts to isolate the impact of grade, sex, rural/urban, and mainlander/Taiwanese distinctions. Future studies might do the same for the impact of intelligence, sibling position, family culture, and other components of the social milieu.

Silin's sophisticated explication (1976) of the general cultural values informing leadership and decision-making within the upper echelons of a large-scale private Taiwanese manufacturing firm provides a valuable reference for students of Chinese political culture. Insisting that organizational sociologists pay more attention to the "cosmologies" individuals bring to bear on their organizational behavior, Silin focuses on the highly political problem of compliance. He describes what he regards as distinctively Chinese about the way Taiwanese managers perform particular compliance-related functions that are universal in large-scale, formal organizations: recruitment, communication, remuneration, leadership, and control. He suggests that compliance processes within an organization are more heavily conditioned by general cultural ideas than by the formal structures of particular organizations. Indeed, the politics of compliance within an organization seem less closely linked to the particular tasks performed by the organization than much Western literature on organizations implies. Although agreeing with Pye and Solomon that dependence on authority is an important theme in Chinese political culture, Silin argues that in the Chinese view the commitment of a follower to a leader should definitely be based not on emotional ties but rather on a rational conviction that the leader represents the most morally correct and practically adequate philosophy available for achieving a common purpose. Since trust between leader and subordinates is in principle contingent on this rational conviction, the leader must continually strive to project an image of himself as the sole source of inspiration, authority, and initiative within the organization. The subordinate must acknowledge the leader's qualitative superiority by manifesting literal fear in his presence, and he must struggle unceasingly to demonstrate that he has correctly grasped the practical implications of the leader's guiding ideas. A political culture predicated on rational conviction frequently produces vain and arbitrary leaders prone to divide-and-rule strategies. It can also produce in subordinates a sense of lonely futility, an unwillingness to communicate bad news, and a propensity to form defensive cliques. However, such a political culture can motivate intense efforts by both leaders and subordinates and can generate secondary structures—particularly personal networks—that partially overcome the culture's dysfunctional effects.

Silin's explication of Chinese concepts of compliance—though more deductive in approach than a "thick" description—persuades the reader and helps interpret other Chinese organizations. However, Silin fails to prove a causal link between values and behavior. Since he restricts himself to enterprises in which control is centralized in the hands of one man and since he relies heavily on one case study, it is impossible to ascertain to what extent the behavior he observes is culturally programmed and to what extent it is a rational adaptation to one-man rule.

For authority relations within kinship groups, we may turn to Emily Ahern's highly political interpretation of ancestor worship. Of the four lineages in her community, one is crippled by factionalism, one is living in relative poverty, one is relatively prosperous with mild internal segmentation, and one is closely integrated with little internal differentiation and few nonlineage residents. These four lineages control progressively more of the ritual activities within their respective settlements. The particular form of ancestral halls, ancestral tablets, and related types of worship expresses not only the underlying cultural and material similarity of the four lineages, but also their differing internal demographic and political composition and their political distinctiveness and rivalry. In general, the greater the opportunity for generating economic benefits from assets owned collectively by a lineage, the greater the lineage's political solidarity and ritual display. However, the ability to maintain control of such resources and to use them productively depends in turn on the lineage members' willingness to cooperate and on the lineage leaders' abilities. Consequently, leaders tend to be not simply those who are older or richer, but those best able to mediate disputes within settlements and to represent settlements to the outside world. Rituals for the dead are charged with ambivalence: not only do survivors feel guilty about obtaining the long-coveted property and authority of the deceased; they also feel chagrined at their inability to claim that property fully and to escape that authority completely. The inclusions of the deceased among the pantheon of lineage ancestors is contingent not simply on the person's death, but on his or her specific contributions to the lineage. It is the maintenance of property or the production of offspring that imposes precise, binding, and enduring obligations on descendants. Ahern's chapters on the social relationships and psychological responses surrounding these dilemmas of authority and succession should provide food for thought to students of Chinese political culture, richly illustrating as they do her general thesis that "the cult of the dead in Ch'inan can be seen as a code that, once deciphered, reveals how groups are articulated and how they are subdivided along economic and political lines" (1973: 91).

Little has been done to probe for possible common denominators between explicitly political and ostensibly economic and ritual behavior (but see Arthur Wolf 1974; Seaman this volume). Certainly the convergence between Silin and Ahern on the calculatedly rational and competitively individual nature of commitments to authority suggests revisions of the affective, collective, passive, and dependent psychocultural model embraced by Wilson. Meanwhile, the residents of Taiwan themselves continue to search for their identity among their evolving political institutions, their prosperous economy, and their Chinese ancestry.

# Government Enterprise and Village Politics

Chung-min Chen

In sugarcane farming communities in southwestern Taiwan, local political leaders have emerged who owe their prominent positions mainly to their close association with the Taiwan Sugar Company—a government-owned enterprise. These local leaders, although unique in certain respects, share a very significant characteristic with local political leaders in other Taiwanese and traditional Chinese rural communities: they can be viewed as "cultural brokers" (Wolf 1956) or as "representative mediators" (Löffler 1971) who achieve their leadership status by occupying a strategic position between the peasants in rural communities and the socioeconomic institutions of the larger society.

## *The Setting*

A brief review of the local setting will provide the necessary background for this discussion. Upper Camp is a village in the southern portion of the Chia-nan Plain, on the southwestern coast of Taiwan. As an administrative unit, the village is a part of Liang-tien township in Tainan county. An elected village mayor (*li-chang*) is the formal head of the village and is expected to manage village affairs, and an elected village representative (*li-min-tai-piao*) is given the authority to represent village interests in the township council (which controls the township government, at least nominally). Upper Camp is also a

This paper is based on fieldwork conducted in a rural village in Tainan county from Dec. 1969 to Feb. 1971. My research was supported by the Harvard-Yenching Institute and by the Institute of Ethnology, Academia Sinica. I am especially grateful to these two institutes for their enthusiastic cooperation. Out of respect for the villagers' privacy, I use pseudonyms for the lineages, village, township, and people mentioned in the following pages.

natural community with clear geographic and social boundaries. Physically, the village is a compact settlement separated from similar neighboring settlements by fields on all sides. It is inhabited by villagers who not only share a strong sense of community but also constitute a social and religious unit, observing the same religious calendar and participating in village-wide ceremonial activities. Furthermore, villagers jointly own the village temple and its property, and share responsibility for its maintenance.

In 1971, 842 villagers lived in the 159 households that formed Upper Camp. The majority of these villagers belonged to one of three localized patrilineages. The largest of these lineages, the Pao lineage, had 542 members and made up roughly 65 percent of the entire village population. The other two lineages were both Kao lineages (they shared the same surname but were not genealogically connected): one had 127 members, the other only 53. In addition to these three lineages, fourteen other surnames were represented in the village by 27 households.

At the first glance, the Pao lineage of Upper Camp seems to fit the model used to describe the lineages found in precommunist southeastern China. The lineage has a very formal ancestral hall where its ancestral tablets are housed and where religious ceremonies are conducted. A well-documented and complete genealogy connects all the lineage members to each other and to their common agnatic ancestor. Moreover, the Pao lineage still possesses a large piece of land that generates a fair amount of income annually to meet ceremonial expenses and to pay for the maintenance of the ancestral hall. However, despite this relatively extensive material base, the Pao lineage is no longer a strong and active sociopolitical unit in the village community, as its counterparts were said to have been in traditional Chinese rural society. There is no lineage activity except for twice-yearly ancestor worship, and even this has been poorly attended in recent years. Unlike those lineage elders often cited in the literature on traditional Chinese villages, elders of the Pao lineage do not play an important role in the community; nor do the elders of the two Kao lineages.

With this brief account of the state of lineages in Upper Camp, let us turn to the village's economic organization. Although not all the households in Upper Camp gain their living from the land, the majority still earn their livelihood in agriculture. Among the 159 households, only 27 can be classified as nonagricultural. The remaining

132 depend either entirely or partly on farming (cultivating sugarcane, sweet potatoes, rice, and various other crops).

Situated in the southwestern coastal plain of Taiwan, where natural rainfall is very unevenly distributed throughout the year and the soil has a rather high saline content, Upper Camp's fields must be irrigated frequently in order for them to produce good crops. Like the other villages in this region, Upper Camp gets its irrigation water from the Chia-nan Irrigation System, which serves the entire Chia-nan Plain. The irrigation system, however, does not have the capacity to supply water to all of the region's 150,000 hectares of cultivated land on a regular and continuous basis. Therefore, a scheme of rotating water distribution was designed when the irrigation system was completed in 1930. Under this arrangement, the region is divided into approximately a thousand "small areas" of about 150 hectares each (150 hectares is roughly the total area of the farms attached to a normal village). These "small areas" in turn are further subdivided into three crop zones of about 50 hectares each. In any given year, only one of these crop zones receives enough irrigation water (three or four months' worth) to cultivate a single crop of wet rice; the second crop zone receives irrigation water on two brief occasions to grow sugarcane (a crop that takes about sixteen months to mature); and the third crop zone depends on rainfall to grow sweet potatoes or other drought-resistant crops. In the following year, the wet rice zone receives no irrigation water (and is therefore used for sweet potatoes); the sugarcane zone (after the cane is harvested) receives irrigation water for one crop of wet rice; and the dry zone receives irrigation water twice (for sugarcane). After three years, the cycle begins again.

This description is only approximate: the actual system of rotation and cultivation is usually more complicated (see Chen 1977: 45–52). But for the purposes of this paper, the description serves to underline the very important fact that this unusual water distribution scheme encourages Upper Camp villagers to continue cultivating sugarcane—a crop that takes longer to mature and earns a smaller cash return than wet rice. Indeed, to understand the role and power bases of Upper Camp's local leader, we must focus our attention on the economics of sugarcane cultivation.

When Taiwan was returned to the Nationalist Chinese Government in 1945, all industries owned by the Japanese Colonial Government or by private Japanese corporations (this included all Taiwan's sugar refineries) were nationalized and placed under the control of various government agencies. In 1947 the Taiwan Sugar Company (TSC) was established to manage the island's sugar industry. Owned jointly by the Nationalist Government of China and the provincial government of Taiwan, the TSC was given a permanent monopoly over the manufacture and sale of Taiwanese sugar. Sugarcane cultivated by villagers in the Chia-nan Plain and elsewhere in Taiwan can thus be sold only to the TSC. Given Chia-nan's peculiar irrigation system and the TSC monopoly, Upper Camp villagers naturally have a strong desire to maintain a close and preferably good relationship with the TSC.

Each year before planting their sugarcane, farmers have to obtain a production contract from the TSC's local agent to make sure that after sixteen months of hard work they will have a buyer for their crop. Among other things, the production contract offered by the TSC specifies the rate at which the cultivator and refinery will share the return on the refined sugar (in 1970 the going rate was 55 percent to the cultivator and 45 percent to the refinery); a guaranteed minimum price for raw canes; the size of the fertilizer loan that the TSC will provide; the size and interest rate of the production loan that the TSC will provide; the cultivator's agreement to ship all his sugarcane to the designated refinery; the refinery's agreement to accept the cane; the cultivator's relinquishment of the right to harvest his crop; and the cultivator's authorization that the harvesting be done at his expense by a work team organized and supervised by the TSC's local agent.

As we can see from the terms of the production contract, Upper Camp villagers are actually working as contract laborers for the TSC when they plant sugarcane in their fields, even though they own their lands and farming equipment. Moreover, they are required by the contract to plant only the special variety of sugarcane selected and approved by the TSC; they must accept the supervision and guidance of the TSC's field agent in the process of cultivating the crop; and they must allow this agent to decide when their crops are ready for harvest. Finally, they have to let the agent's work team do the harvesting for them, paying a fee for such obligatory service. For all these concessions, the cane farmers are given the "privilege" of getting themselves in debt—i.e., they are allowed to apply for cash and fertilizer loans from the TSC.

Although peasants do not really like this arrangement, they have little choice but to accept it given this region's irrigation system and the present economic conditions. Indeed, the TSC's credit policy is designed to make this acceptance still more likely. To encourage the cultivation of sugarcane, the TSC uses fertilizer and cash loans as incentives to get as many cultivators as possible to plant sugarcane in the appropriate crop zone. Although these loans are not very large and the peasants have to pay interest for cash loans (fertilizer loans are given in kind and are interest free), the loans are usually eagerly accepted since peasants are generally short of cash and in need of the fertilizer.

What concerns us here, however, is not the possible exploitation of the peasants but rather the close interdependence of the peasants and the TSC. Just as the peasants have little choice but to cultivate some sugarcane for the TSC, the TSC has to depend on the peasants to produce enough sugarcane to meet its annual production goals. Because of this interdependence, the TSC has had to establish and maintain an effective communications system so that its intentions and expectations can be understood by the peasants, and vice versa. This creates in each of the "small areas" of the Chia-nan Plain a role for a very important middleman.

## *The Commissioner and His Role*

The middleman between the peasants and the TSC is generally referred to as the "commissioner." His formal title is *yüan-liao-wei-yüan* (the commissioner in charge of the raw material). He is selected and appointed by the TSC to function in his native "small area" as the company's local agent. Since a "small area" is frequently also a village, there is one commissioner in most of the villages in this region. The commissioner is not considered an official of the TSC, nor is he classified as a regular TSC employee (since he is not paid a regular salary and not required to keep office hours at the TSC's local office). Instead, he is an agent authorized by the TSC to organize and supervise work teams, and to arrange for the delivery of harvested sugarcane to the local refinery; to persuade all the peasants who own land in the appropriate zone to plant sugarcane and sign a production contract with the TSC; to act as a loan officer for the TSC's fertilizer and production loans by receiving applications and verifying the eligibility of applicants; and to convey the company's instructions to the cultivators and the cultivators' requests and complaints to the company.

In return for performing these services, the commissioner is granted the right to charge each cultivator for the harvesting job that only he is authorized to do. Part of the fee that he receives will of course go to the members of his work team, but about one quarter of it will remain his own. Thus, although the TSC does not pay the commissioner directly, it allows him to charge peasants a fee for an obligatory service. Up to this point, our examination of the commissioner has emphasized his role in organizing and supervising harvests for the TSC. In reality, however, his role is much more complicated than this. As the agent of an institution vitally important to the cultivators' economic well-being, the commissioner has a great deal of influence over the peasants in his community. He is often the real village leader despite the fact that there is a village mayor and a village representative, both elected by the villagers to manage community affairs. Certainly in Upper Camp and in its neighboring villages, the commissioner is the one whom villagers most frequently seek out to mediate disputes or to represent them in dealing with official agencies outside their community. He is also the most respected and persuasive person in the village, and is therefore far more the political boss of the village than either the mayor or representative (if he is not himself the mayor or the representative). His influence is readily illustrated by two cases I recorded during my stay in Upper Camp.

*Case I.* This case exemplifies the commissioner's role as the villagers' protector. Before I go into details, let me first point out that during my stay Upper Camp had a village mayor and village representative who were both relatively young and had been supported by the commissioner when they had run for office. Thus, although the mayor and representative were the formal leaders of the village, in the real political life of the village they were the "lieutenants" of the commissioner.

One day late in the summer of 1970, a man of the Pao lineage who had married uxorilocally five years previously in another village came back to his parents in Upper Camp. He was injured and looked as though he had been in a bad fight. The parents, after taking care of their son's wounds, discovered that he had been beaten by one of his wife's distant relatives in the other village. They were also told that this was not the first time that their son was beaten by the same man.

Very worried and slightly angered, the father asked his son why he did not go to the police. The son answered that the person who beat him was a local hoodlum (*liu-mang*) who would cause more trouble if the police were contacted. The poor man told his parents that since they were poor and did not have any prominent friend who could back them up, the police would not have a real interest in their case; all he would accomplish would be to agitate the *liu-mang* still more and make it much more difficult for him to return to the other village.

The parents, acting on the suggestion of some of their neighbors, appealed to the commissioner of Upper Camp, asking him to intervene on their son's behalf. After listening to the incident, the commissioner told the parents to go home and to keep their son in Upper Camp for a few days. Two days later, the commissioner went to see the chairman of the township council and asked to be introduced to the policeman in charge of the subdistrict where the victim and his wife were living. The chairman obliged and phoned the policeman, casually mentioning that one of his best friends, Mr. Pao, the commissioner of Upper Camp village, would like to visit him and ask him for some help. The next day, the commissioner went to the police station and saw the policeman. He presented the case politely and asked the policeman to see to it that his poor and innocent village friend would not be harassed after returning home. The commissioner was careful not to ask for any retribution, although he stressed that the victim was weak and did not do anything to provoke the incident.

Two days after the commissioner had visited the policeman, the victim's wife came to Upper Camp and told her husband and her in-laws that the *liu-mang* had sent a string of firecrackers to their house (a gesture of apology) and had expressed his regrets. The man went home with his wife, knowing that he would regain whatever face he had lost by exploding the firecrackers in front of his house on his return. He was also very sure that, since the commissioner had intervened, the person who had harassed him would know that he had a strong backer in Upper Camp and would not dare to make any more trouble.

*Case II.* This case concerns the commissioner's role as a mediator. During an argument between two villagers, a 65-year-old man was pushed by his neighbor and fell to the ground. The old man informed the commissioner that he had been beaten and injured by his neighbor, and that he was going to the police station to report the incident. The commissioner calmed him down, promising to look into the case. After talking to the alleged culprit, the commissioner found out that the old man was not entirely innocent: he had struck his neighbor's ox after the neighbor's oxcart had made a deep tire mark in his front yard. It was at that point that the neighbor, who was driving the cart home, pushed the old man. The neighbor insisted that he had not beaten the old man; he was only trying to protect his animal by pushing the old man away.

After determining the facts, the commissioner paid the old man a visit to dissuade him from entering a complaint. The old man agreed not to go to the police if his neighbor would apologize publicly and promise not to mess up his front yard again. A few days later, both parties were asked to go to the village store to meet with the commissioner. The cart driver had agreed beforehand to offer the old man a cigarette as a gesture of apology. Arriving after his offended "victim," the carter bought a pack of the most expensive cigarettes sold at the store and offered them first to the old man, then to the commissioner and everyone else. Afterwards, the carter and the old man sat at the store chatting with other villagers. The one thing they did not talk about was the incident, which was considered resolved because the old man believed that he had regained his lost face.

What we have seen from these two cases is fairly typical of the protector and mediator roles played by the commissioner in Upper Camp. The villagers go to him to resolve conflicts with outsiders because they believe that he has more and better social connections than their elected village officials; and they go to him to settle their disputes with other villagers because they know that he enjoys sufficient respect for people to be receptive to his decisions.

How, then, does the commissioner acquire such influence? The answers are to be found in his close association with the TSC. First of all, the commissioner represents an important source of employment. The work team that he organizes each year is made up of more than forty people whom he alone has the authority to hire. Although these positions are not permanent—they only last four months or so each year—they are regarded as "long-term" jobs with clear advantages over day laboring jobs. In 1970, for example, a cane cutter earning NT$85 per day in the commissioner's work team was supplied with tools and refreshments, whereas a day laborer earning about the same amount for a private household had to work longer hours and furnish his own tools. Thus, villagers are anxious to maintain a good relationship with the commissioner in the hope that they or members of their families will be hired to work for him during the harvest season.

Secondly, the commissioner sets the harvest schedule for all the sugarcane in his small area. Having had their land planted with sugarcane for sixteen months or longer, peasants are understandably eager to have their cane cut at the earliest possible date; and they also want to have it cut on the days that are most suitable to their own work schedule. Indeed, when the harvest season starts or shortly before, the commissioner's house is frequently crowded with villagers who want to be scheduled for particular days. The commissioner's scheduling authority thus adds considerably to his influence.

Thirdly, as noted earlier, the commissioner has a strong influence over production and fertilizer loans. When a peasant signs a contract to plant sugarcane, he is entitled to apply for such loans. In 1970, for each one-tenth *chia*[1] of land under the contract for sugarcane, peasants were allowed to borrow up to NT$550 in cash at the interest rate of 1.25 percent per month and up to NT$700 worth of fertilizer interest free. The fertilizer loan usually has an added bonus: since the cultivator generally receives more fertilizer than he needs for his sugarcane, he is also getting some interest-free fertilizer to use for his other crops. Thus, these loans represent a major source of financial aid to peasants. Of the 79 Upper Camp households that signed production contracts in 1970, all applied for and received loans. Approximately NT$165,200 in cash and NT$260,702 worth of fertilizer were released to these households shortly after the planting season started. This meant that on the average each household received roughly NT$2,090 in cash and NT$3,300 worth of fertilizer. Moreover, the interest rate on production loans has been always much lower than the interest rates charged by other institutions and by private moneylenders. Therefore, virtually all eligible peasants apply for the TSC loans. And as noted, to obtain a loan a peasant must go to his local commissioner for the application forms, complete them, and then submit them to him. Since many peasants in rural Taiwan are still illiterate, they have to ask the commissioner to do the paper work for them. When the applications are submitted, the com-

[1]One *chia* is approximately equal to one hectare.

missioner is authorized by the TSC to verify the information, comment on the trustworthiness of the applicants, and decide what percentage of the requested amount should be granted. Obviously, then, he is in a very favorable position to command the respect of the peasants in his village.

The commissioner is not only sought after and respected by his fellow villagers; he is also well treated by the TSC. As we have seen, the TSC has to depend on peasants to supply raw materials. Therefore, it is vital for the company to encourage as many peasants as possible to plant sugarcane each season. Because the TSC does not have any significant direct contact with the peasants, it has to rely on the commissioner to promote the crop. In order to facilitate the commissioner's task and hence insure an adequate supply of raw material, the TSC has made it an implicit policy to build and boost its commissioners' images in their own communities. The company tries to uphold all decisions made by commissioners about loan applications as well as other matters, hoping that this will enhance the commissioners' reputations. Furthermore, the TSC frequently encourages commissioners, their family members, or their handpicked candidates to run for local political offices, hoping that this added local influence will increase commissioners' effectiveness in carrying out their jobs. Encouragement usually takes the form of assisting the commissioners or their close associates to secure party nomination and run as Kuomintang candidates.

Because the commissioner occupies such a strategic position between the sugarcane farmers and the TSC, it is he, not the lineage elders or the village mayor, who functions as the real leader in Upper Camp. All his counterparts in the seven villages surrounding Upper Camp are powerful figures in their respective communities as well. In 1970, four of these seven commissioners were village mayors, and two were village representatives; the remaining commissioner, an elderly gentleman, was a prominent member of the board of trustees of the Liang-tien Farmers Association.

To be sure, not all of these commissioners became community leaders only after they had become commissioners. Yet it is still very evident that their role as mediator between the peasants and the TSC gave them a high degree of influence. And this influence was frequently consolidated and enhanced by their holding—with the help of the TSC—other official positions in their communities.

### *The Commissioner and the Local Gentry*

Previous studies of local political leadership in traditional rural China have focused largely on the roles of the local gentry. It has been said that there were two types of leaders in rural China, "official leaders" and "lay leaders" (see Yang 1945: 181–92). Official leaders were of lower rank and had less power and influence than lay leaders because they were appointed and paid by the government, and were therefore considered to be government runners. Lay leaders, by contrast, became leaders because of their special qualifications—age, wealth, learning, kin-group status, or personal capacity—and were as a result greatly respected and admired by their constituents (Hsiao 1960: 273).

Depicting lay or informal leaders in this way often gives the impression that they were men of merit who, by virtue of possessing socially desirable characteristics, were sought out by their villagers to lead the community. In some cases, such a characterization may well have been very close to the truth; but it certainly cannot be accepted as a complete explanation of the prominence of the local gentry. Members of the gentry became leaders for far more significant reasons than that they were model members of their communities.

As is well known, in traditional rural China the formal state administrative apparatus did not really reach down to the village level. Without an effective official channel connecting the yamen of the county magistrate to peasant households, there was a clear need for some kind of informal communication link between the "parent official" and his "children people." As educated men who might already have served as officials or were preparing to do so, members of the local gentry were in an ideal position to deal directly with the county magistrate and to command his respect. This enabled the local gentry to represent their villagers and to protect their villagers' interests. In short, gentry leaders in traditional China achieved their positions mainly through their access to administrative power and their ability and willingness to protect and promote the interests of their fellow villagers. Peasants thus looked up to their gentry leaders not merely because they were wealthy and educated, but more importantly because they served as representative mediators between themselves and the administrators who had such a strong influence over their welfare.

There is an obvious parallel between these traditional gentry leaders and the commissioners whom we have just described. Although the commissioner's foremost duty is to serve the TSC, not the peasants, his connection with various government agencies and his close affiliation with the TSC—the only buyer of a very important crop and the largest and the most favorable source of credit in this area—enable him to serve as a representative for his villagers. Moreover, unlike other political leaders such as the village mayor, the commissioner knows very well that he is not in a position to "rule" his villagers. On the contrary, he understands that he has to earn his villagers' respect and support in order to carry out effectively the job entrusted to him by the TSC. Thus, the commissioner has not only the ability but the incentive to help and serve his people. It is primarily due to this incentive that he is willing to help the peasants, thereby becoming the most influential leader in his community.

To conclude, I suggest that the concepts of "cultural broker" and "representative mediator"—introduced respectively by Wolf (1956) and Löffler (1971)—should be used in the study of local political leadership in rural Taiwan. These concepts allow us to go beyond a mere description of the leaders' personal characteristics, such as education, wealth, and personality, and direct our attention to their roles in linking the local community to regional and national institutions. By seeing the leaders as "mediators" and "brokers," we gain a clearer picture of their power bases and motivations. By studying their activities, we can better understand how village communities are integrated into the larger society. Finally, by documenting the changes in the roles and power bases of mediators as well as the emergence and decline of different types of mediators, we can improve our knowledge of the changing relationship between the peasant community and the state.

# Roles Linking State and Society

Edwin A. Winckler

Political anthropology uses many special terms to describe situations not easily captured in the vocabulary of Western political institutions: broker, patron-client, faction, arena, parapolitical, and interhierarchical are some that come to mind. This paper discusses relationships between state and society in Taiwan by distinguishing among *managers*, *contenders*, and *publics*. Although potentially applicable to any political system, these categories of political roles are particularly useful in analyzing the middle levels—subnational-provincial, metropolitan-regional, county-municipal—of authoritarian regimes.[1]

*Managers* umpire political conflict from behind the scenes rather than run for elective office themselves. Managers do, however, compete with each other to impress patrons placed higher in the power structure, hoping for advancement to higher positions. In an authoritarian polity managers are likely to be drawn from a ruling party, security agencies, territorial governments, business circles, or social elites. In Taiwan the principal managers of local political systems are the chairmen of local party committees. They are under the close supervision of provincial and national party headquarters and are backstopped by several competing security agencies. "Graduates" of the local system currently in provincial or national office and senior members of wealthy local families who have good connections

I would like to thank Stevan Harrell, Hill Gates, and Susan Greenhalgh for their helpful comments on this paper. I would also like to thank Sophie Sa for assistance in collating information from newspaper clippings on Taiwan's post-1945 regional electoral politics.

[1]For the classic definition of an authoritarian regime, see Linz 1964; for a recent elaboration, see Linz 1973.

with the national political establishment also advise on important decisions and act as local managers when necessary.[2]

*Contenders* compete continuously for the electoral support of publics whether or not they are candidates for a particular office, and contenders include those who campaign unsuccessfully for nomination as party candidates as well as those with objectives other than election to the offices for which they are candidates. Such aims might include receiving a bribe to withdraw from a race, splitting another candidate's vote, or building support for a later election campaign. In authoritarian polities elected offices usually convey little power for independent public policy initiative. However, they do provide opportunities for attracting the attention of potential patrons higher in the power structure who may then sponsor elected officeholders for the appointed offices through which limited power is actually delegated. In a bureaucratic economy where political power is often the principal ingredient of economic success, elective office may also provide opportunities for the advancement or protection of private business interests. As a result of the changing educational requirements for candidates and the changing occupational composition of society, the background of contenders in Taiwan has shifted significantly in the thirty years of Nationalist rule. The highly educated professionals of the 1950's gave way to less educated older local politicians in the 1960's, and these in turn have increasingly given way to younger businessmen in the 1970's. Nevertheless, the factional networks backing these changing contenders (rival candidates often represent rival networks of political and economic interests) have displayed significant continuity, even though the scale and nature of the stakes have been completely transformed.[3]

*Publics* are groupings of voters within given constituencies whose support or opposition in particular contests in principle determines electoral outcomes. For different offices the relevant constituencies within which publics develop can range from small committees, to the members of local legislatures, to functionally defined segments of the voting population, to all voters of progressively larger territorial administrative units. Kuomintang committees include representatives of occupational as well as territorial groups; the party believes that it represents the interests of all possible publics. Although authori-

[2] For a discussion of the managerial role of the Kuomintang, see Tai 1970.

[3] The best discussion of the behavior of contenders in Taiwan politics is Crissman 1969.

tarian regimes value involvement of publics in politics, the impact of popular participation on electoral outcomes is often highly circumscribed. Many factors serve to reduce—if not to eliminate—the probability of an electoral upset of the ruling party. These include the party's exclusive right to organize, its monopoly of patronage and media, its restriction of choice through intimidation or bribery of potential nonparty candidates, and its control of large blocks of military and other government-affiliated votes. If all else fails, opponents allege, the Kuomintang miscounts the votes. Nevertheless, voters occasionally elect candidates other than party nominees—to as many as one fifth of some types of local office. Although nonparty victories have involved only a small proportion of all offices, they have sometimes included a high proportion of offices actually contested. The Kuomintang regards such upsets as embarrassing anomalies, since if the party were truly in congruence with the public, voters would always support party candidates. To prevent opposition candidates from developing island-wide constituencies, the 21 counties and municipalities into which the island is divided remain the largest units within which most electoral contests take place.[4]

There are both comparative and cultural reasons why distinguishing managers, contenders, and publics facilitates analysis of the relationship between state and society in Taiwan. For purposes of comparison, these categories sidestep preconceptions that the island is a Western-style, electoral democracy, as some of its partisans would like to believe, or that it is simply a cynical police state, as some of its critics conclude. The Republic of China is clearly an authoritarian regime, not only because it manifests the Linzian criteria of diffuse ideology of the leader, limited pluralism within the establishment, and partial mobilization of the people, but also because it is dominated by interests and institutions committed to keeping it that way. To this end backstage managers, screened contenders, and constrained publics remain indispensable.[5]

Culturally, these categories identify components of the political system that the participants know to exist and value as norms. The Chinese have traditionally displayed an acute sense that politics is a troublesome business difficult to bring off gracefully, if at all. Since

[4]Systematic discussions of the formation of publics in Taiwan include Jacobs 1975; Wei n.d.; and Appleton 1970, 1973, 1974.

[5]For these criteria, the different types of authoritarian regimes, and the dynamics of transition between such regimes, see Linz 1975.

the beginning of the twentieth century, their remarkable determination to implement Western-style representative institutions has compounded the difficulty by requiring the political participation of many people of dubious cultivation. Under the circumstances, from a Chinese point of view, it would be irresponsible not to ensure that electoral politics is managed, contenders screened, and publics constrained. This is true not so much procedurally, to ensure that competition remains fair, but rather substantively, to ensure that correct ideas prevail. Rectitude is more important than democracy. After all, the barbarians—communists and capitalists alike—are at the walls.[6]

The body of this paper delineates managers, contenders, and publics in turn. Throughout the paper "national" refers to the Republic of China, which oversees the province of Taiwan, the capital city of Taipei, and miscellaneous other territories. "Provincial" refers to the subnational government headquartered in central Taiwan, which administers most of the island on behalf of the central government. (Taipei has been directly administered by the national government since 1967.) "Regional" refers to the metropolitan areas surrounding the three major cities in northern, central, and southern Taiwan: Taipei, Taichung, and Kaohsiung. Although these regions are not administrative units, they do achieve some political integration through interdependent regional activities and intercommunicating regional elites. "Local" refers to counties and municipalities, and "community" to townships, boroughs, urban districts, and smaller cities. Since this paper relies largely on many small bits of information collated from archives and interviews, and since I have reviewed the existing literature about local politics in Taiwan in another paper in this volume, there are few conventional footnotes. All examples are drawn from northern Taiwan, but the generalizations I hazard are based on materials from the northern, central, and southern regions.[7]

## *Managers*

As noted, managers usually umpire political conflict rather than contend for elective office. The managers most important for elec-

[6] The best recent summary of these dilemmas as they affect local elections is Lerman 1977.

[7] This paper is part of a continuing study of the role of regional political and economic elites in the politics and development of Taiwan. The project involves collating all available government reports, newspaper articles, secondary sources, field studies, and interviews with members of the elite on the subject of post-1945 regional electoral politics. The counties and munici-

toral politics in Taiwan are the party officials dispatched from the central and provincial Kuomintang headquarters to chair county and city party committees. Although the Kuomintang plays the leading managerial role, other political officials also contribute. Appointive heads of provincial government agencies in the locality and even elected local officials are expected to play the disinterested, compassionate role of "mother and father of the people." Difficult conflicts may require that provincial assemblymen, particularly those from the region itself, lend their status to efforts at mediation. Managers may also include exceptionally wealthy and socially established local people whose interests require harmonious local politics. Unfortunately, there is little in the public record about the role of local police chiefs, and virtually nothing about the role of other local security officials.

*Local party organization.* The basic responsibility of the local party chairman is to see that Kuomintang candidates win local elections: a chairman who fails at this is fired. But the chairman also has several secondary responsibilities. He should try to prevent extreme conflicts among local groups, and he should try to impose minimum standards of decorum on local politicians. Where the Kuomintang follows a divide-and-rule strategy, however, a moderate level of conflict among the groups is probably a sign of success rather than of failure, so long as the conflict does not interrupt normal political procedures. The party chairman also has some economic responsibilities, such as stimulating local planning and smoothing the path of local development projects. Finally, his ideological duties include supervising political education for Kuomintang cadres and overseeing public education campaigns on various political and practical themes.

Local party chairmen are perceived by their nonparty challengers as ambassadors plenipotentiary, empowered to invoke the police and courts along with financial and normative incentives to achieve their goals. They are, in fact, probably consulted about important security operations within their jurisdictions. Since they largely determine party nominees for most local offices, chairmen do gain some leverage over local politicians. Also, they dispense some patronage through the local government, assembly, and other organizations.

palities selected for intensive analysis cover the modernizing cores of the northern, central, and southern metropolitan regions of Taiwan. For northern Taiwan, these areas are Taipei city, Taipei county, Keelung city, T'ao-yüan county; for central Taiwan, they are Taichung city, Taichung county, Chang-hua county, and Nan-t'ou county; and for southern Taiwan, they are Kaohsiung city, Kaohsiung county, Tainan city, and Tainan county.

But when interviewed, local party chairmen stress the discrepancy between the major responsibilities they face and the marginal influence they possess. They are expected to settle problems through mediation, not through force or bribes. Yet quite often local politicians are undisciplined, antiparty, or otherwise difficult to persuade, particularly if the next election for which they will need the party chairman's nomination is still far in the future. Moreover, the significant resources are held by the provincial and central party organizations, toward whom the local chairman's relationship is only slightly less petitionary than that of other local leaders. Party chairmen appear to derive genuine satisfaction, however, from successfully obtaining resources to solve local problems.

The local chairmen interviewed all had at least two things in common—party loyalty and political articulateness. They could instantly provide a detailed summary of virtually any local situation from the point of view of current party policy. This articulateness reflects their ability, intelligence, and enthusiasm. But it also reflects the criteria of national leaders for the ideal party official, who should be informed and persuasive in encounters with both party superiors and the general public. Nonparty opponents comment sarcastically—one does not know with what justice—on the ability of local party officials to fool their superiors with glib talk and look out for each others' organizational and career interests.

Over the past thirty years party chairmen have differed considerably in background, having included old mainlanders and young Taiwanese, security operatives and college professors, returned diplomats and local gentry. They have also differed in influence, according to their superiors' confidence in them. A party chairman considered unreliable—for example, the occasional Taiwanese appointee in the 1950's and 1960's—would be cross-checked and backstopped by other party administrators or local security officials. In the late 1960's, Chiang Ching-kuo, working through his key subordinate Li Huan, began to appoint more Taiwanese as local party chairmen. However, in the late 1970's about three-quarters of Taiwan's local party chairmen were still mainlanders, evidently at the insistence of the more conservative party professionals.

Though the responsibilities of party chairmen are local, their perspective is not. In fact, they are in constant communication with the provincial party headquarters, which supervises their work minutely and convenes frequent meetings where chairmen from around the island compare notes and receive instructions. Moreover, local party chairmen are seldom members of the local political system in which they serve. Usually they arrive from outside, serve two two-year terms in the locality, then move on to other assignments. Local notables sometimes serve near their home counties, perhaps to draw on their regional reputations while still conforming to the rule of home-county avoidance. Occasionally, however, a party chairman comes directly from an important organization in the locality—as in the case of a trusted mainlander who happened to be teaching in a local university.

Junior party administrators generally receive their first local party chairmanship only after having served as secretary to an incumbent party chairman. Another pattern suggested by the fragmentary data is that assignments to rural, relatively manageable counties often precede assignments to complex, developing ones. Eventually, experienced local party chairmen are likely to be promoted to supervisory tasks in the provincial or central party headquarters. However, apprentices in the provincial and central headquarters may be sent to gain experience as local chairmen or secretaries, and experienced officials from headquarters sometimes serve as party chairmen in problem localities.

In contrast to the chairman, who usually comes from outside the locality and seldom becomes a contender for local office, the vice-chairman of the local party committee is often someone whom the party is grooming as a candidate for local assembly speaker or for local government executive. In any case, the vice-chairmanship is an advantageous post from which to lobby for nomination to such offices. For example, in the 1950's the Kuomintang chose Huang Ch'i-jui (a Taiwanese lawyer from the historic Wan-hua district of Taipei) to serve as speaker of the Taipei city assembly. In 1954 the party's rather bland candidate for mayor (a Taiwanese general from Taipei county named Wang Ming-ning) was upset—evidently with the help of Taiwanese businessmen from the city's Yen-p'ing district—by the nonparty candidate Kao Yü-shu. The party made Huang vice-chairman of the Taipei city party committee: he then beat Kao in the campaign for mayor in 1957.

A key topic of local politics, and one on which there has been little research, is the membership and role of the local party committee. This is a significant organization for members of the local political elite. It must ratify nominations of party candidates for office, though the more important nominations are largely dictated by the provincial, and occasionally national, party headquarters. Members of the decisive provincial party committee are recruited from local party committees, and competition for influence within local committees often carries over into the provincial committee.

Party members in each county elect representatives, who in turn elect the county party committee from a slate dictated by the local party chairman in consultation with the provincial party headquarters. For example, Taipei county has on the order of twenty thousand party members, two hundred representatives, and twenty committee members. The party maintains its ties to party members through small groups in local and professional associations. In addition, the party targets twenty or thirty notables in each borough and township as key contacts, including both party and nonparty figures. Most people placed on these lists, recruited to the party, or elected to the local party committee are drawn from prescribed social categories—officials, educators, businessmen, doctors, workers, soldiers, and women.

*Local party politics.* One can hardly overstate the impact of the party on local politics. The party designed the political system, staffed it with its own managers, and redistributed resources among the contenders. It picks the candidates, runs the elections, and by many accounts recasts the votes when necessary. Much of this modus operandi, including the general theme of political artifice overriding natural society, follows directly from Sun Yat-sen's formulation of tutelary democracy for China. However, political machines work similarly in many parts of the world, including parts of the United States. On balance, the system has been remarkably successful in maximizing political control while minimizing overt popular dissatisfaction. Regrettably, such an evaluation ignores "what might have been" under other political auspices.

If party control were absolute, at this point we would pack up our notebooks and depart the field. However, different levels and factions within the party sometimes disagree over local candidates and electoral strategies. Even after the party makes up its mind, it does not always have its way. The capital city of Taipei proved one of the most difficult localities to control. The intraparty politics surrounding the nomination for mayor in 1964—the last such contest, because the post was made appointive in 1967—illustrates the complexities.

Huang Ch'i-jui, the Taipei lawyer who had recaptured the mayorship for the Kuomintang in 1957, had been reelected in 1960. However, early in his second term he was removed from office for corruption, and the party appointed as acting mayor Chou Pai-lien, an influential Wan-hua doctor. A member of the provincial party committee, Chou was in a good position not only to stabilize city party affairs, but also to seek the 1964 mayoral nomination for himself. However, his efforts to replace Huang supporters within the city government soon brought him into conflict with the Taipei city party chairman, Loh Cheng-liang. Reportedly this conflict was exacerbated by Chou's condescending treatment of Loh, whom, as a member of the provincial party committee, he outranked.

In August 1962, elections were held within the party to select the more than ninety representatives from local party organizations who would in turn elect the fifteen-member Taipei city party committee. Regarded as a precursor to the mayoral and assembly nominations, these elections attracted much interest. Three groups of approximately equal strength emerged. The first was the incumbent city party committee headed by Loh, a slate of fifteen representatives selected by the provincial party headquarters and responsible to it. The second was the party committee of the city government, headed by Chou. Though it officially had 30 representatives, only ten proved reliable, forcing Chou to take his campaign to the floor of the convention. The third was the "Kiang-Che" group of mainlanders from Kiangsu and Chekiang. This group, which controlled 21 votes and reputedly was the strongest and most united of the three, reflected the large number of people from the lower Yangtze in the city party membership. In the end, Loh's incumbent city party committee won eleven of the fifteen seats on the new committee.

Although Loh had done a good job, he resigned his chairmanship to rejoin the central party headquarters as the 1964 mayoral election approached, perhaps because he could not work with Chou. He was replaced by P'eng Teh, a high-ranking Hakka official in the central party headquarters, who knew both Taipei politics and Chou quite well. P'eng had competed for the party nomination for mayor in 1954, and consequently his job as party chairman was complicated by rumors that he was seeking the 1964 nomination for himself. Allegedly fearing P'eng's competition, Chou did not cooperate fully with P'eng in backing party candidates for the provincial assembly in April 1963, and their relationship began to deteriorate. P'eng requested party permission to resign, partly to dramatize his objection to his superiors' plans to renominate Chou—for whose campaign he did not want to be responsible—and partly to free himself for the nomination. In the end, P'eng and his vice-chairman resigned two days after the party announced the nomination of Chou for mayor.

After failing to persuade P'eng's vice-chairman to become chairman, the central party headquarters sent in the high-ranking mainlander Wang Ch'eng-chang to serve as acting chairman and to put the Taipei city party committee back in shape. Wang, originally from Kiangsi and a graduate of the sixth class of the Whampoa Military Academy, had served in various military posts and as chief of the Taiwan provincial police bureau. Wang had so many local contacts that, until the announcement of Chou's nomination, he himself had been considered a viable candidate. Wang claimed the support of ten groups within the city—party members, Fukienese, military families, various associations, sports groups, national defense personnel, civil defense mobilization units, policemen, militia units, and Wang surname groups—that totaled 370,000 votes. Nevertheless, he was unable to elect Chou. Former nonparty mayor Kao Yü-shu scored an upset victory.

As a replacement for Wang, the central and provincial levels of the party had evidently pushed for Lu Ch'i-huang, a Taiwanese who had headed the education department of the Taipei municipal government and had since run the fourth section of the provincial party headquarters (in charge of elections). However, the city party establishment objected that Lu had been in the party only three years and did not have sufficient experience to handle the contentious politicians in the Taipei government and assembly. This group wanted a tough mainlander. In the end, the party appointed Liang Yung-chang, a native of Shantung who had long been involved in the Shanghai labor movement and had since worked for the Kuomintang central committee. In preparation for future elections, Liang reportedly registered thousands of absentee voters, including many soldiers on duty. However, he proved not smooth enough to maneuver among all the factions in Taipei, and not respected enough by party members to elicit cooperation between the city government and assembly. For much of the time since Taipei city's elevation to provincial status in 1967, the party chairman has been Lin Ting-sheng, a Taiwanese industrial magnate and member of the party central committee.

Several themes emerge from this narrative. One is the party's dilemma over whether to manage local systems through outsiders who are above local conflicts but lack local support, or through insiders who have local support but drag the party into local conflicts. A second is the interlocking of appointments and the exchange of personnel among the central, provincial, and local party organizations. A third is the disagreement between levels over candidates and strategies, with the grand designs of the center generally prevailing over the objections of the party's local representatives. An important recent example of this third theme occurred in the fall of 1977. To maximize the continuity of local leadership, Premier Chiang Ching-kuo and his adviser Li Huan decided that the party would support all incumbent Kuomintang local executives who wished a second term, regardless of how unpopular they had become. As a result, the party lost four of twenty local executiveships, including two of the four remaining county-level municipalities on the island (Taichung and Tainan). Nonparty observers claim that the nonparty candidate also won in Kaohsiung municipality—after Taipei, the largest municipality on the island—but that the Kuomintang could not countenance "another Taipei." Li Huan is currently in political oblivion.

*The regional elite.* The official managers of the regional political system occasionally require assistance from members of the unofficial regional elite. Although hardly disinterested umpires of the region's politics, wealthy and prominent families do frequently respond to party requests for assistance in resolving local problems. They may instruct their lieutenants in the government or assembly to be less intransigent, urge their employees to vote for party candidates, or contribute to particular campaigns or projects. To keep local politicians in line they may dole out expensive favors such as trips, loans, and jobs. They may serve in neighboring localities, or move to the regional central city, demonstrating the regional scale of their reputations and operations. Particularly after protracted local political turmoil, the party sometimes prevails upon respected figures to emerge from private life or return to their localities to serve as local officials because no other suitably prestigious candidates are available. Thus unofficial managers do sometimes assume political office, but with an air of noblesse oblige rather than as nouveaux arrivés, and with little of the uncertainty about the success of their campaigns that surrounds the true contender.

To afford the time and expense required by the role of manager, a family must have a sound economic base that can survive the successive transformations of Taiwan's rapidly modernizing economy. Yet to be motivated to perform this role, the family must either need local political connections to do business or be in some way economically hostage to the Nationalist regime. To exert influence the family must have a significant regional political reputation and many good personal connections with both the Nationalist elite and local politicians. Yet so as not to threaten the Kuomintang, the family's reputation should not be preeminent or island-wide, and its personal connections should be neither too numerous nor too highly organized. To rise above the role of contender, a family should have been socially established for more than one generation and probably should have emerged at least by the end of the Japanese period. Yet it must not have been so committed to Ch'ing values as to have resisted Japanese modernization, nor so pro-Japanese as to have appeared anti-Nationalist. In order to sustain so many functions, it must have had strong patriarchs of long tenure and able sons in each generation. Yet the patriarchs must have been farsighted, and the sons must have been willing to cooperate both with their fathers and with each other. Obviously not many families met all these conditions; and from the Kuomintang's viewpoint, those that did often lost in pliability what they gained in eminence. We shall explore three potential sources of unofficial managers: Ch'ing gentry who survived the Japanese period, émigré Taiwanese who returned to their native localities after 1945, and businessmen who emerged under the Japanese and flourished under the Nationalists.

Some local gentry were too pro-Japanese to continue as local managers. An example in northern Taiwan was the Hokkien policeman and businessman Chien Lang-san, who had kept progressive Taiwanese political movements out of T'ao-yüan county for years. The Nationalists replaced him with a family of Hakka doctors, the Wus. More promising candidates were local gentry who had demanded some autonomy from the Japanese. Although at first the party could not govern without such gentry, it feared their independent political reputations and wished to replace them with returnee Taiwanese or apolitical businessmen as soon as possible. The most prominent such gentry family in northern Taiwan—from the agricultural heartland of the Taipei basin—were the Pan-ch'iao Lins.

The largest landholders in northern Taiwan at the end of the Ch'ing dynasty, the Lins transferred their energies during the Japanese period into banking and commerce in Taipei city and abroad. Of the five branches of the Lin family, only the first and the fifth—the *pen* and *yüan* branches—had sons. These two branches cooperated closely in business under the joint name of Lin Pen-yüan. However the *pen* branch was relatively pro-Japanese, whereas the *yüan* branch, headed by Lin Po-shou, supported moderate Taiwanese demands for greater local self-government. In a straw poll for Taipei prefectural assemblymen conducted in 1932, Lin Po-shou came in first among 24 candidates. After 1945, land reform and, more importantly, bank reform put many Lin assets under government control, but the family remained wealthy shareholders in many major national companies and did not have to lobby for a living. Consequently, like many of the pre-1945 Taiwanese elite, the Lins did not serve as political managers for the Kuomintang, but rather as would-be opposition managers. Lin Po-shou returned to Taiwan permanently only in the mid-1950's and never reentered politics himself. However, he helped finance Kao Yü-shu's antiparty campaign for mayor of Taipei in 1954, aided the independent Taiwanese journal *Wen-hsing*, and backed the unsuccessful movement to form an opposition political party in 1960. Along with members of other prominent gentry families, one of the *pen* branch of the Lin family was appointed by the Nationalists to the provincial historical commission—a curator of the island's political past but not of its political future.

A more productive source of political managers, particularly in the early years of Nationalist rule, were Taiwanese who had left the island during the Japanese period and joined the Nationalist cause on the mainland. There are many types of returnees, with correspondingly different political fates. Some had retained contact with anti-Japanese political movements in Taiwan, and many of these returned to serve as a bridge between the Nationalists and indigenous regional elites. Although some had local political contacts, none had local political bases. And few were rich: had they wealthy families on Taiwan, they would not have had to pursue opportunities on the mainland. However, it was easy to assign them an income from the Japanese and Taiwanese assets that they were needed to manage. The most prominent returnee of this sort in Taipei county was the financier and politician Yu Mi-chien.

Yu was originally from a modest family in Nei-hu township just north of Taipei city, and he had studied in Japan. Though he served as a financial administrator in Hunan and Hupeh, he visited Taiwan during the Japanese period to speak on political reform. In 1945, he was assigned to receive banking operations from the Japanese. From this very influential position—among returnees then in Taiwan, second only to that of the scholar-diplomat Huang Ch'ao-ch'ing—he was able to become the appointed executive of Taipei county during 1946. In 1947 he succeeded Huang as the appointed mayor of Taipei city when Huang took over management of the more important provincial assembly and First Commercial Bank. However, Yu did not survive politically the transition from repressive governor Ch'en Yi to reform governor Wu Kuo-chen. Yu's political empire building alarmed the Kuomintang, and his economic corruption disgusted the public. For the first popularly elected mayor of Taipei, the party chose the journalist and patriot, Wu San-lien instead. In an attempt to regain his political influence, Yu later won control of the Taiwan Paper Company, one of the "four big companies" composed of factories inherited from the Japanese, and the T'ai-an Insurance Company, in which many important Taiwanese businessmen and politicians were involved. He also organized eight voluntary associations for such things as education, culture, charity, aviation, swimming, and tourism. Although his own political fortunes nevertheless continued to decline, many of the Taiwanese whom he had recruited from regional elites around the island (including Chiang Ching-kuo's later principal bridge to the Taiwanese elite, Hsieh Tung-min) became managers not only of local but also of provincial and national politics.

In the long run, however, the most useful source of local political managers proved to be the businessmen and industrialists who benefited from the spectacular economic development engineered under Nationalist rule. Before 1945, undisputed local prominence in the northern cities of Taipei and Keelung was hard for a Taiwanese businessman or professional to achieve, since the Japanese dominated large-scale business; and after 1945, competition among the Taiwanese themselves remained intense. In Taipei city, for example, a real manager emerged only in the 1970's—industrialist Lin Ting-sheng. Lin's father had gotten his start doing engineering and construction work for the Japanese government; and much of the family's plant and equipment after 1945 consisted of Japanese property that technically should have passed to the Nationalist government. Although best known on Taiwan for consumer products such as electric fans and refrigerators, the Lins' Ta-t'ung company is really the General Motors of Taiwan, with involvement in industries vital to the Nationalist state such as metallurgy and machine tools, electrical and electronic equipment, and high technology research. A member of the Kuomintang central committee, Lin reluctantly assumed the job of riding herd on obstreperous nonparty mayor Kao Yü-shu, first as local party chairman and then as speaker of the city assembly. Lin is the perfect local political manager—rich enough to do the job, vulnerable enough to have to do it—and a paradigmatic case of the alliance of Nationalist state power and Taiwanese industrial wealth.

In northern Taiwan the principal industrial resource is minerals—much coal and some gold. The two most frequently mentioned backstage managers of Taipei county politics, the Yens and the Lis, are based in the mining town of Jui-fang, located in the mountains between Taipei and Keelung. Their mines and employees, however, are scattered all over the northern region, providing them with influence and votes in many localities. Yen Yün-nien had received monopoly rights to exploit minerals in part of Jui-fang early in the Japanese period. Subsequently, the various branches of the Yen family displayed an unusual degree of trust and cooperation. When Yen Yün-nien died, family leadership passed to his brother Yen Kuo-nien, whom the Japanese governor-general appointed to his highest consultative council. When Yen Kuo-nien died in 1937, family leadership passed back to the first brother's son, Yen Ch'ing-hsien, who has firmly retained it ever since. The Yens also displayed unusual business acumen. With the commercial skills they developed in mining, transporting, and selling their coal, they diversified into freight shipping, passenger transportation, insurance, and, later, manufacturing. After 1945, Yen Ch'ing-hsien joined not the Kuomintang but rather the Social Democratic Party, serving as its party chairman for Keelung city. He was elected a provincial assemblyman in 1947, but resigned after the Nationalist suppression of the Taiwanese demonstrations of February 1947. He finally joined the Kuomintang in 1959, but declined to assume local office as the party wished. His son and younger brother participated in Keelung city politics, but none entered politics in Taipei county, where their major business interests lie. Nevertheless, they backed some Kuomintang candidates from behind the scenes, including county magistrate Su Ch'ing-po (discussed below). Though not an active manager of party opposition like Lin Po-shou,

Yen was at best a reluctant manager for the Kuomintang, preferring to manage instead his already well-established business empire.

The Lis, unlike the Yens, emerged only late in the Japanese period. Originally employees of the Yens, they acquired coal mines of their own and expanded—not as aggressively as the Yens—into transportation and banking. The Lis were strongly anti-Japanese: two of seven brothers were tortured to death by the Japanese after all seven were arrested during the Second World War for alleged connections with the Kwangsi warlord Pai Chung-hsi. The eldest brother, Li Chien-hsing, ran the family for several decades, maintaining good relations with Chiang Kai-shek. Li remained out of politics himself, but assigned his less able younger brother Li Chien-ho to six terms as provincial assemblyman to advance the family's business interests. When Li Chien-ho died in 1971, two of his sons sought the post, but Li Chien-hsing ruled against both of them in favor of the son of the fourth brother. Despite some electoral successes, however, there have been long periods when both the county executive and the assembly speaker were people ostensibly unacceptable to the Lis. One of their problems was finding suitable candidates. Another of Li Chien-ho's sons served several terms as a county assemblyman, became county assembly speaker, and then graduated to the national legislature: evidently he was not considered able enough to be county executive. The Lis' in-law Hsien Wen-ch'eng, a prominent Hsin-chuang politician in the Japanese period, returned from the national assembly to be elected county executive in 1960, but died soon after his election. The Lis' political protege Tai Te-fa became too successful. A brilliant Jui-fang doctor elected county assembly speaker and then county executive, Tai founded a third Jui-fang faction of his own. Clearly the Lis, though the most cooperative members of the regional elite, themselves verged perilously close to being mere contenders, the subject to which we now turn.

## *Contenders*

As noted, contenders compete for the highest offices accessible through local elections. Information about contenders is voluminous though uneven, and has not yet been exploited systematically. Local executives are the most conspicuous and most discussed.

Though constrained by low budgets and provincial supervision, local executives—and to a lesser extent assembly speakers—dispose of significant patronage. In a largely inert system of public administration, their abilities and preferences can have a significant impact on local development. For political or economic entrepreneurs who have not quite "made it" at the local level, acting as local speaker or executive can advance and consolidate their local gains and serve as a springboard to wider operations. For professional and business entrepreneurs who have already "arrived," however, service as local speaker or executive may be a tax imposed by the Kuomintang in return for opportunities granted earlier. Both types of incumbent gain prestige—though one must ask whether the already successful entrepreneur would pay such a high price for these honors if he had a completely free choice. Nevertheless, a sense of public service often animates such local officials.

*Changing ladders of success.* Contenders may come from either the local or regional elite, depending on the stage of their careers and on the prominence of their families. A typical self-made politician might begin his career with election to the representative body in a borough or township, then serve his community as speaker, and, finally, as executive. During this time, our man-on-the-rise would continue his business or professional career, since community politics does not provide a livelihood, let alone the resources needed for more ambitious political efforts. His next step would be to serve as an ordinary city or county assemblyman for a term or two, hoping to come to the attention of regional power brokers.

Spotting an attractive candidate with the factional connections needed at the moment—or, under Chiang Ching-kuo's more recent strategy, a candidate with no factional connections at all—the party might nominate him for deputy speaker of his city or county assembly. If he were not a party member, this invitation might carry with it the stipulation that he join the party before or after his election. After he had served a term or two as deputy speaker, the party might run him for speaker, particularly if, as under the old rules of the game, it was time for a change in faction. He would then serve as assembly speaker for two terms to balance a government executive of an opposing faction. The party might then nominate him for government executive. Barring mishap, he would be elected and serve for two terms. Since this is a full-time job, he would have to curtail his business or professional activities drastically, leaving them in the hands of family or associates. After that he could run for provincial assembly, or return to a now greatly expanded private career.

This logical progression reflects the stratification of these posts in people's minds, and is, indeed, both the most frequent pattern of circulation through the political system and the career line encouraged by the Kuomintang. However, we should note some significant exceptions and changes. For example, in the late 1940's and the early 1950's local executiveships were largely restricted to Taiwanese who had returned to the island under Nationalist auspices, or to mainlanders with political or security-service backgrounds.

Another departure from the typical career occurs when someone who has already become a provincial assemblyman or an island-wide businessman climbs back down a rung to occupy a leading post at the city or county level. This is most likely when the Kuomintang is in trouble in a particular city or county and needs an impressive figure to help restore control. An important recent example in northern Taiwan is the nationally prominent Taiwanese industrialist Lin Ting-sheng, who served as speaker of the Taipei city assembly. Evidently he was brought in at party insistence to counterbalance the obstreperous nonparty Taiwanese mayor of Taipei, Kao Yü-shu, and to be groomed himself as a possible future candidate for mayor. Perhaps another example from northern Taiwan is the established Hokkien businessman and provincial assemblyman Ch'en Ch'ang-shou, who returned to serve as the executive to T'ao-yüan county. For some years T'ao-yüan had been subject to incessant campaigns to recall speakers and executives, and the party may have had difficulty finding a Hokkien of sufficient standing to serve as county executive.

In the early 1970's the ladder of success began to shorten as Chiang Ching-kuo reached down for young and educated Taiwanese with minimal factional associations. Good examples of such politicians in northern Taiwan are Shao En-hsin, Chang Feng-hsü, Hsü Hsin-chih, and Ch'en Cheng-hsing, who were the executives of Taipei county, Taipei city, T'ao-yüan county, and Keelung city, respectively. It is too early to tell the extent of this shift from factional to "good government" candidates. For example, the Taipei county executive in the early 1970's, Shao En-hsin, was a career official in the provincial government who had headed the civil affairs department in both Kaohsiung and Taipei counties. Though he would appear to have been more a professional civil servant than a local politician, he came from the city of San-ch'ung in Taipei county, the largest single source of local political opposition to the previous county executive, Su Ch'ing-po. A second example is found in T'ao-yüan county. In the early 1970's the county executive was Wu Po-hsiung, whose father, a Hakka, was county executive in the early 1960's. His incumbency directly continues the classic alternation between Hakka and Hokkien incumbents in T'ao-yüan.

The late 1970's have seen more and more nonparty political careers of the sort pioneered by Kao Yü-shu in Taipei city. Traditionally, businessmen bent on furthering their economic interests through a political career within the Kuomintang have found the backroom politics of the provincial assembly the most useful arena for influencing both the allocation of scarce resources and the regulation of economic activity. Such politicians are probably convenient for the Kuomintang because their business interests are vulnerable to just these allocations and regulations. Opposition politicians attempting to make a political point, however, generally find local executiveships the most useful posts, particularly in major metropolitan areas. Such nonparty politicians have often been professional people—doctors, teachers, journalists, lawyers, or engineers—with high prestige, many clients, and little dependence on government economic policy. Other independents are renegades from the Kuomintang. Younger politicians, for example, sometimes become impatient with step-by-step promotions within the party and, when denied the party nomination they desire, run anyway. Since they are then expelled from the party for violating discipline, they automatically become nonparty candidates. Four independent candidates—including one editor of the antiestablishment *Taiwan Political Review*, a journal suppressed by the government in 1975 after only five months of publication—won local executiveships in November 1977. Their success may further weaken party discipline, resulting in more independent candidacies and more nonparty local executives in the future.

*A typical political career.* A good example of the career typical for most regions of Taiwan in the past thirty years is furnished by Su Ch'ing-po, executive of Taipei county for much of the 1960's. Su was born in 1921 in the industrial suburb of Nan-kang, just east of Taipei city. He came from a poor family and received little formal education. After Taiwan's retrocession he worked as a low-level employee of the provincial railway bureau. In 1950 he won election as a representative to the Nan-kang borough assembly, with the ambition, he said, of securing running water and a middle school for that community. While in office he worked for a transportation company, rising to the position of general manager and making a good reputation in business circles. He became associated with the Tan-shui politician Pai Chin-ch'uan, who was also in the transportation business. In 1954 he ran for Taipei county assembly and won; Pai became speaker of the assembly. Su continued to rise in the business world, gradually becoming involved with more and more companies in higher and higher positions.

In 1958 Su was reelected to the county assembly and immediately ran into his first major piece of political luck. The Kuomintang was unable to choose between two candidates for speaker, and turned to Su as a compromise. Pai, much to his embarrassment, ended up as deputy to his former protégé. Nevetheless, with both his business and political fortunes declining, Pai was magnanimous in defeat and continued to support Su. In the meantime, partly because of bad relations between Su's sponsor, Pai, and Li Chien-ho, head of the influential coal-mining family mentioned earlier, Su gradually became aligned with the rival Yen family.

After serving two terms as assembly speaker, Su was lucky once again. Li Chien-ho's son-in-law Hsieh Wen-ch'eng, elected county executive in 1960, died suddenly during his first term in office, opening up the nomination for county executive a term earlier than expected. Perhaps because Li Chien-ho did not have another candidate, the Kuomintang turned to Su, by this time vice-chairman of the county party committee. Despite some complications during the election—a party member named Lin Shih-nan ran for the post in violation of party discipline—Su won handily. His first term was fairly successful, and it was marked by the qualities that were simultaneously his strength and weakness: determination to get things done and frankness in criticizing those he found wanting. Allegedly he showed some favoritism toward Nan-kang in the allocation of development projects.

Su's difficulties began when he sought the party's nomination for a second term as county executive. This nomination was hotly debated for several reasons. First, Su's dynamic approach to administration had offended people. Second, legitimate doubts about the strength of his electoral base had been raised by Taipei's absorption of Su's old constituencies of Nan-kang and Nei-hu. Third and most important, Li Chien-ho strongly opposed Su and threatened to support a non-party candidate if the party renominated him.

The fight over Su's renomination raged in the county and provincial party committees. Even the central party headquarters was indecisive, fearing embarrassment if the party appeared to "bow to the big families." Indeed, if the party gave in, not only would the Li family become even more obstreperous, but the party would probably lose the election because Su's supporters would defect. In the end, the top officials of the central party headquarters explained the problem to Chiang Kai-shek. Told of the Lis' threat to support a nonparty candidate, Chiang said immediately, "Well, in that case, I support Su." Su eventually obtained the support of the Li family by calling on them in Jui-fang and by touring their coal mines, perhaps to help them save face. He won again.

During his second term, however, Su began slipping from the ladder of political success. The city of San-ch'ung, by far the largest and fastest-growing city in the county, remained a poor relation owing to the central government's decision to concentrate resources on Taipei city. San-ch'ung blamed its plight on the incumbent county executive and launched repeated campaigns to recall him. Matters were not helped by Su's bad relations with San-ch'ung's nonparty mayor, Ch'en Chin-p'ao, or by his efforts to tear down what he considered illegal additions to the transport warehouses of the influential San-ch'ung provincial assemblyman Li Ping-sheng. Su later became embroiled in a similar altercation over a construction project in Hsin-tien; here he tore down additions to a structure five times, as a succession of courts alternately ruled for the construction project and for Su. Meanwhile, he was accused of helping county government personnel, including himself, to obtain land for expensive houses at less than market value. The crowning accusation was that he had illegally purchased many hectares of land in a "new town" project in Taipei county and then, along with other land speculators, inadvertently sabotaged the project by mismanaging relations between the project development corporation and the local population. Under the circumstances, he was happy to retire from politics at the end of his second term as county executive. He later served a term in jail on corruption charges.

One feature of Su's political career deserves a final comment. Although Su was basically a self-made man, he is said to have benefited from his wife's relationships with twelve wealthy and influential "sworn sisters." These women included the leader of the Tan-shui women's association, two wealthy women from Lin-kou, a provincial assemblywoman from Ying-ko, the wife of a prominent banker from San-hsia, and several wives of prominent local doctors and politicians. Such fictive kinship relationships appear frequently in political coalitions in Taiwan, though they break up rather easily when they are no longer mutually advantageous.

*Independent contenders.* In some respects the most interesting contests for local office are those in which a nonparty candidate upsets the Kuomintang nominee. This has occurred in northern Taiwan, notably in Taipei and Keelung cities and in T'ao-yüan county. There is no doubt that considerable antiparty sentiment exists among both mainlanders and Taiwanese, and that this sentiment is most concentrated in and around the larger cities. Even given this sentiment, however, upsets usually occur only when local Kuomintang politicians cannot agree on who should be nominated for a post or when local party officials become complacent after a series of victories. As noted, Kao Yü-shu, a Japanese-educated engineer with acute political instincts, capitalized on both Taiwanese solidarity and party disunity to upset the Kuomintang candidate for mayor of Taipei in 1954. Only a massive Kuomintang effort, including the alleged miscounting of votes, defeated him in 1957. He withdrew from the race in 1960 when the Kuomintang would not allow him to station observers at polling places to ensure that votes would be properly counted. A concentrated Kuomintang effort in 1960 also succeeded in defeating two nonparty candidates for the provincial assembly for whom Kao had campaigned.

By the 1964 elections, the Kuomintang assumed that Kao, out of office for seven years, was a political has-been. This time they granted his request for poll observers. Capitalizing on the antiparty sentiment he symbolized and encouraging Kuomintang complacency by running a low-key campaign, Kao won again. Before the next election, partly to avoid further humiliation, the Kuomintang elevated Taipei to the status of a nationally administered city with an appointive mayor. President Chiang Kai-shek then shrewdly kept Kao in the post, much to the outrage of Kao's old enemies in the local party machine.

During his tenure, Kao's establishment enemies brought complex impeachment actions against him for alleged misuses of power. Kao's response was to grant an inconspicuous interview to the English-language *China News*, asking the constitutionally sensitive question "Who can impeach the impeachers?" He went on to suggest that "this is not the time for unnecessary trouble." In other words, if at a time when the Republic of China was fighting to maintain international political recognition the Kuomintang wanted to go into fundamental questions of political legitimacy, he was prepared to take the party on. The Chinese-language newspapers never printed this challenge and the impeachment charges faded gradually from the news. Eventually all pending cases were dropped.

In 1972 Chiang Ching-kuo kicked Kao upstairs to the post of minister of communications in the central government and appointed Chang Feng-hsü, a Taiwanese from outside Taipei, as mayor. A wealthy man who had served as executive of rural P'ing-tung county, Chang was as little involved in the politics of Taipei city as it was possible to be. So ended two decades of Kuomintang attempts to manage the city through its own local elite. Taipei has since been headed by fast-rising Taiwanese technocrats: Lin Yang-kang of Nan-tou county, later the appointed governor of Taiwan, and Lee Teng-hui, a former high official of the Joint Commission on Rural Reconstruction.

Taipei has recently produced the first of a younger generation of nonparty politicians, the national legislator K'ang Ning-hsiang. Running in the 1972 elections to increase Taiwanese representation in the Legislative Yüan, K'ang concentrated his campaign in the old Taiwanese neighborhoods of the city from which he comes. Running again in the 1975 elections, he began to widen the locale and the themes of his campaign to attract independent-minded voters of both Taiwanese and mainlander origins, whether party members or not. Although this cost him some votes in his old bailiwick, it gained him many more votes elsewhere in the city, and he again emerged a victor. In his third campaign, in 1978, he downplayed appeals to "Taiwanese separatism" still further in order to broaden his future political base. K'ang's strategy indicates the high political ground that intelligent, young, nonparty politicians are attempting to occupy.[8]

[8] The northern city of Keelung provides another interesting case of the upset of a Kuomintang candidate for mayor. Beginning in the late 1940's, Keelung politics was dominated by Hsieh Kuan-i, a mainlander from Hunan with a background in political and military affairs, whom the Kuomintang appointed mayor of the city. (He may also have been a military and security aide trusted by the highest levels of leadership to undertake the sensitive assignment of watching over the militarily important port of Keelung.) In any case, the Kuomintang nomi-

Local elections in November 1977 revealed significant shifts in the tactics of both establishment and antiestablishment factions. For the first time in the history of local elections in Taiwan, the Kuomintang scheduled elections on the same day for *all* local officials—local executives, Taipei city councilmen, Taiwan provincial assemblymen, community executives, and community councilmen. Ostensibly this was to spare the voters from having to go to the polls for local elections more than once every four years. However, it also decreased the frequency of disruptive campaigns and made it more difficult for independent politicians to assist each other. For their part, nonparty politicians made unprecedentedly bold, shrewd, and effective demands for a fair election. About six weeks before the election, K'ang Ning-hsiang prepared a speech challenging the Kuomintang's approach to local elections. K'ang's draft argued that if the Republic of China is truly a democracy, the party should recognize the legitimacy of rival candidacies and conduct a fair election. At about the same time, the leading Taiwanese intellectual-turned-politician, Hsü Hsin-liang, broke party discipline after being denied party nomination for the executive post in T'ao-yüan county. He entered the race anyway, letting it be known that he feared a demonstration by his supporters if robbed of an obvious victory. More generally, independent Taiwanese politicians collectively challenged the party establishment to live up to its pretensions of electoral democracy or risk international exposure as just another repressive Asian dictatorship. For a regime preoccupied with maintaining the best possible image in world opinion, such exposure would be a high price to pay for a few local election victories.

Evidently Chiang Ching-kuo persuaded K'ang not to deliver his speech, promising a fair election in return. As a result, independents won four of the twenty local executiveships. Hsü Hsin-liang won in T'ao-yüan. Relying on its control of large blocks of local military votes, the Kuomintang had nominated a rather low-key candidate to oppose Hsü in an effort to play down the importance of his can-

---

nated and elected him for an unusual three terms, which ran from 1951 through 1960. During this time he built up a strong political machine that dominated both the city government and city assembly, another arrangement unusual for Taiwanese local politics. However, Hsieh's departure for Taipei in 1960 greatly weakened his machine. The opposing faction within the Kuomintang, the Tsai faction, never had a chance to develop its position in office, and so was unable to field a strong candidate. As a result, in the 1960 election the local leader of a miniscule Democratic Socialist Party, Lin Fang-wang, succeeded in upsetting the Kuomintang Hsieh faction nominee by running up a huge plurality in the poor central city district of Jen-ai in which he lived.

didacy. This strategy failed, however, when the local party was instructed to allow military personnel to vote as they pleased. Many chose not to vote at all, and, deprived of its electoral ploys, the party lost.

### *Publics*

As noted, publics are those groups in the regional political system whose support or opposition in principle determines electoral outcomes among contenders. Exploring the composition and mobilization of publics provides an opportunity to clarify the practical rules of the political game. It also gives some indication of the impact on politics of the historical and social characteristics of particular localities. Finally, it draws attention to relationships between contests for particular political offices and the development of metropolitan regions. Collecting systematic information about publics would require prying into campaign organization and finances, analyzing election returns, and surveying public opinion. Although field research on publics has not been possible for this paper, some insight into the nature of such followings and audiences can be derived from anecdotes about particular campaigns.

*Size of constituency and strategy of control.* Because electoral districts and ways of counting votes are different for different offices, the relevant constituencies also differ. Party nominations to the local party committee, for example, must be ratified by the party electors in the locality. Assembly speakers are elected by the members of the assembly, though the outcome is virtually always decided by the nomination of the local party committee. Local executives are elected directly by the locality-at-large, though here again nomination by the local party committee is usually decisive. Provincial assemblymen are also elected by the locality-at-large, though they tend to be identified with parts of localities (with groupings of districts in the city, and with groupings of townships and boroughs in the county). County assemblymen are elected within smaller districts, usually six or seven per locality.

In different contests, then, contenders must address different constituencies, and the characteristics of the local population must filter through different aggregation processes. In general, the smaller the constituency, the easier it is for the party to control the outcome. Presumably this explains the party's almost perfect record for elections of speakers within local assemblies. In a rare exception that proves the rule, the Kuomintang candidate Tsai Ta-san lost the race for speaker in the T'ao-yüan county assembly in 1958. However, the party forced the winning candidate Wu Wen-ch'uan to resign through one of T'ao-yüan's notorious recall campaigns and renominated Tsai to run in the supplementary election. Immediately before the election, the Kuomintang took more than two dozen party assemblymen on a sightseeing trip to I-lan, and treated a half-dozen party assemblymen to a visit to the resort town of Pei-t'ou. All returned in a docile mood, and this time Tsai won, 34 to 4.

However, even assemblymen occasionally stage token demonstrations of disgruntlement at party discipline. They may, for example, turn up late or abstain on the first ballot in critical elections. During a particularly complicated election for speaker of the Keelung city assembly in 1964, fifteen assemblymen formed a "sworn brotherhood" and demanded that the Kuomintang nominate their "third brother," Wang Li-ku. Although many of the fifteen were Kuomintang members, they were not able to force the party to give in to them—evidently because one of their number was Liao Han-hua, a longtime enemy of the Kuomintang in Keelung. Since a nonparty candidate had upset the Kuomintang nominee for mayor of Keelung in both 1960 and 1964, the party could not afford any further erosion of its control. In this case, despite the party's best efforts, the "group of fifteen" refused to come to the assembly chamber for the election until the party candidate, Lin T'ai-lang, went to fetch them by automobile. Even then the fifteen cast blank ballots in the first vote, after which Wang Li-ku withdrew, finally allowing Lin T'ai-lang to win on the second ballot. The assembly remained out of party control through the rest of the term, since Lin was outnumbered by fifteen to eleven. In the next election of a speaker, in 1968, only many hours of persuasion on the night before the election—by the local party chairman, a representative of the provincial party committee, and the mayor of Keelung—persuaded Wang Li-ku not to run again.

At the opposite extreme in terms of manipulability are the at-large elections for local executives. The party can bring massive pressure to bear on potential candidates, and it can see that organized publics under its control—principally public employees such as bureaucrats, educators, and servicemen—vote for the party candidate. However, the difficulty of controlling several hundred thousand votes is demonstrated by the remarkable pluralities run up by relatively unknown nonparty candidates on the first ballots of local elections. The Kuomintang's recourse in these cases has been to go to work on the non-party contender himself, attempting to persuade him not to contest the run-off. A successful example of this approach occurred in the 1951 election of Mei Ta-fu as Taipei county executive, after the initially strong showing of Liao Fu-pen, who was persuaded to withdraw. In later elections for the same post, the party appears to have kept its candidate in office by keeping the better-known doctor Li Ch'iou-yuan off the ballot entirely. Li found himself the object of malpractice suits and prosecutions timed to make him legally ineligible to run at election time.

A more systematic way of eliminating undesirable contenders and the opposition that they might arouse is to raise the qualifications for particular offices. This approach has the constructive effect of removing from the political stage many old local leaders and the rivalries that they represent. For example, the son of coal magnate Li Chien-ho might have run for executive of Taipei county in 1968 to oppose the Kuomintang's incumbent, but he did not meet the new educational requirements imposed that year. Changes in election regulations can result overnight in almost generational shifts in the characteristics of candidates.

Finally, when efforts to influence the candidates and the voters have failed, the party has gone to work on the votes themselves. For example, when it became obvious that Kao Yü-shu was winning the 1954 mayoral election in Taipei, election officials stopped the vote count midway on election night. Hurried consultations then took place among local election officials, the central party headquarters, and the country's political leaders. Allegedly what prevented the party from recounting the votes on this occasion was that American observers already knew the real outcome. In 1964 Kao pooled the poll observers he was allowed with those allowed Li Chien-shan, a relative of Taipei county's Li Chien-ho, whom Kao had registered as a dummy candidate for this purpose. He borrowed an auditorium in which he trained his corps of observers, and on election day he fielded an army of runners to feed them so that they could stay on the job.

Kao's 1964 campaign also illustrates how an experienced campaigner in Taiwan recruits the support of community leaders and their followings. Using a political tactic that has since been outlawed, Kao took the opportunity of the lunar New Year early in 1964 to invite each of the 450 ward leaders of Taipei city to dinner, one table of twelve every night for six weeks. Since open campaigning was illegal so long before the election, the guests did not discuss politics but simply made polite conversation about the holiday. Presumably the message got across nevertheless. About a hundred mainlanders and military officers who were ward leaders did not accept Kao's invitation, and presumably Kao wrote off their areas as unreliable.

*Ethnicity and politics.* Contests between party and nonparty candidates attract journalistic and scholarly attention because they reflect basic issues in a one-party political system imposed on the Taiwanese population by mainlanders. However, contests between Taiwanese within the Kuomintang also reflect important facts about the island. For example, the party has achieved most of its objectives in both the government and the assembly of T'ao-yüan county, but the politics of this half-Hokkien, half-Hakka area is anything but dull. The basic line of political cleavage is between the Hokkien in the north and the Hakka in the south. Since 1951, T'ao-yüan has had a perfect record of alternation between Hokkien and Hakka county executives at two-term intervals, with a correspondingly perfect record of electing an assembly speaker of opposite ethnicity to balance the county executive. Although this could have happened by accident, presumably it is one of the Kuomintang's prouder accomplishments of political engineering. It should be remembered that even the existence of T'ao-yüan is an artifact of post-war redistricting. Some Hakka would have preferred to merge southern T'ao-yüan with Hsin-chu county, and some Hokkien to merge northern T'ao-yüan with Taipei county; others advocated setting up the two halves of T'ao-yüan as independent counties.

Nevertheless, the persistence of Hakka-Hokkien animosity does not guarantee solidarity within these ethnic groups. Local rivalries within T'ao-yüan county show up among T'ao-yüan, Kuei-shan, and Ta-hsi Hokkien in the north, and among Chung-li, Yang-mei, P'ing-chen, and Lung-tan Hakka in the south. These geographic cleavages within each ethnic group create opportunities for tactical alliances across ethnic boundaries. In the Hokkien north, leaders of Kuei-shan have repeatedly threatened to field their own candidate against the candidate from T'ao-yüan, thus deliberately splitting the Hokkien vote. A similar split among the Hakka has been one of the strategic determinants of T'ao-yüan county politics since 1951. The Wu family, leaders of one of the principal Hakka factions, supported the first

Hokkien candidate for county executive and later undermined other Hakka candidates, including party nominees. Thus the strategic logic of political conflict overrides even such salient social groupings as Hakka and Hokkien. Whatever the costs of "defection," the strategy seems to have worked for the Wus: both father and son have served as county executive and thus form the only such political dynasty in northern Taiwan. One suspects, however, that this is in part a reward bestowed by the Kuomintang. Despite the Wus' occasional harassment of party nominees, they have helped guarantee the Kuomintang control of the county by providing a swing vote largely responsive to party requirements.

Within T'ao-yüan politics the distinction is explicit between politicians who refuse to ally with politicians of opposite ethnicity, referred to as the "diehard" or "old" clique, and those who are willing to do so, referred to as the "open-minded" or "new" clique. Cross-ethnic alliances and even attempts at statesmanlike behavior give rise to accusations of "Hokkien Hakka" and "Hakka Hokkien" against those who sell out their own group. Sometimes the distinctions between strategy and statesmanship and between old and new political styles are difficult to draw. The first Hokkien county executive, Hsu Ch'ung-te, came from near the city of T'ao-yüan. When he allocated many development projects to Hakka Chung-li, was he attempting to promote intergroup solidarity or was he repaying Chung-li for its support? Evidently most T'ao-yüan politicians took the more cynical view: when his Hakka successor Chang Fang-hsieh of Yang-mei treated the Hokkien north with equal magnanimity, he was nearly recalled. The rising young "new style" Hokkien politician Hsü Hsin-chih appointed many young Hakka to government posts after he became county executive and it turned out that some of them were his schoolmates and "sworn brothers." Was this impartiality or favoritism, people wondered.

Such ethnic crossovers play hob with attempts to maintain strict parity of membership between Hokkien and Hakka on important bodies. For example, in elections to the county party committee in 1962, the party tried to elect four Hokkien, four Hakka, and five mainlanders. Ostensibly the Hakka won five, the Hokkien three, and the mainlanders five seats. However, two of the Hokkien and one of the mainlanders were generally considered pro-Hakka, resulting in the so-called "eight-one-four" committee. This was considered quite a coup for Yeh Han-ch'ing, the Hakka leader who engineered it. As a result, he was able to prevent the reelection to the party committee of the wealthy and powerful Hokkien politician Ch'en Ch'ang-shou, whom the party wished to become vice-chairman. In addition, the Hakka gained significant influence over the nominations of many major county officials in the following two years—provincial assemblymen, county assembly speaker, county executive, and chairmen of both the farmers' and irrigation associations, among others. The Hokkien position was further weakened in 1961–64 by the fact that the ostensibly Hokkien speaker of the county assembly, Yu Yung-shan, was considered a "Hokkien member of the Hakka clique." The Hakka occupied the county executiveship but the Hokkien did not really control the assembly speakership as the party's strategy of factional balance required.

*Sociospatial processes and electoral outcomes.* The most simple and obvious sociospatial process influencing Taiwan's elections is the "locality effect."[9] Political cooperation is more likely among people living near each other than among those living far apart. Different spatial scales involve different social relationships—coresident kinship, neighborhood interaction, common village interests, township solidarity, or multitownship coalitions are all examples.

Elections within Taipei city display locality effects. Candidates from historically defined communities within the city tend to carry their own communities even against very popular opponents. Election returns from Kao Yü-shu's successive campaigns suggest that his opponents carried their own communities, despite Kao's city-wide reputation. Unfortunately, detailed analysis of election returns would not be very illuminating sociologically if the returns have been edited as massively as alleged.

Much of Taipei county politics—and politics elsewhere in Taiwan—is organized around the groupings of two or three townships and boroughs that normally form the electoral districts for provincial assemblymen. Natural units of Taiwanese society during the Ch'ing, and administrative units under the Japanese, these groupings appear to have a historical resonance that makes them effective units for aggregating communities in competitions with other parts of the region. On this hypothesis, county politics becomes a process of coalition building, ticket balancing, circulation of office, and balance

[9] "Locality effects" were first extensively discussed in the political science literature in Key 1950, where they were referred to as "friends-and-neighbors" effects. I adopt the more general term to leave open the question of the nature and scale of the social processes at work.

of power among these contending units. It may be the complexity of this process in the absence of a simplifying ethnic division that prevents any simple spatial pattern from emerging in Taipei county politics.

On a still larger spatial scale, locality effects can extend across related townships in adjacent counties or municipalities. When the nephew of the late independent mayor of Keelung ran unsuccessfully for mayor in 1965, Keelung residents criticized him for bringing people in from Taipei county to help with his campaign. Locals said they did not need outsiders to tell them how to run Keelung politics. Nevertheless, the mineral mines and labor force of the Yen and Li families (which make the families a power in Taipei county politics) straddle the Taipei-Keelung border, making the families influential in Keelung politics. For example, the Lis opposed Hsieh Ch'ing-yun, the party candidate for Keelung mayor in 1964, causing him to lose in the Keelung townships near Jui-fang and consequently to lose the election as well. Ch'en Cheng-hsiung, the vigorous young Taiwanese recruited by Chiang Ching-kuo to run for mayor of Keelung in 1972, came from a poor coal-mining family in this border area. His basic campaign strategy was the exhausting yet successful one of walking through every community in Keelung shaking hands with as many people as possible. This was an attempt to bypass traditional community leaders and extend the "friends-and-neighbors" effect directly to the people of the entire municipality.

A second sociospatial process affecting electoral outcomes is regional modernization. In post-1945 Taiwan this has meant increased concentration of population in cities, increased industrial employment, and the emergence of metropolitan regions. The larger cities have dealt the Kuomintang its most conspicuous electoral upsets: between 1951 and 1977, non-Kuomintang politicians in the five largest cities have served twelve of 37 mayoral terms, whereas in the same period non-Kuomintang politicians have served only seven of 128 county executive terms. The correlation between urbanization and opposition seems obvious. The central government has responded by taking over direct administration of the two largest cities (Taipei in 1967 and Kaohsiung in 1979) and by making their mayors appointed rather than elected officials.

Regional political managers themselves characterize most local political units in terms of an implicit sequence of regional development: agricultural localities relatively untouched by urbanization and industrialization; "half-agricultural, half-industrial" localities; and industrial localities already almost fully developed. Though these categories are most frequently used in characterizing different kinds of development projects, they have implications for electoral strategy as well. The regional elite believe that complex industrial areas are difficult to administer and that relatively mobile urban electorates are difficult to control. No doubt these experienced administrators are aware of many fine distinctions among the communities with which they deal, but the changing proportion of industry to agriculture is how they categorize communities to the outsider and, evidently, to themselves.

Both establishment and antiestablishment advocates of greater Taiwanese political participation have argued that industrialization and urbanization have made the Taiwanese so prosperous and sophisticated that mere "tutelary" democracy is no longer either feasible or appropriate. Nonparty politicians attribute their 1977 victories to the independence of mind of the well-educated young people who make up an increasing proportion of the population and to the ease of reaching this group in urban areas through mass campaign rallies. Since local self-government began, the population of Taiwan has nearly tripled, the proportion living in cities has nearly doubled, and the occupational structure has been completely transformed. It would be remarkable, then, if the limited number of organizational channels and factional networks on which the Kuomintang has relied to get out the vote could continue to dominate completely such a rapidly expanding and drastically changing social field.

A final explanation for the apparent concentration of support for nonparty candidates in the cities is the negative public reaction to Kuomintang attempts at control. As one experienced informant developed this "iatrogenic" argument, people in general—and perhaps the Chinese in particular—are instinctively wary of anyone who exercises unilateral control over them. They resist establishments, back underdogs, and derive satisfaction from influencing the future balance of political forces. In Taiwan this inclination need not stem primarily from antagonism to the Nationalist regime, though it may occasionally focus on the Kuomintang, the regime's agent of electoral control. This antiestablishment inclination, though present in the countryside, thrives notably on two characteristics of urban areas: the ready availability of political information, and the contagious transmission of political excitement. Also, residents of the larger cities are more thoroughly exposed to the obvious one-sidedness of the mass media, and therefore display stronger negative reactions. Since few Kuomintang officials are expert practitioners of competitive multiparty politics, an underdog—when his organization eludes party strangulation for the duration of an urban campaign—may, occasionally, win.

The "urbanity" of individual voters does not fully explain the geographic distribution of opposition success and failure, however. Nonparty provincial assemblymen, county assemblymen, and borough and township executives have been elected in many parts of the island, rural as well as urban, agricultural as well as industrial. In fact for all types of local office the proportion of nonparty candidates elected has been larger in the less industrialized southern third of the island than in the more industrialized northern third. Between 1951 and 1964 (the last mayoral election in Taipei), Tainan and Taipei cities ranked first and second among Taiwan's 21 counties and municipalities in electing nonparty candidates to the four principal types of elective office. However, these two cities are followed by Yün-lin, Chia-i, T'ai-tung, Kaohsiung, Tainan, and I-lan counties, most of which are among the least developed localities on the island. Early industrializing Taipei county and Keelung city (both in the north) ranked eleventh and twelfth, whereas the island's major center of heavy industry, Kaohsiung city (in the south), ranked seventeenth.

These findings suggest the relevance of a third set of sociospatial processes, with greater historical time depth, greater geographic size, and greater organizational scale. Attention shifts from the characteristics of publics back to the interaction of the state and local political elites. Despite the thorough penetration of the island by both the Japanese and Nationalist regimes, the south has remained farthest from Taipei's administrative control and political influence. After the Japanese period, Taiwanese nationalism therefore survived more easily in the central and southern areas of the island than in the north. However, the older central elites have tended to move north, whereas the older southern elites have tended to remain in the south. Thus nationalism and regionalism have combined to give southern politics greater independence from the Kuomintang throughout the postwar period.

In any case, explaining the incidence of nonparty success and failure requires at least as much attention to the organization of elites as to the disposition of voters. Northern and rural voters may be just as willing to vote for nonparty candidates as southern and urban voters—they have enthusiastically supported nonparty candidates when available. However, the Kuomintang may have found it easier to prevent unwanted candidacies in the north and in the countryside. For most of the postwar period, the Kuomintang's strategy has been to control the margin of victory between competing local factions, awarding victory to cooperative local factions in turn. Achieving the necessary balance among factions may have been more difficult where traditional local leaders are more numerous (as perhaps in the south), or where their organizational networks are more dense and complex (as in the cities). In the 1950's and 1960's, opposition victories generally represent either a breakdown in this strategy or a deliberate decision on the part of the Kuomintang to allow a nonparty but cooperative local faction a share of the available offices. Only in the 1970's has the modernity of publics joined the rivalries of contenders as a crucial determinant of electoral outcomes.

A significant example of the recent modernization of publics—and the complexity of analyzing it—is the "Chung-li incident," which occurred in the November 1977 elections. In the town of Chung-li, a local election supervisor allegedly smudged the ballots of an elderly couple voting for Hsü Hsin-liang, thereby invalidating them. The election supervisor maintained, and a government investigation concluded, that all he did was to tell the couple that they had mismarked their ballots, invalidating them themselves. Local supporters of Hsü Hsin-liang got the impression that the Kuomintang was stealing a victory from them, and this touched off a demonstration threatened in the event of any such tampering. Ten thousand citizens of Chung-li poured into the streets, overturned and burned police vans, and burned down the local police station and firehouse. In one sense, the Kuomintang was being punished unfairly for something that—at least in this election—it may not have done. In another sense, of course, the party was reaping the whirlwind sowed in thirty years of electoral manipulation. In any case, Premier Chiang decided to let the demonstration run its course rather than to suppress it by force.

A full explanation of the Chung-li incident requires all three of the sociospatial processes so far discussed. Media commentary on the Chung-li incident focused mainly on the social impact of recent rapid industrialization. Factories, spreading south from Taipei, attracted young people from the countryside. Separated from family discipline, footloose on the town, and sometimes unable to obtain the kinds of jobs they had hoped for, these new urban immigrants seized a political occasion to express their personal frustration. Although this is probably relevant, it does not explain the extent of public involvement and the pointedly political nature of the demonstrators' targets.[10] Chung-li is the traditional capital of the Hakka in southern T'ao-yüan; Hsü Hsin-liang was a Hakka candidate; and his campaign included the covert slogan "Hakka unite!" Thus a "locality effect" helps explain the scale of mass mobilization. Southern T'ao-yüan contains seven major military installations, and block voting by servicemen has been a mainstay of Kuomintang electoral dominance in T'ao-yüan; the Kuomintang candidate was a former policeman and secret service operative; and rumors that the party might steal the election through vote fraud had been rampant during the campaign. Thus, a popular backlash against the obtrusiveness of the state helps explain the crowd's targets.

In any case, the influence of industrialization and urbanization on the changing role of publics in Taiwan deserves further research that systematically takes into account the socioeconomic experience of individuals, the location of their communities in the process of metropolitan development, and the national political forces to which they are subject.[11]

## *Conclusion*

This paper has explored some of the political roles linking the authoritarian state and Chinese society in Taiwan. The roles examined have been those related to the popular election of local executives and representatives, the principal manifestation of Sun Yat-sen's "tutelary democracy" as practiced under what are considered emergency, wartime conditions. These are, however, only some of the roles and transactions between state and society in Taiwan—one should remember that for other purposes, appointed officials, economic policies, or fiscal transfers might be much more important.

The practice of electoral democracy, precisely because it is an alien ideal embraced by the Chinese only within the past hundred years, provides a sensitive indicator of the changing composition of Tai-

[10] Recent migrants in fact tend to remain politically quiescent: see Nelson 1969; and Huntington & Nelson 1976 (especially pp. 116–58).

[11] For a relevant conceptualization of sociospatial processes in Chinese society, see the pieces by Skinner in Skinner 1977.

wan's political system. In many respects Taiwan continues to rely on the combination of bureaucracy and traditional networks that has been the main feature of Chinese politics for thousands of years. However, in both the actual organization of political behavior and the normative expectations about what politics should involve, bureaucracy and networks now coexist with open competition in the electoral marketplace and with a direct exercise of popular sovereignty. Local self-government is regarded as only one among many necessary and worthwhile activities, but one that needs to be hedged, bolstered, and manipulated so that it does not disrupt other institutions.

The particular form of electoral democracy in Taiwan during the past quarter century has reflected not only the mix of internal political forces, but also the influence of Taiwan's involvement with U.S. defense, its foreign trade, and the communist threat. Nonparty candidates and dissident intellectuals have always hoped that Western embassies and world opinion would restrain the Kuomintang from blatant electoral fraud and from harsh postelectoral retaliation. Since the political fate of the island's seventeen million inhabitants continues to depend on how the United States handles its China problems, Americans have some responsibility to understand not only the very great measure of human rights already achieved in Taiwan, but also the lively political aspirations that remain unfulfilled. As the Republic of China's principal experiment in electoral democracy, local self-government, despite its elusive nature, must occupy a significant place in this understanding.

Local politics in Taiwan also offers comparative political sociology a fascinating case of an authoritarian regime sailing as close to the winds of democracy as it dares, with no intention, however, of changing its course in any fundamental way. Whether the managers of the system can continue to maintain the balance between open competition and covert control that they have sustained with increasing subtlety for thirty years is not only of practical significance for the citizens of Taiwan but also of theoretical significance for students of authoritarian polities.[12]

In this paper a focus on managers, contenders, and publics has been used to study a largely authoritarian system, but the same focus

[12] For systematic characterizations of the alternative developmental paths, see Huntington 1968; and Huntington & Nelson 1976.

suggests questions for totalitarian and democratic systems as well. Totalitarian control is seldom so effective that publics are unable to form opinions, politicians unable to contend, and managers unable to intervene.[13] Despite the commitment of capitalist democracies to the principle of an absolutely free political market, it is questionable whether in practice competitive political institutions survive without some management from above.[14] Though democrats are loath to contemplate the ways managers manipulate, contenders are screened, and publics are constrained in democracies, the appropriate comparative concepts may heighten our awareness of such controls. Such comparative reflection would seem in order before passing judgment on, let alone deciding the fate of, alien political systems.

[13] For a systematic theory of fluctuation in the intensity of totalitarian control and alternation in the requisite mechanisms for managing compliance, see Skinner & Winckler 1969: 410–38.

[14] For a provocative argument that the United States is also "managed" by professional party politicians, see Karp 1974.

Part Two

# Local Organization

# The Structure of Local and Regional Systems

Lawrence W. Crissman

This paper attempts to summarize and integrate what anthropologists and other social scientists have discovered about local and regional organization in Taiwan, a topic that, at its broadest, involves all supradomestic social organization having some basis in locality or territory. There are two major difficulties in producing a coherent discussion of such an enormous subject. First, scholarly work on these aspects of Taiwanese society has been predicated on a wide variety of distinct theoretical and disciplinary orientations, which are not necessarily compatible. Thus, the findings of one researcher must be translated into the terms and the underlying concepts employed by another before even basic comparisons can be made. Most anthropologists do this automatically, and even subconsciously, but it must be done explicitly and consistently if this exercise is to be successful. Secondly, every community or locality that has been described in the literature is in many respects unique, having its own special history shaped by a variety of particularistic situations and events. An attempt to generalize over such diversity could easily yield a "lowest common denominator" that was superficial at best and puerile at worst. The temptation to recite numerous details about particular places, leaving it to the reader to induce some general understanding, will also be resisted. The underlying spatial and hierarchical features of Taiwanese social organization will be elicited at the expense of specific ethnographic details of particular communities and regions, and they will be interpreted in terms of a systematic conceptual apparatus.

The analysis will be based on a structural approach that distinguishes different kinds of social relations on the basis of whether they are mere intuitive guides to behavior, whether they have a moral (or normative) basis, or whether they involve jural specifications and authority.[1] The important analytical task is to correctly identify what kinds of relations structure particular social units, and to determine thereby which are corporate and which are not. Much of Taiwanese local and regional organization is in fact noncorporate—i.e., it is not formally organized at all, and to the extent that it is structured in any definable sense, it is governed by normative relations that do not involve legal obligations or formal sanctions.

Much of the factual material in this paper derives from my 1967–68 dissertation research in Chang-hua *hsien*, which dealt primarily with rural marketing systems (1972, 1973, 1976a), but also included work on marriage patterns (1973, 1976b) and local political factions (1969, 1976c). I concentrated my efforts on the southwestern third of the Chang-hua Plain, which is relatively drier, poorer, and less densely populated than the eastern portion, facts that have some significance for understanding local society. Although I extended my treatment of the central-place system to the entire Plain, I know only the townships of Erh-lin, Fang-yüan, Ta-ch'eng, Chu-t'ang, and P'i-t'ou in any detail, and I am far more familiar with Erh-lin town (a community of 10,000) than with any of the outlying settlements. Moreover, I could not in approximately fifteen months of fieldwork gain the sort of intensive knowledge that other anthropologists have acquired of their communities because I had to acquire extensive and

[1]This theoretical approach is developed in an unpublished paper (Crissman 1975), which is available from me on request. I will summarize briefly. Individual understandings of expected and proper relationships are assumed to underlie a person's decisions about acting in particular ways. The relational structures employed to make sense of social behavior compose grammars that people use to interpret other people's behavior and to decide how they will act towards others. A critically significant element of such grammars is the set of beliefs about who ought to obey whom in what contexts. Such *authority relations* define corporations, or "corporate groups" as they are usually known in the literature. All such formal organizations, whether they last five minutes or five centuries, can and usually do specify *jural relations* among their members, which define privileges and prohibitions and thereby establish a variety of rights and duties. Such jural relations must derive from some corporation, since they are in the nature of "standing orders," but they do not in and of themselves compose corporations since they do not directly embody authority and do not generate a governmental system. *Normative* theories about how persons ought to behave produce weaker structural relations, and many Taiwanese interpersonal relationships and social categories have this kind of moral basis. In addition, there are simple expectations about how people are likely to act in various circumstances, and these expectations can provide a minimal kind of structure for social groupings and interactions. Social structures have as their final component *power relations*, which exist after the fact of successful political interaction when one person complies with the communicated desires of another.

quite specific information on my entire field area, which had a total population of around 185,000 distributed among nearly 200 villages and eleven towns. My ideas on Taiwanese social organization thus derive primarily from knowledge of one corner of Chang-hua *hsien*, and may not always be applicable to other regions.

## *Settlements*

The most apparent supradomestic social units in rural Taiwan are local communities, which in most regions correspond more or less to nucleated settlements. We tend to call such settlements villages if they are inhabited primarily by farmers or fishermen, and towns if they have a fair number of commercial functions. I have argued elsewhere (1972: 219–20) that size is not a reliable guide for distinguishing between villages and towns. Indeed, the two categories of settlements are not mutually exclusive, since 90 percent of the population of some towns is not engaged in business, and hundreds of farmers, indistinguishable from those living a kilometer down the road in separate villages, live in all the central towns on the Chang-hua Plain. Nor does life change very much for most residents when a previously agricultural village acquires 50 or 100 businesses (equivalent to standard town status), as has occurred in a significant number of places in Taiwan during the postwar period. Another way to express it would be to say that townsmen can live in villages and villagers can live in towns. Ultimately, the difference between a village and a town depends on one's purposes in distinguishing them, and hence on the criteria one uses. For the purposes of this paper, a settlement's position in the locality defined central-place hierarchy will be employed: thus, a settlement with the necessary number of businesses will be regarded as a town, no matter what size its population is or what percentage of its inhabitants are engaged in agriculture.

The significance of the economic functions of a settlement are discussed below. I am concerned here with the kinds of social structures that they support. A crucial question in this regard is whether or not the inhabitants of Taiwanese villages and towns are organized into corporate groups based on residence. If settlements were corporate, then every resident would be under the authority of some office or governing body that could proclaim laws (jural specifications) governing their behavior and make decisions committing the settlement as a whole to a course of action. The ethnographic evidence[2] is that, in general, Taiwanese settlements are not corporate groups, at least not per se.

It is true that the inhabitants of some villages and even a few small towns are the same as the residents of single subtownship administrative districts (*li* or *ts'un*); that a few townships contain very little apart from a town; and that the largest cities are incorporated as metropolitan areas. However, most districts contain multiple villages or only parts of villages or towns, and most townships contain numerous villages as well as a number of towns. Therefore, it is important to distinguish settlements from official administrative units, the corporate nature of which will be discussed below.

Some Taiwanese villages own public places communally, such as temple grounds or even store sites, and some may from time to time raise small funds of money for minor public works projects. In these cases some corporate structure must exist, since corporations are the only collectivities that can own property or otherwise act as a person in the legal sense; but the settlement itself may still not be a corporation. Many large villages and most towns maintain one or more temples, which have corporate governing bodies composed of a variety of officers, both ritual and managerial. A few Taiwanese villages have corporate patrilineages that own property used to support an ancestral cult (see Ahern 1973). Villages can also support a variety of other corporations, such as the interesting one reported by Pasternak (1972) that manages common property for shareholders. However, in all such cases the authority of the governing officers over the rank and file membership is so limited that these kinds of corporations are not of great significance in accounting for very much of the day-to-day behavior of ordinary rural Taiwanese.

The importance of such organizations is that they can be used to manage a variety of affairs in addition to their ostensible purposes, which is a general feature of Chinese institutions (see Schipper 1977 for an urban Taiwanese example). When some public issue or event arises, be it a quarrel between neighbors or the necessity of repairing a village bridge, any existing organization or its officers can become

[2]Reports based on fieldwork show a consistent lack of evidence for significant authority structures incorporating whole settlements as such. For villages, see Ahern 1973; Cohen 1976; Diamond 1969; Gallin 1966; Harrell 1974; Hsieh 1978; Shu-min Huang 1977; Jacobs 1975, 1976; Jordan 1972; Pasternak 1972; Seaman 1974; P. Vander Meer 1967; A. Wolf 1964; and M. Wolf 1968, 1972. For towns, see Crissman 1973; DeGlopper 1973; Feuchtwang 1972; Kuo 1965; and McCreery 1973.

involved on behalf of the whole community or a part thereof. The principle is the same as in the case of overseas Chinese associations, which provide a kind of informal governance for ethnic communities even though there is no jural basis for such activities (Crissman 1967).

If settlements as such are usually not corporate, and if they support corporate organizations that are at best only intermittently active in communal affairs, what kinds of relations provide the structure of rural settlements? In Taiwan (and, I think, in traditional mainland China as well), local communities are categories of persons defined by coresidence[3] (*t'ung-ti-fang* or *t'ung-chuang*) and linked by affect and morality (*kan-ch'ing*).[4]

Because the locality in question is relative (that is, depending on context it can be a portion of a settlement such as a neighborhood, a discrete settlement, or a collection of settlements), coresidence generates a segmentary system.[5] The additional criterion of *kan-ch'ing*, which in this context defines the way friendly and caring neighbors ought to act toward one another, binds coresidents into normative groups, or communities. Since, as I understand it, *kan-ch'ing* depends on personal acquaintance and successful interaction, local communities as herein defined are not only segmentary and normative, but are also dependent on face-to-face interaction or on the potential for such interaction based on social knowledge of other residents.

There are two concomitants of such a definition. First, all residents of a settlement are not automatically members of the local community. In large settlements with a fairly fluid population (such as a market town) not everyone is known to everyone else, and therefore the moral basis of community membership (*kan-ch'ing*) does not exist between all pairs of inhabitants. However, even in a small and intimate village, declassed or immoral people, entrepreneurs from the outside, newcomers, etc., are usually excluded. The second concomitant is that there are upper limits to the possible size of a local

[3] In this instance, actual coresidence. Among immigrants (like those Yin describes in this volume), co-origin (*t'ung-hsiang*) can also define community boundaries; and such communities can then form corporations to manage common affairs. See my 1967 article for a general discussion of co-origin and its role in shaping communities among overseas Chinese.

[4] See Jacobs 1979 for a lengthy discussion of *kan-ch'ing*, a term that has no ready translation into English.

[5] Such segmentation is asymmetrical, which is the general Chinese segmentary pattern. It also occurs in Chinese lineages (Freedman 1958) and overseas Chinese communities (Crissman 1967).

community. I cannot say what these limits are in absolute terms, but big cities and even places such as Chang-hua city are too large to function as a normative group, although they may contain smaller neighborhood communities. However, even a very large central town such as Lu-kang does constitute a community in the view of most of its inhabitants, even though it contains a number of distinctive subcommunities as well (DeGlopper 1973). In Erh-lin, by contrast, neighborhoods seem not very significant normatively (except for one area along the river with a small temple as its focal point), but the whole town is regarded as a coherent community by most residents. I know of no smaller towns or villages in my field area that do not constitute communities, although some large ones are in addition internally differentiated by sublocality or by political factionalism. It may be that some of the small and markedly heterogeneous settlements on the fringes of the commercial sugar farms do not support any moral sense of community, but I do not know for certain on the basis of firsthand information.

Beyond noting that Taiwanese rural settlements are not significantly corporate but are as a rule normatively structured, I find it very difficult to generalize about them in structural terms. However, some nonstructural features of settlements do need to be discussed. Villages naturally vary greatly in size: some contain a mere handful of households, others have as many as a thousand. In my field area the average village size is around 100 households, but the mean size is nearly half that, falling between 55 and 59. The distribution displays no single modal size: there is a large grouping in the 30–34 household range and minor groupings in the 15–24, 50–64, around 150, and near 200 household ranges. Such figures indicate that there are a fair number of really large villages, but that most are rather small. Towns also vary greatly in size: some have more than four times the population of others with equivalent commercial functions, a result of the fact that the large ones include many farmers, fishermen, and laborers, whereas the small ones consist almost entirely of people engaged in business. (See my 1973 dissertation for more details.)

Size may not be the most significant feature of a settlement, but it is nonetheless clear that life in a small village without even a village store to serve as a social center is structured very differently from life in a large, prosperous village. Exactly how the structure of social relations differs, however, cannot be described without going into considerable detail (as Stevan Harrell does in the next paper).

The age of a village has something to do with its size, since almost all the large villages in my area were founded in the eighteenth century. (The only large villages founded in the Japanese period are those in regions of large-scale land development.) The overall increase in the number of villages in southwestern Chang-hua over the last 150 years or so has not been particularly large—only about 75 percent—and an appreciable amount of that increase is accounted for by settlements of Hakka immigrants from Miao-li (who occupied previously undeveloped land acquired by a wealthy Japanese from one of the Pan-ch'iao Lins), by settlements of Japanese immigrants, or by settlements that grew up after the dissolution of a Japanese sugar farm.

The reasons why some old villages have grown large and prosperous while others have remained small probably have more to do with the amount and productivity of their land than with anything else. If that is so, then it is not surprising that the most often mentioned causes of intervillage fighting (which was severely curtailed under the Japanese but broke out again in the late 1940's) are disputes over land, which I take to refer to disputes over squatting or over "rights" to tenancy, not over ownership of either the subsoil or the surface (Wickberg this volume; Knapp 1976). The next most common causes of intervillage fighting are water (see C. Vander Meer 1971 for a discussion of contemporary water stealing), and then women. (See Lamley's paper in this volume for other considerations.)

During the nineteenth century the major combatants in southwestern Chang-hua are said to have been the Hungs and the Ch'ens, the predominant surname groups in the area, both from Ch'üan-chou prefecture on the mainland. As elsewhere, in the absence of aborigines (who were sinicized and absorbed in Chang-hua very early on), Hokkien and Hakka would normally fight; in the absence of Hakka (some early Hakka settlers along the northern bank of the Ch'o-shui Ch'i were assimilated to the Hokkien majority), Ch'üan-chou and Chang-chou Hokkien would usually fight; and in the absence of Chang-chou people (who were never very numerous in the area) different Ch'üan-chou surname groups would on occasion fight. The largest village in my field area (Lu-shang, with 6,000 persons, which had developed the commercial functions of a standard-level town by 1967) was formed when all the Hsiehs, also from Ch'üan-chou, moved their houses together for mutual protection. If the area had contained only Ch'üan-chou Ch'ens, they could have found a basis for fighting among themselves because they come from three different localities. I do not know, however, what the local Hungs would have done, since their genealogy shows descent from four brothers whose descendants refer to one another in terms of the seasons (e.g., winter Hungs, spring Hungs, etc.). I suppose those lineage branches could have fought, since they quarrel at present. It is interesting that there is no mention of the brothers' father: this may indicate that their common genealogy was constructed after their settlement in Chang-hua.

Homogeneity in surname is more characteristic of villages near the coast, which were primary settlements, than of settlements somewhat farther inland, which were secondary settlements (though still very early ones). However, most large, old villages are dominated by one or possibly two surname groups that compose 70 to 90 percent of the village population and often also predominate (or are very prevalent) in nearby villages. There are normally five to fifteen secondary names in a fair-sized village. (For details, see Crissman 1973: 126–29, 247–49.) According to informants, secondary names were principally introduced through uxorilocal marriages, though sometimes they were introduced when wealthy men rewarded faithful, long-term farm laborers with gifts of enough land to support a family. There are many villages, including some fair-sized ones, listed in the 1831 *Chang-hua hsien chih* that are now completely heterogeneous with respect to surname; however, most villages with a large number of surnames are recent settlements on reclaimed land. The historical facts of settlement—who came, when, and under what auspices—provide the main explanation for the surname composition of most settlements, and these facts resist further useful generalization.

Even in those cases where a single name has predominated in a Chang-hua village from its founding, different lines of descent are usually recognized. Sometimes these descent lines can be linked, as in the case of the Hungs (three branches of whom are usually found living in the same villages), but more commonly no connection is recognized. Nor are there corporate lineages in the region: the only ancestral hall in my field area is an unassuming and dilapidated one in the Hsieh village. In 1967 it still contained a tumbledown pile of ancestral tablets covered by the dust of a decade (in a niche in the back wall partly obscured by a broken china cabinet), but the hall itself was being used variously as an auxiliary schoolroom and a sweet potato storage bin. It was obvious that the Hsiehs were no longer honoring their extradomestic ancestors—but then nobody else was either. In fact, no one knew of any ancestral land in the region. At one point, after a long discussion with a recent college graduate about the relative importance of *ch'in-tsu* (agnates) and *ch'in-ch'i* (other relatives), I wrote in my field notes that "the Taiwanese are *not* patrilineal." I do not believe that now, but it was an interesting lesson in the education of a young anthropologist; and I am still puzzled at the relative unimportance of agnatic kinship in southwestern Chang-hua *hsien*. The significance of surnames for political factions is a different matter, and will be treated below.

There are very significant differences in the reported average landholdings among different villages. Farmers in prosperous villages are said to have an average of one hectare, which is enough to raise a large family and even to maintain a bullock. Some families, however, operate or control several hectares and have in addition business interests in a local town—usually (it is said) the result of prior landed wealth. All villages also have some landless or nearly landless families who either rent the land they work or are employed as agricultural laborers. Others work in the towns, usually at menial occupations.

Villages where average landholdings are as low as one-third hectare are usually located on the fringes of the half-dozen or so Taiwan Sugar Corporation farms that were established under the Japanese and now occupy over 7 percent of the total land area in the five townships that make up my field area. I believe, however, that one reason such villages are poor in land is that they have attracted landless people as wage laborers on the sugar farms. There are sugar company agents like those described by Chen (this volume) in villages near the company farms. However, water for rice is usually adequate in the region and is not rotated, so landowners can freely decide whether to contract with the company to have sugar grown or to grow rice themselves. Given that freedom of choice, it is much more difficult for the agents to dominate village affairs.

A final difference between settlements that has structural implications is the extent and nature of religious activities. An elaborate yearly festival honoring the birthday of a patron deity can help build and maintain a strong sense of community. Rural people take obvious pride in the expense and quality of the puppet or opera troups engaged to entertain their gods, and they lose no opportunity to make invidious comparisons with the poor shows put on by neighboring villages with less ambitious temple organizations. There are also religious associations, like the ones Ahern describes (this volume), that incorporate residents of a number of neighboring settlements. In earlier, less settled times, organizations created ostensibly for religious activities were used for a number of nonreligious purposes, not least among which was the military defense of ethnic or surname groups or local communities (Lamley this volume). Religious associations are still involved with politics; and factional considerations can affect religious organizations and determine participation in certain religious celebrations.

For example, the large contributors whose names are engraved on the walls of the half-dozen or so temples in Erh-lin town are all associated with the same local political faction (one of two in the town). When it was decided by the Erh-lin Ma Tsu Temple directors (i.e., by the leaders of the faction) that a follow-up to a ceremony of cosmic renewal (*chiao-wei*) would be held in 1967, all the town's residents (except the Christians) participated despite their factional allegiances: they displayed offerings in front of their houses and then on tables set up in all the streets and in the school yards; they feted guests from all over the region; and they contributed to the public festivities that were organized by committees (which I believe to have been factionally oriented) in each of the town's four districts (*li*). The most spectacular elements of these ceremonies were "meat mountains" (the largest was 100 feet long and 30 to 40 feet high), which are tiered platforms decorated with halves of headless pigs and goats masked and painted to resemble mythological beasts and surrounded with garlands of plucked ducks and vases filled with flowers and candies.

Despite the involvement of the whole community, the men who participated in the closed ceremonies in the town's Ma Tsu Temple were associated with the faction that organized the celebration. Those men who came from outside the town explicitly represented their districts at these indoor ceremonies, whereas those from the town—the majority—participated as individuals and only implicitly represented their neighborhoods. It is no surprise that the only outlying districts to participate were those most closely identified with, and dominated by, the faction that organized the affair.

The Hakka, who live not too far from Erh-lin town, held their festivities on the day following the celebration in Erh-lin and in other participating districts. It was explained to me that this second date (the 21st of the 10th lunar month) was "special" for the Hakka, and that by choosing it they were emphasizing their ethnic separateness—a point normally downplayed since the Hakka are a small minority that is becoming more and more assimilated. They did not build a meat mountain but gathered in an open field near their numerous small villages, where festivities focused on weighing and displaying gigantic pigs. The winner weighed over 1,400 pounds and was blind from the rolls of fat on its face. Local Hokkien ritual pigs (Ti Kong) are not very big.

Hakka ethnic distinctiveness was manifest in many aspects of their celebration besides the date on which it was held, and I believe that a different day may have been insisted on in order to establish a different kind of distinction. The Hakka tend to oppose the faction responsible for organizing the celebration (though they are by no means united in this respect), and they may have held their part of the festival on a different day in order to disassociate themselves politically from that faction. Of course, they may have just been defying the government's urgings against rotating festivities, or, for that matter, they may in their frugal Hakka way have been merely availing themselves of the opportunity to eat at the expense of their Hokkien friends on the day of the celebration in town.

I have now reached a point where I am no longer generalizing about similarities among Taiwanese settlements. Explanations for differences in the structures of various communities must be sought in particularistic historical circumstances and events, as is well illustrated by Pasternak (1972) and Harrell (this volume) as well as by all the ethnographic accounts cited previously. Something further will be said below about the similarities among rural market towns as well as about the general ways in which such towns can be differentiated hierarchically.

## *Government and Politics*

It is not difficult to describe Taiwan's administrative structure in general terms since it consists of legally constituted corporations and jural entities that have uniform formal characteristics across the levels of the administrative hierarchy. I am often puzzled why anthropologists who study the citizens of contemporary nation-states pay so little explicit attention to formal administrative organization and to the laws established by various organs and levels of government. Nation-states and their constituent units are the most significant corporations to which most people belong, since the authority of a modern government over its citizens is very extensive and its laws are often effectively enforced. As should be expected, therefore, the official administrative system, along with jural specifications with respect to prohibited and privileged behavior, are the most salient components of the structure of contemporary Taiwanese society. The laws of the Republic of China set the boundaries within which individuals and corporate groups are free to act without risking official interference with their activities, and even those who knowingly disobey the law are still acting with reference to it. In addition, many other aspects of social organization, which are not directly stipulated in law, have developed as adaptations to jurally defined systems of behavior. This will be illustrated below with respect to the political factions that operate in the context of elections for public office.

The Province of Taiwan acquired a separate corporate existence as part of the Ch'ing empire in 1887, having been previously administered as part of the Fukien Province. Taiwan was incorporated into the Japanese empire in 1895, and has been a component of the Republic of China since 1945. It has had a variety of internal structures and different laws under the various state-level systems, although the Japanese had a policy of respecting Chinese customary law (especially with regard to domestic affairs), and the present low-level administrative units have evolved out of the ones created by the Japanese.

The Ch'ing government divided the island into *hsien*, which will be referred to as counties. *Hsien* were further subdivided into *pao*, which appear to have been merely bureaucratically defined lists of villages without any formal organization. In any event, the *pao* were not discrete: villages belonging to one were interspersed with those of another in the areas near their approximate boundaries. As in traditional China generally, the county was the lowest level of formal government.

The first decades of Japanese colonial rule saw four or five complete reorganizations of the local administration, which shifted back and forth between very large and very small units. By 1920, the Japanese had settled on a system very similar to the present one at the lower levels. The smallest units were *buraku* (administrative villages),[6] which were grouped into *sho* ("rural" townships) and *gai* ("urban" townships), the difference being the commercial status of the township seat. During the 1930's, a few *sho* were promoted to *gai* because of the growth of the major town they contained. Several townships were grouped together to make a prefecture (*gun*), and a number of prefectures constituted a province (*cho*). During the latter part of the colonial period, elections with limited franchise were held for representatives to advisory councils in the townships. All the appointed officials were Japanese, but Taiwanese staffed the small bureaucracies in the townships and at the prefectural level.

After retrocession Taiwan again became a province of China, but in 1967 Taipei city and its environs became a provincial-level independently administered city, as did Kaohsiung in 1979. The Nationalist reorganization of local government, which was completed by about 1950, dismantled the Japanese provinces and replaced them with smaller counties (*hsien*) created by grouping together the townships that had previously made up a small number of prefectures, which were also abolished. A few county-level municipalities were also established for the largest cities and their immediate hinterlands. These have an internal structure that parallels that of Taiwan's *hsien*, but different names are used for the constituent parts. *Hsien* consist of from twelve to over 30 townships, and some have populations of a million or more people. Each has an elected executive officer or head (*hsien-chang*) and an assembly with several dozen members. *Hsien* assemblies do not have the right to make independent laws, but they do control sizable budgets. Various officials in the *hsien* governments maintain records (of business licenses and the like), run the primary and secondary school systems, and oversee the activities of the township governments; but in general they do not deal directly with the people.

The Chinese did not change the township boundaries, but *sho* were renamed *hsiang* and *gai* renamed *chen*, thus preserving a terminological distinction that will be ignored herein by referring to both as townships (since they are exactly the same except for the impor-

[6] *Buraku* were actually divisions of land established under the cadastral survey of 1898. They are still used for land registration. Under the Japanese, the population was organized under the *hoko* system, which was supposedly a continuation of the Ch'ing *pao-chia* organization. Approximately ten households made up a *ko*, and about ten *ko* made up a *ho*. Initially, the population of a *buraku* constituted a single *ho* unless it had roughly twice the optimum of 100 households. As the population grew, additional *ho* were created by dividing the people living in *buraku*, until there were about two and a half times as many *ho* as *buraku* in 1945.

tance of the major towns they contain). The townships containing municipalities under county administration (*hsien-hsia-shih*), which are typically the capital cities of *hsien*, are called *shih*, but except for having much larger populations and correspondingly larger bureaucracies, they are equivalent to other townships. *Hsiang* and *chen* typically range in size from 10,000 to 40,000 people, and on the average contain two to four market towns at various levels plus ten to forty villages. As in the case of *hsien*, the township head (*hsiang-chang* or *chen-chang*) is elected and is responsible for the activities of his township government, which include minor public works and keeping a variety of records that often do involve dealings with ordinary people. The township council, which consists of a dozen or so elected councilmen, is mainly concerned with allocating the township budget.

Townships are subdivided administratively into *ts'un* (for *hsiang*) and *li* (for *chen* and *shih*), both of which will be referred to as districts. Typically these districts were created by dividing *buraku* that were regarded as having grown too large to be administered as a single unit, although a few were created by combining *buraku* that had not grown proportionately to the overall increase. Thus towns and large villages are almost always divided administratively into a number of districts, each of which typically contains a few small outlying settlements in addition to a portion of the larger settlement. There is a certain amount of confusion in the literature as a result of assuming that *li* and *ts'un* are the same as natural villages, whereas in fact only rarely does a district contain all of a single settlement. Districts range in size from less than 1,000 to over 3,000 people (the latter are found where there has been disproportionate growth since 1950). Each district is divided further into neighborhoods (*lin*), which are the smallest administrative units, having from 10 to 25 member households (*hu*). A roster of the members of each household, who correspond fairly closely to a *chia* (corporate family), is kept by the township government in conjunction with the police.

Administrative units down to the level of the townships are clearly corporate, since they have the ability to act independently, albeit within narrow limits.[7] Whether the districts and their constituent

[7]Very few corporations are completely sovereign—nation-states, the Catholic Church, and the Mafia are some that are. Most corporations occupy positions (offices) in larger corporations or are chartered under the laws of some superordinate corporation. In both cases there are legal limits on the freedom of action allowed to subordinate corporate groups, just as there are on the acts of individual office holders.

neighborhoods are also corporate is an interesting theoretical question, the answer to which illustrates the difference between authority structures and jural structures. Jacobs (1976) does not include *li* and *ts'un* with higher-level administrative divisions, which he says are persons in the legal sense (*fa-jen*). I agree that districts lack the corporate character of the other governmental units, but not because they lack independent budgets[8] and bureaucracies, which are his criteria. Neighborhoods and districts both have elected heads (*lin-chang* and *li-chang/ts'un-chang*) like the higher-level entities, but these officials do not have the right to make regulations governing the behavior of other members or the right to make decisions that commit the unit to a course of action, both of which would be the case if district and neighborhood heads were at the top of independent authority structures. In fact, the elections for these offices are conducted by the townships acting under provincial law, and it is my interpretation that *li-chang* and *ts'un-chang* are positions in township governments and that they themselves do not constitute the minimal independent governments of districts per se. Thus when district or neighborhood heads transmit orders to residents of their units, they do so as officers of corporate townships, not as independent authorities.

District heads are required to perform certain services for residents of their districts, and people should deal with the government through their district heads in certain regards; but these legal responsibilities and requirements define jural relations, not corporations, since authority *stricto sensu* is not involved. The fact that everyone must have a legal residence in some neighborhood, and therefore in some district, also establishes jural identities, and along with the existence of the elected heads, makes neighborhoods as well as districts into jural entities, even though many people do not know who their *lin-chang* is or in what neighborhood they are registered. When they do act, neighborhood heads are regarded as bothersome (or humorous) errand boys for the district heads, who are themselves only somewhat more prestigious functionaries. Some may abuse their office and summarily issue orders or make decisions on behalf of their district, but they are acting as individuals and must rely on bullying tactics rather than legal rights in order to get their way.

The existence in Taiwan since ca. 1900 of corporate administrative units below the level of *hsien* government and of jural entities down

[8] Some districts appear to have minuscule budgets: see, for instance, Pasternak 1972.

to approximately the neighborhood level may have inhibited the development of extradomestic corporations with a basis in kinship, community, or religious activities, various kinds of which appear in the literature on traditional Chinese society. The division of spatially discrete communities into separate districts within which official administrative activities are carried out channels ad hoc corporate organization, and makes it difficult to find a basis for community-wide as well as community-specific cooperation. For example, the four districts into which Erh-lin town is divided put on their own separate entertainment and displays for the *chiao-wei*, and since they are no different from the other districts in the township (except for containing parts of the town itself), outlying districts were not excluded. The statutorily defined districts and townships have become the ready units of reference for most Taiwanese, and now usually serve as the basis for group activities.

The Chinese have traditionally viewed towns and cities as integral though nodal parts of a predominantly rural social fabric rather than attributing to them a fundamentally different nature (as has happened in the postfeudal West). Perhaps as a result, Chinese cities and towns were not corporations, and were administered as parts of *hsien*, as has been the case in Taiwan as well. As a result of the system of local government, which does not recognize natural communities such as towns and villages as single administrative entities, and the segmentary nature of Taiwanese communities in which a town is both a community in itself and a node in a larger, territorially defined community, there is little corporate organization of community activities specific to villages, towns, and *hsien* cities. The same is true of other activities, such as factional politics, which do not exist in the context of settlements or the communities they support, but are generated within units defined by the structure of local government and the system of elections for office within it.

For instance, in Chang-hua each *chen* is grouped together with several surrounding *hsiang* to form an electoral district within which a number of candidates for the county assembly run at large. Named factions (*p'ai* or *p'ai-hsi*)[9] organize slates of candidates within each of these units, which correspond roughly to central-town marketing areas (discussed below) owing to the rather even distribution of the

[9]Groupings of candidates and their supporters are usually referred to in the literature as factions. For additional descriptions, see Crissman 1969, 1976c; DeGlopper n.d., 1969; Gallin 1968; Jacobs 1975, 1976; and Lerman 1972, 1978.

largest towns, each of which is the seat of a *chen*. In southwestern Chang-hua *hsien*, the "four *hsiang/chen*" (as Fang-yüan, Ta'ch'eng, Chu-t'ang, and Erh-lin townships are referred to collectively) is a significant reference category primarily because it is a county electoral district and supports the highest level of locally relevant factions, and not because of marketing habits, religious activities, or official functions.[10]

Other electoral districts in which candidates run at large—collections of districts for township councils and entire counties for the provincial assembly—do not give rise to their own specific factions. The former are too small and the latter are too large, although factional activities occur at the lowest levels and factional alliances form at the highest. Apart from the county electoral districts, townships are the level where factions are most apparent, again because of the offices in the civil government and in the Farmers Associations for which they compete. In southwestern Chang-hua, each *hsiang* has two named factions, but each is more or less permanently aligned with the factions in Erh-lin *chen*, which provide the leadership for, and give their names to, the larger factional groupings that operate at the level of the "four *hsiang/chen*."

Up to 1970, district heads and township councilmen were elected at the same time, followed a couple of months later by elections for township heads and county assemblymen. The election for county head and provincial assembly representatives used to follow in another month or so. From the mid-1970's, however, elections have been consolidated, partly to compress (and hopefully to lessen) factional activities, which are condemned by the national government.

Almost every politically active rural Taiwanese belongs to the Nationalist Party, which regularly used to nominate candidates for elections down to the level of township councilmen and even district heads. The party nominations for township offices were determined at the county level and for county offices at the provincial level, thus giving rise to county-based and even island-wide factional activities. (In 1967, informants could readily identify particular local factions as belonging to Chiang Ching-kuo's faction at the national level.) Up to the early 1960's, candidates who did not win KMT endorsement could withdraw temporarily from the party and run as independents against the party nominee, and then, win or lose, be readmitted to

[10] The four townships also form a police district and are the units in which the Wine and Tobacco and the Salt Monopolies operate.

the party afterwards. However, in the late 1960's this practice was disallowed, and party members who run against the party nominees now lose their membership for a period of years. However, the party simultaneously adopted a policy of neutrality in rural elections, and now usually declines to endorse one party member over another unless it wishes to replace some particularly benighted or corrupt old politician with a young and competent one. Consequently, the KMT has become a less active arena of factional competition. In any event, party ideology never had any significance in local elections, at least in Chang-hua *hsien*. The Nationalist Party is just another source (but not a major source) of spoils for rural Taiwanese politicians.

In addition to offices in civil government and party nominations, the major prizes that the factions compete for are control of the Farmers Associations,[11] which are quasi-governmental agencies organized in each of the townships. These agencies collect land taxes (in kind), exchange rice for fertilizer, contract for cash crops such as fruit, asparagus, and mushrooms, and provide agricultural extension and veterinary services. Decisions by association officers concerning allowable moisture content in rice and acceptability of produce, etc., can make life easy or very difficult for farmers, who are therefore unlikely to oppose them openly. Also, elections for control of the Farmers Associations are held under the associations' own auspices and are far easier to manipulate than civil elections. As a result, each Farmers Association has usually been controlled for a long period (seemingly approaching perpetuity in some cases) by one of the factions in the township. It is normal for the township government to be dominated by the other faction. The KMT was rumored to try to arrange things this way by selective use of nominations and by other means of influencing the outcome of elections in order to preclude the concentration of local power in a few hands. However, given the unstable nature of factional structures, if one faction were to gain control of both power bases in a township, it would be very likely to fission, the two resulting parts absorbing segments of the defeated faction in a general realignment.

The factions in southwestern Chang-hua have their origins in rivalries between different surname groups led by members of the

[11] The Irrigation Associations, which are organized on the basis of canals and branch canals, do not involve the factions, at least in southwestern Chang-hua (a region known throughout Taiwan for pervasive and vociferous factionalism). Perhaps water is too important to be an object of factional competition. See Bailey 1969 for a discussion of collusion between political groups to avoid endangering essential resources.

Ch'ing-period local elite. Under Japanese colonial rule, the nature of competition between surname groups changed from what had often amounted to banditry against each other to less violent but no less remunerative currying of favors from the colonial authorities. The Japanese made use of so-called "go-betweens"—Taiwanese who, by virtue of chance, connections, or Japanese education, were in a position to help them achieve various goals. Those in the best position to serve the Japanese were naturally members of the old elite families (many of whom served personally or by means of surrogates); but there were also many people with rags-to-riches careers resulting from luck or ruthlessness. In any event, during the first part of the twentieth century, a category of men who were the structural equivalents (if not always the direct descendants) of the traditional gentry found benefits in serving as intermediaries of one kind or another between the Japanese authorities and the Taiwanese population.

Such men (or their sons) were in the best position to engage in competition for elected offices under the Nationalists, although most had their wealth diminished by land reform. Others who have made their fortunes from postwar business ventures have joined them as contenders for office. Together these constitute the elite of rural Taiwanese society because of their wealth and their ability to use it to control other men, and not, at least primarily, because of the offices they may hold. (Some of the most important men do not run for office; they simply decide which of their followers do.) In this way, these leaders are similar to Melanesian "big men" who, in the absence of corporate hierarchies, hold sway over others by virtue of the force of their personalities, their control of resources, and their ability to dispense favors.

To be a success in local Taiwanese factional politics, an aspiring big man must first of all have money (since "without money, one can't be seen"), and secondly must invest it in politically relevant ways, such as making generous contributions to temples and to charities—both of which result in the prominent display of donors' names and the amounts given. The most direct ways in which money can be invested in politics is in buying votes or in buying off rival candidates. However, money alone will usually not suffice to control votes, and if leaders are to keep their followers they must provide them with certain services. Big men hold the equivalent of "office hours" when they are freely available to their constituents and clients to hear and settle disputes, to give advice, and to respond to pleas for help in various matters (such as securing free medical treatment, getting a son into school or into a job, or securing or extending a loan). Big men must above all appear to be generous and to be eager to help people with their problems by using their superior connections. It does take money to establish oneself as a big man and to work one's way up in a faction, but the money must be used to gain and maintain people's loyalties so that they will provide political support when support is required. The true measure of a big man's political standing is how many votes he controls.

As far as ordinary people are concerned, factional involvement is usually periodic, being most evident in election years. In fact, very few people will admit to being active partisans, but everyone knows everyone else's past affiliations. Small businessmen usually try to remain neutral or to downplay the importance of factions, since they "need to be friends with everyone." However, at one point the majority of people in Fang-yüan town went without much meat for several months because all the local pork sellers belonged to the opposing faction. Whenever people need to purchase something, particularly something special, they will attempt to find a merchant identified with their faction (provided, of course, that there is no one else with whom they have some more powerful relation that yields better hopes of getting a more favorable deal). The businesses that seem inseparable from factional considerations are those that provide medical services. Sick people, and those with sick relatives, can be very grateful for medical treatment, especially if it is provided free or on credit; as a result, all Western-style doctors and druggists have clear factional affiliations, and often provide medical care in return for political considerations.

Most villages are solidly aligned with one of the two factions in a township, but it is not unusual for different villages in the same district to support opposing factions. In those cases where a village or a district is divided in terms of factional allegiance, I was told that men will not speak to one another, women will not wash clothes together, and youths will fight. The ill feeling generated by such factional divisions runs counter to the normative definition of community, which is one reason why factionalism is widely disparaged. Those people who actually oppose their village's dominant faction usually keep their true loyalties to themselves.

One of the interesting aspects of factions is their territorial basis. Except in some hotly contested heterogeneous regions or border areas, factions are closely associated with discrete localities. Indeed, factions are often named according to north-south or east-west divisions within a township. In southwestern Chang-hua, however, all factions are labeled with surnames (e.g., Ch'en-p'ai and Lin-p'ai), and people talk about them as if they are based on *t'ung-hsing* (same surname) loyalties. Clearly, a history of bad blood between surname groups has contributed to factional feelings in the "four *hsiang/chen*"; but since the major names tend to have rather exclusive distributions, it is somewhat difficult to separate name and locality as bases of factional support.

The factions in southwestern Chang-hua *hsien* in fact took their names from leaders who were responsible for their emergence during the Japanese period. The Lin-p'ai is one of the two major factions in Erh-lin *chen* (yet few Lins live in the township), whereas the Hungs, who have the second most prevalent name in the region, have no major faction named after them. There are three Hung factions in Fang-yüan *hsiang* associated with descendants of three of the four brothers mentioned earlier: one is allied with the Lin faction, one with the Ch'en faction (the Hungs' traditional enemies were the Ch'ens), and one has a bad reputation as a result of fickle shifts from one side to the other. Big men sometimes switch sides, taking their supporters with them, and this complicates matters as well. Consequently, a man's surname is not a reliable predictor of his factional allegiance unless his residence is also known. Even then, fights between brothers usually result in one of them changing his faction so that he can oppose the other, and married-in sons-in-law take on the allegiance of their fathers-in-law, etc., so that the connection between surname and faction is not at all close despite the idiom of common surname often used by the Taiwanese in talking about them.

I am not denying that *t'ung-hsing* and agnatic kinship can have a strong influence on which factional leader a person will support, but many other relationships, such as marriages[12] and friendships, can also be significant in particular cases. Also, factions appear to operate in the same manner in localities with considerable surname heterogeneity (unless this heterogeneity is recent) as they do in areas dominated by a single name. I am therefore of the opinion that the big men who become active in factional politics do so primarily as

[12] I was repeatedly told, although I cannot prove it statistically (see Crissman 1973: 260–62), that marriages are almost always arranged between families that are associated with the same faction. It would without doubt be true for politically active families.

patrons and representatives of local communities (or of collections of contiguous and related communities), and that at the lowest level, the factions are basically territorial phenomena.

When I asked informants why they voted for particular candidates, they gave me a variety of particularistic reasons, such as being from the same community, having the same surname, or having received favors from a candidate or another member of the candidate's faction. No ideological issues were involved, the factions being quite apolitical except in the mere competitive sense, and candidates did not even take stands on matters of local interest except for making pork barrel promises. When asked, ordinary people readily acknowledged that in their view politicians were only after what they could personally get out of winning in terms of prestige or, more importantly, the financial opportunities that public office entailed. But then the voters were not idealists either, and clearly expected special privileges and benefits if the man they supported won. They were not so naive as to sell their votes for mere promises, either. In the late 1960's, virtually every vote was bought and paid for by cash on the barrelhead. The price ranged from a token NT$10 (which was the value of a package of cigarettes) in unopposed elections for district heads, to NT$100 (US$2.50) in the always hotly contested elections for county headships. The sum depended on the degree of competition and the potential spoils of office, which in some cases were enough to make sizable investments in an election well worthwhile.

Vote buying was not done by the big men themselves, but by their lesser followers. Public employees and the staff of the Farmers Associations, for example, were routinely expected to obtain votes (sometimes at their own expense) for the faction to which they owed their jobs, and a variety of other kinds of clients and sycophants were also utilized. Each buyer only needed to procure 25 to 30 votes, and money was only paid to those whom the buyer was certain would come through for him (since there was always the possibility of untrustworthy people selling their votes to both factions or, almost as bad, selling them twice to the same faction). Complicated means were therefore employed to ascertain after the fact just which people had delivered their votes and which had reneged.

Despite the universal buying and selling of votes, there were only a few localities—principally those with considerable postwar inmigration (as a result of the repatriation of Japanese colonists, the establishment of retired soldiers' settlements, or extensive land reclamation)—where voters consistently sold to the highest bidder and money alone could swing an election. Occasionally, when there was a pivotal district that could determine the majority on a township council, strong-arm tactics by organized gangs of bullies might be attempted. A favored tactic in such cases was to obtain identification cards, so that votes that had already been paid for could not be cast. However, as people explained it, in most instances they would only sell their votes to the men they wanted to support anyway, but nonetheless saw no reason not to exact the going rate. I believe that this was largely so, and that only the agents of local patrons, or those acting for the faction that was normally supported, could reliably obtain most people's votes. That was what was meant by saying that so-and-so had 1,000 votes, or that such-and-such a faction had all the votes in some village.

Being able to predict very closely how many votes are at their disposal and what the cost will be allows the leaders of factions to engage in complicated and precise strategies concerning the number of candidates to put up, and how the available votes should be apportioned among them. For instance, in elections for township councils, candidates run at large for a number of seats (usually about three) in electoral districts that are divided in factional strength (they are reorganized if necessary so that this is always the case). If a faction that controls a small majority of the votes in such an electoral district were to try to win all three seats, its votes could be split so evenly that it would lose two of them to the weaker opposition if the latter had only two candidates. It would therefore be better for the stronger faction to put up only two candidates, who would be absolutely guaranteed of winning if the available votes were divided evenly between them. If the opposition were then to put up only one candidate, who also could not lose, there would be no competition, and only a nominal amount would have to be paid for votes. Sometimes it is calculated that paying an opposition candidate to withdraw would be cheaper than contesting an election directly. (Some candidates announce for an election with the purpose of obtaining such bribes, either for personal gain or to turn over to their faction to use in contesting some other office.) As a result of such decisions, most candidates for township councils and county assemblies run unopposed or are assured in advance of a winning number of votes. Usually, only one or two seats are really at issue, and interest as well as serious vote buying centers on them. Elections for district heads are usually not contested (neighborhood headships almost never are), since it is known in advance which faction controls the most votes. There are usually two candidates for township head, but the winner is usually not difficult to predict (although there is always the possibility of surprise shifts by men who control a winning balance of votes). Elections for county head and for provincial assemblymen are more difficult to control as a result of the size and fragility of the alliances necessary to muster the winning number of votes countywide.

The most interesting political competition occurs within a faction as the leaders gather to plan their election strategies and to decide who will be a candidate for what office. Such decisions, as well as the way in which available votes will be distributed among a faction's candidates, are ultimately made by the top man in consultation with his major supporters, who then tell their clients how the votes they control are to be used. The leader of a faction in effect decides which of his followers will win which elections, and he must therefore carefully balance the personal ambitions of subordinates against the overall advantage of the faction. Secret deals are negotiated, promises are broken, and enemies are made as the more important and less important men seek to keep or improve their positions and ultimately to gain high office or enter the elite of a winning faction. Indeed, local-level politics is a fascinating and absorbing game for the Taiwanese, one which is worthy of the interest of wealthy, talented, and serious men.

My analysis of the relations structuring factions leads me to conclude that they are not corporate groups.[13] In describing the operation of the factions, I said that the leaders make decisions and implied at least that they give orders, both of which can be attributes of the government of corporations. However, the critical questions are whether the leaders of factions have authority[14] over their followers, and whether the latter obey because they acknowledge a duty to do what their superiors tell them to do. My answer depends on an interpretation of the beliefs and motives of the actors. But on the basis of what my informants told me, I believe that neither authority

[13] This is not to say that the Taiwanese do not talk about factions in such a way that they would have to be corporate groups if their depictions were to be accurate. Such reification is commonplace, but it has nothing to do with the actual functioning of the factions.

[14] As it was previously defined and as it has been consistently employed in this paper, authority refers only to the jural *right* to give orders. Just because someone tells another to do something and the second person complies, it does not mean that the first has any authority: there are many other bases for compliance (Crissman 1975).

nor jural relations underlie the behavior of members of Taiwanese factions. If that is the case, then they are not corporations, and they cannot act as entities. Nor can members, including the leaders, act on behalf of a faction—they must always act as individuals (or as officers of corporations such as those for which faction members compete).

When the top man in a faction decides that something should be done, he must persuade his followers to go along with his decision. But followers will not do so automatically, and must see some personal advantage (no matter how remote or subtle) before they will comply with the leader's wishes. The same is true of lesser men associated with the factions, right down to the level of common people, who will sell their votes for packages of cigarettes, but not for less. Negotiations are also involved when clients importune their patrons for favors in return for explicit or implicit promises of future support. Obtaining compliance as a result of such interpersonal politics establishes power relations, which combine to form power structures (as when A gets B to get C to do X, or A gets both B and C to do X). Power structures are hierarchical by nature, which is why one can speak of leaders and followers; but since each link in any power structure has to be established separately through specific interaction on each occasion when compliance is achieved, power structures are by nature also ephemeral[15] and nontransitive.[16] Therefore, the factions lack any permanent structure whatever, and as continuing entities are actually only reference categories based on past political support or alliance among particular individuals in particular contexts and on expectations of more of the same on future occasions. Similar factional activity by the same people can usually be generated in the recurrent contexts of elections and of dispensing the spoils of office, but in each instance the power structure underlying the behavior has to be newly created as a result of further political interaction.

There is evidence for a certain normative component to factional relations, but except for general sorts of morality that should govern

[15] Authority relations can be manifest in the same or similar contexts over and over again, and they therefore have a "permanent" quality. (They are actually timeless unless temporal limitations are part of their specifications.) Power relations are generated as a result of actual behavior, and so exist only in the past; they carry over to the present or to the future simply as expectations, unless they result in the creation or acknowledgment of jural specifications.

[16] Authority relations are transitive: if A has authority over B, and B over C, then A also has authority over C. However, if A has to establish power over B, and B the same over C, A does not have power over C. It would have to be established separately in an interaction between A and C.

all social relations, this component has the nature of "honor amongst thieves." Members should of course keep their promises to one another, and really should not put personal advantage ahead of the good of the faction, but such beliefs do not go very far towards explaining factional behavior. In fact, self-interest is the primary basis for factional allegiance, and any loyalties are to persons, not to the group, which explains why, when individual big men do decide to switch sides (in return for advantages from their new friends), they can count on taking their supporters and the votes they control with them into the other camp.

Within each township, each faction consists of fluid hierarchies of big men, their clients, and the common people whose votes they control, but the structures can only be defined with respect to particular events. However, there is usually a recognized top man in each faction who has achieved his prominence by having more control than others over politically relevant resources, such as money, influence, and ultimately votes. But he is rather like a "king of the mountain" in the children's game, because there are others who are desirous of his position and are only waiting for a good opportunity to try to undermine and supplant him. The major checks on their aspirations are the fear of failure, which would cost them much of their accumulated political capital, and the knowledge that if their faction shows signs of weakness the opposition may take advantage of the situation and thus endanger their chances of ultimately achieving their ambitions, which require the backing of a strong faction.

The groupings that exist with respect to the *hsien* assembly electoral districts (a *chen* and several *hsiang*) are the largest hierarchical factions in Chang-hua and are the highest level at which factions are named. In the "four *hsiang/chen*," the top men in these higher-level factions have been the same since the beginning of the Nationalist regime, but I suspect that their long tenure is the result of personal qualities, such as their wealth and their political acumen, rather than of anything fundamentally different about the structure of the factions that operate at this level. These overall leaders are the top men in the factions that operate in Erh-lin *chen*, and they really only act as coordinators of the looser hierarchies that include the factions specific to the associated *hsiang*. Overall strategies for the higher-level factions are necessary to achieve the goals of the township-based factions with respect to offices in the county government, and it is the ability of these two leaders to orchestrate such activities successfully as well as the resources they can allocate to their clients in the *hsiang* that have kept them in control for so long.

The factional groupings at the countywide level, where county heads and provincial assemblymen are elected, do not have the same hierarchical structure as those in lower-level electoral districts, but consist of horizontal alliances among the leaders of the regional hierarchies. Rather than acting as patrons and clients toward each other, they treat one another as equals and often make use of sworn brotherhood to cement their otherwise fragile relationships. The alliances they form shift far more readily than those composing the lower-level hierarchies, and which alliance a local faction will enter into often depends primarily on which one the opposing faction in the township has already sided with for some special reason. Divisions and rivalries at the county level are clearly more complex than eastern Chang-hua versus western Chang-hua, although there can be powerful personal enmities between leaders in different regions because of past failures to deliver promised votes or refusals to lend support in attempts to gain party nominations.

Present-day Taiwanese politicians and factional leaders are in important ways the functional (and even structural) equivalents of the traditional Chinese local elites, and I believe that the foregoing description of their activities and analysis of how their interrelationships are structured can help to fill a gap in our understanding of Imperial Chinese society. It has long been supposed that the operation of the governmental system of traditional China depended heavily on the activities of members of the local elite, who acted as unofficial brokers between officials and peasants. Such gentry were wealthy and usually educated, and were the social and sometimes academic equals (if not the superiors) of the country magistrates with whom they dealt informally. They also represented constituencies that are now believed to be associated with rural marketing communities of the sort described by Skinner (1964). Unfortunately, very few details are known about low-level politics among the traditional rural gentry, but this local elite clearly represented the interests of their own lineages, communities, and localities, and presumably were in competition with one another. They could not have competed for local office or over the votes of the peasants, but they must have been rivals for the favors that the magistrates disposed of, and their power must have depended on their ability to represent and influence the common people in their communities. I therefore believe that traditional Chinese local elites must have formed factions that were basically similar to those which exist in Taiwan today.

## *Marketing Systems*

Since the publication of G. William Skinner's work on Chinese marketing systems (1964), standard marketing communities (which comprise those families that exclusively patronize a particular standard market) have come to be regarded, along with the family and the village, as one of the fundamental units of traditional rural society. These marketing communities effectively set the limits to the social world of peasants, and were the units within which they intermarried. Higher-level markets, which had wholesaling and bulking functions, provided the rural gentry with luxury goods and also with a social setting within which, I now suggest, they engaged in factional politics. Thus the marketing system not only generated the spatial structure of rural China; it also had significant integrative functions, socially and politically as well as economically. My dissertation research was motivated by the need to discover whether rural marketing behavior in Taiwan was the same as that on the mainland, whether it had similar social concomitants, and whether it was as significant a factor in structuring the spatial organization of rural society. I will attempt to provide answers to these questions as concisely as possible in the remainder of this paper.[17]

My analysis of the goods and services available from all of the businesses in southwestern Chang-hua discriminated three functional levels of full-fledged towns, which, following Skinner, I have called standard, intermediate, and central towns.[18] Standard towns have 60 to 100 businesses, which mainly provide inexpensive items that are required frequently. Typically, they have acquired most of their commercial functions since the Second World War, and except for the clusters of shops, they are not very different from ordinary villages. Intermediate towns have from 150 to 300 businesses, and can provide a considerable variety of things that people regularly

[17] I have described the marketing system in southwestern Chang-hua and its historical development in considerable detail elsewhere (1972, 1973, 1976a). Others who have written about marketing patterns and central-place hierarchies in Taiwan are Chen (1953), Shu-min Huang (1971), Ta-chou Huang (1966, 1970), Jacobs (1975, 1976), Knapp (1968, 1971), Pannell (1970), and Yuan (1964).

[18] I do not call them *marketing* towns, which is Skinner's term for traditional mainland rural centers, because Taiwanese towns are rather different—principally in not having periodic markets (there never were any in Chang-hua) and in having many more permanent establishments.

need: some intermediate towns were still villages in 1950, but many grew up as commercial centers after being selected as township seats by the Japanese. Central towns have 500 to 1,000 businesses, some of which can provide luxury or specialty items only occasionally required. Most central towns were commercial centers during the Ch'ing dynasty. There are also minor towns, with 15 to 30 businesses: some have been that size since the 1950's, whereas others have only recently begun to acquire shops. Local cities are much larger and more complex than central towns, and are typically *hsien* capitals. The full seven levels of Taiwan's central-place hierarchy include four regional cities (Keelung, Taichung, Tainan, and Kaohsiung) and one metropolis (Taipei).

I returned to Chang-hua for a month's research in early 1979, and was astonished at the extent to which the island's industrialization had penetrated into the countryside. The largest international shipping containers can be seen on any of the roads, and small factories making such things as shower clogs can be discovered in many villages. The most remarkable large-scale industrialization is along the main highway from Chang-hua city to Ch'i-chou, and along the road from Chang-hua city to Ch'i-hu and on south to Lu-k'ou-ts'u. Real estate development has also been extensive—*hsin-ch'eng* (new cities), which are blocks of from 50 to 250 two- or three-storied shop houses, have been built, are under construction, or are being promoted on the outskirts of all higher-level towns and even some standard towns. Others have been put up in the countryside along the highways. Altogether, I estimate that in rural Chang-hua at least 5,000 business premises have been newly built or are substantially completed, an equal number have been initiated, and thousands more are being advertised. However, 50 percent or more of those completed are vacant, and of those that are occupied, less than 10 percent are being used for business purposes (the remainder are residences). Despite the industrial penetration and the changed look of things, the actual number of businesses in the towns has not grown very much since 1967. The kinds of businesses and the variety and quality of goods for sale have changed enormously, as could be expected in conjunction with the astonishing economic growth that has occurred in the last decade. But I was also surprised that the existing towns had not grown commercially to the same extent, and that, if anything, there had been a decline in the number of minor towns. Only one, Wa-tzu, had become a standard town, and this was an exceptional place in 1967. The only other town in Chang-hua that had grown disproportionately is Yüan-lin, which was the largest central town and now rivals nearby Chang-hua city in complexity as well as in size.

The relationship between the commercial and the administrative hierarchies in Taiwan is not straightforward, especially at the lower levels. All *hsien* capitals are local cities, but there are other places, such as Yüan-lin, which have also reached that level. *Chen* seats are all central towns (except for Yüan-lin) because of the aforementioned fact that the Japanese designated some townships as urban and others as rural on the basis of the size and complexity of the major towns they contained, and the towns in the upper levels of the rural central-place hierarchy have not changed much relative to one another since. *Hsiang* seats are usually intermediate towns, but some such as Ch'i-chou are central towns, others such as Fang-yüan are standard towns, and still others such as Fu-hsing have their township offices in the outskirts of central towns or, like P'u-yen, have them located in places that are not even proper minor towns. There are a fair number of intermediate towns that do not have any governmental functions, whereas standard towns rarely have any.

As far as marketing areas are concerned, once functional levels of goods and services are discriminated, it can be determined that the boundaries between the hinterlands of adjacent towns at the same level are roughly halfway between them, whereas marketing area boundaries for goods associated with a lower level are rather closer to the smaller places and further from the larger places. Lower-level places are themselves contained within the higher-level marketing areas belonging to neighboring larger places. Consequently, the marketing areas of central towns for standard-level goods are several times as large, in area and in population, as the marketing areas of standard towns, whereas central town hinterlands for intermediate-level goods are approximately twice as large as those belonging to intermediate towns. The latter, in turn, have hinterlands for standard-level goods that are about twice the size of standard-town marketing areas.[19]

How many towns particular villagers patronize depends on the levels of surrounding towns. At one extreme, people living far from a

[19] Such arrangements are difficult to visualize. There are maps of actual hinterlands in Crissman (1972, 1973) and Knapp (1971), and formal models of such systems in Crissman (1973, 1976a).

central town will shop at their village store for convenience items not worth a trip to town; will go regularly to a nearby standard town for things they need fairly often or that are readily available there; will visit a more distant intermediate town for more expensive, less frequently required goods not available at their standard town; and when necessary, will travel to the nearest central town for things such as specialized medical care, entertainment, and other high-level goods and services not available any closer. At the other extreme, people living in a small village near a central town will do all of their shopping in the central town, since their village may not even have its own store. Slightly more than half the marketing needs of Taiwanese farm families are usually provided at the standard level; thus, even those people who normally shop at three different places do at least 50 percent of their marketing at their standard town. Central-level goods only account for 10 to 20 percent of rural needs, and intermediate-level goods account for the remaining 30 to 40 percent.[20]

Skinner, following Christaller's general theoretical formulations (1966), has produced models that have all standard marketing areas equal in size despite the rank of the town around which they are centered. However, there is evidence from the mainland for differences in the size of standard marketing areas that are as large as the differences in Chang-hua, where the standard-level marketing areas of central towns can include as many as 60 villages, and the hinterlands of standard towns average only eight villages. The difference in population (approximately 50,000 versus 8,000) is significant with respect to *kan-ch'ing*; and by extension it can now be estimated that as many as 10 percent of traditional Chinese standard marketing areas (those served by central marketing towns, which would have contained as much as 25 percent of the population) were too large to have functioned as communities that depended on interaction or social knowledge of other members.

Marketing areas in Taiwan do not constitute communities as they were defined earlier in this paper. In this respect, they are like the "trading areas" that Skinner (1965) describes as the result of modern change on the mainland, the only difference being that in Taiwan trading areas exist at all levels of the rural central-place hierarchy,

[20] What I have depicted as primary marketing areas (1972: 217) are nearly equivalent to standard marketing areas, the only difference being that they do not take into account the small proportion of standard-level goods provided by minor towns (or nearby standard towns) to villages in the primary areas of larger, more distant places that supply most standard-level goods, which are purchased on multipurpose trips.

not just at the intermediate and higher levels. As Skinner hypothesized for modernized trading systems, there is no evidence for communities any larger than individual villages and towns; indeed, in southwestern Chang-hua marketing areas do not even serve as reference categories (that function is provided by townships or higher-level election districts, as previously discussed). Marketing areas do, however, define "social horizons," as Skinner puts it, since social relationships are established and maintained in the course of marketing activities.

Although towns provide the locus for some organized activities, including religious cults, martial arts clubs, and rotating credit associations (all of which involve only a few individuals, anyway), they generally foster dyadic relationships—individuals meet old schoolmates and other acquaintances, run into relatives, and visit shopkeepers or political patrons. Although sets of such personal relationships do not define social units, their importance should still not be underestimated. For instance, their role in determining marriage patterns has been shown by Jacobs (1975, 1976), Knapp (1968, 1971), and myself (1973, 1976). I found, for example, that an immediate effect of changed marketing habits, as occurs when a new standard town develops, is a disruption of existing marriage patterns, which is often followed in a decade or so by the emergence of new marriage patterns within the new marketing areas. Both Jacobs and Knapp demonstrate a link between marketing and marriages, but both unfortunately describe it in terms of endogamy, not frequency of intermarriage. Also, Knapp's figures refer to townships and not to marketing areas per se.

Marriages depend upon and create interpersonal relations, but such dyadic relations do not necessarily derive from larger social units of any kind, nor do they in turn generate any. Marriages in rural Taiwan result from decisions taken by corporate families or (increasingly today) by the prospective partners themselves; but choices still depend on social knowledge of prospective partners and their families. Such knowledge can be obtained through relationships that derive from marketing activities, thus creating a link between marketing areas and marriage patterns. Mapped distributions of marriages show that brides are usually acquired within regions roughly the size of—though rarely corresponding to—intermediate marketing areas. This means that persons living in standard town marketing areas go outside them for a sizable proportion of brides, whereas people living in central town primary marketing areas tend to get brides within the surrounding portion of the town's entire marketing area. My statistics show that simple propinquity is consistently the strongest predictor of rates of intermarriage (see also Gallin 1960). Other factors such as surname exogamy, factional allegiance, and hypergamy (which involves geographical movement away from the poorer coastal regions and up the central-place hierarchy, as well as social class mobility) also have their effects, even if they do not show up statistically in any coherent manner. However, the spatial distribution of affinal relatives of the residents of a settlement does create a pattern that must be accounted for in part by the local marketing system. Beyond that, nothing very interesting can be said from a structural perspective about rural Taiwanese marriage patterns.

The rural towns in Taiwan correspond only approximately to those in traditional (or modernized) mainland China, and marketing areas do not have the same consequences for rural social organization since they developed as trading hinterlands while Taiwan underwent modernization. However, the rural marketing system in Taiwan does have profound influence on the spatial structure of rural society, mediated only by the administrative system described previously. As with structural analyses generally, the understanding of spatial organization requires formal models, which must then be related in a logical way to information about real systems. The basic theory about retail marketing structures comes from the work of Walter Christaller (which was only fully translated into English in 1966), who invoked a "marketing principle" to account for the distribution of rural commercial and service centers. He also discussed the operation of a "traffic principle" (which really only involves a constraint on the marketing principle) and described an "administrative principle" (which has less deductive rigor and, I suspect, less relevance to real world systems). To describe his models as concisely as possible, the marketing principle produces a hierarchical distribution of market centers with optimal convenience of access for a dispersed rural population, whereas the traffic principle produces a different theoretical distribution based on an optimal transportation network between towns. The administrative principle has lower-level centers and their hinterlands entirely within the hinterland of a single higher-level center, a pattern that also occurs in Chinese city systems, as opposed to rural marketing systems (Skinner 1977). Skinner's models A and B (1964) are versions of Christaller's general formulations adapted to Chinese society, and my alternative general models (1973, 1976a) are essentially further modifications of Skinner's necessitated by my discovery of systematic differences in the size of standard marketing areas in Taiwan and on the mainland as well as by logical difficulties with Skinner's geometry.

Initially I analyzed the distribution of market towns on the Chang-hua Plain in terms of models derived from the traffic principle (1973, 1976a); but I was troubled by the numerous gaps in the pattern and the number of places that required special explanations in terms of unique circumstances and histories. I have since discovered that the distribution fits a marketing principle model almost perfectly, and that there are only a few instances where the actual road system does not match the predicted pattern of traffic principle routes through marketing principle locations. The theoretical implications of this discovery have yet to be completely worked out, and its demonstration necessarily requires highly technical and detailed explanations that must be developed elsewhere. However, I can now demonstrate that the marketing principle explains why some villages on the Chang-hua Plain have grown into towns and some have not, and why some towns have grown more than others. The network of roads that has been built and maintained between the towns is all that can be accounted for in terms of the traffic model.

However, what do such spatial structures have to do with social structure? The two are clearly very different, yet they are also clearly interdependent. The marketing principle, after all, predicts for a carefully defined hypothetical universe the optimal central-place patterns that will be produced by entrepreneurial investments and consumer choices based on economizing in space. Correspondingly, in the real world investors start shops in places that they believe will have good businesses; and shoppers frequent different places according to convenience and costs. In both instances, spatial and behavioral factors are involved.

As I view it, social structure governs individual decisions about how to behave, and in the aggregate these decisions result in spatial systems. Yet existing spatial systems have a considerable influence on the structural relations that generate behavior. There is thus not only feedback between social and spatial systems; more importantly, there are also synergistic effects resulting from the distribution of social relationships over the landscape. I am not arguing that there is no distinction between social structure and spatial structure—I think that knowledge of both is equally necessary for understanding how social systems occupy landscapes, and how individual people decide what they will do where. On the one hand, at the lower levels (settlements and their equivalent) I think that anthropologists tend to take spatial influences very much for granted, and that perhaps we should pay more explicit attention to the local effects of spatial distinctions and distributions on social behavior. On the other hand, at the intermediate levels I think that there is too much emphasis on the spatial aspects of social and administrative units, when in fact social structure, consisting of different kinds and arrangements of relations among people, is often the most significant in accounting for what people do.

When we discuss regional systems—like those supported by the Chang-hua Plain—I believe that we leave the domain of anthropology, strictly speaking, and enter the domains of geography, economics, and political science. Descriptions of large-scale economic or administrative systems, especially if the systems are differentiated spatially or hierarchically, can be useful in ordering and interpreting our anthropological data, but are not themselves of primary interest. For instance, it is certainly valuable to be able to explain the arrangement of towns on the Chang-hua Plain in terms of the marketing principle; but what does this tell us about what is going on in the minds of the Taiwanese—who are themselves ignorant of (or indifferent to) such spatial structures, at least as we portray them? Then again, what does it gain us to be able to assign a particular settlement to a hierarchical position in such a structure? We may thereby be better able to understand the whole system and make predictions about future growth; but can we on that basis say whether a wealthy local man desiring to go into some business will actually invest his money there? I cannot even say with assurance which town a farmer will visit on any given occasion. In order to say such things, we would have to know much more about particular individuals and what enters into their decisions apart from their (presumably uniform) perceptions of spatial arrangements. However, we often end up knowing so much about the people and the communities with which we usually deal, that their particulars become far more interesting and meaningful for our anthropological analyses than the generalities about their placement in spatial systems.

On the basis of these final observations, I can urge that more attention be paid to locational and territorial aspects of social structures without suggesting that anthropologists become social geographers. The sort of explanations we are seeking for Taiwanese social behavior—explanations phrased in terms of culture—will at the most general level need to assume that spatial factors are constant (however variable they may be in reality), just as topographical and cultural factors must be held constant in order to elucidate spatial structures.

# Social Organization in Hai-shan

Stevan Harrell

Close by each other in the area just southwest of Taipei known as Hai-shan, and centered around the market towns of Shu-lin, Ying-ko, and San-hsia, lie a number of very diverse rural communities. The great majority of the inhabitants of this area trace their origins to eighteenth- and nineteenth-century settlers from An-ch'i county, Ch'üan-chou prefecture, Fukien province. Thus, they all speak Hokkien with nearly identical accents, and they all are familiar with the same customs and traditions. Despite this similarity in language and customs, however, the social organization of these rural communities is exceedingly diverse. We find single-lineage villages, multilineage villages, and villages with no lineages at all. We find communities arranged along streets, rather as towns are arranged; we find communities consisting of discrete smaller hamlets; and we find areas of dispersed housing where it is difficult to define any bounded local communities at all. In some communities, families are in large measure subordinate to lineages in matters of ritual organization and politics, whereas in others, where there is no lineage organization, families are more independent. These differences in social organization are in turn reflected in differences in religious organization on both the community and family levels.

The aim of this paper is to suggest some explanation for these dif-

This paper was also presented at the China Colloquium of the Institute for Comparative and Foreign Area Studies, University of Washington, and to the Ecology Seminar in the Department of Anthropology, University of Washington. Several people made extensive and helpful comments on the first draft: Cynthia Anson, Peter Chase, Charles F. Keyes, and Burton Pasternak. I am grateful to all of them for their suggestions. Something resembling the present version was presented to the China Seminar at the University of British Columbia in February 1977, and I also wish to express my thanks for this opportunity.

ferences in social organization in a region having a common language and common customs. This, I think, is a manageable task. There is nothing random about the variation between villages, and we do not need to posit different origins or different cultural values to explain differences in social organization. Indeed, the most satisfactory way to account for these differences is to see them as adaptive responses to different environments by people with largely identical cultural backgrounds. If by "environment" we mean the combination of a community's physical setting and its relationship with a wider social system, then the environment of each community is clearly different from those of its neighbors. Differences in social organization can be explained as different adaptive responses to the varying environments; and differences in ritual organization, in turn, can be seen as reflections of differences in social organization.

To back up this thesis, I will examine in detail three communities: Ch'i-nan, Hsi-yüan, and Ploughshare.[1] I will occasionally refer to other communities, known either through published accounts or through personal knowledge, but my systematic comparison will concern the three communities named above. In keeping with the thesis that adaptive responses to varying natural and social environments produce differences in social organization, and that religious differences result from differences in social organization, I will begin with a description of the natural setting and economic activity of the three communities, then go on to describe their spatial and social organization and its reflection in religious rituals.

## *Environment*

Ch'i-nan, nestled between the San-hsia and Heng-ch'i rivers and the foothills of one of the northern spurs of Taiwan's central mountain range, is a group of four discrete, nucleated settlements, each inhabited primarily by members of one patrilineage. According to Ahern, the first settlers here probably arrived from An-ch'i county sometime around 1740 or 1750, though large-scale migration to the area does not seem to have begun until well into the latter half of the same century (Ahern 1973: 10–11). The original settlers probably began growing wet-field rice within a few years of their arrival; and for

[1]Ch'i-nan has been studied by Emily Ahern (1973, 1976). I have studied Hsi-yüan (1974a), where I spent the summer of 1970, and Ploughshare (1974a, 1974b, 1976), where I conducted my dissertation research in 1972–73.

this they needed to construct small irrigation systems, each lineage irrigating the fields surrounding its own settlement with water from a separate small stream, many of which flow into Ch'i-nan from the adjacent mountains. These mountains, though a welcome source of irrigation water, were at the same time a source of worry: they were inhabited by hostile aborigines who raided Chinese settlements until their eventual "pacification" by the Japanese colonial government in the early decades of this century. As a result, the early settlers cooperated in building a bamboo stockade and in setting up a common defense system; the latter was incorporated before 1800 into a larger defense line extending many miles in each direction, which remained in use until after the Japanese arrival (Ahern 1973: 12–15).

Most Ch'i-nan villagers apparently continued to grow rice throughout the nineteenth century. Most of the village land was owned by individual families, though some was owned by the lineages collectively. In this period and under the Japanese, the villagers also supplemented their income with work in the camphor industry in neighboring Ch'eng-fu (Ahern 1973: 15) and by growing tea in the nearby mountains. The Japanese occupation of course ended the danger of raids by aborigines, but it appears to have brought few economic changes: some villagers became coal miners after 1920, but most seem to have continued their traditional agrarian life. Since the establishment of Kuomintang rule, the economic activities of villagers have diversified somewhat: it is particularly noteworthy that members of all four lineages have been successful in business enterprises both in Ch'i-nan and farther afield. In addition, members of the Li lineage, nearly all of whose land was sold sometime before the beginning of this century (Ahern 1973: 42–43), have generally taken up other occupations (as wage laborers, cottage industry knitters, tea processors, etc.). On the whole, however, the striking thing about Ch'i-nan is that most families in the other three lineage communities are still actively engaged in agriculture (Ahern 1973: 22–23), although their income is generally supplemented by the nonagricultural wage earnings of the younger generation.

Hsi-yüan *li* is an artificially delineated administrative district on the floodplain between the San-hsia and Tokoham rivers. Together with the neighboring districts known as Kan-yüan, Tung-yüan, Pei-yüan, and Nan-yüan, it forms a geographical entity known to natives as Shih-t'ou-hsi. In contrast to settlement patterns in Ch'i-nan, settlement patterns in Hsi-yüan and, with the exception of Kan-yüan town, in Shih-t'ou-hsi as a whole, consist of scattered compounds and groups of compounds, each holding from one to ten or more families. These families are usually agnatically related, just as the inhabitants of several nearby compounds are often agnatically related (see below). The earliest ancestors of the area's current inhabitants settled here around 1780 or 1790, though there is evidence of earlier habitation by Chinese, either Hokkien from Chang-chou or Hakka. Whoever these original Chinese settlers were, their numbers along with the distance and rivers separating Shih-t'ou-hsi from the mountains on both sides apparently removed any threat of attacks by aborigines quite early on.

During the nineteenth and early twentieth centuries, the economy of Shih-t'ou-hsi, like that of Ch'i-nan, seems to have remained overwhelmingly agrarian. In the case of Shih-t'ou-hsi, even such cash crops as camphor and tea were never important: the flat floodplain between the two rivers seems to have always been devoted almost entirely to rice cultivation. Before the land reform program, a large portion of the land was owned by one absentee landlord family, the fabulously wealthy Lims of nearby Pan-ch'iao; and a smaller portion was owned by local landlords. The majority of the inhabitants at this time were probably tenant farmers. As in the case of Ch'i-nan, a large number of people have left the area in recent years, and there are many businessmen in San-hsia and Taipei who still trace agnatic links with Hsi-yüan lineages. Nowadays, those who remain in the area almost all continue to grow rice; but again most families supplement their agricultural income with wages, and cottage industry (knitting mills) is an important source of cash for some local families.

In stark contrast to both Ch'i-nan and Hsi-yüan is the village of Ploughshare, a nucleated community of 101 households situated on a point of land high above the confluence of the San-hsia river and a smaller, unnamed stream that flows into it. Between Ploughshare and the mountains stands a small plateau, given over mostly to rice cultivation and known as Cap-sa:-thi:. One of the most important influences on the history of Ploughshare is the fact that Cap-sa:-thi:, despite its being closer to the mountains and to the hostile aborigines, was settled before Ploughshare—in about 1820, according to the genealogy of the large lineage inhabiting one of Cap-sa:-thi:'s two nucleated settlements. By contrast, I cannot trace Chinese habitation in Ploughshare back much beyond 1840, at least on the basis of my fragmentary information. The poor settlers who first built on

Ploughshare point were thus for the most part not rice farmers, since most of the nearby land was already being farmed by people living on the plateau above. Although a small number of Ploughshare families became tenant farmers, the great majority took up occupations far less prestigious and secure: some became agricultural laborers; some grew tea on the mountainsides or picked tea on others' estates; some sold charcoal made from wood cut in the mountains.

Under the Japanese (who burned Ploughshare to the ground in 1895 in retaliation for the villagers' resistance), the occupations of Ploughshare workers gradually changed. By the 1930's most workers were either coal miners in the nearby mountains or laborers on the pushcart railway that transported coal to river ports on the floor of the Taipei basin. But these jobs, like those of the agricultural laborers and the charcoal burners before them, were low-prestige, temporary, and not very lucrative, so Ploughshare continued to be a community with two landowning families, some tenant farmers (perhaps a quarter of the village families), and a large number of laborers, whom the natives called *than-ciaq-lang* ("people who earn wages to eat"). The latter group had considerable village-to-village mobility, probably continuing a pattern of the pre-Japanese period (though I have no direct evidence of this).

With Taiwan's recent economic growth, the circumstances of many villagers have improved: though villagers continue to move elsewhere in considerable numbers, many have found without moving lucrative employment in nearby factories and in the cottage-based knitting industry, a factor that has become very important in the village economy. There are still a few farmers (who have owned their land since the Land-to-the-Tiller program of the early 1950's), but Ploughshare remains primarily what it always has been—a rural community of nonfarmers.

Already we see a striking difference among these communities that appears to be a product of environmental and economic influences—the difference in settlement patterns. Ch'i-nan consists of four nucleated settlements, originally surrounded by a common stockade; Hsi-yüan contains no nucleated settlements at all, but simply a widely scattered collection of compounds; Ploughshare is a single, nucleated village. We can explain these differences without even examining the villages' social organization. The case of Ploughshare is particularly simple: very little land was left for the laborers who settled there, since the neighboring plateau had already been claimed by absentee landlords and owner-farmers. As a result, Ploughshare's settlers clustered their houses together in the only available space. The settlers of Ch'i-nan were encouraged to live in nucleated settlements, even though they could have built dispersed housing, because of the threat of raids by aborigines. Not only was a palisade built around the whole of Ch'i-nan, but Ch'i-nan's four constituent settlements formed clusters as a protection against surprise attacks. In Hsi-yüan, however, there was plenty of land on which to spread out, and the danger of raids appears to have ended before the ancestors of the current inhabitants settled there. But we must still ask why the inhabitants, having a choice between nucleated and dispersed housing, chose dispersed housing. One reason may be that, unlike the inhabitants of either Ch'i-nan or Ploughshare, the inhabitants of Hsi-yüan (until quite recently) relied almost exclusively on agriculture for their livelihood; and unlike the inhabitants of Ch'i-nan, most were tenant farmers until the 1950's. With approximately half the crop going to landlords as rent and with no supplemental sources of income, these tenant farmers needed to farm quite large parcels to earn a living, and the larger the parcels, the longer the average distance from a nucleated settlement to a farmer's fields. So it must have seemed convenient to spread habitation out over the plain, producing a settlement pattern that contrasted sharply with those of Ch'i-nan and Ploughshare.

## *Social Organization*

We have seen how physical setting and outside pressures vary greatly for the three communities under study, and how this variation is reflected in the arrangement of housing. As we turn to social organization, we will likewise see three different patterns, each apparently the result of adaptation to a different environment. These variations in social organization are discussed on two levels: first at the level of the structure and the political leadership of the communities themselves; then at the level of the family (as a component of the community).

Ch'i-nan is a discrete natural and administrative unit, and is in turn divided into smaller, discrete units. A formal administrative district since Japanese times (Ahern 1973: 4) and an informal geographical community before that, Ch'i-nan is clearly separate from the neighboring districts of Ch'i-pei and Ch'i-tung, which, together with it, make up the larger unit known as Heng-ch'i. This sense of definition of Ch'i-nan vis-à-vis its neighbors is clearly expressed in the organization of several annual rituals performed to honor locally prominent deities. In the rites celebrating the birthday of the twin gods known as Ang Kong, for example, the responsibility for organizing the festival rotates yearly among all three Heng-ch'i communities (Ahern 1973: 5–6). For the other two major yearly festivals—celebrating the birthdays of Tho Te Kong, the Earth God, and Co Su Kong, the powerful god enshrined in the main temple in the market town of San-hsia—Ch'i-nan has its own celebration, with its own procession and its own opera performances. Though the other Heng-ch'i communities also worship these two deities, their celebrations are conducted independently of those held in Ch'i-nan (*ibid.*: 6–9). Moreover, Ch'i-nan has its own temple to Tho Te Kong: all the villagers and no outsiders participate in its yearly festival. The organization of religious rituals thus supports geography and formal administration in defining Ch'i-nan as a discrete community, separate from its neighbors.

Similarly, the internal organization of Ch'i-nan reveals discrete building blocks. Each of the four settlements in the community is inhabited primarily by members of a single lineage; thus the four settlements are called, after their inhabitants, Ong *chu*, Li *chu*, Lou *chu*, and Ui *chu* (Ahern 1973: 4). These four settlements are rivals within the larger unity of Ch'i-nan, a fact revealed not only in their self-conscious competition in the building of ancestral halls (*ibid.*: 99–102) but also in past conflicts, particularly between the Lous, who were employed as policemen by the Japanese, and their long-standing opponents the Uis, who appear to have been among the leaders of resistance to the Japanese. To this date, there remains a prohibition on intermarriage between the Lous and the Uis (*ibid.*: 71–74). This internal segmentation into discrete territorial/kinship units is mirrored in ritual in two ways. First, in the celebrations for local gods' birthdays (including the celebration for Ang Kong, which Ch'i-nan sponsors once every three years), responsibility for the festivities rotates among the four settlements (*ibid.*: 4–9). Second, the foci of ancestor worship for nearly all inhabitants of the community are the lineages' ancestral halls, which contain the memorial tablets of former lineage members. These ancestral halls ordinarily admit tablets of lineage members only; ancestors with other surnames are relegated to altars in family homes (*ibid.*: 121–25). Thus territorial subcommunities, each a solidary agnatic kin group, form the next level of social organization in Ch'i-nan.

Within each lineage, there are further discrete subdivisions. The Ong lineage is divided into two mutually antagonistic groups called *thau* and *be*, or head and tail, each descended from one of the two brothers who founded the lineage (Ahern 1973: 21). These two groups are generally at odds, though they have been known to cooperate when the interests of the whole lineage are threatened (*ibid.*: 31–34). The other lineages are also internally segmented, albeit to a lesser degree: here the internal divisions are branches, or *fangs*, descended from the sons of each lineage's first Ch'i-nan settler. These divisions are primarily relevant, however, for rotating the responsibility for rituals that are paid for by the proceeds from collectively owned land: only in the Lou lineage are people often identified in terms of their *fang* membership (*ibid.*: 50). Indeed, since no subgroup of a Ch'i-nan lineage owns corporate land or an ancestral hall, these internal divisions, with the exception of the *thau/be* cleavage, are often given far less emphasis than the unity of each lineage vis-à-vis the others.

Political leadership in Ch'i-nan seems to reflect community organization quite closely. Though there appears to be no leader for the village as a whole, there are recognized leaders for each lineage except the Ongs, who have rival leaders for the *thau* and *be* groups. In the case of the Lis, two men work together harmoniously as leaders, settling disputes among members and often representing the lineage in its dealings with outsiders. (Ahern 1973: 23–26, 45–46, 50–53, 58–59.)

Local organization in Shih-t'ou-hsi is very different. Here we find no neat territorial units of the sort that make up Heng-ch'i. Instead, though Shih-t'ou-hsi forms a discrete social whole, there appear to be no significant rural communities within it. For administrative convenience, the Nationalist government has divided Shih-t'ou-hsi into five *li*: Kan-yüan (which includes Kan-yüan town and the immediately surrounding countryside) and four purely rural *li* in a ring around Kan-yüan (Hsi-yüan, Nan-yüan, Tung-yüan, and Pei-yüan). With the exception of Kan-yüan, however, none of these *li* contains anything resembling a nucleated village; instead, they contain dispersed compounds. And the units of cooperation for religious ritual—usually indicative of natural community organization—do not coincide in most cases with the artificially drawn *li*. In the yearly festivals for Ang Kong and Co Su Kong, all Shih-t'ou-hsi worships on the same day, but there are three subdivisions, each with its own procession and opera. The first of these subdivisions, Chhiu:-chhiu Khut, consists of the western half of what is now Hsi-yüan *li*, between the main road and the Tokoham River. The second subdivision is Nan-yüan *li*, formerly known as Tho-a-kha. The third subdivision lumps together the remainder of Shih-t'ou-hsi, but is itself divided into four further subdivisions or *ko*, each of which assumes responsibility for organizing local ritual on a rotating annual basis.[2]

It might at first appear that preexisting natural units, defined by ritual, have been superseded for administrative purposes by newly drawn districts. But closer observation suggests otherwise: these preexisting units seem to have been as arbitrary as the present ones, and it is highly unlikely that they ever formed solidary communities. The evidence from Hsi-yüan, at least, bears this out clearly: though there is a decrepit little Tho Te Kong shrine at the southern end of the district, there is no festival organized for Tho Te Kong's birthday; and Hsi-yüan residents, when asked where they worship Tho Te Kong, usually answer "at home." If pressed to state which temple they patronize, they answer in a manner that suggests a division along the center of the *li*. Those closer to Kan-yüan town visit the temple there; those at the southwestern end of the *li* visit that area's small shrine. Thus the division between Chhiu:-chhiu Khut in the west and Khei-ki:-chu in the east does not apply to Tho Te Kong worship at all; rather, the division here is between north and south. Since Tho Te Kong is the god of the local community, the fact that Hsi-yüan has no organized celebration of his birthday serves to emphasize the fact that in Shih-t'ou-hsi, outside of Kan-yüan town, there are no rural communities that correspond in size with the villages of Ch'i-nan and Ploughshare.

In addition, agnatic organization in Shih-t'ou-hsi shows that the lack of territorial communities is not made up for by the existence of solidary localized lineages; there are none of these either. In Hsi-yüan, for example, there are several groups that might be legitimately described as patrilineages: in particular, there is an Ong lineage of

[2] A summer's fieldwork in the southwestern corner of Shih-t'ou-hsi was insufficient to determine the boundaries of these *ko*, which appear to have survived from Japanese times. One of these *ko* includes the eastern part of Hsi-yüan *li*, formerly known as Khei-ki:-chu, along with Kan-yüan town.

25 households (inhabiting four large compounds and one smaller house) and a Li lineage of 46 families (inhabiting six compounds and two single-family houses). Both these lineages hold small corporate rice paddies (used to finance ceremonies honoring founding ancestors), and senior men in each lineage are aware of the genealogical relationships between themselves and their near and their distant agnates. But the lineages are not localized; their compounds, houses, and fields are scattered all over the plain, extending in one case to the outskirts of Kan-yüan town. Thus the lineages do not now seem to act as corporate bodies, except in ritual. Whether they did so in the past, I am not sure. But the dispersal of lineage members across the plain must be associated with the weakness of the lineages: people have always had good reason to cooperate with their neighbors or with people with whom they shared irrigation water rather than with agnates three compounds away.

To find a solidary agnatic or local group in Hsi-yüan, we must look at compounds. These usually consist of a maximum of ten or twelve closely related families living together. Families in such compounds tend to cooperate informally and are often identified by the names of one or two dominant senior males. But compounds cannot be considered the basic units of society here, since many people live in isolated one- and two-family houses.

Thus we see that in Hsi-yüan, cooperation within a compound is often quite close. However, little cooperation is expected between members of neighboring compounds or between lineage-mates living in different compounds: people cooperate in specific situations with whoever shares their particular interests. Thus neighborhood and agnatic ties may figure prominently as bases for association between individual families; but they do not seem to be the bases for the formation of solidary groups, as in the case in Ch'i-nan.

I was not in Hsi-yüan long enough to learn much about local political leadership, but my impression is that there are a number of important Hsi-yüan men, some of them quite bitter rivals, who compete for the political allegiance of less prominent families and who are consulted in matters of importance. Agnatic ties are one basis for these leaders' political backing, but they are certainly not the only basis.

Thus we find that in Shih-t'ou-hsi, at least in the rural areas outside Kan-yüan town, there are no solidary communities larger than compounds or smaller than Shih-t'ou-hsi itself. There are no villages—only the compound at one end of the scale, and the whole of Shih-t'ou-hsi at the other. The intermediate levels consist of networks of relationships between particular people, not of divisions that form discrete groups. In this light, we can understand better the great discrepancy between the administrative divisions of the Japanese period and those of today: both governments needed some unit at this level, and both created them essentially arbitrarily. Neither group of administrative divisions corresponds with natural villages, because there are no natural villages.

The local organization of Ploughshare contains features common to both Ch'i-nan and Hsi-yüan: Ploughshare is a discrete unit in relation to other communities, but it contains no discrete internal divisions whatsoever. In Japanese times, Ploughshare was a local administrative district (*chuang*) by itself, but since 1945 it has been combined for administrative purposes with Blacksmith Gulch (directly across a small, unnamed stream) and with the nearby mountain area known as Pai-chi. However, in terms of community consciousness and ritual, Ploughshare is still very much a unit vis-à-vis the surrounding communities. The festival for Co Su Kong, though celebrated the same day in Blacksmith Gulch, is organized separately in Ploughshare: each village has its own procession and its own opera. Ploughshare also has its own Tho Te Kong temple, which all villagers attend and which even has a circulating incense plaque (a board that passes daily from household to household, with the household having it responsible for presenting offerings and tidying up around the temple before passing the plaque on to a neighbor).[3]

Not only ritual, but certain kinds of group feelings distinguish Ploughshare from its near neighbors. Many people told me of the village's special characteristics, ranging from its primarily *than-ciaq-lang* population to the general honesty of its inhabitants. "We here in Ploughshare" was a phrase commonly heard.

A concomitant of Ploughshare's distinctness as a community is its lack of formal internal divisions: the village has no recognizable neighborhoods or patrilineages. Though many villagers bear the surname Ong, for example, only one group of eight families and three groups of seven families can claim (in each case) a common ancestor.

[3]This plaque, however, does not visit every household in the community on its rounds. Nobody in the village seemed to know why it skipped some people, and those skipped were certainly not marginal to the community in any other sense. This illustrates the danger of depending too heavily on outward forms, such as ritual, to determine social organization.

Moreover, none of these groups holds corporate property (with the trivial exception of common burial plots); none has an ancestral altar (let alone anything resembling a hall); and none appears to act in concert, to have a recognized leader, or to be referred to by name. This lack of internal divisions is expressed in ritual by the fact that each of the three annual religious celebrations is organized by the village as a whole, with the master of ceremonies (*lo-cu*) chosen by lot each year—without recourse to any sort of rotation system—from all the family heads in the community.

But the fact that there are no formal village divisions does not mean, of course, that there is no strife, conflict, or informal alliances. These exist in great profusion, but are all based on networks of dyadic ties. Many kinds of ties can be important for building such networks—agnation, affinity, matrilateral filiation, sworn kinship, neighborhood, and patron-client relations all come to mind. And indeed, so thick is the net of dyadic relationships that it is possible to connect nearly all the village's 102 households into a single web by drawing the dyadic connections between them.

Political leadership in Ploughshare seems to be a matter of having the largest network of connections, both inside and outside the village—not of having formal or informal leadership over any particular group. Thus the three most important men in the village in 1972 were Tiu: Ong-lai, a man who had married uxorilocally into a prominent village family but who was a section head in the local township government office; Ong Chin-hieng, the village head or *li-chang*, who had few agnates (only two brothers) in the village but a large number of affines, sworn brothers, and employees in his prosperous knitting mill; and Kou Pou-kim, a township representative and the owner of a textile factory in the nearby market town of San-hsia, who was successful in mobilizing his kinship ties with people who had complaints against Ong Chin-hieng. The story of village politics, then, is largely the story of these men and their attempts to mobilize diverse networks of villagers in their support.

The key thing to remember here is that these networks do not coalesce into permanent factions; indeed, many villagers maintain reasonably good relationships with all three leaders. Thus allegiance is flexible, and the village—though divided internally—is able to present a united front to outsiders.

Two important differences in social organization may be noted from the foregoing descriptions of Ch'i-nan, Hsi-yüan, and Ploughshare. First, solidary village-level communities are not always present; second, the internal organization of communities below the village level is not always the same. We see, for example, that Ploughshare is a solidary village; that Ch'i-nan, also a village, is made up of four distinct, solidary settlements; and that Hsi-yüan is but a collection of small compounds and isolated residences (where the various artificial administrative divisions that have been imposed from time to time simply reflect the absence of appropriate natural territorial units). As communities, Ploughshare and Ch'i-nan resemble each other more than either resembles Hsi-yüan; yet the natural resources of Ch'i-nan and Hsi-yüan resemble each other more than the resources of either resemble those of Ploughshare. For this reason, then, we must look beyond ecology for an explanation of the differences in social organization.

In my view, the explanation lies in the degree to which each community was threatened militarily and in the degree to which each was homogeneous in social class. During the late Ch'ing period, military defense, important in Ch'i-nan and Ploughshare but not in Hsi-yüan, not only required nucleated settlements, but also tended to promote feelings of community solidarity. And class homogeneity—not always present in neighboring settlements, but present in both Ch'i-nan and Ploughshare—continued to be a factor in village solidarity throughout the Japanese period. In Hsi-yüan, where both landlords and tenants were scattered about the plain, and where there were neither obvious natural boundaries nor occupational differences, there were never any strong economic bases for community organization and solidarity. (The one exception was, of course, Kan-yüan town.) In Ploughshare and Ch'i-nan, however, the economic bases for community solidarity have always existed. In the nineteenth century, nearly all the land in Ch'i-nan was held either corporately by the village's four lineages or individually by lineage families; little if any land was owned by absentee landlords. Right across the Heng-ch'i River in Ch'i-pei, however, most of the land was owned by outsiders—primarily by the famous Lim family of Pan-ch'iao (Arthur Wolf, personal communication). Aside from their common military concerns, then, Ch'i-nan villagers all through the Ch'ing and Japanese periods must have felt a solidarity as owner-farmers successfully defending their holdings from the paddy-gobbling Lims.

Ploughshare, like Ch'i-nan, was relatively homogeneous yet different from its neighbors. A collection of day laborers, tea pickers, charcoal burners, and a few tenant farmers, all living on rented land (indeed, to this day most of the building sites in Ploughshare are owned by a religious association controlled by a former landlord family in San-hsia), Ploughshare's inhabitants also forged a community, and one that still takes a certain pride in its distinctiveness.

Freedman has usefully argued (1958: 127–29) that the critical variable explaining the existence and strength of lineage organization in China is the presence and extent of corporate property. Detailed field studies by Baker (1968), Potter (1968), and others have corroborated this view with ethnographic reports of lineages and lineage segments that owe their solidarity and their political importance to the possession of land. The data presented here also seem to lend some support to this view: in both Ch'i-nan and Hsi-yüan (where rice farming has enabled groups of agnates to set aside corporate property in the names of focal ancestors), lineage organization has resulted from common ownership. In Ploughshare, however, no available property has meant no corporate property, and even those small groups of agnatically related families that are found in the village show no sort of corporate consciousness or activity.

This apparent link between corporate property and lineage organization is further supported by the social structure of the farming community of Cap-sa:-thi:, located on the plateau directly above Ploughshare. The plateau contains a few scattered compounds, but most residents of the area live in one of two nucleated settlements—Ong *chu* and Sa:-te-chu. Ong *chu*, as its name implies, is exclusively inhabited by twenty-some families of the Ong lineage, whereas Sa:-te-chu is inhabited by about an equal number of families without lineage or surname ties. This difference between two similar farming communities is explained by the fact that prior to land reform in the early 1950's, the Ongs owned about one-fourth the land in Cap-sa:-thi:, whereas the inhabitants of Sa:-te-chu were all tenants of wealthy absentee landlords living in San-hsia.

But, as Ahern points out, common property is not everything. In a recent article (1976), she argues that written genealogies indicate that lineage members themselves consider shares in a corporate property holding to be less important for lineage structure than common residence in a local lineage community. Thus the genealogies of the

Ch'i-nan lineages all pay close attention to lineage members' migrations and to new lineage settlements; but three such genealogies make no mention whatever of corporate property holdings, even though each of the lineages holds some corporate land. Ahern suggests that the importance of migration and new settlement lies in the risky nature of frontier development and in the pride of having successfully migrated and set up a new and prosperous local lineage (1976: 13). Though accepting Ahern's contention that locality is extremely important for lineage solidarity, I would like to suggest, on the basis of the comparative data presented in this paper, that there is a more sociologically compelling explanation for this than the danger and hardship of migration. In brief, a compact community can more easily act as a solidary group. If we compare the lineages of Ch'i-nan with the Ong and Li lineages of Hsi-yüan, we find that all are roughly similar in the number of their households and in the extent of their corporate property, with the exception of the Ui lineage of Ch'i-nan, which owns far more corporate property than any of the other lineages in either place (Ahern 1973: 23). But, as mentioned, the localized Chi-nan lineages are the most important social groups in the community; and it is not going too far to say that they are the basic units making up the village. Dispersed lineages of similar size and with similar holdings in Hsi-yüan, however, do not act as solidary groups, and though cooperating from time to time in the performance of rituals, are far from being primary building blocks of the community. Compounds, as we have seen, often contain families that cooperate with each other more frequently, but they are too small to dominate an area the size of a village. Hence we find that any migration, no matter how short the distance involved, creates a potentially solidary, local, agnatic group and at the same time divides a group already in existence. Because migration occurs so much sooner in the normal development of lineages in Shih-t'ou-hsi than in the normal development of lineages in Ch'i-nan, the local agnatic groups of Ch'i-nan have grown to a size where they are significant segments of the community. In Shih-t'ou-hsi, by contrast, localized groups have never reached a significant size; and dispersed groups have had little opportunity to develop much corporate solidarity. This is true in spite of the fact that the corporate landholdings of all the groups are roughly equivalent.

But if the genealogies record data on migration in great detail because locality of settlement is very important, this does not explain why they fail to record data concerning corporate estates. The answer here, I think, is that in nearly all the lineages in question, corporate estates are actually not very important. Except in the case of the Ui lineage of Ch'i-nan, the amount of land corporately held is so small that its primary use is in financing yearly festivals for lineage ancestors. In Ch'i-nan, these festivals seem largely a reaffirmation of a solidarity stemming from geographical and political factors. And in Hsi-yüan, similar festivals are generally pro forma affairs, as there is little lineage solidarity to contribute to. The fact that the lineages of Ch'i-nan are localized and those of Hsi-yüan are not is much more important in explaining the strength and importance of the lineages than is any comparison of corporate landholdings. The Ui lineage perhaps provides the exception that proves the rule. This lineage holds considerably more corporate land than any of the others (four hectares—the Ch'i-nan Lou lineage and the Hsi-yüan Ong lineage are next with about one hectare each), and it is the only lineage that apparently uses the income from its corporate lands for purposes other than ritual: it has built additions onto the settlement itself, purchased a community water pump, and established an education fund for the brighter children of its members (Ahern 1973: 58–61). Moreover, the Ui lineage generally displays the highest level of corporate solidarity (*ibid.*: 87). It is not surprising, then, that the Ui genealogy is the only one that mentions the location of corporate lineage property: the Uis are the only lineage whose members gain substantively from the income of such property.[4]

Thus we see that the presence of corporate land and the localization of residence both contribute to the political strength and the importance of lineages. But, whereas localization seems nearly always to make a lineage into a discrete social unit, corporate property does not seem sufficient to create such solidarity unless there is enough property to bring direct benefit to lineage members.

There remains the question of why Hsi-yüan's dispersed lineages exist at all, since they have very little function. They seem to have held a bit more corporate land during the Japanese period, but it is unclear how much more. Indeed, one must assume that they were

[4] I have examined the genealogies of two large Chekiang lineages that contain detailed records of corporate property holdings: in both cases, the holdings were very extensive and were used for such purposes as financing schools and paying the travel expenses of examination candidates (Liang 1922; Ho 1893).

once organized for some sort of activity and have continued to exist even though they have outlived their practical value. The original purpose of their organization, however, remains unclear.

## *Family, Community, and Ritual*

In all three communities, the family, or *chia*, remains the basic unit of production and consumption (as it does throughout the rest of China). Nearly all productive property is held by families; family members and only family members share a common household budget; and when family members are living in the same community, they reside in the same house. In each village, families normally go through a cycle of growth from the nuclear form to the stem form, and then in many cases to the joint form, before dividing (*fen-chia*) and starting the cycle all over again (Cohen 1970). But I am not concerned here with the form, developmental pattern, or economic function of village families. Instead, I am interested in the political role of families within the community, and in the extent to which families are seen as independent units. When larger independent groups, in this case lineages, exist and operate within the community, the independence of families is compromised; families are seen not just as individual entities but also as members of kinship-based groups. As noted, in Ploughshare families are linked only by dyadic ties; in the Hsi-yüan, compounds and lineages sometimes cooperate; and in Ch'i-nan, lineages are the basic political units in the community. This variation is reflected in both behavior and ritual (particularly in ancestor worship).

On the behavioral level, this variation is especially apparent in the degree to which family heads customarily represent the interests of other families to outsiders. In Ch'i-nan, recognized lineage leaders seem to be able to speak for other family heads in their lineages. For example, the leaders of the *thau* and *be* segments of the Ong lineage represented their entire followings when they worked together during a dispute with an outsider over water control (Ahern 1973: 31–35). Similarly, the most active leader of the Ui lineage was able to elicit cooperation from all lineage members, even though some were opposed, when he organized a project to construct a new water-pumping system (Ahern 1973: 59). In Ploughshare, however, no such representative leadership seems possible. In a telling case, when the community was involved in discussions about a government grant (*she-ch'ü*) for material improvements to the village, there was daily haggling among a large group of senior men over what was to be constructed where; and several months later, people were still expressing resentment that their path had not been widened or that they had not received compensation quickly enough for some land that had been used to improve a roadway. In a community like this one, it is still possible for a leader or leaders to represent the whole village against a threat from outside. But in internal affairs, it is rare for anyone to speak for anyone else.

The differences between communities where households are virtually independent of large groups and those where households are partially submerged in lineages is nowhere more graphically expressed than in stove god and ancestor worship. The stove god is usually seen as the embodiment of the family, as, indeed, the family can be referred to simply as a stove (*cau*). It is striking, then, that in Ch'i-nan few families worship the stove god in his usual abode—the brick stove where they traditionally prepare meals. Instead, almost all current worship of the stove god (and some families seem to have abolished the stove god altogether) takes place in the ancestral hall. As Ahern expresses it, "It is as though the ritual idiom for delineating the distinctness of households is used to demonstrate their common place within a single lineage" (1973: 95). In Hsi-yüan, the stove god's birthday is also celebrated collectively in the main room of each compound, where ancestral tablets are housed; but in addition, most households seem to post the stove god's name in the kitchen and worship him there. And in Ploughshare, where no family is submerged in a larger group, worship of the stove god is carried out solely in the kitchen.

When we turn to ancestor worship, we find similar variation—from emphasis on the lineage rather than the family in Ch'i-nan, to full emphasis on the family in Ploughshare. This difference in emphasis can be seen in both the location of tablets and the degree to which true agnatic ancestry is a criterion for the inclusion of tablets at particular altars.

In Ch'i-nan, ancestor worship normally takes place in the four lineage halls. Freedman's distinction (1958: 81) between domestic and hall ancestor cults is blurred here, since the tablets of near and distant ancestors alike are included on the communal altars in the halls (Ahern 1973: 91–98). Domestic altars are only maintained when families have tablets of ancestors of other than the lineage surname (see below), or when families who have built new houses inconveniently far from the hall move their ancestors' tablets to their homes for reasons of convenience (*ibid.*: 135). Ordinarily, however, people who set up domestic altars for lineage ancestors include on these altars only the tablets of near ancestors to whom only they are obligated. Tablets of ancestors whose worship is shared by more than one family remain in the hall (*ibid.*: 132). And in the most solidary of the four lineages, the Ui, no household has domestic tablets for any Ui ancestor, even though worshiping at the hall involves considerable inconvenience for some of them (*ibid.*: 137). The subordination of household to lineage in Ui ritual is further illustrated by the fact that when a Ui man takes a bride, the ceremonial red draperies—in most Taiwanese communities, hung over the door of the groom's household—are hung over the main gate to the lineage compound: in ritual at least, even marriage is seen as something concerning the lineage as a whole rather than its component households (*ibid.*: 61). The place of lineages in Ch'i-nan is also illustrated clearly by the fact that almost all worship of near and distant ancestors goes on in the hall: only nineteen of 113 lineage households in the four main settlements have domestic altars; and these altars include only tablets of ancestors to whom those households alone are obligated.

Another manifestation of Ch'i-nan's strict emphasis on lineages is the degree to which tablets of outsiders (ancestors of other surnames) are excluded from ancestral altars in the main lineage halls. With one exception—an unrelated man who died without descendants and who left all his land as corporate property to the Ui lineage—only male lineage members who did not marry out, their wives, and female lineage members who married uxorilocally can be worshiped in the halls. All other tablets, including tablets of men with other surnames who married into the lineage uxorilocally, and tablets brought by women at the time of their marriage with a lineage member, must be placed outside the hall on domestic altars (Ahern 1973: 130–38). And even on domestic altars, it is necessary to separate lineage ancestors from nonlineage ancestors, at the very least by placing a wooden board between their tablets (*ibid.*: 132). Lineage hall altars are for lineage members only: others eligible for worship as ancestors receive offerings outside the ancestral hall, the main focus of the lineage's ancestor cult.

In Hsi-yüan, the situation is looser, reflecting the weaker position of lineages. Generally, ancestral tablets are located in the central room (*tua-thia:*) of each house or compound. Since some large compounds contain up to twelve families, there is considerable variation in the number of people who worship their ancestors at a particular altar. In the large compounds, one finds something resembling a weak version of Ch'i-nan's subordination of household to lineage: people do not have separate domestic ancestral shrines unless they have ancestors whose tablets are not admissible at the compound's main altar. However, several large compounds have ancestral tablets of more than one surname on their main altars; indeed, of 41 ancestral shrines in the community, eight have ancestral tablets of two or more surnames. Of these eight, only one, a large compound, relegates secondary ancestors to a separate altar; six content themselves with placing boards between two sets of tablets; and one simply has two sets of tablets sitting side by side on its altar with no symbolic divider.

In the nonlineage community of Ploughshare, we reach the other extreme: here ancestor worship consists of the domestic cult pure and simple. (For a more detailed discussion, see Harrell 1976.) Not only does practically every family in the village worship its ancestors separately; but there is also only a minimal attempt to separate direct agnatic ancestors from other ancestors to whom families are obligated. Thus, even though there are groups of seven or eight agnatically related households in the community, none of these has a common ancestral altar. In fact, usually as soon as brothers divide their households, they set up separate ancestral altars with tablets of all their ancestors from the first settler in the village to their own parents. Thus, the 91 families who worship their ancestors in Ploughshare do so at 85 altars: only very recently divided families or coresident families with but one place where ancestral tablets might be suitably enshrined ever share altars. This rigorously domestic ancestor cult reinforces the emphasis on household independence that is visible in other aspects of Ploughshare's social organization and ritual.

The importance of the household in Ploughshare is also revealed in another aspect of ancestor worship: the willingness of villagers to include tablets of ancestors of other surnames, often without even symbolic separation, on domestic altars. Of 85 domestic shrines in the village, 41 include two or more sets of ancestral tablets; but in only one case are separate altars found. (In eleven of the remaining cases, a board separates two sets of tablets; in the other 29 cases, two or three sets of tablets are simply placed side by side on the altar.) In fact, many villagers use double cabinets that have places for two sets of tablets in one box. When each household is an independent unit in the village's social organization, the principle of agnatic descent clearly becomes much weaker; households are not tied to each other in agnatic groups, and the agnatic descent principle does not retain its usual importance in defining either the household or its ancestors.

We can see, then, that the place of families in the community—subordinate (to strong lineages) in Ch'i-nan, more independent in Hsi-yüan, and almost entirely independent in Ploughshare—derives from other aspects of the community's economy and structure. Indeed, differences in ritual and worship are testimony to the fact that the organization of ritual is highly dependent on the nature of the community performing the ritual.

In this paper, I hope I have made a small contribution to the field of intracultural and intrasocietal comparison. To the present, the most ambitious and rigorous attempt at such comparison for Chinese villages has undoubtedly been the work of Pasternak (1972). Pasternak argues that differences in the social structure of two villages in southern Taiwan are explained by differences in the need for cooperation in constructing irrigation works—differences that are in turn traceable to the ecological variables of rainfall and terrain. Yet despite his closely reasoned and extensively documented argument, one is troubled by the fact that one of his villages is Hakka, the other Hokkien. I think, however, that this paper implicitly strengthens Pasternak's argument, because differences in environment are shown here to lead to sociostructural differences in villages whose ethnic identity is the same: all were settled by immigrants from the same county in Fukien. At the same time, this paper extends the comparative method beyond the realm of purely agricultural villages, and demonstrates how the categories of analysis that Pasternak uses to explain differences between two agricultural villages can also be used to explain differences between agricultural and laboring communities.

Because my study deals in part with a laboring community, it also invites comparison with studies of other nonagricultural communities—as, for example, with the studies of Taiwanese fishing villages done by Diamond (1969) and Wang (1971), or with the study of communities of boat people done by Anderson (1970). All these communities, like Ploughshare, are noteworthy for their lack of lineage organization: only Diamond's study of K'un-shen provides any evidence of such organization, which in this case has taken on a nearly unrecognizable form (1969: 68–73). In general, the absence of lineage organization can be traced largely to the difficulties involved in collective ownership of property (usually fishing boats and equipment). Also relevant may be the fact that migration is easier (and lineages thus weaker) when one's livelihood is not based on stationary resources such as land. Certainly Ploughshare has been very unstable in its membership over at least the last 80 years, and such instability makes the formation of large groups of agnates improbable.

My corroboration of the findings of Pasternak, Diamond, Wang, and Anderson must be seen, however, in the context of Ahern's argument (1976) that lineages see their main role as organizing local communities, not as exploiting corporately owned estates. Ahern's view may be true, but it still seems unlikely that a lineage would develop to the point where it could be an effective political influence unless there were something—even individually owned rice land—that served to keep a core of agnates from leaving the area altogether.

This paper also bears out Arthur Wolf's hypothesis (1974) that some aspects of Chinese folk religion are more or less direct projections of the earthly social order onto the supernatural plane. The fact that ancestor worship is so different in Ploughshare and Ch'i-nan, and the fact that no organized community cult of Tho Te Kong seems to exist in the rural parts of Shih-t'ou-hsi, are further proof that common principles about gods, ghosts, and ancestors are shaped to suit the forms and needs of particular communities.

Finally, I hope this study and others like it will contribute to a sensible evaluation of the place of village studies in Chinese anthropology. Initially, the field consisted almost exclusively of village studies (Fried 1953 is a rare exception), and this tended to place far too much emphasis on the village, which is, after all, only one of the levels of social organization relevant to the life of most Chinese. Skinner's delineation of Chinese central-place hierarchies (1964, 1965a, 1965b) effectively ended this one-sided preoccupation with the village by suggesting that the standard marketing community was perhaps a more relevant unit for study. But village studies have continued, and it should by now be clear why: works such as those by Baker (1968), Potter (1968), Ahern (1973), Pasternak (1972), Watson (1975), and others have again demonstrated that understanding village organization is often indispensable if one wants to obtain a clear picture of rural Chinese society. What I hope this paper will do is help put this in perspective: in some places the village is important, in others, not. Nowhere is the village a paramount unit of social organization, more important than all others—but then neither is the family, the lineage, nor the standard-level marketing town. To understand Chinese social organization, even in modern times, we must take a more open-minded view and recognize that the rural Chinese peasant, landlord, fisherman, or worker always has been and still is a member of many different kinds of social units.

# Part Three

# Economic Organization

# Economics and Ecology

Burton Pasternak

The variety of Chinese customs has long intrigued scholars in China—witness the discussions of local custom that are part of most local histories. But this interest has been mainly descriptive and has not led to attempts to explain why customs are as they are. Western knowledge of China, initially unsystematic and abstract, until recently lacked even this degree of sophistication (see Fried 1954).

With the accumulation of descriptive studies, and reflecting a general resurgence of nomothetic concerns in anthropology since the 1950's, Western and non-Western scholars alike have become increasingly interested in the causes of intracultural variation. Why do we find different forms of marriage, adoption, family structure, descent groups, cross-kin association, community integration, intercommunity relations, migration, religious practices, and ideological beliefs all within a single society? Since many of us are interested in the material circumstances that produce or encourage such diversity, economic variables are naturally receiving increasing attention.

## *Economic Aspects of Family Organization*

Reflecting the traditional concerns of Western and Chinese scholars, much anthropological work on Taiwan has focused on various aspects of kinship. We already know much about the conditions under which different forms of the family emerge and endure, and I suspect that we will soon know much more about the conditions that favor different forms of marriage and adoption as well (see Cohen 1967, 1968, 1970; Chuang 1972; A. Wolf 1966, 1968; M. Wolf 1968, 1970, 1972). Systematic study of the causes and consequences of different patterns of marriage and adoption requires an ability to isolate economic and ecological variables—an ability well within our grasp for Taiwan. With respect to the relationship between economic and ecological factors and family life, the recent study by Cohen (1976) is probably the most exhaustive and detailed account produced to date. For this reason (and also because it builds upon the work of so many others), Cohen's study will be considered at some length.

Variation in family form[1] and in family relations cannot be predicted or accounted for simply in terms of differential adherence to a supposedly common Chinese ideal; nor can we hope to achieve satisfying results if we attempt to link family form with some generalized notion of wealth and gentry status, or poverty and peasant status. In a subsequent paper in this volume, Sung proposes that family form is substantially affected by the nature of the family estate: joint families may be more common among the wealthy than among the poor because a larger proportion of wealthy families' estates are likely to be inherited (thus allowing the father to exert more control over his sons). However, whether property is inherited or acquired may not be as vital to family extension as the nature of the family's business interests (Cohen 1976: 218). Even where the family estate contains a large proportion of acquired wealth, there could be strong economic motives for avoiding partition.

The key to variation in family form is probably to be found, as Cohen indicates, in the "degree of interdependence that characterizes the family economy" (1976: 218). It is not wealth or poverty per se that engenders or precludes certain family forms; rather it is the way wealth is invested and used or the way poverty is dealt with that affects family dynamics. The tendency of Chinese families, poor and wealthy, to optimize their security by diversifying their investment of human and material resources has been noted by many writers (see, for example, Chow 1966: 113; Ho 1962: 291; M. Yang 1945: 84). Cohen, indeed, gives special attention to the effects of diversification on family form and family dynamics. The wealthy are in a position to increase their resources through multi-enterprise investment, and the poor may stave off destitution by diversifying their limited resources.

[1]Chinese families are minimal corporate kin groups. They may be coresidential units, or they may consist of discrete but economically interdependent households. They may be simple conjugal units (husband, wife, and their children), or they may be extended. The most common extended form is the stem family, with a conjugal unit in two successive generations. Joint extended families (statistically uncommon, but traditionally the most valued in China) have at least two conjugal units in the same generation.

Sons can be sent out in all directions, underwritten to the best ability of the family, in the hope that their efforts will ultimately improve the lot of the entire family. If they succeed, they can send home remittances; if they fail, they can retreat to the security of the family. If wealthy families are more often joint in form than poor families, it may be because they are in a better position to diversify their capital and labor investments.

Diversification is usually achieved through some degree of family dispersion. Anthropologists now generally appreciate the difference between the family (a minimal corporate kin group) and the household (a residential unit)—an apt distinction for Taiwanese society, where migration, urbanization, commercialization, and diversification of family investment sometimes result in extended families composed of discrete households. A number of studies carried out in Taiwan suggest that the coincidence of family and household may be becoming less frequent and that extended families may prove especially durable as a result. There are definite benefits to dispersion. As Cohen argues (1976: 115), dispersion "can be employed as a strategy for advancement in the absence of pressures within the estate, and it can benefit a *chia* [family] precisely because the economic efforts of its members are individualized while the unity of the group is maintained. The noninclusive economy is thus one expression of the diversification strategy; and like others it may be motivated by hardship, ambition, or a combination of both." The perpetuation of the joint family, in Cohen's view, depends on whether inclinations to separate are overridden by the economic disadvantages of partition. Family division would be particularly disadvantageous where the family estate consists of separate enterprises managed by specialists. Only with families that remain an economic unit can capital and labor be shifted easily and economically.

There is now considerable evidence that economic factors other than dispersed investment and labor may also discourage family partition. The cultivation of certain crops, for example, seems to have this effect. In Yen-liao (Cohen 1967, 1968, 1970, 1976), the tobacco crop is associated with an unusually high and steady demand for female labor. Owing to the nature and timing of this crop, labor cannot easily be obtained through exchange or hiring. Families must depend upon themselves for workers, and anything that diverts them from their tobacco interests—such as partition and the associated proliferation of domestic units—is therefore to be avoided as much as possible. Tobacco families are indeed less likely than others to seek income away from the farm, and they are also more likely to create and perpetuate joint families.

My own work in Chung-she village (1972a, 1972b) also indicates the impact of economic factors on family form. In this case, aspects of the supply and demand for labor affect both the form of the family and the nature of interfamilial and intercommunity cooperation. Initially, rainfall-dependent agriculture meant high demands for labor (in this instance male labor) during relatively short periods of the year—a circumstance that reduced the feasibility of exchange and encouraged family (and community) self-reliance. The introduction of irrigation lengthened the period of labor and reduced its intensity. Interfamilial (and intercommunity) cooperation then became possible, and a former impediment to family partition was removed. The proportion of joint families in the community swiftly declined as a result.

What, however, can one say about the effects of migration to Taiwan's developing urban centers? Speare suggests that migration to Taichung "usually resulted in the division of existing extended families" (1974: 319). However, since Speare does not distinguish clearly between households and families, his conclusion is not entirely convincing. Moreover, like many of us, he is inclined to accept emic expressions at face value and is persuaded, perhaps too easily, that migrants tend to embrace "modern" values about the family more readily than nonmigrants. By relying upon expressed rather than actual values, Speare assumes that extended families are uniformly valued in Taiwan, and he believes that people will maintain such families if they can. He is therefore primarily concerned with conditions that discourage family extension. It seems to me, however, that since not all people who could form extended families actually do form them (Speare 1974), the more important problem may be to identify conditions that favor extension.

In fact, it is quite possible for migration to reduce intrafamilial conflict and at the same time make possible a more diversified investment of a family's labor and capital, thus delaying partition. Indeed, Speare himself notes that the "cohesion of an extended family can be maintained after division through frequent visitation and the exchange of aid" (1972: 326–27), and his figures on remittances to relatives at home (*ibid.*: 327; cf. Marsh 1968; Wang & Apthorpe 1974:

13) suggest that the extended family may frequently continue to exist as an economic unit despite the migration of some of its members.

Bernard and Rita Gallin (1974) also investigate the social and economic correlates of rural-to-urban migration, and some of their findings are relevant to our discussion of the impact of migration on family form. They note, for example, that short-distance migrants tend to come from families of relatively high socioeconomic status, often to diversify the family's economic base—a motive that encourages the maintenance of extended families. Such migrants commonly work in small-scale business or manufacturing, or work as technicians or craftsmen. Some are even professionals or civil servants. Once again we should think about the advantages that often accrue to families who maintain close economic ties with such people.

Whereas the urban migrants studied by Speare also tend to be relatively wealthy and well educated, the long-distance (urban) migrants studied by the Gallins tend to be the opposite. Yet the Gallins suggest that migration, even among the relatively poor, may actually delay family partition by providing greater diversity for the family economy (1974: 340; cf. Wang & Apthorpe 1974: 13, 25, 32, 38–39). Indeed, urban employment often reduces pressure on family resources and, at the same time, provides new possibilities for increasing those resources (in a setting where both the risk and cost of failure are reduced). In such cases, then, we should expect migration to encourage the existence of extended families with rural and urban components. At any rate, there are very good reasons for taking a closer look at the economic relations between urban and rural households.

Even for city-based families, we should not assume that urban life is incompatible with family extension. There is already abundant evidence from all over the world that—under certain circumstances—the urban extended family is far from obsolete (see Pasternak 1976: chap. 7). The Gallins note (1974: 351) instances in Taipei where "two or more families of [immigrant] cart drivers have jointly rented a large apartment; each family is assigned a bedroom, while the sitting room and other facilities are shared. In at least one such case, the sharing families, all Huangs, are agnates. In virtually all such cases, the Hsin-hsing migrants happily note that living together in this manner is like being in a large family situation once again." Though such arrangements are reportedly rare, it is possible that they may correspond to the joint-family households formed among the urban poor to save on domestic labor and living costs.

In an article on businessmen in Lu-kang, DeGlopper concludes that joint families are rare in the business community: "Most partners in Lukang businesses are brothers, or fathers and sons. Such partnerships do not represent large, complex families that have postponed the usual division of the family. Large, undivided households are rare in Lukang, and those few that exist are regarded more as curiosities than as status-generating realizations of a cultural ideal. In almost all cases brothers who are business partners have separate households, each with its own budget, often dwelling in different houses." (1972: 317; cf. Mark 1972.) But before we accept DeGlopper's conclusion, we should recall that families and households need not coincide. We should, for example, see whether separate households constitute residential components of larger, multi-enterprise family corporations (i.e., extended families). And we should look for connections between merchant households in town and households in the countryside. Given complementary work cycles, such links could provide many advantages—capital and labor, for example, could be economically shifted from farm to factory or store.

Closer attention to the economics of urban family life may reveal a greater number of extended families (whether living in close proximity or far apart) than any of us expect. Certainly more work needs to be done to determine the number of such families and the circumstances that favor their formation and perpetuation. And work is also required to determine the impact of rural-to-urban migration on those family members left at home. How, for example, does the departure of men affect those who stay behind? Is the adjustment different when the migrants are women? Are rural marriage networks affected? Do urban men and women tend to find urban or rural spouses? And what is the effect of male employment outside the village on the position and functions of the women left behind? Do wives assume, as Wang and Apthorpe suggest (1974: 18–19), an increasing managerial role when their husbands are gone? We must also look closely at the way relationships within urban families are structured. There is already some evidence that the nature of these relationships may be quite different from what we have been led to expect (see Diamond 1975).

Although a number of scholars have already studied relationships within the Taiwanese family (e.g., A. Wolf 1970; Chu 1970; M. Wolf

1968, 1972), a new perspective on this subject is provided by Cohen (1976). Cohen argues that the economics of family life have a dynamic and variable influence on intrafamilial relationships; and he focuses on the distinctly economic processes that affect the distribution of authority and also produce changes in the jural status of family members.

Disagreeing with Freedman (1966: 49), for example, Cohen proposes that sons are not automatically joint heirs of the family estate but rather grow into that status (since it is always possible that they may be adopted or married out before they achieve it). Prior to adulthood, a son is either a legal "dependent" (a person with no rights) or what Cohen refers to as an "expectant" (a person with limited privileges, such as the right to have one's marriage financed from family resources).

Precisely because adulthood confers coparcenary rights, it generates centripetal and centrifugal forces: brothers can either remain together or demand their share and leave. At this point the disadvantages of partition have to be balanced carefully against the advantages. And the possibility of maintaining the joint family now requires particularly impartial use of family resources (Cohen 1976: 144).

Most China scholars have attributed family partition to strife generated by women—a reasonable enough interpretation in view of the fact that the Chinese themselves usually attribute family partition to this cause. Recently, however, there have been some second thoughts. Margery Wolf proposes, for example, that the roots of family partition may reside in the lenient treatment of younger brothers during their upbringing—a treatment ultimately incompatible with later requirements for their submission to the eldest brother. In Wolf's view, conflict among wives only exacerbates tensions associated with their husbands' adjustment to adult roles (1970: 61–62). Yet Wolf tends to see the relationship among adults as more or less static, and therefore concludes that "had the younger brother been trained from infancy to submit to the elder, the Chinese joint family might be less of a myth" (*ibid.*: 61).

Speare's view (1974: 313) of relationships within the Chinese family is even more static. He uncritically accepts the standard view that "in the ideal family, the relationship between father and son was the strongest, that between brothers the next strongest, and that between husband and wife the weakest. The relative unimportance of the husband-wife relationship was due in part to the fact that marriages were usually arranged by the parents." Formulations such as this one divert us not only from developmental changes, but also from the forces that generate such changes. The work of Margery Wolf (1970) and Cohen (1976) suggest that where the conjugal relationship is relatively weak, it is not simply because the marriage has been parentally arranged. Cohen, for example, goes on to show that there are also various economic factors that encourage or discourage strong husband-wife bonds.

In Cohen's view, marriage establishes new economic roles and property relationships that alter the character of intrafamilial relations. His very detailed description of the transactions associated with the marriage ceremony reveals that certain allocations endow (within the extended family) a new category of property as well as a new property-owning unit—the conjugal unit. Moreover, there are allocations of "private money" to the bride alone for the benefit of her conjugal unit and, especially at the beginning, for the benefit of what Margery Wolf calls her "uterine" family (herself and her children). This "private money" obtained in marriage transactions is subsequently increased through prudent investment and hard work.[2] Within the joint family, only women own private property on an individual basis. During the solidary phase of a joint family, according to Cohen (1976: 196),

> the very commitments and sharing practices that express continuing solidarity among brothers are those which at the same time constrain each from acting on behalf of the particular interests of his "*fo*" [conjugal unit]. A brother's wife is thus sharply defined as the isolated guardian of "*fo*" welfare, and she is drawn into conflict with her sisters-in-law owing to redistributive practices within the joint family which assure that each "*fo*" will fare differently from the others.[3]

Since conjugal units usually vary in size, jural equality among brothers usually means inequalities in consumption; and when dif-

[2] Wang and Apthorpe observe that in Hsing-fu village, after the domestic requirements have been satisfied, a wife is allowed to retain the surplus proceeds from the sale of poultry and livestock; and they suggest that this practice is an important incentive to production (1974: 44).

[3] M. Wolf similarly underscores the special importance of the "uterine family" (1972: 37). It is interesting to note that the importance of this group is also reflected in burial practices. Freedman notes (1966: 131) that the sons of different mothers in polygynous families seek their "separate paths to fortune through their several maternal tombs." My own work among the Hakka of Mei-nung provides support for Freedman's observation. When a man's several wives

ferent consumption requirements become fully apparent, each wife strives to defend the interests of her own "uterine" group (cf. M. Wolf 1972: 36–37). Husbands, however, may not act in the interests of the conjugal unit without jeopardizing the stability of the joint family; and so long as they have reason to maintain the solidarity of the joint family, their relationships with their wives will be strained. Indeed, the husband's energies serve the joint family economy; the wife's serve the interests of her own uterine group. The marital tie is not similarly strained in stem families, since in such cases "family unity is not compromised by hostility between the father and his married son" (Cohen 1976: 199).

The maintenance of joint families taxes relationships between spouses only so long as relationships among brothers and between brothers and parents are relatively strong. The well-known hostility between a woman and her daughter-in-law is understandable in terms of their respective loyalties to different uterine families. But whereas the competition of women is more or less predictable, the relationships of men to their wives, parents, and to each other, depends upon the economic health of the joint family (Cohen 1976: 195). When the advantages of remaining together appear to be outweighed by the attractions of partition, men begin to take the complaints of their wives more seriously. When partition is imminent, fraternal strife and marital solidarity take over as conjugal units anticipate their independence.[4]

## *Economic Aspects of Intracommunity and Intercommunity Relationships*

Many studies of Taiwan discuss the ways families are integrated into communities, and communities into systems of communities. Active in the process of integration are formal groups (like descent and cross-kin groups), temple hierarchies, and a variety of official and semiofficial government agencies; but there are also integrating

are buried separately, their children provide sacrifices together at their father's tomb, but provide sacrifices separately at the tombs of their respective mothers (Pasternak 1973).

[4] Sung describes (this volume) some of the considerations that affect the allocation of shares at the time of family partition, and he indicates how the way the Taiwanese classify property rights makes it possible for tensions to reach a climax during partition. Antagonisms are especially likely to become intense if coparceners disagree about whether particular items are to be considered as inherited property (and hence to be divided equally) or as acquired property—a distinction that is not always clear-cut.

bonds of a more particular nature, such as those based on marriage, friendship, or business association. In this section we will consider the relations between family and family, village and village, and between village and urban area, highlighting some of the things we have learned about the economic and ecological factors that shape those relations.

*Descent and the community.* Anthropologists have long been interested in the nature and functions of descent groups and in the factors that shape them. The variety of descent groups available for study in Taiwan provides a convenient microcosm of those on the Chinese mainland: some are localized, others dispersed; some include entire settlements, others parts of settlements; some are internally segmented, others unified; some have considerable influence over their members, others little influence. The literature on Taiwan sheds some light on the factors responsible for producing such variation.

Virtually all community studies about Taiwan pay some attention to the organization, functions, and economic management of descent and cross-kin groups. Since most anthropologists who have worked in Taiwan have done fieldwork in the countryside, the ethnographic record is richer for rural lineages and cross-kin groups than for their urban counterparts, although some start has been made to correct this imbalance (see Fried 1966; Yin this volume). We now have some insight into the political and social functions of urban-based descent groups; but we know little about their economic foundations and even less about how they relate to rural-based descent groups.

Because of the variety of Taiwan's descent groups, the mainland work of Freedman (1958, 1966), Potter (1968, 1970), Baker (1968), and others is naturally relevant. Some years ago, for example, Freedman tentatively proposed a link between strong and elaborate lineages, rice cultivation, extensive irrigation, and frontier conditions. The work of others subsequently lent support to this speculation: Potter, for instance, attributed lineage elaboration to the production of agricultural surpluses, the exigencies of frontier life, the absence of strong government control, and the presence of commercial development (1970). Several researchers have attempted to test these hypotheses for Taiwan, the last Chinese frontier.

After comparing the two Taiwanese communities where I did fieldwork (Ta-tieh and Chung-she) with others described in the literature, I proposed (1972a) several modifications to the formulations of

Freedman and Potter. It seemed to me that when frontier settlement involved neither conflict, competition, nor a need for cooperation, descent groups were usually able to prosper in relative isolation (as they did in Chung-she [Pasternak 1972a]). However, under different frontier conditions (like those in Ta-tieh [Pasternak 1972a]), the development of descent groups was no doubt often initially inhibited—as when resources or geography encouraged mixed settlements and extensive cooperation across surname lines. In such cases, however, the subsequent pacification and development of the frontier often released competitive forces that eventually led to the growth of strong descent groups.

In his reconstruction of settlement patterns on the I-lan Plain, Hsu observed that whereas the region met the conditions Freedman and Potter said would encourage elaborate lineages, such lineages failed to develop. His explanation for this failure, like my own, points to ecological and economic aspects of frontier life:

> The various needs which required some corporate effort to provide a solution actually were met by means other than lineage organization. The hired Hakka guards provided I-lan farmers as well as travellers with effective protection against the adversary activities of the hostile aborigines. The local order was kept by the headman (Chieh-shou) who was leader of the reclamation band. The expensive cost of irrigation construction was financed by outside investment. And many such activities were carried out by concerned parties who signed formal contracts [with] well-spelt rights and obligations. What Freedman viewed as favorable conditions to create strong lineages seemed to have endorsed the growth of local ties and the commercialization of agriculture. Very few strong lineages appeared in I-lan in the 19th Century. I-lan people erected scores of temples in the 19th Century. Even today, when I-lan is sufficiently wealthy to maintain no less than two hundred temples for various kinds of deities, there are only three lineage temples in the whole region. (Hsu 1972: 66.)

Another illustration of territorial development and integration taking over the functions of descent groups on a Taiwanese frontier (Chu-shan) is provided by Chuang. Chuang notes (1973) that the need for cooperation in subsistence activities was very important, especially with respect to irrigation and cultivation. But cooperation was primarily achieved in terms of territory rather than in terms of kinship; and temples were more important to community and intercommunity integration than were ancestral halls.

These studies seem to confirm that where agnatic groups had a need for common defense and cooperation, bonds based on territory were likely to take precedence over bonds based on descent. But not all Taiwan's frontier areas were of this sort. The ethnography of Taiwan reveals communities ranging from multisurname (Diamond 1969; Gallin 1960; Pasternak 1972a; Wang 1967) to single surname (Ahern 1973; Harrell this volume; Pasternak 1972a). Chung-she village on the Chia-nan Plain (Pasternak 1972a) is one of the latter sort. Here there were neither hostile aborigines, ethnic rivalries, nor significant competition for critical resources like land or water. The ecology was such that there was little need for cooperation, and, under these circumstances, the community was dominated by an internally segmented lineage.

Falling somewhere between Chung-she and the various multisurname communities described in the literature are the four lineage-dominated settlements that together make up Ch'i-nan (Ahern 1973). Although Ch'i-nan's four lineages differ in terms of their corporate resources, their degree of political integration, and the extent to which their constituent families are economically differentiated, they do not consist of segments focusing on different ancestral trusts; and there are no rituals that serve to clearly distinguish lineage segments. The correspondence between descent group and community is suggested in a variety of ways: each of the four adjoining settlements focuses not on a community temple but on an ancestral hall; families of different surname are excluded from one or more community rituals; in some cases gods are worshiped in ancestral halls; regional surname rituals involve parades around the community; etc. What, then, accounts for the fact that descent groups in Ch'i-nan are more active than those in Ta-tieh (Pasternak 1972a), yet less elaborate internally than those in Chung-she? Ahern attributes the distinctive character of Ch'i-nan's four lineages partly to the way Ch'i-nan developed:

> The founding ancestors of the four lineages settled there at about the same time. They were bound together physically by the rivers and mountains that make Ch'inan into a natural amphitheater; they were bound together socially by the experience of constructing irrigation works and defending themselves against the aborigines. In these circumstances, the settlements came to view each other as four like units. They competed for prestige through their ancestral halls, yet at the same time cooperated through the

Tho-te-kong temple. . . . But in Ch'inan [these] groups of like order are separate lineage communities, not segments within a single lineage. (1973: 113.)

The special relationships that developed among the four lineage settlements of Ch'i-nan are manifested in regard to ritual by the rotation of responsibility for organizing several annual festivals. However, Ch'i-nan's settlements probably cooperated less fully among themselves than Ta-tieh did with her Hakka neighbors. Once irrigation facilities had been constructed in Ch'i-nan, little cooperation was required to maintain them or to allocate water. The nature and extent of fighting with nearby aborigines evidently did not require multisurname settlements in Ch'i-nan, but subsequent competition among lineage groups has sometimes led to violence (Ahern 1973: 71–74). The fact that descent groups in Ch'i-nan were not linked to corporate branches in other communities may indicate that there was little need here—in contrast to the situation among Hakka on the P'ing-tung plain—for vast territorial alliances. And the lack of segmentation within local descent groups may reflect the fact that wealth was not, as in Chung-she, concentrated in particular lines. In the face of competition among descent groups, then, the unity of individual groups (settlements) in Ch'i-nan probably took precedence over differentiation within them, especially after the menace of conflict with the aborigines had abated under Japanese rule.

The part played by ecological and economic factors in lineage and community organization is underscored by Harrell (this volume). Harrell compares Ch'i-nan with two villages where he did fieldwork—Hsi-yüan and Ploughshare. The three communities differ in terms of settlement patterns, family relations, lineage organization, community integration, and even religious behavior. Harrell attributed differences in social organization to ecological and economic factors, and he attributes differences in religious behavior to differences in social organization. Moreover, he suggests that a comparison of lineage organization in the three localities lends some support to Freedman's assertion that the presence of corporate property accounts for lineage strength: in both Ch'i-nan and Hsi-yüan rice farming enabled groups of agnates to establish lineage estates, whereas in Ploughshare the lack of available property precluded the development of such estates. The fact that Ch'i-nan's lineages are more solidary than those of Hsi-yüan is attributed to their greater localization. In short, Harrell proposes that the development and solidarity of lineages—supposing that they have the economic potential to form lineage estates—depends upon the degree to which they are localized, and that this in turn is a function of land use and problems of defense.

Harrell may be a bit too eager, however, to endorse Freedman's views about lineage property. Though lineage solidarity may require a corporate focus of some sort, strong agnatic ties can be the impetus for such a focus as well as its result. A lineage does not create corporate estates simply because it can; and the fact that the size of such estates is not a good predictor of lineage strength suggests the importance of the ecological factors Harrell outlines. The problem, after all, is to account for the strength of agnatic ties in the first place.

*Community systems and descent.* Rarely are communities or settlements on the Chinese mainland isolated; instead, they are invariably integrated into complex hierarchies. It is now well known that Taiwanese communities are similarly linked by hierarchies based on kinship, ritual, marketing practices, and political or administrative organization. The nature and extent of these hierarchies varies from place to place, as does the degree to which they overlap and reinforce one another. Indeed, we are only beginning to appreciate the range of Taiwan's community systems, and we are still far from understanding how they work and why they differ. Some understanding of the economic factors that shape such arrangements is therefore essential.

One of the things we have learned from the study of Chinese descent groups is that such groups often include people in separate communities. In Freedman's view, higher-order lineages (i.e., lineages with corporate branches in more than one community) were often promoted by terrain that could not accommodate large aggregations of agnates. Such terrain forced groups of agnates to migrate; and when this did not end the migrants' corporate ties with their original community, higher-order lineages resulted (1966: 36–37). But what conditions encouraged migrants to retain corporate ties? This question is important since broken terrain and migration have not invariably led to higher-order lineages in China or in Taiwan.

Cohen and I both describe higher-order lineages among Hakka on the P'ing-tung plain. Cohen considers such lineages largely a response to surname heterogeneity and to conflict among small agnatic groups. In turn, he attributes the small size of local agnatic groups to the recent date of Hakka settlement on the plain—a factor, like broken terrain, that has the effect of limiting the number of agnates available in any given locality (1969: 177–79). My own fieldwork among Hakka at the other end of the P'ing-tung plain suggests another impetus for the formation of nonlocalized corporate descent groups. Higher-order lineages provide an efficient way to organize and perpetuate alliances on a vast territorial scale when local agnatic groups are small and when the threat of external warfare is great (1972a, 1973). The threat of ethnic violence may have been the major cause for the surname heterogeneity of Hakka settlements throughout the plain and for the emergence of higher-order lineages. The scale and persistence of ethnic confrontations affected the size and distribution of these lineages as well as their internal development.

Freedman proposes that higher-order lineages are likely to be confined to areas that can be crossed on foot in a couple of hours—areas he refers to as vicinages (1966: 23, 37). Skinner argues that lineage organization above the village level probably conforms to the standard marketing area of the lowest-level market town (1964: 36–37). The two positions have much in common. As Freedman observes, the vicinage and the standard marketing area are mostly congruent (1966: 25). Both scholars also agree that when lineages span more than one vicinage or standard marketing area, they probably reflect and serve gentry commercial and political interests; indeed, it is not difficult to find examples of higher-order lineages that serve special interests in connection with market centers of various sizes (see Hsiao 1960: 353; Fried 1966). One reason lineages are often confined to single vicinages or standard marketing areas may be that once agnatic organization extends beyond such units, it invites counter-pressure from the government (Hsiao 1960: 354).

Yet, as Cohen and I indicate, the Hakka lineages of the P'ing-tung plain expanded to include members in many vicinages and marketing areas. Two related factors are probably largely responsible for this: on the one hand, the government was not strong enough to prevent the expansion; on the other, antagonistic Hokkien were a common and persistent menace. Local Hakka responded to the threat of warfare not only in terms of their lineage organization, but also in terms of their social organization more generally: higher-order lineages were only one of many means by which Hakka throughout the plain were lastingly and profitably integrated. Hakka hamlets were combined into neighborhoods or villages that in turn formed higher-level systems, though these systems did not necessarily coincide with the administrative units established by government authorities. These higher-level systems (or vicinages, to use Freedman's term) were linked together in still larger aggregations. At each level, social, religious, political, and military factors furthered Hakka integration. The highest level of organization was the total area of Hakka habitation on the plain—the region of common peril.

Descent groups vary not only with respect to whether they are confined to single communities, but also with respect to whether members live contiguously. At one extreme, core members (i.e., those who stay put after marriage) live in compact, unmixed communities; at the other extreme, core members live interspersed with people of different descent groups. However, the physical distance between agnates and the degree to which agnates live contiguously are not the same thing. Interspersion, for example, is probably often a reflection of the nature of local warfare. Usually, local warfare induces patrilineally related males to live contiguously. But if the fighting takes place mainly or exclusively against other societies or against other ethnic groups, tight clustering of agnates is not as necessary, and interspersed settlement patterns may develop (and may even be strategically advantageous). A recent cross-cultural study (Ember, Ember, & Pasternak 1974) in fact provides some confirmation of a link between contiguity and internal warfare on the one hand, and interspersion and external warfare on the other. Interestingly, the Hakka of south Taiwan formed agnatic groups of both the contiguous and interspersed varieties—perhaps because pressure from an external enemy outweighed internal squabbling without eliminating it altogether.

There are other illustrations of Taiwanese communities forming links for common defense or for other forms of cooperation. For example, Ch'i-nan's four lineage-based settlements are linked hierarchically through temple (and to a lesser degree, surname) ritual, reflecting their common problems of defense. Ch'i-nan is in turn similarly bound through ritual to three neighboring groups of villages, reflecting their economic and social ties. At a still higher level, the entire region is integrated through ritual (Ahern 1973).

*Marketing, technology, and the integration of communities.* Thus far we have mainly been talking about how communities and systems of communities are integrated through descent. For the most part, we have been considering rural communities and their relationships to one another, and we have noted that kinship networks may or may not mirror commercial networks. Let us now turn to the latter.

Skinner's application of central-place theory to Chinese marketing networks (1964, 1965) provided a new perspective on Chinese behavior and society, and further illuminated the local impact of larger economic systems. On the basis of mainland materials, Skinner constructed a hierarchical model of markets, classified in terms of their size and functions; and he showed that villages in what he called a "standard marketing area" themselves form a community characterized by relatively intensive social interactions (marriage, ritual exchanges, friendship networks, etc.) and often even by its own dialect and customs.

Owing to China's remarkable cultural diversity, it was only to be expected that subsequent researchers would elaborate and modify Skinner's models. In this connection, Taiwan has turned out to be of considerable importance. My own work among Hakka in the south indicates how ethnic confrontation may prevent what Freedman believed to be the natural correspondence between vicinage and standard marketing area. Ahern's work also shows that this correspondence need not be perfect (Ch'i-nan apparently constitutes a vicinage but not a standard marketing area). Of particular interest is the work of Crissman, which confirms a number of Skinner's predictions about a modernizing marketing system yet suggests the influence of factors other than those mentioned by Skinner (Crissman 1972, 1976). Crissman describes a marketing system on the Chang-hua plain where the development of rural and urban industry provides a source of cash in the countryside. Owing to Taiwan's modern system of transportation, this cash can be spent outside standard marketing areas (for goods, services, and entertainment). Thus distance—one of the critical factors in central-place theory—does not limit marketing behavior as it does in more traditional settings.

Huang looks at Taiwanese marketing networks in terms of economic activities rather than in terms of geography. His concern is with "the whole process of productivity, transportation, transaction, and information input for further production" (1971: 211), which is what he means by the term "marketing network." Interested in the factors shaping marketing networks as well as in the relationships between them, he is aware (as is Crissman) that Taiwan's developed system of transportation enables farmers to participate in market networks that are larger than their political and social networks (1971: 211). Not only does the highly efficient system of transportation lead to marketing behavior comparable to that predicted by Skinner's model (of modernization), but it also contributes to peculiarities in patterns of migration (see Gallin & Gallin 1974). Finally, Huang provides some insight into the relationships between middlemen—whose roles have been created by the increasing commercialization of Taiwanese agriculture—and producers and wholesalers.

We have considered only some of the strands connecting rural villages to one another as well as to towns and to cities. A number of studies show how technology also shapes relations between families and communities. The cultivation of certain crops, for example, may encourage special relationships. We have evidence of this from Huang's discussion (1971) of the marketing behavior of vegetable growers, and from Cohen's descriptions (1967, 1968, 1969, 1976) of the ties binding families of tobacco growers. (Future studies of tea cultivators, banana growers, orange growers, and others will also undoubtedly reveal special patterns of interfamilial cooperation.) A number of researchers indicate that irrigation practices likewise affect the nature of interfamilial and intercommunity relations. Hsieh, Vander Meer, and I show how areas of cooperation and conflict may expand or contract as the necessity for cooperation in irrigation expands or contracts (Hsieh 1973; Vander Meer 1971; Pasternak 1968a, 1972a, 1972b); Gallin reveals how cooperation in irrigation may shape marriage networks (1960, 1966); and Wang describes how agnatically related families in different communities may be bound together for generations by their common interest (a lineage estate) in a major irrigation system (1972). Several scholars also note the impact of power tillers—recently introduced in Taiwan—on the timing of crops, on labor supply and demand, and on interfamilial relations (Pasternak 1968b, 1972b; Wang & Apthorpe 1974). Others show how Taiwanese fishing communities create distinctive and appropriate kinds of interfamilial and intercommunity relations (Diamond 1969; Wang 1967).

More work needs to be done on the networks that link families by marriage and by friendship. What, for example, are the factors that lead to and shape friendship networks? There is already evidence that affinal networks vary extensively in Taiwan. As indicated earlier, the nature of irrigation may influence patterns of marriage (Gallin 1960, 1966). The nature of crops may have a similar effect: tobacco cultivators tend to marry tobacco cultivators (Cohen 1967, 1968, 1970, 1976). And surely it is of interest that some communities and groups of communities are endogamous, whereas others are not. Why, for example, should intravillage marriage be more common in Ta-tieh (Pasternak 1972a) than in Hsin-hsing (Gallin 1966)? And why should Ch'i-nan's four settlements compose an essentially exogamous unit, whereas those that make up Mei-nung do not? From what has already been said, it seems obvious that answers to such questions will undoubtedly require the isolation of economic and ecological variables—a procedure that we are already in a position to carry out for Taiwan.

## *Economic Aspects of Religious Behavior*

There is now a rich and extensive literature on various aspects of ritual and religion in Taiwan. We have, for example, fine and detailed reconstructions of where and when temples were built, and we have excellent descriptions of festivals, marriage customs, ancestor worship, burial practices, mourning practices, cosmological systems, beliefs in ghosts, etc. But as yet we have little information on the economic aspects of any of these topics. Although temples form hierarchies that parallel social hierarchies, we have no published study on the financial management of a Taiwanese temple or on the financial links between temples. Nor do we have a systematic study of the activities of temple members, one that examines the kinds of people who involve themselves at various levels in the building, maintenance, management, and rituals of temples. Again, though we have some excellent discussions of the functions and activities of religious practitioners, we know next to nothing about the economic advantages of temple membership for businessmen. A few of us are now beginning to fill these gaps. I have already mentioned Cohen's (1976) detailed study of the economics of marriage; and there are other works that highlight economic aspects of various ritual practices.

Ahern's perceptive and detailed study of ancestor worship in Ch'i-nan (1973) is particularly interesting because of the light it sheds on economic factors. Consider, for example, the criteria for lineage membership and for a place in the lineage hall after death. Contrary to what most scholars have assumed, lineage membership and the right to have a commemorative tablet in the ancestral hall are not rights automatically inherited at birth; both privileges may be acquired or lost subsequently. In fact, both depend upon "an actual or potential contribution to the property or membership of the lineage [along with] possession of the lineage surname" (1973: 121).

By highlighting the part that inheritance plays in the ancestral cult, Ahern resolves a number of puzzling questions about the way ancestral tablets are handled—as, for example, why uxorilocally married men are denied a place in their own lineage hall as well as in the hall of their spouses; why the death of children often precludes their right to have tablets in the ancestral hall; and why the tablets of women who die before marriage are commonly excluded from the altars of their own lineage halls. Inheritance also has a lot to do with the responsibility for preparing ancestral tablets and for worshiping the dead; both obligations are closely related to benefits descendents have received (1973: 147–49). In fact, descent may be a less critical determinant of these obligations than inheritance: "Just as property inheritance accompanied by descent entails the obligation to worship, so also may property inheritance in the absence of descent require worship. Weakening the relationship between the parties still more, we find that mere use of a deceased person's property may entail the obligation to worship him." (*Ibid.*: 152.)

This link between ritual obligation and inheritance is noted by others. Wolf indicates that garments worn during a funeral reflect privileges connected with the estate of the deceased, and he notes that claims upon this estate may sometimes be expressed by wearing garments appropriate to a son (1970: 205; cf. Ahern 1973: 153). My own work on tomb sacrifices in Mei-nung (1973) indicates a similar connection between inherited benefits and ritual obligations. Deviations from normal ritual practices, for example, are often attributable to inheritance. Indeed, as in Ch'i-nan, the responsibility for offering tomb and tablet sacrifices is sometimes the result of nonagnatic inheritance (see also Wang 1972: 173–74).

Ahern's paper (this volume) is also of particular interest. Her general discussion of the political and educational functions of Taiwanese *pai-pai* (religious festivals) is both perceptive and correct, as is her explanation of government attempts to curtail *pai-pai* expenditures. I am troubled, however, by her discussion of why the pig is singled out for sacrifice. Her view is that pigs are better suited than other barnyard animals for conveying an "internal message" about achievement, improvement, and success.

Ahern's analysis focuses on several themes supposedly expressed in the fattening and sacrificing of the pig. For one thing, pigs are set apart from other domestic animals because they depend extensively on humans for care and nourishment. Yet they are often portrayed in Chinese literature as embodying undesirable human qualities and are often seen as slightly malevolent. If rituals dramatize themes that preoccupy people, Ahern argues, then perhaps using the pig dramatizes the possibility of transforming something ugly, useless, and malevolent into something beautiful, useful, and lofty.

It is possible that sacrificing the pig conveys the message Ahern suggests—though I am not convinced that this message is as clear to those who sacrifice the pig as it is to Ahern. However, what I find most problematic is Ahern's account of why pigs are chosen in the first place. Of all the animals on the Chinese farm, the pig is probably the most efficient source of protein and calories. Like buffalo and oxen, pigs transform inedible products into edible products. But unlike other animals, pigs require relatively little housing and foraging space to do this. Moreover, pigs are a form of stored capital with a highly visible and easily transferable monetary value. Finally, pigs are an important source of fat—much valued in China—and in this regard they cannot be rivaled by poultry or cattle. Chinese festive fare would not be the same without them.

The value of an offering need not be measured solely in terms of size or weight (although Chinese farmers, in my experience, admire larger pigs and recognize their greater monetary value). Rarity, cost of production, and value to other participants may also help to determine the selection of sacrificial offerings. Perhaps the fattening of a Ti Kong pig simply reflects the local inhabitants' own view of the festival as an infrequent and especially important regional activity worthy of a large display and sacrifice of wealth. And because of the festival's importance, there are more people to be fed. Moreover, in many societies where pigs are ceremonially sacrificed and eaten, such events function partly as ways of redistributing surplus wealth.[5] The reciprocal feastings associated with Taiwanese community and intercommunity festivals (as well as with weddings and funerals) clearly form redistributive networks through which wealth and food flow. Indeed, as Ahern points out, these festivals are periodic stimuli to

[5] Wang and Apthorpe refer to the redistributive nature of temple-sponsored "ritual competitions" involving pigs in Hsing-fu (1974: 63). The prize of success, they point out, is prestige. But they also recognize the intrinsic value of pork: fat pork is said to be an important luxury in Hsing-fu, and I believe that this is the case in most of China.

production and saving, the end product of which is in large part consumed by the communities participating in the ritual cycle. In brief, offering the pig may convey the message suggested by Ahern; but the choice of the pig may be dictated by more mundane considerations.

## *Development Studies*

Taiwan provides an almost unparalleled opportunity for observing at first hand the consequences of deliberate tampering. Indeed, agrarian reform, industrialization, and urbanization are all relatively recent phenomena. Moreover, Taiwan has been affected by an enormous infusion of foreign capital and investment—forces that many believe are, like Green Revolutions, generally counterproductive (see, for example, Frank 1969; Havens & Flinn 1971; Myrdal 1971; Singer 1971; Griffin 1974). Change and development in Taiwan, then, should be of interest to general anthropologists as well as to anthropologists with particular concerns in this field.

*Rural development.* Taiwan's modern rural development began in the 1920's and 1930's when the island became the site of one of the earliest Green Revolutions (see Myers & Ching 1964; Wang & Apthorpe 1974; Wickberg this volume). As Wickberg points out, Green Revolutions traditionally mean that large and prosperous landlords become more so, that less land is available for the less well-off, that confrontations between owners and laborers become frequent, that mechanization increases rural unemployment, and that these unemployed flock into urban areas ill equipped to absorb them (cf. Griffin 1974). Interestingly, none of this appears to have taken place in Taiwan.

Griffin suggests that one of the main reasons why Green Revolutions are so often disappointing is that "land tenure, market structure, and government policy combine in such a way that most of the incentives to innovate are directed toward the large landlord" (1974: 54–55). In most of Asia, according to Griffin, government policies have discriminated in favor of the large landlord; but in Taiwan, land reform made it virtually impossible for policy to be biased in this way (*ibid.*: 52, 80). Wickberg, however, offers a different perspective on Taiwan (this volume)—one that leads us to question Griffin's stress on land reform. Wickberg's reconstruction of land tenure conditions between 1900 and 1940 suggests that long before land reform the Taiwanese tenure system was particularly suited to a successful

Green Revolution. First, the traditional separation of cultivation and ownership rights meant that people who were not interested in improving cultivation could transfer cultivation rights to those who were. Secondly, Taiwan's fixed (rather than share) rent system served to stimulate production. Thirdly, because commercialization was already well developed when the Japanese colonial authorities introduced their Green Revolution, farmers adapted easily to new cash demands. Finally, most tenants cultivated relatively large landholdings. (The deposits associated with some tenancy arrangements suggest that tenancy was not necessarily associated with poverty; in fact, a desire to make up for deposits placed could have been one incentive to production. In short, the high rate of tenancy was not in this case an impediment to development.)

Under the Nationalists, Taiwan has continued to benefit from highly successful land reform and from various technological and infrastructural innovations. Land consolidation, for example, has been under way for some time now; and there have even been experiments in collectivization. In addition, there has been a rapid development of Taiwanese industry, not only in cities, but in smaller towns as well. An enormous literature documents these changes in detail. Most of this literature, however, focuses primarily on the effects of specific changes on income, investment, and production. One of the most comprehensive and anthropologically sophisticated studies of agricultural development in Taiwan is the recent volume by Wang and Apthorpe (1974). Though this is primarily a discussion of the rural economy of three Taiwanese villages, it gives serious attention to the nature and social consequences of changes introduced from Japanese times on. As far as I am aware, this volume contains the only anthropological field reports of local responses to land consolidation and farm cooperatives. Apart from this excellent work, there are few studies that trace the consequences of recent developments very deeply into the Taiwanese social fabric.

The various stages of land reform and their general consequences have been documented in numerous government and scholarly publications. It is usually claimed that by 1949 (when the program was initiated) high rates of tenancy, small-sized holdings, high rents, and tenant insecurity had so intensified that further improvements in productivity would not be possible without a thorough restructuring of the land tenure system. To complicate matters, rural areas were expected to play a major part in supporting the large number of recently arrived mainlanders and also to help underwrite the costs of rapid urban and industrial development. The land reform program was to make all this possible by increasing the labor and capital invested in agriculture. Incentives would be generated, it was hoped, by equalizing access to land, by improving technology and credit, by providing cultivators with greater security, and by permitting cultivators to enjoy a larger share of the products of their labor.

A few anthropologists discuss the consequences of land reform from the perspective of particular communities (e.g., Gallin 1963; Bessac 1964; Pasternak 1968b). Most of these researchers point to the effects of land reform on the nature of leadership, the distribution of power, and the pattern of rural investment. All indicate that the various stages of land reform reduced the political influence of traditional former landlords and resulted in the diffusion of power and influence among a new and more diverse group of leaders. A less often noted consequence of land reform, however, is the tendency for some wealth (along with political and social commitments) to be diverted from local communities to new kinds of investments in towns and cities (see Gallin 1963).

Land reform is not the only development to have helped reshape leadership in the Taiwanese countryside. Chen describes sugar commissioners as "cultural brokers" (this volume); the Gallins describe vegetable merchants in similar terms (1974); and Kung portrays the rural school principal as a source of urban industrial employment (this volume). The growth of an official and semiofficial administrative network reaching into every Taiwanese village has also created its brokers (leaders).

Traditionally, rural Taiwanese leaders owed their influence to wealth, cultivation, and community support. It was the last criterion that kept private ambition within bounds: community support depended on an ostentatious and consistent demonstration of commitment to community well-being. It was thus no coincidence that local leaders were often prominent members of temple management boards. An ambitious village leader, for example, was likely to be prominent in the organization and conduct of village ritual; and a leader whose influence extended over an entire region was likely to be involved in temple activities throughout the region. In the past, then, ambition usually required maintaining a balance between individual aspirations and community needs: the latter tempered the former. But as social and economic mobility becomes increasingly dependent on activities and investments outside the community, and as outside opportunities more and more attract rural talent and energies, it is possible that community commitment may become a less important prerequisite of political success than it once was. To the extent that this occurs, we may anticipate significant changes in the nature of community and intercommunity integration and in the character and functions of local leaders. The emergence of new sources of influence and authority in the Taiwanese countryside, the proliferation of opportunities for greater numbers of people, and the movement of population into towns and cities—all suggest the value of research into social change and its cultural correlates.

*Rural-to-urban migration.* The development of new opportunities in commerce, public administration, and industry has stimulated a flow of people from the rural areas to the urban areas of Taiwan, a flow that has been strengthened by a widespread belief that the limits of agricultural profitability have been reached. We now have a number of studies that deal with the reasons, patterns, and consequences of this migration.

In a recent study, Speare observes that migration in Taiwan has generally been less disruptive than migration in most other Asian countries. The rapid development of Taiwanese industry has enabled urban areas to absorb rural migrants, though partly because the migration rate itself has been restrained by the steady improvement of agriculture and by industrial growth outside the largest cities (1974: 304). Speare's main concern is the effect of urbanization, industrialization, and migration on the Chinese family.

In their study of migrants from Hsin-hsing village, the Gallins, like Huang, suggest that the efficiency of Taiwan's transportation system has modified the familiar pattern of rural-to-urban migration (Gallin & Gallin 1974; Huang 1971). The traditional piecemeal movement from village to town to city (cf. Speare 1974) is now easly short-circuited because migrants can go directly to distant cities. The Gallins also note that Taiwanese migrants have changed in terms of who goes when and to what: early migrants to Taipei, mostly males, went into available service trade positions; later migrants, mostly females, went into the expanding industrial sector. Furthermore, the Gallins draw attention to the various phases of migration that are associated with changing urban opportunities—a theme developed further by Yin (this volume), though the stages Yin describes are different from those the Gallins describe, as is the nature of the adaptation Yin sees.

The Gallins tell us that the earliest migrants from Hsin-hsing to Taipei were often married; that they usually became laborers in the vegetable section of the central market (though some eventually became vegetable merchants); that they frequently worked hard to find jobs for other Hsin-hsing villagers; and that they established formal associations based upon their Hsin-hsing origins. Hsin-hsing migrants are now younger and less often married; more likely to find jobs for city friends than for fellow villagers; and not likely to be involved with fellow villagers in formal associations (though they do participate in "informal coalitions" and reportedly help each other). It appears, moreover, that Hsin-hsing villagers in Taipei are now divided into two groups—merchants and workers—linked in a symbiotic relationship (1974: 354). Merchants, for example, act as mediators between laborers and the local government, a role analogous to that of many rural leaders (cf. Chen this volume). Mutual aid among Hsin-hsing migrants usually means providing occasional small, interest-free loans and also helping during various life-crisis rituals. But village-based ties require special nurturing in the city because they are purely voluntary and because social relationships naturally extend beyond kinsmen and fellow villagers.

Yin describes (this volume) migration from the P'eng-hu islands to Kaohsiung. Unlike the migrants described by Speare or by the Gallins, P'eng-hu migrants initially came to the Taiwanese mainland to escape hardships at home (where ecological conditions had limited agriculture and the mechanization of fishing had resulted in a depletion of marine foods). Before 1950, most migrants had been male, in their teens, poorly educated, and unskilled. They came to the mainland in response to the demand for unskilled labor, especially in Kaohsiung, where they settled in specific precincts (as Hsin-hsing villagers did in Taipei). Since 1950, however, more migrants have been women, their educational level has been higher, they have tended to have more work experience, and they have secured more diverse employment. They have also been upwardly mobile and have not as often settled in particular precincts.

Since the reasons for migration and the backgrounds of migrants have changed over time, it is not surprising that the adaptive structures of P'eng-hu migrants have also changed. During the initial phase of migration, religious associations were very important: these efficiently served the needs of migrants from the same village, all of whom normally lived in the same area of the city, and most of whom were either friends or relatives. Need for financial aid resulted in the organization of mutual aid associations that included people of the same township (rather than simply people of the same village). A regional association was later formed to link all P'eng-hu migrants; and still more recently, younger businessmen have formed a club to further their business interests. With the passage of time, the earlier forms of voluntary association lost popularity as newer ones were organized to meet more up-to-date needs.

Enough has been said to indicate that reasons for migration, patterns of migration, and modes of subsequent adaptation are diverse. Yet we have a long way to go before we can discern general patterns or predict critical variables. The increasing number of women joining the stream of migrants, for example, deserves special study. The only scholars to deal with women migrants are Diamond (1975) and Kung (this volume). Kung focuses almost entirely on attitudes toward work in a T'ao-yüan factory, suggesting that factory work generates new attitudes that extend beyond the workplace. Though her study describes the predicament of many young women in Taiwanese factories, it needs to be seen in the context of information (available in her 1978 dissertation) about the conditions under which women migrate, how they settle, how they live, the nature of their relations with families at home, whom they marry, whom they go to for help and support, etc.

Rural-to-urban migration has reduced the availability of labor in the Taiwanese countryside and increased its costs. In some locations, this has lowered rice-farming profits and land values as well. We must still investigate, therefore, how migration has affected labor distribution, land tenure, and crop choices, and how changes in these areas have affected interfamilial and intercommunity relations.

*Life in town and city.* Apart from the few studies we have on migrants, we know little about the people who live in Taiwan's towns and cities. What has been the impact on them of urban conditions, industrial and commercial development, increasing dependence on wages, etc.? There have been a few attempts to uncover (through questionnaires) the attitudes and values of specific urban groups. Unfortunately, some of these studies lack methodological rigor, and, in this circumstance, it is impossible to assess their relevance to actual behavior. Furthermore, many urban studies tacitly assume that urbanization, industrialization, and modernization produce similar effects everywhere—that people inevitably become more "Western."

In Taiwanese towns and cities, therefore, we should expect traditional forms to disappear after an appropriate period of transition. But do families always decrease in size and complexity in urban circumstances? Does urban life automatically free the young to choose their mates? Does the conjugal relationship really come to allow a more open expression of feeling? Do women in cities really achieve greater equality and more voice in the management of family affairs? These are empiricial questions, and the answers should not be assumed a priori. As Diamond (1975: 4) points out:

> If we choose to ignore the developing political and economic scene, we are reduced to explaining ongoing behaviors and values either as continuities from the traditional past, real or spurious, or as changes lumped under the catchalls of "acculturation" and "modernization." Both these terms are useful and even relevant to some extent . . . but they are not wholly satisfactory. We cannot deny that some of the content of present-day Taiwan life reflects the influence of Japanese and American/European thought and practices. But selective borrowing from other societies can only be understood in the total context of the receiving-culture's experiences and organization.

Adjustment to urban life will thus depend on the way "modernizing" forces work on behavior and expectations. But Chinese people in towns and cities do not automatically fall in step with any general program of urban development. Their towns and cities are distinctive to begin with, and inhabitants bring to them their own inventory of behavior and expectations.

There have been a number of studies on urban attitudes toward marriage and the family, and on changes in these attitudes that apparently reflect the influence of modernization. Marsh and O'Hara, for example, interviewed college students about their attitudes toward "modern" patterns of marriage and the family (1961); and O'Hara subsequently conducted a survey among Taipei students on this matter (1962; see also O'Hara 1967). Comparing Taipei students to American students, O'Hara found that "Chinese and Americans are nearly equally modern in respect to love as basis of choice of mate, the desire to choose one's mate independently, preference for the new (Western) style of marriage, interaction between the sexes at social gatherings, coeducation at the primary school and university level, and engagement before marriage" (1962: 59; cf. Marsh 1968; Tsai 1964).

O'Hara, like many others, infers from expressed attitudes a change from "traditional" to "modern" values, and he attributes this change to industrialization, urbanization, and changes in ideology and law (1962: 60–61). Apart from the difficulty of inferring actual values and behavior from values expressed in questionnaires, there remains the problem of determining the extent to which even expressed values are the products of industrialization, urbanization, etc. One way of shedding light on this latter issue is to question rural Taiwanese. M. Yang did just this (1962) and obtained results strikingly similar to those obtained by O'Hara, Marsh, and Tsai. Yang reports that young people in the countryside aspire to simpler families based on a more intimate conjugal relationship. He also assures us that free courtship is on the increase and wifely submission on the decline.

In a recent study of women's life-styles among Taiwan's new urban middle class, Diamond finds that urban life and a household economy based on a salary leads to intrafamilial relationships dramatically different from those most of us have observed in the countryside (1975). Accustomed as we are to the assumption that migration to the city liberates the young and allows more equal marital relationships, we are surprised to learn that the opposite is true. Though Marsh indicates that urban Taiwanese interact with friends more often than their Danish or their American counterparts (1966: 575–76), Diamond shows that urban housewives are very often isolated and bored. The marital relationship is no more rewarding or intimate in cities than it is in the countryside, and in fact, may be far less so. If one compares Margery Wolf's description (1972) of female social networks in the countryside with Diamond's description of the social life of urban women, the relative isolation of the latter is obvious. That life in cities transforms rural expectations—sometimes in a way that only exacerbates features of rural life that city life is supposed to do away with—is also indicated by Kung (this volume).

One of the most impressive studies of urban social structure and attitudes has been done by Marsh. In 1963, Marsh administered questionnaires to a group of urban, male household heads (20 to 69 years of age) in an effort to elicit data on social stratification, social mobility, family patterns, work, rural and urban exposure, and attitudes toward various social issues. Contrary to what expressed values might lead us to believe, Marsh concludes that household heads in Taipei are more likely than their counterparts in Japan, Denmark, or the United States to have large households with extranuclear kin (1968: 572). He also finds that considerable help (financial and otherwise) is exchanged between parents and children, and that such help is independent of the distance between them (*ibid.*: 574). This last fact may reflect the ability of the Taiwanese family to endure despite residential discontinuity. Finally, Marsh finds that in terms of expressed values Taipei household heads endorse sexual equality and believe that social prestige is and ought to be based on achievement rather than on inherited position or influence (*ibid.*: 578).

Though upward mobility in Taipei is similar to that in other cities (in Japan, Denmark, and the United States), class consciousness seems to have a special form. The Taiwanese, according to Marsh, perceive class differences; but they see their society as being rather less differentiated by class than the Danish see their society, and tend to view class conflict "more in the 'common sense' context of employers' treatment of employees than in the abstract context of 'class interests'" (1968: 582). Generalizing from the responses of household heads, Marsh argues that the Taiwanese, like the Japanese, do not infer an inexorable opposition between workers and capitalists from the fact that employers sometimes take advantage of their workers. Urban males in Japan and his Taiwanese respondents express the view that workers and capitalists should cooperate rather than clash. Since the Japanese hold this view despite their government's tolerance for radical labor unions, Marsh concludes that the view must be a reflection of "East Asian, and more specifically Confucian, cultural values and norms favoring 'harmony,' 'compromise,' and the like" (1968: 583). I am troubled by this conclusion because, for one thing, Taiwan does not share Japan's alleged tolerance for radical labor unions. But also, if we accept this belief in harmony as the product of a Confucian value system, then we are very hard put to explain the directions recently taken by Chinese, Korean, and Vietnamese peoples on the Asian mainland.

If changes in the Taiwanese countryside increase rural ideological and behavioral heterogeneity, the still greater differences among city dwellers should all the more generate urban ideological and behavioral heterogeneity. Indeed, the different social and economic conditions that shape the lives of factory workers, carpenters, bankers, industrialists, restaurateurs, and college students should produce a mosaic of adaptive responses; and since Taiwanese cities and towns vary considerably, their particular mosaics should also vary considerably. In short, as worthwhile as it may be to study urban attitudes and values in general, the efforts of scholars like Diamond, Kung, Olsen, and Marsh all indicate the importance of being very cautious about generalizations. Are the family structures, social networks, religious activities, and value systems of vegetable merchants in the Taipei market, for example, like those of the market's cart drivers? Do female factory workers adapt to urban life as male construction workers do? Are department store salesgirls more like female agricultural workers than like airline stewardesses?

One study that highlights values shared by a particular segment of the urban population is Olsen's essay on how economic values are transmitted in Taipei business families (1972). Olsen's evidence confirms that a very elaborate system of values is passed on from one generation to the next in such families. His data also suggest that there may be variations within this general system linked to specific types of business commitments.

As noted, inherent in many urban studies is the belief that what people say they value and do, and what they actually value and do, are the same thing. If someone says he would allow his daughter to choose her own husband, then it is often assumed that he has "modern" values and that his convictions will, to some extent at least, be translated into action. But educated and relatively well-to-do urban dwellers may simply be responding in a way they consider appropriate for people of their status and education. Though I would not argue that expressed values never influence behavior, I would urge that this influence be demonstrated empirically whenever possible. All people reflect internalized attitudes and values in their behavior. But the critical question, it seems to me, is why people develop different attitudes and values. In what ways are artisans, butchers, or female factory workers different from one another, if indeed they are? By attributing behavior largely to values, one runs the risk of settling for a rather poor predictor of behavior.

Apart from DeGlopper's article (1972) on Taiwanese business relations in Lu-kang, the work of Huang (1971) and the Gallins (1974) on vegetable transport and marketing enterprises, and Knapp's work (1970, 1971) on itinerant merchants, there are virtually no studies that focus on the economic, political, and social aspects of particular business enterprises. (Mark's doctoral research [1972] on "entrepreneurial lineages" in Taipei will soon be added, one hopes, to the list of published works.) This is an area ripe for development.

DeGlopper's primary interest is in business practices, contractual relations and obligations, relations among businessmen, and relations between employers and their employees. Although he is unable to provide the level of economic detail that would allow a finer analysis of how Lu-kang businesses actually work and relate to one another, he succeeds in providing us with preliminary insights into the operation of particular businesses and into the social adaptations they promote. With respect to merchants, artisans, industrial workers, government employees, the urban unemployed, and other analogous groups, we will need to accumulate more quantitative data about families, marriages, businesses, and social and religious behavior, before we can hope to discern general patterns and variations within Taiwan's urban population.

## *Conclusions*

As anthropologists, we do not study Taiwan simply for the sake of understanding the Taiwanese or even, for that matter, the Chinese. Precisely because Taiwan is so excellent a laboratory for evaluating a wide range of hypotheses, we have a special obligation to relate our work to concerns and problems in the field in general. Indeed, it may not even be possible to account for behavior in Taiwan or in China without taking the behavior of other peoples into consideration. Yet if we survey the work done on Taiwan to date, we find that attempts to fit our findings into general theory have been modest and hesitant. We seem to be suffering from a parochialism—though this parochialism may stem in part from the intellectual preparation and commitment that goes with the area. Still, if our work is to have the most value possible, we must make a greater effort to show the general significance of our findings and to benefit from the work of others elsewhere. And these observations apply not only to economic and ecological anthropology but to all anthropology. What is the relevance of what we have learned about Taiwanese families and descent groups to our understanding of family and descent in general? Is it possible in other societies to predict characteristics of ancestor worship on the basis of knowledge about inheritance practices, or to predict forms of family and interfamily relations on the basis of knowledge about crops or irrigation systems? Would a commitment to cultivating sisal in Taiwan result, as it did in Brazil (Gross 1971), in malnutrition as well as in greater socioeconomic differentiation? In what ways might development theory benefit from our research in the countryside, towns, and cities?

Finally, more attention in Taiwan needs to be paid to the area where physical and cultural anthropology overlap. Although studies are available that address folk definitions of (and attitudes toward) disease and curative processes, little attention has been given to the empirical consequences of different practices. Judging from work in progress, however, I believe that we are on the threshold of extending our knowledge in this direction. Attempts are being made to relate cultural practices and beliefs to fertility and infant mortality. A fuller appreciation of the relationships between biological and cultural phenomena, however, will require the isolation of economic variables. I hope that some of us will get around to investigating these relationships, making use of analogous studies conducted elsewhere.

Life in the rapidly developing urban and industrial centers of Taiwan presents one of the most important and inviting areas for future research. Variations in the Taiwanese countryside are magnified and multiplied in towns and cities as differences of class, occupations, ethnic background, living patterns, domestic circumstances, production, and consumption widen and interlink. Urban centers may also differ from one another in terms of the kinds of social adjustments they encourage. With a few notable exceptions, most of us have preferred to work with the relative quiet and simplicity of the countryside, justifying our choice on the grounds that most Taiwanese are rural. As DeGlopper points out, however, urban Taiwanese are becoming less and less a minority.

We have reached the stage where our efforts can and should become more consciously comparative. Data collected in various parts of Taiwan are unusually compatible, so that hypotheses formulated in one area can be tested in another. Greater collaboration is thus essential not only among those of us working in Taiwan, but also with specialists working elsewhere.

# Perceptions of Work among Factory Women

Lydia Kung

Over the last fifteen or so years, Taiwan has experienced a rapid proliferation of factories engaged in food processing and in the manufacture of garments, textiles, plastics, and electronic products. These enterprises, ranging from firms employing thousands of workers to family-run businesses employing a handful of neighbors, have provided young women with wage-earning opportunities that were previously unavailable.[1] From ethnographic accounts of Taiwan and from more specific works such as Margery Wolf's *Women and the Family in Rural Taiwan*, we already know a good deal about the background from which the majority of these factory women come. However, we have less information about their working conditions and about the interaction that takes place within the factory milieu. For the women themselves, one important change resulting from wage earning is a change in their status within the family. This is a central and complex subject, however, that I will not discuss here.[2] Instead, I will try to describe how factory women experience work and how these experiences alter their perceptions of factory employment.

[1] Out of a total 1972 population of over fifteen million, there were an estimated half-million female factory workers (Liu 1972: 25). The majority of factory women with whom I worked were aged 15 to 30.

[2] The mere fact of wage earning has not conferred upon daughters the right to control their incomes. Because the family's interests are being served when a daughter goes to work, decisions concerning the proper disposal of her income are in the hands of the family head. Women in dormitories allot approximately half their earnings to living expenses; but this is not equivalent to having full control over the disposal of their income. It is true that women are allowed spending money; but with the exception of working students, these sums are not large enough to improve women's future options. Nor have factory women come to regard their occupations as a viable or desirable alternative to marriage. They may speak of themselves as self-supporting, but they do not see this circumstance as extending very far into the future.

My premise is that the experience of work may well be as important as the fact of earning an income in affecting a woman's status or her understanding of that status. In the words of the women themselves, what is new is their coming "outside" (regardless of whether they live in company dormitories or continue to live with their families); and although this change is the result of economic necessity, it appears to have a more direct and immediate impact on their lives than earning an income.

This paper, then, will focus on relationships formed at work, on the interaction of women with their co-workers and superiors, and on the women's views of management. Rightly or wrongly, much of what female workers learn in the factory and many of the conclusions that they form there about personal relationships and about their own social roles are generalized to the larger society. Chang, who had worked in a factory for two years, commented: "You can learn things here in the factory that you can't learn at home. The most important is learning how to get along with people. People in school are simpler, whereas in society you see all kinds of people; it's more disorderly. At home it's no problem getting along with people, but here outside, as in the factory, you have to be very careful in how you deal with people. Sometimes a very small matter can offend somebody." The way factory women see their work and their relations with other workers is, of course, determined in part by the positions they occupy in the company hierarchy. But by examining these matters, I hope to say something about how the attitudes women bring to the factory are reinforced or transformed into new attitudes, and how these new attitudes then constitute the social context in which women work. This approach also gives us an effective means of exploring concepts such as "work commitment," "work involvement," and "job satisfaction."

I gathered most of the data for this paper during six months' research at a T'ao-yüan factory I shall call Western Electronics. There I was allowed to conduct informal interviews during working hours, live in company dormitories, and also have limited access to various personnel records. An American-owned firm employing approximately 4,000 female workers, Western Electronics operated three manufacturing plants (two for television parts, one for solid-state components), and was thus one of the largest factories in Taiwan. In addition, I also gathered data on working conditions and work relations from women employed by other firms in the San-hsia area who lived at home and commuted to work. Throughout the following discussion, then, it should be remembered that my sources have been working women and that I am not attempting an objective analysis of industry or industrial relations in Taiwan.[3]

When women enter a factory they bring with them certain expectations about the job and perhaps even about the firm that employs them. As they acquire broader exposure to different companies and greater work experience, they often find that their initial attitudes are modified by experiences in different positions. But before turning to this interplay between expectations and work experience, I want to touch briefly on several factors that shape women's initial attitudes toward factory employment.

The sight of young women waiting for company buses in the mornings and being dropped off in the early evenings is now commonplace in many villages and small towns in Taiwan; it attests not only to the increasing number of factories in the outskirts of urban centers, but also to the widespread acceptance of factory work as a respectable occupation for young women. This new attitude presents a marked contrast with the prevailing view in prerevolutionary China, when the reputation of women factory workers was often questionable,[4] and with the prevailing view in the period Margery Wolf describes, when factories were just being built in Taiwan, and when many parents were reluctant to permit their daughters to go outside to work. Though factory work does not bring a woman prestige, it is conceded to be more acceptable than work as a shopgirl, ticket collector, or waitress, since these occupations involve contact with the public and mean a working environment that is often said to be too complex. I discuss in further detail elsewhere (1978) how occupations are selected for young women. Here it is sufficient to note that for a large majority of factory women, factory work was a virtually automatic step after primary school or lower middle school.

Even after the 1969 extension of compulsory education through the ninth grade, the cost of lower middle school remains too high for many families. For these people, it makes much more sense to have a

[3]I conducted fieldwork in northern Taiwan between January 1974 and January 1975, and was supported by grants from the National Science Foundation, the Yale Concilium on International and Area Studies, and Sigma Xi. A grant from the American Association of University Women permitted preliminary analysis of the data.

[4]See, for example, Fong 1932: 147; Lieu 1936: 167.

daughter bringing home an income than being a drain upon family resources, especially since she will eventually marry and leave. The choice between continuing school or beginning work is customarily not one for daughters to make; and by the time young women face this decision, they are familiar enough with their family's economic situation to have already become reconciled to the idea of entering a factory after primary or lower middle school. Indeed, foreseeing this and aware that she is expected to assist her family financially, a young woman enters factory work with attitudes that are already realistic.

Although her alternatives are limited, a new factory worker may still have varying expectations about her work as a result of several additional factors. First, a girl in her teens, recently out of school, is inevitably less well informed and assertive than her workmate who has been working for several years and may have had experience in several factories. Second, fluctuations in the job market naturally affect a woman's assessment of her current position. If another job can be easily found, a dissatisfied worker will have no qualms about leaving one factory and "trying out" another; if the demand for workers drops, however, a worker may be willing (as in the fall of 1974) "to put up with more and not complain about it." Third, increasing numbers of women regard factory work as a means of attaining an education (generally at the high school level). These women, who attend school on a full-time or part-time basis and work a regular eight-hour day, obviously have somewhat different perspectives on their jobs than women who cannot look forward to the time when a high school diploma will enable them to leave the factory. Finally, some women perceive a factory job primarily as an opportunity to leave home, to see more of the world, and to gain greater independence; they too bring a special perspective to their work.

This has been an abbreviated summary of some of the factors that shape women's expectations about factory work. Given that educational attainments confer prestige, that manual work carries low status, and that a daughter usually does not have much say about whether she continues in school or goes to a factory, one does not expect unskilled women to have high expectations about the satisfactions or benefits of their jobs. This is an oversimplification, but it is a starting point for asking what features of factory work provide satisfactions, and what features lead to frustration.

I begin with a brief description of the socialization process by which newly hired women gain familiarity with the factory and with their new roles. I then consider the relations between female workers and their supervisors and the way women characterize these relations and supervisory roles. Finally, I examine the bases on which women evaluate their jobs and review workers' perceptions of management.

Newly hired workers, in contrast to older and more knowledgeable workers, are seen as naive, as "not knowing anything." To understand how such women become more experienced, one must begin with a woman's first introduction to factory work. By discussing some of her initial reactions, I hope to give some idea—albeit impressionistically—of the difficulties women customarily encounter.[5]

The way a young woman comes to Western Electronics in the first place determines to some degree the ease with which she adjusts. Whether she comes alone or with friends, or whether she joins acquaintances already at the firm, can make a considerable difference. For a company as large as Western Electronics (with its commensurately large demand for workers), routine recruiting procedures include sending company representatives to middle schools, particularly in areas distant from industrial zones.[6] Friendly, carefully cultivated, and mutually beneficial contacts between these representatives and school teachers and principals ensure that a pool of workers is always available. Indeed, since rural schoolgirls and their parents are not likely to have extensive knowledge about particular factories in the north, it makes sense for them to follow the advice of teachers and principals. Other women are recruited to Western Electronics by newspaper advertisements—though information provided by one's friends is considered the most reliable.

Orientation sessions for newly hired workers at Western Electronics consist of two-day programs (separate for men and women) that include some technical training (intended more for reducing anxiety than for promoting proficiency) and a tour of the factory premises. The orientation is conducted by one of three trainers, who were formerly assemblers themselves. Each trainee is asked to introduce herself and encouraged to volunteer information about her

[5] I do not claim that Western Electronics represents a typical industrial organization in Taiwan. However, the firm is one of a handful of well-known firms for which many factory women have worked at one time or another.

[6] This is not a new method of recruitment. Fong, for example, described similar conditions in China between 1912 and 1930 (1932: 118–19).

background.[7] A reluctance to speak and a flustered manner are the most telling characteristics of young women starting their first jobs. I excerpt the following cases from my notes.

Chen Hsiao-ping and Chen Hsiao-lan were sisters who came to Western Electronics together and lived at home in T'ao-yüan county. Hsiao-ping had been out of school for two years and her younger sister for one year. When the trainer asked what they had been doing during that time, neither was willing to offer any information; and both remained silent when asked whether they had worked before. Only after more prompting did they mention that they had operated knitting machines for about half a year, having heard that such jobs pay well and allow a person to learn a skill. They subsequently decided that the work was too strenuous.

Lin Mei-hua and P'eng Su-fang were classmates and said only this about themselves: "We're just out of lower middle school and feel very ignorant about the world outside." Under the mistaken impression that the company paid for all meals, they brought very little cash with them, and, as a result, they said they could not afford to buy enough to eat.

Originally from Kaohsiung, Hsü Kuo-ying had worked in the north and came to Western Electronics because she had a friend there. She was particularly eager to know the section to which she would be assigned, since she was apprehensive about soldering. [Most women had heard about the deaths that had resulted from soldering fumes in a factory some years ago.] She went on, "I'm not afraid of hard work; I only worry if it's harmful to my health." [Women are also apprehensive about the eyestrain and resulting harm that may come from extensive use of microscopes.]

The trainers can all recount anecdotes about employees who thought that they were joining a toy factory or who held wildly inaccurate notions about wages and benefits. The central purpose of the orientation session is thus to correct such misconceptions. Trainers begin with the proper pronunciation of the company's name, then run through a gamut of company regulations concerning hours, time cards, holidays, leaves of absence, welfare benefits, and, most important, pay. (To the base pay are added a food allowance, a transportation allowance, and, if one qualifies, various annual bonuses and attendance bonuses; and from this wage are deducted the employee's contributions to the union and to medical insurance costs.[8])

[7]The trainers explained the reluctance of most women to speak about their former work experience this way: "They are afraid that if they admit to having worked before, it will mean more questions and trouble. Besides, previous experience won't get them a better position."

[8]In 1974, NT$38 = US$1.00. Wages for assemblers in electronics factories then averaged between NT$1,600 (US$42) and NT$1,900 (US$50) per month for beginners. (Workers in gar-

Since no one takes notes during the presentation, it is hardly surprising that most new workers remember little more than how much they will earn and their work schedules. Yang works in one of the largest garment factories in Taiwan, and had this to say about starting work with a new company:

> The more you know—about wages, about how often you get paid, about meals—*before* you go to work, the better. But not all girls think to make inquiries beforehand. Even then you still only get a general idea of conditions in a factory; only gradually do you learn more from your co-workers. As for how much is deducted for medical insurance and so on, you know only by looking at your pay slip; and the same goes for union dues. Actually, no one pays much attention to these little matters; the only thing we really notice is the net pay.

Similarly, when I asked Lim, who works in an electronics plant outside San-hsia, about the company union, she replied: "I know I'm in the union but don't know much else about it; everyone knows this because you can see the deduction on the pay slip. I heard the union explained once, but I didn't pay much attention; and even if I had been listening, I would have forgotten long ago."

During the time I was at Western Electronics, an experimental program was devised to better ascertain new workers' reasons for resigning. It is generally not easy to persuade young women to give their true reasons for leaving a company.[9] Nonetheless, some of the reasons new workers offer suggest discrepancies between what women expect and what they actually find. When first asked by a trainer why she wanted to leave, one newly hired worker said that her father had written asking her to return home. Only after much probing did she admit to being out of funds—again, because she thought that meals and lodging were free. (She had written home for money, but

---

ment factories, generally paid by the piece, could earn well over NT$3,000 a month, if experienced.) At Western Electronics, a beginning assembler's base wage was NT$1,350, with a monthly food allowance of NT$180 and a monthly transportation allowance of NT$180. (The base wage for an evening shift worker was NT$1,480.) After thirty days, there was an increase of NT$25; after ninety days, an additional NT$50; after six months, an additional NT$50; and after one year, an additional NT$100. Annual increments thereafter were NT$100. Finally, there was a monthly charge of NT$50 for the use of dormitory facilities.

[9]This is an understatement: women find it very embarrassing to resign, and only rarely give the true reasons. In part, this has to do with not losing face. If a woman admits that the wages are too low, she seems to imply that she desperately needs the money. The aim is to be able to leave with as little fuss as possible. One worker in a garment factory explained that women "want to leave behind a good impression in case their next job doesn't work out and they decide to return."

none was sent.) When she spoke to the trainer, she had no more money for food, had had no breakfast, and had packed her belongings; she remained only because she had no money for a train ticket. (Subsequently, the trainer arranged for a temporary advance on her wages, and she stayed.) Another group of four women came to the factory with work experience, but this was their first time away from home. Predictably, the reasons each woman gave for wanting to leave matched those given by her companions: she was homesick, thought the dormitories too noisy, suspected thefts of her personal belongings, was not eating enough because food was too expensive, and was unable to tolerate the fumes and smells in the plant.

Since the technical training portion of the orientation program does not try to bring new workers' skills up to the level required on the assembly lines, many women are not prepared for the rapid pace and strict discipline that the job actually entails. Thus, women who view a factory job as a means of liberation or as a new and exciting experience—but who have never visited a factory—are often ill equipped to make the adjustments required of them. One worker said:

> When we first came to be trained, everything was so different. The room [where orientation programs were held] was carpeted, air-conditioned, and quiet. Then when we actually began to work in the plant, it was such a disappointment. The plant is noisy, and it's usually too warm. It's so far from what I used to think about when I was in school. At this job, each worker is more like a machine than a person. Before, I could not have imagined myself using tools such as these.

This description comes from a trainer: "Before, at home or at school, these girls always had a teacher or parents to look after them, and at first many become dependent on us. They often treat their work like play, toying with the parts, and then they are unable to fill their work quotas. Then when their group leader or foreman scolds them, they're ready to walk off the job."

The unwillingness of many workers to ask for information only exacerbates their difficulties. A group leader cited the following case as an example: "A girl on my line burned her hand with her soldering iron but didn't tell anyone. She was afraid she would get into trouble and would be scolded. It wasn't until the next day when I noticed the swelling that I sent her to the nurse. That's how it is with many of them who come to work for the first time; they're young, they don't have their parents here, and they don't have the nerve to say anything."

Given the authoritarian character of Taiwanese schools, the timidity of new workers should not be surprising. Indeed, the factory hierarchy is far more complex than the school hierarchy. Each of the three plants operated by Western Electronics has a plant manager, manufacturing managers, superintendents, foremen, and group leaders, before one gets to the various grades of workers themselves.

New workers generally become assemblers; and inspectors, testers, quality-control workers, and group leaders are usually promoted from experienced assemblers. Women with high school diplomas, particularly from vocational schools, stand a slightly better chance of being placed in tester and quality-control positions more quickly. Group leaders (who receive an additional NT$250 per month) may have to supervise up to thirty assemblers, though the average number ranges between fifteen and twenty. Foremen are responsible for approximately eighty to a hundred workers, and they in turn report to superintendents. (During the time I was at Western Electronics, there was one "forewoman" in the factory.)

Because of the size of Western Electronics, women frequently admit that they do not even know who the managers in their plants are. Although female workers form opinions of managers and superintendents, they have direct contact only with group leaders and foremen, who, almost by default, are perceived as extensions of the company management. In our conversations about supervisors, women rarely mention superintendents. And the few unsolicited comments they do make are similar in content: "A superintendent might know the names of some of the group leaders in his section, but there's no point in even talking about managers. When we see a manager coming, most will quickly act as if we're very busy at work. A superintendent may have something to say to a group leader, but never to us workers."

Women naturally form a clearer image of their foreman than of their superintendent or their manager; and they hold very firm opinions about the foreman's authority and responsibilities. Indeed, the foreman knows the names of the women on the lines he supervises—though his direct contact with them is in fact infrequent. In the women's eyes, then, he is known primarily by his manner of interacting with their group leader.

Unlike trainers (who are more solicitous of new workers' well-being), foremen are perceived, at least initially, as no-nonsense supervisors whose sole concern is meeting production quotas.[10] Foremen are in fact expected to be strict and "mean." Tseng, the only forewoman at Western Electronics, remarked that many women still find it odd that she holds her position: "Many feel that a foreman should be a man, and that any woman who does a foreman's work must be a very mean person indeed." For some workers, though, this image is merely a stereotype. After one month on the job, Chang described her foreman as "not really a bad person; sometimes he'll joke around with us, although not all the time, because that way no one would be scared of him." And when I asked whether workers in fact found him intimidating, she laughed and said "no, not really."

Women complain frequently, however, that their foremen are too strict. Su, a Western Electronics employee for five years, was one of three women in the entire factory who had worked her way up from an assembler to a trouble-shooter. She thought that the tendency of many foremen to be excessively strict was one of the causes of the firm's high employee turnover rate: "Sometimes, especially when they are under a lot of pressure from their superiors, foremen demand too much from the girls; they expect everything to be perfect. Many workers see their foremen as being too concerned with following regulations to the letter. Many women find this hard to take. If there are other jobs available, they wonder why they should have to put up with this, and so just quit on the spot."

The relationships between workers and their foremen are not simple, and the expectations women have in this regard are frequently ambiguous. Moreover, workers judge their foremen differently, according to their own positions and temperaments. But despite these differences, it is still possible to cite some of the factors that often influence relationships between workers and foremen.

Factory women invariably address their foremen by title, since to address them by name would connote a level of familiarity that does not exist. (Foremen, though, address workers by name.) Yet the job

[10]Toward the end of my research year, Western Electronics began a series of training sessions for foremen in which groups of foremen were asked to list their most urgent problems in order of priority. I have information for two of these groups. In the first group's list of eight needs, "how to motivate and encourage assemblers" was given last. This need was also listed as number eight by the second group, though in this case it was followed by ventilation problems, equipment shortages, and safety.

hierarchy is not the only factor that limits familiarity. "There's no point in taking our problems to the foreman," one group leader said; "we're all women, and he's a man." Age is also a factor: older foremen (40 and above) are seen as laconic, stern, and distant; and women readily attribute to age any peculiarities in their foremen's temperaments. By contrast, regional origin seems to have very little effect on relationships between workers and foremen.

The limited interaction between foremen and workers is easily observed at the plants: foremen are often seen hovering over assembly lines, but they only occasionally have direct contact with workers. This is largely a consequence of the way work is organized in the factory, and the women know this. Moreover, with group leaders acting as intermediaries between foremen and workers, there is little need for foremen to pay much attention to individual workers, so long as they are doing an adequate job. Assemblers comment that the foreman only comes "if there's a problem or a mistake. When there are few rejects, you won't find him coming over to say something nice."

Though many women say they would like their foremen to show more concern and feeling, they also do not want to be "bothered" by someone who is seen to be a representative of management. This independent attitude is a reflection of the vertical relationship between worker and foreman—a relationship that contrasts, for example, with the one Dore found in Japan (1973: 250) where a foreman and his workers together constitute a team. Workers' ambivalent expectations thus present difficulties for foremen, who often find themselves on precarious and ill-defined footing in their informal dealings on the plant floor. Genuine concern for a worker's welfare, for instance, can be misinterpreted as unwelcome attention. And since women rarely seek out their foreman, the burden of establishing the "proper" relationship rests upon him. As one worker explained: "Actually our foreman is pretty nice; he isn't overly strict and he kids around with us. Once he said, 'If there's something on your mind, don't be afraid to come and see me.' But what difference does saying this make? Who would actually go see him on her own?"

Since women are largely unable to make their wishes known directly to their foreman, the foreman must be able to sense what he may legitimately do and also understand the consequences of his behavior (since inconsequential acts may appear to have serious implications for workers). Chang had this to say about a foreman and the women he supervised:

Of course, each person likes to know that someone is concerned about her. For example, when my younger brother came to Taipei, my foreman asked about him and what he was doing here. But this would depend on the girl herself; some don't like to mix work matters and personal affairs. For instance, if a worker were an adopted daughter, she would not want to talk about her family. She would find a foreman's questions annoying, as if he were prying. In any case, a foreman is most interested in production.

Group leaders, since they must deal with both foremen and workers, are most apt to appreciate that a comfortable, friendly relationship between foremen and workers can often improve work performance. A group leader gave this example from her own experiences: "When a new foreman comes, there are bound to be some rough spots and differences in opinion about how the job ought to be done, and often a person will take such disagreements personally. But if everyone is on good terms, if there's a need to work overtime, for example, it wouldn't be a problem; whereas now, it's almost as if overtime were forced on us."

Most women agreed that it would not do for a foreman suddenly to initiate a more familiar relationship; he ought instead to begin by complimenting a worker on her performance or taking an interest in her work, and only later proceed to more personal matters. And such matters need not concern major issues. Inquiring after a worker's health after she has been ill, notifying her family after something has happened, treating workers to ice cream for achieving a high work quota, asking if a worker has eaten or has done well at her school examinations—all indicate that a foreman has "human feeling" and takes an interest in his workers' welfare. Few workers, though, actually claim to have (or even conceive of having) a close relationship with their foreman. If they converse with him at all, the subject is usually production.

As noted, a fine line separates a foreman's efforts to be kind and actions that could be interpreted as improper and unwanted advances. Experienced workers described as too friendly a foreman who patted everyone on the shoulder (considered too forward), another who liked to talk when his workers preferred to be left alone, and others who were considered to be playboy types. "Our foreman is always trying to take advantage of the girls. He's a very slippery person; that's why girls who come out to work cannot be too trusting." This works the other way as well: women who are on familiar terms with their foreman are accused by their co-workers of "kissing-up." But with favoritism viewed as inevitable, women concede that those who know "how to talk" come out ahead.

Factory women value warmth in their relations with a foreman more highly for its own sake than for the sake of its possible work-related advantages. This feeling is largely sustained by the women's realistic awareness of the limits of what a foreman can achieve in terms of working conditions and benefits for his workers. As one worker said: "No one pays any attention to our opinions. We could tell our foreman but it's not likely that he would speak to those above him for us, because he does not want to jeopardize his job. You can't blame him; everyone wants to move up. He's afraid that he might be considered too much of a busybody." Though some women claim that workers on friendly terms with their foreman stand a better chance for promotion, the final decision to promote a worker to group leader is in fact made by the superintendent.

Greater dissatisfaction is caused by a foreman who underlines the distance between his position and his workers' position by flaunting his higher status. Because women perceive it to be the foreman's responsibility to introduce a personal dimension into their relationship, they are apt to interpret even a casual remark or gesture as a sign that their foreman is putting on airs. According to one group leader, "All it takes is just one time if he happens not to respond to or acknowledge a girl, and she'd think that he looks down on her."

The sensitivity of many factory women about their status as manual workers and about their low educational level makes them especially prone to such interpretations. As one trainer remarked: "Some girls may be on friendly terms with their foreman, but if he should ever yell at them, their reaction is stronger than you might expect, because they assume that he looks down on them because they are only primary or lower middle school graduates." This same trainer recalled her own attitude when she was a group leader: "I admit now that I was wrong to think that way, but as a high school graduate, I didn't want to associate with primary or lower middle school graduates. I preferred to talk with other high school graduates and the foreman, since they were better educated." In addition, when women say that the "spring of their youth has been sold to the company," they refer not only to the amount of time spent in the factory but to the fact that they are only able to interact with a group leader and a handful of co-workers. The foreman is thus a member of a larger and more varied circle of people whom a worker may wish to have the opportunity to know.

Although a foreman is not categorized as a member of the managerial class, he is not regarded as a laborer either, since giving orders is a legitimate part of his authority. A group leader is different; she resembles her assemblers in background and in previous work experience, but she also supervises them. Her social identities as worker and as supervisor inevitably generate ambiguity about her status.[11] One worker, after her group leader refused her request for a day off, complained: "All I was trying to do was do *her* a favor by telling her ahead of time; otherwise, I could have just not come to work at all. Who does she think she is, acting as if she's got all the authority!"

Not surprisingly, factory women frequently have ambivalent feelings about becoming group leaders themselves. Their reluctance to move up to this position tells us something about job commitment and job satisfaction (since becoming a group leader is a promotion), and it also indicates the importance of the perceived contrast between a timid, uncertain woman entering her first factory, and a woman who, perhaps after a few months, oversees fifteen or twenty women much like herself.

Older workers at Western Electronics told me that four or five years previously there had been more opportunities for assemblers and group leaders to be promoted, because the company's expansion had created a demand for more clerical workers. (They could point to women in the offices, including the three trainers, who were formerly assemblers.) The prospect of such mobility, however, no longer exists; and even though the company has a policy of promoting from within, all agree that few openings materialize. The status of group leader, then, is the highest that an assembler can hope to attain; and when I asked assemblers about positions to which a group leader could be promoted, their answers either indicated that there were none or alluded to "the way things were four or five years ago." As one working student put it, "Here I feel as if I will always be a group leader. Even if I had more schooling, it wouldn't be any use; there're no chances for promotion beyond group leader." (Moreover, the opportunity to become a group leader arises only when another de-

[11] There is less ambiguity about relations between office women and factory women (see Kung 1976). Office women are in a different class altogether in status and identity; and though their higher educational level justifies their superior positions, it does not justify, in workers' eyes, the superior airs some of them display.

parts.) The tendency for workers to flock to new factories thus reflects the realization that one's chances for promotion are better with a growing company.

New workers generally first address their group leader by title, though after a few days they call her by name as the other workers do, a practice group leaders apparently prefer. One group leader said, "I would feel funny hearing someone calling me a group leader; it'd be as if I were a level higher, so I ask them to call me by name." Most assemblers and group leaders, however, acknowledge their difference in status. Yet this difference is often specific to the work situation: "It's not something that you would feel away from work or that you would take with you off the job." Nevertheless, the title itself carries some prestige: "Being a group leader just sounds a lot better than being an assembler; if you tell someone outside the company that you work as a group leader, it sounds nicer." To one woman, a group leader is still a "factory girl," although she is "higher than we are by one level"; to another, a group leader is in a position of honor because "then she is no longer just a manual worker."

Though a group leader may insist in the abstract that all women are workers and that she does not want special treatment, she may be reluctant in practice to accept reassignment as an assembler. In the fall of 1974, the production of several television models ended, and a number of group leaders were switched to other sections as assemblers. Although their wages remained the same, the move was distressing: "After all, the positions are different; before, you were the one telling people what to do, and now someone else is giving you orders." At a smaller electronics plant, a group leader was sick for three weeks and returned to find another woman in her place. The situation was awkward for both women and their foreman, with the new group leader feeling that she could not be expected to supervise her predecessor. Her predecessor, however, felt that she could not bear to remain on the same line, and was subsequently transferred to another section.

To many women, however, the added prestige that the title group leader bestows seems empty, and even the extra NT$250 does not seem sufficient compensation for a thankless job. A new worker is apt to notice only the more comfortable and superficial features of a group leader's day: "I certainly wouldn't mind being a group leader; all they do is walk around and talk, and they don't have very much work to do." A far more frequently heard assessment, though, is that a group leader's work is light but her responsibilities heavy.

By definition, a group leader is required to deal with people, and she is constantly placed in the position of being an intermediary between workers and their foreman.[12] The difficulties of being an intermediary, however, cause some workers to think twice before accepting a promotion to group leader. In the opinion of one woman who has been both a group leader and a forewoman, the former position is the more demanding: "Foremen do not always have to deal with every worker directly, but a group leader has to cope with all matters relating to every worker." The following comment summarizes the group leader's predicament: "Being a group leader isn't easy. If you really follow company rules to the letter you'll have all the girls against you; no one will like you. But if you bend the rules too much, you're in trouble with the foreman and the superintendent. You can't please both sides. But many workers are still interested in becoming a group leader; you can't blame them; everyone wants to climb up, only they don't realize how bitter the job can be until they actually begin it."

Though group leaders are expected to perform supervisory tasks that are similar (in nature if not in extent) to those foremen carry out, they lack (or feel they lack) the right to exercise that authority—authority, they believe, that their mere title does not legitimize. A group leader cannot treat her workers in the way a foreman might and still remain an effective group leader; yet she must nonetheless answer to her foreman.

> It's easy for a foreman to scold us group leaders, but what methods are we to use to get the girls to listen to us? If a group leader does what a foreman tells her to do and resorts to his methods, the girls wouldn't stand for it, and you would have an even worse situation. Sometimes when a worker's performance isn't good enough, a foreman will want to get rid of her, but how is one supposed to say such things? It's hard to criticize your workers since you know them well, and since we were all doing the same job once.

An assembler can usually count on the inspector on her line to catch her mistakes, but a group leader is held accountable not only

[12] On one occasion, I was speaking with an informant while she was working; shortly thereafter, her group leader came over and said reluctantly that the foreman wanted to know what I was doing there (he was new and had not seen me before, and I was not in uniform). My informant later said that her group leader had felt very uneasy about having to do this, but another

for the quality of the assembled parts (a responsibility that sometimes leads to conflict between group leaders and quality control workers) but also for the conduct of her workers on the line. Faced with an uncooperative worker, a group leader must find her own solution, and this usually involves encouragement rather than scolding. Some group leaders, in fact, consciously exploit the close relationship they have with assemblers. One group leader claimed that "a more complex relationship develops between workers and their group leader because of the greater contact between them. A worker who does poorly, therefore, might feel embarrassed toward her group leader, whereas it matters less with a foreman since she doesn't have much of a relationship with him anyway." Indeed, difficulties often arise when a group leader is not close to a worker—as, for example, when she is much younger and consequently finds it awkward to assert her authority. Differences in education can also lead to difficulties. Group leaders with only a primary or lower middle school education, for instance, frequently attribute some of their problems to this factor: "That girl thinks that because she is a high school graduate, I have no right to supervise her."[13]

The importance factory women attach to educational level, and the fact that promotion from assembler to group leader does not hinge on education, together undermine group leaders' self-confidence. Though most workers concede that group leaders are experienced, few workers see much else to justify their elevated status. Predictably, however, better educated workers are nearly unanimous in asserting that educational level should be taken into account for promotion, whereas workers with less schooling emphasize the greater relevance of work experience.

A none-too-thorough understanding of company policy concerning the selection of group leaders for the very few available openings also promotes ill feeling (which is sometimes directed at the group leader herself). A group leader may recommend workers for promotion, but the final decision is made by the superintendent, who reviews suggestions from the foremen. Selection is based on seniority,

---

group leader gave a different interpretation of the episode: "The fact that he sent over the group leader already means that he was giving you 'face' [sparing me embarrassment]. If he had come over himself, no girl would dare to come back and talk to someone in his section."

[13] I have discussed the divisions among factory women in greater detail in an earlier paper (1976). A double standard operates here: a lower middle school graduate might feel superior to an elementary school graduate, but might resent being looked down upon by an office worker or by a high school graduate.

performance, and "leadership ability." But since only one of these factors can be measured objectively, there are inevitably suspicions of favoritism. And though many factors come into play, it is widely agreed that knowing the right people is essential for attaining any desirable job: "There aren't many openings anymore; all the promotions I know of depended on connections. If one foreman knows another foreman well, and a worker is on good terms with one of them, she can flatter him to get a better position. So the girls who are smooth talkers come out ahead."

Thus, although women at times deny that they attach much value to a group leader's title, they do make assessments about group leaders according to their moral character, work experience, or educational level. The friction that such assessments may generate between workers and group leaders represents only part of a larger pattern of discrimination that can interfere with smooth relations among factory workers.

Factory work is undeniably monotonous. As a consequence, many women look to the social opportunities that the factory provides as the most rewarding aspect of their work (though new friendships are sometimes harder to form at the factory than at school). If satisfying social relationships are not often the primary consideration when women take a factory job, these relationships soon become very important. As one worker (in this case, not from Western Electronics) put it, "I've been at this company for almost three years; the best part of going to work day after day is being able to be with friends. With this sort of work, it'd be impossible for anyone to just sit there for eight hours; talking makes the work easier to tolerate."

Yet despite the satisfactions of companionship, perhaps the most anxiety-producing part of adjusting to work is learning to deal with a new set of people. Workers must do this fairly often, since the high turnover rate and the dismantling of obsolete production lines necessitate shifting women from one part of the factory to another.[14] But other forces also affect friendship patterns. Common educational background, for example, leads to a relatively clear division between the friendship networks of workers who attend school and the friendship networks of workers who do not.

Women are critical of those who emphasize status distinctions,

[14] When workers resign, they rarely do so individually; instead, they leave with a friend or two (to insure that adjustment to a new company is not too difficult).

and their criticisms extend to all levels of the company hierarchy. Although distinctions between white-collar and blue-collar workers cause the greatest frustration, women complain more generally that "there are far too many levels in this company." One woman said, "Even the restrooms are separated, different ones for office staff and for us; that's just going too far."[15] Some women, of course, acknowledge that a multitude of levels is necessary in a firm as large as Western Electronics and that the firm's size makes certain patterns of interaction virtually impossible. But if this knowledge leads women to lower their expectations, it does not modify the environment in which they work. Status distinctions, conflicting job demands, and the heterogeneity of the work force inevitably produce an atmosphere not altogether conducive to the type of warm relations that workers value.

Many women thus discover that there are drawbacks to leaving home for a factory job—drawbacks that go beyond the impersonality of a large factory and reflect the opportunism and conflicts that pervade work relations (facts "one cannot learn from books or in school"). For this reason, workers emphasize the importance of choosing friends carefully: it is "too easy to learn bad ways in an environment as complex as the factory." Female workers, for instance, are reluctant to participate in loan clubs because there is the problem of "finding people who are reliable," and because "it would be too risky here." The claim that human feelings run "shallow and thin" in the factory has become a cliché; and though new workers may be merely repeating what they hear, experienced workers are able to cite specific causes for the problem. "Things are less complicated at school; at work people do things with ulterior motives. Work can disrupt relationships. For example, if two girls are assemblers and there is a chance for a promotion for one, each will hope inside that the other will not get it, and suspect the other of thinking the same thing. This puts distance between two people who might have gotten along well in the past."

Opportunism and self-seeking are by no means confined to the factory ("many people are this way nowadays," as one worker put it). Yet workers' recognition of these traits has a very clear effect

[15] At Western Electronics, the most conspicuous signs of status, aside from titles, are in dress (different color uniforms). Workers must also punch time cards and are paid according to hours worked. Dining rooms are not formally segregated, but the higher cost of meals in one section serves to keep most workers in other areas.

within the factory. In company dormitories, for example, women are often unwilling (or unable) to get to know their next-door neighbors—a reflection of their cautiousness about personal ties.[16] "A person who comes out to work must be 'round and slippery' in order to maintain smooth relations with everyone; but then, if you think about it, this is hardly a good trait to have." "Girls who come out to work have to let others know that they cannot be taken advantage of; for instance, if someone knows you won't stand up to him or talk back, he'll treat you even worse."

Workers also charge the company management with opportunism, especially in its "take it or leave it" attitude toward jobs. Women claim, for instance, that the company only rarely makes efforts to persuade a departing worker to stay. "The company is only concerned with what's good for it at any particular moment. When they need workers, they'll even offer a bonus if you introduce someone to work here, but when you're no longer needed, they make it so that it's very hard for you to stay on." Though women can cite examples of company opportunism from various periods, they most frequently cite examples from the fall of 1974 when an island-wide recession forced many factories either to close or to reduce their work force, often substantially.[17] At Western Electronics, the number of employees who were actually laid off was small in comparison with the numbers laid off at other factories, but the threat of layoffs and the knowledge that jobs could not be had elsewhere produced a quick and visible change.[18] Reading, eating, and napping on the job were definitely frowned upon previously, but during this period, the increased anxiety that many women felt was reflected in a distinctly new level of conscientiousness. The absence of a clear-cut company policy accelerated this change.

The company should have a specific policy stating how workers will be laid off, such as by seniority, by quality of performance, or by section. Instead,

[16] Thefts are the most worrisome problem in dormitories, and they are rarely solved.

[17] The situation has changed markedly since 1974. Newspaper reports indicate that factories in the Taipei, T'ao-yüan , and Hsin-chu areas need 70,000 women; that the largest factory in Taiwan is short 600 workers; that a garment factory in another market town needs an additional 300 women; etc. One factory in Chang-hua county resorted to making compulsory deductions from its workers' wages as "savings," thereby creating an additional obstacle for workers who consider leaving (*Lien He Pao*, May 3, 1976, p. 4).

[18] At Western Electronics, approximately 200 male workers were laid off and given severance compensation. Two weeks later, some 300 women were laid off, also with compensation. By contrast, one television factory in Tan-shui cut its work force from 3,000 to 900, and another television firm in T'ao-yüan county laid off 700 workers. (Personal communications.)

what the company does is to make it hard for you to stay on; it amounts to forcing you to leave. That way, they don't have to pay you any severance compensation. For example, things have become much stricter—no books, no food, no loud talking, no walking around—so that if you're caught violating even a small rule, they have reason to dismiss you. Another method of forcing workers to leave on their own is by reducing the number of buses [and routes served] for commuting workers, so that those who find it too inconvenient to come to work will just quit.

To be sure, the economic problems of 1974 heightened workers' propensity to detect purely instrumental motives on the part of management (sometimes mistakenly); but for many women, the supposed policies of the company during the crisis only confirmed what they had known all along. ("In any case, all factories just use our labor to make money.") The small annual wage increases, for instance, had long signified to many women that the company had little interest in retaining its more experienced workers, since new workers came at a "cheaper price."

One might expect that the company's opportunism would result in alienating many members of the labor force. But factory women, particularly the more experienced ones, characterize their relationship with management as simply the exchange of cash for labor. "All I feel is that the company has the money to employ me. I will work for them to earn that money and will do what is assigned me. For myself, I don't see this work as necessarily improving my future in any way. For now, only the wages matter."

An awareness that the obligation between employer and employee is primarily instrumental encourages women to try out different factories and also sets limits to their expectations. Women without a high school (or college) diploma know that significantly better jobs are out of reach, that a comparable position paying more is bound to involve a greater amount of "bitter" work, and that cumulative, on-the-job experience does not guarantee a woman a higher rank at another firm. Finding an ordinary job (i.e., as an assembler or something comparable in a garment or textile factory) is not difficult, but the widely shared views that "a factory girl is just a factory girl" and that "factories aren't all that different" eventually make constant job switching appear pointless and self-defeating.

Yet despite their fairly realistic appraisal of the job market, many factory women still aspire to better working conditions.

Of course, our expectations cannot be too high, but the company should recognize that the efforts of the workers are very important. After all, if the products are good, it's the workers who make them that way, not the managers. But we rarely get any praise and receive no encouragement. All the firm seems to care about is saving money, and their attitude is "if you don't like it here, there's nothing to stop you from leaving." For example, the new schedule [longer hours on weekdays and no work on Saturdays] is especially hard on students; and for those who only have a year of school before graduation, all they can do is try to put up with it. No one pays any attention to our opinions, so we girls just talk among ourselves and let it go at that.

The reminder that expectations cannot be too high, therefore, does not prevent women from wishing that things might be better; and in part, the tension between these attitudes may stimulate some women to make their way from factory to factory.

The cynicism and passivity revealed in the quotation above are typical: factory women perhaps share this ambiguous viewpoint more than they share any other attitude. The consensus is that the opinions of mere assemblers do not count for much. Rather than seeing themselves as the largest class of employees in the factory, women see only the factory's size: "There're so many people in the company, why should they listen to us? We're just one among many." Although some argue forcefully that they deserve more recognition for their work, they would not dare to be so presumptuous as to voice their criticisms to anyone but themselves. Even a worker in a small company that employs about twenty women (outside San-hsia) expressed a similar view: "It's true that we have meetings, and I admit it sounds better here than at other factories. But if we were really to speak out about our dissatisfactions, we would only be reprimanded." The majority of workers are thus resigned; they recognize that submitting suggestions or complaints is futile because there are no effective channels for transmitting them. In the words of one woman, "Whom would we tell? Everyone wants to move up: if we tell the foreman, he's not going to tell the superintendent, since the superintendent is even more afraid of the manager." There are, of course, union representatives;[19] but despite a general understanding

[19] According to Liu (1974: 29), there are now some 635 unions in Taiwan. (By law, factories with more than 50 workers must organize their own unions.) At Western Electronics, the manufacturing managers are the union's standing directors. The factory's approximately 100 union representatives (who meet once a year) are elected by the workers in the various sections of the factory. Union membership for office workers is optional. Because Taiwan is still officially under martial law, strikes are of course illegal.

that the union's purpose is to protect workers, few workers could tell me who their union representatives were. The idea of seeking out a union representative was inconceivable to most women: "The way the system works now, the union only knows the opinions of the foremen and the people above them and hears nothing from the women workers themselves. So how can it do anything for us?"

For many women, therefore, being left to work in peace takes priority over seeking improvements in company policies. One group leader simply advises her workers not to let little things bother them. Indeed, a woman may be dissatisfied with certain features of her job or with her working conditions, but in the end she is apt to shrug and say, "I do my work and the company pays me for it; what else needs to be said?"

But as we have seen, women often do have much to say about the improvements they would like to see. Working students, for example, would like special consideration to help them solve problems posed by awkward examination schedules and rising tuition costs. A wage scale linked to seniority rather than to merit leads many more workers to conclude that good performance simply goes unrecognized. As one woman said before leaving Western Electronics, "The company gives no special attention to a good worker; it need not give a big reward, but it should do at least something as an indication that it appreciates extra efforts." More generally, workers believe that management does not express sufficient appreciation for the work they do. And this appreciation does not need to be expressed in money terms—a point clearly illustrated by the one worker who volunteered a high opinion of her employers. (This woman worked in a garment factory near San-hsia that employed approximately two hundred workers.) "The managers are good to us workers; they'll come over to our work areas and talk with us. They even remember the names of those who have been here longer. They also ask those of us who've been here awhile if there are any problems or if we have suggestions."

The factory where this woman worked was owned by three brothers. This is significant: good relationships between workers and managers are most frequent in family-run enterprises. Such an enterprise, workers claim, is itself much "like a family." As one woman in a small knitting factory put it: "Even in a [large] factory a person doesn't get to enjoy that many benefits; and if *we* go on outings, our boss pays for everything. Few people here would even think about medical insurance; generally, if you become sick, it's just a matter of buying some medicine and getting some shots. If a person is seriously ill, our boss wouldn't let us down and would help out." But relations can still be complex in a small factory. A woman from San-hsia left one knitting business because the owner repeatedly asked her to go out with him. Another worker pointed out: "In a large factory, if you argue with someone it doesn't matter much; it won't be hard to stay on because this sort of thing happens all the time. But it would be more difficult to stay on in a small company; it'd be too awkward if you didn't get along with someone."

Women prefer the company to establish programs for the benefit of its workers on its own initiative. However, they do not always regard existing amenities and fringe benefits as adequate to their needs. (One important exception at Western Electronics is the designation of one room on each floor of the dormitories as a study hall for students. Previously, limited desk space and early lights-out in the rooms severely restricted study time for students.) Factory women know that only relatively large enterprises like Western Electronics have the resources to provide a full range of welfare benefits, educational programs, and recreational facilities. Yet except for concern about the quality of a company's dormitories, considerations about the availability of medical coverage, company-sponsored outings, sewing classes, etc. are rarely the deciding factors in determining whether a worker remains with one company or opts for another. "It's true that the welfare programs in a large company are more varied, but if it's a choice between programs and more money, I would rather have the money; it's something you can take with you." Similarly, women criticize singing contests, popular at several large factories, as wasting funds that might be put to better use. Moreover, except in cases of serious illness, workers' medical coverage sometimes appears to inconvenience them rather than to provide them with adequate care. Women claim that they are given inferior treatment and are subjected to the rudeness of doctors and hospital personnel, who "don't like to see workers' insurance slips" (because the fees they collect are smaller). Therefore, women often spend their own money to obtain proper and more courteous medical attention.

In the opinion of some factory women, many company programs exist only for show (much as the union and the suggestion boxes are provided largely for the sake of appearance). Other examples cited to corroborate this view range from ventilation units that are supposed to remove soldering fumes but do not to examinations for clerical positions that are irrelevant because the promotions have been determined by connections beforehand.

Added to these suspicions is an often imperfect understanding of company policies, leading some workers to conclude indignantly that the company is always trying to "put one over on us." Rumors about the contrived way the firm dismisses rather than lays off workers are one example. At times, even more serious charges are made. One group leader from another television factory, for instance, speculated that union representatives had helped themselves to funds from workers' contributions. One group of roommates at Western Electronics declined to submit entries for a company-wide art contest, claiming that such competitions are always "fixed" in favor of office employees.

Part of the problem stems from the difficulty of disseminating accurate information on a myriad of subjects to all workers in a factory the size of Western Electronics. One worker who had spent four years in a smaller electronics firm stated that in such a firm "a worker has more opportunities to know and has a better idea of what's going on in the company—whether, for example, the company is having financial problems, or whether it's doing well. Having such information, a worker will more likely feel that what is good for the company is good for workers as well." At Western Electronics, company bulletins are of course issued; but these often appear too late to undo rumors. Lack of information also affects hiring practices. In the case of company examinations, for example, one personnel manager admitted: "Sure, there's a promotion-from-within policy; the problem is that there is no communications supervisor, so how are women to know when and what positions become open?"

Factory women thus vacillate between resignation and indignation; they accept their low status and modest expectations, yet they become angry over the company's failure to provide better treatment and due recognition of their efforts. Not surprisingly, supervisors complain that workers do not adequately appreciate the company's needs. In the eyes of many trainers, group leaders, and foremen, workers leaving the firm seldom give much thought to the obligation that they may owe to the firm or to the inconvenience that they may cause to others.

*

Economic necessity, educational background, the job market, low expectations about the intrinsic interest of an assembler's job, and the expectation of only a few years' work before marriage—all shape the attitudes women bring with them when they enter a factory.[20] More experienced workers characterize their newer workmates as impressionable ("like a blank sheet of paper"), naive, timid, and obedient; and they see themselves as more outgoing and assertive. But learning to manage for oneself in the factory milieu does not signify greater certainty about goals, especially since one "must keep a proper perspective on one's own qualifications." Factory women widely share the beliefs that the days a woman spends in the factory should be taken one at a time, that there is no particular goal ahead (except in the case of working students), and that things will take their own course.

Factory women's perceptions of work, therefore, involve factors that go beyond the nature of the tasks they perform; and the satisfactions that they find in work derive in large part from the social context they themselves create (a context that may not have very much to do with the company itself). But at the same time, the work environment reduces the chances that a woman's high social expectations will be met. Women in factories certainly share enough of the same disabilities to permit the development of class consciousness; but rather than developing class consciousness, women direct their resentments at group leaders, supervisors, co-workers, or office staff. Women are more concerned about opportunism in social relations and fine gradations in status and rank (concerns that undermine their solidarity as workers) than with the union and how it actually might be made to serve them.

On the basis of a study of several industrial firms in Taiwan (one intensively researched), Silin concludes that in the day-to-day operations of most firms there are few appeals to employees to contribute to Taiwan's social and economic progress—though training manuals contain a "well-developed argument in which workers and lower-level managers are reminded of Taiwan's need to industrialize" (1976: 170). The effect of these entreaties on factory women is difficult to ascertain, since the women are asked to reconcile two conflicting

[20] The idea that a factory job is temporary gives rise to the notion that it is easier for women to find jobs than it is for men to find jobs. Since a man's job will be more permanent, it must not be an unpleasant one.

messages—that their labor is essential to their nation's growth, but that it is rewarded with neither high wages nor respect.

As for why their wages are low, female workers invariably point to the obvious fact that theirs is a job anyone can do. They recognize that small firms, even though they might not be financially secure, will offer high wages in the hope of attracting women willing to work long hours; but beyond this, women have little conception of the limits within which their wages may be raised or of the determinants of the overall wage scale of workers. During the 1974 recession, one Western Electronics worker told me: "I never did believe that Americans could buy *all* those television sets year after year!" Women, however, are less cognizant of the fact that international capital could easily move from Taiwan to other areas. In addition, as long as "the less education a woman has received, the greater chance she has to be employed," and so long as the largest number of unemployed women are those who have senior high school diplomas (Tsui 1972: 353–54), women will remain at an economic disadvantage. As a largely unskilled, technologically ignorant labor force, factory women thus acquire some measure of economic independence only as members of a class that is economically disadvantaged. Women employed in factories often must work because of economic necessity, but their job options are in fact few in number. Because most of the industries employing women are labor intensive, workers can easily move from one firm to another; but the absence of a high demand for skilled female workers and the high employee turnover rate discourage the organization of training programs and keep women from moving to significantly better jobs. It is little wonder, then, that factory women regard themselves as easily replaceable and that they see their job security as dependent on the fortunes of their employer (which some women at least recognize to be subject to the whims of foreign consumers).

Writers who predict that wage earning will substantially improve the position of women are thus only predicting what may happen when there is adequate economic mobility in the society generally. Simply put, factory work does not automatically make women better off.[21] Moreover, firms in Taiwan usually prefer to employ young women, thereby further reducing the already limited career oppor-

[21]Though women become wage earners, they find that their place in the family and their familial responsibilities are not substantially altered. Thus, women are encouraged to take part in production, but they are still subject in practice to the traditional kinds of discrimination.

tunities that they make available. The way women perceive factory work in Taiwan thus sensibly reflects the modest benefits that such work brings. The women are aware that their employment is largely temporary and that they are "only factory girls"; but they are not aware of (or, at any rate, they cannot articulate) the importance of their contribution to Taiwan's economic growth. As one worker summed up, "But then, like so many things, if one doesn't have a choice, one should just try to adjust; once a person becomes accustomed to something, then things will be all right."

# Continuities in Land Tenure, 1900-1940

Edgar Wickberg

## *Late Ch'ing Land Tenure in Taiwan*

When the Japanese assumed control over Taiwan, the agricultural land tenure system of the island was already highly developed. A massive Japanese land survey of 1898–1903 and parallel surveys of customary law and economic institutions provide us with our most detailed information about the Ch'ing land system—information, in fact, that is the most detailed available for any part of China.

Four major influences shaped Taiwan's tenure system: frontier colonization, lineage development, commercialization, and population pressure. By 1900, Taiwan was well past its frontier stage, but the institutions that had proved useful in colonizing the island were still visible. The prevailing hierarchical system of land rights was similar to that found in much of South China from the Ming period onward and known as the "one-field, two-owner" or "one-field, three-owner" system. In the Taiwanese version of this system, a person of wealth was granted a patent to bring new lands under cultivation. He then recruited farmers to do the actual work, providing them with the considerable funds necessary for land reclamation and for defense against aborigines and other hostile groups. The patent holder, eventually called the "big rent householder" (*ta-tsu hu*), received in exchange for his contribution the right to a perpetual income from

I wish to thank Shen Shih-k'o, the Director of Taiwan's Provincial Bureau of Lands, for giving me permission to use materials on a number of villages in northern Taiwan. I also wish to thank Lin Hsin-hsiung and Ti Chin for research assistance, and especially Arthur Wolf for the opportunity to use the P'eng-fu land and household records that he has collected. Finally, I am indebted to Wang Sung-hsing and Norma Diamond for their criticisms of the draft version of this paper.

the land for himself and for his heirs and assigns. This income was usually fixed at about 10 percent of the gross produce of the land, payable as "big rent" (*ta-tsu*). Once the patent holder had supplied the initial expenses for opening the land, his only other responsibility was to pay the land tax, which was not a heavy burden. Moreover, his claim upon the land could be sold or mortgaged.

Meanwhile, the man who opened the land acquired what almost amounted to co-ownership. He paid no land tax, but he was responsible for remitting the "big rent" to the patent holder. Otherwise, he had more or less permanent rights to cultivate and dispose of the land—rights that he in turn could sell or mortgage. This meant that he could lease the land to a tenant, and grow upon it whatever crops he or the tenant wished. Since the opener of the land was often an entrepreneur who did not actually farm ("Tochi ni kansuru" 1901: 6–7), he frequently rented his land out in this way. On paddy lands, where this practice was most common, the rent he collected from the tenant was a fixed amount of rice, usually set at between 40 and 60 percent of the year's production. This fee was called "little rent" (*hsiao-tsu*), and the opener of the land to whom it was due came to be known as the usufruct holder (*hsiao-tsu hu*). If the usufruct holder did not live near the land or if the land were difficult and expensive to bring under cultivation (thereby requiring extra effort and expense by the tenant), the tenant would often acquire a permanent right of tenancy upon the land. This historical experience, then, led to a two-tiered and sometimes three-tiered system of multiple "ownership" in which each "owner" had his own set of claims and rights (Tai 1963: 1–47).

Evelyn Rawski, following Niida's analysis, suggests that this system originated in mainland reclamation practices developed during the Ming period (1972: 14–24), and Ronald Knapp shows the system's appropriateness to the frontier conditions of eighteenth-century Taiwan (1975). Indeed, reclamation was expensive, and frontier colonization arduous and dangerous; hence a system of multiple rights provided strong incentives to both investors and workers. One of the most important consequences of this system was a high rate of tenancy. We see this, for example, in the Taipei–Hsin-chu area of northern Taiwan. My analysis of the land records of twelve villages scattered throughout this area shows that in 1900 an average of 75 percent of the cultivated land was worked by tenants (1970: 80). A survey of the whole island carried out in 1910 (*TCTY* 1946: 513) in-

TABLE 1
*Percentages of Tenanted Land and Tenant Households*

| Location and date | Tenanted land as a percentage of all cultivated land | Tenant households as a percentage of all farming households |
|---|---|---|
| Localities in East and South China, ca. 1930 | 40% | 25%[a] |
| Localities in six provinces in South China, ca. 1888 | unknown | ca. 50% |
| Canton Delta region, ca. 1930 | 75% or more | 70–85%[b] |
| Taiwan, ca. 1900 | 75% | 43%[c] |

SOURCES: Buck 1937: 194–95; Freedman 1958: 16; Jamieson 1888: 97–113; Wickberg 1970; *TCTY* 1946: 513.
[a] Another 33 percent are owner-tenants.
[b] Includes owner-tenants.
[c] Another 24 percent are owner-tenants.

dicates that 43 percent of all farming households were tenants and that another 24 percent were owner-tenants (i.e., people who owned part of their farmland, but were tenants on the rest). If we regard as high a tenancy rate of 50 percent (measured either by the percentage of tenant households among farming households or by the percentage of farmland cultivated by tenants), then we may reasonably conclude that Taiwan had a high tenancy rate at the start of our period. This matter may also be placed in a comparative context. Though analogous data for the Chinese mainland are crude and incomplete, there are some useful sources—notably missionary reports published in 1888 (dealing with selected localities in six provinces in South China) and Buck's survey conducted around 1930 (dealing with selected localities in East and South China). This material is summarized in Table 1.

Lineage development was a second major influence shaping Taiwan's tenure system. Though lineages were unevenly distributed in Taiwan (Pasternak 1972), where they were strong they frequently owned large tracts of land. This corporate land was then leased to lineage members and others, further contributing to Taiwan's high tenancy rate.

Commercialization was a third major influence on Taiwan's tenure system. Although earlier commercialization in Fukien had some influence on Taiwan (Rawski 1972: chaps. 3, 4; Azuma 1944: 62–93, 289–317), commercialization in Taiwan itself was largely a phenomenon of the last four decades of the nineteenth century. Between 1860 and 1900 Taiwan was opened to international trade, which stimulated the production of sugar, tea, camphor, and other agricultural commodities—production that in turn led to a modest increase in urbanization and also to an increase in agricultural land values. Those who profited from commercial development were able to invest in land, and this circumstance probably had the effect of concentrating landownership in fewer hands. More importantly, however, the commercialization of this period had a bearing on certain forms of tenure and on certain ways of using labor that will be discussed below.

Population pressure was the final major influence on the tenure system. According to one estimate, there were approximately 300,000 farm households in Taiwan in 1900 cultivating about 550,000 hectares[1] of farmland, thus creating an average farm size of 1.8 hectares per household (Lee 1971: 35–36). This farm size may be compared with rough estimates for the mainland. According to Jamieson's 1888 data for localities in six provinces of South China, the average farm size was only 1 hectare per household; and according to Buck's 1930 data for localities in East and South China, the average farm size was only 1.2 hectares per household (Jamieson 1888: 97–113; Buck 1937: 269).

Several things, then, are evident from the available comparative figures, even allowing for their necessarily approximate nature. First, Taiwan's tenancy rate in 1900 was apparently higher than the rates in almost all the localities in East and South China studied by Buck and others in 1930, except for the Canton Delta region. Second, the average farm size in Taiwan (again in 1900) was somewhat larger than the average farm size found by Buck, and apparently much larger than the average farm size suggested by Jamieson's South China informants in 1888. Indeed, the Taiwan figure of 1.8 hectares is well over the 1.0 hectare minimum household subsistence holding recognized for the island (*Keizai* 1905: 574–77), and perhaps applicable to rice-producing regions on the mainland as well. It is probably safe to say, therefore, that although there was some population pressure on the most desirable lands in Taiwan in 1900 (evident in rent levels and tenant competition), there was still much land that could be reclaimed. Moreover, the average farm size in Taiwan was larger than the average farm size in most of the rice-growing areas of the mainland—a fact that was to remain true throughout the Japanese period.

[1]For convenience, 1 *chia* is taken as equivalent to 1 hectare.

Population pressure no doubt had some effect on tenancy rates. But its greatest effect was on the conditions and forms of tenancy—on such things as lengths of leases, forms of payment, levels of rent, contributions of landlords and tenants to production costs, and special conditions relating to adjustments. Leases, for example, were either short-term (one to five years) or long-term (permanent or nearly so). Earlier we noted how tenants became virtually third "owners" of their land by acquiring a permanent right of cultivation. By 1900, however, this right was becoming less common as a consequence of tenant competition—competition that encouraged the usufruct holder to change tenants frequently, with consequent bidding up of the rent at each change.

The usufruct right itself was an object of competition as population growth and commercial development took place. Between 1850 and 1900, the sale price of the usufruct right tripled; and one Japanese investigator observed that holders of this right were the ones who made the largest profits from the land (Tai 1963: 23; *Taiwan shihō* 1910: 287–88, 337–38; "Tochi ni kansuru" 1901: 4–5). In 1889, the Taiwan provincial government moved in the direction of recognizing the usufruct right as superior by requiring the usufruct holder (rather than the patent holder) to assume the tax burden and by reducing by 40 percent the "big rent" he was required to pay. Although this measure was implemented effectively only in northern Taiwan, it made clear the government's policy of considering the usufruct holder the most important claimant to the land. The patent holder's claim seemed to be a residual one, which the usufruct holder often did not even bother to pay (*Provincial Report* 1902: 74, 78; Lin Account Books). Given the patent holder's original relationship to the land, the passage of time, and the salability of his rights, it is not surprising that he often did not live near the land and, if he resided in another part of Taiwan or in Fukien, that he might not even know where the land was located. When the patent holder did live in the locality, however, he might well have been a patent holder on some lands and a usufruct holder on others. Since both rights were salable, we are not talking about separate classes of people, only about separate rights to land.

The most important tenure relationships were coming to be those between the usufruct holder (who by 1900 was called the landowner) and the tenant. The trend toward short-term contracts mentioned above reflects both the general population growth and the gradual disappearance of new land that could be brought under cultivation. Where there were still new lands to be reclaimed, long-term or permanent contracts and share rent (which spread the risk between owner and tenant) were common. But once a piece of land had a stable yield, the contract became short-term, and share rents were replaced by fixed amounts of grain usually set at about 50 percent of the usual yield. On lands with a stable yield and a short-term contract, the landlord usually paid the land tax and the "big rent"; the tenant normally paid only the water fee. The owner sometimes furnished a house on or near the land; but all production expenses were normally the tenant's, and he functioned as an independent manager. Among the special conditions included in contracts, two are of particular interest. In years of bad harvests, a tenant had the right to negotiate for a reduced rent. In cases where the usufruct right was sold before the tenant's contract had expired, the tenant had no right to continue on the land and he could only hope for an opportunity to negotiate a contract with the new owner (Wickberg 1969: 3–5).

Thus, in the most heavily settled and cultivated parts of Taiwan, the trend was towards shorter leases and more frequent changes of tenant. As the usufruct holders emerged as owners and as tenant competition for land increased, the tenant's position became less assured than before. There were, however, ways in which a tenant could strengthen his position—if he were wealthy enough.

Naturally there were owners who needed cash to pay off debts or to use for investments. In many cases, these owners could not or did not wish to sell their lands. The land, for example, was perhaps corporately owned and hence very difficult to sell. Or an absentee owner may have acquired many of the most valuable lands in a given locality and was therefore reluctant to dispose of them. An ordinary family, for prestige or filial reasons, may have been reluctant to sell its land outright. Yet renting out the land in the usual way would not have yielded immediate cash in the amount needed. There were several solutions to this problem.

One was the *tien* or "pledge" (McAleavy 1958: 403–15), an institution dating back at least to the T'ang period. Through the "pledge," the landowner conveyed to a creditor full rights to the use and the income of his land, in exchange for an interest-free loan. The lender, therefore, derived his profits not from interest but from the productivity of the land while it was under his care. The amount of loan was commonly about 80 percent of the market value of the property. Once the owner repaid the loan, the lender was required to return the land. The time period during which redemption was possible was often very vague. The Ch'ing government attempted to impose a limit of 30 years on pledge contracts, but in Taiwan, as on the mainland, many contracts continued in force long past that point (*Taiwan shihō* 1910: 651–710).

A second method of raising cash was through the *pao-p'u* or *tsung-p'u*[2] (general contractor tenancy). In this system, a large contractor—perhaps a major landowning family corporation, such as the famous Lin family of Pan-ch'iao—leased a sizable amount of land from the owner, then subleased it to others (who in turn either hired laborers to work it or let it out in smaller parcels to tenants). The owner received the cash he needed from the contractor's fee, and the contractor made his profit from the difference between that fee and what he collected from lessees below him (*Taiwan kyūkan* 1906: 611–14). Thus, landlords and merchants were able to become tenants as lease contractors with various levels of lessees beneath them. This system is similar to the one reported by Chen Han-seng for the Canton Delta in the 1930's (Chen 1936: 47–49).

A third form of raising cash in exchange for cultivation rights was through deposits or "caution money," properly called *ai-ti yin*[3] (hindrance fee) or *fang-tsu yin* (protection fee) in Taiwan. Providing "caution money" was a common practice on heavily cultivated rice lands, especially in northern Taiwan. As the name suggests, "caution money" served as a guarantee of rent payment and of actual cultivation of the land by the tenant. In cases of defection or default, the owner retained all or else the appropriate portion of the money deposited. This money was paid by the tenant in advance of cultivation. The amount varied widely, anywhere from 10 percent to 100 percent of the cash equivalent of one year's rent. During the period of cultivation, the owner had the deposit to use as he wished, paying no interest to the tenant and having only to return it when the contract was terminated. If the required deposit were very large and the tenant had to borrow the sum (as was often the case), the tenant then had to pay 9 or 10 percent interest, though he received no interest from the

[2] I have been unable to find the word *p'u* in any Chinese dictionary. It is a Taiwanese word ("*bok*") used to refer to various forms of tenure in Taiwan. *P'u* would be the probable pronunciation of the word in Mandarin.

[3] *Ai-ti yin* was often rendered *ch'i-ti yin*. The word *ch'i* suggests rocky or sandy land, but the term *ch'i-ti yin* was used as an equivalent of *ai-ti yin*, apparently referring to cultivated land of any character. (*Tochi kankō* 1905: 85–86; Kobayashi 1905: 13–19.)

landlord (*Keizai* 1905: 566–74; Wickberg 1969: 5; Kawada 1928: 90; *Tochi kankō* 1905: 85–86).

The most extreme form of raising cash through advance deposits was the *chao-keng tai-chieh*, which may be translated as "to summon a cultivator and bring a loan." Here, a would-be tenant acquired long-term cultivation rights to a piece of land by presenting the owner in advance with an interest-free loan many times the amount of a year's rent (Kobayashi 1905: 13–15). I have not had time to examine in detail the contracts of this kind available in print. I have seen a case from about 1900, however, in which a Taiwanese tenant described as a typical "middle-class farmer" paid ¥4,000 of "deposit" money for the right to cultivate land that rented for the grain equivalent of ¥1,000 per year. He thus paid four years' rent in advance in the form of an interest-free loan—money that he had to borrow at a cost of ¥350 per year in interest (*Keizai* 1905: 566–70).

How common were these four practices in Taiwan at the start of this century? The evidence from twelve villages in northern Taiwan indicates that the pledge was not very common: only 6 percent of the cultivated land was under pledge (Wickberg 1970: 86–87). It is not yet possible to estimate the frequency of the *pao-p'u* and *chao-keng tai-chieh* arrangements. However, all sources note that deposits were a regular feature of rice cultivation, especially in northern Taiwan; and we know that similar practices were common on the mainland. In Kwangtung, for example, Chen reports that the practice was widespread on lineage lands as well as on family lands (Chen 1936: 44–47). Although Chen's data are from the 1930's, it seems reasonable to assume that the practice existed earlier since we know of similar institutions in other parts of nineteenth-century China. In the middle Yangtze region, deposits—called there, as elsewhere on the mainland, *ya-tsu*—were common from at least the middle of the nineteenth century. Kubota finds examples of such deposits in Szechwan from the eighteenth century (1967: 260–72). There the deposit was often much larger than one year's rent (making it seem much like *chao-keng tai-chieh* in Taiwan), though if it were very large, the rent was lowered. Similar cases of a low rent accompanying a large deposit are noted for Taiwan (*Taiwan shihō* 1910: 600). In the Taiwanese example of *chao-keng tai-chieh* mentioned above, the rent was 40 percent of the total crop, and hence certainly at the lower end of the rent range.

Deposits are often thought to have originated from the attempts of middle Yangtze landlords to oppose the antirent movement of the T'ai-p'ing period (1850–1864). Drawing on eighteenth- and nineteenth-century evidence from Szechwan, however, Kubota sees deposits less as a measure to insure rent payments than as a way for landlords to obtain needed cash. As Szechwan and other parts of China developed commercially, this need for cash became greater. Landlords could of course count on tenant competition to bid up rentals, if they wished. But if cash were their main interest, they could raise it more quickly through deposits. Indeed, there were many would-be tenants, often former landlords or merchants, who had access to cash and were prepared to pay handsomely for long-term cultivation rights (especially when rental rates were kept low because the landlord was interested in cash, not rent). In Kubota's view, then, *ya-tsu* deposits reflected Szechwan's commercialization and expanding need for cash far more than they reflected landlord-tenant friction (Kubota 1967: 247–96).

In the case of Taiwan, there are several important conclusions suggested by this pattern of advance payment for the right to cultivate. First, the amount of good land available on the market must have been decreasing significantly in relation to demand, thus forcing the purchasers of cultivation rights to pay high prices. This conclusion seems to be supported by the comments of one investigator who said that the right to cultivate as a tenant frequently involved paying a bribe, and that on certain government lands the successful bidder was usually the one who offered a bribe of decisive proportions ("Tochi ni kansuru" 1901: 9–12). Second, the fact that people were prepared to pay high prices for the right to cultivate suggests not only the high profitability of at least some Taiwanese farmland, but also the existence of an affluent class who were anxious to make profits. Third, if we accept Kubota's argument about deposits and tenant borrowing practices, we may infer that at least the north of Taiwan (where these practices were most common) was fairly commercialized.

Before turning to a case study, however, let us summarize our discussion to this point. Land tenure in Taiwan in 1900 may be characterized by the following features: a high rate of tenancy; a moderate concentration of lands; a hierarchical system of ownership in which the usufruct holder was emerging as the real owner; a trend toward tenant leases of short duration despite the continued existence of means by which long-term leases could be obtained by those who were able to pay the price; and a set of institutions that made it easy to alienate cultivation rights without disposing of ultimate ownership.

## *P'eng-fu*

In 1900, P'eng-fu was an administrative village that included a natural village and the adjacent market town of Shu-lin. It was located in the river basin area of northern Taiwan then known as Hai-shan. The agricultural products of this locality were almost exclusively rice and vegetables; special products played little if any part in the economy.

The materials on which the following discussion will be based are of two kinds: records of the Japanese land survey of 1898–1903 for twelve villages in northern Taiwan; and land and household records of the period 1900–1910 for the administrative village of P'eng-fu.

The Japanese survey and the post-1905 Taiwanese land records have been described elsewhere (Vander Meer & Vander Meer 1968: 144–50), and I shall not duplicate that discussion here. Briefly, however, such records allow us to determine levels of tenancy, kinds and grades of tenant-cultivated lands, rates of rent and other charges, and patterns of land distribution (according to types of owners, sizes of holdings, and owners' surnames). In the case of P'eng-fu village, we also have the names of 80 percent of the tenants of nearby lands.

A few methodological issues deserve mention at the outset. It is well known, for example, that joint ownership was sometimes registered as individual ownership, and that some lands (especially lineage properties) were occasionally registered in the names of deceased ancestors. This creates problems for the user of post-1905 land records. But the user of the 1898–1903 survey records and of the 1905 household records is better off: the Japanese surveyors were aware of Taiwanese registry practices and demanded documentation and witnesses ("Tochi ni kansuru" 1901: 9). For their part, Taiwanese owners, knowing that these efforts on the part of a new and more vigorous administration would be the basis of future policies, had every reason to insure that land they might wish to pass on to their heirs or sell was registered under the appropriate name. In the case of the P'eng-fu records, we can settle nearly all the registration ambiguities by reference to the explanatory sections of the registry sheet and by use of the household records.

The household records are the product of Japanese-instituted civil registration practices starting in 1905. Using them, we can discuss owner households, tenant households, and households of neither owners nor tenants in terms of their size, composition, and members' occupations.

The major problem here is to reconcile information from the household registers of 1905 with information from the land survey, which passed through P'eng-fu in 1900. There is necessarily some imprecision about the exact number of households and persons in P'eng-fu in 1900. Although there was much moving about in this part of Taiwan, the households involved were about the same size and structure—that is, all were small households moving in search of work. Hence, for our purposes, imprecision about which households were present in 1900 is not a major problem. The number of households I use for the purpose of my discussion represents the households known to be present on December 31, 1905, along with those not present then but having P'eng-fu addresses in the 1900 land survey and those who lived in nearby villages but owned P'eng-fu property. This method, though including nearly all households that lived in P'eng-fu in 1900–1905, produces results—302 households and 2,023 persons—that are probably slightly larger than P'eng-fu's real figures for 1900. However, my analyses and comparisons of households, done by percentages, will not be seriously affected by this slight exaggeration of size. Of these 302 households, we have detailed information on 248, or slightly over 80 percent.

As indicated above, 2,023 persons lived in P'eng-fu in 302 households, for an average of 6.7 persons per household—a household size considerably larger than the 5.2 persons per household determined for the island as a whole by the 1905 census (Barclay 1954: 175). Since P'eng-fu included the market town of Shu-lin, we may reasonably view it as a microcosm of Taiwan. Thus, by using the 1905 census conclusion that two-thirds of Taiwan's households were engaged primarily in agriculture (*ibid.*: 57), we may assume that about 200 of P'eng-fu's roughly 300 households were so engaged. Of these 200 agricultural households, 49 (according to survey and household records) were usufruct holders, recognized in the 1900 survey as landowners. Of the 49, only five were owner-cultivators pure and simple; another nine can be fitted into various combined categories of owner-tenant, landlord-tenant, landlord-owner, and landlord-cultivator; and the remainder all rented out their land to others (as landlords). Approximately 100 households were agricultural tenants pure and simple—a figure derived by adding the tenant households identified in the land survey records with 30 additional households whose recorded occupation was agriculture but who were not registered as landowners. Finally, we may conclude that there were about 50 households of landless agricultural laborers (a figure obtained by subtracting the number of owner and tenant households from the total of 200 households assumed to be engaged in agriculture), and another 100 households of people in nonagricultural occupations (a figure inferred from the 1905 census average for all of Taiwan and from P'eng-fu's marketing and administrative functions). I strongly suspect, however, that within the 200 agricultural households, a substantial number—perhaps 75 or more—regularly moved back and forth between farm labor and small tenancy on the one hand, and urban labor on the other. Indeed, the occupation of "day laborer" is common in this locality, and it refers to both rural and urban employment.

P'eng-fu was supported by 233 hectares of cultivated land. Thus, each of the village's 150 owner or tenant households had an average of 1.5 hectares of farmland—an area somewhat smaller than the 1.8 hectares per household calculated for Taiwan as a whole. Landownership, however, was relatively concentrated. A single absentee family with no local kin, for example, owned about 30 percent of the village's cultivated land. Moreover, another 30 percent of the village's land was owned by other absentee owners without any local kin, and an additional 13 percent of the land was owned by absentee owners with local kin. (See Table 2.) Local ownership was thus comparatively weak, and lineage ownership apparently very weak.

Thirty-two surnames were represented in the village. Wang, the most common of these, was shared by 13 percent of the population;

TABLE 2
*Distribution by Owners of Cultivated Land in P'eng-fu*

| Owners | Approximate percentage |
|---|---|
| Lin family of Pan-chi'ao ($N$ = 1) | 30% |
| Other absentee owners with no local kin ($N$ = 24) | 30 |
| Local owners ($N$ = 49) | 19 |
| Absentee owners with local kin ($N$ = 6) | 13 |
| Surname organizations ($N$ = 7) | 5 |
| Temples and religious organizations ($N$ = 3) | 1 |
| Business investors ($N$ = 2) | 1 |
| Public ($N$ = 1) | 1 |

SOURCE: P'eng-fu land records and household records for 1900–1910.

and the leading nine surnames (each shared by at least ten households) provided the surnames for 63 percent of the population. Not all the households included in this segment of the population owned land. Nevertheless, almost all the major local owners of cultivated land came from the six largest surname groups: the Wangs (whose members owned nine hectares), the Lais (with sixteen hectares), the Chous (with six hectares), the Changs (with five hectares), the Chiens (with three hectares), and the Liaos (with three hectares). Despite the substantial numbers of households with common surnames, however, lineages and other surname organizations were not strong. As noted, only 5 percent of the village's land was owned by surname corporations—in this case, by two Chang and five Chien corporations. Indeed, we would expect, for example, that the Wangs would have corporate property: like the Changs, they arrived early, occupied good land, and drew income (individually) as patent holders. The Lais, however, are even more puzzling in this regard. They owned more land than any other surname group; and, unlike any other surname group, they lived together in one part of the village surrounded by their own lands, furnishing few tenants to other owners. Yet they had no surname organization and no corporately owned lands. After 1905, all the Lai lands were passed on to heirs according to a pattern of equal shares for each of a family's sons. And since there is no Lai genealogy available (a circumstance true for several important surname groups), it is impossible to trace inheritance patterns before 1900. But even if all the Lai lands and all the lands owned by the other five large surname groups had been held corporately, the total of corporately held land in the village would only have been 20 percent (42 hectares). The picture of weak lineage ownership and of domination by outside owners would thus not be changed.

Of P'eng-fu's 233 hectares of cultivated land, 219 hectares (or 94 percent) were farmed by tenants (a figure substantially higher than the 75 percent average [Table 1] for Taiwan as a whole). As noted, about 100 (or 50 percent) of P'eng-fu's 200 agricultural households were tenants (a figure somewhat higher than the 43 percent average for Taiwan as a whole [*TCTY* 1946: 513]). Thus, the average farm cultivated by P'eng-fu tenants was about 2.2 hectares per household (a figure that is very close to the 2.26 hectares per household for the village's owner-cultivators). A more detailed picture of farm size according to class of tenants is presented in Table 3.

TABLE 3
*Average P'eng-fu Tenant Farm Size by Type of Owner*

| Type of owner | Number of tenants | Tenant farm size (hectares per household) |
|---|---|---|
| Absentee surname corporations ($N = 3$) | 1 listed | 1.28 |
| Local owners ($N = 35$) | 29 | 1.37 |
| Absentee owners with local kin ($N = 6$) | 9 | 1.59 |
| Local surname corporations ($N = 4$) | 4 listed | 1.64 |
| Absentee owners with no local kin ($N = 24$) | 24 | 2.93 |
| The Lin family of Pan-ch'iao ($N = 1$) | 20 | 3.93 |

SOURCE: P'eng-fu land records and household records for 1900–1910.

Table 3 shows significant differences among the average sizes of tenant holdings. With very few exceptions, locally owned lands were let out in small parcels. The same was true of surname corporation lands and lands belonging to absentee owners with local relatives. If a tenant wished to farm more than two hectares, then, he usually had to go to an absentee owner with no local kin—to a member of the Lin family, whose branches controlled much of the best land in northern Taiwan, or to one of the other absentees, who lived in Taipei, Hsin-chuang, or Pan-ch'iao. It is also worth noting that wild plains land, which could sometimes be brought under cultivation or used for other income-producing purposes, was almost entirely owned by the Lins and by one other absentee owner. Finally, Table 3 shows us that the largest tenants farmed more land than the average P'eng-fu owner-cultivator (who held only 2.26 hectares). This fact, however, can be misleading: tenants paid about half of their crops in rent, whereas owner-cultivators paid only about a quarter of their crops in taxes and fees. Thus, tenants farming 2.93 hectares had less net income than owner-cultivators farming 2.26 hectares. (A tenant would have had to farm 3.39 hectares to retain the same income as an owner-cultivator with 2.26 hectares—and only tenants of the Lin family held this much land.)

Let us now take a brief look at P'eng-fu households, tenant and otherwise. An important point to bear in mind here is that these households usually consisted only of family members; hence, we are essentially looking at families. Table 4, based on information about 248 of P'eng-fu's 302 households, shows the relationship between various types of households and their respective sizes. (This group of 248 includes the 69 tenant households for which we have reliable information.)

TABLE 4
*Average P'eng-fu Household Size by Type of Household*

| Type of household | Average number of persons per household |
|---|---|
| Landless villagers ($N$ = 139) | 5.6 |
| Local owners ($N$ = 40) | 7.5 |
| All tenants ($N$ = 69) | 8.6 |
| Tenants farming 2.0 or more hectares ($N$ = 23) | 12.1 |
| Tenants farming 3.5 or more hectares ($N$ = 14) | 12.1 |
| Lin family tenants farming 3.5 or more hectares ($N$ = 8) | 13.4 |

SOURCE: P'eng-fu land records and household records for 1900–1910.

Since the largest farms were cultivated by tenants rather than by owner-cultivators, it is not surprising to find that tenant households were larger than owner-cultivator households. Nor is it surprising to find that the larger the tenant's farm, the larger his household. Thus, the familiar generalization that household size increases as landownership increases should be amended in the case of a village like P'eng-fu (where owner-cultivators were rare) to state simply that the larger the farm, the larger the household. (And in P'eng-fu, only tenants were able to have large farms.)

The importance of household size relative to farm size can best be understood by looking at household labor power. Since women did not regularly do farm work in Hai-shan, it is most convenient to consider only full-strength male workers (i.e., men between the ages of 16 and 60). The average number of these in various households is shown in Table 5.

From the foregoing data, I draw three general conclusions about P'eng-fu. First, within P'eng-fu the size of a tenant's holdings was probably a good indication of his prosperity. The very largest tenant families (those who farmed 3.5 or more hectares) were thus probably the most prosperous agricultural families in the village. Indeed, their households were not only the largest, but the most likely to be complex. Landless families, for example, were typically small nuclear families. Owner and small tenant families were probably in roughly equal numbers nuclear, stem, or joint families. But among the 23 families farming 2.0 or more hectares, stem and joint families clearly predominated: there were only four nuclear families, whereas there were nine stem and ten joint families. It may be objected that family size and complexity are not necessarily reliable indicators of prosperity. In this case, though, the argument for the prosperity of these tenants is strengthened by the fact that their lands were generally the best available. The owners who controlled these lands—notably the Lin family of Pan-ch'iao—were in a position to choose as tenants applicants with the best stock of resources and skills. Unfortunately, we have no information about the assets of P'eng-fu tenants other than the lands that they rented. They might, for example, have owned or rented land elsewhere (perhaps in a nearby village). And it is also possible that some or all of the large tenants were engaged in other economic activities in addition to farming. Nevertheless, on the basis of the information we do have, we can conclude that these large tenants were probably successful farmers. Before the 1920's, success in farming depended upon (1) having an adequate amount of good land; (2) having a favorable contract with a good landlord; (3) having the means to keep labor costs fairly low; (4) having a modicum of managerial skill; and (5) having sufficient capital. At present, we only know about (1) and (3) in relation to P'eng-fu's large tenants; their land was very good, and their households were large enough to ensure adequate low-cost labor. These factors seem sufficient, however, to assure us that these large tenants were indeed prosperous by P'eng-fu standards.

My second general conclusion about P'eng-fu concerns the local

TABLE 5
*Average Numbers of Adult Male Workers in P'eng-fu Households by Type of Household*

| Type of household | Average number of adult male workers per household[a] |
|---|---|
| Landless villagers (*N* = 139) | 1.7 |
| Local owners (*N* = 40) | 2.5 |
| All tenants (*N* = 69) | 2.4 |
| Tenants farming 2.0 or more hectares (*N* = 23) | 3.7 |
| Tenants farming 3.5 or more hectares (*N* = 14) | 3.9 |
| Lin family tenants farming 3.5 or more hectares (*N* = 8) | 4.7 |

SOURCE: P'eng-fu land records and household records for 1900–1910.
[a] Refers to men between the ages of 16 and 60.

economy: here, where over 90 percent of all farmland was rented, leases, not ownership, were the critical economic determinants. Myron Cohen's recent book (1976) provides a useful comparison. Cohen explains the prevalence of large, complex families among ordinary peasant cultivators in a region in southern Taiwan by pointing to the labor-intensive demands of the area's major crop, tobacco, and to the peasants' skill at diversifying their sources of income. Our information about P'eng-fu does not permit us to generalize about the diversification of income-producing activities. But we can see how P'eng-fu's leasehold economy shaped the village's growth. Since two-thirds of P'eng-fu's farmland was let out in units of more than 2.0 hectares—i.e., in units significantly larger than the average P'eng-fu holding of 1.5 hectares—the important thing for a family was to have enough wealth and labor to rent lands on this scale. Thus, just as Cohen's region was shaped by the circumstances of tobacco cultivation, P'eng-fu was shaped by a leasehold economy dependent on absentee owners. Since local owners did not have land to let out in large holdings, absentee owners therefore made it possible for P'eng-fu's most successful cultivators to maintain large and complex families and—probably—prosperity.

My third general conclusion about P'eng-fu is that it was probably more developed commercially than one might have expected it to be on the basis of previous literature about Taiwan. Indeed, long before the Green Revolution brought about by the Japanese in the 1920's and 1930's, northern Taiwan as a whole was, I believe, a commercialized area. This conclusion merits more extended discussion.

To begin with, it appears that P'eng-fu had a fairly large number of agricultural laborers and others who were neither owners nor tenants. The average P'eng-fu household size was 6.7, as compared with the island-wide average of 5.2. How, then, could a preindustrial economy support households of this size when only about half the households in the village were owners or tenants? A fairly large number of the heads of households gave their occupation as "day laborer" in 1905. These villagers usually had small households and some of them showed up in the 1900 land survey as small tenants (though I suspect that they moved in and out of agriculture and between small tenancy and labor). We know, of course, that the market town of Shu-lin was part of P'eng-fu. We can see urbanization there from 1850, visible in the conversion of a row of high quality rice lands into the shops and houses that by 1900 made up the main business street. Urban construction, then, absorbed some labor. Of more importance, a winery employed 100 or more persons, and 30 or 40 persons were engaged in the river transport business.

We have already noted that small families moved around within the area a great deal. They also moved into and out of the area regularly. (By contrast, large families rarely moved, though young males sometimes went away seasonally to work in Hsin-chuang, Panch'iao, and Taipei.) I suspect, therefore, that the small families who moved were often looking for day laboring jobs—a conclusion that points to the existence of a fairly extensive market for hired labor. What jobs made up this market? In northern Taiwan as a whole (according to an economic survey of 1905), owner-cultivators were rare; far more common were tenants, both large and small, who often hired farm labor to work their rice lands (*Keizai* 1905: 512, 566–68). Tea farms provided another market for hired labor. The tea boom of the 1860's and 1870's had declined by 1900, but there were still many opportunities for both men and women as seasonal wage laborers picking and processing tea. Finally, surveys of the household economy of over 100 farmers taken in 1920, when cultivating practices were still much like those of 1900, show that both tenants and owner-cultivators made much use of hired labor. In the 1920 samples, from 13 to 35 percent of the labor on farms in the rice-growing region was hired (*NKCS* 1923: 18)—a somewhat higher figure than the 15 percent Buck found in 1930 for the East and South China rice regions he surveyed (1937: 293).

Moreover, even before the Green Revolution of the 1920's and 1930's, Taiwan marketed a surprisingly large percentage of its rice production. Lee, for example, found that 48 percent of the rice crop was marketed during the period 1911–15 (1971: 71). A Japanese study of 1920 found that 65 percent was marketed (*NKCS* 1923: 16). The contrast with mainland China is thus striking. In the East and South China regions studied by Buck (1937: 263), at most 36 percent of the rice crop was sold (this takes into account the 15 percent sold by the grower and all of the 21 percent that went to the landlord as rent). Buck's coverage of the rice-growing regions of mainland China leaves something to be desired; yet it still seems evident that Taiwan, even in 1911 (and so, presumably, in 1900), was a good deal more commercialized than the rice-growing regions of the mainland.

Finally, the existence of the leasehold deposit in its various forms, common in some commercialized parts of mainland China, also argues for commercialization. The fact that for a given piece of Taiwanese land there might be "caution money," an additional deposit, and a payment to a bondsman suggests that commercial interests were involved, not just concern with keeping tenants on the land or insuring rent payments (Wickberg 1969: 5).

Kubota shows that the "big tenants" of Szechwan were those who were able to afford the large deposits necessary for obtaining large units of land. To raise this deposit money, these tenants usually had to engage in some activity that further stimulated commercial development. This might have involved cash crops, wage labor, craft work, commerce, or moneylending (Kubota 1967: 260–96). It is perhaps premature to attempt to apply Kubota's analysis to northern Taiwan and to P'eng-fu. The largest units of tenant cultivation in P'eng-fu were not really very large—only comfortably larger than average. Moreover, we lack a great deal of information about the economic activities of P'eng-fu's large tenants. Nevertheless, the similarities between tenancy arrangements in northern Taiwan and those in Szechwan are sufficiently intriguing to make further investigation along the lines of Kubota's argument seem very worthwhile.

How typical of northern Taiwan was P'eng-fu? And how typical of all Taiwan was northern Taiwan? We observed earlier that in Taiwan as a whole 43 percent of agricultural households were tenant households, whereas the analogous figure for P'eng-fu was 50 percent. If we examine data for all of Taiwan from later in the Japanese period, however, we find that the expenditures of owner-cultivators, owner-tenants, and tenants suggest that owner-cultivators had the largest incomes and tenants the smallest (Chang 1969: 35–62)—seemingly quite unlike the situation in P'eng-fu in 1900. It appears likely, though, that P'eng-fu's unusually low number of owner-cultivators, its somewhat high number of tenants, and its probably high percentage of wage laborers can be explained by tenure patterns and by the inclusion of Shu-lin in P'eng-fu's administrative jurisdiction. The extremely high rate of tenancy as measured in terms of land (over 90 percent) does not seem so very abnormal when one remembers that in twelve villages (some commercialized and some not) in northern Taiwan, the average tenancy rate was 75 percent. P'eng-fu was thus an extreme case in several ways, but it still fits well within the northern Taiwanese spectrum. Furthermore, Hai-shan and various other parts of northern Taiwan were probably reasonably similar to the several commercialized areas in central and southern Taiwan. The generalizations made above, therefore, may not necessarily apply to all of Taiwan, but they should at least apply to the other commercialized, rice-growing parts of the island.

### *Institutional Continuity under Japanese Rule*

Under Japanese rule, Taiwan enjoyed half a century of political stability and agricultural development. During the first 25 years, the Japanese completed the job of pacification, began organizing the economic infrastructure, and opened the island to agricultural investment by Japanese corporations. Relying on this base, the Japanese attempted to bring about during the 1920's and 1930's what would later be termed a Green Revolution in Taiwan's rice and sugar production. The general goal of these decades was to bring about agricultural change without industrial development and without major social or political change. The specific goal was to produce cheap, reliable exports of rice and sugar to supply Japan's needs.

Japanese business firms, mostly sugar corporations, eventually owned almost one-fifth of the cultivated land in Taiwan. In order to ensure a certain level of raw materials, supply areas were assigned to each mill. Contracts between mills and growers (whether the growers were tenants of the mill or independent owner-cultivators) became an important part of agricultural life in southern Taiwan. The effect of this Japanese corporate landlordism on tenancy remains to be studied. We have had several broad suggestions on the subject (Yanaihara 1929; Asada 1968: 13–66; Jo 1975: 464–74), but much more detailed research is needed.

The most widely felt aspect of Japanese influence on rural Taiwan was the Green Revolution of the 1920's and 1930's. Students of the Green Revolutions of the 1970's are well aware that such phenomena depend not only on the introduction of high-yield seeds but also on the application of improved technology and organization. From this standpoint, modern students would not be disappointed by the Japanese efforts in Taiwan. The chief programs of Taiwan's Green Revolution included the creation of (1) an infrastructure of transportation, standard currency and markets, and credit assistance; (2) associations to distribute technical information and production aids (including seeds and fertilizer); (3) irrigation systems; (4) agencies to promote approved methods of cultivation (work in which even the police were involved); and (5) tax and pricing policies designed to encourage agricultural development. Some of these programs had begun before 1920; but new and old programs alike were given high priority in the 1920's as the Japanese directed their efforts specifically to the goal of creating Taiwanese rice and sugar surpluses.

The results of the Japanese programs were impressive. The new varieties of rice and sugarcane introduced in the 1920's took hold in the 1930's; and by the end of the 1930's, yields in both rice and sugar were more than double what they had been before 1920. Taiwanese farmers adopted increasingly scientific cultivation methods. The new high-yield varieties required more careful farm management and larger amounts of fertilizer, water, and labor. Moreover, commercial fertilizer had to be used: whereas previously the major costs of farming had been land and labor costs, fertilizer now became a third major expense. Increased production costs naturally increased farmers' needs for credit and hence the need for accessible credit institutions.

Green Revolutions are supposed to be neutral in respect to scale: that is, they should profit equally small and large cultivators. But in fact, Green Revolutions are often accompanied by growing social differentiation. Some farmers—usually the larger ones—do far better than others. The usual explanation is that these farmers have greater access to critical resources: they have the most or the best land, the easiest access to capital, the readiest access to information, and so forth (Griffin 1974: 46–91). Studies of recent Green Revolutions indeed suggest that they have had four common results (Griffin 1974; Frankel 1971; Rosen 1975). First, large and prosperous owners frequently become even more prosperous and increase their landholdings. Second, the tendency of prosperous owners to increase their holdings leads to a greater concentration of land in fewer hands. Third, the increased demand for farm labor often encourages laborers to demand higher wages, which in turn leads to confrontations between owners and laborers and brings to an end previous patron-client relationships. Fourth, increased wage demands by laborers stimulate owners to try to mechanize agricultural production (when they can afford to do so), thus reducing the number of farm laboring jobs available.

How do these general results fit with Taiwan in the 1920's and 1930's? If larger owners were widening the distance between themselves and smaller owners, we would expect to find this manifested in a growing concentration of owned land among a smaller number of owners. This, in turn, should increase the rate of tenancy. We might also expect to find some changes in the terms of tenancy, such as increased rental rates reflecting the competition of a growing number of would-be tenants for the opportunity to cultivate lands held in a smaller and smaller number of hands. If there were changes in laborers' status, we would expect to see these reflected by changes in the wage level or by a farm laborers' political movement.

In fact, it is surprisingly difficult to find evidence for Taiwan of any changes of the kind predicted above. No doubt the statistics presented here conceal movements of individual families as well as a number of differences in families' abilities to cope with change and to adjust to what may have become a much more competitive atmosphere. We will not know about these issues until a closer examination of the economy of individual farm households is possible. But the general picture that emerges is one of continuity and minimal disruption.

If one looks, for example, at changes in the pattern of landownership between 1920 and 1939, one is surprised by the relatively small magnitude of the changes that took place. In 1920, 64 percent of Taiwan's owners of farmland owned less than one hectare, 34 percent owned between one and ten hectares, and 2 percent owned over ten hectares. In 1939, the figures were exactly the same. Again in 1920, 15 percent of Taiwan's cultivated land was owned by owners with less than one hectare, 50 percent was owned by owners with between one and ten hectares, and 35 percent was owned by owners with more than ten hectares. In 1939, the respective figures were 14 percent, 45 percent, and 41 percent (Wang 1964: 45–46). It is thus apparent that the largest landowners slightly increased their proportion of Taiwan's cultivated land (from 35 percent to 41 percent). But this increase was not at the expense of the smallest owners. Nor is it at all clear that it was related to the Green Revolution. Japanese land policies after 1903 made it possible for Japanese corporations and private individuals to acquire large tracts of land that had been declared public or government land. Japanese sugar corporations and other businesses also purchased privately owned land in sizable parcels. This process of acquisition continued throughout the Japanese period. Although the land involved represented no more than one-fifth of all cultivated land on the island, the purchasers were among the largest landowners (those with more than ten hectares), and so their efforts must account for much of the overall change. A lesser influence was the continued reclamation of new lands up to the early

1930's. If this was done in accordance with past practices, it probably means that large tracts went to individuals who were able to finance the reclamation.

As noted previously, we would expect that any massive concentration of landownership would be reflected in tenancy rates—in particular, in a sharply increased rate of absentee ownership. Although one can find assertions that this increase took place (Jo 1975: 473), one is inclined to have serious doubts about such assertions in view of the already high rates of absentee ownership in 1900 (Wickberg 1970: 82–86). The one significant change in fact evident from official figures is an increase in the proportion of owner-tenant families within the landed agricultural population: owner-tenant families made up 24 percent of all landed agricultural families in 1910, 29 percent in 1922, and 32 percent in 1938 (*TCTY* 1946: 513). By contrast, the proportion of tenant families for the same years declined from 43 percent, to 41 percent, to 38 percent; and the proportion of owner families declined from 33 percent to 30 percent, where it remained. There are several possible interpretations for the substantial increase in the proportion of owner-tenant families. The most optimistic one is that the Green Revolution made possible increases in tenant family incomes, thus allowing tenants to purchase some land and become owner-tenants. The most pessimistic explanation is that some owner families, finding it difficult to cope with the demands of the Green Revolution, were forced to sell some of their land and become tenants on it (thereby becoming owner-tenants). There are other possible interpretations, and in the end the explanation may make use of several at once, including the two apparently opposing interpretations cited above. We will not know the answer to this until more detailed research has been done. The problem is complicated because the term owner-tenant is a legal term, not a social or economic one, and because the statistical totals do not show how families became owner-tenants or how their lands were divided between owned land and rented land. Finally, one last point needs to be made: much of the increase in the proportion of owner-tenants took place before the Green Revolution, indicating that other forces were at work.

Tenancy rates thus do not reflect any massive increase in the concentration of landownership. But what about farm size? We would expect, for example, that if large owners increased the size of their holdings, tenants might have increased the size of theirs also. This, however, does not seem to have happened. In 1920, 45 percent of all Taiwanese farms were less than one hectare, 39 percent were between one and three hectares, and 16 percent were over three hectares. By 1939, 46 percent were less than one hectare (up 1 percent), 39 percent were between one and three hectares (unchanged), and 15 percent were over three hectares (down 1 percent). Naturally, some of these farms were in the hands of owner-cultivators; but the great majority were in the hands of tenants, so the conclusion—that the size of tenant holdings did not substantially increase—still holds true (Ho 1978: 42, 349–52).[4] Moreover, the average farm size remained in the 1.8 to 2.0 hectare range throughout the Japanese period (JCRR 1956: 7, 8, 11).

Also, there were no major changes in the terms of tenancy. Rents remained between 40 and 60 percent of one's crop. In the case of rice, the introduction of the *p'eng-lai* high-yield variety resulted in greater productivity, which in turn resulted in higher land values. Rents may have gone up slightly as a consequence (since tenants paid fixed rents rather than share rents); but the evidence of Japanese surveys indicates no increases that were out of proportion to the land's increased productivity or that would fundamentally alter relationships between tenants and owners (complaints about high rents during the 1920's notwithstanding).

Tenure was probably less secure in the 1930's than before. The limits of cultivable land had been reached by then, yet Taiwan's population was growing faster than ever. Tenant competition encouraged some owners to shorten leases, thereby allowing them to raise rents more frequently—a trend visible from 1900. As before, contracts were usually oral, so neither party had documents to prove a violation if one party dissolved the contract without notice. Tenant complaints about insecurity were common in the 1930's. But we still cannot be certain that these were related to the Green Revolution. We have already mentioned increased tenant competition, which would have existed simply because of Taiwan's expanding population. Furthermore, some of the complaints of the 1930's may have been related to short-term influences, such as Japan's depression. And even if these complaints were a result of the Green Revolution, the picture is still mixed. Along with speculating landlords only interested in making a quick profit out of rising land values, there were landlords

[4] Ho's discussion of the 1920 data is vital to my argument.

who encouraged their tenants to plant *p'eng-lai* rice by negotiating written contracts with them stipulating that they grow this variety. Some landlords of the 1920's also began paying water fees for their tenants or helping them with other production costs when they were willing to grow *p'eng-lai.* For landlords who took the longer view, there was every reason to want to retain skillful tenants who could realize the full potential of *p'eng-lai.*

The deposit, or "caution money," remained in use throughout the Japanese period. One might have expected the Japanese to abolish this, since they were anxious to offer incentives to cultivators. They did not, however—perhaps because it had its uses (as we shall see). In fact, the Japanese made no attempt to limit rental rates, to insist upon written contracts or minimum lease periods, or to intervene in more than a tentative way in relations between owners and tenants. Owners were encouraged to help tenants grow *p'eng-lai* rice, to sign written contracts, and to join with tenants in an association to help resolve tenancy disputes. Beyond this, though, the Japanese did not interfere (Wickberg 1969).

No large-scale confrontation between owners and laborers is visible from the materials at hand. And laborers' wages show no striking increases or decreases in the 1920's and 1930's of the sort that would suggest dramatic changes in demand. In fact, their wage levels followed general wage and price trends (*TCTY* 1946: 844–46; Lee 1971: 57). Changes in the demand for labor should also be apparent in the occupational and residential statistics of the censuses; no such changes, however, can be found (Barclay 1954). There was a labor movement in Taiwan during the 1920's, and it may have been related to the problems of farm laborers. But there was no mechanization of farming that would have dispossessed agricultural laborers; and the agrarian movement of those years was not one of laborers in confrontation with owners. Taiwan's Peasant Movement was instead concerned with farm rent, security of tenure, use of cultivated lands, and marketing organization (Wickberg 1975).

It appears, then, that Taiwan's Green Revolution caused very little disruption and only slightly altered patterns of land tenure. Part of the reason for this was of course the Japanese administrators' desire to avoid major social change. But a more important cause of Taiwan's agricultural continuity during the Japanese period may be ascribed to the nature of Taiwan's preexisting land tenure system. Let me suggest three reasons for this.

First, the land tenure system developed in late Ch'ing Taiwan made it relatively easy to transfer farmland from people who were not interested in developing it to people who were (through ordinary tenancy, the "pledge," etc.). This was very much harder to do, by contrast, in societies where cultivation and ownership rights were largely inseparable (Barrows 1974). The Japanese, then, had only to tinker with Taiwan's tenure system to make it a bit more flexible—primarily by putting an end to the patent holder's right, thereby simplifying claims to farmland and providing clear title (and unambiguous responsibility for taxes) to the usufruct holder as the full owner. This measure greatly facilitated Japanese agricultural goals (Myers & Ching 1964). But the Japanese also ended permanent tenures by establishing a twenty-year limit, a change that assured tenants a sufficient period to develop the land without freezing cultivation rights (Wickberg 1969: 9).

Second, Taiwan's system of fixed rents for agricultural land paved the way for a successful Green Revolution. In countries with a share rent system, tenants sometimes lacked sufficient incentives to make Green Revolutions work: although share rents spread the risks of cultivation, they did not greatly reward tenants for increased production since increases had to be shared with owners. Fixed rents, then, meant that Taiwan's tenant farmers had every reason to support innovation. Furthermore, Taiwan's owners were not overlooked: the Japanese allowed owners to dominate the agricultural development associations that the government sponsored, and they made development activities worthwhile by not limiting the rates of rent or the amounts of "caution money" that owners could ask for (Wickberg 1969: 23; Lee 1971: 78–79, 89, 126–27). Even the continuation of "caution money"—at first glance a likely hindrance to agricultural development—may have aided progress because it excluded tenants who did not have the resources to farm effectively and provided an additional incentive to tenants who did.

Third, the level of commercialization already existing in Taiwan before 1920 was a good preparation for the Green Revolution. Griffin points out, for example, how easily commercial farmers can adapt to the cash demands of a Green Revolution (1974: 73, 188). In Taiwan, cultivators were long accustomed to putting a large percentage of their rice crop on the market, so the Japanese did not have to use much persuasion about the benefits of a market economy. Such an economy was especially well established in areas with high rates of tenancy and absentee ownership. (As a general rule, high concentrations of landownership are associated with high rates of marketing.) Moreover, Taiwan's many moderate-sized farms meant that tenants as well as owners had rice left over to put on the market. (On very small farms, tenants had no experience of markets since they had to consume all the rice that remained after they had paid their rents.) Finally, the very largest tenants were probably skilled entrepreneurs. The Japanese encouraged landlords to innovate; and this process was greatly facilitated by the entrepreneurial skills already developed among Taiwan's most successful tenants.

This does not mean that the Green Revolution was carried out by landlords and tenants only. Up to 1930 the Japanese relied upon police and landlord persuasion, and most of the rice was marketed by landlords. After 1930 income incentives became important, and the largest proportion of the rice was marketed by tenants and by owner-cultivators (Lee 1971: 73–80). Clearly, all groups marketed their rice by the 1930's. But in a high-tenancy society—and Taiwan was that, since throughout the Japanese period no less than 50 percent of cultivated land was cultivated by tenants (Ho 1978: 354)—much of the success of agricultural innovation would have depended upon the quality of the tenants, and the presence of some successful large tenants may have been important in that context.

The preceding picture of successful development with few dislocations is derived from statistical and other materials at a national level. It may conceal a great deal. It is difficult to believe, for example, that the Peasant Movement was unrelated to the Green Revolution, although no relationship has yet been established. The very existence of such a movement suggests pressures and dislocations that need study on a local level. It is equally clear that we will not thoroughly understand the effect of the Green Revolution on Taiwan's land tenure institutions until we have made detailed studies of the spread of high-yield seeds, locality by locality and, if possible, farm by farm. The foregoing argument, therefore, can be no more than preliminary and suggestive.

# Part Four

# Ethnicity

# Ethnicity and Social Class

Hill Gates

## *Aims of the Paper*

The existence of two major ethnic blocs in Taiwan is a fact obvious to everyone from the greenest tourist to my elderly Taipei landlady, who spends many cheerful hours slandering "those hillbilly Chinese" for cutting out the Taiwanese-language soap operas. Social scientists, however, have been cautious in exploring the social significance of ethnicity in Taiwan. This caution has resulted both from an unwillingness to analyze such a potentially sensitive topic and from the inability of ethnicity theory to provide more than superficial insights into an immensely complex issue. Both these difficulties are now being overcome: research interests in Taiwan are broader than ever before, and progress is being made in understanding ethnicity as an informal political system within a complex society. Taiwan is a modern state whose macrostructure, politics, and economics provide the parameters within which the people of families, villages, and neighborhoods must operate. Ethnicity appears—to me, to the tourist, and to my landlady, at any rate—to be a factor that operates throughout Taiwanese society, influencing and being influenced by national-level events.

Chinese society is indisputably characterized by broad cultural

The data on which this paper is based were gathered in Taipei—in 1970 with the assistance of Miss Ch'en Fu-mei, and in 1974–75 with the assistance of Miss Wang Ch'un-hua. Both Miss Ch'en and Miss Wang deserve my sincerest thanks. Their resourcefulness and determination were in large measure responsible for the success of my fieldwork (though they bear no responsibility for my conclusions). I am also grateful to the Wenner-Gren Foundation for Anthropological Research for a research grant in 1970, and to the Research and Creative Endeavors Committee of Central Michigan University for a research grant in 1974–75.

variations. Names of languages and of dialects within languages are often used as labels for groups of people who may share some other objectively determinable identifying characteristics—cuisines, costume variations, etc. The Chinese accept—though they could not possibly all agree on the details of—the existence of regional provincial and local stereotypes that express subjectively perceived subcultural differences (see Eberhard 1965). These subjective and objective differences may appear significant enough under circumstances of segmentary opposition to be termed "ethnic." In recent years, such usage has become common for describing subcultural variation within Taiwan; this can be seen in Hsu (1976) and Ahern (this volume) though Lamley (this volume) prefers to use "subethnic" in this context.

In this paper, I will focus on ethnic differences between the "Taiwanese" (the native born and their descendants) and "mainlanders" (post-Second World War immigrants and their Taiwan-born offspring). My primary aim is to analyze the functional and historical causes of Taiwan's present bi-ethnic organization, an organization that has been created and maintained by specific structures and interests. Some of these structures and interests are the result of historical accident, but others derive from the ongoing processes of political interaction in an industrial state. As anthropologists, we may properly inquire into these processes. How does the state, with all its power to influence, categorize, and educate its populace, perceive and implement ethnic policies? What interests are served by the maintenance of ethnic boundaries, and what interests are harmed? To what degree are insiders' perceptions of ethnic relations congruent with observable, measurable behavior, and to what degree are they mystifications, convenient illusions?

If these questions are to be answered, a theory of ethnic group behavior must be formulated. A second aim of this paper, then, is to review and criticize existing theories of ethnicity in order to find and apply the most powerful theory to Taiwan. Without anticipating too far the results of this analysis, I will note that any attempt to explain ethnicity in a complex society must take social class into account.

Consequently, the third aim of this paper is to provide a description and analysis of the relationship between Taiwan's social classes and ethnic groups. This attempt is far from final, since it is limited both by the length of this discussion and by my own inadequate knowledge. It appears to me, however, that no progress can be made on either ethnicity or class until they are examined together.

## *Theories of Ethnicity: Historical-Idealist and Functional-Ecological*

Until the Second World War, the main anthropological arguments about ethnicity were concerned with the degree to which race, language, culture, and "nationality" could be said to be biologically determined. From Boas (at least) to Beals and Hoijer, liberal-minded anthropologists were kept so busy putting out racist brushfires on this thorny perimeter that they found little time to do more than demonstrate that ethnic groups were not distinguished from each other by sets of genes. In 1956, Wagley and Harris presented an original analysis of ethnicity in Latin America that included as its most important new element an emphasis on the role of the state and on the significance of differential power in ethnic relations (see Wagley & Harris 1964). Harris later developed this theme more fully in his 1964 *Patterns of Race in the Americas*. But this strong and—for anthropology—even radical analysis of the political and economic bases of ethnicity was generally ignored in favor of continued emphasis on historical-idealist approaches.[1] The latter viewpoint continues subtly to influence many social scientists' perceptions of ethnic relations in Taiwan.

Essentially, the historical-idealist position is based on the assumption that ethnic groups have a tendency to persist regardless of circumstances in which their members find themselves. An ideology of ethnic separateness is treated as an independent variable that "causes" other patterns of behavior without itself being susceptible to causal analysis. Such an approach, though not generally made explicit by contemporary anthropologists, can occasionally deflect attention from a potentially interesting problem: ethnicity can be misinterpreted as a given where it is in fact a consequence of another difference unrelated to ethnic peculiarities. This paper, for example, is intended to refute the widely accepted notion that mainlander and Taiwanese differences result from the persistence of patterns of behavior characteristic of these groups' respective areas of origin, by

[1]A quick survey of recent major works on this subject (Cohen 1974b; Barth 1969; De Vos 1975) does not reveal a single reference to the pioneering work of Wagley and Harris.

showing that the groups' relationships with each other and with other exogenous variables are in fact responsible for much of the cultural and social variation between them.

Even when the historical-idealist approach is made explicit, however, it is difficult to prove incorrect, for disproof depends on negative evidence. When ethnic groups are examined cross-culturally, they appear in a bewildering variety of settings. The incautious or idealist observer can easily conclude that the only constant in all this variety is that ethnicity persists. To analyze properly the reasons for ethnic continuity, however, we should take into account not only the groups that have persisted, but also those that have not. The disappearance of ethnicity thus shows the weakness of the historical-idealist explanation, since according to this explanation, ethnic groups—short of being the victims of genocide—should never disappear. Yet they obviously do, as one Taiwanese case is sufficient to show: there are "Hakka" in the Chang-hua Plain who think that they were always as "Hokkien" as they now appear to be (Hsu 1976).

Easier to find (but no less relevant) are cases where ethnic groups have nearly disappeared. The Lu-kang Muslims were clearly losing their distinctiveness before an active body of Muslims from the mainland revitalized their traditions (Pillsbury 1973); many seventeenth- and eighteenth-century Chinese migrants to Southeast Asia merged almost completely with native populations before the large immigrations of the nineteenth century created new roles there for ethnic Chinese; Mexico contains sprinklings of people of Chinese and Korean ancestry (now collectively known as "chinos") who have been absorbed into local mestizo culture with only their names and descriptive epithet to distinguish them from other Yucatecans.[2] The assumption that ethnic groups tend inherently to persist, then, cannot be valid. It seems wiser always to assume that the existence of ethnic groups in a society implies a good deal more than that parts of the population have had different historic origins.

Frederik Barth's functional-ecological theory of ethnicity, set forth in his introduction to *Ethnic Groups and Boundaries* (1969), influences much recent anthropological work on ethnicity. Barth's arguments represent a significant theoretical advance over the histor-

[2]Dr. Alice Littlefield has described to me examples of lower-class ethnic assimilation in Mexico involving blacks, Koreans, and Chinese; in all these instances, the numbers of those assimilated were too small (in comparison with the numbers of the native lower class) to permit ethnically based communities. (Personal communication.)

ical-idealist tradition, but they also present a number of problems of application to a society such as Taiwan's. Barth rejects earlier notions that ethnic groups result from the inevitable preservation of accidental differences in culture. Ethnic groups are maintained "not only by a once-and-for-all recruitment but by continual expression and validation"; thus, "the critical focus of investigation from this point of view becomes the ethnic *boundary* that defines the group, not the cultural stuff that it encloses" (1969: 15).

Reduced to its essentials, ethnicity for Barth is a means of maintaining solidarity among people who share the same ecological niche. Self-ascription, not "cultural stuff," is the basis for ethnic identity. Adjusting to ecological resources is possible because individuals (and groups) can change their ethnic identity by adopting some of the characteristic "markers" of the group they wish to join, then claim a new identity. Boundary-maintenance mechanisms, such as endogamy, food taboos, and linguistic forms preserve the structure of ethnic groups, despite changes in personnel and in cultural traits.

Barbara Pillsbury skillfully applies Barth's idea of boundary-maintenance mechanisms to the analysis of the Hui (Muslims) in Taiwan (1973). Self-ascription as Muslims with a "different blood," endogamy, and a taboo on eating pork have preserved the distinctiveness of the group for many centuries in China and continue to do so today in Taiwan. Pillsbury documents the pressures for assimilation that deeply concern the mainlander Hui community, and describes the onetime nearly complete assimilation of the Lu-kang Hui by Hokkien culture. However, she does not deal extensively with the issues of dissociation and assimilation: with why (not how) the mainlander Muslims opted to maintain boundaries against Han inroads, and with why the Taiwanese Hui succumbed to these pressures. There appear to be two reasons for her failure to account for these differences. Both are implicit in (and constitute major flaws of) Barth's functional-ecological framework.

This framework assumes a relatively free flow of personnel across ethnic boundaries, because ethnic groups are in essence ecologically based communities. People's perceptions of their group membership conform closely to their actual social membership, a function of their economy. This is frequently not true, however, in state societies. Barth's arguments, then, are not readily applicable to Taiwanese society.

We should distinguish clearly between the "ethnicity" developed by essentially autonomous, though interrelated, tribal social systems, where social relations *may* derive directly from ecological factors, and the "ethnicity" that is found in state societies. In state societies, political power—though never divorced from its material base—takes forms wholly unlike those that emerge in tribal settings. Indeed, it seems appropriate to use "tribalism" (*pace*, Morton Fried) in the former case and to reserve "ethnicity" for certain kinds of groupings found within state societies, where political power over people and resources is more concentrated, and where approximation to ecological homeostasis is less likely. The connection—whatever it may be—between economy and polity is not the same. To generalize simultaneously about ethnic groups in tribal and state settings, then, appears to me unwise.

Barth also focuses on the way people move between ethnic groups by adopting and abandoning various kinds of behavior. From Barth's own work on Southwest Asia (and even more vividly from Edmund Leach's description of the same phenomenon in Highland Burma [1954]), one sees cases of people "becoming" something they formerly were not and, apparently, being accepted in their new roles. The question of acceptance is touched on where Barth notes that "the critical feature [of a definition of ethnic groups] . . . becomes . . . the characteristic of self-ascription and ascription by others" (1969: 13). Yet his discussion ignores the extent to which "ascription by others" means that ethnic identity can be imposed on or denied to people by conditions beyond their control. Recent research on the Chinese in the United States, for example, demonstrates how much supposed Chinese "clannishness" and ethnic separateness is a result of the refusal of other Americans and the state to permit them to settle at will, engage in many occupations, intermarry, and become citizens (see Light 1973; Nee & Nee 1973). The ethnic identity of the American Chinese in fact owes a great deal to official exclusion. Attempts by Chinese to find new "ecological" or economic niches in American society assuredly did not follow the laws of homeostatic resource allocation, which may operate in some tribal settings: such "laws" were set aside by the state in order to maintain inequality in favor of non-Chinese. Similar arguments go far in explaining the ethnic separateness of Southeast Asian Chinese (see Willmott 1970). In the case of Taiwan, the behavior of the two main ethnic groups is likewise shaped to a great extent by the different statuses the state awards to each.

In short, for Taiwan I find that much of Barth's analysis is unhelpful because of Barth's own failure to recognize clearly the differences between the political economies of state and nonstate societies. States, with their capacity to centralize power, are inherently nonegalitarian; in them, one should expect to find not the ecological chess game of the tribe, but considerable conflict among inescapably unequal competitors.

For our purposes, Barth has made his most useful contribution in his acute analysis of ethnic boundaries and their dependence on a shared perception of common identity rather than on biological or cultural continuities. A Hakka can be a Hakka whether or not she wears a black-fringed hat; a person born in Taiwan who has never seen Shantung, cannot speak its dialect, and does not like *man-t'ou* (steamed buns), can still be Shantungnese. Barth's reliance on the idea of self-ascription leads him to an essentially emic analysis of ethnic relations that excludes from serious consideration etic evidence—i.e., those factors that can be "identified and studied independently of the natives' cultural judgments" (Harris 1975: 160).

Emic views of ethnic relations in a state society are especially interesting, however, because the state is likely to propagandize its official policy on the subject with considerable effectiveness. The result is that insiders' perceptions of socially important categories may differ significantly from those formed by cultural outsiders who have not been influenced by the views the state has instilled in its people and who analyze ethnic relations on the basis of etic categories.

## *Ethnicity, the State, and Social Inequality: A Dialectical View*

I have dealt with Barth's ideas extensively because though they are influential, they avoid a number of essential issues and thus lead to a misunderstanding of the political role of ethnic groups in state societies. An anthropologist who deals much more directly with the politics of ethnicity in state societies is Abner Cohen. Cohen argues that "the central theoretical problem in social anthropology has been the analysis of the dialectical relations between two major variables: symbolic action and power relations" (1974a: 13). It is useful to characterize symbolic acts as reifications of collective understandings, a kind of group "emics"; power relations, however, are data susceptible to etic analysis. Cohen sees clearly the effects of highly concentrated state power on the dialectical relationship between symbolic acts and power relations; and his own work explicitly focuses on state-level formations. The concentration of power inherent in states and the resulting inequalities of state-level societies make it advantageous for some social groups to camouflage and mislead other groups about their existence and function. In a chapter on "invisible" organizations, Cohen sets forth views on ethnicity that are directly applicable to Taiwan.

Ethnic groups are described as "collectivities of people who share some patterns of normative behavior or culture, and who form part of a larger population, interacting within the framework of a common social system like the state" (1974a: 92). Further, they are interest groups that "exploit parts of their traditional culture in order to articulate informal organizational functions that are used in the struggle of these groups for power within the framework of formal organizations" (*ibid.*: 91). This definition, Cohen admits, does not allow us to distinguish ethnic groups with perfect clarity from some other interest groups, notably elites. However, a recognition of the many similarities between elite groups (and social classes in general) and ethnic groups is one of the features of Cohen's analysis that makes it a clear theoretical advance over those analyses that conceive of ethnic groups and social classes as alternative ways of conceptualizing social structure (e.g., De Vos 1975: 6, 20).

Elite groups—Cohen cites the delightful example of London stockbrokers—resemble ethnic groups in many ways. Why, then, do we distinguish between the two? Cohen supplies the answer: "City men are socioculturally as distinct within British society as are the Hausa within Yoruba society. They are indeed as 'ethnic' as any ethnic group can be. But they are not usually described as an ethnic group because the term 'ethnic' connotes to many people lower status, minority status, or migrancy. Numerically, City men are literally a minority. But largely because of their high and privileged status they are referred to as an 'elite' not a 'minority.'" (1974a: 101.)

The conclusion underscored by Cohen's analysis is that an essential semantic component of the concept of ethnicity is an asymmetrical distribution of power. It is curious that Cohen fails to pursue the implications of the notion that ethnic groups, as interest groups competing informally for political advantage within a state, are themselves likely to be unequal in their capacity to accumulate and hold power. This is important, particularly because people do not move freely between ethnic categories in state societies, as argued above.

My analysis of Taiwan's ethnic groups and their relationships will rely, then, on Barth's ideas about boundary maintenance (with the provision that we should not expect a free movement of people across these boundaries); on Cohen's understanding of ethnic groups as competitors within a formal political system, in this case the state; and on the premise that considerations of structural inequality among socially defined groups are essential to the analysis of a state society such as Taiwan's.

## *The Concept of Social Class*

Before proceeding further with Cohen's analysis of the political functions of ethnicity, I must turn briefly to the subject of social class. Ethnic groups cannot be understood in state societies, especially industrial ones, outside the framework of social class. The principal factors I shall take into account in assessing social class are the relationships of occupational groups to the means of production, the family as a social and economic unit, and class consciousness.

The first factor—the relationships of occupational groups to the means of production—is the most important. A group's niche in the economy powerfully affects its opportunities for social mobility, its life-style, and its ideology. Thus a group's range of occupations, role in the wider economy, and prospects for capital accumulation and ownership of the means of production are the main matters I shall consider under this heading.

The second factor—the social and economic roles of the family as a unit—is easily stated, but produces endless practical problems for the social analyst. As I hope to show, however, the coresident family and not the individual is the appropriate unit for class analysis in Taiwan. Since a typical family has more than one worker, there are sometimes difficulties in assessing individual cases. In most families, though, the status gap between workers is not broad; and if it becomes so, the excessively mobile subgroup will probably "divide the family."

The third factor—class consciousness—is an emic one. Must a social group have a sense of itself as a group to be called a class? From a behaviorist perspective, the answer seems obvious. In societies where power is unequally distributed, it would be positively dangerous not to have a good cognitive map of the social structure: knowing when to display deference or superiority is a basic survival skill. People always know, then, that other people fall into at least three categories—superiors, equals, and subordinates. A consciousness of class may not be developed beyond this rudimentary level, however, if only because of the normal limitations of each person's experience. Moreover, modern nations often maintain an official ideology of classlessness, one that stresses racial or ethnic divisions in society rather than class divisions or in some other way obscures popular perceptions of economically based social differences.

In this paper, then, assignment of families to social class will take into account their objective status with respect to the means of production and, secondarily, behavior that reveals perceptions of differential position within society.

## *Cohen's Two Cases*

Having presented some preliminary ideas about social class, I will now turn to an analysis of ethnic groups in this context. Abner Cohen describes two hypothetical sets of consequences for the mingling of ethnic groups in a complex society. In Case I—a society newly formed by the merging of two ethnic groups—socioeconomic cleavages coincide with previously existing ethnic distinctions. Here "cultural differences between the two groups will become entrenched, consolidated, and strengthened in order to articulate the struggle between the two social groups across the new class lines. Old customs will tend to persist. But within the newly emerging social system they will assume new values and new social significance." (1974a: 96.) In Case II, economic and political cleavages cut across ethnic lines, with the result that people from each ethnic group are found in the upper and lower classes. In such a situation, if class differences are very sharp, ethnic differences will tend to disappear and the classes may evolve subcultural styles of life as far apart as those of the rich and the poor in Victorian England.

These two hypothetical relationships between ethnicity and social class provide us with a starting point for our analysis. Cohen's discussion of both models, however, fails to take into account the full effects of inequality between ethnic groups, classes, or both. In Case I, assume for the sake of simplicity that we are talking about two ranked ethnic groups forming distinct social classes. Though corresponding lines of class and ethnic cleavage present a formidable barrier to social mobility, pressures for upward mobility from the lower class and against downward mobility from the upper class are relentless—especially in a society experiencing moderate economic growth. If what is actually a class distinction is popularly perceived as an ethnic distinction, we should expect continual attempts to move upward on the part of the lower class, and heightened vigilance against such movement by the upper. We may then predict the development of strict control over hypogamy, elaboration of social ritual, refinement of dialect, and stress on cultural attainments that validate status.

In Case II, where class lines cut across ethnic ones, it may be to the advantage of the members of the upper class to bury their ethnic differences and merge into a culturally unified elite. The best strategy for members of the lower class, however, is by no means as clear. Though a strongly united lower class would be able, by sheer weight of numbers, to influence society on its own behalf, such unity is difficult to achieve. For many, maintaining useful ties to persons on a higher stratum may offer a more immediate path to success. Claims of kinship, common origin, and shared culture are common ploys in this game. As a result, ethnic self-consciousness is likely to persist among the lower class even as it erodes in the upper. A shrewd elite may encourage ethnic differences within the lower class in order to prevent the formation of a class unity that would threaten their power. Because the two emerging classes in this hypothetical case are not equal in power, they will stress and manipulate in unlike ways the symbolic ties that cut across class lines.

Under some circumstances, as in societies where elections are a means to power, members of the upper class may choose to maintain an ethnic identity that will assure them lower class ethnic support. A tradition of ethnically conscious electioneering by upper-class candidates or by candidates co-opted from the lower class is a highly respectable way of vitiating lower-class power in a multi-ethnic state.

A further characteristic of structural differentiation between two emerging social classes is the obvious one of size. Elites are usually small, whereas the poorer people whose surplus production makes possible the elite's higher standard of living usually constitute a majority. Returning to Cohen's hypothetical Case I, we see that the socially and ethnically dominant group may have to be whittled down in numbers before it will constitute an efficient ruling class. What is to become of the superfluous members of this group in a society where ethnic and social status are presumed to be congruent? Such people will be socially problematic—and emically ambiguous—to both upper and lower classes.

In Taiwan, Cohen's hypothetical case where "two ethnic groups join together and interact politically and economically and establish a new political system" (1974a: 95) has been realized. The interaction of native Taiwanese and mainlanders has had an almost experimental clarity to it: we know about the economic and organizational structures that the Japanese left behind, and we know that the Japanese themselves disappeared and had very little influence on Taiwan again until well after the KMT had established its rule; we also know that the mainlander immigration lasted only five years, then virtually ceased, and that the KMT was able to establish itself, after a little skirmishing, as one of the strongest, most heavily manned, and most irresistible governments of the twentieth century.

Fundamentally, there were few significant cultural differences between the Han Taiwanese and the mixed Han mainlanders in 1945, though their recent social, economic, and political histories had diverged widely during the period of Japanese rule. There was considerable enthusiasm in Taiwan at the end of the war for a reunion with the Chinese people to whom many Taiwanese felt they properly belonged. If Taiwanese-mainlander ethnic distinctiveness exists now, it has arisen in response to recent conditions. Ethnic relations as we see them in today's Taiwan are almost solely the result of the political, social, and economic interaction of Taiwanese and mainlanders since the war. During this time, the mainlanders' virtual monopoly of state power—though not of other kinds of power—has created asymmetries in the way ethnicity is used in political competition. Consequently, a strong sense of ethnic separateness, felt by both groups, has been created where it formerly did not exist and strengthened where it did. The two main ethnic groups in Taiwan are thus part of a currently evolving political process.

A problem arises, however, when we try to apply Cohen's analytical framework to Taiwan: Taiwan appears to fit both Case I and Case II. I will briefly discuss the basis of this apparent contradiction before attempting to resolve it.

### *Case I: Congruence of Class and Ethnic Cleavages*

If we examine primarily emic data, Case I seems to bear the closest resemblance to Taiwan's social conditions. In Case I, it will be remembered, two previously separate ethnic groups become part of a single political system, with one group clearly superior in power and social status.

It is extremely easy to elicit emic data, generally in the form of stereotypes and prejudices, in support of this view of Taiwan's social structure. Replete with invidious comparisons, the view emerges as the cognitive model underlying much behavior on both sides. Taiwanese and mainlanders typically agree, though in different emotional keys, that the mainlanders have a cultural advantage in being more directly derived from the Han homeland (which is bigger and more important than Taiwan) and that the Taiwanese language is hopelessly scatological, impossible to reduce to writing, and perhaps (as many university students of both groups insisted in my husband's linguistics classes) not a real language with form and order at all. Taiwanese life-styles, cuisine, and religious beliefs are likewise described as inferior by many members of both groups. The Taiwanese sometimes indicate the higher socioeconomic status of mainlanders by describing them as "people with money" (in contrast to themselves, who are "poor"). Mainlanders underline the contrast by stressing the idea that they are educated people and that the Taiwanese are not. The Taiwanese are understandably less willing to see the distinction in these terms, and often question mainlanders' claims to social status based on education: they believe that many high school and college "degrees" were granted on board ship coming to Taiwan or simply manufactured in registry offices thereafter.

There are a few areas in which the Taiwanese do claim superiority (cleanliness of person and environment is a notable one), and there are a few groups of Taiwanese who are especially likely to claim it. Upper-class Taiwanese feel at an advantage in dealing with mainlanders because of their conformity to Japanese ideals of education and culture. In fact, Japan continues to exercise great influence on members of this class: many were educated in Japan, and most look to Japan for cultural leadership in literature, the arts, and living styles. Moreover, many members of the Taiwanese elite frequently travel to Japan on business or to see relatives. By contrast, middle-class, upwardly mobile Taiwanese often achieve social superiority by acculturating partly to American or European patterns. Pride simply in being Taiwanese is rare, at least in the urban areas where mainlander values are most pervasive.

Most Taiwanese, however, are willing to grant many of the status claims made by mainlanders and to see themselves as participants in a "lower" culture. But this does not mean that they readily abandon their identity as Taiwanese. I do not have, and never expect to have, enough data on the private feelings of the Taiwanese to analyze the psychocultural dynamics of ethnic identity that appear so significant to some students of ethnic groups. That the Taiwanese have complex feelings about their ethnic status is obvious; but I do not believe that superficial methods, such as handing out survey questionnaires or spending a few years with the Taiwanese, will reveal them. Literary sources may provide some insights, however. A recent article on the mainlander author Pai Hsien-yung suggests the richness of such materials (Lau 1975).

There is, however, an abundance of evidence that many Taiwanese try to shed their ascribed position, and that most fail in the attempt. In most social situations, strangers can place each other immediately as native born or not on the basis of speech, dress, and the like. Many middle-class Taiwanese are fairly successful at eliminating obvious ethnic signs from their behavior. Yet such people are not invariably permitted to become members of a generalized upper-status group, for however completely one alters one's speech, ritual practices, and life-style, mainlander associates will continue to respond to one's Taiwanese background. Among school teachers and civil servants, the aspiring Taiwanese is gently but incessantly reminded of his origins by his colleagues. In the course of introductions to such people, new acquaintances were usually "placed" for me—a foreigner who might miss the significant obvious—as Taiwanese or as mainlanders. The common social chat among strangers attending dinner parties begins by establishing the origins of all persons present with jocular references to foods, speech peculiarities, or personality traits supposedly characteristic of each ethnic group. Polite interest in each other's family (number of siblings, living parents) also quickly reveals one's origins. Statements such as "I don't even know where my co-workers or schoolmates come from" are, in general, graceful ways of saying "I don't *care* where they originate, I am not prejudiced"—which is quite another matter. Taiwanese who would like to be identified primarily as "middle class" rather than as "Taiwanese" are readily hindered from doing so. It is obvious, though still noteworthy, that the reverse situation—a mainlander wishing to be accepted as a Taiwanese—is much rarer. A poor, wifeless, retired soldier clings to his only social advantage, his ethnic status, which in and of itself makes him superior. By contrast, however, the sons of very poor mainlander families sometimes find it advantageous to be socially acceptable to the Taiwanese among whom they must expect to find jobs, wives, and their futures.

These examples of prejudice and stereotyping show that many people in Taiwan perceive their society as one in which mainlanders are at once an ethnic group and a class that is superior to the ethnic group and class of Taiwanese—that is, a Case I society. This view is corroborated, moreover, by objective data. Ethnic group membership for example, is based on one's father's place of origin, and this information is a necessary item on the identity cards carried by all persons aged fifteen and over. Children are socialized by the state to accept ethnicity as a primary identity: in many elementary and high schools, children are asked publicly to state their province of origin at the beginning of the term, and the census of students by province is posted. Finally, mainlanders are heavily overrepresented in the higher levels of government service. Only 12 percent of the population are mainlanders; but of the 88,873 civil service functionaries of Taiwan province, including those in the provincial government, provincial enterprises, and public schools (and excluding persons in similar positions who work for *hsien* and municipal governments), 31,592, or 36 percent, are mainlanders. If we include only government officials and school employees, the total is 40,768; of these, the number of mainlanders is 19,801, or 49 percent. (*Chung-hua Min-kuo t'ung-chi t'i-yao* 1974: 721.) These aggregate figures in fact conceal a much higher degree of concentration of mainlander power in policy-making branches of government. According to Tien, there are still "few convincing signs of a genuine sharing of political power with aspiring Taiwanese" (1975: 617).

These and other data suggest that Cohen's Case I model applies well to Taiwan's social structure. However, his quite different Case II model also appears to apply.

## *Case II: Multiclass Ethnic Groups*

In Cohen's Case II model, lines of socioeconomic cleavage cut across ethnic boundaries, giving rise, in time, to a society where the poor of all ethnic groups merge, as do the rich, to form a two-class society. I have already suggested some reasons why such intermixing is unlikely for the lower class, although it might occur among the elite. In a relatively new state such as Taiwan, the shift from ethnic to class stratification generally creates a society where people respond to both class and ethnic membership. Under these circumstances, both ethnic groups contain members in each of the two (or more) classes.

This is a better model for Taiwan's society than the simpler Case I, even though it does not fit as well with dominant popular perceptions. Informants for both groups, if prodded, will allow that there are rich and powerful Taiwanese with high social status, and that there are poor mainlanders to whom many Taiwanese feel socially superior. In my experience, these views come more readily from mainlanders; Taiwanese are likely to invoke the Case I model by observing that even poor mainlanders have "connections," are better cared for by the government, and are consequently in a position of greater social advantage. In addition, elite Taiwanese are often differentiated from elite mainlanders by their supposed lack of education and tendency to be found in less worthy occupations like trade and industry. It is nevertheless generally possible to elicit grudging verbal confirmation of the multiclass structure of both ethnic groups; and a great deal of nonverbal behavior similarly demonstrates that everyone takes both class and ethnicity into account as separate variables. A bare-chested cart puller does not share betel nut with a black-suited bureaucrat caught in the same doorway during the rain, no matter what the bureaucrat's ethnic background.

Other data support the multiclass model. In a population that is (as noted) approximately 12 percent mainlander, there is a large Taiwanese elite as well as a large mainlander one (see Cole 1967); the 1974 edition of *T'ai-wan 500 kung-shang jen-ming-lu*, published by a private consulting firm, listed 500 major business people in Taiwan, of whom 68 percent were Taiwanese and 32 percent were mainlanders. (That nearly one-third of the country's biggest private entrepreneurs were non-Taiwanese surprised many mainlanders to whom I

TABLE 1
*Government Employees and School Teachers of Taiwanese Descent at the Provincial, County, and Municipal Levels*

| Date | Number employed[a] | Percent who are Taiwanese |
|---|---|---|
| 1946 | 42,467 | 77% |
| 1950 | 49,798 | 74 |
| 1954 | 72,405 | 62 |
| 1958 | 86,260 | 63 |
| 1962 | 108,041 | 61 |
| 1966 | 124,193 | 63 |
| 1970 | 126,566[b] | 66 |
| 1973 | 151,851[c] | 69 |

SOURCE: *T'ai-wan sheng cheng-fu jen-shih t'ung-chi t'i-yao* 1974: 38–39.
[a] As government employees and school teachers at the provincial, county, and municipal levels.
[b] Does not include 4,666 people employed in Taipei city.
[c] Does not include 5,397 people employed in Taipei city.

mentioned the statistic, since their belief that the Taiwanese monopolize big business was strong.)

The existence of large and expanding upper-class suburbs outside Taipei hints at a recent expansion of the wealthy classes. According to data supplied by a 1973 statistical abstract of Taipei city (*T'ai-pei shih t'ung-chi yao-lan* 1973: 35–36), 73 percent of those who moved between 1968 and 1973 into the relatively affluent suburbs of Shih-lin, Pei-tou, Ching-mei, and Mu-chia were Taiwanese.

Government employees and school teachers at the provincial, county, and municipal levels constitute a very large middle-class stratum. And the Taiwanese have held a majority of the jobs in this stratum since 1946, as Table 1 indicates. What Table 1 does not indicate, however, is that Taiwanese employees have predominated at the less prestigious county and municipal levels; at the provincial level, by contrast, they have held a much lower percentage of the jobs (in 1974, for example, only 55 percent of provincial school teachers and 49 percent of provincial government employees were Taiwanese). Moreover, the figures show an overall decline in the percentage of jobs at all three levels held by Taiwanese employees (though this decline was most marked in the first decade after the war).

Though the Taiwanese share of the jobs considered in Table 1 has declined since 1946, the decline has been offset by the obvious growth in the number of middle-class Taiwanese who have attained a new level of affluence and social status on the basis of commercial activities (usually small businesses). A 1971 commercial census of Taiwan (and also of the Fukien area, although the figures for this area are negligible) contains data on 278,965 private enterprises. Of these, 90.1 percent employed 1 to 10 persons; 7.7 percent employed 11 to 49 persons; 1.1 percent employed 50 to 99 persons; 0.9 percent employed 100 to 499 persons; and 0.2 percent employed 500 or more persons (*T'ai Fu ti-chü kung-shang yeh p'u-ch'a pao-kao* 1973: 74–75). The first two categories, containing 97.8 percent of all enterprises, include a range of owner-operated businesses that support moderate to upper middle-class styles of life. Unfortunately, no data are supplied about the ethnic background of owners of firms in these categories. I must therefore fall back on my impression that in cities like Taipei and Kaohsiung—where mainlanders are most numerous—mainlanders own and operate less than 15 percent of the small private enterprises. In heavily Taiwanese areas, mainlanders have little business success; and even in military communities (such as those found in parts of T'ao-yüan and Chia-i), mainlanders are not likely to achieve middle-class status through business activities.

Both ethnic groups are also represented among wage laborers and still poorer segments of Taiwan's society. The large number of retired mainland soldiers, isolated by prejudice, language, lack of kinsmen, old age, and ill health, is one of the most obvious anomalies for those who would apply Case I.

There does not appear to be a new generation of extremely poor mainlanders growing up, however. Young mainlander women, much in demand in a distorted marriage market, can usually contract hypergamous marriages within their own ethnic group, as long as they remain respectable. One hears of very few who are prostitutes or beggars, and few take menial jobs as domestics or as factory hands (though their mothers may have). Young mainlander men from poor families have more difficulties in establishing a minimally "respectable" standard of living, though as long as mainlanders control the enormous patronage of the civil and military bureaucracies, these young men will have a slight ethnic advantage in gaining access to secure jobs.

By contrast, among lower-class Taiwanese there are a substantial number of prostitutes, gangsters, beggars, opera players, and the merely poor. David Shak, in as yet unpublished materials, has evidence for the existence of many impoverished and unregistered Taiwanese households that have maintained their low status for many decades (personal communication). It would appear, then, that very poor mainlanders are disappearing as the older generation dies and its successors take advantage of their ethnic ties to rise socially, whereas poor and socially deviant Taiwanese remain a relatively fixed proportion of the population.

For the moment, both ethnic groups can be subdivided into an elite, a middle, and a lower class. We can also divide the middle class, for reasons I will give in greater detail below (see also Rohsenow 1973), into a "traditional" middle class oriented toward commerce, and a "new" middle class dependent on managerial roles and on government service. In terms of Cohen's two-part model, Taiwan's class structure consists of a largely urban elite made up of upper and new middle-class workers in government, the professions, commerce, and industry; and a lower class made up of the traditional middle class (of small craftsmen, shopkeepers, and peasants) along with laborers, the deviants, and the very poor. Taiwanese and mainlanders are present in both strata.

It is thus possible to draw together data conforming to both of Cohen's cases, though neither case provides a wholly adequate model for Taiwan's social system. An additional and perhaps key factor is given by Cynthia Enloe, who points out the different potentials for political revolution in societies where class and ethnicity combine in the ways postulated by Cohen. Enloe notes that Case I societies (her "vertically stratified societies") may easily become unstable under modernization as sharp ethnic barriers to upward social mobility promote revolution. Case II societies ("horizontally stratified") are less likely to undergo revolution because the emerging class structure weakens the solidarity between elite and lower-class members of an ethnic group before the lines of ethnic cleavage dissolve (Enloe 1973: 28–30). All governments are sensitive to the possibility of revolution, and we might expect a government that had recently experienced a massive rejection by its populace to be especially sensitive. This analysis, then, must necessarily inquire into the role that the state, with its enormous power to control and educate, plays in stressing ethnicity and/or class.

The contradiction between the emic view that Taiwan is a Case I society and the etic view that it is largely a Case II society can be resolved without discarding either native perceptions or economic data. Taiwan was founded in 1945 as a Case I society but began to shift in the late 1950's toward a Case II society. The persistence of ethnicity results from the fact that the maintenance of strong ethnic identities serves the varied political ends of both ethnic groups and of the government.

### *Structural and Historical Origins of Ethnic Separateness*

I shall turn first to the years between 1945 and 1955. Further research by economists, historians, and political scientists would contribute much to the understanding of this murky period, but from the perspective of the present, the main outlines are clear. During that decade, Taiwan came very close to being structured along the lines of Cohen's first ideal type. The reasons for this are historical, political, and ideological.

The role that mainlanders were to play in Taiwan was definitively conditioned by Taiwan's history as a colonized island. The Japanese had conquered a virtually ungoverned congeries of local communities and outposts of a distant and faltering empire. They created in its place a two-sector society of small private farmers on the one hand, and a modern plantation economy dependent on Taiwanese labor supervised by Japanese administrators on the other. Political, social, and ideological institutions necessary to maintain Japanese control were developed in the first turbulent decades of Japanese rule and continued in force until the end of the Second World War.

These institutions and policies included a Japanese monopoly on high-ranking positions in the civil and military bureaucracies, in government economic enterprises, in schools, and in much else. By the time of the War, many Taiwanese had been trained for lower posts, but the Japanese remained in charge of policy. When the Japanese left, the KMT did not promote low-ranking Taiwanese but placed mainlanders in the higher posts. Since many of these mainlanders had little technical expertise, the successful operation of the office or enterprise depended not only on methods and practices inherited from the Japanese but also on the de facto leadership of trained Taiwanese personnel. Internal structure, paperwork, and social relations continued in patterns originally set by the Japanese.

Such patterns have sometimes changed very slowly. Two national-level agencies where my husband and I taught English daily for over a year and several municipal offices with which I am familiar show similar patterns at present. One of the national-level agencies, which has considerable importance for Taiwan's export trade, is especially interesting. Though the high-ranking managers are in general mainlanders, Taiwanese remains the language of common use among the lower-ranking bureaucrats. When technical matters are being discussed, however, Japanese is used. Much of the bureau's well-used reference library consists of Japanese materials, and the actual day-to-day managers of departments—some of whom speak no Mandarin at all—are elderly Taiwanese. When I asked a Taiwanese what would happen if a young mainlander came to work in the office, he appeared amused: "We would all speak the national language to him, of course. But I do not think he would want to work here."

Taipei city ward offices (*ch'ü kung so*) are often managed in a similar way, though Japanese is no longer the technical language. The ubiquitous household registration form, its method of use, and much of the administration of household records follow closely the patterns developed by the Japanese. The typical organization of personnel places mainlanders in positions of responsibility and Taiwanese in clerical or technical ranks. Naturally there are variations in this pattern. In the *ch'ü kung so* of Ta-an, for example, there appear to be many more mainlanders (including women clerical workers) at all levels. Ta-an is, of course, a heavily mainlander ward of Taipei. And some national-level and many provincial-level government organizations are known to be dominated by Taiwanese—as, for example, the Bureau of Forestry. Detailed studies of the ethnic composition of Taiwan's government agencies would thus prove valuable for understanding both social structure and politics.

For our purposes, however, it seems adequately clear that the distinctions originally made by the Japanese to separate themselves from the Taiwanese were carried over into the new state developed by the KMT, and that much of this separation persists today. Such a policy naturally fosters a consciousness of ethnicity, especially among the Taiwanese.

De facto residential segregation was another legacy of Japanese rule that influenced mainlander-Taiwanese ethnic relations. This segregation resulted from new housing constructed for Japanese administrators and their work force, including civil servants, teachers, and employees of large organizations. When mainlanders replaced the Japanese as Taiwan's rulers, their employees, not surprisingly, often

TABLE 2
*Ethnic Clustering by Ward in Taipei*

| Ward | 1968 | | 1973 | | 1968–73 |
|---|---|---|---|---|---|
| | Percent Taiwanese | Percent mainlander | Percent Taiwanese | Percent mainlander | Percent change of Taiwanese |
| Taipei city | 62.8 | 37.2 | 66.0 | 34.0 | +3.2 |
| Sung-shan | 50.4 | 49.6 | 61.0 | 39.0 | +10.6 |
| Ta-an | 36.4 | 63.6 | 41.3 | 58.7 | +4.9 |
| Ku-t'ing | 50.4 | 49.6 | 52.9 | 47.1 | +2.5 |
| Shuang-yüan | 80.7 | 19.3 | 83.8 | 16.2 | +3.1 |
| Lung-shan | 79.7 | 20.3 | 86.7 | 13.3 | +7.0 |
| Ch'eng-chung | 52.7 | 47.3 | 58.1 | 41.9 | +5.4 |
| Chien-ch'eng | 88.7 | 11.3 | 90.5 | 9.5 | +1.8 |
| Yen-p'ing | 83.2 | 16.8 | 84.3 | 15.7 | +1.1 |
| Ta-t'ung | 84.8 | 15.2 | 86.4 | 13.6 | +1.6 |
| Chung-shan | 65.2 | 34.8 | 70.9 | 29.1 | +5.7 |
| Nei-hu | 64.3 | 35.7 | 62.9 | 37.1 | −1.4 |
| Nan-kang | 72.7 | 27.3 | 72.3 | 27.7 | −0.4 |
| Mu-chia | 56.5 | 43.5 | 52.2 | 47.8 | −4.3 |
| Ching-mei | 59.1 | 40.9 | 57.2 | 42.8 | −1.9 |
| Shih-lin | 71.4 | 28.6 | 75.6 | 24.4 | +4.2 |
| Pei-t'ou | 68.2 | 31.8 | 71.8 | 28.2 | +3.6 |

SOURCE: *T'ai-pei shih t'ung-chi yao-lan* 1973: 35–36.
NOTE: Only the Chinese populations of these wards were used in calculating the above percentages; foreigners were not included.

moved into housing vacated by the Japanese. The colonial era's tendency toward residential segregation was thus carried over into the new state. As Americans know all too well, residential segregation perhaps most strongly influences long-term ethnic relations by leading to segregated schools. It is easy to find mainlanders born in Taiwan who never learned Taiwanese in childhood because they had no Taiwanese schoolmates. Further inquiries often elicit the fact that these mainlanders are the children of state employees; thus they grew up and attended school in neighborhoods that were previously Japanese or were built after 1949 for mainlanders. This problem was not confined to Taipei: other cities had similar though smaller residential areas constructed for the Japanese. But residential segregation is clearest in Taipei, where—despite decades of social mobility—patterns of ethnic clustering are still very apparent (see Table 2).

In 1973, Taipei's population was about one-third mainlander and two-thirds Taiwanese. If we look at the population ratios of the city's wards, however, we see that this general ratio was not evenly distributed. Though I shall pursue this issue no further here, the reader familiar with Taipei will quickly note that concentrations of mainlanders are most striking in sections of the city with large amounts of government housing, such as Ta-an and Ch'eng-chung. In the suburbs (Nei-hu, Nan-kang, Mu-chia, Ching-mei, Shih-lin, and Pei-t'ou), a great deal of upper-class housing has been built since government controls on the import of private autos were relaxed in 1970. Much of this housing has been occupied by mainlanders; and in four suburban wards, the percentage of mainlanders has actually increased, despite the fact that mainlander population growth is substantially lower than Taiwanese population growth. This suggests, then, that mainlanders now find some of the wealthy suburbs as attractive as the older central districts that have traditionally housed them.

Extensive interviewing of older residents throughout Taipei in 1974–75 reinforces the view suggested by the statistics. More casual inquiries in other cities reveal a similar pattern of residential segregation, again inherited from the Japanese period. The policy of housing government functionaries, however innocent, has thus tended throughout Taiwan to emphasize a distinction between Taiwanese and mainlander that has come to be seen as an ethnic one.

Language was a third major factor in the division that appeared between the two groups immediately upon Taiwan's return to China. In 1945, the two communities were necessarily separated by a simple inability to talk to one another. This situation was not easily remedied, of course, and it has taken time to introduce a wide familiarity with Mandarin into Taiwan's countryside and into the back alleys of her cities.

Effective bilingual communication could have been established much more readily, had this been the only goal, by teaching the smaller group of generally literate mainlanders to speak Taiwanese instead of obliging, as the KMT decided to do, millions of relatively unschooled Taiwanese to learn Mandarin. When we consider this fact, some of the political functions of making Mandarin the national language become more evident. Even if the KMT had not been committed to a northern China language identified with the traditional capital, the maintenance of Mandarin as the official tongue would still have provided a rationale for excluding or demoting Taiwanese from responsibility. It placed the burden of effort, of awkwardness, and of linguistic ineptitude on a group that was already coming to be categorized as inferior because it was culturally different and politically impotent.

Even now for Taiwanese in the urban lower class and in the rural population, there is little need to speak Mandarin except to officials; and for such people, contacts with officials are rare, though they can be important when they occur. For urban and higher-status Taiwanese during the 1940's and 1950's, however, the inability to use the official language was a catastrophe: Japanese-educated Taiwanese school teachers and civil servants found their small degree of upward mobility blocked or reversed; and a large proportion of the Taiwanese elite lost status as the substitution of Mandarin for Japanese gave them a primary identification as Taiwanese rather than as members of a middle or upper class.

Taiwanese are now more generally bilingual, but as David Jordan points out (1969), they use the second language in restricted spheres, retaining their native tongue in home, community, and religious contexts, and showing little resentment at this arrangement. The official meetings of one Taipei neighborhood citizens' association (*li min ta hui*) always began in 1970 with an announcement by the KMT representative that the association's head, a monolingual Taiwanese, was too unwell to act as chair. This spared the old gentleman's feelings, since all agreed that such official events should properly be conducted in Mandarin.

However, there are areas of life where mild conflict over language arises. Entertainment is one of these. Television and radio stations are governed by large numbers of ad hoc edicts emanating from the central military and educational authorities; Taiwan still has no clear-cut broadcasting law. Decisions about language are therefore subject to a constant struggle between advertisers, who favor Taiwanese, and government bodies, who wish to promote Mandarin. Changes in programming, especially cuts in the number of hours permitted for Taiwanese-language shows, provoke bitter comments and a good deal of resentment. Taiwanese sometimes justify their objections to this policy by appealing to that highest of traditional values, filial piety. "We don't care for ourselves, since we can speak Mandarin," say the young; "But what about my old grandmother, who can't understand Mandarin and doesn't like their modern programs anyway?"

It is interesting to look at the linguistic behavior of upwardly mobile Taiwanese. Such couples not uncommonly refuse to speak Taiwanese to their infants and toddlers so as to prepare them better for the "good" preschools, kindergartens, and elementary schools—i.e., those schools that educate children successfully for entrance into middle schools and colleges. There is considerable concern that children learn the "correct" Mandarin accent: a strong local twang is an immediate ethnic giveaway that an aspiring Taiwanese may try to shed and that a mainlander does not want his child to acquire. Taiwanese independence literature, however, frequently exhorts readers, mostly Taiwanese living abroad, to teach their children their native tongue rather than Mandarin (e.g., Lo Hoai-un 1975: 8).

The official language policy of the state has thus been a prime determinant in creating a society in which class and ethnic status coincide by claiming superiority for a tongue not native to the majority of the population.

A fourth pattern of behavior that has promoted the popular view of two separate and unequal ethnic groups in Taiwan is found, paradoxically, in intermarriage. This pattern parallels (though it also differs from) the Japanese-Taiwanese relationship,[3] but is not a direct outgrowth of it. Common Han identity and a belief in shared blood and culture made intermarriage relatively easy even during the 1940's and 1950's. Furthermore, the mainlanders arrived in Taiwan not with boatloads of women and children, but with a great preponderance of wifeless men. Had the social status of Taiwanese and mainlanders been perfectly equal in the 1940's, the mere addition of so many single men would have upset the marriage market and led to conflict.

As any Taiwanese family knows, acquiring a wife for a son is expensive. There were only 3,003,333 women for the 3,060,527 men in Taiwan in 1946 (*Chung-hua Min-kuo t'ung-chi t'i-yao* 1974: 42–43); hence, the influx of hundreds of thousands of soldiers with assured incomes and social power guaranteed that the chances of Taiwanese men getting a bride were greatly reduced. Nor was it possible for a Taiwanese man to improve his chances by marrying a mainlander woman, as such women were eagerly sought after by their compatriots.

In 1974–75, I compiled data from household registers on 755

[3] Intermarriage during the Japanese period was generally between Japanese women and Taiwanese men. This is difficult to explain, unless many of these "Japanese" women were born and raised in Taiwan (perhaps in mixed families) and were not considered sufficiently Japanese by Japanese men. Unlike present-day mainlander men, Japanese men could always send home for orthodox brides.

marriages in twelve neighborhoods within three Taipei wards (Ku-t'ing, Ta-an, and Chung-shan).[4] These neighborhoods were chosen for their relatively high proportion of mainlanders (one could hardly expect to find much intermarriage in areas with no mainlanders) and for their relatively high proportion of middle-class residents (though the areas included a squatter settlement and a cluster of expensive condominiums). Of the 755 marriages, over 57 percent were Taiwanese-Taiwanese marriages, 20 percent were mainlander-mainlander marriages, and slightly over 22 percent were mixed mainlander-Taiwanese marriages. Of the mixed mainlander-Taiwanese marriages, however, nearly 92 percent were between mainlander men and Taiwanese women; just over 8 percent were between Taiwanese men and mainlander women. Inequality between ethnic groups is clearly revealed by these statistics.

In four critical areas—government employment, residential segregation, language use, and intermarriage—postwar Taiwan was a society where ethnic and class lines closely coincided. The two principal reasons for this were the social patterns the KMT government inherited from its predecessor and the historical circumstances of the mainlander migration. I will turn now to a discussion of the ethnic significance of the KMT's official national ideology.

## *The Official Ideology and Ethnicity*

Since 1945, the KMT has been officially committed to the reunification of China. After 1949, this meant a policy of mainland recovery. This policy has had a powerful effect on state organization, politics, economics, and indeed all social life in Taiwan. One of its probably unintended consequences has been to build an emphasis on ethnic differences into the whole structure of society.[5]

[4]I hope soon to make available the complete data from this survey. The figures presented here aggregate marriages throughout the postwar period. Though my analysis of the data is incomplete, there is no apparent trend over time either for an increased level of intermarriage or for a more balanced exchange of women.

[5]I hope that none of my readers will misunderstand the following analysis of the relationship between the mainland recovery policy and ethnicity. I am in deep sympathy with the feelings of the thousands of mainlanders whose warmest wish is to return to their homeland. No one can fail to share the pain of friends who left mother and father in Shantung "for a few months," and find themselves, thirty years later, in a still alien outpost, not knowing at New Year's whether they should address prayers to their parents' spirits. These personal tragedies lend an emotional color to the mainland recovery policy and make it difficult to view objectively. This highly important policy, however, supplies a necessary key to understanding the persistence and even increase of ethnic sentiment in Taiwan.

Mainland recovery is often referred to in Taiwan as a "sacred trust," a categorical imperative that should engender a deep, personal, emotional commitment. Though some citizens feel this commitment less than others, and though even in the most steadfast the desire for its implementation may have weakened over the years, the commitment still remains a fundamental cornerstone of national policy.

Recovering the mainland is the principle on which the legitimacy of the present government rests. The KMT maintains its authority within Taiwan primarily because of its claim to represent the unity of all China and because of its promise that this unity will be translated into reality once again. Without this claim and promise, its standing in Taiwan would be dubious indeed. The KMT symbolizes its claim to rule all China by maintaining a national-level government that includes representatives of mainland provinces, and it symbolizes its promise to retake China by maintaining a large military establishment headed almost exclusively by mainlanders. Neither of these institutions would be necessary for a small, independent Taiwan; they make sense only in the context of a commitment to mainland recovery.

Political power in Taiwan is heavily concentrated in the national government and in the military; high-ranking members of both groups form the apex of Taiwan's status pyramid. If the national government is to represent all of China, it must of necessity be made up overwhelmingly of mainlanders. It would appear less imperative that the military leadership be drawn from this same ethnic group; but it can still be argued that senior mainlanders are the only men available who have experience in fighting the Communists. A correlation between ethnicity and social power follows inevitably from this logic. Any attempt to make the national government more representative of the local population automatically undermines that government's legitimacy, a result no state can be expected to view with equanimity. In an extreme extension of this logic, attempts by the Taiwanese to gain an equal share of political power at the national level can be seen as subversive of the whole system.

There have been, of course, many attempts at political subversion in Taiwan: the 1947 rebellion was an isolated case only in respect to its violence. Some of the best-publicized efforts have involved criticisms of mainlander political exclusiveness or of the mainland recovery policy (Tien 1975: 628–30; Appleton 1972: 34–35). For the years between 1945 and 1955, one pro-Taiwanese writer accepts the estimate that 90,000 political prisoners were detained, of whom half were executed (Mendel 1970: 120). Though probably exaggerated, these figures suggest a high level of discontent. Nevertheless, the very large military and police establishment has successfully maintained as a guiding principle the mainland recovery policy with all that it implies for ethnic relations.

Societies structured as Taiwan's was in the 1940's and early 1950's are likely to be politically unstable because private aspirations for upward social mobility are blocked by ethnic boundaries. Taiwan's government sometimes attempted to soften the distinction between ethnic groups (to which their policy committed them) both because of the revolutionary potential inherent in such a situation and because its leaders probably shared the common Chinese view of Taiwanese and mainlanders as Han. In the 1970's, however, the government's interest in ethnic equality has been far more pronounced, with some Taiwanese, newly elected or promoted to high office, serving as symbols of the change in emphasis.

We should not be surprised by the government's ambivalence about ethnicity. At one extreme, we could imagine the official position to represent a sincere desire for unity along with blindness to the ethnically divisive effects of the mainland recovery policy. At the other extreme, we could imagine the position to represent a sophisticated strategy for thwarting the emergence of class consciousness and preventing an outright ethnic confrontation. It is extremely difficult to gather valid data on this subject from members of the elite; moreover, both viewpoints (as well as others) are and have been reflected by policy-making bodies.

Nevertheless, mainlanders have long benefited from ethnic separation. Between 1945 and 1949, when class and ethnicity were highly congruent, even the poorest mainlanders enjoyed several advantages over wealthy and formerly powerful Taiwanese. Under martial law and in the confusion of troubled times, mainlanders claimed goods, residences, and high-status employment; mainlander men married Taiwanese women in vastly greater numbers than Taiwanese men married mainlander women; and low-ranking mainlander soldiers and police forcefully asserted considerable power. When more orderly rule returned after 1949, many abuses were corrected, but the status advantage still lay with the newcomers, however low in rank.

During the first decade after retrocession, the Taiwanese elite of landlords and urban middle class suffered drastic reductions in their ranks and wealth. Executions resulting from the 1947 rebellion decimated the class; and the loss of investments in Japanese companies, the severe inflation of the 1940's and 1950's (see Koo 1973: 402–6), and the land reform program all undercut its economic base. Those who had attained some political influence or social prestige through acculturation to the Japanese found their advantages wiped out overnight, leaving them in a poor position to compete for resources with mainlanders. In the economic boom of the 1960's, however, previously absolute ethnic advantages and disadvantages became relative as poor mainlanders and rich Taiwanese became part of the social landscape. Indeed, a potential political problem emerged when some mainlanders became part of the lower class: on the mainland, after all, a coalition of peasants, workers, and soldiers (in which ethnicity was irrelevant) had driven the KMT from power. Keeping mainlander soldiers separate from the Taiwanese lower class by strong ethnic sentiments thus provided clear benefits for a government desirous of retaining political stability and firm control of the population.

### *Economic Development and the Emergence of Class*

Economic improvement came with a rush in the 1960's. This widened the social differences within each of Taiwan's ethnic groups and produced a shift away from a social system in which class and ethnicity were largely congruent toward a system organized primarily by class. Unfortunately, anthropologists have not yet paid adequate attention to these two related changes.

The most obvious way that economic improvement influenced these changes was through the unequal distribution of new wealth. On the one hand, there was so much more wealth in Taiwan by the end of the 1960's than during the first postwar decade that living standards rose noticeably among almost all social groups. (Even for the few people whose jobs, income, or housing did not improve markedly, social measures such as easier access to primary education, better public transportation, and more widely available health care made conditions considerably better nonetheless.) Yet on the other hand, some segments of the population—as we would expect—benefited more than others from the newly available wealth. Different economic opportunities and hence different degrees of social mobility led to a widening of the class range over the whole society. A particularly striking change is found within the middle class. In the first decade, when the Taiwanese middle class was undergoing a decline in its fortunes, only middle-class mainlanders had sufficient capital and government contacts to pursue lucrative middle-class occupations. But subsequent economic development led to the growth of a Taiwanese middle class whose occupations were tied to the boom in private enterprise (see Cole 1967). The island's elite thus expanded as a Taiwanese upper class reemerged, drawn not only from newly rich Taiwanese entrepreneurs but also from a number of formerly wealthy families (especially landowning families) who had made a successful transition to industrialists after land reform.

The broadening of the social range of mainlanders came chiefly from the downward social mobility of military personnel (as more and more of the rank and file retired on inadequate pensions) at a time when many young and middle-aged mainlanders were able to enhance their social status (by capturing a disproportionate share of middle-class occupations in the civil service and public schools). This has resulted in a class distribution among mainlanders where more families now belong to the middle class than to the soldiery, and where there is a distinct group of very poor people whose class status and chances for upward mobility are significantly inferior to those of middle- and upper-class Taiwanese.

I have briefly outlined how and when this transition took place; it remains to consider why. With the massive political advantage mainlanders had in their first decade in Taiwan, it would appear that they could easily have channeled economic development so as to benefit themselves alone. In the mid-1950's, many of Taiwan's largest industries were those inherited from the Japanese or brought over from Shanghai and Chungking. The companies whose stock compensated major Taiwanese landlords for the land reform redistribution—Taiwan Cement, for example—were and are government controlled. Moreover, the state sector of the economy remained larger, in terms of total assets, than the private sector.[6] In 1971, for example, only 0.1 percent of Taiwan's enterprises were government owned; but these

[6]Economists tell me that value added is a better measure here; on this basis, Taiwan's state enterprises produce about one-fourth, and private enterprises about three-fourths, of the total value added. However, when we consider the capital investment that state enterprises have in the spheres of heavy industry, mining and metals, petrochemicals, electric power, fertilizer, export agricultural products, and finance, there appears to be some basis for the use of the total value of assets as the relevant measure.

enterprises employed almost 9 percent of Taiwan's work force, produced 24 percent of Taiwan's total value added, and held 52 percent of Taiwan's assets in operation (*T'ai Fu ti-ch'ü kung-shang yeh p'u-ch'a pao-kao* 1973: 74).

Given the government's tight control on all aspects of life, and given its desire to accumulate and hold in trust resources for the nation's use after a projected return to the mainland, we may speculate that it could easily have moved in the direction of a kind of state capitalism in which the primary means of industrial production were controlled by the state and, ultimately, by mainlanders. The degree to which exports and imports, even of consumer goods, are still supervised in the interest of overall economic and social policy tends to give weight to this speculation.

As we know, Taiwan did not develop a Soviet-style state capitalist economy, but rather one in which an exuberant private sector soon flourished. Why would the government, if its aims and policies were as I have described them, free the economic sphere, thereby enabling the Taiwanese to develop considerable economic and social power? Remember that in the 1950's the national leadership believed very strongly in the importance of maintaining sufficient resources and political authority to recover the mainland. Would not these ends have been better served by continued mainlander and government ownership of the means of production? The Taiwanese population could then have been brought—largely as industrial workers—into state enterprises geared to national needs and cost-effective criteria.

There are naturally many reasons, including the frequently stated ones, why private enterprise was encouraged, despite its foreseeable social consequences. One reason, for example, was the belief that private enterprise was the most efficient path to economic development—a belief doubtless attractive to mainlanders with private capital to invest. A second reason was the democratic commitment to the betterment of all Taiwan's citizens embodied in Sun Yat-sen's Three Principles of the People. A third reason was the fear of a revolution if the Taiwanese ethnic majority were excluded from the island's growing middle class. All these reasons, then, assuredly played some part in shaping Taiwan's policy of encouraging private enterprise.

But there was an additional and perhaps more important reason that is less often cited: Taiwan's place in the international political economy. The KMT encouraged private enterprise in Taiwan as strongly as it did, I suggest, because of Taiwan's peculiar relationship with the United States. As the major supplier of economic and military aid (see Jacoby 1966) and as the KMT's main ally in its continuing war with China, the United States was able to influence the direction of Taiwan's economy. An open door to private enterprise and foreign capital has allowed U.S. corporations to take advantage of a labor force that is described in a recent Taiwan government advertisement as "the best bargain in Asia, if not the world, when efficiency as well as cost is taken into account. And the island workers are well-disciplined; there is practically none of the costly labor strife that characterizes the industries in many parts of the world. There are no strikes." ("Free China Salutes the American Bicentennial," *New York Times*, July 4, 1976, p. 20.)

Initially, the United States may have found it necessary to exert considerable pressure to bring about the change of policy from state control of industry to encouragement of private industry. For small nations, massive foreign investment can have very harmful consequences, as critical commentators have noted (e.g., Magdoff & Sweezy 1971: 109). Foreign investment in Taiwan is now heavily American, with about US$2.5 billion to date lent or invested by U.S. firms (*New York Times*, July 11, 1976). Japanese investments, formerly very significant for the economy, have dropped sharply since 1971 (*Foreign Trade of Japan* 1974: 87).[7]

Much of this investment leads to the building of factories in "our" villages and neighborhoods, and results in subtle and not-so-subtle changes in family structure, the status of women, and other areas of life. Foreign investment not only results in cheaper television sets and larger dowries; it also produces military and other internationally strategic goods. A large advertising brochure was recently sponsored by the Chinese Information Service of the Republic of China, paid for by firms and institutions whose interests have been served by Taiwan's enthusiasm for private enterprise (*New York Times*, July 4, 1976). Very few of these advertisements were for producers of consumer goods; the bulk came from banks and from manufacturers of producer goods, military hardware, advanced electronic gear, and petrochemicals. U.S. financial, military, and industrial relations in Taiwan are complicated and often secretive. Thus as we ponder the nature of the real relationship between the gods Ma Tsu

[7] A complete analysis of Taiwan's class and ethnic structure would deal extensively with the continuing Japanese connection.

and Kuan Yin, we should remember that when David Rockefeller opens a branch of the Chase Manhattan Bank on Taipei's East Nanking Road, that too is part of Taiwanese culture.

### *The Present Class and Ethnic Structure*

I shall now describe the main outlines of the social system produced by the interrelationship of class and ethnicity in Taiwan. Taiwan is a society where economic change has produced several conceptually distinguishable social classes. It is fair to assume that most people desire to maintain or better their social position and that they make plans and decisions for themselves and their families with this in mind. Not everyone is successful at raising or even maintaining class status, and massive downward mobility often presents acute social problems. In the rising curve of Taiwan's recent economy, however, most people have had reasonable expectations of some absolute improvement in their living standards, and many have had hopes of a relative improvement as well.

In this situation, ethnicity becomes a stratagem that groups may use to further their competitive ends. That there is still a perception in Taiwan of mainlander superiority or advantage and Taiwanese inferiority or weakness reflects continuing inequality between these two groups. In particular cases, however, ethnicity is to a greater or lesser degree significant as it becomes to a greater or lesser degree useful in creating a competitive advantage through group solidarity. Indeed, social classes that are distinguishable largely on the basis of their occupations and life-styles differ in the degrees to which the solidarity created through ethnicity can serve the ends of status mobility. Perhaps the clearest example of this comes from the bifurcation of Taiwan's most heterogeneous social stratum, its middle class. Most social mobility involves movement into or through this class; and the class may be characterized most easily by bracketing it between a lower and an upper class.

The lower class consists of the great body of industrial workers, landless agricultural workers (such as those who supply labor for the Taiwan Sugar Corporation), salespeople, peddlers, and small-scale craftsmen. Low and uncertain incomes, poor educational opportunities, no prestige, and very restricted access to political power shape their lives. Similarities and variations within this class are as yet poorly studied, since only factory workers have received much attention from researchers.

Members of the upper class are sufficiently wealthy to have easy access not only to the goods and life-styles that money can buy, but also to the finest educational establishments, to political power, and to the social prestige that derives from all of these. Upper-class families in Taiwan are of two sorts: elite government and military personnel, often wealthy as well as politically powerful, and big industrial and commercial entrepreneurs, whose sometimes greater wealth is often the basis for nearly equal political power. In general, the former are ethnically mainlander, the latter, Taiwanese. The close interaction between these two groups is a subject of the utmost importance for understanding Taiwan's society. Like the elites of other modern countries, however, Taiwan's elite recognizes that its goals are served best by inconspicuousness and secrecy (Cohen 1975a: 129; Domhoff 1974). As a result, this group generally escapes the attention of anthropologists.

The middle class appears thus far only as a residual category. It is, however, a distinct conceptual entity; and the confusion about its characteristics arises from the fact that there are actually two middle classes. These overlap substantially in income ranges, but differ sharply in occupations, life-styles, and aspirations. One, which I have labeled the "new middle class" (Rohsenow 1973: 12), resembles the class of "salary men" in Japan (Vogel 1963) and the bureaucratic "new class" in some state capitalist societies (Djilas 1957). The heads of new-middle-class households are typically employees of large bureaucratic organizations—government institutions, schools, large industries—and their principal income is in the form of salary and fringe benefits (housing, rice allowances, special insurance plans, wholesale buying co-ops). The security, fringe benefits, and opportunities for making useful contacts that such jobs offer are generally what make them attractive and prestigious, even at the lower end of the salary scale.

New-middle-class jobs are attainable only by those who can first meet certain educational criteria. And these criteria remain essential, even though civil servants, teachers, and managers are sometimes chosen from the pool of formally qualified applicants on the basis of more particularistic considerations. Education, long-term career commitment to a single institution, and individual achievement are thus the factors around which members of the new middle class shape their plans for maintaining or improving their social status. People from the lower class who hope to rise in the class hierarchy must compete in these terms. Finally, an extremely successful new-middle-class career can take a person into the upper class through promotion to a national-level post.

Salaried bureaucrats, technicians, and teachers, however, do not own or exercise control over the means of production; they are hired, as laborers are hired, by the state or by large private corporations. Skills derived from specialized and competitive training allow them to command salaries and conditions of work that set them apart from workers, who sell only their strength or more readily acquired expertise. For people within the new middle class, then, the maintenance or improvement of their position naturally depends in part on the continued power of the institutions that employ them. Consequently, they develop loyalties to and identifications with these institutions. Thus, their perception of their class status—their class consciousness—helps set them apart from the lower class.

The other part of the middle class I have called the "traditional middle class." Its occupations are typically in owner-operated farms, commerce, and small industry. These are all enterprises with a potential for capital accumulation, though this potential is most commonly realized in commerce and industry. Table 3 provides some insight into the size and economic importance of this class.

Of Taiwan's (nonfarm) private enterprises, 86 percent employ one

TABLE 3
*Numbers of Firms in Taiwan by Work Force Size*

| | Numbers of firms | | |
|---|---|---|---|
| Number of employees | Government | Private | Total |
| Small: | | | |
| 1–3 | 25 | 202,454 | 202,479 |
| 4–6 | 30 | 36,719 | 36,749 |
| Medium: | | | |
| 7–9 | 19 | 12,299 | 12,318 |
| 10–19 | 39 | 12,911 | 12,950 |
| 20–29 | 18 | 4,478 | 4,496 |
| 30–49 | 28 | 4,002 | 4,030 |
| 50–99 | 79 | 3,046 | 3,125 |
| Large: | | | |
| 100–499 | 40 | 2,377 | 2,417 |
| 500+ | 44 | 407 | 451 |
| TOTAL | 322 | 278,693 | 279,015 |

SOURCE: *Chung-hua Min-kuo t'ung-chi t'i-yao* 1974: 196.

to six people (see Table 3). These are mostly small owner-operated businesses that do not make enough profits to allow for significant social mobility. Technically, families who own such businesses (like peasants) are part of the traditional middle class by virtue of their owning some of the means of production. Their chances of accumulating capital from business savings, however, are slim. But if the living standards of such families often differ little from those of propertyless people, their aspirations and self-perceptions are similar to those of the rest of their class. Businesses with more than six employees have some potential for capital accumulation and growth. A business employing from 7 to 99 workers is classified by Taiwan's commercial and industrial census takers as "medium," a classification that we shall use (albeit arbitrarily) as a cutoff point. In this category are found 13 percent of Taiwan's private enterprises. These enterprises may be considered middle-level enterprises capable of sustaining a secure traditional-middle-class position for their owners' families.

Entry into the upwardly mobile segment of the traditional middle class is generally contingent on success in a very small business. Peddlers, fruit-stand operators, and people with permanent family shops (whose businesses make up the first and largest category of enterprises in Taiwan) are the most likely to be successful in this way, though some industrial workers and farmers are also able to accumulate enough capital to become small businessmen. Once established as a growing concern, many of these businesses, if economic conditions are good, can aspire to a pattern of continued growth and eventual entry into the world of really big business. There is a folklore about such businesses—the Shao Mei ice-cream concern, for example, was built from a tiny operation into a national distributionship by a hardworking widow and her three sons—that encourages competitors in what statistics show to be a gamble with poor odds.

Success depends not only on business experience, but also on other factors including frugality, long hours of hard work, family cohesion, good contacts, good credit, and a reliable reputation. In contrast with the new middle class, the traditional middle class finds that success—although requiring good managerial ability—does not depend on technical expertise beyond limited bookkeeping and other simple business skills; in fact, extended education for children robs the family of workers and money that could otherwise provide the wherewithal for business success. Nor do the frugality, cohesion, and community ties of the traditional middle class offer many advantages to the aspirant to the new middle class, who most of all needs a carefully supervised education, a childhood free from all duties except homework, and a small family whose members will not prove an encumbrance should he succeed.

The paths that lead through the traditional middle class to the commercial elite and through the new middle class to the bureaucratic elite are quite distinct. Both Taiwanese and mainlander informants described these two "roads" to me when I asked about possible careers for young men of different backgrounds. Commerce is often referred to as a "crooked road"; of less worth to society than public service, it is held to compromise honesty and oblige one to "kill" or "be killed." In general, "being Taiwanese" helps one's success on this path, but is a hindrance on the other. "Being Taiwanese" involves having roots in a family and in a community, which gives a person a solid, reliable reputation in business. It also means maintaining at least some ritual traditions and ties with a temple as a public demonstration of prosperity. Ethnic affiliation helps create the network of kin, friends, and business associates on whom relatively small businessmen rely in lieu of banks and advertising agencies.

"Being mainlander," by contrast, means being free of the ties of kin and community. Nuclear families are common across the entire social range of mainlanders, but they are especially well suited when the maintenance of status depends on early and unremitting attention to children's education (see Diamond 1973: 223–25). Mainlanders also make use of contacts with people already in bureaucratic jobs, of course; and here widely dispersed provincial ties are more helpful than closely knit community ties.

Not all the traditional middle class is Taiwanese, nor all the new middle class mainlander. Many traditional-middle-class businesses are owned by mainlanders: the Hui manage butcher shops and *chiao-tsu* (meat dumpling) parlors; the Cantonese run restaurants; the Shanghainese operate dry goods stores. In fact, many of the smaller mainlander businesses are typically "ethnic" and depend heavily on mainlanders for success. By contrast, Taiwanese who move into the new middle class generally give up folk religion, found nuclear families, and sometimes cease to speak Taiwanese even at home.

Emphasis on ethnicity varies, then, according to the social class a family finds itself in or aspires to. Where a local, small business career is the aim, ethnic identity is stressed; where government service or important management posts are sought, people try to drop all symbols of ethnic inferiority. The variable that explains why ethnic identification is sometimes important and sometimes not is social class, not some quality inherent in ethnicity itself.

In the past few pages, I have concentrated on the usefulness of ethnicity for enhancing social opportunities for individuals and families. The same analysis, however, can be applied to larger groups as well. Taiwanese political candidates speak in folk temples, symbols of their ethnic group; mainlanders of different provincial origins lobby at the national level through provincial associations; and the Foochow community of Taipei puts on a massive eight-day folk ceremony (a *p'u tu*) to demonstrate its closeness to the Taiwanese community with which it is uniquely allied.

## *The Five Social Classes*

Thus far, my survey has focused on urban life, especially in Taipei. I have identified five social classes: the lumpen proletariat of the "deviant" and unemployed, the lower class, the traditional middle class, the new middle class, and the upper class. The ranges of the two middle classes overlap widely in terms of social prestige and wealth; and middle-class families, in their attempts to diversify their occupations and resources, may have working members in both.

If this analysis were based solely on income and occupational ranges, we would speak simply of a middle class. I am convinced, however, that there are both subjective and objective differences between the traditional and the new middle classes, and that their dissimilar uses of ethnicity are evidence that this is so. The critical variable that distinguishes these classes is their relationship to the means of production. The traditional middle class constitutes a petty bourgeoisie that owns and tries to expand capital; the new middle class is made up of salaried functionaries hired by the state and by the large corporations that the state allows to exist. The new middle class, owning no means of production, sells its labor like the lower class, but at so much higher a price that it has achieved a totally different life-style, class identity, and set of loyalties.

Relationships to the means of production are much clearer for the lower and upper classes. The lower class sells its labor or combines the value of that labor with the capital of tiny enterprises or minimal farmlands to maintain a steady social position. The upper class, through public and private enterprise, controls the means of large-scale production as well as the legal and economic conditions under which its own and smaller businesses operate. The fifth class, the lumpen proletariat (of the chronically unemployed and of criminals, prostitutes, etc.), is unproductive and "parasitical."

How do we connect urban social structure with the social realities of the countryside and the small towns? Diamond (1969), Feuchtwang (1972), and others provide class analyses of local communities, but their conclusions are difficult to relate to the wider society because they concentrate on fine distinctions within a narrow class range. There are two conceptual bridges across the gap that separates urban and rural social organization, however. The first comes from migration studies (e.g., Gallin & Gallin 1974; Hsieh 1972). These demonstrate the fairly obvious point that a move to the city is seen by migrants as generally offering improved living standards, improved social opportunities, and perhaps improved social status. We know who moves, for example, and we know what kinds of positions they move into: migrants from poor farms usually go into industrial work; those from farms large enough to allow for capital accumulation often go into small businesses. This tells us about the relative social statuses involved. Small shopkeepers and artisans slightly outrank self-sustaining farmers; industrial workers outrank poor farmers and agricultural laborers. The agricultural worker or peasant from a farm that simply sustains the family belongs to the lower class, somewhat below his urban laboring counterpart. The farmer whose capital enables him to accumulate profits is equal or slightly inferior to a middle-class shopkeeper or craftsman in town.

The second conceptual bridge between rural and urban social organization comes from the work of Feuchtwang (1972). There is, Feuchtwang notes, a tendency for the rich to move out of small and unimportant towns via a hierarchy of central places that culminates in Taipei. Herein lies a useful clue to the relative position of merchants, government employees, and professionals throughout the society. Members of both the traditional middle class and the new middle class are present in smaller cities and towns, where they form the apex of the local status pyramid. Their standing within their classes (as conceived on a national basis) is contingent on their distance in the central-place hierarchy from the capital. Members of the national-level upper class are not found outside Taipei and a few other major cities.

## *Summary and Suggestions*

This paper has been wide ranging and, in parts, highly speculative. Its aims have been to examine the way anthropologists have treated ethnicity in Taiwan and to criticize and (if possible) supplant those treatments with a more comprehensive one. The political uses of ethnicity have been seen to differ according to social class. Class and ethnic relations have been shown to emerge from a process in which historical, ideological, and economic factors all play their parts. The current (though continually changing) end product of this process is the division of Taiwan's society, urban and rural, into five identifiable classes. The brief discussion of Taiwan's economic and political relations with the United States hints at the role that an internationally oriented theoretical framework could play in the analysis of this neither unique nor isolated country.

In examining ethnicity and social class in Taiwan, I have come to feel that the gaps in our anthropological knowledge lie in two major areas: in economics and in politics. There have been four economic periods in Taiwan's modern history, beginning with the Japanese colonial era. For the latter, much work remains to be done on the effects of building an industrial and export-oriented system of production. We must look at the effects of modern technology, of better communications, of a large and elite Japanese presence, and perhaps even of Japanese values and bureaucratic methods. The period from 1945 until the late 1950's is, as I have said, murky. This tense and economically straitened era set the tone for much that we still observe. What was happening in the city and countryside during those years? The prosperous 1960's created the economic basis for middle-class expansion. But what else happened? Presumably, people left the land, entered factories, and started businesses in droves—just at the time when much early anthropological fieldwork was being done. Then the slump of the 1970's occurred, so visible and so painful during my visit in 1974–75. Families who had seen nothing but good times for ten years found themselves out of work or back on the farm, overstocked with overeducated teenagers, their plans for the future in disarray. If the middle class remains static or contracts, what will become of already noticeable ethnic tensions? What other effects does a depression have?

Politics is another matter. Hard as it is to squeeze reliable economic data out of people, it is still harder to obtain reliable political information. Yet the political framework of laws and national customs has an enormous effect on people's lives. Though anthropologists have examined politics at the grass roots, they have expended little effort on state-level politics and on the policies that constrain politics at this level. Much of what these authors describe happens as it does precisely because the state—and the KMT—sets the ground rules for others to follow or evade. Distinction among groups of different provincial origins is official policy, deriving from state-level goals of the greatest ideological importance. The Taiwanese-mainlander dichotomy is thus fostered, even if unintentionally, by the highest circles of power. Ethnicity, in turn, affects the emerging pattern of social class.

In the past, the unintended consequences of state power were perhaps less profound because of the relative inability of premodern states to enforce their policies efficiently. Chinese states have long claimed the right and shown the desire to monopolize education, to control totally such things as religion and commerce, and to reach into the most intimate familial settings by equating household relationships with political relationships. Yet the state's capacity to implement these grandiose ambitions has often been small. Repeatedly over the millennia, whole regions fell into the anarchy of clan warfare; peasant rebellions involving millions lasted for decades; tax and census data became so routinely fraudulent that only a tiny percentage of legal revenues trickled into Peking. The government of Taiwan, by contrast, claims less all-encompassing power over its people, but with the aid of an extremely large military and police arm and very modern technology it enforces more stringently those powers that it does claim. Ethnic identity and social class relations respond readily, if often in unanticipated ways, to the exercise of this pervasive force.

Anthropology has produced valuable work on Taiwan. However, we should not perpetuate in this work the errors of an earlier generation of anthropologists, many of whom, in the midst of the most massive social revolution of this century, ignored the complex connections between their field sites and the wider society and reported only placid villages and traditional Chinese families.

# Subethnic Rivalry in the Ch'ing Period

Harry J. Lamley

Over the 212-year period of Ch'ing rule in Taiwan (1684–1895), interaction among diverse groups of inhabitants had a marked effect on local socioeconomic development and cultural change, an effect still discernible on the island today.[1] This paper deals with one major type of Ch'ing-period ethnicity: the interaction among rival Chinese groups in settled portions of Taiwan.[2] Although these groups shared a common Han Chinese background, they came from relatively isolated areas of southern Fukien and eastern Kwangtung. In Taiwan, they tended to form discrete communities and perpetuate the diverse customs of their native subcultures. The term "subethnic," as used in this paper, refers to such subcultural distinctions.[3] It is also useful in distinguishing Chinese *intra*ethnic competition from the better-

[1]Interethnic relations in Taiwan have been recorded for even earlier times. In the seventeenth century, Dutch and Spanish colonists came into contact with local aborigines as well as with early Chinese settlers and traders and a number of Japanese residents. More extensive Chinese relations with the aborigines developed between 1662 and 1683 when Taiwan was controlled by the Ming-loyalist Cheng family. This earlier and less pervasive ethnic interaction, however, was not of such importance in the historical development of present-day Taiwanese society.

[2]Ethnicity is construed here as "essentially a form of interaction between cultural groups operating within common social contexts" (Abner Cohen 1974: xi). I am indebted to Hill Gates and T'ang Mei-chun for their comments on the original draft of this paper, which was submitted to the Conference on Anthropology in Taiwan. Other conference members also offered valuable insights and suggestions. I am particularly grateful to G. William Skinner and Edgar Wickberg for their help and encouragement.

[3]Cynthia Enloe has attempted (1973: 23–25) to distinguish different categories of ethnic groups by referring to the origins of their separate identities. She points out that tribal, national, and racial ethnicity are the most prevalent forms of ethnicity. However, in China—as in other parts of the world where pervasive cultures or civilizations with "great traditions" have existed—major subcultural distinctions have often led to separate ethnic identities apart from tribal, national, or racial ascriptions. Hence "subcultural ethnicity" may also be recognized as a widespread type.

known Chinese-aboriginal *inter*ethnic contention, the other major type of ethnicity that prevailed on the island throughout the Ch'ing period.

Taiwan's Chinese subcultural groups differed primarily in dialect and provenance. In Ch'ing times, most of the island's Chinese inhabitants were Hokkien and Hakka speakers, whose dialects remained mutually unintelligible. The Hokkien speakers, locally referred to as "Hoklo" (*Fu-lao*),[4] hailed mainly from Ch'üan-chou and Chang-chou prefectures in southern Fukien and areas peripheral to these prefectures. The Hakka (*K'o-chia*),[5] by contrast, came chiefly from eastern Kwangtung. Thanks to a further division of the Hokkien speakers into rival Ch'üan-chou and Chang-chou subgroups there developed in effect three, extensive, mutually exclusive subcultural groups in Taiwan. Within these groups, especially the Ch'üan-chou group, there was a further tendency to divide into communities based on county (*hsien*) origins. Except among some Ch'üan-chou communities, however, competition among county-level subgroups never seems to have been intense.

Subethnic feuding in Taiwan during the Ch'ing period has recently attracted the attention of a number of scholars.[6] This paper assesses more fully the background and nature of this intense and pervasive rivalry. It also attempts to demonstrate that the study of subethnicity may be of value in gaining a clearer perception of change and development in a heterogeneous Chinese society—in this case a premodern one that arose during the late imperial era.

[4]Hokkien speakers who migrated from southern Fukien to coastal areas farther south probably as early as the ninth century (and eventually to areas overseas) became known as "Hoklo"—i.e., "People of Fukien" (Skinner 1957: 37). In eastern Kwangtung as well as in Taiwan, other speech groups referred to these people as Hoklo in Ch'ing times. The Hokkien (i.e., "Fukienese") originally hailed from Honan and other regions of North China, and first began to settle southern Fukien extensively during the seventh and eighth centuries (Lo 1971: 169).

[5]*K'o-chia* means "guest families," indicating that the Hakka were latecomers in regions of southeastern China. Like the Hokkien, the Hakka originally came from North China, began to advance southward in the seventh and eighth centuries, and started to enter eastern Kwangtung at the end of the Southern Sung. Chia-ying, the chief center of Hakka culture in Ch'ing times, became a purely Hakka area during the latter half of the fourteenth century when heavy concentrations of emigrants from T'ing-chou (in southwestern Fukien) and southern Kiangsi converged there (Wen 1903: *chüan* 7, 85b–86b).

[6]Anthropologists who have recently called attention to Ch'ing subethnic strife in Taiwan include Hsü Chia-ming (1973) and Shih Chen-min (1973); historians who have lately expressed specific interest in the rivalry and feuding include Chang T'an (1974, 1976), Fan Hsin-yüan (1974), Huang Hsiu-cheng (1976), and myself (1977a, 1977b). Maurice Freedman has dealt with comparable strife involving feuds among lineages and surname aggregates in Fukien and Kwangtung (1958: 105–13; 1966: 104–17). Prevalent in the home region, this form of communal strife is discussed below.

The first part of this paper presents general background information on Taiwan and the southeastern mainland region from whence Taiwan's population came. The second discusses the major subcultural groups that emerged on the island. The third focuses on the settlement of Taiwan and the processes by which local communal groups of different home-area provenance were established and then acquired more cohesion as intercommunity rivalry intensified. The fourth deals with the phase of exceptionally severe subethnic strife that lasted from the 1780's to the 1860's, and contrasts communal feuding in Taiwan during this period with that in the home region. This final part also considers the response of the Ch'ing government to subethnic feuding in Taiwan and treats briefly the island's late Ch'ing turbulence and rivalry.

### *Taiwan and the Fukien-Kwangtung Home Region*

Southern Fukien and eastern Kwangtung have an area of about 33,340 square miles. The entire region is set apart from most of the rest of China by massive mountain ranges. The five prefectural-level administrative territories into which southern Fukien was divided under Ch'ing rule were also generally set off from one another by mountain peaks and ranges. The rugged borders of Ch'üan-chou and Chang-chou bounded separate river systems. Similarly, the three principal administrative territories that made up eastern Kwangtung were separated from one another by spurs of the Nan-ling ranges that extend across much of South China.

The region's physical features tended to divide it into highland and lowland sections. In the highland Hakka country of Chia-ying and T'ing-chou, the population was thinly scattered in small villages. There were few large towns and cities. Farming was generally restricted to narrow strips of cultivated fields in the valleys or along the terraced hillsides, except in the upland basins. Similar conditions existed in other interior areas, Hakka and Hokkien alike. By contrast, the Hokkien-dominated lowland areas supported more extensive agriculture and a much denser population. Here, there were many large villages and urban centers, and shipping flourished at downriver and coastal trading ports.

Taiwan, an area of 13,884 square miles, is only a little over one-third the size of the home region. Moreover, much of the island is rugged: hills, tablelands, and high mountains occupy an estimated 76 percent of the total area; plains and basins merely 24 percent (Hsieh Chiao-min 1964: 29). The narrow alluvial plains along the western coastline were quite extensively settled during the Ch'ing period, as were the Taipei Basin in the north and the I-lan Plain in the northeast. Foothills rise sharply from the coastal plains and Taipei Basin, then spread inland to elevations of over 3,000 feet before giving way to the lofty central mountain ranges that run north and south the length of the island. Many of the habitable foothill areas were also settled during the Ch'ing period, as were the larger interior valleys. In these upland areas, where cultivable land was not as plentiful and the soil generally less fertile than in the lowlands, Chinese settlement tended to be sparser.

Contrasts in Taiwan's terrain tended to divide the island, like the mainland home region, into highland and lowland sections. In the hilly areas, where agricultural output was limited, the Chinese inhabitants depended on the lumber and camphor industries and, to a lesser extent, on mining. The coastal plains and lowland basins supported most of the island's rice and sugarcane production; in addition, salt fields operated in tidal flats, and offshore fishing flourished. Port towns located along Taiwan's flat western coastline, the northeastern Keelung and I-lan seacoasts, and the navigable Tanshui River in the Taipei Basin served as central markets and commercial outlets for their respective hinterlands.

During the Ch'ing period, only a few Chinese settled along Taiwan's inhospitable east coast, and even fewer in the mountain areas that until 1875 were reserved by Ch'ing policy for the "wild aborigines" (*sheng-fan*). The great bulk of the Chinese population was concentrated in the western and northern portions of the island.

*Speech groups and local society.* In the home region, as we have seen, the population consisted mostly of Hokkien and Hakka speakers. The Hokkien spoke varieties of the Southern Min dialect, most of which were to some extent mutually intelligible.[7] On the whole the Hakka spoke a more uniform dialect. However, the predominantly Hakka areas were relatively isolated from each other, and there were

[7]According to natives of southern Fukien, each county in Ch'üan-chou and Chang-chou supported variations in Min-nan speech (Li Han-ching 1974: 1099). Even in a single county, such as Hui-an in Ch'üan-chou, the local vernacular varied with respect to intonation and idiom (Chang K'ai-ch'üan 1963: 6). Examples of differences in Hokkien speech in Ch'ao-chou and Hui-chou are listed by Li Yung-ming (1959: 1–5) and by Liu Kuei-nien (1881: 842–43). The Hokkien in Ch'ao-chou (who call themselves "Teochius" and are also referred to as "Hoklo") resembled the Chang-chou inhabitants in their speech.

several Hakka subdialects, plus many local variations in speech. Moreover, Hakka in areas of Hui-chou accessible from central Kwangtung were influenced to some extent in their speech by contact with Cantonese speakers (Liu Kuei-nien 1881: 842–43).

During the Ch'ing dynasty (1644–1911), the distribution of the Hakka and Hokkien populations within the Fukien-Kwangtung home region remained relatively fixed. In eastern Kwangtung a zone of mixed habitation, dividing the more purely Hakka highlands from the Hokkien lowlands, followed the contour of the mountains that rise from the coastal plains and stretch northeastward from Hai-feng county in Hui-chou. After crossing into the southern Fukien highlands, this zone formed a less distinct Hakka-Min dialect boundary that extended inland in a northerly direction through rugged areas of Chang-chou and western sections of Lung-yen, then crossed the northern portion of mountainous T'ing-chou.[8] This entire zone apparently remained stable in Ch'ing times. Although disorder was rife throughout Fukien and Kwangtung, severe Hokkien-Hakka conflicts similar to the Hoklo-Hakka contention in Taiwan were not reported in areas of mixed habitation along this sociolinguistic boundary.

Neither was there widespread conflict between the Hokkien populations of Ch'üan-chou and Chang-chou. These inhabitants of southern Fukien were connected by intimate ties, and had long shared similar customs and practices. Even in areas where they associated together, people from these adjacent prefectures or counties within them did not exhibit the mutual antagonism that came to prevail among Hoklo groups in Taiwan. After Amoy (Hsia-men) was reopened to maritime trade in 1684, for example, Ch'üan-chou and Chang-chou people resided together there in relative peace amid a growing community that reflected the customs of the nearby counties of both prefectures (Chou K'ai 1839: 317–18, 639). Subethnicity, then, was not a critical factor in the home region under Ch'ing rule as it came to be in Taiwan.

Coastal and highland populations differed, however, in respect to economic well-being and modes of livelihood. The Hokkien speakers dwelling along the seacoast had been dependent on trade and seafaring activities for many centuries, and suffered great hardships when

[8] The general Hokkien-Hakka boundary in eastern Kwangtung is shown in a map entitled "Swatow Mission Field" (drawn by Rev. W. Riddel) in Gibson 1901. Professor G. William Skinner has kindly provided me with a map showing his own estimate of Hakka boundaries in eastern Kwangtung and southern Fukien. I have relied on both maps.

they were ordered to move ten to fifteen miles inland at intervals from 1661 to 1683, the period in which Ch'ing imperial forces fought against Taiwan-based opponents—the Ming-loyalist Cheng Ch'eng-kung (Koxinga) and his successors (Hsieh Kuo-ching 1932: 589–90). After Taiwan was surrendered, the coastal populations of southern Fukien and eastern Kwangtung soon reverted to their familiar maritime pursuits, the inhabitants of Ch'üan-chou and Chang-chou profiting from the flourishing trade that developed at Amoy. Local merchant and shipping interests made this sheltered island harbor of T'ung-an county their base of operations, and reestablished trading links with Luzon in the northern Philippines and other Nan-yang (South Sea) areas. They also engaged in extensive coastal shipping (Fu 1948: 43–46).

Southern Fukien merchant-shippers came to dominate trade with Taiwan. They cooperated closely with local Ch'ing officials during the period from 1684 to 1783, when Amoy served as the only designated port for both government and merchant shipping to and from the island. They established *chiao* (literally, "outskirt") guilds at An-p'ing (serving the prefectural center at Tainan) and subsequently at other Taiwan port towns as well. In 1784, a Han-chiang port near the Ch'üan-chou prefectural center was also opened for legitimate trade with the island, as was Wu-hu-men (serving Foochow to the north) in 1792. Yet Foochow merchants were unable to gain much advantage from direct trade with Taiwan by way of this northern port. By then, southern Fukien commercial interests, particularly those of Ch'üan-chou, were in nearly complete control of the cross-channel junk trade. Their monopoly on the Taiwan side was handled by the *chiao* guilds that had begun to control nearly all major aspects of maritime trade and shipping.[9]

Meanwhile, those inhabitants residing in the more distant highland districts of the home region gained few commercial advantages from the resettlement along the seaboard. The Hakkas, in particular, still controlled only small trading areas and established few if any discrete merchant guilds in major urban centers beyond the bounds of Chia-ying and T'ing-chou (Liang 1956: 152). Even in recent times, the Hakka dialect has been recognized as "not being a language of

[9] Fang Hao has recently written a series of articles dealing with the *chiao* guilds at various port towns in Taiwan. For an idea of their general nature and operations, see especially Fang 1971: 21–27. Fang believes that the Amoy *chiao* associations mentioned by Fu (1948: 55) were similar to many of those in Taiwan.

commerce" (Forrest 1948: 238). To compensate for the relatively low remuneration from trade and agriculture in their highland districts, many Hakka men sought to advance themselves by earning academic degrees (Lin Yün-ku 1956: 30, 32), while Hakka women, who did not bind their feet as was customary among the Hokkien, replaced them in the fields.

In the main, however, both the Hakka and the upland Hokkien labored to wrest a meager living from their poorly endowed mountainous surroundings. Ming and Ch'ing accounts portray both populations as sturdy and thrifty highlanders (Hu 1923: *chüan* 4, 8). In fact, Hakka and Hokkien populations, no matter whether of highland or lowland residence, shared many of the same traditions, beliefs, and forms of social organization.

Both people were also characterized by the prevalence of powerful kinship and surname groups, except in the poorest and most sparsely inhabited districts. Frequently, large lineages occupied sections of villages and towns and suburbs of walled administrative seats. Single-lineage villages were also common, and common descent groups of a more inclusive sort prevailed as well. Extensive Hakka clans were formed during the late eighteenth or early nineteenth century in Chia-ying, where local agnatic groups established joint ancestral halls (*tsung-tz'u*) in county seats and higher-level "great halls" (*ta tsung-tz'u*) at the departmental center. These clan buildups apparently occurred when the fashion of communal feuding spread upriver from Ch'ao-chou (Huang Chao 1899: 157–58, 166). Surname aggregates of a less structured nature were also widely formed, usually on a more or less temporary basis for some particular purpose, often a feud (Lamley 1977b: 9–10, 17). Since a majority of the inhabitants in most districts bore the same few surnames, such loosely knit aggregates could, if need be, embrace sizable portions of the local population.

Surname aggregates also became widespread in Taiwan during the Ch'ing period. Immigants who settled in newly opened areas sometimes regrouped along common-surname lines (Chou Hsi 1832: 284). Settler bands that migrated from other parts of Taiwan often organized themselves on a surname basis as well.[10] Through the gradual fusion of small agnatic groupings, local surname aggregates contin-

[10] For example, the various bands of settlers that migrated to newly opened areas in the I-lan Plain and the P'u-li Basin (in central Taiwan) are usually identified in Ch'ing sources by their predominant surnames rather than by their subcultural or home-region extraction.

ued to form and expand. Powerful aggregates, or "great surnames" (*ta-hsing*), were established in Taiwan's major port towns (Huang Ch'i-mu 1953: 57). Similar groupings, composed of lineages and extended family groups, played dominant roles in rural communities and appear to have wielded proportionally more power within areas where subethnic feuds had subsided and contending enclaves were weaker and less cohesive. In localities where subethnic rivalry was not prevalent, aggregates at times formed rival alliances and spawned surname feuds resembling the large-scale conflicts waged by surname confederations in the home region.

When circumstance allowed, both Hoklo and Hakka agnatic groups established ancestral estates in common and, in effect, developed into corporate lineages. These lineages tended to be less powerful than the local lineages that spread in Fukien and Kwangtung by natural fission, as Burton Pasternak (1969) has pointed out. Nor did they become as extensive and highly structured as the clans that formed in Chia-ying. Nevertheless, within their respective communities corporate lineages throughout Taiwan proved to be relatively strong and wealthy and helped support subethnic rivalry.

Ch'ing authorities generally regarded southern Fukien and eastern Kwangtung as disorderly regions and the inhabitants as rapacious, greedy, and vindictive. After the Manchus extended their sway over South China in the mid-seventeenth century, the inhabitants of the region experienced several more decades of turmoil, especially in areas where Ming loyalist forces contended with Ch'ing troops and along the seaboard, from which the population was periodically evacuated.

After the coastal areas were resettled, disputes arose among the inhabitants over property boundaries and tideland rights. By the Yung-cheng reign (1723–35), frequent outbreaks of well-organized feuds, described as "lineage fights" (*tsu-tou*) and categorized officially as *hsieh-tou* ("armed affrays") were reported in Ch'üan-chou and Chang-chou (Lamley 1977b: 17). The spread of communal feuding from these two prefectures to other portions of the home region was accompanied by a resurgence of other types of disorder—coastal piracy, pervasive banditry, secret society activity, and occasional uprisings.

Conditions in Taiwan were generally even more turbulent during the Ch'ing period than conditions in the home region. Violence was particularly common in frontier areas, where relentless Chinese pressure to reclaim lands and exploit wilderness resources was countered by reprisals from aborigines. Banditry and offshore piracy were rife, making travel hazardous. Vagrant bands and dissident settlers, including secret society members, added to the trouble by fomenting disturbances and insurrections. According to a popular adage, Taiwan could expect "an uprising each three years, a rebellion every five."

*Government.* The problems of governing southern Fukien and eastern Kwangtung were compounded by the region's isolation from Foochow and Canton, their respective capitals. Following the capitulation of the last Ming loyalist forces in 1683, provincial authorities in Foochow and Canton, together with the Ch'ing court in Peking, attempted to normalize conditions in the region by allowing civil functionaries stationed there to exercise greater authority. Meanwhile, Green Standard (*Lu-ying*) units, consisting mainly of local Chinese troops and their officers, were redeployed about the coastal and interior areas to help maintain order.

In Taiwan, the form of government resembled that in the home region for most of the Ch'ing period. The island was placed under Fukien jurisdiction in 1684, and a prefecture with three counties was then established in the west coast sections where scattered Chinese settlements already existed. The two highest officials, an intendant and a brigade-general both stationed at the prefectural center (present-day Tainan) in the south, were at first assigned duties related to defense; but as the needs of an expanding population increased, they were eventually granted much broader authority than their counterparts in southern Fukien and eastern Kwangtung. Additional Green Standard troops were also gradually assigned to Taiwan and new military posts established, primarily in the northern half of the island where the population growth was most rapid. Moreover, units of civil authority continued to be created in newly settled areas until another county, along with three subprefectures (*t'ing*), had been established in the west-central and northern portions of the island by the middle of the nineteenth century.

Sweeping administrative reforms were initiated in Taiwan during the last two decades of local Ch'ing rule, mainly in response to the incursions of foreign powers. Yet these reforms helped to alleviate some of the worst domestic problems. In 1875, obsolete restrictions on immigration and settlement were removed, and formal Ch'ing authority was extended over the entire island including remote aboriginal territories now opened to Chinese settlers. Also, semimodern Chinese forces began to be stationed in Taiwan in partial replacement of the ineffective Green Standard troops. Again, a second prefecture was established in the north and three counties created there in lieu of the Tan-shui and Ko-ma-lan (I-lan) subprefectural administrations. Finally, in 1886, Taiwan was made a separate province, and Taipei, the center of a third prefecture newly established in the northernmost portion of Taiwan, came to serve as the provincial capital.

All in all, however, Ch'ing rule tended to be relatively ineffective in Taiwan, due in part to the poorly trained Green Standard land and water forces that were assigned to posts in Taiwan at three-year intervals. These troops were rotated from brigades and regiments stationed throughout Fukien and at Nan-ao in eastern Kwangtung. Those hailing from Ch'üan-chou and Chang-chou proved the least reliable, since they were inclined to side with belligerent island inhabitants from the same home area (Li Ju-ho 1970: 4). Corrupt mandarins and yamen underlings also provoked rather than alleviated local discord, as did the restrictive regulations that Taiwan officials were obliged to enforce until the final two decades of the Ch'ing period. As argued below, subethnic rivalry in its most virulent form was essentially a phenomenon of an era of weak and restrictive government in Taiwan.

## *Major Subcultural Groups in Taiwan*

The main flow of Chinese settlers to Taiwan took place during the eighteenth century. As noted, this flow came largely from southern Fukien and, to a lesser extent, from eastern Kwangtung: up to 1895, in fact, 98 percent of all Taiwan's Chinese immigrants had come from these two areas (82 percent of the total were Hoklo, and 16 percent were Hakka).[11] This cross-channel migration fluctuated in

[11]The population percentages and ratios that appear in this section are based mainly on Ch'en Han-kuang's summary (1972: 85–104) of the 1926 census survey of Taiwan's Chinese inhabitants and their home-region registries. However, since only southern Fukien and eastern Kwangtung origins are given in this survey, the Hoklo and Hakka percentages presented here are not calculated entirely on the basis of the figures shown in the survey. (Relatively small numbers of Hoklo and Hakka came from other regions of southeastern China, including areas of Fukien north of the Min-nan speech region: Ch'en Chi-lu, for example, mentions (1972: 130) Fukien emigrants who belatedly crossed over from the Hsing-hua and Fu-chou coastal

volume, but never assumed the massive proportions of some of the great interregional migrations of the Ch'ing dynasty (Ho 1959: 136–65). Nevertheless, considerable migration occurred: Taiwan's Chinese population increased from about one hundred thousand in 1683, after Ch'ing forces assumed control of the island, to almost two million by 1811. By 1895, this population had risen to nearly three million, although natural increase rather than immigration accounted for much of the later growth (Ch'en Shao-hsing 1964: 117, 164–66).

Though Hoklo and Hakka people were principally distinguished by their mutually unintelligible dialects, they could also be differentiated by other features. Hakka women, for example, did not bind their feet and favored distinctive hair styles. There were also religious differences in regard to festivals, temple names, and deities. Veneration of San Shan Kuo Wang, for instance, was generally a characteristic of Hakka settlers from eastern Kwangtung. Distinctions in dress, architecture, and eating habits likewise led Hoklo and Hakka to associate with their own kind and to discriminate against others.

Although there were fewer Hakka in Taiwan than Hoklo, the Hakka came from nearly as many prefectures and departments. By 1895, Hakka from Chia-ying made up almost 8 percent of Taiwan's Chinese population; Hakka from Hui-chou about 4 percent; Hakka from Ch'ao-chou (unfortunately not distinguished from Hoklo from Ch'ao-chou in population records) probably about 3 percent; and Hakka from T'ing-chou (in southwestern Fukien) at least 1 percent. Immigrants from these areas reportedly spoke four separate Hakka subdialects (Chung 1973: 19–20), yet each of the subdialects could be understood by all Hakka-speaking people (Wang Ta-lu 1920: 14b). The Hakka dialect thus seems to have had a unifying effect on Taiwan's Hakka, allowing them to band together as a solidary minority group. Indeed, there is no evidence of massive confrontations between Hakka of different backgrounds, whereas there is evidence of such confrontations between rival Hoklo groups.

Throughout the Ch'ing period, Ch'üan-chou and Chang-chou Hoklo made up the overwhelming majority of Taiwan's Chinese population. By the end of the period, Ch'üan-chou people constituted al-

---

prefectures and generally engaged in the "three blades" (*san-tao*) trades as cooks, tailors, and barbers.) In this section general population estimates are based on the two most accurate Taiwan population surveys of the Ch'ing period, those of 1811 and 1893. (See Ch'en Shao-hsing 1964: Tables X-2 and X-3, pp. 159–62.)

most 45 percent of this population, and Chang-chou people more than 35 percent. During the seventeenth and eighteenth centuries, the combined Ch'üan-chou and Chang-chou population was proportionately larger. However, a marked decline in Hoklo immigration together with a small but steady stream of nineteenth-century Hakka immigrants eventually reduced the relative sizes of the Ch'üan-chou and Chang-chou groups.[12]

Like the more inclusive Hoklo and Hakka identities, Chang-chou and Ch'üan-chou identities were also fostered by differences in speech and mainland provenance. In general, however, religious distinctions proved most effective as cultural markers setting off Chang-chou from Ch'üan-chou communities.[13] The inhabitants of Chang-chou communities tended to worship K'ai Chang Sheng Wang, a patron deity peculiar to their home prefecture. Again, Chang-chou and Ch'üan-chou immigrants are reported to have made offerings to their ancestors at different hours during the prescribed days of the lunar year and to have offered different meats and delicacies.

In areas of Taiwan where a Ch'üan-chou population was predominant, the inhabitants tended to form more discrete communities reflecting their different home-county origins. Such Ch'üan-chou subgroups generally worshiped major deities brought over from their home areas. Thus Three Counties (San-i) people (from Chin-chiang, Hui-an, and Nan-an) venerated Kuang Tse Tsun Wang as a principal communal god; and people from T'ung-an and An-ch'i counties honored Pao Sheng Ta Ti and Ch'ing Shui Tsu Shih (or Pao I Ta Fu) respectively (Wang Shih-ch'ing 1972: 12–13, 19).

*Hakka and Hoklo group formation.* In general, one finds relative solidarity among the Hakka and relative disunity and divisiveness among the Hoklo. Such a contrast does not mean that Hoklo groups were incapable of achieving unity or of creating effective alignments when the need arose. Accounts of subethnic feuds show that the in-

[12] At the end of the Ch'ing period, the approximate ratio among Taiwan's Ch'üan-chou, Chang-chou, and Hakka populations was 47 : 37 : 16. The approximate ratio among Taiwan's three major Ch'üan-chou subgroups (Three Counties, T'ung-an, and An-ch'i), who together made up almost 45 percent of the island's Chinese population, was 40 : 33 : 27. (These estimates are based on the 1926 census: see Note 11.)

[13] This, of course, is an oversimplification owing to the variety of mainland deities worshiped. For example, Hoklo communities of diverse prefectural origins tended to establish Ma Tsu temples; Ch'üan-chou inhabitants worshiped a number of different Wang Yeh deities; and some groups or subgroups enshrined special territorial gods brought over from ancestral community temples. Shih Chen-min briefly lists (1973: 198) a few home-county or prefectural deities.

volved groups functioned cohesively and became adept at forming alliances with their neighbors. Large Hoklo alignments emerged in areas where the Hoklo inhabitants were pitted against adversaries of at least equal strength. For example, in the Hsia-tan-shui River basin of southern Taiwan, Ch'üan-chou, Chang-chou, and Ch'ao-chou Hoklo cooperated to oppose Chia-ying, Ch'ao-chou, and T'ing-chou Hakka. In contrast, where both Ch'üan-chou and Chang-chou Hoklo outnumbered local Hakka—as in most areas of western Taiwan from Chia-i northward—separate Ch'üan-chou and Chang-chou aggregates generally contended against Hakka groups (Tai 1963b: 213). In these areas, Hakka survival depended on cooperation and unity to counter more powerful but disunited Ch'üan-chou and Chang-chou foes.

Throughout Taiwan, in fact, local conditions encouraged Hakka community and intergroup solidarity. In many areas Hakka settlers were latecomers, or else a distinct minority, and had to endure great hardships in opening only moderately productive wilderness lands. Consequently, Hakka communities were generally smaller and poorer than Hoklo communities and had to face almost continuously a level of insecurity that Hoklo communities experienced only during periods of extreme turbulence. Even the inhabitants of the island's most extensive Hakka enclave, the Liu-tui confederation in the Tung-kang River area of southwestern Taiwan, felt continually threatened by nearby Hoklo and aboriginal populations (Chung 1973: 82–83, 265–66).

Various socioeconomic factors also fostered Hakka unity. Hakka communities, for instance, had few exceptionally wealthy families of the sort that often dramatized disparities of wealth and divided people in Hoklo communities.[14] Hakka solidarity was also encouraged by large Hakka investments in corporate estates and religious societies, institutions that provided for community needs and undertakings. Chung Jen-shou claims (1973: 270) that various *chi-ssu kung-yeh* (ancestral estates) and *shen-ming-hui* (religious societies) held from 50 percent to 70 percent of the cultivated land within the extensive Liu-tui confederation. The managers of such holdings decided which community projects merited support from these investments.

[14]See Chung 1973: 265–71. Burton Pasternak has discovered similar contrasts between Hakka and Hoklo villages in present-day Taiwan. The households of the Hakka village that he studied frequently acted in concert, coordinating their efforts at the village level to achieve common objectives; in the Hoklo village, by contrast, there was "no comparable stress on ways of unifying the community or reinforcing alliances between communities" (1972: 128).

Related to the practice of forming *shen-ming-hui* was the Hakka inclination to build community temples in lieu of ancestral halls (an inclination initially shared by Hoklo settlers). These temples became local political centers and served as symbols of unity, centers of self-government, and (in times of strife) headquarters for local militia. Some community temples—like the Lin-chao Kung and Yung-an Kung in Chang-hua county—not only provided numerous services for their own settlements but also administered to many neighboring villages (Hsü Chia-ming 1973: 171–85). Other temples assumed highly specialized paramilitary functions within local alliances and confederations. The Chung-i Tz'u, which served as the command center of the Liu-tui confederation from 1721 to 1895, is the foremost example of this type of Hakka temple.

*Shen-ming-hui* and *chi-ssu kung-yeh* were also formed in Hoklo communities and became principal sources of communal wealth. Besides defraying the costs of religious worship, such corporate enterprises met a variety of local needs, including those associated with sustaining armed feuds (Ssu-fa hsing-cheng pu 1969: 608–9, 612). In both Ch'üan-chou and Chang-chou communities, these organizations helped to maintain local subethnic identity and also, through temple affiliations, occasionally rendered support to larger aggregates. The well-endowed Lung-shan Ssu (a Kuan Yin temple) in the northern port town of Meng-chia provides an example of this type of support. Built in 1740 from contributions by early Three Counties immigrants, this temple was initially patronized by local merchants. Later, it served as a military command center for Three Counties people during their feud with newcomers from neighboring T'ung-an. Not long after this feud ended in 1859, the temple became the main command center for a Ch'üan-chou aggregate drawn from a much wider area that was fighting against a similarly large Chang-chou force (Huang Ch'i-mu 1953: 55–57).

Some Hoklo temples performed specialized military roles akin to those performed by the Hakka Chung-i Tz'u. The latter temple, in fact, was the first of a number of *i-min* ("righteous commoner") shrines dedicated to local militia members who sacrificed their lives in wars against rebel, aboriginal, and subethnic opponents. After the Lin Shuang-wen Rebellion of 1786–87, both Hoklo and Hakka *i-min* shrines were founded throughout Taiwan. Some of these shrines even served as centers of resistance when Japanese forces entered the island more than a century later. However, most *i-min* shrines—

including the well-known Pao-chung shrines near Hsin-p'u in Hsin-chu county and near Chung-li in T'ao-yüan county[15]—were established by Hakka.

Because Taiwan's Hoklo and Hakka shared many social institutions and practices (as they had in their home areas), they responded to rivalry and disorder in largely similar ways. But whereas Hakka communities depended upon close cooperation and cohesiveness almost continuously, Hoklo communities relied on these factors only occasionally as circumstances warranted.

## *Immigration and Settlement*

From the beginning of Ch'ing rule in Taiwan in 1684, cross-channel migration was subject to a variety of restrictions. These included traditional controls on trade and travel abroad as well as new restrictions imposed by a Ch'ing court more interested in keeping Taiwan as a protective shield than in developing it as a region for further settlement. Neither women nor the families of settlers already in Taiwan, for example, were allowed to immigrate there. Although these restrictions were set aside for brief periods during the eighteenth century, they were not relaxed on a continuous basis until the 1790's and not rescinded until 1875 (Chuang 1964: 1, 50). Moreover, Fukien authorities in Taiwan discriminated against Hakka settlers (labeled "Yüeh" or "Kwangtung" people) until the end of the Chu I-kuei Rebellion of 1721, when, in return for Hakka assistance against Hoklo rebels, they began to treat immigrants from eastern Kwangtung on a more or less equal basis with those from southern Fukien (Huang Shu-ching 1736: 92–93).

Troublesome restrictions, however, did not stop large numbers of immigrants from entering Taiwan in response to the attractions of virgin land and commercial opportunities. The earliest Ch'ing immigrants hailed largely from Ch'üan-chou and Chang-chou, though a few came from the coastal areas of Ch'ao-chou and Hui-chou. During the eighteenth century, Hoklo people from further inland within southern Fukien (including Yung-ch'un and Lung-yen highlanders) crossed over as well. The Hakka exodus to Taiwan from Chia-ying

[15] These two shrines have been treated briefly in recent articles (Ts'ai Mou-t'ang 1976; Lin Hui-ling 1977). The term *pao-chung* refers to a decoration for loyalty conferred by the Ch'ing emperor—in this case to honor Hakka braves (*yung*) who perished while fighting against rebels.

and adjacent areas in Hui-chou and Ch'ao-chou seems to have peaked during the late eighteenth and early nineteenth centuries. This migration mainly followed the Han River route to the seacoast, where arrangements were made for secret crossings. However, various Chia-ying officials tried to encourage Hakka emigration from the eastern Kwangtung highlands by facilitating transit through southern Fukien. There was thus some legitimate Hakka migration by way of overland routes and sailings from Amoy.[16] But ineffective supervision of shipping and stringent immigration restrictions encouraged the great majority of both Hakka and Hoklo migrants to enter Taiwan illegally (Chuang 1964: 40–42, 50).

Government restrictions on shipping and immigration had a profound effect on settlement in Taiwan because they made the simultaneous migration of large lineages and village groups impossible. Immigrants were forced to cross over in small and often diverse bands to Taiwan, where they formed new communities that depended on a variety of ascribed relationships. Moreover, during the seventeenth century and the first half of the eighteenth century, the island's Chinese population remained predominantly one of male settlers without local family ties. Consequently, social conditions in all but the oldest settled areas continued to be frontierlike for years after the lands had been cleared and the threat of attack from aborigines had ended (Chang T'an 1970: 25–27).

Migration to Taiwan resembled Chinese overseas emigration in other respects. During the early decades of the Ch'ing period, for example, many male settlers evidently hoped to retire to their native mainland villages. However, except for immigrants engaged in seasonal or temporary labor, most remained in Taiwan—the normal circumstance in overseas Chinese communities. Migration to Taiwan also frequently resulted in the familiar chain pattern: early settlers induced others from their home areas to join them.[17] Such locally in-

[16] Huang Chao 1899: 117, 153. Huang (1789–1853), a Hakka scholar of Chen-p'ing (present-day Chiao-ling) county in Chia-ying, complained that emigrants from his county seeking legal entry into Taiwan had to secure certificates from both the Chen-p'ing authorities and the subprefect stationed at Amoy. Thus they had to pay two sets of customary fees (*lou-kuei*) in order to move from eastern Kwangtung to Taiwan via Amoy.

[17] For example, kinsmen of a Chou-surname lineage in An-ch'i crossed over to Taiwan after two brothers had migrated there and eventually opened a shop in the Taipei area. These Chou kinsmen proceeded to establish a shipping company (Huang Shih-ch'iao 1971: 103). James L. Watson, discussing Chinese chain migration overseas in more recent times, notes that "the lineage is ideally suited to the needs of large-scale *chain migration*" (1975: 101). However, the extent of continuous chains of migration to Taiwan among lineage members or single-lineage

tensive migration eventually contributed to the growth of discrete, homogeneous communities that were set apart from one another by differences in speech, customs, and provenance.

Ch'ing-period migration to Taiwan was socially as well as subculturally diverse. Though many of the immigrants who opened up new land were destitute peasants, many of those who initiated land reclamation projects or who invested in commercial enterprises were wealthy. Increasing numbers of merchants and tradesmen (sometimes from areas outside the home region) also migrated to Taiwan and established guilds and shops in towns and in administrative centers. Moreover, outlaws and outcasts entered Taiwan illegally, resulting in a sizable vagrant (*liu-min*) population of often desperate men without local household registry or means of livelihood (Tai 1963b: 204–6).

The initial restrictions on immigration, however, inevitably favored the wealthy, who were able to enter Taiwan legally. These privileged immigrants included landed proprietors and large-rent holders (*ta-tsu yeh*) dependent on the goodwill of Taiwan's authorities for land grants and tax concessions, and large merchants and shipping magnates dependent on official endorsements and protection. Importantly, wealthy immigrants and their descendants often maintained strong links with their native areas and thereby helped to perpetuate Taiwan's subcultural heterogeneity.[18]

Immigration from southern Fukien to Taiwan slowed down markedly around the end of the eighteenth century after the island's western lowland areas and the Taipei Basin were fully opened and the choice lands reclaimed. Although Hakka from eastern Kwangtung continued to cross the channel in appreciable numbers, the great majority of emigrants from both eastern Kwangtung and southern Fukien went to Southeast Asia. This modern era of Chinese emigration to Southeast Asia had little effect on subethnic relations in Taiwan

villagers is difficult to assess. Besides, there was a high degree of risk and uncertainty involved in cross-channel migration to Taiwan. In 1814, for instance, a sizable group of Huang-surname kinsmen from Chin-chiang departed for Taiwan on two junks. One junk arrived at the northern port of Pa-li-fen, but the other was driven southward by strong winds and tides to the mid-island port town of Lu-kang. The men from this second junk settled nearby on the Chang-hua county border (Huang Shih-ch'iao 1968: 122).

[18] Little attention has been paid to migrants who returned to the home region. Some could afford to retire at home as a matter of preference, but others were forced home by rebellions or feuds (Huang Shih-ch'iao 1968: 128), by family or lineage orders, and by jobs—for example, to copy genealogical records (Huang Shih-ch'iao 1969: 108, 112). Those returnees who went back to Taiwan undoubtedly contributed to the cultural enrichment of their particular island communities.

or on the nature of the diminished flow of cross-channel migrants. Ch'ing-period migration to Taiwan, like the subethnic rivalry it helped to spawn, remained essentially a product of premodern political and socioeconomic conditions.

*Settlement.* Prior to the establishment of Ch'ing rule in 1684, Chinese settlement in Taiwan was concentrated on the southwestern coastal plains in portions of present-day Tainan, Chia-i, and Kaohsiung counties. A few isolated settlements were scattered along the west-central and northern coasts. During the latter part of the seventeenth century and the first half of the eighteenth, the already colonized areas in the southwest acquired much denser populations. From early in the eighteenth century, west-central areas also began to attract considerable settlement; and from the second half of that century (following the opening of the Taipei Basin and additional northern coastal areas), the north received a substantial influx of settlers as well. Upland areas and interior mountain basins—usually held by aborigines—tended to be settled later, often during the nineteenth century. Finally, steady settlement in the island's southern tip and along its rugged eastern coast did not begin until late in the Ch'ing period, except in Keelung and I-lan. (The first permanent settlers arrived in I-lan in 1796.)

Maps prepared by Ch'en Cheng-hsiang (1959: 24, no. 39; 119–25, nos. 153–64) indicate the general distribution of Taiwan's subcultural groups at the end of the Ch'ing period. They show Ch'üan-chou and Chang-chou populations in the old, established areas of the southwest, early Hakka settlements in the interior of what was once Feng-shan county (Kaohsiung and P'ing-tung), and later Hakka settlements in the mountainous areas of present-day T'ao-yüan, Hsin-chu, and Miao-li counties. The maps also show heavy concentrations of Ch'üan-chou people (mainly from T'ung-an and the Three Counties) along nearly the entire western coastline. Chang-chou people dominated stretches of coastline only in Kaohsiung, Tainan, Yün-lin, and T'ao-yüan counties, along with the northeastern coastline around Keelung and I-lan; and Hakka groups occupied only a few western coastal areas in Miao-li, northern T'ao-yüan, and P'ing-tung counties.

These maps tend to support the standard view of Chinese settlement in Taiwan. According to this view, Ch'üan-chou immigrants arrived first and established villages and towns near harbors and mouths of rivers; Chang-chou immigrants arrived next and settled farther inland along the western plains; and Hakka immigrants arrived last and were forced to settle in less productive hilly areas (Ch'en Chi-lu 1972: 87). The problem with these generalizations is that they are accurate only for certain areas of Taiwan and do not do justice to the complexity and diversity of settlement patterns. The first settlers along parts of Yün-lin's coast, for example, were Chang-chou immigrants, who were subsequently pushed inland by larger groups of Ch'üan-chou immigrants. Similarly, various groups of Hakka settlers were forced inland by the arrival of larger groups of Hoklo settlers. Moreover, the standard view of settlement does not take into account local conditions. Few areas in the plains and basins, for instance, came under the exclusive control of one subethnic group—a fact made clear by the extensive subethnic feuding that occurred in many parts of Taiwan from the late eighteenth century until well into the second half of the nineteenth century.

Taiwan's history of subethnic conflict is not merely evidence that most parts of the island were ethnically mixed; it also indicates that settlement patterns changed. Internal migration—whether forced or simply in response to newly opened land—was frequent and important. Lien Wen-hsi shows (1971: 9–24; 1972: 6–7) that Hakka laborer and settler groups often remained highly mobile, not only reclaiming lowland areas but opening up mountainous tracts as well. Many Hoklo likewise remained mobile. Chang-chou people, for instance, made up a majority of the more than forty thousand inhabitants of northern Taiwan who poured into the I-lan Plain during the first decade of settlement there. Similarly, in the middle of the nineteenth century Chang-chou and Ch'üan-chou settlers opened up the mountainous P'u-li Basin in central Taiwan. Feuds broke out among subethnic groups in both I-lan and P'u-li; in I-lan, the feuds escalated into local warfare when the Chang-chou majority fought allied Ch'üan-chou, Hakka, and aboriginal opponents (Hsu Cho-yun 1972: 53–54). The subethnic strife in I-lan and P'u-li is especially significant because it shows how easily intense rivalry developed during the eighteenth century could later spread to frontier territories, often necessitating still further internal migration and making Taiwan's settlement patterns even more complex.[19]

[19] In I-lan, for example, the Chang-chou majority succeeded in driving Ch'üan-chou and Hakka settlers from the central part of the plain to localities as far south as Lo-tung (Lamley 1977a: 181). In Yün-lin, Ch'üan-chou immigrants drove both Chang-chou and Hakka settlers from the coast, not only seizing their lands, but installing different community and surname

*Towns and walled cities.* Taiwan's market and port towns were often affected by the same kinds of subethnic rivalries that affected the countryside. Indeed, as the population grew and as competition over trade and resources increased, subethnic rivalry naturally assumed an urban dimension. In fact, subethnic feuds sometimes dramatically changed the composition of town populations and even altered towns' sizes and locations. For example, the Chang-chou townspeople of Pei-kang moved east and formed a new market town at Hsin-kang because of friction with Pei-kang's more numerous Ch'üan-chou residents.[20] In southwestern Miao-li, recurrent feuds among Ch'üan-chou, Chang-chou, and Hakka groups during the middle of the nineteenth century led to the formation of three separate port towns (Ts'ai Chen-feng 1897: 118).

Although there was a tendency for towns to become the exclusive territory of one or another local subcultural grouping, this was not always the case. As a result of a feud between Three Counties and T'ung-an townspeople in Meng-chia, for instance, the T'ung-an inhabitants fled downriver and joined with Chang-chou people to develop Ta-tao-ch'eng as a rival port. Accommodation, then, was an alternative to separation as a response to subethnic strife. Successful efforts to survive by means of accommodation also took place in rural areas—as in parts of Chang-hua county where neighboring Chang-chou and Hakka communities learned to live together (leading to the eventual assimilation of the Hakka) as a result of pressure from powerful Ch'üan-chou alignments (Hsü Chia-ming 1973). In the turbulent Tou-liu area of Yün-lin county, Hakka inhabitants similarly acquired the speech and religious practices of their dominant Chang-chou neighbors (Ni 1894: 30).

Conditions in Taiwan's walled cities—its prefectural, subprefectural, and county seats, largely postdating pioneering settlements—also favored accommodation. In these protected localities, the inhabitants generally enjoyed relative peace and order, except in times of uprisings and urban riots. The "guest" residents, including offi-

---

deities in their abandoned temples (Yün-lin Record 1972: 120). Again, most Hakka settlers moved southward from the Taipei Basin when menaced by intense Chang-chou and Ch'üan-chou rivalry during the middle part of the nineteenth century. These Hakka even abandoned their major commercial and religious center at Hsin-chuang (Lien 1971: 21–24; 1972: 13–14).

[20] Thereafter, animosity continued between Pei-kang Ch'üan-chou and Hsin-kang Chang-chou. Pei-kang Ch'üan-chou would not marry their daughters to Hsin-kang Chang-chou, but they would accept wives from them. Such discriminatory practices led to subethnic feuds between the two townspeople (Yün-lin Record 1972: 120).

cials and their entourages, hailed from many mainland areas besides the home region, and this helped to create a cosmopolitan environment in which local elites often developed interests and ties that transcended particular communities and subethnic groups. However, Taiwan's administrative centers contained mainly mixed Hoklo populations. Sizable Hakka communities rarely formed in the walled cities and their suburbs.

The literature of the period, in fact, suggests that Hakka were discriminated against in some walled cities by the Hoklo populace and, at times, by local officials. Around 1720, for example, Tainan residents were cautioned by the authorities not to rent to Hakka so as to stop them from becoming too numerous within the city's four wards (Lien 1971: 5). Thereafter, with the exception of wealthy individuals and outstanding gentry-scholars, the island's Hakka appear to have been treated as outsiders in that prefectural center. This seems to have been the case in Hsin-chu city as well. Hakka went there for business and scholarly purposes (Huang Chung-sheng 1960: 16), but were denied the full advantages of city or suburban life because of their dialect, troublesome reputations, and relative lack of commercial experience.[21]

*Subethnic rivalry and island development.* In order to understand more clearly how settlement and subethnic rivalry were related, we may envision three general stages of development for the areas of Taiwan settled during the Ch'ing period. First was a pioneering stage in which wilderness territories were opened for cultivation; next came an intermediate stage of economic growth; and finally came an advanced stage in which local society more closely resembled that prevailing in long-established communities in the home region.

Although subethnic conflict sometimes occurred when diverse settlers converged on the same wilderness areas, cooperation was often the rule during the pioneering stage. Settlers worked together on land reclamation and water control projects and fought together against hostile aborigines. Many settler bands were naturally close-knit groups of kinsmen and associates with "common locality" (*t'ung-hsiang*) ties. But at other times, tenants and laborers of diverse

[21] At the Chang-hua county seat, where a predominantly Chang-chou population existed, Hakka residents were apparently tolerated. The Chang-hua gazetteer (Chou Hsi 1832: 289) mentions that both Min (Fukien) and Yüeh (Kwangtung) family schools (where learning was carried on in separate dialects) were located within the city as well as in county market centers and villages.

origins had to be collected to gain sufficient manpower for large-scale undertakings. Such cooperative ventures were usually arranged through proprietorships established to open up specific localities. In lowland areas, Ch'üan-chou and Chang-chou proprietors officially authorized as "reclamation householders" (*k'en-hu*) sometimes recruited mixed Hoklo bands. They also appear to have employed Hakka laborers who had no tenancy privileges. Lien Wen-hsi lists (1971) many instances when Hakka and Hoklo together reclaimed lands in wilderness areas from Chia-i northward. The pioneer settlements that evolved from these joint ventures generally housed Hoklo and Hakka workers in close proximity (sometimes in separate neighborhoods, sometimes "roof-to-roof" within the same villages).

Hakka proprietors normally operated apart from their Hoklo counterparts and formed settler bands from among their own people. Beginning in the late eighteenth century, however, a number of joint Hoklo-Hakka proprietorships were established to open up mountainous terrain in northern Taiwan. Though the Hoklo and Hakka partners (or major shareholders) cooperated directly in management, they generally recruited separate bands of tenant-settlers, who lived and worked apart. These joint proprietorships proved especially effective in coordinating land reclamation projects in sections of the island already beset by subethnic tension. The most outstanding proprietorship of this nature—bearing the corporate name Chin Kuang Fu—was formed in 1834 and partly subsidized by the Tan-shui subprefect. This proprietorship enlisted around twenty-four bands of Hoklo and Hakka settlers (mostly the latter), and in thirteen years succeeded in opening sizable areas of rugged terrain southwest of the subprefectural center in present-day Hsin-chu county (Lien 1971: 17).

The intermediate stage of development began in each area after the better lands had been reclaimed and more immigrants had arrived on the scene. This second stage was marked by the spread of new market centers, the construction of irrigation systems (coupled with increased agricultural production), the attainment of more balanced age and sex ratios, and the appearance of new kinds of local leaders in keeping with significant cultural and commercial advances. Moreover, population growth and economic expansion led to more competition for land and other limited resources as well as to more commercial and social rivalry—all factors that tended to intensify subethnic conflict. This increase in local discord occurred as pioneer settlements segmented or disappeared, leaving in their stead communal groups based largely on shared provenance, dialect, and religious customs.

The competition that disrupted older mixed settlements in turn fostered solidarity within these more discrete communal groups. Indeed, as local discord assumed the guise of intercommunity strife, people's interests and loyalties became closely linked with the welfare of their respective communities regardless of their status, wealth, and kinship affiliations. At the same time, conflict among rival communities impeded the development of full and open intercommunity relationships, which remained precarious and strained.

Under tense and unstable conditions rivalry between such subculturally discrete communities led to subethnic feuds. Communities at feud often created alliances with other communities within their local subcultural grouping or with "friendly" communities nearby, thus spreading their feuds over much larger areas. In time, intermittent feuding turned territorial groupings into belligerent enclaves with enduring boundaries. This escalation of violence also forced "neutral" communities to choose sides, causing isolated Ch'üan-chou, Chang-chou, and Hakka inhabitants to seek protection among people of their own kind. The highest degree of rural "coercive closure"—to use G. William Skinner's term (1971: 279–80)—thus became normal for the polarized communities and enclaves in feud-afflicted areas of Taiwan.

Feuding of such magnitude occurred mainly during one long and severe phase of subethnic strife—a phase that began in 1782 when an affray between Ch'üan-chou and Chang-chou villagers in Chang-hua spread northward into Tan-shui subprefecture as well as south into Chia-i county. The problem was exacerbated in 1826 when Hoklo-Hakka feuding became widespread in the wake of a subethnic disturbance in the Chang-hua countryside (Inō 1928: 931–32). Thereafter, Ch'üan-chou, Chang-chou, and Hakka adversaries intermittently battled in feud-afflicted areas throughout the west-central and northern portions of the island. Elsewhere, extensive Hoklo-Hakka affrays, following feud patterns developed at the time of the Chu I-kuei Rebellion (1721), became commonplace in districts of Feng-shan in southern Taiwan. This virulent phase of subethnic strife, lasting roughly 81 years (from 1782 through 1862), largely coincided with the intermediate stage of Taiwan's development.

Though plagued by subethnic conflict, the intermediate stage (as noted) was economically constructive. During the 81-year period of severe strife, a number of irrigation systems were built through private or community endeavor (Hsieh Tung-min 1954: 228). Large city-building projects, also requiring considerable local capital and labor, were undertaken as well. Much of this development took place in the west-central and northern areas of Taiwan where economic growth was most evident despite the prevalence of subethnic feuds. It is apparent, however, that extensive subethnic feuding had an adverse effect on social development at levels higher than the discrete community or local enclave. Social intercourse and cultural interchange were impeded and marketing often severely constricted in the segregated countryside. Local government tended to become (or remain) ineffective and remiss. In sum, persistent large-scale feuding disrupted the many ties that customarily linked the villages, market towns, and walled cities together within a central-place hierarchy.[22]

Feuding gradually subsided and tension lessened during the mid-nineteenth century. In the 1860's, the last of Taiwan's great epidemics of subethnic fighting came to an end, and a more stable and open society evolved—an indication that the third stage of development had begun. Signs foreshadowing this more mature stage had in fact appeared earlier when Taiwan's gentry-scholar class had begun to assume more active leadership about the island (Lamley 1964: 92–124). Subsequently, reforms in civil and military government and improvements in administration helped to make society in Taiwan increasingly resemble that in the home region.

## *Subethnic Feuds and Government Response*

In several important respects, Taiwan's subethnic feuds seem to have been patterned after the home region's feuds among lineages and surname aggregates. For one thing, feuds in both areas were highly organized—in fact, almost with the formality of ritual. For another, temples commonly served as headquarters for feud preparations. Moreover, the armed bands issuing forth from Taiwan's com-

[22] G. William Skinner has distinguished (1977: 275) two hierarchies of central places for late imperial China: a formal one created and regulated by the imperial bureaucracy, and an informal one reflecting the natural structure of Chinese society ("a world of marketing and trading systems, informal politics, and nested subcultures"). The two were interrelated. Extensive local feuding directly affected the informal hierarchy; but the formal hierarchy also suffered when officials became overburdened and, along with their underlings, were denied free access to towns and village localities in a state of war.

munity temples and *i-min* shrines (with banners, images of local deities, etc.) reflected community and temple influence in much the same way that the armed bands issuing forth from the home region's lineage temples manifested the strength of local lineages or of larger buildups of surname aggregates. Then, too, temples in both areas were important in financing feuds. In Taiwan, funds from local ancestral estates (*chi-ssu kung-yeh*)—formed by kinship groups to support ancestor worship—were frequently used for feuds. In the home region, proceeds from nearly identical "sacrificial land" (*cheng-ch'ang-t'ien*) associations were misappropriated for the same purpose (Liu Hsing-t'ang 1936: 37–39). This form of support was less substantial in Taiwan than it was in the home region because Taiwan's kinship groups had less corporate wealth. Nevertheless, local lineages with common property (though not always of demonstrated common descent, according to Wang Sung-hsing [1972: 175]) supplied funds and leaders for feuds, as did Taiwan's great families and surname aggregates.

However, *chi-ssu kung-yeh* did not become numerous in Taiwan until well into the nineteenth century. The extensive subethnic feuds of the eighteenth and early nineteenth centuries appear to have been financed largely by local religious societies (*shen-ming-hui*). These societies were usually organized to support the worship of particular deities and to finance the upkeep of these deities' altars and temples, although some served as organizations for supporting ancestor worship or as professional or artisan associations.[23] By and large, the versatile *shen-ming-hui* provided a network of mostly nonkin connections in communities lacking extensive agnatic ties.

The support that temples and religious associations provided for feuding groups was not limited to men and money but extended to supernatural aid from gods, ghosts, and ancestors. In Taiwan, for example, the ghosts of local braves who had fallen in previous subethnic feuds (or in battles against rebels or aborigines) were cared for in *i-min* shrines and called upon by shrine communities for help against common enemies. More often, gods and ancestors were appealed to for their aid and blessings and requested to "witness" oaths and contracts made in preparation for armed affrays.

[23] These remarks about Ch'ing *shen-ming-hui* are based mainly on descriptions by Sun Sen-yen in the compilation Ssu-fa hsing-cheng pu (1969: 605–48). For an account of *chi-ssu kung-yeh* in Taiwan during this period and thereafter, see Tuan Sheng-feng's discussion in the same compilation (1969: 693–820).

Taiwan and the home region differed, however, with respect to those who participated in the fighting. In the turbulent areas of southern Fukien and eastern Kwangtung, where lineage feuds were frequent, the fighting often led to the development of a professional mercenary class dependent on feuds for a livelihood. In some counties, powerful rival bands of mercenaries were able to extort vast amounts of lineage wealth, with a ruinous effect on the feuding lineages and on local society in general. Nineteenth-century accounts, for example, cite many cases of lineage leaders who were unable to control or stop the feuds that they had started: reportedly, wealthy lineage members became impoverished and powerful lineages grew weak as a result (Cheng 1887: 621).

Feuding was most destructive, of course, when entire villages or market towns were plundered and burned, and the survivors killed or forced to flee. In Taiwan, feuds on this scale were sometimes incited by bandits and vagrants merely anxious for an opportunity to pillage. Taiwan's authorities were appalled by the ease with which feuds could begin, intensify, and spread to distant areas with similar alignments of subethnic rivals. This matter was particularly serious because large-scale feuds posed a direct threat to governmental authority. Sometimes, in fact, subethnic feuds gave rise to rebellions, although more often rebellions (dependent on subethnic alliances) gave way to feuds. Taiwan's most serious rebellions of the Ch'ing period—those of Chu I-kuei (1721), Lin Shuang-wen (1786–87), Chang Ping (1832), and Tai Ch'ao-ch'un (1862)—all involved subethnic strife (Inō 1928: 937–40).

In the long run, however, it appears that Taiwan's subethnic feuds did not have as ruinous a local effect as the home region's lineage and surname feuds. Growth and development, at least, continued in those parts of Taiwan most affected by recurrent subethnic strife. Large projects that required considerable local organization and cooperation between rival communities were even carried out, some as joint community ventures (such as the construction of irrigation systems), others as projects initiated by Ch'ing officials and gentry leaders. In northern Taiwan, the building of the Ko-ma-lan subprefectural seat and the reconstruction of the walled Tan-shui subprefectural center were accomplished by gentry-managed bands of mutually estranged Hoklo and Hakka workers. Again, the wall-building project at Taipei, the site of the new northern prefectural center, was undertaken in the early 1880's by rival Ch'üan-chou and

Chang-chou managers and laborers who still bore grudges stemming from the feuds of previous decades (Lamley 1977a: 186–93, 199–200).

The ability of estranged rivals to work together helps to explain how a period of severe subethnic strife could also be a period of economic growth. Feuds, then, did not stop all productive pursuits, and did not even rule out some kinds of cooperation between enemies. The notion of "peace in the feud" (see Gluckman 1956: 1–26) is appropriate for this situation in Taiwan. Tightly organized "closed" communities imposed peace in their immediate locales, as did larger enclaves in their respective territories. Other factors besides in-group cohesion, however, helped to bring about this peace. The establishment of new and exclusive market towns, the departure of weak groups from strife-ridden localities, and the formation of extensive "religious spheres" tended to reduce friction within closed-off territories and to create more clearly delineated boundaries.[24] However, these same factors also helped to uphold the status quo among belligerent groups.

These observations suggest that Taiwan's local communal groups, as parts of larger enclaves, fared better than lineage communities in the home region did during prolonged periods of strife. Taiwan's communal groups were more sheltered within the island's closed off and subethnically homogeneous territories, and hence had a better chance of maintaining their strength and solidarity. Nor do they seem to have been as susceptible as feuding lineages in Fukien and Kwangtung to exactions by mercenaries. Also, organized bandit and vagrant bands tended to be treated as outcasts in Taiwan no matter what their provenance: such dissidents were rarely able to derive status and power by inciting violence and seldom gained access to corporate sources of community wealth. Moreover, island communities usually exercised more effective control over their fighting braves, enlisting mainly their own young men and usually demobilizing them—sometimes with the encouragement of wary local officials—when their services were no longer urgently required (Lamley 1977b: 25–26; Li Ju-ho 1970: 4–5). Similarly, the presence of discrete rival

[24] For reference to "religious spheres", see Shih Chen-min's recent work on Chang-hua (1973). There, during the Ch'ing period, the worship of home-region Hoklo deities was extended to neighboring villages, thus forming religious territories or spheres that amounted to subcultural ritual units. A complementary study by Hsü Chia-ming (1973) indicates that small Hakka communities under the threat of attack by Ch'üan-chou people joined Chang-chou villages in communal worship. Ultimately, the Hakka were assimilated.

communities and enclaves in so many settled areas of Taiwan tended to limit secret society activity.[25]

Extensive feuding in Taiwan, as in the home region, tended to occur in periods of chronic local disorder. Indeed, Taiwan's 81-year phase of severe subethnic strife coincided with a period of island-wide turbulence highlighted by serious rebellions.[26] The animosity bred by feuding and insurrections set the stage for further violence, so that even minor incidents were sufficient to spark great epidemics of subethnic strife. In such a troubled environment, the "peace in the feud" often proved frail and short-lived, and local Ch'ing rule was frequently imperiled.

*Government response.* Ch'ing authorities acted harshly, though not always effectively, to suppress subethnic feuding in Taiwan whenever armed affrays spread and threatened to engulf entire localities. In the eyes of the government, such feuding was tantamount to local rebellion. The precedent for dealing with large-scale feuding was established in 1782 in response to the first major outbreak of fighting between Ch'üan-chou and Chang-chou settlers. Officials quickly dispatched troops to pacify troubled areas and ordered the execution of rival leaders. The onset of extensive Hoklo-Hakka fighting in 1826 provoked a similar response, even prompting the governor-general, stationed in Foochow, to tour Taiwan and to devise a plan for bolstering local defenses in the northern half of the island (Lamley 1977a: 186–87).

Military efforts, however, proved insufficient to curb local violence, largely because such efforts did nothing to lessen the intense animosity that gave rise to the violence. In fact, this animosity was sometimes exacerbated by local civil and military functionaries who regarded Hakka settlers as "outside provincials" from Kwangtung. Moreover, the actions of the Green Standard troops stationed in Taiwan constantly posed a problem. These rotated troops shared backgrounds and traits with the island's Ch'üan-chou and Chang-chou

[25] When rebel leaders with secret society affiliations fomented uprisings, subethnic friction invariably occurred among subordinates and followers. Moreover, rival communal groups not represented in local rebel forces often sided with the government or else remained neutral. During the Lin Shuang-wen Rebellion, for example, Ch'üan-chou and Hakka alignments in disturbed areas formed *i-min* units to oppose predominantly Chang-chou rebel forces (Chang T'an 1974: 82–83). In the Ch'ing period, Taiwan's Hakka never fomented large uprisings, although members of Hakka communities occasionally joined rebellions.

[26] Lists of disturbances in Taiwan under Ch'ing rule are given in Chang T'an 1970: 35–43; and Ch'en Shao-hsing 1964: 190–93. Together, these lists indicate that the period 1782–1862 was highly disorderly in respect to both feuds and uprisings.

inhabitants and were therefore apt to take sides in feuds rather than act impartially to stop the fighting (Li Ju-ho 1970: 18–19). Furthermore, officials, officers, and yamen runners often tried to extract bribes or fees by offering to intervene in feuds or in litigation following outbreaks of violence. With unreliable subordinates and underlings, even the best officials were unable to maintain order, much less devise means of reducing subethnic tension.

The makeshift solution to which local officials most frequently resorted was to pit rival groups against each other, "using the people to control the people" (*i-min chih-min*). The government's formal recognition of armed Hakka bands as a legitimate militia in southern Taiwan and the awards bestowed on these "righteous commoner" (*i-min*) forces for their stand against rebels during the Chu I-kuei Rebellion provide a notable instance. Thereafter, Hakka forces were deployed as far north as Chia-i in later engagements with Hoklo rebels.

Spurred in part by the fear that internal disorder might invite foreign intervention, Taiwan's authorities experimented with other forms of local control during the early nineteenth century. Local directors (*tsung-li*) and overseers (*tung-shih*) were selected from commoners living in rural communities, charged with keeping the peace, and reprimanded whenever subethnic fighting took place in their localities. The authorities also began to introduce collective security measures based on the existing *pao-chia* system under which registered households were organized into small units and the inhabitants held accountable for each other's actions. In 1833, a united *chia* (*lien-chia*) system was briefly established in central areas of the island to unite "law abiding people" (*liang-min*) within much larger units made up of towns and nearby rural localities. In other parts of Taiwan, officials initiated "united village compacts" (*lien-chuang yüeh*) that embraced entire rural districts. Under these compacts, large villages were required to protect small villages, and powerful kinship groups were obliged to defend weak ones. United militias were also formed to guard against local uprisings, banditry, and feuding.[27]

These early experiments in collective security were not very successful in curbing subethnic strife. United *chia* and united village systems functioned only as long as dedicated officials were on hand, and

[27] For discussions of the various forms of militia and local control that operated in Taiwan under Ch'ing rule, see Inō 1928: 941–46; and Tai 1963a: 77–82. The Ch'ing *pao-chia* system and its different functions (including those related to police and militia operations throughout many areas of China) are dealt with in Hsiao 1960: 43–83.

even then were introduced in only a few areas. Furthermore, in most instances such security measures called for the inclusion of rival communities within the same units. During the latter half of the nineteenth century, however, local officials assumed a more realistic view of Taiwan's deep-rooted subethnic rivalry and allowed separate Hoklo and Hakka confederations and militia bands to maintain order within their own territories (Inō 1928: 941–42, 946).

Taiwan's officials also tried to persuade rival communal groups to refrain from violence—sometimes, by calling upon local leaders to mediate disputes in their areas (Huang Hsiu-cheng 1976: 82). The problem with this approach was that subethnic conflict frequently involved competition between the leaders of rival groups. Indeed, the power and prestige acquired by leaders provided direct benefits to their respective groups—such as more favorable treatment from local civil and military functionaries. Ch'ing authorities fully understood this kind of competition among rival elites and attempted to make use of it. One way of doing this was to give gentry status to local notables. Throughout the Ch'ing period, in fact, the government was generous in granting academic and expectant-office titles (conferring gentry status and privileges) to eminent members of all three major subcultural groups as rewards for services. Moreover, special Yüeh (Kwangtung) quotas were established for civil and military *sheng-yüan* degrees in 1741 in an attempt to appease Taiwan's Hakka population. Thereafter, the competition became so keen among Hoklo and Hakka scholars about the island that quotas applicable to both groups were gradually enlarged. Early in the nineteenth century, a separate Yüeh quota was also introduced for island Hakka competing in the provincial examinations held in Foochow (Chuang 1973: 80–84, 474).

As an expanding and privileged class, Taiwan's gentry came more into their own as leaders and community spokesmen during the first half of the nineteenth century. Hence, Ch'ing authorities began to rely more heavily on them to intercede in subethnic disputes. Fengshan officials, for example, made headway in reducing long-standing tensions between Hoklo and Hakka in the Hsia-tan-shui River area after encouraging local gentry from both sides to act jointly as managers of local irrigation systems and ferry services (Inō 1928: 949–50). Such members of the gentry had much to gain in terms of wealth and influence from helping to alleviate chronic local disorder. As the gentry gradually formed wider ties and interests, they naturally tended to take a firmer stand against subethnic strife—not only in their own localities but in other areas as well. One well-known result is the discourse "Exhortation for Peace" (*Ch'üan ho lun*), delivered by a northern gentry-scholar in an effort to end feuding between Ch'üan-chou and Chang-chou communities in the Tan-shui subprefecture (Inō 1928: 950–51).

By the middle of the nineteenth century, officials in Taiwan were making even greater use of the gentry in their efforts to maintain order. Hoklo and Hakka militia units, under local gentry commanders, proved effective in quelling uprisings and in curbing subethnic violence (Lamley 1964: 102, 108). Even when these units were not actively deployed, power still gravitated into the hands of the gentry commanders, whose interests and responsibilities increasingly transcended the confines of their own communities. As a result, this gentry elite was able to play a major role in curtailing subethnic strife on an island-wide basis from the 1860's on.

Comprehensive reforms in government policy and administration during the final decades of Ch'ing rule also helped to reduce subethnic tension in Taiwan by allowing reform-minded gentry to serve the state in various managerial capacities and to become advisers to the island's new senior officials. Moreover, Taiwan's gentry leaders began to foster a wider sense of provincial identity that tended to override local prejudice. Finally, the arrival of semimodern troops recruited outside the home region also helped to bring about more orderly conditions in areas of mixed settlement. Their presence on the island also allowed the opening of remote coastal and mountainous areas by mixed bands of settlers without subethnic strife.

*Late Ch'ing turbulence and rivalry.* Despite late Ch'ing reforms and the lessening of subethnic tension, local conditions remained turbulent in Taiwan. Banditry was still rife, and conflict with aborigines increased as greater numbers of Chinese troops and settlers entered wilderness areas. Above all, conflict involving kinship and surname groups became more widespread and intense. Previously, serious conflict between such groups had been limited mainly to port towns and to those rural localities where there was little subethnic rivalry. However, as subethnic tension lessened in areas of mixed settlement, massive affrays among bellicose lineages, great families, and surname aggregates began to take place, and communal feuding revived. Hence, in rural areas where powerful enclaves had fragmented and created more open conditions (especially in mixed Hoklo localities), neighboring villages turned against one another, and new feud patterns and cycles of "community closures" set in. Countryside affrays (*hsiang-tou*), sustained by the predominant surname groups of rival villages, proved awesome and destructive in both Hoklo and Hakka localities.[28]

Meanwhile, rivalry among the island's three major subcultural groups assumed new dimensions when prominent Hoklo and Hakka gentry leaders began to represent their respective groups at the prefectural and provincial levels of Taiwan's much revised government. Competition arose over the familiar issue of quotas in Taiwan's enlarged examination system as well as over efforts to obtain patronage and official favors. From time to time, hard-pressed authorities also endeavored to secure the cooperation of important rival leaders.[29] Such high-level competition among subcultural elites generally transcended intercommunity rivalries and precluded the subethnic feud strategies of the past.

Though subethnic conflict persisted, it was increasingly confined to fights between Hoklo and Hakka groups—local affrays evident even during Taiwan's resistance to the Japanese in 1895 (Lamley 1970: 30, 51). On an island-wide basis, subethnic strife was largely overshadowed by escalating kinship and surname disturbances, which came to resemble the extensive lineage and surname-aggregate feuds in Fukien and Kwangtung. This escalation took place as aggressive common-surname groups formed networks of affiliations over wider areas (Huang Hsiu-cheng 1976: 82). Thus in the late Ch'ing period, the authorities were confronted with a familiar but grave type of disorder that threatened to equal or exceed the bounds of previous epidemics of subethnic feuds, for at that period most of the nearly three million Chinese inhabitants of Taiwan shared only a

[28] See, for example, a Chang-hua scholar's description of the widespread damage caused by these rural feuds in the 1880's (Hsü Tuan-fu 1970: 2723–24). Other evidence of this strife is still at hand. Myron Cohen (1969: 179) translates a circular written sometime during the latter part of the nineteenth century announcing a meeting of lineage members to prepare for an affray in the Hakka district of Mei-nung (then in Feng-shan county). David Jordan (1972: 20–26) describes the "great" surname wars that took place in at least seven Hoklo villages north of the Tainan prefectural center sometime between 1855 and 1870.

[29] For instance, when provincial officials undertook to bolster Taiwan's defenses against Japanese attack in 1894–95, they appointed an influential Chang-chou gentry leader to head an island-wide militia system. But because almost all the enrolled militia units consisted of Hoklo bands, the officials subsequently called upon the island's most prominent Hakka gentry-scholar to form a supplementary force composed of local Hakka braves and *i-min* bands (Lamley 1970: 35).

few common surnames.[30] Moreover, native-place ties within Taiwan, rather than subethnic identities per se, became increasingly important, particularly as north-south political rivalry developed between Taipei, the new provincial capital, and Tainan, the old prefectural center. This factor, too, had the effect of diluting subethnic feelings and limiting their influence.

Subsequently, Japanese rule over Taiwan (1895–1945) hastened the growth of a more distinctively Taiwanese perspective among the island's Chinese inhabitants. This perspective greatly reduced the significance of subethnic divisions. Furthermore, the Japanese had much more effective military and police forces at their disposal than their Ch'ing predecessors had, and were therefore more successful in curbing subethnic strife as well as kinship and surname violence. In most areas, the orderly conditions under Japanese rule led to the peaceful merging of Ch'üan-chou and Chang-chou peoples. Today, in fact, the descendants of Taiwan's Ch'üan-chou and Chang-chou settlers seem much less aware of their different mainland origins; often, they are only able to distinguish their backgrounds on the basis of slight distinctions in speech. A degree of Hoklo-Hakka discord has continued, however, nourished by long-standing differences in dialect, customs, and attitudes. In areas where sizable communities of Hoklo and Hakka coexist, subcultural boundaries are still evident despite the many modern influences that encourage assimilation.

## *Conclusions*

Subethnic rivalry arose in Taiwan during the Ch'ing period as a result of heterogeneous Chinese immigration and settlement. Generally manifested through intercommunity competition among the three major subcultural groups that emerged on the island, this widespread form of rivalry in turn influenced internal migration and local patterns of settlement. In the case of Taiwan, however, subethnic rivalry cannot be construed simply as a product of the pioneer stage in which diverse settler bands contended with each other in an effort to survive and improve their lot. Such rivalry spread and intensified

[30]Li Tung-ming estimates that 97 percent of the Taiwanese (not counting aborigines and mainlanders) share 100 surnames. However, 53 percent share just ten of these surnames; and almost 20 percent share the two most common ones, Ch'en and Lin. That is, about one out of every nine Taiwanese is a Ch'en, and one out of every twelve is a Lin (1976: 75–76). Hence, through rival surname networks among the ten most common surnames (especially the Ch'ens and Lins), it was possible to foment massive and extensive local strife.

during an intermediate stage of development, and persisted to a lesser degree (and also at higher levels of political competition) even after Taiwan had reached a relatively mature stage in the final decades of Ch'ing rule. Viewed over the course of many decades, subethnic rivalry may be seen to have been a factor that, to a greater or lesser extent, continuously affected socioeconomic development in many of the island's areas of mixed Chinese settlement.

Subethnic rivalry also affected cultural change, particularly when intergroup competition increased locally and communities of a more discrete sort formed as a consequence. From this point on, settlers and their descendants appear to have made concerted efforts to re-adopt customs and practices native to their home areas in southern Fukien and eastern Kwangtung. Their selective borrowing of religious traits proved especially significant: distinctions in home-area deities and religious observances (reinforced by differences in speech and other traditional customs) served as key cultural markers that imparted exclusive identities to rival communities and more clearly defined and reinforced the cleavages between them.

In a similar vein, the borrowing and adaptation of home-region practices was evidenced by the organized feuding that lent such a violent tone to subethnic rivalry in Taiwan. Preparations for costly armed affrays (*hsieh-tou*) entailed essentially the same institutional procedures as those preceding the outbreak of lineage and surname affrays in Fukien and Kwangtung. When the familiar *hsieh-tou* fashion spread among local bodies of Ch'üan-chou, Chang-chou, and Hakka adversaries, alarmed officials designated this version of armed feuding as *fen-lei hsieh-tou* (literally, "armed affrays among diverse types"), a term denoting the distinctively subethnic character of Taiwan's communal feuds (Lamley 1977b: 10–11).

The feud seems to have been an appropriate form of conflict for rival communities contending in an insecure environment plagued by disorder and weak government. Communities at feud tended to balance off each other, thus allowing for a relative status quo and for brief periods of peace. Moreover, feuding brought about a high degree of community organization and cooperation under "closed" conditions, factors that enabled local economic development to proceed. However, intermittent feuding also intensified and perpetuated local tensions and consolidated the boundaries between contending communities and enclaves, thereby enabling subethnic rivalry to become an enduring and deeply rooted phenomenon in Taiwan.

Feuds also tended to spread and spark subethnic disturbances in other localities. As a result, extensive feud patterns formed among subcultural groupings in many parts of Taiwan during the island's 81-year period of severe subethnic stife. Subcultural configurations of this magnitude were in turn important in creating the rudimentary framework of a plural society—a society segmented into three groups with parallel structures and class hierarchies. Later on, however, a well-defined plural society did not take shape, for the lines between Taiwan's major subcultural groups became blurred by both peaceful and violent proceedings: namely, social integration among local groupings at peace, and widespread kinship and surname violence that revived intercommunity rivalries on the basis of common descent instead of ethnicity per se. Nevertheless, each major group continued to have representation by way of contacts between their respective gentry elites and local Ch'ing authorities.

The state, in fact, played a ubiquitous role in the development of subethnic rivalry in Taiwan. Ineffective restrictions and weak government helped to bring about the heterogeneous immigration and settlement that gave rise to Chinese subethnicity. Subsequently, weak governmental control allowed and, indeed, encouraged the formation and preservation of bellicose rival communities. The discrimination and prejudice shown by civil and military functionaries further stimulated subethnic contention. Finally, official concessions to one or other subcultural group or local grouping not only fostered subethnic rivalry but set precedents for competition of an economic, social, and political sort. Only when subethnic strife posed an immediate threat to local order did Ch'ing authorities normally take much heed of the disparities and tensions that made nearby communities such bitter rivals.

Despite the general negligence of Ch'ing officials, their reports about subethnic rivalry in Taiwan help to keep historical issues in proper perspective. One finds, for instance, that subethnic conflict eventually involved much larger segments of the island's population and occupied more time than did Chinese-aboriginal contention. Again, the divisive influence of ingrained rivalries among local communal groups usually hampered the spread of secret society and rebel activities during even the most serious uprisings. Ch'ing records also serve to refute the commonly accepted idea that subethnic dissension prevailed only among frontier settlements adjusting to a new environment.

Research on Ch'ing-period subethnic rivalry not only provides a better understanding of Taiwan's past, but sheds light on the present. Popular religion, for example, is still deeply rooted in the turbulent past when territorial boundaries also served as religious boundaries and when subethnic feuds were staged as religious wars. Something of this fierce and competitive legacy is reflected in the conspicuous consumption that accompanies Taiwanese religious festivals today. Other reminders of earlier subethnic dissension are the divine guardians and supernatural enemies figuring in local religious ritual. In addition, community graveyards and rural *i-min* shrines, devoted to the spirits of fallen village braves, commemorate subethnic disturbances of the past and vividly call to mind subethnic feuds and their grim consequences.

One discovers that Taiwan's subethnic rivalry had other long-lasting effects. The absence of periodic standard markets may be attributed, at least in part, to subethnic feuds and to the "closed" communities that prolonged conflict brought about (Crissman 1972: 253–54). Again, settlement patterns were affected, as were marriage patterns—the latter perhaps permanently in some localities. Above all, the prejudice against Hakka still apparent in Taiwanese society is a carry-over from the Hoklo-Hakka rivalry of the Ch'ing period.

Finally, the more general study of subethnicity in Taiwan may serve as a basis for comparative historical analysis of the interaction of immigrant groups within China as well as within (and among) Chinese settlements overseas. For over two millennia, groups of Han Chinese with different backgrounds and local origins have migrated, then intermixed along frontiers and in areas undergoing resettlement. As in Taiwan, these mainland immigrant groups often adjusted to their new environment and to other subcultural groups without losing their subcultural identities.[31]

For anthropologists and historians dealing with Taiwan's subethnicity, the prospects of comparative research on the immigrant backgrounds of the Nan-yang Chinese may be especially fruitful. In Ch'ing times, the majority of these overseas Chinese hailed from southern Fukien and eastern Kwangtung, like the Taiwanese. Also, there are historical resemblances with the Taiwanese in their overseas migra-

[31] Abner Cohen (1974: xiv) has called attention to similar situations in which immigrant groups, rather than losing their cultural identities through integration, have reorganized their own traditional customs or developed new customs under traditional symbols in an effort to become more distinct. He has called this process "ethnic continuity" or "revival."

tions, mixed settlement abroad, and closely knit communal groups based on common dialects and home-area provenance. Comparative research on this vast scale—encompassing mainland China, Taiwan, and Chinese settlements abroad—should yield valuable insights about the character of Chinese subethnicity and its manifold effects under varied conditions ranging from traditional to modern. Of course, comparisons of Chinese subethnic interaction with ethnic or subethnic interaction among non-Chinese groups should be highly rewarding as well.

# Voluntary Associations and Rural-Urban Migration

Alexander Chien-chung Yin

## *Theoretical Orientation*

This paper deals historically and statistically with the adaptation of P'eng-hu migrants to life in Kaohsiung, a fast-growing industrial city in southwestern Taiwan. Since the early part of the twentieth century, the people of P'eng-hu have been migrating to Kaohsiung, where they have relied largely on voluntary associations to solve problems, cope with economic and ideological demands, elevate their political and social status, and maintain contacts with their place of origin. The primary aim of this study of Kaohsiung voluntary associations (common interest groups) is to suggest that different periods and patterns of migration strongly affected the process of adaptation.

Kenneth Little provides a useful African model for the study of voluntary associations. He employs the concepts of adaptation and integration in studying the function of voluntary associations in social change, selecting for study a formerly "backward" area where industrial growth was fully under way. A subsistence economy had been replaced by a market economy, disturbing traditional ideas of status and creating new social roles. People in these new roles tended to interact with others on the basis of common economic, educational, religious, and political interests, rather than on the traditional basis of common place of origin and common descent. Little found that West African migrants in the urban areas adjusted to their new environment by adopting selected Western values, technology, and

This study began in 1967; fieldwork was conducted in both P'eng-hu and Kaohsiung in 1968–69 and 1972–73. See also Yin 1969, 1975, 1976, 1978a, 1978b, and 1978c.

economic practices (1965: 85). He also found that voluntary associations were used as adaptive mechanisms (1957: 591; 1973a: 414–19). These associations became cultural bridges enabling migrants to move from one kind of social universe to another (1965: 1–2, 87).[1]

Maurice Freedman and Marjorie Topley both demonstrate that Chinese migrants in Singapore have also relied on voluntary associations (based on religious, territorial, linguistic, occupational, surname, and other criteria) to help them adapt to an alien environment (Freedman 1967: 35–48; Topley 1967: 59–62). Many other overseas Chinese regional associations have been studied—by T'ien in Sarawak (1953), by Li in Malaysia (1970), by Skinner in Thailand (1958), by Willmott in Cambodia (1969), and by Crissman in Southeast Asia (1967). Within China itself, Tou provides much data on the historical background of regional associations and the reasons for their emergence (1943); and Ho adds to this body of material (1966).

In Taiwan, at least one well-known migration (described by Bernard and Rita Gallin) did not immediately result in the formation of voluntary associations. Here, an imbalance in the population/land ratio was the major cause of the migration of "excess labor" from Hsin-hsing village in central Taiwan to Taipei in the late 1940's (Gallin 1966: 120, 121). Most of the migrants were males above the age of sixteen, who usually found jobs as pedicab drivers, unskilled laborers, or store clerks. Job information was often provided by relatives, friends, and fellow villagers before migrants left the village (*ibid.*: 122). Migrant communities were formed in the Wan-hua precinct of Taipei, and members frequently went home to participate in the ritual and social activities of their village (*ibid.*: 123). The pattern of socioeconomic incentives in the city, the relatively successful adaptation of early migrants, and the continual exchange of information between home village and new residence thus initiated a process of chain migration (in which already settled migrants encouraged others from their home communities to follow them). In two recent articles, the Gallins argue that the limited number and lower-class background of Hsin-hsing migrants made it difficult for them to organize a cohesive, mutual aid group outside their occupational network (1974a: 242; 1974b: 352, 357). As a result, they participated in a Vegetable Merchants' Association and in the more broadly based

[1]A number of similar studies have been done. See Banton 1957; Barnes & Peil 1977; Dewey 1968, 1970; Doughty 1972; Freedman 1967; Gallin 1966; Gallin & Gallin 1974a, 1974b; Kerri 1977; and Little 1957, 1965, 1973a, 1973b, 1975.

Chang-hua *hsien* Regional Association to advance their economic and sociopolitical ends (1974a: 242; 1974b: 351–53). In addition, the Gallins note that kinship and localized relationships continued to be significant (1974b: 354, 358).

The major purpose of my P'eng-hu–Kaohsiung migration study is to use the methods of demographic anthropology to distinguish different historical patterns of migration and to emphasize the role of voluntary associations in the migrants' adaptation to urban life.

## *The Setting*

*The P'eng-hu islands.* The P'eng-hus (or Pescadores, as the Portuguese called them) are a group of 64 islands, 21 of which are inhabited, in the Taiwan Strait southwest of Taiwan. The total land area is 126.9 square kilometers, and the largest island is P'eng-hu itself with 64.2 square kilometers (Taiwan Provincial Governor-General's Office 1946: 51). In 1971, the islands' total population was 118,744, creating a population density of 936 people per square kilometer (*Taiwan Demographic Fact Book* 1971: Table 26). The islands' economic and political center is Ma-kung, a port city 88 miles by sea from Kaohsiung. Together, the islands form one of Taiwan's sixteen *hsien*; and P'eng-hu *hsien* is in turn divided into six administrative subunits. The islands' most striking topographic characteristic is that they are low, flat, and without forestation—like lotus leaves floating on the sea.

Three outstanding features of the climate of the P'eng-hus—strong wind, sparse average rainfall, and what islanders refer to as "salty rain" (*hsien-yü*)—restrict agricultural development and make living conditions difficult. The strong wind blows almost daily from the end of September to the end of March, eroding the topsoil and reducing agricultural productivity. P'eng-hu farmers use low walls of broken coral to protect the available arable land, and they construct their homes compactly with small windows to protect themselves against the strong and damaging wind. Also because of the heavy wind, many P'eng-hu fishing boats have to go far from home to fish and to sell their catches. Seasonal out-migration during this period has been common, especially before the 1950's. Usually these seasonal migrants worked as servants in Tainan and Kaohsiung (Suzuki 1918: 42; Inō 1928: 670; P'eng-hu t'ing 1936: 10; Yin 1969: 5–7).

Rainfall is not abundant and is unevenly distributed throughout the year. The dry season—from late September to early April—lasts just over half the year. Though summer typhoons usually bring heavy rains (Ch'en Cheng-hsiang 1955: 79), strong wind and meager rainfall during the rest of the year make the islands very dry. Moreover, windblown ocean spray—the islands' notorious "salty rain" —causes heavy damage, withering the islands' crops (including peanuts, sorghum, millet, and sweet potatoes).

The P'eng-hus have always been one of the major centers of Taiwan's fishing industry, and residents depend on this industry as their main source of income for purchasing products from the outside (rice, flour, salt, sugar, canned goods, gas, oil, soap, batteries, fruit, etc.). In 1971, 62.2 percent of the employed population (aged 15 and over) were engaged in the agricultural and fishing industries, which are combined in official occupational censuses (though agricultural production has been only a minor source of family income). Only 4.7 percent of the 1971 population worked in mining, manufacturing, water purification, gas refining, and construction; and the remaining 33.1 percent worked in commerce, transportation, industrial and commercial service, finance, government, and community and other individual services (*Taiwan Demographic Fact Book* 1971: Table 29).

There are many reasons—ecological, economic, and social—for out-migration from the P'eng-hus. Ecological reasons are naturally very important. As early as 1894, Lin noted that the imbalance in the population/land ratio had pushed thousands of P'eng-hu people to Taiwan proper. Earlier, in July 1881, the P'eng-hus had three occurrences of "salty rain" in one month, and "many thousands of the starving masses" were sent to Taiwan by the government. In that year, the total number of starving people reached 49,000 out of a total population of about 65,000. Lin also noted that the P'eng-hus had suffered from 28 years of famine, 14 years of serious damage from "salty rain," 19 years of serious damage from typhoons and strong winds, and two invasions (one by pirates and one by the French)—all within the 90-year period from 1805 to 1894 (1894: 368–79). Such conditions naturally encouraged both permanent and seasonal migration. Inō, for example, noted in 1928 that more than half the male population of the islands normally went off to Taiwan to earn their living (1928: 670). However, neither Lin nor Inō gave the destination of P'eng-hu migrants. According to the testimony of my contemporary informants, most of these migrants went to the Tainan area, at least during the period 1850–1908.

The environment of the P'eng-hus is thus a major handicap to agricultural development. But in addition, there is a shortage of arable land—a problem aggravated by the use of some of the best land for graveyards. In fact, almost 10 percent of the total land of the islands is used for graveyards (a legacy of Chinese settlement dating back at least to the twelfth century), and on one of the smaller islands this figure climbs to 46 percent (Ch'en Cheng-hsiang 1955: 5). As a result of the shortage of arable land, agricultural production can only provide food for four or five months of the year. In 1950 and 1954, the average caloric intake of P'eng-hu residents from local agricultural and livestock products was only enough to satisfy half their minimum needs (Ch'en Cheng-hsiang 1955: 60–61, 133–34). Even at the present time, agriculture plays a minor role in the economy.

In 1949, when the Chinese government retreated to Taiwan, P'eng-hu became a military base; as a result, the government launched many programs to improve the local economy. In 1950, there were only twelve motorized fishing boats in P'eng-hu; by 1971, the number had increased to 1,546 (P'eng-hu *hsien* Government 1950: Table 73; 1971: Table 44). Nature did not provide, however, for a corresponding increase in the number of fish available in the vicinity. Consequently, the ever-increasing number of boats has all but wiped out schools of fish in nearby waters. P'eng-hu fishermen must go farther out to sea to make their catches. Many of them therefore leave the islands to join international fishing fleets or to seek other work in Taiwan.

Though a large number of P'eng-hu natives still migrate to Taiwan to secure a better living, many now go to obtain an education or to gain social prestige. Indeed, the possibility of upward social mobility is becoming a strong motivation for migration. Many P'eng-hu migrants now living in Kaohsiung are successful businessmen. Some own companies; others have invested in hotels and transportation facilities; many even own industrial firms. Former P'eng-hu residents also seek political office in Kaohsiung: one became mayor, and others at one time held nearly one-third of the city council seats.

Almost all P'eng-hu natives now living in Kaohsiung contribute to the support of the parts of their families remaining at home. Many also send contributions for religious celebrations or return to the islands to participate in religious activities. These successful migrants are always treated with great respect, and their home villages share their prestige. The mass media in P'eng-hu like to report stories of former residents who have become successful in Kaohsiung. Thus, news stories, visits of successful businessmen to their home villages, and gifts and correspondence from migrants in Kaohsiung all encourage P'eng-hu residents to consider migration.

Many residents who are forced to remain on the islands complain bitterly about their situation. These are often people who feel that they must stay to support aging parents or relatives or their own families. This does not mean, however, that all P'eng-hu residents are anxious to leave: some still prefer life on the islands and consider starting a new life in Taiwan as either unappealing or too risky. Yet the younger generation now seeks new opportunities for improvement, and most often this means leaving P'eng-hu (Yin 1975: 208–10, 213, 215). Recently, many young P'eng-hu natives have begun to travel abroad to study. Most of them attend vocational schools, colleges, or universities in Taiwan proper. A few even go on to other countries after they complete their studies in Taiwan.

The traditional pattern of P'eng-hu migration to Tainan ended in 1908, the year in which the Japanese began construction of the first stage of a new harbor at Kaohsiung. This project marked the beginning of substantial migration to Kaohsiung, a migration that can be roughly divided into two periods—the first from 1908 to the 1950's, the second from the 1950's to the present. During the first period, Kaohsiung needed a massive labor force to complete the harbor project and related development. During the second period, however, migrants broadened their aspirations, taking new jobs, moving to parts of Kaohsiung not previously inhabited by people from P'eng-hu, and even deciding to leave Kaohsiung for other parts of Taiwan or for other parts of the world.

Unfortunately, no official published data are available to indicate rates of permanent migration or migrants' destinations. For the period from 1923 to 1939, however, we do know that the average seasonal migration rate was 48 percent for adult males and 24 percent for adult females, and that the overall seasonal migration rate was 36 percent. Informants in P'eng-hu, Kaohsiung, and Tainan all agree that most of these seasonal migrants went to Kaohsiung in search of temporary and part-time work (Yin 1975: 93–96).

It is also clear that the demographic characteristics of P'eng-hu migrants changed dramatically from the first period to the second. In the first period, most migrants were teenaged males with little education or previous work experience. Consequently, they tended to end up in low-wage, low-prestige jobs, mainly in construction, and they tended to cluster in certain precincts of Kaohsiung. Their migration, in short, was principally in response to the demand for cheap labor created by large-scale industrial development.

In the second period, by contrast, more migrants have been female, more have been educated, fewer have come from fishing and agricultural backgrounds, more have moved into Kaohsiung neighborhoods that have not been the traditional homes of P'eng-hu migrants, and fewer have been involved in chain migration. (And as a natural result, this more varied group of migrants has found its way into a wide variety of new occupations.) We may thus classify the first pattern of migration as *homogeneous* and the second as *heterogeneous* (Yin 1978a: 1–26).

*Kaohsiung.* Kaohsiung was opened as an international port in 1863, mainly as a secondary port for Tainan. Later, when the ports around Tainan silted up, Kaohsiung became the major port for southern Taiwan. Aware of the city's commercial and strategic importance, the Japanese instituted a major harbor redevelopment program that lasted from 1908 until the end of the Second World War. The Japanese also encouraged industrial development throughout this period as part of their plan to make Kaohsiung a military and economic base for their operations in Southeast Asia (Kao-hsiung shih wen-hsien wei-yüan-hui 1958: 15, 22–45).

At present, Kaohsiung is Taiwan's second largest city and includes Taiwan's largest commercial harbor. It is also a center for much of Taiwan's heavy industry—for petroleum refineries, fertilizer plants, aluminum factories, steel plants, shipbuilding yards, sugar refineries, and cement factories. Two large export processing zones have also been established recently with substantial investments of domestic and foreign (including overseas Chinese) capital. In 1971, only 11.5 percent of Kaohsiung's employed population (aged fifteen and over) worked in primary industry (agriculture, fishing, and extractive industries); 31.8 percent worked in secondary industry (manufacturing and construction); and 56.7 percent worked in tertiary industry (*Taiwan Demographic Fact Book* 1971: Table 29). The city itself—which includes ten precincts divided into 385 basic administrative units (*li*)—covers 183.8 square kilometers (Kaohsiung City Government 1972: Table 1). The 1971 population of the city was 871,824, creating a population density of 7,664 people per square kilometer (*Taiwan Demographic Fact Book* 1971: Table 26). Kaohsiung is thus an ur-

TABLE I

*Distribution of Kaohsiung P'eng-hu Regional Association Members by Area of Origin in 1972*

(Percent)

| Kaohsiung precincts | Area of Origin | | | | | | |
|---|---|---|---|---|---|---|---|
| | Ma-kung town ($N = 2,999$) | Hu-hsi township ($N = 1,998$) | Pai-sha township ($N = 1,776$) | Hsi-yü township ($N = 863$) | Wang-an township ($N = 1,274$) | Chi-mei township ($N = 725$) | Total ($N = 9,635$) |
| Industrial (Nan-tzu, Ch'ien-chen, Tsu-ying) | 9.8% | 6.1% | 5.2% | 4.4% | 2.6% | 1.1% | 6.1% |
| Business and harbor (Yen-ch'eng, Ku-shan) | 42.2 | 35.3 | 42.7 | 46.3 | 55.7 | 13.5 | 40.9 |
| Small business, etc.[a] (Hsin-hsing, San-min) | 22.7 | 38.0 | 32.4 | 29.5 | 13.4 | 2.4 | 25.5 |
| Gov't, school, and dormitory (Ch'ien-chin, Ling-ya) | 24.5 | 19.5 | 18.5 | 19.4 | 13.8 | 3.0 | 18.9 |
| Fishing and boat-building (Chi-chin) | 0.8 | 1.1 | 1.2 | 0.4 | 14.5 | 80.0 | 8.6 |
| TOTAL | 100.0% | 100.0% | 100.0% | 100.0% | 100.0% | 100.0% | 100.0% |
| Percent of total membership ($N = 9,635$) | 31.1% | 20.7% | 18.4% | 9.0% | 13.2% | 7.5% | 100.0% |

SOURCE: Data supplied by the Kaohsiung P'eng-hu Regional Association.

[a] These precincts include schools and hospitals.

ban and industrial center whose growth since the early part of this century has depended upon attracting large numbers of nonlocal workers.

Traditionally, P'eng-hu migrants have tended to select their Kaohsiung residences and occupations according to the residences and occupations of relatives and friends from P'eng-hu. Migrants from Ma-kung (an urban and business area in P'eng-hu), for example, have tended to live in and start their businesses in Yen-ch'eng precinct, the oldest and most prosperous area in Kaohsiung, as have migrants from the township of Hsi-yü, many of whom were fishermen and farmers who are now engaged in various small business enterprises (often furniture making). People from Hu-hsi township, an agricultural area in P'eng-hu, have tended to go to Hsin-hsing precinct, a secondary business area of Kaohsiung, where they operate lumber mills and construction businesses. Migrants from Wang-an and Chimei townships (both areas where fishing predominates) have generally settled, respectively, in Ku-shan and Chi-chin, where fishing and light industry are popular.

This pattern of settlement results from the kind of chain migration that has been observed in many overseas Chinese communities (T'ien 1953; Dewey 1962; Crissman 1967; Li 1970; Watson 1975), a fact suggested by Table 1, which shows the distribution by precinct of the members of Kaohsiung's P'eng-hu Regional Association. Two-thirds of the members of this association, for example, live in four precincts (Yen-ch'eng, Ku-shan, Hsin-hsing, and San-min—in general, the oldest areas of Kaohsiung); and a great proportion of this group are second-generation migrants.

Though the difficulties of migrating from P'eng-hu to Kaohsiung are eased for migrants who settle in neighborhoods with other P'eng-hu migrants, many difficulties still remain. Life in P'eng-hu, for example, is very strongly affected by traditions (in ways of thinking, conducting business, dressing, spending leisure time, etc.). Life in Kaohsiung, by contrast, is far less encumbered by traditions, in part because of the city's urban and industrial character, and in part because of the heterogeneous origins of the city's residents. Many P'eng-hu migrants in fact complain that urban life is too impersonal to allow them to make good friends and too commercial to allow them to lead simple lives. Yet when they return to P'eng-hu, they often find life there to be too conservative, too monotonous, and not sufficiently modern. These people often strongly believe that the young should go to an urban area to develop their skills and widen their horizons—a sign that they have adapted with reasonable success to Kaohsiung. We now turn to some of the agencies that have helped make this adaptation possible.

## *Voluntary Associations*

P'eng-hu migrants formed various sorts of traditional voluntary associations and common interest groups to help them cope with life in Kaohsiung. I will discuss three of the most important types: religious associations, mutual aid associations, and regional associations.

*Religious associations.* Kaohsiung's P'eng-hu religious associations differ from those in P'eng-hu itself in four ways. First, they are not based on kinship: members of the steering committee may be chosen (though they need not be) from various surname groups in a given area. Second, migrants' temples and their activities are not village based. Third, the steering committees of some P'eng-hu migrants' temples now include outsiders (people from Kaohsiung and Tainan). Fourth, a Taoist temple has been founded that all P'eng-hu migrants may join.

Of the 112 Buddhist and Taoist temples in Kaohsiung, 33 were built and managed by P'eng-hu migrants. These temples were formed when new communities of migrants "divided incense" (*fen-hsiang* or *fen-ling*) with their home area temples, thereby founding branch temples linked spiritually with temples at home in P'eng-hu.[2] Most of the P'eng-hu migrants' temples are located in the four oldest Kaohsiung precincts, where the majority of P'eng-hu migrants can be found.

A few decades ago these temples provided P'eng-hu migrants with protection (spiritual and physical), education (in military tactics and writing), meeting places, places for recreation and entertainment, and places for negotiating disputes. Older people thus usually have great confidence in the temples and in their steering committees, and believe that temple associations are useful organizations for satisfying their needs. However, the younger generation, including many newly arrived migrants, feel quite differently. In the past, the temples

[2] Seven of Kaohsiung's 112 temples were built by migrants from other parts of Taiwan (information supplied by the Kaohsiung city government in 1973). Usually, part of the religious paraphernalia (incense pot, etc.) of a branch temple is granted by the main temple in a special ceremony to formalize the temples' connection and relationship.

and their associations provided many services; but during and especially after the Second World War, the entire society underwent a radical change that reduced the temples' attractiveness. Some temple functions have been replaced by the work of government agencies, private businesses, and other kinds of voluntary associations. Newly arrived migrants and the younger generation now tend to join various secular associations rather than religious associations or temples.

Yet religious associations continue to exist, and two factors seem significant in explaining this. First, even today many of the men active in religious associations are also executive members of Kaohsiung's P'eng-hu Regional Association. This suggests not only that the leaders of Kaohsiung's migrant community are very active, but also that they feel they must be active in many social spheres. Second, many P'eng-hu migrants in Kaohsiung still feel that they are outsiders in need of an organization that unites all P'eng-hu migrants spiritually and socially. Indeed, in 1925—after twenty-five years of real and imagined discrimination—P'eng-hu migrants formed the Wen Wu Sheng Tien (the saints of literature and martial arts temple) to foster such unity. The two major deities worshiped here—Confucius (god of literature) and Kuan Yu (god of war and strategy)—are not worshiped in village or township temples in P'eng-hu. P'eng-hu migrants' sense of being struggling outsiders is clearly reflected in a slogan to which they attached considerable importance: "One who wants to create his own heaven and earth should have two abilities—writing and fighting." This slogan, which has been called the spirit of the P'eng-hu people, provides apt symbolic expression of the predicament that migrants have felt and continue to feel themselves to be in. Religious associations, then, are still useful in helping migrants cope collectively with this predicament.

*Mutual aid associations.* The mutual aid associations established by P'eng-hu migrants in Kaohsiung were designed to provide financial aid and were based on ties of common P'eng-hu origins. Like migrants' religious associations, they were not based on kinship. Since they had written constitutions and rules but still preserved local divisions, they are best understood as a stage in the evolution of a formal P'eng-hu regional association (*t'ung hsiang hui*). In this paper, I will consider only those mutual aid associations that functioned like modern credit unions (these differ from traditional *ch'ien hui*[3] and

[3]For the organization of traditional *ch'ien hui*, see Wu 1974; Fei 1939: 263–74; Ch'en Juit'ang 1969: 525–55; Lang 1968: 69, 73, 168; Diamond 1969: 23; and Potter 1968: 156.

*ho hui* by virtue of their more formal structure and organization). My example will be the Wang-an Mutual Aid Association, or Wang-an Yi Chi Hui (though in fact Kaohsiung had five such associations, reflecting P'eng-hu's five Japanese administrative units).

The data on the Wang-an Yi Chi Hui were provided by one of the association's former executives, Mr. Ch'en Wei. Mr. Ch'en—82 years old in 1973—was the owner of the Taiwan Transportation Company and was the Kaohsiung representative of four Japanese shipping lines. After coming to Kaohsiung in 1907 at the age of sixteen, he was hired by the Jih-tung Company of Osaka, Japan, when it recruited workers in P'eng-hu. Because of his background as a janitor in the Japanese-run Wang-an police station (and hence a man who spoke Japanese), he was promoted by the company very quickly. He also became one of the original executives of the first P'eng-hu Regional Association.

The Yi Chi Hui was originally organized by port construction workers from Wang-an township in P'eng-hu. Newly arrived migrants joined this organization (and others like it) primarily to get financial help for special occasions. As well as having a common region of origin, the early members of the Yi Chi Hui were alike in having low incomes. In its later years, the Yi Chi Hui became more structured, and its financial procedures became more complex. According to the 1925 constitution, all Wang-an Yi Chi Hui members had to pay a monthly fee of ¥0.50 on the fifth day of each month. If a member wanted to borrow money, he would have to pay 12 percent interest and repay the amount of the loan within four months (Wang-an Yi Chi Hui 1925: Articles 8, 12). The maximum amount that could be borrowed by a member was ¥20—at that time, almost equal to a worker's monthly income.

Each member was issued a membership card that expired if he did not pay his membership fee for a period of eight months or more; and a member also lost his membership if he disobeyed the constitution or incited other members to make trouble (Wang-an Yi Chi Hui 1925: Articles 9, 17). Membership benefits included (1) the right to borrow money; (2) job placement assistance; (3) burial aid of ¥5;[4] (4) a wedding gift; (5) financial aid at the birth of a son; and (6) sick benefits after two months' illness.

[4]If all the brothers in a family joined the association, burial benefits would be paid not only for themselves, but also for their parents, grandparents, and other close relatives.

The Wang-an Yi Chi Hui no longer exists, although other credit associations organized along similar lines do. Like its four counterparts in Kaohsiung, the Yi Chi Hui eventually merged with the more inclusive P'eng-hu Regional Association—the P'eng-hu T'ing Min Hui.[5] This association now serves as the mutual aid association for all Kaohsiung's P'eng-hu migrants.

*Regional associations.* As noted, the P'eng-hu T'ing Min Hui was established in 1927 to provide Kaohsiung's P'eng-hu migrants with a single organization to help them fight discrimination and obtain jobs. Help in these two areas, of course, was not a pressing need at the outset of P'eng-hu migration to Kaohsiung: the migrants had come to Kaohsiung in direct response to the urgent demand for unskilled laborers. By the mid-1920's, however, increasing numbers of P'eng-hu migrants had improved their financial situation and had begun to enter various kinds of businesses. This naturally placed them in competition with Kaohsiung natives and migrants from other parts of Taiwan, which in turn gave rise to discrimination and even violence.

An additional problem at this time was the attitude of the Japanese police, who often routinely favored Kaohsiung natives in disputes, even when P'eng-hu migrants were clearly in the right. In such circumstances, the migrants needed physical protection, especially since a significant section of their community was no longer young (and physical protection was not something that could be provided by a mutual aid association). Moreover, this problem affected all P'eng-hu migrants without reference to place of origin. Since an effective response did not have to depend on family and community ties (ties that were essential for mutual aid associations), P'eng-hu migrant leaders were able to start an organization for all P'eng-hu migrants. This organization, it was hoped, would not only protect migrants and help raise their social status, but also reduce rivalries and tensions within the migrant community.

The men most active in creating and promoting the P'eng-hu T'ing Min Hui were men who had already achieved positions of considerable influence within Kaohsiung's P'eng-hu migrant community (often as heads of mutual aid associations or as leaders of workers from their home districts). Ch'en Kuang-ts'an, a Kaohsiung busi-

[5] P'eng-hu *hsien* was called P'eng-hu *t'ing* from 1926 to 1945; hence the name P'eng-hu T'ing Min Hui.

nessman and the son of a P'eng-hu migrant, provides a good example. Appointed by the Japanese as a councilman in Kaohsiung *chou* in 1922 (a post he kept until 1944), Ch'en also served as the head of the Wen Wu Sheng Tien. His good relationship with the Japanese, his wealth and business success, and his leadership in the religious association all made him a natural leader for P'eng-hu people in Kaohsiung and thus an influential figure in the founding of the Hui. He became the Hui's first president, and kept this office until 1946. Another influential figure in the founding of the Hui was Wu Ch'ien. Wu came to Kaohsiung in 1904 at the age of 27, and eventually became a manager of a group of harbor construction workers from his native Ma-kung. He earned a high reputation among P'eng-hu migrants by serving his workers not merely as a manager, but as—in effect—a village elder. He became one of the Hui's first vice-presidents as a result.

Four major functions were listed in the first constitution of the Hui, published in 1928: (1) to unite people from P'eng-hu in times of trouble; (2) to provide financial aid for the needy; (3) to eliminate conflicts among the P'eng-hu migrants themselves; and (4) to represent the membership in negotiations with older groups. The last was particularly important, I was told, in migrants' dealings with the Japanese Colonial Government.[6] The association was also to provide nursing for the sick, encourage the increase of knowledge, and establish a moral code—though these aims were subordinate to the first four.

In 1929, the T'ing Min Hui used its funds to build a huge new hall. From 1937 to 1945, however, the Hui temporarily ceased its activities because of the Sino-Japanese War: P'eng-hu migrants feared that the Japanese would charge the Hui with acting against Japanese interests. In 1946, the association resumed its activities and changed its name to the Kaohsiung P'eng-hu T'ung Hsiang Hui (P'eng-hu Regional Association of Kaohsiung). The membership at this time was approximately three hundred. In 1966, the hall was remodeled into the form of a modern movie theater, and the association changed its constitution to provide a more effective administrative structure. Currently, the association has a general assembly with 400 representatives, each representing approximately twenty members. Each

[6]In his study of Chinese migrant communities in Southeast Asia, Willmott concludes that the authority conferred on indigenous Chinese leaders by national or colonial rulers was extremely important in the maintenance of coherent regional associations (1969: 282–301).

TABLE 2
*Age and Sex of Members of Kaohsiung's P'eng-hu Regional Association in 1972*

| | Males | | Females | | Total | |
|---|---|---|---|---|---|---|
| Age bracket | No. | Pct. | No. | Pct. | No. | Pct. |
| 19–29 | 1,280 | 18.4% | 702 | 26.2% | 1,982 | 20.6% |
| 30–39 | 2,066 | 29.7 | 748 | 27.9 | 2,814 | 29.2 |
| 40–49 | 1,694 | 24.4 | 597 | 22.2 | 2,291 | 23.8 |
| 50–59 | 1,082 | 15.6 | 352 | 13.1 | 1,434 | 14.9 |
| 60–69 | 482 | 6.9 | 179 | 6.7 | 661 | 6.8 |
| 70+ | 125 | 1.8 | 75 | 2.8 | 200 | 2.1 |
| Unknown | 222 | 3.2 | 31 | 1.1 | 253 | 2.6 |
| TOTAL | 6,951 | 100.0% | 2,684 | 100.0% | 9,635 | 100.0% |

SOURCE: Data supplied by the Kaohsiung P'eng-hu Regional Association.

basic administrative unit in Kaohsiung has one regional officer, and each basic administrative unit in P'eng-hu has one representative. The assembly elects three of its members as a supervisory committee and nine as an administrative council. The members of the administrative council choose one of their own members to act as the council's president.

Four departments under the administrative council conduct the association's business: the Department of General Affairs, the Department of Education, the Department of Welfare, and the Department of Social Affairs. The last department is the newest, and its major function is to organize P'eng-hu migrants (including nonmembers) during political campaigns. All four of these departments help the Hui render effective services.

Membership in the association is open to adult men and women. The figures in Table 2 indicate that in 1972 women made up nearly a third of the membership and young people from 19 to 29 about a fifth. Nine-tenths of the members were under 60, with the majority distributed evenly through the years of active adulthood. Though such figures tell us little about the degree of members' involvement, they do suggest that young adult members are by no means difficult to enroll.

In 1967, the annual income of the association was NT$815,210 (US$21,453), with funds totaling NT$1,155,456 (US$30,406) at the end of the year. In 1970, the annual income was NT$1,313,724 (US$34,572), with funds totaling NT$3,862,900 (US$101,655) at the end of the year. The association's financial reports for 1967 and 1970 reveal much about how the organization puts its ideals into practice. In 1967, 22 percent of the association's income was paid out for members' welfare,[7] 16 percent was spent on the association's administrative costs, and 62 percent was added to the general fund. In the 1970, only 13 percent was paid out for members' welfare, 16 percent was spent on administrative costs, and 71 percent was added to the general fund.

Why was so little money spent on members' welfare benefits in comparison with the money deposited in the bank and the money spent on administration? We must turn to politics for an answer. In 1967, for instance, many members complained about unnecessary meetings and banquets when a full 5 percent of the association's income was spent on meetings of the executive board. But the board had a clear goal in mind: political victory in the 1968–69 campaign. From the financial report, we can easily see that the main interest of the association was to save money for the general fund. It thus seems likely that the association was trying to create the image of being wealthy to make a political impression on both P'eng-hu migrants and local people.

Such political motives were not factors in the early period of migration. Then, the primary concerns of P'eng-hu migrants in Kaohsiung were job security and improved living conditions. However, in Kaohsiung's 1946 elections for temporary city councilmen and precinct heads, six P'eng-hu migrants were elected. In 1950, new city council elections were held, and in the following year, elections began for provincial councilmen and for mayor: a P'eng-hu migrant was elected the first mayor of Kaohsiung, following the election of eight P'eng-hu migrants to the 28-member city council. Kaohsiung natives, Tainan migrants, and P'eng-hu migrants had become the three major political groups in the city, each group considering the other groups as potential enemies.

At local elections today, these three groups oppose each other strongly. P'eng-hu migrants combine to vote as a "bloc," and it is evident that the T'ung Hsiang Hui plays a very significant role in assuring this. The association supports all candidates from P'eng-hu, regardless of their party affiliation, and takes as its major objective the goal of persuading uncommitted voters to vote for these candidates.

Let us review the history of this political involvement. The years

[7] Money spent under the heading of members' welfare benefits includes money spent on public relations efforts as well as money spent for charity, burial aid, scholarships, and financial aid for weddings.

TABLE 3
*P'eng-hu Migrants on the Kaohsiung City Council, 1951–77*

| Term | Council members | | Percent of seats held by P'eng-hu migrants |
|---|---|---|---|
| | P'eng-hu migrants | Total | |
| 1951–52[a] | 8 | 28 | 29% |
| 1953–54 | 6 | 30 | 20 |
| 1955–57 | 6 | 33 | 18 |
| 1958–60 | 3 | 38 | 8 |
| 1961–63 | 4 | 36 | 11 |
| 1964–67[b] | 6 | 41 | 15 |
| 1968–72 | 7 | 45 | 16 |
| 1973–77 | 7 | 51 | 14 |

SOURCES: Figures supplied by the Kaohsiung P'eng-hu Regional Association and by the Kaohsiung city government.

[a] From 1951–52, the deputy head of the city council was a P'eng-hu migrant. From 1951–54, the mayor was a P'eng-hu migrant.

[b] In 1966, the Regional Association was reformed and its general assembly created. This did not produce a dramatic change in the level of P'eng-hu representation on the city council because of the influx of migrants from other areas of Taiwan into Kaohsiung.

from 1946 to 1956 were the high tide of P'eng-hu migrants' political success in Kaohsiung, a golden period that resulted from the efforts of P'eng-hu migrants to unify their community and to improve their social status. (The P'eng-hu T'ung Hsiang Hui was a product of these efforts.) By contrast, the years from 1956 to 1965, according to my informants, were a period of "low tide." P'eng-hu migrants lost much of their political influence, and many migrant leaders called for a reform of the T'ung Hsiang Hui. My informants explained that the main purpose of this reform—which took place in 1966—was to create an efficient communications channel between the association and its members and thereby regain the unified support of P'eng-hu migrants. Some people who were not from P'eng-hu claimed that the major goal of the reform was to rebuild P'eng-hu political influence within Kaohsiung. In the 1968 election for city councilmen, P'eng-hu migrant leaders did not succeed fully in this goal (assuming it to be their goal), though the results of their campaign were better than the results of their efforts in 1956, 1958, 1961, and 1965. P'eng-hu migrants' participation in the city council is summed up in Table 3.

Migrants with political interests have often sought administrative and executive posts in the regional association. However, this tendency has caused resentment: association members and other P'eng-hu migrants have felt that the association's political activities often serve only the interests of a small group of people (who are usually already wealthy). The majority of members no longer think that the regional association can solve their real problems, which are felt to be largely economic. Such adverse opinion suggests that the association has lost touch with the needs of the majority of its members. This is probably one reason why many P'eng-hu candidates failed to win office in the 1972–73 election—a failure that was an important factor in the founding of a Wisdom and Friendship Club, a new kind of voluntary organization that someday may prove to be as significant for P'eng-hu migrants as the three types of associations analyzed in the preceding pages.[8]

## *Conclusions*

This study has focused on several of the voluntary associations established by P'eng-hu migrants in Kaohsiung as a way of helping them adapt to an alien environment. As one would expect, the changing role of these voluntary associations mirrored the changing nature of P'eng-hu migration to Kaohsiung as well as the changing status of P'eng-hu migrants within Kaohsiung. In the period from 1908 to the close of the Second World War, most P'eng-hu migrants were young men with little formal education who came to Kaohsiung in response to the demand for unskilled laborers. The voluntary associations started by these early migrants reflected their basic needs and were based largely on traditional and P'eng-hu models. Since the end of the War, P'eng-hu migrants have been more heterogeneous (in terms of age, sex, education, and socioeconomic status) than their predecessors, and as a result they have been able to move more quickly into diverse niches in the urban environment. This change along with the improved status of successful members of the early migrant community has strongly affected the development of traditional voluntary associations and led to the creation of new associations suited to new needs—a process that is certain to continue. Indeed, the younger generation and newly arrived migrants at present evince no strong desire to limit their voluntary association membership to a single organization based primarily on local ties and trying to serve a wide range of needs. Instead, they tend to combine mem-

[8] The Wisdom and Friendship Club limits its membership to men between the ages of 20 and 40, and it holds regular monthly meetings. To date, there is not enough information about the club and its activities to permit any detailed analysis. The club's primary purpose, however, appears to be to assist younger P'eng-hu migrants to develop their businesses. Its most striking feature is obviously its age restriction. The club thus contrasts markedly with the regional association, in recent years dominated by older migrants.

bership in the P'eng-hu Regional Association with membership in more narrowly focused voluntary associations—such as sports clubs, school societies, political organizations, and professional groups—that are based on shared enthusiasms, shared ideological viewpoints, and shared professional concerns.

Although this study concerns P'eng-hu migrants in Kaohsiung, its findings can be used to furnish a comparative model for studying internal migration in other societies, Chinese and non-Chinese. More work needs to be done, and many potentially fruitful approaches come to mind. One could focus, for example, on individual adaptation and maladaptation, on migrant fertility patterns, on migrants' influence in their home communities, on migrants who have returned to their home communities, on delinquency among migrants, on the relative effects of poverty and wealth, on occupational adaptation in factories, on the formation of interest groups among first- and second-generation migrants, or on the impact of urban change on migrants and migration.

But as anthropologists continue to investigate these and analogous topics, I hope that they will not lose sight of the fact that they are studying parts of larger cultural wholes. In respect to my own area of interest—the anthropology of Chinese societies—I especially hope that anthropologists will remember that Chinese culture is not tribal, that it is affected by various ideologies both traditional and modern, and that it should be studied within a broad framework incorporating overseas as well as mainland Chinese and traditional as well as nontraditional forms.

# Part Five

# The Family

# Domestic Organization

Arthur P. Wolf

In 1957 I went to Taiwan convinced that there was nothing new to be learned about the Chinese family. Looking back on the work done there over the past twenty years, I now feel that the study of the Chinese family has just begun. It is as though we could not see the complexity of our subject until we were forced to focus our attention on one segment of China's vast landscape.

My task in preparing this paper was very much eased by the recent appearance of Myron Cohen's masterly *House United, House Divided.* By way of a meticulous analysis of family life in Yen-liao, a Hakka village in southern Taiwan, the book disposes of many misunderstandings, sums up Cohen's important contributions to Taiwanese studies, and sets forth a challengingly fresh interpretation of the Chinese family. I will therefore begin my review of the literature with Cohen's book and trace the brief history of our field in reverse order.

In his preface, Cohen tells us that he did not begin to ask the questions his book addresses until he had settled in Yen-liao and "discovered that the so-called 'large,' 'extended,' or 'joint' form of the family was commonplace, to the extent that more than half of the village's population were members of such units" (1976: xiii). Forty years earlier this finding would not have been a "discovery" and would not have stimulated further inquiry. It was assumed that the joint family, or what I prefer to call the grand family, was the typical form throughout China. By 1950, however, it had become "almost customary . . . to begin discussions of the Chinese family system with a round denunciation of the older view that the 'large' or 'joint' family is the typical family of China" (Freedman 1958: 19). Complex families were only to be found in the homes of landlords, great merchants, and officials. The typical farm family consisted of a married couple and their unmarried children. As a result, Cohen was "unprepared for Yen-liao's families; that they even existed was a puzzle, [which] I spent much of my time in the field trying to solve" (1976: xiii).

By the early 1940's, when the families Cohen studied were taking shape, mortality in Taiwan had dropped precipitously but fertility remained as high as ever. Most families raised two or three sons and saw them all survive to marry. Thus, with "at least two men able to go their separate ways, the basic question is why in some families they stay together for longer periods than in others" (Cohen 1976: 230). The originality of Cohen's answer is best seen by contrasting his analysis with that offered by Maurice Freedman (1963 and 1966). In Freedman's view, everything hangs on the ability of the father to exercise his authority as *pater* and *chia-chang* (head of household). The father has, on the one hand, to suppress the rebelliousness of those of his sons who would supersede him, and, on the other, to hold in check the fierce competition of his sons with one another. Large families emerge and endure among the wealthy where the father, politically and economically strong, can dominate his sons; small families are the rule among the poor where weak fathers cannot suppress rebellion or impose domestic peace.

Whereas Freedman assumed that the authority of the father is only dissolved by death, Cohen is of the view that it ends when a son is married. Overtly, and particularly in public, a married son has to defer to his father; but with respect to the most critical of all resources, landed property, he enjoys jural equality with his father. "Each is a coparcener to the estate and can demand its partition" (Cohen 1976: 99). If brothers remain together after they have married, it is not because they are cowed by their father's authority. It is because they see some advantage in pooling their resources. Cohen naturally recognizes the possibility of rivalry among brothers; but he argues that rivalry is consciously suppressed when cooperation is economically advantageous. For Freedman's "competition . . . potentially of a fierce kind" (1966: 46), Cohen substitutes calculated self-interest.

In Freedman's analysis, a strong father attempts to hold in check his rebellious and competitive sons. Whether he succeeds or not depends largely on the extent to which his authority as a father is buttressed by his position in the society at large. In Cohen's revision, the father is reduced to jural equality with his sons and the fraternal relationship loses much of its competitive character. The fate of a family is decided by all of the adult men individually and rationally in search of economic advantage. In Yen-liao, married brothers commonly remain together because they grow tobacco, a labor-intensive crop, or because diversification has created several interdependent family enterprises. In most other areas of China, the sons of farmers go their separate ways within a few years of marriage because there is little opportunity for diversification and their farms are "neither so commercialized nor so demanding in labor as those of the Yen-liao tobacco-growers" (1976: 236).

Having begun with the problem of why Yen-liao's families are so much larger than those of the typical farming community, Cohen concludes by insisting that "the basic uniformity of practices most important for family organization . . . has not been sufficiently emphasized by scholars" (1976: 230). By this he means that differences in family size and complexity cannot be explained with reference to rules, norms, or ideals. Basically, the Chinese family is the same everywhere; all that varies are the conditions that make large families more or less advantageous. If the families of the wealthy are larger than those of the poor, this is not because they are governed by different ideals. It is only because wealth encourages diversification and thereby makes cooperation mutually advantageous.

Three years prior to the publication of Cohen's *House United, House Divided*, another major work appeared—a book greeted as a "splendid study of ancestor worship and lineage organization" (*TLS*, February 22, 1974). I refer, of course, to Emily M. Ahern's *The Cult of the Dead in a Chinese Village*. Superficially, the two books appear to have little in common: one deals with family economy, the other with domestic worship. In fact, they develop the same theme, demonstrating once again that ancestor worship is but another aspect of family organization. When Cohen insists that "it was crucial to *chia* [family] organization that ties between persons were associated with common ties to an estate" (1976: 231), he is applying to the living a point that Ahern had already made in discussing the dead. In her study of Ch'i-nan, a Hokkien village in northern Taiwan, Ahern demonstrates that we must overcome "the common conception that ancestor worship among the Chinese is essentially a matter of obligations between agnates created by descent" (1973: 154). The man who leaves no estate is not honored with a seat on his ancestral altar and cannot expect to receive offerings from all of his children and grandchildren. It is only when the living receive property that they are absolutely obligated to provide for the welfare of the dead. "In every other situation, there is room for interpretation, contention, and debate" (*ibid.*: 155).

Ahern and Cohen agree that Chinese domestic relationships can only be understood with reference to property rights, but they sharply disagree about how these rights are passed from one generation to the next. Cohen insists that a married man stands as his father's jural equal and can demand division of the estate. Ahern tells us that she found "a very strong feeling against sons' dividing the property of their father before his death" (1973: 196). After he marries, a young man and his wife may provide themselves with their own stove and eat separately, but "the land . . . is still legally owned by the father and is not divided until his death. . . . When I asked why sons do not divide the land before their father's death, I was told, 'The land belongs to the father and mother; how can the sons take it away from them?'" (*Ibid.*: 196–97.)

Do rights that pass at marriage in one village remain with a father until death in another? If so, are these differences characteristic of the north as against the south, Hakka as against Hokkien, or what? These questions are intriguing and become all the more so when one reads Ahern's account of Ch'i-nan ancestors. Those ancestors do not fit Freedman's characterization of Chinese ancestors as "essentially benign and considerate of their issue" (1967: 93); instead, they are "fierce, often capricious, and occasionally malicious" (Ahern 1973: 203). Moreover, there is evidence that in the eyes of their descendants the Ch'i-nan dead are extremely reluctant to give up their authority and never relinquish all of it. Are these harsh and demanding ancestors a product of the senior generation's control of property? Does a son's impatience make his father appear larger and more authoritarian the longer he lives? A careful comparison of Ch'i-nan and Yen-liao could provide a clear answer.

By now the reader will understand the spirit of my opening paragraph. When I wrote that "the study of the Chinese family has just begun," I did not intend to deprecate the work of the 1920's, 1930's, and 1940's. My point was rather that whereas twenty years ago there appeared to be little need for yet another study of the Chinese family, it now appears that there is more need for such studies than there are qualified people to carry them out. Taiwan has provided us with new data, new questions, and a new vitality.

We come now, in our backward track through time, to Burton Pasternak's 1972 *Kinship and Community in Two Chinese Villages*. In addition to the contribution it makes to a wide range of substantive questions, this book stands as a model for future field studies. Anthropologists have long held that field studies as well as library research ought to be comparative. Pasternak is one of the few to have put this ideal into practice. *Kinship and Community* provides a systematic comparison of Ta-t'ieh, a Hakka village in Ping-tung *hsien*, and Chung-she, a Hokkien village near Chia-i. The book focuses on community integration and particularly on the integrative role of agnatic ties, but it has much to offer those whose primary interest is domestic institutions. Pasternak's discussion of uxorilocal marriages illustrates the very diverse character of Taiwanese villages and at the same time suggests a way of explaining this diversity.

Prior to the completion of the Chia-nan Irrigation Project in 1930, uxorilocal marriages accounted for approximately 40 percent of all first marriages in Chung-she.[1] After that, the frequency declined sharply to something less than 15 percent. In Ta-t'ieh, uxorilocal marriages appear to have been "a rarity" from at least the turn of the century. Why did the frequency of uxorilocal marriages in Chung-she decline so rapidly after 1930? And why was this form of marriage common in one community and rare in the other? The answer Pasternak gives suggests that in some contexts Chinese domestic institutions are like a box of tools. People use those that suit the job at hand but do not discard the others. In both Ta-t'ieh and Chung-she, uxorilocal marriages were sometimes used to preserve lines when there were daughters but no sons. In Chung-she, however, this form of marriage appears to have served an additional purpose. Before the Chia-nan irrigation system provided Chung-she's farmers with an adequate, controlled water supply, the farmers were largely dependent on rainfall, wryly referring to their fields as *k'an-t'ien t'ien*—"fields that depend on the heavens." One consequence of this circumstance was that "farm families had to be largely self-sufficient with respect to labor; when it rained, all hands were needed at the same time for work on the family holdings" (Pasternak 1972: 48).

[1]The precise figures are given in Table 1. They are drawn from my analysis of Chung-she's household registers but agree closely with the estimates given by Pasternak.

Often the result was that even when a family had a son of their own, they were forced to arrange an uxorilocal marriage for a daughter as a means of supplementing an inadequate labor force. In Ta-t'ieh this was not necessary because a developed irrigation system allowed farmers to stagger major agricultural tasks and exchange labor.

In Pasternak's analysis, the shape of Chinese families is primarily determined by external forces—by the economy, by physical facilities like irrigation systems, and by the government. Another book published the same year as *Kinship and Community* takes a very different view of the matter. In *Women and the Family in Rural Taiwan*, Margery Wolf argues persuasively that like any living thing the Chinese family is as much a product of what goes on within it as what happens outside it. Though not presented in these terms, her thesis can be read as a response to a point made by Maurice Freedman in introducing *The House of Lim*. In that book, Margery Wolf suggested that the solidarity expected of brothers in China is seldom achieved because of the quarrelsomeness of their wives. Freedman noted these remarks and wrote: "I should suggest (without foisting my opinion on Mrs. Wolf) that, while the quarrels precipitated by women are often seen as the major causes of the disruption of Chinese families, it is to the brittle relationship between brothers that we must look for an understanding of why, in spite of the great pride taken in large families, they are nonetheless very rare" (M. Wolf 1968: xiv–xv).

The argument developed in *Women and the Family* proceeds from the assumption that women, like men, want to control their own lives and the lives of others. The difference is that whereas men depend on authority and property rights, women are forced by their status as women to make what they can of their relationships with their children. Taking advantage of their roles as mothers, they forge the solidary group Wolf refers to as the uterine family. This family "has no ideology, no formal structure, and no public existence. It is built out of sentiments and loyalties that die with its members, but it is no less real for all that." (1972: 37.) When this group's interests or its integrity are threatened by other members of the larger household, the woman whose security it represents responds as fiercely as the man whose property rights are transgressed. If the threat comes from a sister-in-law or brother-in-law, the woman reacts by trying to draw her husband out of the family. If the danger comes from a daughter-in-law, she looks for faults that will give her an opportunity to assert her authority. In either case, quarrels that have little to do with the interests of male family members can escalate and eventually force a division of the family. In Wolf's view, the "pillow ghost" (i.e., the self-serving wife) is not a chauvinistic myth. It is a frightful representation of the forces that destroy most joint families.

In Freedman's view, the "quarrelsomeness of Chinese women" is "a reflex of their position as the representatives of their husbands in inner-domestic life" (1963: 98). Wolf agrees that Chinese women are quarrelsome but insists that they fight on their own account and to achieve their own goals. Why this difference matters and deserves further attention will be apparent to anyone who studies Cohen's *House United, House Divided*. Cohen first notes that "in Yen-liao it is almost inevitable for persons of either sex to blame women for the domestic discord that causes the partition of families" (1976: 196), then argues that the prominence of women in family conflicts "in fact testifies to the inability of women to threaten family unity." "Women are accused of harboring a mutual antipathy which threatens the relationship between the men when it is the men who by keeping the family together set the women against each other" (*ibid.*: 201). Are women inconsequential? Is the shape of the Chinese family nothing more than a representation of the interests of men? Is the native view that attributes family division to women merely a myth? These are some of the questions I had in mind in suggesting that research on Taiwan has revitalized an old topic.

The last book I wish to discuss is Bernard Gallin's 1966 study, *Hsin Hsing, Taiwan: A Chinese Village in Change*. This was the first study of a Taiwanese community to be published in English, but that is not the only reason it commands our attention. Again and again, Gallin's observations, modestly offered, have been confirmed by later research. I think, for example, of his discussion of minor marriages[2] and the reason for their decline, of his interest in the significance of affinal ties, and of his passing comment on women and private property in joint families. There is, however, one aspect of Gallin's work that we have largely ignored. In preparing this paper, I was struck by the fact that Gallin's book is still the only major work addressed to the problem of social change. The rest of us write as though the so-

[2] What I term minor marriages were very common in some parts of China, particularly northern Taiwan, southern Kiangsi, and Fukien. A woman who married in this fashion was removed from her natal family as an infant or small child and raised by her future husband's parents, the result being that husband and wife grew up under conditions as intimate as those experienced by siblings. For further details, see Wolf 1974.

ciety under scrutiny came to a dead halt about midway through our first field study. When we return to the field, we go back to our aging informants and take up where we left off. If we do not actively regret what has happened in the meantime, we at least ignore it, with the result that some of us are in danger of becoming historians without ever having taken an active interest in the subject. Perhaps it is time that we followed Gallin's lead in this matter as we have in others, even if it means leaving the comfortable countryside for the bleak reality of Taipei or Kaohsiung.

Since my concern in this paper is less with what we know about the Chinese family than with what we make of what we know, I will not attempt to push this brief review of major works back into the Japanese period. Important as the work of Japanese scholars is to those who are interested in reconstructing Taiwanese society in the first half of this century, the questions asked by such men as Okada Yuzuru (1949) and Ikeda Toshio (1944) are no longer of interest. They have been either answered or reformulated in a new idiom. However, I would neglect the most important part of my subject if I did not say something about three widely read though still unpublished works: Wang Sung-hsing's "Pooling and Sharing in a Chinese Fishing Economy: Kuei-shan Tao," Sung Lung-sheng's "Inheritance and Kinship in North Taiwan," and Sophie Sa's "Family and Community in Urban Taiwan: Social Status and Demographic Strategy among Taipei Households, 1885–1935."

Wang's "Pooling and Sharing" may well be the most important anthropological work from the pen of a Chinese scholar since Fei Hsiao-tung's classic *Peasant Life in China*. All I can do here is note one aspect of Wang's richly detailed account of life in Kuei-shan. In Yen-liao, Cohen found that a labor-intensive crop makes it economically advantageous for married men to swallow their differences and pool their resources. Wang, however, shows us that in Kuei-shan precisely the opposite situation holds. The mobility required by seasonal changes in the organization of fishing teams makes it impossible for large families to work together as units. Under these conditions, sons set up separate households as soon as they marry. This would be an important finding in any case, but it takes on a special significance when Wang also shows us that though the families of fishermen are smaller than those of farmers, they are governed by the same principles. Descent passes from father to son; brothers take equal shares out of their father's estate; and people provide regular offerings for their lineal agnatic ascendants. To me this suggests that in the realm of kinship, rigidity of principle is entirely compatible with flexibility of organization.

Sung's "Inheritance and Kinship" marks a clear departure in the methodology of field studies in Taiwan. Rather than examining a community at a point in time, Sung traces a small number of families from the 1770's and 1790's (when they arrived in Taiwan) to the early 1970's. This unusual perspective brings out a number of interesting points, including the very important distinction between the property a man inherits and the property he acquires through his own and his sons' efforts. With the exception of a small share granted the son of the eldest son, inherited property is always divided equally among brothers. Acquired property, by contrast, is divided according to individual effort. This distinction is important for many reasons (as Sung demonstrates in his contribution to this volume), not the least of which is the suggestion that the power of a Chinese father has been highly variable insofar as it has depended on his control of landed property. At one extreme have been men whose estates have consisted solely of land acquired through their own efforts. These men have enjoyed personal control of their property and could, if necessary, threaten to disinherit a rebellious descendant. At the opposite extreme have been men whose property has been purchased with money earned by their sons. Their position has been weak because their sons have been partners with the right to demand division at any time. And finally, intermediate between these two, have been men whose estates have consisted of land inherited from their own fathers. As trustees of estates owned by corporate descent groups, these men have not been as strong as men who have been sole owners, but they have been much stronger than men whose land has been acquired by sons. Strong fathers, harsh ancestors, and large families may go with one kind of estate; weak fathers, mild ancestors, and small families with another.

Sophie Sa's "Family and Community in Urban Taiwan" is unique, but one hopes that it will not long remain so. It demonstrates how much an anthropologist can learn by taking history seriously and by comparing the practices (rather than the ideas) of an elite with those of common men. The study consists of a meticulous comparison of the changing marriage and adoption strategies of 483 families chosen to represent an urban elite of officials and wealthy merchants, a middle class of shopkeepers, businessmen, and teachers, and a lower class of manual laborers, street vendors, and rickshaw drivers. Since I cannot do more than provide an example of Sa's many findings, I will choose the one that interests me most. In my own work with the source used by Sa—Japanese household registers—I found that at the turn of the century many farm families in the Taipei area chose to raise their sons' wives. Of a total of 1,491 women born in Hai-shan in the years 1891–1910,[3] 41.4 percent made what I term a minor marriage. Does this mean that these families were impoverished? Did they choose the minor form of marriage because they could not afford the bride price and the festivities required by a major marriage (i.e., a marriage involving a woman who joins her husband's family as a young adult)? In part, yes. But Sa's data from Taipei suggest that there was an additional motive. Minor marriages were less common in the city than in the country; yet this form of marriage was chosen by wealthy merchants and comfortable shopkeepers almost as often as it was chosen by laborers and street vendors. Minor marriages accounted for 23.1 percent of 216 lower-class marriages, 18.8 percent of 287 middle-class marriages, and 11.0 percent of 317 upper-class marriages (Sa 1975: 208). Sa reports minor marriages even at the very top of the social hierarchy. My guess is that families who could easily afford a major marriage sometimes chose to raise a son's wife because it was easier to educate a child than reeducate a young adult. A daughter-in-law reared from infancy could be taught to accept her mother-in-law's authority and thus did not urge family division as a way of escaping that authority.

I would confine this review to the work of professional anthropologists were it not that the decision would force me to ignore an important series of papers by Nancy Olsen. The first examines the relationship between family structure and the way that independence is inculcated in children in Pei-ho-tien, the village in northern Taiwan familiar to many as the home of the Lims. Olsen shows that women who live apart from their mothers-in-law demand more independence of their small children than do women who live with their mothers-in-law. Since the presence of adolescent daughters does not affect a woman's attitude toward independence training, this dif-

[3] I use the old place name Hai-shan to refer to the southwestern corner of the Taipei Basin, specifically to Pan-ch'iao *chen*, Shu-lin *chen*, San-hsia *chen*, Ying-ko *chen*, and T'u-ch'eng *hsiang*.

ference cannot be attributed to a tendency to indulge children when there are adults to do the work. In Olsen's view, it is more likely that the explanation is to be "found in the conflict which is a very characteristic feature of the relationship between mother-in-law and daughter-in-law in Taiwan. [Margery] Wolf has observed that one outcome of this conflict may be competition for the affection and loyalty of children. Doing things for the children and keeping them dependent on her are certainly among the tactics that a mother might employ in this context." (1973: 518.)

Anthropologists who suffer acute psychophobia as a result of an early experience with the culture and personality school need not avoid Olsen's work. Far from attempting to explain society as the product of child-training practices, she examines child training in terms of ideas drawn from the study of class relations. In her second paper, she argues that the position of a young mother in an extended family is analogous to that of a working-class man employed in a large factory. "In both cases, rewards are contingent upon following the directions of one's superiors, rather than upon organizing and carrying out work on one's own" (1974: 1396). Olsen therefore predicts—and in fact finds—that "mothers in three-generation households . . . resemble working-class men in the high value they place upon conformity and obedience in children, while mothers in nuclear families . . . place more emphasis on autonomy and self-reliance" (*ibid.*: 1396).

In her third paper, Olsen compares the child-training practices of four groups of women. These women were chosen to represent upper-, middle-, and working-class families in Taipei, and farm families in a village in Chang-hua *hsien*. Accustomed as we are to attributing much of the variation we find in China to social class, we are not surprised to learn that Olsen finds clear differences among these four groups. High-status urban women emphasize self-reliance and employ "love-oriented" forms of discipline; low-status women and rural women emphasize conformity and control of aggression and favor "power-assertive" disciplinary measures. The surprise is that though this apparently class-based difference in behavior patterns holds for both modern and traditional women, the difference is largely eliminated if one groups the women according to their level of education (1975: 672). Since Olsen takes as her measure of class standing the occupation of the head of each household, her finding suggests that occupation alone does not affect child-training practices and that wealth and social status may not either, at least directly. Perhaps, then, we need to look more closely at the presumed differences in the family life of farm laborers, tenant farmers, country landlords, and great merchants. The well-known differences in family size may have led us to infer too much.

I turn now from particular studies of family life in Taiwan to look at some of the characteristics these studies share. The most obvious is the heavy emphasis placed on property rights. Ahern makes inheritance the basis of ancestor worship; Cohen argues that "it was crucial to *chia* organization that ties between persons were associated with common ties to an estate" (1976: 231); and Sung finds unforeseen complexity in the rules governing the division of landed property. All three scholars raise questions that must be pursued, but the answers will not mark an end to this line of inquiry. So far most Taiwan researchers have viewed property from a jural perspective. Little attention has been paid to the relationship between family organization and the timing, frequency, and direction of property transactions. This is all the more a shame in light of the opportunity afforded by Taiwan's magnificent household registers and unusually detailed land records.

To make my point, I have reconstructed from these records the history of what I call the Ong family. On December 15, 1905, when the household registers were instituted in the Ong's home village, the family was as shown in Figure 1. In the course of the next twenty years, their membership grew from 22 persons to 40 persons as I, J, K, O, P, and T all married and fathered children. At the same time, purchases of property in 1907, 1908, 1909, 1913, and 1915 greatly enlarged the family estate from a total taxable value of ¥83.69 in 1905 (including paddy, upland, and house sites) to a total of ¥131.30 in 1924. Then on August 20, 1924, the elderly matriarch, A, died at 77 years of age. Seven months later, on March 18, 1925, the family segmented. The senior branch received a share valued at ¥35.70, while the three junior branches headed by C, E, and G received shares valued at ¥31.59, ¥38.52, and ¥25.13, respectively.

Before the year was out J and K had sold their shares in four separate transactions; in 1929 their elder brother, I, sold a large portion of his inheritance; and in 1928 and 1932 the head of the fourth branch of the family, G, sold first part, then all, of his estate and moved away. Only C and E managed to retain all the property they

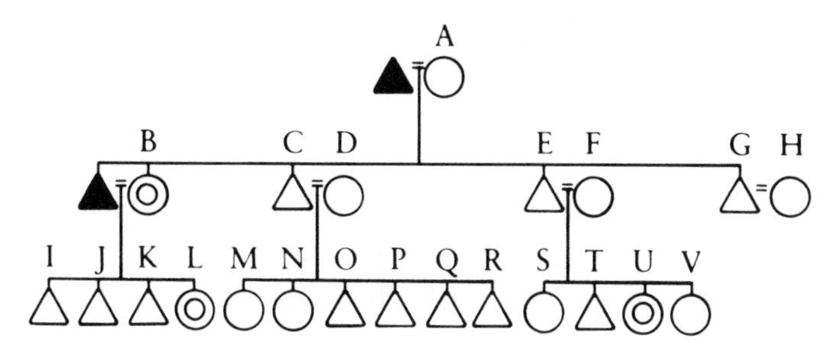


FIG. 1. The Ong family in December 1905. (B, L, and U are adopted daughters.)

took out of the original estate; and only C was able to increase the size of his farm. He and his sons purchased land in 1934 and 1939 to bring the total taxable value of their estate to ¥46.03.

It is my impression that the high frequency of land transactions by the Ong family—seven purchases and seven sales in forty years—was not unusual. Estates were not enduring entities, passed on intact from generation to generation. They expanded and contracted in sympathy with the growth and decline of the families that owned them. What, then, was the link between family and estate? What enabled growing families to purchase land? And what forced declining families to sell? The history of the Ong family suggests that for farmers the critical variable was the size of their domestic labor force. In 1905, the Ong family had only four able-bodied males. During the course of the next twenty years, they added nine men to their labor force and nearly doubled the size of their estate. Then in 1925, the family division partitioned the labor force into six very unequal units. The segments headed by I, J, K, and G had one adult male each; the segment headed by E had three adult males; and the segment headed by C had six adult males. Within a few years, I, J, K, and G had sold most of their land; E held onto all of the land he inherited but did not purchase additional land; only C, with five adult sons, was able to regain the momentum lost in the process of division.

Putting land records together with household registers, one can determine the social relationships involved in land transactions as well as their frequency and value. We learn that four of the Ongs' five purchases were from agnates and that six of their seven sales were to agnates. Since the Ong lineage was neither large nor isolated, such a high frequency of transactions within the lineage suggests a circumscribed land market. Members of the lineage must have enjoyed rights of first refusal with respect to one another's property. What emerges, then, from this brief excursion into the archives is a picture of a community in which land changed hands frequently but within a limited social sphere. Were communities of this kind common? Was the frequency of land transactions as high elsewhere as it appears to have been among the Ongs? Did a high frequency favor a more or less equitable distribution of land? Did these transactions occur because no family could maintain a large labor force for long? These are only a sample of the many questions for which there are answers in Taiwan's wonderful records.

A second characteristic of recent Taiwan research taken as a whole is a new interest in social class and a new view of class differentiation. Cohen is the only author to argue that in the family life of "dirt farmers" and the "traditional elite," "we see one system in operation" (1976: 237). But the same conclusion could be drawn from Sa's work with marriage or from Olsen's study of child-training practices. They too find that the distance between classes is not as great as it was once assumed to be. What makes this so interesting is that as research has narrowed the gap between social classes, it has lengthened the distance between communities. Ahern and Cohen report profoundly different attitudes toward parental authority and inheritance in Ch'i-nan and Yen-liao, and Pasternak makes the differences between Chung-she and Ta-t'ieh the subject of a book-length study. I am now convinced that class differences did not emerge as the fundamental dimension of Taiwanese society until after 1930. Before that, regional differences were more profound than class differences.

Allow me to provide one bit of support for what the reader may regard as an extreme position. In her study of marriage and adoption in Taipei, Sa compares three groups of families, two of which were chosen to represent the top and bottom rungs of the social ladder. Most of her upper-class families were prominent and powerful, the elite of the capital city and hence of Taiwan. Her lower-class families supplied coolies, street vendors, and rickshaw drivers. My conviction that class did not differentiate social groups as profoundly as region came when I placed Sa's comparison of the first marriages of these two classes next to a table I had made to compare Yen-liao, Chung-she, and Hai-shan. I found (see Table 1) that regardless of whether one made the comparison in terms of the frequency of major, minor,

TABLE 1
*Relative Frequency of Major, Minor, and Uxorilocal Marriages in Three Communities and in Three Classes*

| Location/class | N | Type of marriage | | |
|---|---|---|---|---|
| | | Major | Minor | Uxorilocal |
| Community comparisons[a] | | | | |
| Yen-liao | 90 | 96.7% | 1.1% | 2.2% |
| Chung-she | 71 | 46.5 | 14.1 | 39.4 |
| Hai-shan | 1,491 | 43.2 | 41.4 | 15.4 |
| Class comparisons[b] | | | | |
| Upper | 317 | 87.7 | 11.0 | 1.3 |
| Middle | 287 | 70.4 | 18.8 | 10.8 |
| Lower | 216 | 61.6 | 23.1 | 15.3 |

SOURCES: Cohen 1976: 32–34; Sa 1975: 208; Wolf & Huang 1980: 125, 318.

[a] All three sets of figures refer to the marriages of women born in the years 1891–1910. The figures for Chung-she and Hai-shan are based on household registers and are as accurate as can be obtained. Those for Yen-liao are estimates but cannot err by more than a few percent. See Cohen 1976: 32–34.

[b] Sa's figures for Taipei classes refer to marriages occurring as early as 1876 and as late as 1945, but the great majority are for marriages occurring in the years 1886–1925. Thus, the figures refer to approximately the same period as the figures for the three communities.

or uxorilocal marriages, the range of the variation across communities was twice the range of the variation across social classes.[4] On the question of how their sons were to marry, the Taipei merchant and the Taipei coolie were far more likely to agree than the Yen-liao farmer and the Hai-shan farmer.

Recognition of Taiwan's regional variation helps solve some puzzles. For example, after noting that in the early years of this century fertility was considerably higher in the south than in the north, George Barclay comments: "This is surprising to find, especially since Taiwan is small in size and new in its settlement, and Taiwanese displayed little variation in demographic characteristics among prefectures. One would not expect to find 'regional' differences, which would most likely stem from long tradition and established usage. Yet this pattern was present, and lacks any apparent reason to explain it." (1954: 252.) Putting the evidence I have collected together with that provided by Okada (1949) and Kajiwara (1941), I have lit-

[4] At the Wentworth conference, this conclusion was challenged on the grounds that the comparison of communities does not take social class into account. It was suggested that the differences among the three communities might reflect class rather than locale. I reject this argument for two reasons. First, the ethnography leaves no doubt but that the residents of all three communities were farmers and that the distribution of wealthy and poor farmers did not differ strikingly. Second, were we to attribute the greater part of the community differences to social class, we would be forced to the patently ridiculous conclusion that, as regards social precedence, the farmers of Yen-liao, Chung-she, and Hai-shan were separated by a gulf wider than that separating the urban elite from the men who pulled their rickshaws.

tle doubt but that minor marriages accounted for something more than 40 percent of all first marriages in northern Taiwan. The situation in the south is less clear, but the best evidence we have (presented in Table 1) suggests a frequency of not more than 10 percent. Given, then, that the fertility of minor marriages was 25 percent less than the fertility of major and uxorilocal marriages (A. Wolf: 1975, 1976), the solution to Barclay's puzzle is obvious. There were more births in the south because there were fewer "little daughters-in-law."

But the problems solved when one sees the significance of regional variation look like molehills compared to the mountains that then appear on the horizon. One can only agree with Barclay when he argues that marked regional differences are not likely on an island as small and as recently settled as Taiwan. Yet the differences are there, and the anthropologist must ask why. Why was parental authority firmer in Ch'i-nan than in Yen-liao? Why were uxorilocal marriages rare in Ta-t'ieh but commonplace in Chung-she? Why was the frequency of minor marriages so much higher in the north than in the south? Put in an historical perspective, the questions we face are clearer but no less daunting. During the past several years, Huang Chieh-shan and I have spent considerable time collecting information about the relative frequency of major, minor, and uxorilocal marriages on mainland China. Since we view Taiwan from a northern perspective, we were not surprised to find that minor marriages were a common feature of family life in southern Fukien, the homeland of Taiwan's Hokkien-speaking majority. For us the surprise came when we discovered that minor marriages were even more important in the Hakka districts of southern Kiangsi and northern Kwangtung. Late Ch'ing and early Communist sources agree in estimating the frequency of such marriages at somewhere between 60 and 80 percent of all first marriages.[5]

We know that during the early years of this century minor marriages constituted 40 percent of first marriages in Hokkien-speaking villages in northern Taiwan; less than 15 percent in Chung-she, a Hokkien-speaking village in southern Taiwan; and no more than 1 or 2 percent in Yen-liao, a Hakka-speaking village in southern Taiwan. We also know that during these same years minor marriages ac-

[5] The evidence for this statement is too unwieldy to present here. It is presented in Wolf & Huang 1980.

counted for approximately 33 percent of all first marriages in the Hokkien areas of southern Fukien and something like 67 percent of all first marriages in the Hakka areas of Kiangsi and Kwangtung. Thus, there is no escape from the conclusion that the marriage customs of some of these groups changed radically in the space of less than two hundred years. In the case of the Hakka, there could have been a sharp rise in the frequency of minor marriages on the mainland or a sharp decline in the frequency of minor marriages among the immigrants to Taiwan; in the case of the Hokkien, there could have been a rise in the frequency of minor marriages on the mainland and in northern Taiwan, or, what is more likely, a decline in the frequency of minor marriages among those immigrants who settled in Chung-she. Present evidence does not allow us to decide between these possibilities, but it leaves no doubt that there was a dramatic change.

This brings me to the last point I have to make concerning the accomplishments of Taiwanese research on the family. Beginning with Gallin's discussion of social change in Hsin Hsing, one sees an ever-increasing emphasis on the basic uniformity of Chinese domestic institutions. This assumption is strong in Pasternak's *Kinship and Community* and is made explicit by Cohen when he chides us for not paying sufficient attention to what he terms "the basic uniformity of practices most important for family organization." Had each new field study turned up yet another Hsin Hsing, this trend would not be very surprising or very interesting. The fact is, however, that from my own research onwards, every study has found some new combination of family size, marriage forms, inheritance rules, or ritual usages. The discovery of a basic uniformity has occurred in the midst of a surge of evidence reporting unimagined diversity. What I take this to mean is that Chinese domestic institutions are extraordinarily flexible. A few basic ideas provide coherence and continuity without interfering with people's ability to adapt to a wide variety of situations.

Assuming that this view of the Chinese family is approximately correct, we are left wondering how such a combination of uniform ideas and diverse behavior could long endure. In many Taiwanese communities, the frequency of major marriages fell below 50 percent and stayed there for at least five generations. Even the elite of these communities did not always marry their sons in the major fashion. How did the idea that major marriage is the right and proper way to marry survive the pull of precedent? Wang Sung-hsing shows us that in some fishing villages sons hived off to establish independent households as they married. How did these communities preserve the rules that Myron Cohen finds at the basis of joint family organization? In a word, we must now ask how Chinese culture survived in Chinese society.

I will conclude with three recommendations. The first is the familiar plea for more historical studies. If we are to understand the present development of the Chinese family in Taiwan, we need to know more about the family under the Japanese; and if we are to understand the family under the Japanese, we need a clearer picture of the family in the nineteenth century. Perhaps an example will convince the reader that more history means better anthropology. During the Japanese period, the average age at which girls were adopted for minor marriages was nine months. Since there is strong evidence that early and intimate childhood association arouses an aversion to sexual relations, I once assumed that the rapid decline of minor marriages after 1930 was primarily the result of social and economic changes set in motion by the Japanese: given opportunities for wage employment in new industries, young people revolted against a particularly distasteful manifestation of parental authority. Recently, new evidence from the household registers has forced me to reconsider. I discovered that prior to 1890 the average age at adoption was two or three years and that in the 1860's and 1870's it was seven or eight years. Given, then, that couples who are not brought together until after five years of age do not experience strong sexual aversion, it could be that the revolt of the 1930's was a result of the pressures generated by the decline in the age of adoption rather than a result of the changes brought about by the Japanese. Perhaps the tendency toward earlier and earlier adoption would have brought the system to disaster without Japanese intervention.

My second recommendation is that if we must choose between empirical elegance and grand theory, we should choose the former. Again my point is best made by way of an example. In Myron Cohen's view, the transition from stem to joint family "brings changes . . . such that tensions in the husband-wife relationship are now encouraged" (1976: 235). In essence, the reason for this is that in the joint family fraternal solidarity must take precedence over conjugal solidarity. For Margery Wolf, the critical transition is from stem or joint family to elementary family. In her view, the force that pulls a man away from his wife is his mother, not his brother. By generalizing from these authors' views on other subjects, it would be easy to turn this difference into a grand confrontation between androcentric and gynecocentric theories or, worse, between theories of "techno-environmental-determinism" and psychology. What is needed is empirical confrontation, not verbal confrontation. For Cohen, the critical contrast is between joint families and elementary and stem families; for Wolf, it is between elementary families and stem and joint families. Let us assume that fertility will be higher where the conjugal relationship is relaxed than it is where the conjugal relationship is tense. We can then put the question to a test by comparing the total marital fertility[6] of women in elementary, stem, and joint families. The result for a large sample of women in Hai-shan is an average of 7.83 children for elementary families, 6.51 for stem families, and 6.59 for joint families.[7] The evidence is not definitive, but it certainly favors Wolf's position over Cohen's. The next step would be to repeat the test with data for Yen-liao. It could be that the differences between Wolf's and Cohen's positions reflect regional differences in family life rather than different views of human behavior.

My third recommendation concerns the need for comprehensive and hence long-term studies. Once again, I turn to an example—in this case, to illustrate why it is extremely difficult to arrive at sound conclusions on the basis of one or two years of work. On my first field trip to Hai-shan, I discovered that among women married prior to 1930 minor marriages were almost as frequent as major marriages. From this I concluded that the two forms of marriage—however different—were equally attractive. I was of course assuming, without ever thinking about it, that if a family married their son in the major fashion, they had chosen this fashion of marriage. It was not until fifteen years later that I discovered my error. On analyzing the frequency of the various forms of female adoption, I found that 30 percent of all female children were retained by their natal families as insurance against not bearing sons, and another 30 percent were adopted by childless families in the hope that the adopted daughter would "lead in a younger brother." Only then did I realize that the

[6] Total marital fertility is obtained by summing age-specific marital fertility rates. This figure represents the number of children a woman would bear if she married at the age of 15 and survived through age 45, bearing at each stage of life the average of the number of children borne by her peers.

[7] These figures are based on a sample of 689 women born in Hai-shan in the years 1891–1900.

frequency of minor marriages was controlled by the supply of female children available for adoption. Because that supply was limited, many families did not have a choice. Hence, the relative frequency of the two forms of marriage did not say anything about people's preferences. The point is familiar but worth repeating. One cannot accurately interpret the parts of a system until one understands the system.

I will close with one remark concerning the problems of future research. Surveying the history of the Chinese family in Taiwan, we now see marked diversity but suspect that underneath it all there were shared principles. Increasingly, then, Taiwan's recent past is seen to have been a good deal more homogeneous than early observers understood it to be. But history has recapitulated this movement: Taiwan has in fact become far more homogeneous than it once was. If those of us who look back from this point have to find out what held a heterogeneous society together, those of us who look forward may need to ask what holds a homogeneous society together. In the past, diversity concealed a more fundamental uniformity; in the future, this circumstance may be reversed.

# Property and Family Division

Lung-sheng Sung

The family, or *ke*, is the fundamental social unit in Chinese society.[1] In the rural areas of northern Taiwan, the family is a corporate body, forming an independent property-owning group: its members, sharing a common economy and a common budget, have exclusive (though not always identical) rights of inheritance. The composition of a family varies according to its phase in the developmental cycle, its estate arrangements, and its economic situation.

The Taiwanese distinguish two critical phases in the developmental cycle: *pun-ke* (family division) and *ke-sieng* (inheritance). Although these phases represent distinct socioeconomic activities, they are sometimes coterminous. *Pun-ke* can occur under several circumstances: when a family rearranges its social and productive activities, when younger sons marry, when family members squabble, when the head of the family dies, or when a brother takes a job in another town. In each of these cases, brothers have a right to ask for a division of the family. Thus *pun-ke* may take place before or after the death of the father, since it is a matter of rearranging family life for social and economic purposes in such a way that the independence of each family subunit (*pang-thau*)[2] and its members is increased. At the time of *pun-ke*, inherited property is divided equally among agnates, and acquired property is divided equally among all family

[1]For romanizing Hokkien words and names, I follow the system outlined in Bodman 1955.

[2]In the Shu-lin area of the Taipei Basin, the composition of a family varies at different stages in its development. Daughters normally marry out, whereas sons, provided with wives, continue their membership in the original family group. Ideally, a fully developed extended family consists of a family head (usually the senior male member of the family), his wife, their unmarried children, their married sons, and their married sons' wives and children. I refer to a married son and his wife and children within an undivided family as a *pang-thau*.

members. The principle of equal division among the eligible applies to both kinds of property and is assured by the supervision of relatives and village leaders. Generally, the division is worked out through a lottery to make certain of fairness. After the division, each son establishes a separate stove for his own household. If the parents are still living, the sons reserve some fields for their use, pay them a regular income of money and food, or take turns inviting them to live in their own newly independent households.

In contrast to *pun-ke*, *ke-sieng* can only occur at the death of the family head, who is usually the senior male member of the family group. *Ke-sieng* is thus a matter of succession involving the transfer of certain rights and duties (including obligations of ancestor worship) from a deceased senior family member to a junior family member or members.

This paper is concerned with the interrelationships between forms of ownership, the domestic cycle, and descent among Chinese living in the Taipei Basin in northern Taiwan. My thesis is simply that certain aspects of Chinese family life can be clarified by recognizing that Chinese customary law distinguishes two forms of ownership. My argument is based on an examination of land records and on fieldwork conducted among farmers living in the rural area around the town of Shu-lin.

## *The Family*

Traditionally, scholars have used residence to define four types of families in China: elementary or nuclear families, joint families, stem families, and fraternal joint families. Much early research on the Chinese family concerned the relative frequency of these types—the consensus being that joint and fraternal joint families were in a minority (Lang 1946). Unfortunately, the bare frequency of these family types tells us little about the dynamics of kinship, inheritance, or even marriage. More recent studies have described the developmental cycle of the domestic family (Freedman 1958, 1963, 1966) and studied its workings (Cohen 1970, 1976). In describing the family as a property-holding unit, Cohen distinguishes three components: the family estate (the holdings subject to division), the family group (those persons who have rights of one sort or another to the family estate at the time of division), and the family economy (the exploitation of the family estate and the estate's benefits). These components can be concentrated or dispersed, and the connections between them can assume a variety of forms. Cohen's analysis is useful in explaining the Chinese family system. But he fails to explain how and why different kinds of rights to different kinds of property come into play at the time of family division.

Maurice Freedman constructs models to identify some of the principles underlying family organization in China. Because of the diversity within Chinese society, Freedman believes that a single model of the domestic developmental cycle cannot be applied. Instead, he suggests (1963: 100) separate models for the rich and large family and for the poor and small family: "The model families must move within numerical ranges of these two different orders. But a real family can, as it were, commute between the ranges when it is moving up or down the social scale. As it grows richer and more powerful, having begun as a fairly simple unit, it can realize the complexity for which it has the children. Contrariwise, a move downwards can shatter a complex unit into many new and simple ones." Freedman explains the need for two models (1958: 28–30) by noting that rich families tend to be larger than poor families (owing to a lower infant mortality rate) and also more cohesive (owing to larger capital investments in buildings and agricultural equipment and to greater political influence—strong inducements for members to cooperate and to live in close proximity).

Francis L. K. Hsu, who also posits two models, suggests that rich and poor families emphasize different relationships: the rich emphasize the father-son relationship, the poor emphasize the husband-wife relationship (1943, 1949). Families grow large or remain small according to the adjustment they make between these conflicting relationships. I do not think, however, that this is an adequate explanation of the variation in the size of the Chinese family. Hsu sees two very important relationships in opposition to each other, but he does not seem to recognize that they rest on separate social principles. The father-son relationship is basic to the continuation of the descent line; it is a relationship of filiation that emphasizes the descent principle. The husband-wife relationship is basic to the creation of the family; it is a relationship of affinity that emphasizes the conjugal principle. However, the descent line is dependent on conjugal relationships for its continuation. Although these two relationships may come into conflict, or one relationship may be stronger than the other, the principles basic to both exist in all Chinese families, rich and poor, large and small.

It seems to me that the time has come to sort out a single set of principles capable of explaining the Chinese family system. Positing separate models of development for families in different economic situations serves only to polarize the rich and the poor without indicating the basic unity of Chinese society. Once we have sorted out the rules that customarily govern the inheritance of property, I think we will have gone a long way toward resolving some of the confusion presently surrounding our understanding of the Chinese family. In my research, I have found that inherited property and acquired property are passed on to subsequent generations according to very different principles. Since rich families inherit most of their property and poor families acquire most of theirs, the division of property inevitably seems different for the rich and for the poor. But this difference is only apparent. The principles of division do not vary, merely the circumstances. A poor family with only a bit of inherited property will follow the same principles in dividing it as a wealthy family, and a wealthy family will divide its acquired property in the same way as a poor one.

## *Family, Descent Line, and Property*

Before turning to the problem at hand, I would like to make clear what I mean by the term "family." In an unpublished paper entitled "Line, Lineage, and Family," Arthur Wolf draws a distinction between the family and what he calls the "descent line" (1973: 2–13). In his view, "a line consists, for any given man, of all his lineal agnatic ascendants, as far back in time as his imagination can carry him, and all his lineal agnatic descendants, including, aside from his living sons and grandsons, all men of future generations who will someday look up to him as their common ancestor." Wolf argues that the family is not just "a contemporary manifestation" of the line. The two institutions recruit their members in different ways and serve different purposes. Whereas "a line recruits its principal members, the males, by way of birth or adoption, the family recruits members by birth, by adoption, by a variety of forms of marriage, and simply by assimilation." Whereas "the line serves as the primary property-holding unit and is responsible for the rites of ancestor worship, the family is the primary unit of production and consumption and is concerned with the worship of such tutelary deities as the T'u Ti Kung."

The force of Wolf's distinction is readily illustrated by an example. In 1953 Ch'iu Tun came north to Shu-lin, where he married uxorilocally the Tai family's only child—their daughter, Tai Shu-mei. The couple eventually produced four sons. In accordance with terms specified in the marriage contract, the eldest of the sons took his descent from his maternal grandfather and was named Tai Han-chia; his three younger brothers took their descent from their father and were named Ch'iu Ping-huang, Ch'iu Lai-fu, and Ch'iu Ming-i. The result was one family incorporating two lines of descent. Ch'iu Tun and his three younger sons worship the Ch'iu ancestors, and the sons will inherit the property held by the Ch'iu line; Tai Shu-mei and her eldest son worship the Tai ancestors, and the son will inherit the property held by the Tai line.

Although I accept Wolf's distinction and base my analysis on it, I believe that Wolf is mistaken in describing the descent line as the primary property-holding unit. Both the line and the family hold property in the communities I studied. Lines hold what I call "inherited property," whereas families hold what I call "acquired property." I use the term "inherited property" for the Hokkien expression *co-thuan giap-san* (literally, "property inherited from the ancestors") and the term "acquired property" for the Hokkien expression *chiu-ti giap-san* (literally, "property acquired by the family members"). These expressions clearly suggest that in the first case we are concerned with rights based on descent, whereas in the second we are concerned with rights acquired as a result of family membership and family effort.

Inherited property, which in rural areas consists mainly of land and buildings, exists to sustain men so that they may fulfill the duty of perpetuating their descent lines. As a general rule, only those members of a family who are also in the descent line have rights to the proceeds of this part of the estate and rights to inherit it. Inherited property is corporately owned by the descent line, whose membership extends to deceased ancestors and future agnatic descendants. Theoretically, then, the father—as the head of this corporate group—is the trustee and not the owner of the property. All members of a family may have the right to use inherited property (to work the land or live in the house), but they cannot dispose of it. Equal rights to inherited property are shared by the living members of a descent line on a per stirpes basis.

Acquired property may be defined as the property acquired through the efforts of family members while the family maintains itself as a corporate group. Rights to such property are shared by all family members on a per capita basis. However, acquired property may be transformed into "inherited property" if it is acquired exclusively through the efforts of the head of the family. Under these circumstances, the head of the family has the right to transfer his accumulations of property into the inherited category if he wishes. For the Chinese in Shu-lin, land and the security it provides are intimately connected with the perpetuation of the descent line and the lineage. As a result, there is a strong tendency for all real estate to be classified in the inherited property category. Women, however, are not excluded from claims to the property held by the family. It is a father's duty to provide his daughter with a dowry at marriage, and her dowry is considered her share of the common (acquired) property of the family.

Let us see some of these principles in operation by considering the case of a family consisting of two married brothers (both of whom take their descent from their father) and their wives and children. Suppose that the brothers' father had inherited two *ka*[3] of land and that this land is divided after the father's death. Let us suppose further that the division takes place shortly after the harvest. Since inherited property is normally divided equally on a per stirpes basis, each brother would receive half the land, or one *ka*. But they would not necessarily receive equal shares of the harvested grain. Whereas inherited property is divided equally between the branches of a line, property acquired through the efforts of the living members of a family is normally divided on a per capita basis. Thus, if the family segment headed by the elder brother had twice as many members as that headed by the younger brother, the elder brother would receive two thirds of the harvest, and the younger brother would have to be satisfied with one third. Also, what applies to grain and other movable property acquired through the joint efforts of family members applies also to landed property. Only inherited property is subject to division on a per stirpes basis; acquired property is divided in such a way as to allow all people to enjoy the fruits of their labor. Let us

[3] 1 *ka* = 1 *chia* (about 2.40 acres).

return for a moment to the case of Ch'iu Tun and imagine that after he had married into the Tai family he and his father-in-law purchased two *ka* of land with money earned by means of a joint effort. This property would then be divided equally by Ch'iu's sons regardless of descent. Those sons who took their descent from their father would not be entitled to a share of the land held by the Tai line, but they would be entitled to an equal share of the land purchased after their father's marriage. Their right would rest on the fact that all members of a family enjoy rights in land acquired by the family.

Because the division of acquired property is calculated with reference to effort rather than to genealogy, there are no precise rules that govern the process. In some cases, the adult males of the family divide acquired property on a simple per capita basis, whereas in others they make an effort to agree on a formula that recognizes the relative contribution of each party. One naturally has to know a great deal about the history of a family to predict how its members will divide acquired property, but this does not in any way qualify the main point—that the principle involved is not the same as that governing the division of inherited property.

Many authorities on the Chinese family claim that a daughter is not entitled to a share of her father's land, whereas others note that wealthy families sometimes include land in a daughter's dowry. What appears to be a contradiction merely results from confusing inherited property with acquired property. Because the dead retain rights in inherited property, a man cannot give land to a daughter without risking their displeasure. But the dead have no interest in acquired property. A man is thus free to give his daughter a share of any land that he has acquired through his own efforts. Indeed, a daughter may even claim a share of this land if she has made a substantial contribution to the effort that made its purchase possible.

## *Family Division and Inheritance*

The distinction between the family and the descent line has already been noted. But another important distinction should also be made—between the family (*ke*) and the household (*ho*). In the rural area around Shu-lin, the membership of the *ke* usually coincides with the membership of the *ho*; but whereas the *ke* is a property-holding unit, the *ho* is not. It is not necessary for all members of the *ke* to live under one roof, to eat from the same stove, or to worship the same stove god. (Wherever there is a stove, there is in theory a god who guards the hearth and protects the members of the household.) In this part of Taiwan, it is in fact quite common for a family to split up into two or more *ho* before a final division of the family property. Thus, the *ke* may be defined as a family group whose members share common property. The *ho*, by contrast, is merely a residential unit; though the *ho* usually coincides with the *ke*, it can also be a subgroup of the *ke* before the final division of the *ke* and its property. An outsider would naturally be hard put to distinguish between the *ke* and the *ho* in this kind of arrangement.

A large family of the Cheng lineage in T'ao-tzu-chiao provides a good example of the differences between the *ke* as a property-holding, cooperatively run economic unit, and the *ho* as a non-property-holding, residential group. In 1972, the three-generation extended Cheng family was headed by Cheng Piao, who was then 70 years old. He and his wife had seven married sons and 40 grandchildren. The family was dispersed in three separate houses. The first house, located in the old farm compound, sheltered the *pang-thau* of Cheng's first, third, and sixth sons. The second house, built in 1962 about half a mile south of the first house, was occupied by Cheng and his wife along with the *pang-thau* of Cheng's fourth, fifth, and seventh sons. The third house was a new two-story building on Shu-lin's Kan-yüan street; this was the home of the *pang-thau* of Cheng's second son. There was a stove in each of these houses, so each residential group constituted a commensal unit. The three wives in the first house rotated cooking responsibilities on a five-day cycle, as did the three wives in the second house. The inhabitants of the third house ate by themselves. Although the members of the *ke* were dispersed in three households, ate from three stoves, and worshiped three stove gods, they were still one family group. Their rice came from the family storehouse, and their vegetables came from the family garden. Cheng Piao went grocery shopping every day, and delivered meat, fish, and other foods and necessities to each house on a per capita basis. He also controlled the income from the family's land and knitting machines, and he disbursed the wages his sons earned in the slack seasons. His first son was a part-time bricklayer in the vicinity, and his second son was a foreman in a coal mine and the manager of a small variety store. All the money these sons earned was handed over to Cheng. At the end of each year, Cheng gave a sum of money for new clothes and shoes to each *pang-thau* according to the numbers and ages of the children in each. He also paid all marriage and educational expenses.

The Cheng family, then, was clearly a property-holding unit with a single, inclusive economy. Not surprisingly, the family's corporate character extended to ancestor worship: there was only one ancestral altar, which was located in the first and oldest of the family's houses. (Even had the Cheng brothers divided the family, however, it is not likely that they would have set up separate ancestral altars. In this area of Taiwan, separate altars are generally formed only by family branches that move away.) The three *pang-thau* living in the first Cheng house took most responsibility for worshiping the line's ancestors, and the three *pang-thau* living in the second house took care of the daily needs of Cheng Piao and his wife. Family members regarded performing ancestral rites and providing for Cheng and his wife as equivalent duties. Obligations to the line's senior dead and senior living members were thus similar: the matter called for nothing more than a simple division of family labor.[4]

Another arrangement that leads to confusion between the *ke* and the *ho* is the so-called independent household set up by a man and his wife and children before the formal division of the old *ke*. Such a household has an independent economic life, and its members eat apart from the other parts of the family. But the *ke* of which it is a part has not yet reached the point of division. In this situation, when the brothers talk together, the *ke* they refer to is the *ke* of their parents. To them, the *ke* must include their parents and their brothers and their dependents. Before the division of the family, a brother can differentiate his residence from his brother's residence only by saying *gua-hia* ("my side") and *lin-hia* ("your side"). The terms change immediately after division: *gua-hia* becomes *gun-tau* ("my home"), and *lin-hia* becomes *lin-tau* ("your home").

Independent households are sometimes set up before the final division of family property to avoid conflict among large and active *pang-thau*. In such cases, family division becomes a gradual process. The Chien family of Shu-lin provides a good example. In 1972, the head of the family was Chien Wu-ming, then 74 years old. He had inherited 0.4 *ka* of land from his father in 1931 and had later ac-

[4]Divided families with a common ancestral altar usually rotate the responsibility for performing rites. Undivided families usually assign this responsibility to a single member (most often, the oldest brother), even though the offerings and incense are purchased out of the family's common budget.

quired another 2 *ka*. Chien and his wife lived in the original farm compound along with his youngest son and the son's *pang-thau*. Five other sons lived independently in households outside the compound. From the outset, Chien had encouraged his sons to be independent: he had built separate houses for the five older sons and had made them depend on their own efforts to earn a living. He had also offered each of his sons the right to use 0.4 *ka* of the family's land. Only Chien's second and third sons, however, had taken full advantage of the offer and had become full-time farmers. Except for the sixth son, who tilled no land for himself, the others made partial use of their rights while they engaged in other businesses. The first son tilled 0.1 *ka* of land; the fourth used 0.15 *ka* of land for a fish pond; and the fifth tilled 0.1 *ka* of land. Chien did not provide any capital for his sons' businesses, because he felt that this might lead to disputes over whether the profits should belong to the whole family; moreover, he did not have enough capital to set each son up in business. On their own, then, Chien's sons found various sources of income: the first son became a butcher with a meat stand in the new market in Shu-lin; the second became a vegetable gardener; the third became a rice farmer; the fourth became the owner of a neighborhood grocery store; the fifth became a rice merchant and fruit peddler; and the sixth got a job at a local pharmaceutical factory. Each son kept the profits or wages that his efforts brought in. The family rented 0.4 *ka* of land to a man who raised fish, and Chien saved this rent for family emergencies and for expenses connected with ancestor worship. The remaining 0.85 *ka* of land was worked by the family as a whole to produce the rice and vegetables that they consumed daily. All the sons were obliged to work on this part of the land. Chien did not ask his sons for money, since he owned three small houses that brought him a total monthly rent of NT$1,800. Chien ate breakfast and supper at the farm compound, but had lunch with his fourth son's *pang-thau* because it was convenient for him to stay at the grocery store to chat and drink with friends. Chien told me that he could eat at any of his sons' homes; to him, these were also his homes. The sons, however, saw only the compound as a common home; their own residences were for their own *pang-thau* (an attitude naturally shared by their wives). Chien controlled all the family's common property and enjoyed what he thought of as an undivided family. Nonetheless, he was glad to have his sons separate, independent, and living in harmony.

The father—the senior member of the family—holds a pivotal position in relation to his sons and symbolizes the family for younger generations. When the father dies and there is no person of comparable status to succeed him, final division of the family becomes necessary. Sometimes, however, such a division is made during the father's lifetime. This is likely to happen when a family's *pang-thau* grow so large (or ambitious) as to make economic cooperation difficult, or when a father simply loses control over his sons. When the father is still alive, family division is sometimes an unhappy matter for the poor. Parents can be left almost helpless if they divide their scanty property among their sons and their sons are unwilling to support them. Family division while the father is still alive is much easier for the rich: when the estate is divided, a share of land is usually reserved for the parents' exclusive use as *lau-pun* ("pension land"). Only when the parents die is the *lau-pun* divided up among the sons.

Whether the parents of a well-to-do family reserve pension land for themselves at the division of the family estate depends in part on their attitude and in part on the nature of the estate. If there is land that has been acquired through the parents' own efforts, then the father has an absolute right to set aside this land (or any part of it) as pension land; indeed, he is free to dispose of this land however he wishes, even by selling it. In general, most wealthy parents do reserve *lau-pun* to support themselves in old age and to pay for their funerals. (Few parents, after all, want to become a burden on their children.) Some wealthy parents, however, do not reserve any *lau-pun* on the assumption that their children will not mind taking care of them. What children think about this is another matter: some daughters-in-law had no hesitation in admitting that parents without pension land are a burden; and many people agreed that parents who do not reserve such land are gambling. But whether or not pension land is set aside, there is always an agreement among sons to take turns inviting their parents to stay with them after the estate is divided. When family division takes place after the death of the father, however, no pension land is set aside for the mother. Landed property belongs to the descent line, so responsibility for supporting the mother falls directly on the sons and their families.

The Chinese family is conventionally described as patriarchal: the senior male member is its head and has authority over all of the other members; he controls the family economy and makes the final decisions. All or some of these statements may be true at various times in the family's developmental cycle, but they are not necessarily true for the entire cycle. The authority of a line's (or a family's) senior member over the junior members changes throughout the senior member's life. Sometimes the older generation's authority is transmitted smoothly to the younger generation; at other times, a struggle is necessary. In short, there are different kinds of rights and duties vested in the members of the family and descent line appropriate to the members' status in these groups. I have argued that all members of the descent line have an equal right to inherited property; they are thus heirs apparent. While these potential heirs are still young, the head of the line assumes complete management of the property. His position is more like a trustee than that of an owner since he shares ownership with the junior members. As time goes on, the right of the junior members to claim their individual shares gradually increases, and the degree of control over those rights by the head of the line gradually decreases. When the junior members reach maturity and are ready to assume their shares of the inherited property, the property can be divided among the members, shifting the balance of power in favor of the now adult junior members. After the death of the head, division is of course inevitable. When division is delayed this long, it is generally because the head of the family has been unusually capable or has acquired most of the property himself. Since these two factors reinforce each other, there is often a considerable imbalance in power between fathers and adult sons.

In a family with only inherited property, a father can easily lose control of his estate because his position is essentially that of a trustee. He is still, however, in a stronger position than the father of a poor family in which the sons have acquired most of the property. In both situations, adult sons often press for their shares to establish independent households. The case of Chan Ping-ying illustrates the difficulties that can arise when the bulk of an estate consists of inherited property. Chan had five sons, who, in 1971, wanted to divide up the inherited estate. At first, Chan refused. However, his oldest grandson needed a loan for a business investment, and the bank refused to grant the loan because the grandson did not have any property in his own name. The grandson took the matter to a court in Taipei, arguing that his grandfather had no right to retain control of the family's inherited property when the successors were ready for their inheritances. The judge ruled, however, that the case could not be decided by formal law, and he ordered the Chans to settle the dispute themselves by compromise.

At this point, several local leaders were called in as mediators. They classified the problem as one of *pun-ke-he* ("dividing up the family estate") among the title holders, rather than as a case of inheritance in the narrow sense. Chan was talked into giving up control of the estate and allowing his sons to establish independent households; in return, the sons agreed that they would support their parents (on a rotating basis). The estate was then divided equally among the five sons, since Chan did not feel that it was necessary to reserve any *lau-pun* for himself and his wife.

Chan told me that old people are of no use at all. He pointed out that once a father loses control of the family estate he loses his power in the family and sooner or later becomes a burden to his sons. He complained that feeding one's children when they are young is not the same thing as being fed by them when one is old. Eating in a son's home, for example, "shows you that to receive kindness from sons is more difficult than to give kindness to them. For in your sons' families, you have to watch and listen for what they want you to do. You are not the boss at all. Only when they call you to eat, do you go to eat." Moreover, as soon as one son has taken his turn at taking care of his parents, he expects them to move immediately to another son's household. Indeed, a father raises his sons from a sense of social responsibility and from a self-interested desire to perpetuate his line. But showing filial duty to aging parents is only a matter of social responsibility; it is not reinforced by self-interest. As a result, sons are generally a bit less happy about caring for their parents than their parents were about caring for them.

The most powerful fathers—those who retain firm control of wealthy estates—are usually men who have acquired large amounts of property themselves. Cheng Piao and Chien Wu-ming provide good examples of men of this sort (see Sung 1975). They controlled not only the family property and economy but also the lives of family members. Here we see the components of the ideal Chinese family: an extended household, a powerful father, and subordinate sons (who do not seek a division of family property until the father dies or wants a division himself). At the very least, a father must preserve inherited property intact if he wishes to avoid having a family division forced upon him. But even this is not enough to guarantee his dominant position forever. As soon as his sons are ready to inherit their shares of the estate, his position as the estate's trustee becomes precarious. To be genuinely powerful, then, a father must be the owner of his property instead of merely its trustee: his sons must be his heirs, not just his successors.

Common interests and uncommon leadership, however, sometimes keep families together in circumstances where one would expect a division. The Liu family of Shu-lin illustrates this point. In the space of little more than a year in the mid-1890's, the father of the Liu family and his three oldest sons all died. Funeral expenses then plunged the family deeply into debt. At age 26, the only surviving son, Liu Kuei-ti, succeeded his father as the head of the family (which included the adult sons of Liu Kuei-ti's older brothers). Fellow villagers expected that the Lius would soon be forced to divide the family estate to avoid what appeared to be imminent financial disaster. However, the Lius decided instead to remain under one roof with one manager—a decision taken by Liu Kuei-ti and his adult nephews. The decision was a very good one. By 1900, the Lius had acquired 13 *ka* of land to add to the 15 *ka* that they had inherited, and they had become one of the richest families in the area. When Liu Kuei-ti died in 1906, his oldest nephew, Liu Hou-lien, succeeded him as head of the family. Though Liu Hou-lien was in fact two years older than his late uncle, he was less successful as the head of the family: after only a year, he lost his authority and the family estate was divided up among the four *pang-thau*. In this instance, then, exceptionally able leadership and perceived common interests delayed family division for just over a decade.

Cohen and Pasternak are thus right in claiming that families usually delay division because of the economic advantages of pooled capital and labor (Cohen 1976: 216–18; Pasternak this volume). The important point, however, is that after the death of the father this delay is always a voluntary matter; family members retain the right to claim their share of property whenever they want to.

Although property acquired through individual effort theoretically belongs to the family as a whole, the person responsible for acquiring the property often feels that he should be able to keep some part of it for his own benefit. Such feelings become stronger as people get older, particularly if the family has dispersed. In the families I studied, the man or *pang-thau* most directly involved in an enterprise generally claims the largest share of it at the time of family division. The division of the wealthy Chan family in Ch'i-ch'ien-ts'o village near Shu-lin provides a good illustration of this point. Chan Tsai-tan inherited 0.7 *ka* of land from his father in 1919. His family later acquired 25 *ka* of land: 12 *ka* in Chiao-tzu-t'ou village in Ying-ko township, 5 *ka* in Ta-kuai-ch'i village in T'ao-yüan county, and 8 *ka* in Ch'i-ch'ien-ts'o. Chan had three sons. The first son died at the age of nineteen without a wife or an heir. Chan Ping-kun, the elder of the surviving sons, was said to have acquired most of the family land. However, all the land was registered in the father's name (as the head of the household) except for 2 *ka* of land in Ch'i-ch'ien-ts'o village, which was in Chan Ping-kun's name. Nonetheless, this 2 *ka* of land was always considered to be the family's common property. After the parents died, the brothers continued to live together for eight years. Then in 1953, under the Land-to-the-Tiller Program, the brothers lost all their land in Ying-ko and T'ao-yüan to their tenants. Soon afterwards, they decided to divide up the remaining 8.7 *ka* in Ch'i-ch'ien-ts'o. Theoretically, the land should have been divided into two equal shares. However, Chan Ping-kun refused to agree to this, insisting that only the 6.7 *ka* of land in his father's name should be divided equally. His case rested on three strong arguments. First, 2 *ka* of the land was already in his own name. Second, most of the estate was acquired through his efforts. Third, his eldest son was the senior grandson of the family, and as such (according to customary law) had an independent claim to a share of the estate. Though angry, the younger brother had little recourse but to give in: he got 3.35 *ka* of land and Chan Ping-kun got 5.35 *ka*.

There are other circumstances in which family property is not shared according to the strict rules and schedules of per capita or per stirpes division. To find employment, for example, a family member may have to move to another town before family division. In such cases, it is accepted practice for him to set up an independent household; he then keeps a portion of his income to maintain his own *pang-thau* and sends the rest home to his parents. In a rich family, if a son's income away from home is not sufficient to support him, his parents send him money. He retains his membership in the family and shares rights and duties with other members until the family is divided or until he has received his share of the estate. Sometimes it is even permissible for members of an undivided family still living together to accumulate personal savings and belongings. This is most likely to occur in the third generation of an extended family. The money and belongings that a son and his *pang-thau* accumulate become their exclusive property when the family is divided. Therefore, it is possible for differences in wealth to emerge among *pang-thau* before the final division of the family property. The richest of the Chien brothers, for example, is the eldest brother, and the poorest is the third brother. The greater right of brothers who contribute most to an estate tends to be forgotten by those who contribute least, particularly when it comes time to divide the income from the estate. Quarrels and the eventual division of the family are the usual result. Currently, a man who accumulates private savings while still living with his brothers is severely criticized by his fellow villagers. It is felt that as a member of his parents' family, he should show that his first loyalty is to the family as a whole.

## *Conclusions*

The distinction between inherited property and acquired property is also relevant to the study of Chinese domestic cycles. Freedman argues persuasively that the researcher needs to distinguish, at a minimum, between "rich and poor versions of the Chinese family":

> A poor family might in the extreme be unable to raise a son to marriageable age and ensure that he stay at home to recreate the domestic unit. The chances were that at most one son would marry and continue the family in the same house. As soon as this son begot a child three generations were present, but the senior generation, represented by the elderly parents, were very unlikely to see a fourth emerge. As soon as these parents died a two-generation family appeared again. The process was repeated: elementary family grew to stem and was reduced once more to elementary. Even though there might be two married brothers at any stage in the evolution of a family, they rarely lived together, with the consequence that no joint family appears in the typical cycle.
>
> A rich family produced several sons and retained them, perhaps adding to their number by adoption. The sons remained in an undivided family as long as the parental generation survived. And since these sons married young and the seniors might live long, a joint family of four generations could appear. (1966: 44–45.)

Freedman recognizes that a crucial question is why partition occurs earlier among poor families than among rich families. His answer is based on the assumption that the inherent equality of brothers creates fraternal competition that can only be held in check by a powerful father. In poor families, the father is politically and economically weak, so partition occurs quickly (*ibid.*: 45–47). Though I agree that fraternal competition is always present and that the father's ability to control his sons varies, I would suggest that an important part of the difference between rich and poor families is that the estate of a rich family is likely to include a larger proportion of inherited property. This is relevant for two reasons. First, acquired property is more likely to lead to jealousy (and hence early division) than inherited property, simply because the principle governing the division of acquired property leaves more room for disagreement. Brothers are less likely to quarrel if they are guaranteed equal shares by descent and do not need to negotiate the division of property acquired through joint but not necessarily equal efforts. Second, a father is better able to control his sons if he has inherited his estate than if he has acquired it with his sons' help. His position as father is then reinforced by his position as the head of the line that holds the estate. In the case of an acquired estate obtained through the joint efforts of father and sons, the father's authority rests solely on his position as father. In respect to the property, the father is only another member of the family: his sons can demand partition of the estate on the grounds that they have helped acquire it.

I therefore believe that family patterns are more strongly affected by how families obtain their property than by whether they are rich or poor. Hsu, as noted, argues that wealthy families stress filial relationships and that poor families stress conjugal relationships (1943: 556–59; 1949: 775). In my view, this difference is readily explained by the fact that wealthy families are more likely than poor families to have large amounts of inherited property: filial relationships are naturally more important than conjugal relationships when the bulk of the family's property is owned by the line, not by the family. Wealth per se, then, is not as significant in shaping the Chinese family as the principles that govern its control and distribution—principles that differ for inherited and acquired property.

This difference is even relevant to attitudes about the supernatural. In her important study of ancestor worship in Ch'i-nan, Emily Ahern found (1973) that village ancestors are thought of as powerful, punishing spirits. I think that this may well reflect the fact that most of the property in Ch'i-nan is inherited property and hence property to which ancestors have a legitimate claim. In communities where the great majority of the population before land reform consisted of tenant farmers, ancestors do not appear to be powerful and interfering. My guess is that where land is owned primarily by the descent line, ancestors are conceived of in far more vivid terms than they are where recently acquired property makes the family rather than the line the main unit of ownership.

# Part Six

# Religion and Ritual

# The Sexual Politics of Karmic Retribution

Gary Seaman

*This brings us to a final question. If, as I believe to be the case, women do not deliberately use their capacity to pollute against men, what happens when the shoe is on the other foot? Do men deliberately use beliefs in pollution as a weapon against women? Many of the most polluting substances emanate from a woman's reproductive organs, the source of her greatest power over her husband's family—her ability to produce descendants. Once the polluting nature of the sex act, . . . menstrual blood, . . . and childbirth . . . is established, the source of a woman's power is obscured, if not rendered invisible, by a layer of negative sentiment. While this line of thought is suggestive, I know of no evidence that men intentionally and self-servingly perpetuate these beliefs.—Emily Ahern*

I hope to show that men do, indeed, encourage the perpetuation of negative beliefs surrounding women's sexuality, and that men are quite aware of the need to rationalize the socially inferior position of women. I will also take up another of Ahern's contentions: that there is a paradox in men's participation in the ritual performed at women's funerals called the "Ceremony of the Bloody Pond" or "Breaking the Blood Bowl" (*phau-hueq-phun*), a ritual that shows gratitude and pity for women's fate on the one hand while dramatizing women's pollution on the other. I hope to explain some of the

I would like to thank Barbara Pillsbury for her criticisms of the first draft of this paper and Lydia Kung for pointing out that in Taiwanese "black dog" means a ladies' man. I very much appreciate Emily Ahern's extensive editorial suggestions. The epigraph is from Ahern 1975: 213–14. Hokkien terms are spelled according to the orthography in Bodman 1955.

elements of this dramatic juxtaposition of filial devotion and horror of pollution and perhaps to make their association less paradoxical.

My sources are diverse: the Ceremony of the Bloody Pond and the ritual text (*Tz'u-pei hsüeh-p'en-ch'an*) associated with it; the seven-syllable verse lines so popular in Taiwanese ballads concerning "moral matters" (*khuan se*); and my own experiences attending many funerals in the P'u-li Basin of central Taiwan from 1970 to 1976.

The most basic assignment of social roles is on the basis of sex. Not only is everyone categorized on the basis of his or her physical attributes and consequent reproductive role, but the historical "facts" of parentage determine one's access to material wealth and to the services of others. In societies like China, where descent is based almost exclusively on the male line, women's rights and the way women are incorporated into their husbands' lines are fraught with danger, threatening male solidarity. To preserve the solidarity of the male-oriented agnatic line, a rationalizing ideology develops that subordinates the role of women to that of men. After all, a reproductive unit is formed by people from alien and potentially hostile agnatic lines. For husbands, who are parties to the difficult political negotiations involved in taking brides, the absence of "wives' rights" in the agnatic line is not difficult to rationalize. However, for sons, who owe their very being and consequently their membership in the line to their mothers, the implicit mistrust and hostility towards all women (including their mothers) is much harder to explain. One way of rationalizing the inferior position of women vis-à-vis men within the line, as Ahern has observed, is to obscure those points of a woman's sexuality that differ from a man's with a "layer of negative sentiment." The basic political unit in Chinese society is traditionally depicted as a band of brothers—from the pious peasant family struggling to keep its patrimony undivided, to the sworn brotherhood of the heroes of the oath in the peach garden celebrated in the *Romance of the Three Kingdoms*. A group of determined men—whether related by blood, oath, or conviction—can build an empire if they remain true to each other. Loyalty is the supreme political virtue. Indeed, it is a favorite task in popular literature and history to document the baleful effects of women in government and to deplore the effects of the families of empresses or royal concubines who mix in the business of ruling.

I scarcely need to add argument to the calumny that Chinese social commentators have heaped upon wives for their disruptive role in relations between brothers. Not surprisingly, relations between affines are hedged about with strong avoidance conventions. Moreover, marriage negotiations are dangerous and are conducted at arm's length through indispensable go-betweens. The dangers that haunt a man in his marital relations have been made legend by the incident in the *Romance of the Three Kingdoms* where Liu Pei narrowly avoids being eliminated by his rivals who try to use the "fair damsel ruse" to lure him to his death.

In terms of property as well as kin-group affiliation, women represent a threat to the male-oriented family unit. The rules of estate inheritance insure an equal share for each male sibling; but the dowry property managed independently by each wife places a strain on the continuity of the patrilineal estate. It is impossible for a family to avoid the repeated introduction of unknown influences in the form of new brides. Thus the Chinese make moral exemplars of men like Kuan Yü, who avoid even the appearance of familiar behavior with their brothers' wives. However, the potential for illicit and disruptive sexual relationships between brothers-in-law and sisters-in-law is always present. All in all, one has not far to look for the threat that women pose to the social fabric of China (see especially Wolf 1975).

But if women are a threat in some ways, they are essential in others. It is probably unnecessary to develop elaborate proofs of the importance of children in Chinese society. Even the most perfunctory experience of China creates an awareness of the immense social and cultural pressures for procreation. To have no children is still the most unfilial of things; and to have children, men must depend upon women. The rules of marriage, descent, and property thus all converge to define a woman's role in terms of exchanges between successive male protectors. For a male, political rights are stable and focused on the same agnatic lineage throughout his lifetime. The position of a female is indicated by the saying that every woman has three names in her lifetime: her father's when a child, her husband's when married, and her son's when grown old. No wonder that Chinese women have organized resistance to marriage from time to time in the past (Topley 1975).

If women—despite their essential role in procreation—present a threat to the male sodalities that wield political and economic power, it is no surprise that the very presence of women in some ritual contexts is enough to shatter the positive power of divinity and change the gods' benevolence into vengeful spite. Wedded to the perception of women as social disrupters is a parallel perception of them as ritual polluters, capable of destroying the harmony between men and gods. Ahern analyzes the relationship of women to gods in terms of pollution: primarily concerned with taboos against women's proximity to and participation in various rites of worship (1975: 202–8), she rightly points to the difficulties that these taboos put in the way of women approaching the higher gods. In the present context, I would stress that women's access to the gods is a political matter as well as a function of traditional taboos.

As a result of the carefully defined hierarchy of purity and virtue among the various heavenly beings, the right to perform various roles in rituals is an important expression of political rights and power. For example, it is the prerogative of the emperor alone to carry out certain sacrifices to heaven, and their performance epitomizes the ruler's right to his throne. Since pollution usually disqualifies women from participating in rites directed to the higher deities, women cannot achieve for themselves the benefits that a regular relationship with the gods can bring. As a result, they must depend on men to act as their representatives or intermediaries in most important religious matters.

Men's monopoly of religious rights is revealed in an especially clear light by spirit mediums. Although, as Ahern points out, there are some spirits that are worshiped almost exclusively by women, these are mostly of low rank and have little community-wide importance (1975). Politically important cults, by contrast, almost always have male mediums—a nearly inevitable consequence of the way mediums are recruited and trained. Though some mediums apparently develop their talents spontaneously, most mediums (especially in well-established cults) develop their talents through a process called "cultivating mediums" (*lian ki*). In this process, a space is purified (a room in a temple, a cave, or perhaps a hut constructed for the occasion), and the prospective medium is confined in it, usually along with a medium who has already achieved contact with the gods. For a fixed period of time, the candidate and the trained medium observe certain taboos that purify their bodies and make them fit vessels for the spirits of the gods. Their diet is commonly restricted to water, rice, and fruit; sex and bowel movements are prohibited; and chanting and breathing exercises are often required. The length of time spent in this "cultivation" varies, however, from just a day or so to much longer. The temple that I studied, for example, holds that 49 days are necessary for attaining the requisite degree of purity. In cases like this, of course, some relaxation of the rules is permitted (in respect to confinement, bowel movements, etc.); but if certain forms of pollution occur (e.g., contact with menstrual or birth blood), then the "cultivation" is terminated. Obviously, such circumstances make it difficult for women to achieve sufficient purity to act as mediums.

What is there about women's nature that is so different from men's? I remember once overhearing a discussion among several men about the nature of the Boddhisattva Kuan Yin, a goddess most Taiwanese pay homage to regularly. These men performed as actors in funeral rites and were probably all familiar with the text of the Blood Bowl Sutra (*Tz'u-pei hsüeh-p'en-ch'an*) used in women's funeral rites. One man held that since Kuan Yin had the physical body of a woman and had existed historically as a woman (as is the case in the popular myth of Kuan Yin's origin), there was no obstacle to a woman becoming a Buddha, just as Kuan Yin had. All the other men present opposed this view, insisting that Kuan Yin was not really a woman at all, but a Buddha who chose to manifest himself in a female form. They argued that physical limitations made it impossible for a woman to become a Buddha. In the great tradition of Buddhism, these physical limitations—not much discussed in the general literature—are known as the "five obstacles" (*go-ciang*). Basically, the five obstacles are defects of a woman's physical nature that prevent her from being directly reincarnated as a Buddha or other higher being. A woman can only become a god or a Buddha by being first reincarnated as a man, living a meritorious life as a man, and then passing on to a higher plane of existence.

In China, the "five obstacles" are seen as closely related to women's purity, or rather to her relative lack of purity. We may then ask, if men are purer beings than women, what is it about women that makes them unclean and polluting? Ahern has answered many aspects of this question and provides a useful typology of the different ways in which women may pollute (1975). It is my intention to concentrate on the etiology of pollution—that is, on the unique processes within women's bodies that differ from those within men's bodies and make women polluting. I begin by translating two passages from the text of Blood Bowl Sutra, apparently a purely Chinese rite (no Indian original is known: see Soothill 1937: 221) that is performed only at the funerals of women. In present-day funerals in Taiwan, most of the text is paraphrased by professional actors hired for the occasion, who usually put the content of the sutra into a popular form of verse.

> From time immemorial till now, we men have never been able to escape this mortal world. So much the less can women, who have the Five Obstacles. Dwelling in the way of the unrighteous, they have about them filth and evil. Whether moving, stopping, sitting, or sleeping, they are disturbed by the sensations of the six sense organs, which arouse in them the five desires, and lead to the committing of innumerable sins.
>
> What are the five desires?
>
> The first desire is of the eyes, which desire to gaze upon sensual forms. Whether male or female, forms good and beautiful, things jeweled and precious. Or wondrous colors, black, yellow, red, and green. The heart engenders pleasure and thus arises the joy of loving. Selfish thoughts arise in one's innermost heart. Be firm and think! Do not give in to this desire! Giving vent to reckless rage arouses the Obstacle of Confusion.
>
> The second desire is that of the ear to hear sounds. The rustling of silk or bamboos, or the tinkling of jades. Whether man or woman, singing, chanting, humming, tolling bells, clashing cymbals, gongs, and drums, every kind of sound. Because they all come from the external world, they arouse material desires, and by setting the heart in turmoil, they hide the entrance to the way, thus creating the Obstacle of Ignorance.
>
> The third desire is to smell. The smell of male and female scents, of things to eat and drink, and all grass, trees, flowers, fruit, and forests. All kinds of scents lead the mind to take delight. Thus arises the attachment of desire, which can obstruct the way to enlightenment. Tumultuous thoughts are aroused, and thus is engendered the Obstacle of Confusion.
>
> The fourth desire is tasting. Sensuous eating and drinking, of milk, sauces, fishes, and meats: boiled, fried, steamed, or raw. Turtle, carp, shrimp, goose, duck, chicken, whether from the water, the land, or out of the sky, sweet, smooth, spicy, soft. In order to feed mouth and stomach—painful slash of the fat flesh—death at knife's edge upon the chopping block, and passing to the boiling fire, the cause of suffering extreme.

Linked in eternal enmity, through eons and untold eons, hate is harbored in the heart. After death, these feuds and fights are resolved by rebirth, to be fought out in another form, alternately sent to chew and tear at one another.

And there is no end to it.

These five obstacles all derive from the six sense organs, the six causes of impurity that cast the pall of the eighty-four thousand mortal distresses, obstructing the mind that seeks enlightenment, obscuring the karma of good deeds, so that people drift back and forth between birth and death, forever bound to the wheel of transmigration. When one karma is exhausted, the soul must sink into hell among animals and hungry ghosts, suffering untold pain.

If ye can but awaken to these facts, may ye fear and tremble!

How can ye not repent?!

Our bodies, born of our parents, are made up of three hundred and sixty bone joints, ninety thousand pores, nine thousand sinews and blood vessels. But only a woman's body has the five hundred worms that leech onto her joints. When all these worms are active, her body is listless and weary.

Moreover, a woman has within her the eighty thousand *yin* [female] worms, which collect in her vagina. These worms have twelve heads and twelve mouths. When they feed, each sucks raw blood. Day and night they move about, wearying muscle and bone. Midway through the month, they slough unclean fluid. Each of these worms vomits pus and blood out of its mouths. Each exudes blood and pus that has a red color. These ulcerous worms: their mouths are like sharp needles, and they regularly afflict women, eating raw blood, irritating each other, ceaselessly crawling, disturbing a woman, making her body unable to calm itself. This is the result of karmic retribution, for which there is no surcease. (Vol. 1, chaps. 5–7.)

For our present purpose, the important part of the above text is its description of the etiology of the female condition. The female body is condemned to ceaseless imbalance because of the presence of worms within it. These worms are of two kinds: worms that afflict the joints, and *yin* worms that eat blood. This bipartite division of forces calls to mind Topley's description (1974: 237) of the course of pregnancy in women in Hong Kong: "She herself is polarized in the direction of cold and the fetus in the direction of hot. The woman is considered cold because internally she is losing blood to the fetus. Each month women move from cold toward hot, which they reach in the middle of the month, and then back to cold when blood is passed as menstrual fluid."

The text of the Blood Bowl Sutra differs from Topley's analysis in that the menstrual discharge is ascribed not to abstractions like cold and hot but to the biological rhythms of specific organisms. And the discharge is seen as the result of worms eating both bone and raw blood. Female menstruation is thus related to eating food and eliminating waste rather than to the clash of abstract forces.

The obstacles that prevent a woman from achieving the higher planes of existence can hinder those close to her as well. The polluting states of women—childbirth, menstruation, and sexual receptivity—are all strictly avoided by men who take part in rituals aimed at communicating with the gods. For example, a man will not enter a room where a birth has taken place for at least a month after the event, on pain of exclusion from any normal communication with the spirits. Merely passing under a bamboo pole where menstrual cloths are hung can make a man vulnerable to misfortunes caused by malicious ghosts. The by-products of birth and menstruation are typically the ingredients of the most potent "charms" (*hu-a*) in the magical arts. Paradoxically, the same polluting items call forth from men the ultimate proof of their filial piety: during a mother's funeral rites, a son must drink the blood of his birth.

Funeral rites in China are often highly dramatized, with professional actors performing as Buddhist saints and mourners incorporated in appropriate roles. For women's funerals, the drama-*cum*-ritual called "Breaking the Blood Bowl" is an adaptation of the story of Mu-lien's descent into hell to save his mother. In the ritual, the sons and daughters of a dead woman mime a descent into hell. A set is built representing the fortress in hell where their mother's soul is imprisoned, and a bowl of wine, dyed red, is placed in the fortress to symbolize the pool of blood in which she is drowning. After the actor who plays the part of Mu-lien vanquishes the jailers of hell (who would keep the woman's soul imprisoned), the bowl of red wine is portioned out to the children of the dead woman. Each of them drinks, wipes the bowl clean, then presents it to Mu-lien for a final purification. Indeed, it is highly suggestive that in some Chinese dialects the word for "blood bowl" (*hueq-phun*) also means "placenta." (For performances of the rite, see my films *Breaking the Blood Bowl* [1974] and *Journey to the West* [1977].)

Given the utter disgust with which men regard the pollution connected with childbirth, it is hard even to imagine a circumstance that would induce a Taiwanese man to touch birth blood, much less drink it. But this is the symbolic act that men regularly perform at their mothers' funerals. In spite of the fact that they are drinking only wine dyed red with food coloring, most men can barely bring themselves to sip and swallow. Indeed, they are performing in public the most degrading of acts. What brings a man to swallow the symbolic remains of his birth? He may have feelings of pity for women along with feelings of gratitude to his own mother. But he also has a self-interested motive arising from the workings of karmic retribution (*giap-po*): if he does not make amends for the pain he has caused his mother at his birth, he will be forced to live with this wrong in his future lives. Thus, he drinks the blood of his birth to free himself (and his mother) from future karmic conflict.

Let us look at another section of the Blood Bowl Sutra. This section examines the relationship between women's bodies, pollution, and karmic retribution.

> What are the five unclean things?
> Birth is unclean.
> Intercourse is unclean.
> The body is unclean.
> The ego is unclean.
> Death is unclean.
>
> Birth is an unclean thing: a woman's body is an unclean collection of worms' pus and filth, which comes together and collects.
> Ten months it ripens between the two viscera, entrapped, pressed into a female prison.
> One thing should be known: this body is not the Pure Land. No lotus is to be seen, nor wafting sandalwood incense.
> There is only the stench of shit, where the fetus develops for so long.
> And this life can only enter and leave through a woman's vagina.
>
> The second unclean thing is intercourse: the two drops of red and white matter from the parents' bodies collect, and it dwells within.
> Its soul comes from the woman's breath, which goes in and out.
> Thus it receives its body at the time of intercourse.
> And it is therefore unclean.

The third unclean thing is the body: all the six parts of the body, from head to foot, are nothing but filthy matter. For example, a dead dog is cast into the sea to wash it clean.
But when it is washed, only the smallest particle will have been removed, and even that will still stink.

The fourth unclean thing is the ego: for it is the seat of the senses.
Proceeding from an impure karma, it is consigned to be born amidst filthy things.
After long development it arises, but its nature is self-centered and cannot be altered.

The fifth unclean thing is death: when a karma is ended, the body is discarded in the grave like a piece of rotten wood. Every bit of it is unclean.
Out of the grave overflow thoughts and emotions, and the desires of those wanting life or coveting wealth.
Unharmonious emotions: hatred not dissipated, quarrels not yet resolved, or shame harbored in the heart.
These souls do not dissipate: those who complain of having no land, and those involved in feuds or in seeking vengeance. Instead, these are consigned to the womb to be reborn.
When the time of birth has come, whether full or soon, their birth is fitful, lacks smoothness, and is brought forth with difficulty.
Their hands and feet grapple and obstruct, so that the fetus does not come out. Now sticking, now smashing around in the womb, they cause their mother great suffering. Sometimes they cannot come forth at all, so that the birth channel has to be cut apart.
The mother meets with the extremity of pain, and the child suffers deeply.
Life is ended and breath extinguished.
The soul is benumbed and dies.

Because of karmic retribution, the fates of mother and child are bound together.
How can there be an end to it all?
Because of the cycle of karmic retribution, we here today must also meet with death. And to move the Buddha's compassion, we repent of everything.

All women, when they give birth, draw water from the well, or from the river or pond, to wash the birth cloths or to wash the body. The bloody water overflows and spreads to cover the ground—the veins empty their contents into the well.

Taking water to brew tea, it is then offered to the gods, and in it is this unclean thing, this blood.
It is a blasphemy to offer this disgusting filth to the gods, so the divine officials in charge of recording good and evil deeds will note the woman's name; waiting until she dies, the malevolent demons of hell will take up iron forks and pierce her innards, and iron hooks will grapple her cheeks.
They will force stinking pus and loathsome blood down her gullet.
They will take molten copper to quench her thirst and iron balls to stop her hunger.
There is not one of these dead souls who is not scorched with thirst.
In the space of one day and one night, she will have died ten thousand deaths, gone through ten thousand rebirths.
Her muscles, veins, bones, and marrow will throb with pain unceasing.

Thus we and those present here reflect on hell's miseries to move the Buddha's heart, and rely on the Great Merciful Father for salvation.

It is evident from the above passage that souls in conflict—"former resentments," to use Topley's term (1974: 245)—are intimately connected with the suffering brought about by the physical nature of women. And if one dies without somehow reconciling these conflicts and resentments, it is inevitable that one's soul will come back in the same way, locked forever in "cosmic antagonisms" (again, Topley's term).

I have thus far concentrated on popular conceptions of the physical causes of female pollution. However, since women are not merely organisms but also social animals, I will now consider popular conceptions of the social characteristics of women. In the popular arts and literature about birth, death, and the pollution of women, there is a persistent theme associating the behavior and nature of women with the behavior and nature of dogs, especially black dogs. For example, at funerals black dogs are frequently encountered in dramatic renditions of the Mu-lien story. The following is one of the earliest extant versions of the story.

Mu-lien was obliged to go back once more to Buddha who explained that not till the Avalambana Festival had been celebrated could his mother eat. On the fifteenth day of the seventh month he held the first celebration of this festival and out of the Avalambana bowl of offerings his mother was at last able to eat her fill. After this, however, he lost sight of her and on making enquiries was told by Buddha to go through the city begging at random, not choosing one house rather than another. In this way he would come to the house of a certain man of substance. A black dog would run out at the gate, tug at his cassock, and begin to speak in human language. "That dog," Buddha said, "is your mother."

It turned out as he had predicted. "As you saved me from the dark ways of Hell," the dog said, "why do you not save me from the misery of living in a dog's form?" "Kind mother," said Mu-lien, "it was entirely owing to my lack of filial piety that you got into trouble and dropped into Hell. Surely, however, you are better off as a dog here than you were in the world of Hungry Ghosts?" "Filial son," the dog said, "it is true that in this form of existence I can go or stay, sit or lie as I choose. If I am hungry I can always eat human excrements in the privy; if I am thirsty, I can always quench my thirst in the gutter. In the morning I hear my master invoking the protection of the Three Treasures [Buddha, the Religion, and the Community]; in the evening I hear his wife reciting the noble scriptures. To be a dog and have to accept the whole realm of impurities is a small price to pay for never so much as hearing the word 'Hell' said in my ear." (Waley 1960: 232–33.)

By itself, this episode does not suggest much. But its significance grows when other dramatic versions of the story of Mu-lien are considered. In the versions acted out at Taiwanese funerals, Mu-lien's mother is accused of earning her damnation by feeding the fetus of a black dog (*o-kau-the*) to her husband's brother, causing his death. In these funeral dramas, the reference to the fetus of a black dog is often understood to mean a human fetus—a much used ingredient in black magic potions. Similarly, the term "black dog" is found in the expression "black dog's blood" (*o-kau-hueq*), which refers to human menstrual blood—the most potent ingredient in magic charms that give power over other people. Black dogs are thus associated with unclean sexuality: in fact, a ladies' man in Taiwan is called a "black dog" (*o-kau*).

Black dogs also figure prominently in the imagery used to describe some political events. In the village where I worked in central Taiwan, kin groups are not important political units (except on a very small scale). Religious cults generally provide the organization and wider networks for political activity. These religious cults correspond to the sworn brotherhoods and "secret societies" so often linked with popular movements in China. An illuminating story is told about the destruction of one such local cult just after the Second World War. The agent of the destruction was a demon called the

Black Dog Demon (*o-kau-cia:*). In this area the Black Dog Demon is frequently associated with the black-magic tradition of the area's flatland aborigines, whose magical powers are said to derive from committing tabooed acts, such as throwing good cooked rice in the latrine, sucking menstrual blood, etc. Significantly, one of the most prominent features of social organization that distinguishes the flatland aborigines from the surrounding Chinese is the aborigines' willingness to allow persons of the same surname (*kang-se:* or *kang-kut:* "of the same bone") to intermarry. This violates one of the strongest Chinese incest taboos.

Just after the Second World War, members of a local Chinese cult associated with the god Chen Wu went on an "incense cutting" trip ("incense cutting" is the colloquial term for a pilgrimage to a temple or other center believed to be the spiritual home of a given cult). The group visited the main center of the Chen Wu cult, and also took a side trip to the temple of the mother goddess Ma Tsu in Pei-kang. When they returned, mass hysteria broke out, with scores of men possessed at once and a great deal of frenetic ritual activity. The hysteria was brought about by a man newly possessed, who accused another family in the village of serving false gods. Eventually the image of one of these false gods was burned. But shortly thereafter, the accuser himself was denounced as falsely possessed: he was not possessed by a true god at all, but by the Black Dog Demon. He had introduced this devil into the cult by means of a votive plaque of Ma Tsu that he had acquired in Pei-kang "under the banana trees" (*kin-ciou-kha*). In this context, "under the banana trees" means "in the bushes" (with the sexual connotation intended). Not only did this plaque come from one of the female spirit mediums associated with the cult of Ma Tsu, but the man who brought it back was a native of a nearby village known to be heavily populated by flatland aborigines. My informants even suggested that the plaque could have been purposely contaminated with *o-kau-hueq* (menstrual blood). In any event, the pollution of the votive plaque drove away the pure, orthodox, and benevolent spirits that had previously been in residence with the cult group and allowed impure, heterodox, and malevolent spirits to take their place.

The Black Dog Demon's intrusion into the cult, even though it was eventually exorcised by "boiling in oil" (*ci:-iu-tia:*), so contaminated everything and everyone that the gods no longer came to possess the cult's spirit mediums. As a result, the cult was unable to play an effective spiritual role in the community, and it declined as a social and political force. This was a serious matter for the villagers: since the times were troubled, the quarrels and factionalism resulting from the eventual dissolution of the cult weakened the ability of the villagers to defend their interests. Even though the demon was exorcised, its baleful influence succeeded in destroying a vital part of the village social structure. As one man put it: "It is very important to have a 'united hall' [*kiet-tng*—i.e., a strong cult group or secret society] in the community. If you don't, then you don't have a center where people can get together, and outsiders will think that the people have no spirit. And the place will have no power [*be chut si-thau*]." The Black Dog Demon thus can be seen as the apotheosis of the destructive potential of female sexuality: when this sexuality destroyed the bond between the men in the cult, it also destroyed the political unity of the community at large. (For a fuller treatment of the events described above, see Seaman 1978.)

Every society must come to grips with the facts of sex, birth, and death, since these are among the basic components of individual (and social) identity. In the case of China and Taiwan, the rite called Breaking the Blood Bowl provides an expression of the society's division of labor and political power and an explanation of the ultimate sources of individual fate and identity. Women are portrayed as impure, imperfect, and even immature because of the "worms" that attack their innermost being. Because of their polluting nature, women cannot approach the deities who could help them to overcome the ties of karmic retribution caused by their sexuality. Women need men to act on their behalf, and the story of Mu-lien is thus perfectly apropos of women's condition in China and Taiwan. The production of sons is what defines a woman's place in the ancestral cult, but the process of producing them destroys male solidarity: as brothers take wives and produce sons, their primary loyalties shift from each other to their own heirs and uterine group, thus weakening the bond of brotherhood.

The term the Taiwanese use to describe the maturation of a boy into a man is *tng-kut* ("the change of bone"). When this change happens at adolescence, a boy becomes a full member of the descent group into which he was born. If he dies thereafter, he will have his name inscribed on the tablets kept in memory of dead ancestors. The same can never be true of a woman. It is only through marriage and the production of sons that she can become a full member of any descent group (i.e., an ancestor). While she lives, a woman's status is always unclear, since her body, and the bone and blood that compose it, is derived from one group, and yet she lives with another.

A woman's fate is to bear within her body worms that eat her bone and blood. This is the source of her monthly discharge, as the worms attack her body. When a woman conceives, these fluids are no longer discharged but nurture the fetus. The end result is that the bone of the mother, which she inherited from her own agnatic ancestors, is transformed into the body of a child, who is a member of a different agnatic group—that of her husband. We may conclude that the power of birth and menstrual blood to pollute and destroy the purity of male-oriented cults is derived from a horror of the process that produces the blood. Since the female body has within it the power to destroy the bone of one agnatic lineage and transform it into the bone of another, it is no wonder that men shrink from contact with such a potent substance. And yet every man derives his very being and his social identity by passing through the pollution of birth. Even though mere contact with birth blood is a sin and offends the gods, only the women who produce the blood are punished by imprisonment in special hells. Hence every man is given the opportunity at his mother's funeral to perform a deed of great merit and mercy. By symbolically drinking the blood of his birth, he can feee his mother from the bonds of her existence as a woman and allow her to be reincarnated as a higher being. By performing this act, men achieve merit on their own behalf, qualifying their own souls for reincarnation as gods, saints, and the pure spirits of orthodox cults.

If sexuality is a destructive force stimulated by the female body, then it is not hard to understand why men try to cast a film of negative sentiment over the processes and very being of the female body. Simply put, women are the most dangerous threat to the solidarity of male-centered groups, and it is small wonder that the rites occurring at death should insist upon the resolution of all conflict, and particularly conflict between mother and child.

It often happens, however, that not all a woman's offspring are present at her funeral, for they may have predeceased her. The logic of karmic retribution would demand that she be linked to these unfilial souls in future generations, since they are not present to drink the blood. Yet there remains a means of salvation. The ritual specialist, acting in his role of Mu-lien, the paragon of filial piety who braved the pollution of hell to save his mother, raises his staff above his head—then smashes the empty bowl that lies on the ground. With this act, he breaks the karmic bond of antagonism engendered by the physical processes of sex, birth, and death. Man saves woman from her fate. But to be saved, she must have sons, for how else would there be someone to drink from the bowl?

# The Thai Ti Kong Festival

Emily Martin Ahern

One of the most elaborate festivals in San-hsia, a township in northern Taiwan, is the Thai Ti Kong festival, or "The Slaughter of the Honorable Pig." The festival (*pai-pai*) honors the god Co Su Kong, said to have been a powerful physician when he lived on the mainland in the eleventh century. To secure Co Su Kong's patronage during the difficult settlement of northern Taiwan, the first Chinese immigrants from An-ch'i county (Ch'üan-chou prefecture in Fukien) brought his image along; to show their gratitude for his aid and protection over the centuries, the present descendants of those An-ch'i settlers stage a magnificent Thai Ti Kong festival each year to commemorate his birthday.

In what follows, I argue that certain messages are expressed obliquely in this festival: some deal with the nature of social mobility and the character men must have to achieve it; others deal with local political and economic opposition to the state. My analysis attempts to provide a counterbalance to those who argue that rituals and the beliefs underlying them conceal the true, oppressive nature of political power from those subject to it, thus serving the interests of those

Unfootnoted material in this essay is based on field data gathered in 1969–70 and during the summers of 1972 and 1975. I am grateful to Liu Hsiou-yüan for help during all three periods of research and to Wang Ch'un-hua for help during the most recent period. I am also grateful to the Fulbright-Hays Fellowship Program, the Department of Epidemiology of the University of Washington, the Social Science Research Council, and the National Institute for Mental Health's Small Grant Program for financial support. I owe thanks to participants at the Conference on Anthropology in Taiwan (especially to Harry Lamley and Hill Gates) for various suggestions and references. Discussions with Susan Bean were very helpful as were comments received in seminars at Johns Hopkins University, the University of Maryland, Oxford University, and the School of Oriental and African Studies at the University of London.

Hokkien words are spelled according to the system outlined in Nicholas C. Bodman's *Spo-*

who govern (Bloch 1974: 79; Feuchtwang 1975: 80; Godelier 1977: 69; Rappaport 1971: 35–36). Some aspects of this festival—those extolling the possibility of social and economic mobility—may tend to lull the populace into accepting the existing political status quo. But other aspects of the festival—those delineating a cleavage between central rulers and local populace—reveal with precision the true nature of political power in Taiwan and thus serve the interests of those who are governed.

## *Organization*

Seven groups known as *ko* (shares) rotate responsibility for the Thai Ti Kong, each group providing in turn specially fattened pigs to offer to the god. Five of the *ko* are formed by major surname groups in the area; one is formed by "miscellaneous surnames"; and one is formed by the present and past residents of a village called Chung-chuang. The geographical area of the festival's participants is roughly coincident with the marketing area of San-hsia, an area dominated by Taiwanese of An-ch'i origins. This area includes all of San-hsia township and parts of the neighboring townships of Ying-ko, Shu-lin, and Ta-ch'i.

Knowledgeable people in the area frequently note the ties between Co Su Kong and Taiwanese of An-ch'i origins. One man told me that everyone who lives up the valley of the Tan-shui tributary toward Taipei—from San-hsia as far as the northern limits of a town called Ting-p'u—is of An-ch'i origin and therefore worships Co Su Kong. Beyond that boundary, he said, live people whose ancestors came from Chang-chou prefecture, and they do not pay homage to Co Su Kong.[1] He clinched his point by adding that the boundary is marked by a Tua Bong Kiong (a shrine for bones of the unknown dead), a result of the frequent battles between Ch'üan-chou and Chang-chou people in the last century. The people of Ting-p'u no longer participate in the *pai-pai* for Co Su Kong held at the San-hsia temple, but

*ken Amoy Hokkien* (1955), except that tone marks have been omitted. Mandarin is used for place-names. Surnames mentioned in the text are pseudonyms.

[1]The most important ethnic division among Taiwanese is between Hakka and Hokkien. Hokkien are divided according to the two prefectures in Fukien that they came from: Ch'üan-chou and Chang-chou. Ch'üan-chou and Chang-chou Hokkien are also subdivided according to their place of origin within these prefectures. The most important for our purposes is An-ch'i, a county in Ch'üan-chou.

only because they have built their own temple to Co Su Kong in Ting-p'u itself. The Ting-p'u temple's manager told me that the new temple (built 60 or 70 years ago) made everything more convenient; in the old days, villagers had to carry their pigs and other offerings all the way to San-hsia (a distance of four miles along a difficult trail), and this meant that they had to limit significantly the size of their fattened pigs.

Another clue to the importance of An-ch'i origins for participation in the Thai Ti Kong festival is provided by the *ko* for residents of Chung-chuang. Most people I asked were puzzled by the fact that this *ko* was based on residence rather than on surname. One informant was able to point out that Chung-chuang, located in neighboring Ta-ch'i township, is an An-ch'i enclave in otherwise Chang-chou territory; he regarded this as the original reason Chung-chuang was given a share all to itself.

Though participation in the *pai-pai* at the San-hsia temple is largely confined to those of An-ch'i origins, the festival does not encompass all An-ch'i Taiwanese who honor Co Su Kong. As noted, the An-ch'i people in Ting-p'u seceded from the San-hsia temple and established their own. Furthermore, the San-hsia temple itself is a branch of an older temple located in a Taiwanese section of Taipei known as Wan-hua. The manager of the Wan-hua temple told me that his was the oldest Co Su Kong temple in Taiwan: it was built where Co Su Kong's image was first permanently located by the settlers who brought it from An-ch'i. This temple has an annual *pai-pai* for Co Su Kong, and responsibility for putting it on rotates among residents of three areas adjacent to Wan-hua, all of whom trace their ancestry to settlers from An-ch'i.

The Co Su Kong *pai-pai* throws into relief two of the broadest social groupings in Taiwanese society—the clan, whose members share a common surname but cannot demonstrate common descent, and the ethnic group, whose ancestors are all from the same mainland county. The *pai-pai* also throws into relief one of the most important small social groupings in Taiwanese society—the family that shares a single purse, stove, and household. Such families, in fact, are generally responsible for saving the money and raising the pigs for the *pai-pai*. (Sons still attached to their fathers' households usually do not raise their own pigs; sons who have started independent households usually do.) When two households cooperate in raising a pig (generally for reasons of economy), they tend to be linked by friendship rather than by close kinship.[2]

Intermediate-sized social groupings (i.e., groupings that would combine households but divide the ethnic group and clans) are not emphasized by the *pai-pai*. Although lineage ancestors and territorially based earth gods are worshiped in the course of the festivities, people do not organize themselves in these terms: members of different lineages and residents of different villages worship Co Su Kong side by side at the temple in San-hsia. In no case is a pig for the festival regarded as the cooperative product of a lineage, lineage segment, village, or neighborhood. For example, when one household of Ongs won the important honor of taking their pig to the temple in San-hsia in 1970, they were accompanied by a distinctly miscellaneous collection of people—some kinsmen, some neighbors, some neither—with whom they had cordial, cooperative relationships.

In February of 1970, when I was living in the Ong settlement in Ch'i-nan (a village in San-hsia township), responsibility for the Thai Ti Kong fell to the Ong surname *ko*. This meant that all of the more than sixty Ong households in the settlement had begun to raise a Ti Kong ("Honorable Pig") at least a year in advance of Co Su Kong's birthday (on the sixth day of the first lunar month).[3] A short time before the birthday, any household that believed its pig was heavy enough registered at the San-hsia temple. Then, just before the sixth, a temple committee visited each registered household to weigh its pig, often an extraordinarily difficult task since the heaviest pigs weighed eight hundred or nine hundred pounds (and had to be dragged, struggling, onto a flatbed scale). One pig in Ch'i-nan placed among the twelve heaviest pigs in the *ko* and so was slaughtered, decorated, and taken to the San-hsia temple to be offered to Co Su Kong there. The other eleven pigs were slaughtered and decorated also, though less elaborately, and offered to an image of the god borrowed from the temple and temporarily installed in the village.

After completing offerings to Co Su Kong and other gods, each household butchered its pig and began to prepare food for feasts held

[2] Of the three pairs of households that raised pigs cooperatively in the Lou settlement in Ch'i-nan in 1975, only one pair involved brothers. The other two pairs were composed of households in different major branches of the Lou lineage.

[3] People say that there are two kinds of pigs: Ti Kong (raised with special care and slaughtered for the gods) and *chai-ti* (fed on garbage or purchased feed and slaughtered for sale). The word "Kong" in Ti Kong is an honorific often appended to the names of spiritual beings and to kinship terms for certain male ascendants. *Chai-ti* literally translates "food pig" and refers to the ordinary leftovers fed to these pigs.

the same evening or the next day. The disruption of normal domestic routines was enormous: trestle tables were set up in living rooms to provide space for preparing food, and as many beds as possible were arranged in other rooms for overnight guests. By the end of the festivities, each Ong household in the village had spent a minimum of NT$10,000, had entertained dozens (friends, affines, and business associates), and had paid an impressive homage to the gods.[4] As a kind of compensation, the Ongs were able to look forward to taking their turn as guests in the households of members of the other six *ko* during the following six years.

## *Offerings*

Since the organization of the *pai-pai* marks off a wide range of social groups, it is not surprising that the *pai-pai*'s offerings are distributed to a wide range of spiritual beings. After the pig is slaughtered, disembowelled, shaved, and decorated, it is placed alongside other offerings and presented first to Thi: Kong, the highest god, and then to Co Su Kong. Next the pig is butchered and its flesh cooked, with shares going first to Tho Te Kong, the earth god, and then to the celebrants' ancestors. Finally, even the ghostly subordinates of the gods and dangerous hungry ghosts receive their shares: Co Su Kong is said to give them a portion of what is offered to him. Thus, representatives of all the major categories of spirits receive offerings, from the highest ranking god down through ancestors and ghosts.

It is well known that the Taiwanese offer different kinds of foods and ritual money to different gods and spirits.[5] The pattern of offerings changes, however, for the Thai Ti Kong festival (see Table 1). This change is systematic and clear-cut: each spirit moves up one level in the spiritual hierarchy, receiving the offerings ordinarily appropriate to the being above him. Thi: Kong and (in the case of food offerings) Co Su Kong move off the normal scale, receiving offerings ordinarily not used at all.

Upon inquiry, I was told that the same elevation of food and ritual money offerings occurs on other occasions: at engagements, winter solstices, New Year's celebrations, and celebrations held after the birth of the first son.[6] These are all classified as "happy events" (*hi-*

[4] In 1970, NT$40 = US$1.00.

[5] See Ahern 1973: 167 and Arthur Wolf 1974: 177–81 for two interpretations.

[6] On these occasions, the elevation only affects ancestors and Tho Te Kong. A pig is not usually killed, and no raw offerings are made.

TABLE 1
*Food and Ritual Money Offerings*

| Offering | Usual recipient | Thai Ti Kong recipient |
|---|---|---|
| Food | | |
| Whole raw animals | none | Thi: Kong and Co Su Kong |
| Fruit and dry foods | Thi: Kong | Co Su Kong |
| Five uncut, cooked items[a] | Co Su Kong | Tho Te Kong |
| Three uncut, cooked items[a] | Tho Te Kong | ancestors |
| Cut, cooked, seasoned food | ancestors | none |
| Money[b] | | |
| *Ciok-pik siu-kim* (gold) | none | Thi: Kong |
| *Gou-ci:* (gold) | Thi: Kong | Co Su Kong |
| *Siu-kim* (gold) | Co Su Kong | Tho Te Kong |
| *Hok-kim* (gold) | Tho Te Kong | ancestors |
| *Siou-gun* (silver) | ancestors | none |

[a] These include such things as chickens, ducks, fish, slabs of pork, and pork livers.
[b] To simplify, I list only the highest value money offered to each being. With the exception of *siou-gun*, lower value money can be offered to any being entitled to money of a higher value.

*su*). Thai Ti Kong thus shares with these *hi-su* an emphasis on growth and prosperity; in fact, many people say that the most important reason they participate in a Thai Ti Kong is so that they can display their accumulated wealth.

Though it is possible to see why Thai Ti Kong festivals should be grouped with *hi-su*, it is far from evident why gods and ancestors should be elevated in rank. Two likely answers come to mind. The first is that this elevation is intended to increase the probability of future favors. Gods are seen as the source of desired events, and the higher their rank, the more efficacious (*lieng*) they can be in bringing such events about. Thus, when people attribute a higher rank to gods and ancestors through their offerings, they may be expressing the hope that the gods will be even more *lieng* than usual. This answer, however, does not explain why people should express such a hope at a time when the gods have thoroughly demonstrated their efficacy rather than at a time when the gods are perceived as withholding succor. A second likely answer (and one that may complement the first) is that elevating the rank of gods and ancestors is a way of expressing appreciation for gifts already received. Since *hi-su* are highly valued, it is obviously appropriate for highly valued offerings to be made in return. I shall supplement these two possible answers with a third in the next section of the paper.

In discussing the offerings made to gods and ancestors, however, I have underplayed an important aspect of this *pai-pai*: the presence of danger, demons, and death at its very heart. This fact is surprising because most rituals either celebrate life-affirming events (birthdays, engagements, weddings, births of sons, the building of new houses) or are related to death (funerals, death-day anniversaries). Most rituals associated with *hi-su* are occasions when people fete (*pai*) gods or ancestors, offering them homage and respect; most rituals associated with death (*song-su*) are occasions when people propitiate (*ce*) spirits lest they cause trouble. The term *ce* is explained as being the opposite of *pai*; though variously interpreted, it is usually said to imply the placation of dangerous spirits (*kui* or ghosts).

Aside from Co Su Kong's birthday, most occasions when people slaughter Ti Kong are unambiguously linked with *hi-su*—as, for example, decennial birthday celebrations for the elderly (these begin at the 50th birthday), births of first sons, and completions of pledges to a god for his help in the successful accomplishment of some goal (such as building a new house or starting a new business). Co Su Kong's celebration clearly belongs in some ways with this class of events: it is the birthday of a god; it is often also used to celebrate the birthdays of people or the completion of pledges; it is commonly called a *hi-su* or a big *pai-pai* (*tua pai-pai*); and it involves traditional symbols of a *hi-su* celebration such as gold ritual money and red hangings over doorways.

In other ways, however, Co Su Kong's celebration belongs to the class of events during which people propitiate potentially dangerous spirits.[7] For example, when I asked why a raw pig and raw fowl were offered to Co Su Kong, who is known to be a vegetarian, I was often told that Co Su Kong accepts the raw meat, cooks it, and distributes it to the hungry ghosts. One man said that the raw fowl is for the hungry ghosts and that the Ti Kong is for the "mountain spirits" who are also the soldiers of Co Su Kong. (Soldiers of gods are *kui* in character and have to be bought off frequently with offerings lest they cause sickness and trouble.) When I asked one man why this Thai Ti Kong is called a *pai-pai* if ghosts are involved, he said "Actually people do not '*pai-pai*' [pay respect]; they '*ce*' [placate]. The meat is used by Co Su Kong to *ce* ghosts in the underworld." The

[7] Most people in the San-hsia area know that another Thai Ti Kong—performed by Hakka in neighboring Hsin-chu county—is also intended to propitiate dangerous spirits: the hungry ghosts of Hakka slain while resisting an eighteenth-century uprising. In Hsin-chu itself, this event is regarded as a *pho-to* (exorcism) and focuses on the grave containing the bones of those Hakka slain in their efforts to support imperial troops against the forces of the rebel Lin Shuang-wen in 1786–88 (Michael Moser, personal communication).

most elaborate explanation I heard was offered by a woman of the Lou lineage whose household's pig had won the eighth prize in 1975. When I referred to the Thai Ti Kong as a *pai-pai*, she stopped me, saying:

It is not an occasion for *pai-pai*; it is an occasion for *ce*. We *ce* to placate the spirit of an enormous bird who destroyed the soldiers of Koxinga in Ying-ko [a nearby township] about three hundred years ago. After Koxinga killed the bird, a search was made for its body, but no body could be found. Just then a large stone in the shape of a bird appeared on the mountain. A hole opened in the stone, and mist came out. People feel that this bird's soul may still be around causing trouble; so we follow Koxinga's advice and kill a pig every year to prevent it from causing harm. Because we don't know how to *ce*, we ask Co Su Kong to help us. He acts for us just as Taoist priests do, by helping to manage the ghosts.

The intrusion of ghostly elements in this *pai-pai* is shown in another way: people are divided about whether a Thai Ti Kong can be held when there has been a recent death in the family. According to one Ong woman, this is the only *pai-pai* that a family may participate in even if a recent death has occurred. Some people, the woman claimed, combine the Thai Ti Kong feast with the feast that takes place after the funeral. Other people were certain, however, that they could not take part in a Thai Ti Kong after a death. One family had raised a pig for twenty months when a death occurred: they gave the pig away to another family (who saw it win fourth prize) because the death made them "unclean" and because death, a *song-su*, cannot be mixed with a Thai Ti Kong, a *hi-su*. Others were very uncertain whether they would take part in a Thai Ti Kong if they were in mourning. This indecision—whatever the outcome—is another manifestation of the ambiguous position of the Thai Ti Kong *pai-pai* in comparison with other *pai-pai*. (No one, for example, would think of holding a wedding or a grandfather's birthday celebration while in mourning.)

Some of the elements of danger and death in the Thai Ti Kong stem from the slaughtering process itself. An Ong man said: "Killing the pig is a very dangerous matter. Certain people shouldn't be present at that time because their birth date makes them vulnerable. Just the other day a man watched who shouldn't have. He went home and fell very sick. But the butcher made a drink using the red patch of paper from the knife that had been used to kill the pig, and as soon as the man had drunk it, he recovered." Other measures are taken to protect against danger at this time: wine is poured over rice, and this rice is given to the pig just before the slaughter (an exorcising technique in other contexts); the rope used to tie the pig's legs, the slaughtering knife, and the butcher's apron are all marked with patches of red (often used as a prophylactic); and the pig is offered ritual money. This offering is called *ce-suaq* ("placate evil"): it is designed to keep the pig from being angry at being killed.

In part, the danger of slaughtering a Ti Kong comes from the danger of slaughter in general. There is an antivenin factory in Ch'i-nan where buffalo and horses are frequently slaughtered. People in the community were so fearful of the dangerous spirits of the slaughtered animals—it was said that one could hear their screams at night—that the owner of the factory built a special Tho Te Kong temple on the premises to control them.

The broad scope of San-hsia's Thai Ti Kong festival is thus emphasized by its associations with death, danger, and ghosts. Other Taiwanese rituals are much more specific in their thrust and limited in their participants: a family may exorcise a ghost; a lineage may commemorate an ancestor's death day; or a village may pay homage to its patron deity. But this Thai Ti Kong involves a wide range of groups and provides for the celebration of gods and ancestors as well as for the propitiation of ghosts and gods' subordinates. The frequency of a ritual is also a very good clue to its scope. Rituals organized by families, lineages, and villages tend to require (respectively) daily, monthly, and yearly participation. The panoramic nature of Co Su Kong's Thai Ti Kong is therefore clear from the fact that its period is longer than most other rituals in this part of Taiwan: responsibility for raising a pig comes to each household only once every seven years.[8]

## *Pigs*

The care lavished on Ti Kong makes it obvious that they are of central concern in Co Su Kong's *pai-pai.* Why should pigs, rather than other animals, serve as the central offering? To answer this, we must look at the characteristics of ordinary pigs and at the special characteristics of Ti Kong—in both cases, in relation to human beings.

Consider first ordinary domestic pigs. They are set apart from

[8] Temple *chiao* (esoteric Taoist rituals to renew a temple's charter) have an even longer period: ideally they should be performed once every 60 years (Saso 1972: 33).

other domestic animals by the extent to which they depend on humans. Their sties are usually inside the house, adjoining the kitchen and toilet. Their food is often prepared. One old man who spent hours chopping and boiling sweet-potato leaves for pigs told me that he did this despite the recommendation of the Farmers' Association not to cook pigs' food. Although he agreed that not all pigs' food had to be cooked (vegetables and meat scraps as well as purchased feed were offered uncooked), he felt that pigs fared better on cooked food. But cooked or not, everything a pig eats is provided by its owner: pigs in this part of Taiwan do not scavenge for their food.[9] Other domestic animals such as water buffalo, chickens, ducks, cats, and dogs may likewise live under the same roof as their owners. Except for dogs, however, these animals are capable of obtaining their own food and are expected to do so, at least in part.

Pigs are also set apart from other domestic animals by the frequency with which they appear in proverbs, folksongs, and metaphors epitomizing behavior undesirable in humans. Some examples follow, taken from a wide variety of sources.

*Pigs are sexually licentious.* Chu Pa-chieh, the pig figure in the novel *Hsi-yu chi*, is often a prominent character in village dramatizations of the journey of Monkey and Tripitaka. He is characteristically lewd and licentious, exactly as he is in the written tradition (Dudbridge 1970: 197; Wu Ch'eng-en 1958: 153).

Hong Kong farmers disapprove of boat people because in boats several couples (even including brothers) may sleep side by side: "They don't know the shame of it. It is like the pigs." (Osgood 1975: 108–9.)

A riddle is phrased, "I wear black clothes; I cross hills and mountains searching for girls; everyone calls me a playboy; I only go home after earning a lot of money." The answer is, "Older brother pig (stud pig)." (Wu Ying-t'ao 1969: 277.) My informants said this was a name for a boy who lusts after girls too much; it calls to mind the slobbering of pigs.

[9]The feeling that pigs should eat cooked food is common in other parts of China (Cohen 1976: 147; Gallin 1966: 60; Osgood 1975: 131–32). Writing about a village in Hong Kong, Osgood notes that one sow's unusual toleration for uncooked kale was "attributed to the fact that [the] sow was not of the common Chinese breed, but one with mixed Australian ancestry" (1975: 132). Gallin's informants in Hsin Hsing spent much time preparing cooked food for pigs: despite the Farmers Association's insistence that pig food need not be cooked, they persisted in saying that "pigs will not grow fat on raw sweet potatoes" (1966: 60).

*Pigs are weak and stupid.* The phrase "a sow turns into a tiger" is interpreted to mean "the weak become strong" (Wu Ying-t'ao 1975: 173).

In physiognomy, a person whose face resembles a pig's face is "just plain stupid" (Burkhardt 1955: 94).

*Pigs have immoderate appetites for food.* The proverb "When a pig comes, you are poor; when a dog comes, you are rich; when a cat comes, you can build a house" (Wu Ying-t'ao 1975: 175) was interpreted by my informants as "pigs eat too much, dogs guard the house, a cat eats rats and saves grain."

A person who overeats can be called Ti Ma (mother pig) or Ti Kong in jest.

The proverb "Before a man takes a wife he has a lot of money to spend; before you raise a pig, you have a lot of feed" implies that afterward, in both cases, one's resources are consumed (Wu Ying-t'ao 1975: 57).

*Pigs are lazy and useless.*[10] A person who sleeps all day is called a "sleeping pig" (*khun-ti*).

A children's song (Wu Ying-t'ao 1975: 606) compares the activities of pigs with the activities of other domestic animals:

"Chicken, oh chicken, we are going to slaughter you."
"What are you going to slaughter me for?"
"Because you don't lay eggs."
"On the first day I laid a hundred; on the second I laid a basketful.
If you want to slaughter, slaughter a duck."

"Duck, oh duck, we are going to slaughter you."
"What are you going to slaughter me for?"
"Because you don't lay eggs."
"On the first day I laid an incubator full; on the second I laid a cupboard full.
If you want to slaughter, slaughter a cow."

"Cow, oh cow, we are going to slaughter you."
"What are you going to slaughter me for?"
"Because you don't plow the fields."
"I plowed the upper hill; I harrowed the lower hill.
If you want to slaughter, slaughter a horse."

[10]The pig figure Chu Pa-chieh labors very strenuously in the novel *Hsi-yu chi*, but this is before he takes on the physical form of a pig (Wu Ch'eng-en 1958: 149).

"Horse, oh horse, we are going to slaughter you."
"What are you going to slaughter me for?"
"Because you don't walk."
"I've traveled the upper road; I've walked the lower road.
If you want to slaughter, slaughter a dog."

"Dog, oh dog, we are going to slaughter you."
"What are you going to slaughter me for?"
"Because you don't guard the house."
"I've guarded the roof; I've watched the house.
If you want to slaughter, slaughter a pig."

"Pig, oh pig, we are going to slaughter you."
"What are you going to slaughter me for?"
"Because you don't eat the garbage."
"I've eaten a batch of your spoiled garbage; I've eaten a batch of your bad rice-washing water.
If you want to slaughter me, go ahead. If you want to cut me up, go ahead."

The above song contrasts the pig's usefulness and willingness to help out with other domestic animals' usefulness and willingness to help out. The pig is obviously deficient in both areas: his work is minor and self-gratifying, and his lackadaisical attitude about dying shows that he is not ardent in the service of his owner. Indeed, pigs are even seen as faintly malevolent. One family, for example, was told by a ritual expert that their present difficulties stemmed from the fact that a pigsty had once existed underneath their kitchen. Unless they unearthed all the stones that the pigs had lived on, their difficulties would continue.

In fact, pigs are often described as the "worst" animals—a description corroborated by the supposition that bad men are sometimes punished by being reincarnated as pigs. In "A Wicked Merchant Turns into a Pig" (a story circulated by a San-hsia religious sect), the merchant's son dreams that his dead father tells him: "In the past, I was so extremely wicked that I let three people living in a hut burn to death. It was really a crime deserving of ten thousand deaths. The King of the Underworld did not permit me to go into the world of men again, but compelled me to enter a pig's womb." Because pigs are the "worst" animals, they are frequently used to symbolize undesirable people. During the 1891 mainland campaign against foreign missionaries, for example, pictures were distributed showing pigs—representing Christians—being attacked by Buddhist priests (Chesneaux 1971: 98–99). This was also a fine visual depiction of a pun: the word for pig in mandarin (*chu*) differs only in tone from the word for Jesus.

If the pig's character is seen in a negative light, his economic role is not: pigs are (and are recognized to be) extremely efficient machines for disposing of refuse and for producing both fertilizer (manure) and highly valuable meat. In this sense, then, pigs are maligned. Indeed, pigs are thought to combine a number of characteristics found together only in one other sort of being—hungry ghosts (the spirits of those who die violently or without descendants). Like hungry ghosts, pigs depend on people to feed them, are capable of causing harm, and die violently (since they are invariably slaughtered). And both pigs and hungry ghosts embody qualities undesirable in humans: sloth and greed in one case, loneliness and isolation in the other.

In many ways, then, pigs are foils for desirable human conduct. But when pigs are raised as Ti Kong their relationship to humans becomes more complex: in certain ways, they become similar to humans. Like humans, for example, they are sensitive to pollution. One woman told me that Ti Kong take offense if anyone in a polluted state tries to feed them—so much so that they bite in displeasure. Indeed, they object to pollution from any source, including funerals, births, and menstruation. Like some human children, Ti Kong are said to be *kui-khi* (expensive and difficult to raise).[11] This means that they must be treated very carefully—not in the casual way ordinary pigs are. Most families who raise a Ti Kong consult Co Su Kong at his temple whenever the pig loses his appetite or shows any signs of illness; and many families regularly bring home incense ash for the pig to eat in much the same fashion that they would for a *kui-khi* child.

Ti Kong also have abilities not found in ordinary pigs. They understand human speech, and so one must be careful about what is said within their hearing. If a Ti Kong hears people arguing, for instance, he will lose his appetite. To avoid this situation, only one person in the household is usually assigned to tend the pig. (The one time I was allowed into a Ti Kong's presence, I was warned not to say anything.) Also, like humans, Ti Kong have distinct personalities. One family

[11] See M. Wolf 1972: 63–64 for a discussion of *kui-khi* children.

told me that the Ti Kong they raised seven years ago was extremely sensitive: he would only accept food from one person, and he became very upset if strangers came into the house and spoke loudly. This year's Ti Kong was very different: he did not object to strangers at all.

Much of the human-like treatment accorded to a Ti Kong revolves around his food. Ti Kong have definite food preferences—informants often said "Ti Kong are like people; they like some things better than others"—and their preferences are respected. Wheat, rice, bran, sweet potatoes, eggs, chicken, fresh fruits, and vegetables are some of the foods Ti Kong are given, and all this food is prepared exactly as if it were for human consumption. "Ti Kong aren't like ordinary pigs, who don't care whether or not food is spoiled." Ti Kong are also usually given their rice or grain separately from other parts of the meal: it is cooked so that it can be formed into sticky balls and fed to the pig by hand. Some people provide their pigs two or three "regular meals" of grain each day as well as snacks of fruit and vegetables between meals. Often the pigs are offered clean water to drink at the end of each feeding. And no Ti Kong ever seems to receive the homogenized slops that are the fare of ordinary pigs.

The physical conditions under which Ti Kong live also emphasize their human-like position and set them apart from ordinary pigs. A fastidious owner will provide his Ti Kong with several baths a day, an electric fan in hot weather, a layer of sand to serve as a soft bed, an electric light during the evening, and a spraying of insecticide whenever mosquitoes are about. Furthermore, a Ti Kong's sty is cleaned each time he urinates or defecates, and his mouth is wiped after each meal.

Even though it is clear that Ti Kong are given special treatment, one might object to my analogy between Ti Kong and human beings. Yet there are a number of ways in which Ti Kong become strikingly human-like. Prize-winning pigs (and any others whose owners care to take the trouble) are decorated and placed on elaborate scaffolds decked out with colorful hangings, flowers, and lanterns. Sometimes replicas of old-fashioned "ancient-style" houses (made of paper and bamboo splints) are mounted on the scaffolds. These scaffolds are explicitly compared to houses: "If you look at the pig from the front, he appears to be inside a house." Ti Kong are, then, pigs who have moved from their sties into houses of their own with all the privileges thereof.

A more fanciful but inescapable point is that a decorated Ti Kong in some ways resembles a human: all his bristles are shaved off except for a dark patch on his head, and he has a pale-colored body. Indeed, it is common to see people bent over a slaughtered Ti Kong, laboriously plucking out every last hair from his face and ears. A hairless face is evidently as much a sign of beauty among such pigs as it is among people.[12]

A related fact is that households identify very closely with their Ti Kong. In 1970, when cameras were scarce in the countryside, I was kept very busy taking pictures of people standing alongside their decorated Ti Kong. It is small wonder that owners are proud of their Ti Kong, since the pigs are literally embodiments of their own resources. Not only are pigs usually raised at great financial cost (one prize-winning family spent NT$100,000), but they absorb untold time, effort, and concern.

The argument that Ti Kong attain nearly human status can be made even stronger. My informants, for example, frequently insisted that Ti Kong are treated better than people. One woman told me that her household's Ti Kong often took two or three hours to finish each of his three meals of grain: "You cannot rush the pig or force him in any way. If he is slow to eat or refuses food, you must not get angry or irritated at all. We bought all kinds of things to offer him—papaya, plums, and apples, canned and fresh—so that if he didn't want one thing, we could switch to another." At this point, my assistant noted that the pig received better treatment than people. The woman laughed and readily agreed. Another informant volunteered, "Ti Kong are really better off than people are. We are satisfied with any old thing to eat, but Ti Kong have to have special care. There was a family who fed their pig oily rice, prepared very well with meat and other delicacies.[13] Once the family had unexpected guests. Since there wasn't enough ordinary rice, the host said, 'Bring out the pig's rice.' The guests were horrified at the thought of people eating pig's food, but when they saw it, they said, 'It's actually better than the food we were just eating!'"

Some informants stressed that Ti Kong are "greater" (*khaq-tua*)

[12] See Schreider & Schreider 1969: 16 for a photograph of a man plucking hair from a Ti Kong's head. The color contrast between hair and flesh makes apparent the similarity between pig and man.

[13] "Oily rice" (*iu-png*) is a special food eaten by women after childbirth. It is a rich delicacy, considered nourishing and delicious.

than people because they are offerings to the gods. "We respect the gods by respecting what we offer them." Indeed, a sacrificial animal bridges the gap between humans and gods, and thus in a sense is "greater" than humans (Leach 1976: 84). Ti Kong, then, have somehow acquired a most extraordinary position: they are animals ordinarily notable for their sloth, stupidity, and greed; yet as Ti Kong, they are accorded comforts and privileges not available to most men. It would perhaps not be going too far to suggest that Ti Kong are allowed to live as if they were members of the leisured upper class. The indolence pure and simple of ordinary pigs is turned into the indolence of wealth and status, thanks to constant human attention, physical comfort, and culinary delicacies on demand.

A ritual may be seen as a dramatization of themes that preoccupy the ritual's participants. If such an approach is adopted here, one theme that strongly emerges is the transformation of something ugly, ghostly, lazy, hurtful, and lowly into something beautiful, godly, purposeful, helpful, and privileged. People explained, for example, that virtually all the pig's decorations—the red cloth on its back, the necklace of old coins around its neck, the two gold foil "flowers" stuck in its head, the fruit in its mouth—contributed to its beauty. It may be that an aspect of this beauty is the aura of the upper class mentioned earlier. One informant tentatively suggested that the gold "flowers" stuck in the pig's head are like the hat decorations worn by Ch'ing magistrates; and it is a fair guess that people may associate the necklace of old coins (each coin marked with the seal of an earlier dynasty) with the political authority of a past era. An indolent animal, like a ghost in its dependence on others and in its aura of malice, has thus become a creature "greater than men" (or more precisely, "greater than ordinary peasants"). The Ti Kong is now fully pleasing as an offering for the gods and capable of helping men confirm their status in society.[14]

If pigs are transformed by the *pai-pai* in all these ways, men are also altered in no small measure. Not only does the pig demonstrate a household's ability to hold its own in a stiff financial effort, but it stands as proof that the household is in a favored relationship with the god Co Su Kong. I was told over and over that the most impor-

[14] In one obvious way the pigs' standing is not improved: after the slaughter, they are dead. Gary Seaman's informants in central Taiwan explained that Ti Kong are actually better off after the slaughter because they are reincarnated as women (personal communication).

tant factor in raising a Ti Kong is to have sincere respect for Co Su Kong: only if you have this respect will the god protect the pig and help it grow; if you lack respect, it matters little what you feed the pig, for it will not grow fat.

If the most obvious, overt message of the ritual deals with the transformation of the bad, low, and useless into the good, high, and useful, there are other messages that are, as Geertz put it, "disquietful," presenting life in a light one normally ignores or holding up for contemplation experiences normally repressed (1972: 24). The ritual depicts the bad traits of pigs being turned into good traits. If it also presupposes a close identification between people and pigs, then it follows that some rather pointed messages about human character are being conveyed.

The ritual shows us the transformation of a creature that is like all men in some ways and like lazy and immoderate men in others. The point is not merely that such traits are undesirable but that even creatures with such traits are capable of changing their character and status. If a pig can become "better" than a man, then surely a man can become a better man. But there is more. If pigs are felt to be the most appropriate animals to represent this transformation, it must be *in part* because people can be a lot like pigs. The transformation of pigs and the potential transformation of humans in the *pai-pai* does not obscure this basic similarity. Indeed, a recognition of improvement implies a recognition that there is something to be improved. I do not wish to argue here that animals always serve as foils for human ideals in the way, for example, that the aggressive, furious cock illustrates for the Balinese the behavior most removed from ideal human behavior (Geertz 1972: 25). But if the dominant concerns in Taiwanese rural society are (as I think most observers would agree) hard work and frugality—both dedicated to bettering one's lot in life—then it is not surprising that a major ritual should express themes of betterment and that the slothful, dissolute pig should be used to demonstrate the antithesis of desirable human conduct.

There is also a practical reason why the pig should be the central offering in a festival preoccupied with transformation of the useless into the useful. Pigs, be they *chai-ti* (ordinary pigs) or Ti Kong, daily transform substances useless to humans (garbage and roughage) into a most precious substance: manure. The pig's contribution to the fertility of grain and vegetables (a contribution that was critical before the availability of chemical fertilizers) means that in this basic, material way pigs perform the same function that they are given in ritual: waste becomes treasure, and the bad and useless becomes good and useful.

### *Participants*

The hypothesis that a Thai Ti Kong ritual displays themes of improvement would be strengthened if people believed that their participation in the ritual actually brought about improvement in their lives. Tales of families offering pigs and then being lifted out of abject poverty are not uncommon. Many people in Ch'i-nan knew the story of an old woman who was so poor that she could hardly feed her pig. Nonetheless, her Ti Kong grew to such an enormous size that it won the weight competition. People said that Co Su Kong's strength must have made the pig grow, so the pork (imbued with the god's efficacy) sold for a very high price. With the money from the sale, the old woman was able to build herself a house in place of her former straw hut.

Participation in a Thai Ti Kong festival with the hope of improving one's economic and social mobility is not impossible even for the very poor. I asked many people whether any household might be too poor to offer a pig. The consensus was that this was nearly inconceivable. One woman said, "If you are very poor, you can cooperate with a relative or friend and contribute half the cost. If you are too poor even for that, you can borrow the money and pay it back later with interest. If you didn't kill a pig, everyone would laugh at you." She thought it likely that a household would go to any lengths to finance a Ti Kong.

In a time of general prosperity in this part of Taiwan, it is difficult to find poverty-stricken rural households. In 1975, for instance, all Lou households in Ch'i-nan killed pigs for Co Su Kong except a vegetarian household, a household in mourning, and four households who purchased all the pork they needed (an even more expensive undertaking than raising a Ti Kong).

People insisted that even in the old days when poverty was widespread anyone could raise a pig, because Co Su Kong would lend assistance. My former landlady told me: "Co Su Kong is very efficacious. No matter how poor you are, he will help you raise a pig. Even in the Japanese period when everyone was poor, a piglet could be purchased very cheaply. If you could just give it any old thing to eat so it grew to two hundred or three hundred pounds, that would be fine. In those days, everyone raised vegetables, chickens, and ducks, so it wasn't too expensive to invite guests. There may have been some who didn't kill a pig, but they were very few."

It is clear from the remarks just quoted that along with the hope of improving one's material condition goes a concern with avoiding loss of face in the community: "The pig is connected with your face, so you can't avoid offering it. Since you live here in Ch'i-nan, you have to go along with the local customs. It's like the saying 'Lose to an individual, not to a whole group: if you lose to a whole group, your face looks terrible.' People laugh when they see you don't have the resources to kill a pig. The only way to avoid this laughter would be to move to another place to live."

By not offering a Ti Kong or by doing it poorly, people clearly risk losing considerable status within the community. In 1975, villagers were still talking about the Peqs' 1973 Ti Kong feast. Only after the feast was over did the guests discover that the pork they had eaten had not come from a Ti Kong: it had come instead from a pig that had died of natural causes, which the Peqs had purchased to save money. Many guests said that they were so disgusted they vomited; others said that they would never be guests of the Peqs again; and all agreed that poverty was no excuse for such behavior. It would have been, they insisted, far better (though still unwise) for the Peqs to have done nothing at all.

By offering a Ti Kong well, people can gain status or at the very least maintain status. But people's needs to improve or defend their status vary. As one woman in Ch'i-nan's Ong settlement put it,

> There are two kinds of people who kill a Ti Kong for Co Su Kong. First are those who are afraid that other people will laugh at them if they don't, saying that they don't have the ability. You just can't avoid spending less than NT$10,000. The second kind are those who hope to get the god's protection. But other people don't offer pigs at all. Last year, the mayor of Sanhsia didn't kill a pig. He knew he would have to invite an enormous number of guests, so he avoided the problem by offering the god an ordinary piece of pork. Smart people don't kill pigs; only dumb ones do.

In this woman's mind, the display of wealth associated with killing a Ti Kong was unnecessary for those whose social position was very secure. "Smart people" were those whose ability to offer a pig would never be questioned (or who would not feel insecure in the face of such questioning).

Part of the reason some people feel secure with regard to Ti Kong competition is of course that they are no longer competing for status within the local community, but are looking elsewhere—to urban centers like Taipei or even to national or international arenas. Outside San-hsia, moving up (in politics, commerce, or the professions) calls for education, money to invest, and political connections. In this world, pig-raising competitions are totally irrelevant. Still, nothing prevents people who are trying to move upward in the larger world from demonstrating their competence within San-hsia: in 1970, many tales were told of the enormous feast that the richest Ong family offered to over two hundred guests.

The Thai Ti Kong ritual, then, does not display the possibility of improvement merely for aesthetic reasons. As the proverb has it, "Raise a daughter and you lose your reputation; raise a pig and you gain fame." Despite the enormous expenditure, participants believe that through a Thai Ti Kong they stand to win, lose, or maintain important social and economic status. This fact can lead us to a fuller understanding of the systematic elevation of offerings that the festival calls forth. If successfully raising a Ti Kong often brings increased status, then elevating the rank of ancestors and gods makes good sense: only in this way can the distance between men and spirits be kept the same. The ritual may allow people to better their position, but not at the expense of narrowing the distance between men and gods.

## *Politics*

It would be a gross distortion to leave the impression that Co Su Kong's festival is performed solely for the edification of An-ch'i Hokkien in and about San-hsia. For some time, the festival has been a subject of contention between the Nationalist government dominated by mainlanders and the township population dominated by Taiwanese.[15] The government's concern stems in part from its long-

[15] See Tien 1975: 626–28 for a discussion of mainlanders' domination of positions in the categories of "public administration" and "military, police, and national security." The following discussion deliberately simplifies the local political situation, but see Gates and Winckler, this volume, for amplification. Because the matter is too complex to discuss here, I do not elaborate on the role of elected officials (such as the mayor of San-hsia) who are Taiwanese. Many ordinary citizens see Taiwanese officials as caught in a difficult position: they must promulgate policies originated by their superiors in the government, but if they promulgate unpopular ones, such as those directed against *pai-pai*, they will lose local support.

standing policy of discouraging Taiwanese religious customs, especially *pai-pai*. I cannot review the history of this policy here (see Rohsenow 1973: 84–96); but suffice it to note that on my first field trip in 1969 Ch'i-nan villagers were upset over a government tax on each performance of a folk opera for the gods and over mounting government pressure to combine what were traditionally separate *pai-pai* for the god Ang Kong (held by different districts in sequence). Even at that time, resentment toward these policies was common. One elderly man said:

We work hard every day. We are up early every morning at 5:00 A.M. and don't sleep until late at night in order to get everything done. Why does the government begrudge us a few days' rest? The aborigines have their *pai-pai* in the mountains; why can't we have ours? Every year the government spends untold dollars celebrating national holidays like Double Ten. If they can spend money on their *pai-pai*, why can't we spend money on ours? No, they insist on interfering with our customs by imposing fines and taxes on opera performances. There is absolutely no chance we will ever combine our *pai-pai* for Ang Kong with others.

The San-hsia Thai Ti Kong came in for special attention from the government as early as 1974. A newspaper article congratulated the people of San-hsia for putting on an "economical *pai-pai*":

At times there have been over one thousand Ti Kong, the largest exceeding one thousand pounds. This certainly absorbs people's energy and wastes their money terribly. It has been estimated conservatively that the amount of money wasted offering pigs and giving banquets in one year would be enough to rebuild the bridge from San-hsia to Ying-ko. (Altogether, NT$15,000,000 is spent.) Anyone who is surprised that there is this much waste can think about it and realize that it is so.

This year, just as it came to the Peqs' turn to slaughter the pigs, the government enforced their policy of stabilizing prices. In accordance with the government's policy, a lot of people in the township tried not to extend the waste, some even to the point of not killing a pig at all. Because of this, the number of pigs participating in the pig contest this year declined sharply. There were only slightly more than one hundred pigs. This was the smallest number of pigs at any recent Co Su Kong temple *pai-pai*. (*Lien He Pao* 1974.)

In 1975, the government stepped up its efforts to discourage participation. It was reasoned that if the Lous (whose turn it was and who held the first of the seven *ko*) could be persuaded to desist, the other six *ko* would follow suit. Numerous newspaper articles exhorting economy appeared before the *pai-pai*, and government representatives met with village heads to ask for their support. Afterward, a newspaper article claimed that only about one hundred pigs had been killed:

> The policy "Simplify Customs and Save Waste" actively promulgated by the township government office has had obvious success. It is said that the Mayor called a meeting at the government office for the Co Su Kong temple committee and other local concerned persons to encourage the township populace to follow the government's policy of "New Government" and to avoid wasting their resources. They found ways to make the believers understand that the government's main goal concerning the Thai Ti Kong is that each believer will not continue to waste resources through religious practices. They do not intend to influence the people's "belief that one should respect the gods." This is because to believe, it is only necessary to respect the gods in your heart. The gods will know it and will absolutely not take account of whether you have killed a big pig or bought a lot of fruit to offer them. (*Chung Kuo Shih Pao* 1975a.)

In all its forms, the government's message stresses saving money instead of wasting it on things to offer the gods. But local people respond by saying that if one thinks the *pai-pai* wastes money, one has completely missed its point. "It is inconceivable that you could be worse off after the *pai-pai* than before. If we pay our respects to Co Su Kong, he will protect us and help us earn the money we need to buy offerings. If we didn't worship, we wouldn't earn the money and be able to save it anyway. So telling us to save instead of celebrating is useless." Co Su Kong's protection, moreover, is not the only benefit of the *pai-pai*. "Thai Ti Kong is not wasteful. Even those old people who insist on killing a pig every year really work very hard to earn money so they can feed the pig fine things. This is not wasted effort because it teaches people to be diligent and work hard at honest labor." And the most practically minded of all emphasize the absurdity of the juxtaposition "don't celebrate, save instead." "The *pai-pai* does not waste money. First, pork from a Ti Kong sells for a very high price, so you can make money selling what you don't need. Second, the government itself makes money from the slaughter of each pig by extracting a very high tax. Their exhortation to 'stop the *pai-pai* and save' makes no sense at all."

These responses all share an insistence that the government fails to understand the central concern of this *pai-pai*. We have seen that the internal message of the ritual concerns improvement, achievement, and transformation. Yet the government insists that the *pai-pai* is wasteful and squanders resources. A more fundamental misapprehension of its point could scarcely be imagined.

It is difficult to say what impact these government policies have had on people's behavior. Opinion in San-hsia is divided, for example, about whether participation in the *pai-pai* has increased or decreased. Those who see the festivities only in their villages often insist that participation has increased along with the population. As households divide and multiply, they say, the number of pigs killed increases. Others (also speaking from a village vantage point) say that the total number of people participating has stayed the same, though the *ko* have changed in size. Still others claim that participation has fallen off, citing as evidence that crowds near the temple are smaller and that fewer pigs are taken to the temple.

It is likely that there has been some reduction in the overall magnitude of the celebrations, though it is impossible to say whether participation has indeed fallen off or whether people are simply less likely to go to the temple with their pigs (perhaps in order to keep the number of participants less visible).[16] The township government office said in 1975 that its records of the numbers of pigs killed prior to 1972 have been destroyed; but by their rough estimate, the numbers have decreased drastically. The Co Su Kong temple has records beginning in 1947 of how many people in each *ko* registered to have their pigs weighed—a measure only of the most thoroughgoing kind of participation. But even these records are inconclusive: since 1947, the numbers of people registered have almost doubled for three *ko*, have decreased for three other *ko*, and have stayed about the same for the remaining *ko*.

The question of changing participation aside, it is clear that certain local leaders are acting resourcefully to protect the *pai-pai* from further attack. The government may discourage the slaughter of Ti

[16] It would be interesting to analyze the changes in the extent of participation (and size of offerings) over time. If Skinner's suggestion (1971) that Chinese communities are sometimes relatively open and sometimes relatively closed can be applied to Taiwan, then we might expect that during open periods—characterized by stability, prosperity, and high mobility—participation would be extensive, offerings large and generous, and attendance at the temple common. During closed periods—characterized by disorder, poverty, and restricted opportunity—participation would be correspondingly less and offerings modest and more likely to be presented to the gods in villages rather than at market-town temples. If this were so (and there is not space to attempt such an analysis here), the smaller and fewer pigs offered during closed periods would reflect not merely (and obviously) a lack of resources, but also people's perceptions of their restricted mobility. This would not be inconsistent with my suggestion that Ti Kong dramatize betterment.

Kong as wasteful, but recently it has strongly encouraged the raising and selling of pigs to offset the high price of pork. It should come as no surprise, then, that from 1976 the Co Su Kong *pai-pai* has been jointly sponsored by the temple and by the Farmers Association. "Since the government is always encouraging people to raise pigs, the *pai-pai* can pose as a contest to raise the biggest and the fattest pigs possible. Of course, the contest will take place as usual in front of the Co Su Kong temple." Most local people saw this move as a minor adjustment in the *pai-pai*'s traditional organization, but one that would "sound better" and give local leaders "something to say" to their superiors in the government.[17]

Before this recent tactic, Co Su Kong worshipers explicitly communicated their political loyalty to the Nationalist government, perhaps hoping that this would forestall interference of the kind that is threatened today. As early as 1970, pigs offered to Co Su Kong in town and countryside alike fairly bristled with colorful additions to the traditional decorations: miniature red, white, and blue Nationalist flags.

It is clear that people are not willing simply to stop offering pigs. Nor are they willing to consider simplifying the *pai-pai* as the government has sometimes urged by offering a bowl of fruit instead. In part this reluctance must stem from the complex set of associations surrounding pigs: offering just anything to Co Su Kong would not convey the same messages. Nor could a lesser offering secure one's status in the community.

Another reason people resist simplification may be that Ti Kong have become ethnic symbols for Taiwanese (as opposed to mainlanders).[18] This possibility first occurred to me when I read a Taiwanese folktale in a newspaper article about Thai Ti Kong festivals. The tale explains why a large orange is placed in the mouth of a Ti Kong when he is presented to the gods.

In former times, on the ninth day of each lunar month, the big feast day of Yü Huang Ta Ti [the Jade Emperor, also known as Thi: Kong], every household customarily put on an extensive ritual. Whole pigs and goats were the

[17] Pressure against the *pai-pai* did not stop in 1976. Several newspaper articles decried the expense and waste (*Lien He Pao* 1976a, 1976b, 1976c; *Chung Kuo Shih Pao* 1976). The *hsien* government reportedly decided to suspend temporarily local development subsidies to San-hsia, pending *pai-pai* reform (*Lien He Pao* 1976a).

[18] This has occurred despite the popular Taiwanese habit of referring to mainlanders as "pigs" when contrasting them with Japanese "dogs."

most important offerings.[19] So everywhere pigs and goats met with disaster. Then Ti Kong's and Iu: Kong's [Honorable Pig's and Honorable Goat's] representatives in heaven plotted together to get rid of this custom. In order to make people stop killing pigs and goats, they spread the idea everywhere that worshiping Thi: Kong made no sense. Everyone believed the wicked words of Pig and Goat and gradually began to simplify the "Worship Thi: Kong" festival, even to the point of not having pigs and goats as offerings on the sacrificial table.

On subsequent birthdays, Thi: Kong began to notice that people in the world below were producing poorer and poorer *pai-pai* for him. Then one year he asked some other gods what the reason was. Thus he came to know for the first time that everyone had believed the evil words of Pig and Goat.

When Thi: Kong heard this news, he was very angry and immediately summoned the representatives of pigs and goats. He scolded them severely and forbade them to go around speaking nonsense thereafter.

For the first few years, Pig and Goat did not dare to contradict these sacred orders, but they did not alter their former evil ways. After a few years, they again began spreading the depraved argument that it wasn't necessary to worship Thi: Kong. This time Thi: Kong was not able to forgive them; so to prevent them from talking he ordered all people from that day forth to put large oranges in the mouths of the pigs and goats they sacrificed. After this, the pigs and goats had no way of moving their mouths. From this time forth, Thi: Kong's birthday was held every year according to custom, and no one dared again to be lazy. (*Chung Kuo Shih Pao* 1975b.)

Would it be too farfetched to suggest that people might see the attempts of the Heavenly Pig and Goat to simplify offerings as analogous to the attempts of the earthly government to do the same? If such an analogy can be drawn, it should immediately make us ask whether there is self-interest behind the efforts of the government as there obviously is in the case of Pig and Goat in the tale.

There is certainly, for example, at least some difference between national and local interests. Pigs offered to the gods are eventually consumed as are pigs sold in the ordinary fashion. But pork from a Ti Kong can be used directly by the owners to build social relationships that they highly value through feasting and through gifts of meat. Everyone says that the pork from a Ti Kong is efficacious, and this is clearly one sense in which the claim is true. Marketed pork

[19] In San-hsia, goats are rarely offered; when they are, they are regarded as inferior substitutes for pigs. Elsewhere in Taiwan, pigs and goats are offered, the goats astride the pigs' backs. Where this is so, one could analyze the role of goats in the same fashion I have done for pigs.

may bring its owner monetary profit, but it also serves the ends of the government by reducing inflated prices. Curbing inflation may eventually benefit the original owner, but it only does so indirectly through the national-level economy. The government, in short, would like to extract pork through local markets to aid the national economy. But the household with a Ti Kong would like to concentrate its pork's usefulness in the service of its own local goals.

Similarly, the government urges expenditure on public works (especially roads and bridges) with the funds that they imagine would be freed by simplifying the *pai-pai*. Naturally public works would benefit local communities as well as traveling government officials or marching armies; but people regard public works as only distantly related to their face-to-face contacts with kinsmen, friends, and neighbors. As one old woman put it, "Of course roads and bridges are good for everyone, and if you have money you can contribute to these things. But you absolutely must kill a pig or people will laugh. If you don't give money for roads or bridges, no one will laugh."

The government may also feel that its interests would be served by reducing Taiwanese allegiance to gods like Co Su Kong, its protestations to the contrary (as in the newspaper article above) notwithstanding. We now have several impressive studies that confirm the extent to which the Taiwanese supernatural hierarchy is fashioned on a bureaucratic model (Arthur Wolf 1974; Jordan 1972; Feuchtwang 1974). But we know little about how this hierarchy relates to the political personnel of present-day Taiwan. We know that in late Ch'ing China (and Taiwan) gods and officials formed a single hierarchy of power, some gods ranking over lower officials, and some officials ranking over lower gods. In Taiwan today—where the government is largely seen as an interest group and ethnic group separate from the general population—it is worth considering whether ruling officials see Taiwanese gods as threatening or competing forces. In tales of the Japanese period still told in San-hsia, competition between the occupying Japanese and local gods is a prominent theme. In most accounts, the Japanese, outright foreigners, are trounced. It might be that another version of this kind of competition is going on today: elaborate *pai-pai* honoring efficacious gods and circulating wealth in local systems may represent victories for native Taiwanese; simplified *pai-pai* paying perfunctory respect to weakened gods and releasing resources to circulate nationally may represent victories for mainland officials.

There is some evidence that a partly parallel situation existed in nineteenth-century mainland China where leaders in market towns often recognized that locally focused festivals kept goods in local marketing systems—a recognition that led them to encourage such festivals enthusiastically (Hsiao 1960: 234; Skinner, personal communication). Then as now, local festivals would have tended to emphasize and define local interests in contradistinction to outside interests (and also then as now, government officials would have been at best unenthusiastic outsiders).

To return to the tale of Pig and Goat in heaven, we must ask whether simplifying local *pai-pai* is as serious a matter for the government as it obviously is for pigs and goats. I would like to suggest that it is—not only because of the factors already mentioned, but also because offering Ti Kong has become a vital marker of Taiwanese ethnic identity.[20] I am convinced of this for two reasons. First, a great many Taiwanese practice Thai Ti Kong, but no mainlanders do. The newspaper article containing the story of Pig and Goat in heaven states that raising Ti Kong has become one of Taiwan's universal customs, practiced by Kwang-tung Hakka as well as by Chang-chou and Ch'üan-chou Hokkien. Informants confirmed that these three major subgroups of Taiwanese all raise Ti Kong. Asked whether mainlanders do, people responded emphatically "No."

Second, the way the Taiwanese prepare and offer Ti Kong—unlike the way they prepare and offer most other ritual items—is strikingly uniform across ethnic boundaries. Informants in Ta-ch'i, a Chang-chou area south of San-hsia, assured me (and produced photographs to prove it) that their pigs are decorated in exactly the same way as pigs in Ch'üan-chou San-hsia: in both areas, a Ti Kong has a coin necklace around its neck; "gold flowers" on its head; a patch of hair left on its scalp; a cleaver smashed into its forehead; a red cloth on its back; a live fish, entrails, and raw fowl hanging from its neck; and a pineapple or other fruit in its mouth.[21] San-hsia residents also insisted that all Taiwanese Ti Kong, whether offered by Ch'üan-chou, Chang-chou, or Hakka people, were decorated in just the same fashion.

Such an emphasis on uniformity must be significant in a setting where people often call attention to the considerable variation in so-

[20] Rohsenow (1973: 18) makes a similar point with regard to *pai-pai* in general.

[21] The cleaver smashed into the pig's head is a ritual detail for which I could obtain little exegesis. One informant said it was to cut the pig up for Co Su Kong.

cial custom and ritual even from village to village. It seems to me, then, that this uniformity is best explained by the fact that Ti Kong have become associated with the Taiwanese as an ethnic group (as opposed to mainlanders). My informants certainly believed this to be true: though Ch'üan-chou people in San-hsia offer Ti Kong to Co Su Kong, Chang-chou people in Ta-ch'i offer Ti Kong to K'ai Chang Sheng Wang, and Hakka in Hsin-chu offer Ti Kong at their I-min temple, the form of the offering is thought to be precisely the same, much as all three groups see themselves alike as Taiwanese. As one San-hsia merchant said, "Thai Ti Kong festivals are a custom that belong to us Taiwanese."

The Hakka perspective is more complex. I interviewed a few Hakka who were natives of Hsin-chu township (west of San-hsia) but long-term residents of San-hsia. They assured me in a mischievous way that Hakka and Hokkien Ti Kong are different in only one way: Hakka Ti Kong are bigger than Ch'üan-chou or Chang-chou Ti Kong.[22] But Michael Moser's Hakka informants in Hsin-chu itself would disagree:

> While pigs in Pei-p'u do wear a necklace of coins strung with red thread like their San-hsia counterparts, they are *never* adorned with the entrails of raw chickens and ducks. My informants all thought the latter practice (which they readily identified as being Hokkien) was disgusting at worst and simply ugly at best. They also felt that having a live fish suspended from the pig's mouth was quite gauche: something a Hakka just wouldn't do. (In the words of one of my informants, this was something that a Hokkien would also invariably do because all Hokkien people are either "rich" or "do a lot of fishing.") Again, slamming a cleaver into the forehead of the pig was looked upon by my informants as disgusting, "excessive," and almost "wrong" in the moral sense. (Personal communication.)

I can only speculate about why these Hakka are so concerned with differentiating between Ti Kong. Their view could derive from their awareness that Hokkien stereotype Hakka as inferior: Hokkien like to think that their pigs set the standard, whereas Hakka want to make it clear that they have their own aesthetic and moral standards. Also, the Hakka view could reflect an earlier period in Taiwan's history when there was no government suppression of *pai-pai* and hence more local and regional rivalry. If this second speculation is

[22] In 1974, the largest Ti Kong in Hsin-chu weighed 1,436 pounds (Ts'ai 1976: 31). In the same year, the San-hsia Co Su Kong temple records show that the heaviest pig weighed 951 pounds.

accurate, we would expect residents of San-hsia and Ta-ch'i—falling more within the sphere of government influence radiating from Taipei—to close ranks and emphasize their common Taiwanese identity before residents of Hsin-chu would feel the need to do this.

The specific content of offerings to Co Su Kong obviously matters. Offering a pig, rather than some other animal, enables people to communicate what might be called an internal message about achievement, improvement, and success—a message that is internal because it is understood by all those who participate in the ritual. But offering pigs and decorating them as one imagines all other Taiwanese do also enables people to communicate what might be called an external message about the ethnic identity of Taiwanese and the power of their gods—a message that is external because it is made in reference to a distinct, outside group. Similarly, Rohsenow concludes that *pai-pai* in a Taipei community are "directed toward the government as an audience, forming as they do one of the few modes of collective expression available to the Taiwanese" (1973: 140). At the very least, these external political messages suggest that we may always be advised to consider whether rituals performed in complex nation-states have a political content. This question arises even with Geertz's masterful analysis of Balinese cockfights: the cockfights have been outlawed by the government and must be held surreptitiously (1972: 2).

The external messages of the Thai Ti Kong clearly suggest that people subject to powerful governments sometimes use ritual to talk about politics from their own vantage point. Whether or not the local population is consoled or placated (and the interests of the government advanced) by the Thai Ti Kong's messages about social and economic betterment, the local population is potentially served simply if the ritual helps them to see that the Taiwanese form a single group whose interests may not be identical with those of the mainlander-dominated government. Many things make it clear that the Thai Ti Kong *pai-pai* has a panoramic scope—its inclusion of all levels of spirits from hungry ghosts to Thi: Kong, its organization around households as well as around ethnic and surname groups, its requirement of sponsorship only once in every seven years. I would argue that its scope is even greater than these features indicate: whereas worshiping Co Su Kong marks worshipers as An-ch'i Hokkien, offering Ti Kong marks them, simply, as Taiwanese.

# Afterword

Sidney W. Mintz

During the meetings at which these papers were presented, there was a justifiable insistence upon the anthropological obligation to observe with care, to confirm or dispute findings, and, when possible, to set forth—so as to be able to test by some process of falsification—particular hypotheses. Dr. DeGlopper struck this note with some force when he spoke of laboring over minute particulars. Who would dare to disagree? A combination of care for detail on the one hand, and capacity for making sense theoretically of profuse data on the other, have brought the anthropology of China into the discipline firmly and irrevocably.

But even with the most narrowly conceived and rigorously conducted fieldwork, there are problems of selection and, at some later point, problems of interpretation. The data neither leap up at us in the field, nor leap into our faces from the printed page—at any rate, this writer's data never have. On even the narrowest stage, there is always an infinity of particulars:

> First of all, we begin, as in any science, with observation. We see such and such events going on. Many things are always happening at the same time, however. How are we to determine whether or not those things which happen at the same time are related to one another? For it is obvious that they may be contemporary events, or even serial events, not because they are related to one another but because their determinants, unknown and unobserved, have caused them to happen at the same or subsequent times. In

I am very grateful to Professor Emily Ahern and her colleagues for inviting me to participate in the SSRC Conference on Anthropology in Taiwan, and to all of the participants who criticized and advised me on earlier drafts of this paper. Jacqueline Wei Mintz also commented very usefully on early versions. Its persisting faults, however, are my responsibility alone.

short, contemporary or associated events may be merely coexistences. Culture, at any one time, is first and foremost a mass of coexistent events. (Lesser 1935: 392.)

The selection of what we choose to call a "problem" and the development of adequate analytical devices to understand that problem—what we call an "interpretation"—do not depend on the magnitude of the relationships we choose to explain; those relationships can be as difficult to explain adequately on a modest scale as on a large one. Accordingly, the deliberate reduction of the scale of a problem need not be correlated with any increase in our ability to solve it. This assertion, of course, affects in no way the need for careful, replicable, and falsifiable research hypotheses; nor is it a plea for methodological imprudence. All the same, the idea that small is good can be oversold in anthropological research.

It may be useful to begin in this way, since a critical commentary by an outsider on the work represented here must be viewed in terms of the commentator's own outlook: how he or she evaluates developments in anthropology at large. What are some of the general changes occurring in social and cultural anthropology against which developments in the China field may be assessed? First, there is the recognition that the great chasm supposedly dividing the so-called primitive from the so-called modern, civilized, or nonprimitive was probably never so wide nor so deep as our predecessors sometimes made it seem. Whether in the field of law, religion, kinship, or economics, the last half century of anthropology has consisted in good measure of battles, first, about where that chasm lay, and second, whether indeed it existed at all.[1] These battles have resulted in the successive repudiation of concept after concept, each once thought to measure or mark the differences between primitive and modern, either in kind or in degree.

Second, there is the ever-increasing understanding that so-called primitive or non-Western enclaves within large, complex polities have been neither so primitive nor so insulated as they have often been represented in anthropological studies to be. Correspondingly, the features that appeared to separate one segment of a national society from another have sometimes turned out to be more political

[1] A Pandora's box, surely. But one thinks here, for instance, of Pospisil on law (1958), Horton on religion (1967), Leach on kinship (1954), and Cook on economics (1966, 1974). This writer is by no means convinced by all of the arguments; it is striking, however, that these arguments continue with such vigor.

than cultural in etiology, as recent developments in the theory of ethnicity strongly suggest.[2] Moreover, we have gradually learned that villagers and townsmen may be as intrinsically interesting and as theoretically important to anthropological enterprise as those seemingly more exotic peoples living a thousand meters higher up or on the other, more remote, side of the valley. Not until the end of the Second World War did studies of "nonprimitive" groups within large societies begin to win approval from the anthropological establishment as professionally legitimate. Before then, the Kachin in Burma, the Todas in India, the Veddas in Ceylon, the Lolo in China, the so-called Montagnards in Viet Nam were anthropologically okay; their neighbors were not. In the case of North American anthropology, where nearly all the research done by our predecessors concentrated on Native Americans, the cost of legitimacy was an overwhelming concentration on the past and a determined detachment of the people under study from the large, modern, industrial society in which they lived and to which they were subject. One may read scores of superb papers and monographs about Native American peoples without encountering a pickup truck, a pair of blue jeans, or even a flashlight. Only in the decades immediately preceding the War did the present shyly reveal itself, together with the neighbors of the "primitives," in the work of our illustrious forebears (e.g., Spier 1929; Redfield 1930; Mead 1932; Lesser 1933).

Third, there has come the recognition, albeit slowly, that the last five centuries have witnessed the rapid permeation of all the world's societies, however small or remote, by Western influences. Thus, almost any local study must, on one level or another, take into account those wider political, social, and economic systems within which most human groups are now inextricably embedded. If such an assertion is persuasive, then the end of anthropology's oldest—and, one suspects, most misleading—dream, the uncontaminated McCoy, marks the beginning of a world anthropology, truly an anthropology of humankind.

Finally, there is the acknowledgment, still grudging, and arising in some degree from the acceptance of the foregoing assertions, that anthropological techniques—given substantial modifications in both methodology and perspective—might be useful in studying large, populous, complicated societies. Thirty years ago, Julian Steward

[2]For instance, Barth 1969; Vincent 1974; Nagata 1974; Cohen 1969, 1974; Mintz 1978; Schildkrout 1978.

pointed out the dangers implicit in attempts to transfer anthropological methods and expectations uncritically to the study of groups or "communities" within larger sociocultural systems (Steward 1950). Though his warnings were not unheeded, few scholars tried hard enough at first to cope with the conceptual problems such transfers engendered. Indeed, Steward's caution accompanied his own aspirations to see a large, complex society studied by anthropological methods.

When Steward first projected a series of simultaneous studies of several Puerto Rican communities with the objective of attaining a synthetic rendering of all of Puerto Rican society—a whole that would exceed the sum of its parts—he pioneered (and to the extent that he succeeded, he legitimized) a new domain of anthropological inquiry. "His was a pioneering recognition," Robert Adams tells us in an important paper (1977: 271), "that higher level systems of integration modified the character of their components through the forms of functional dependence that they imposed." Though the product of Steward's pathbreaking cooperative effort (Steward et al. 1956) failed to escape the limitations of its time in the view of some (including this writer), it has apparently attracted more attention, not less, as the time of its writing recedes.[3] If one asks why this should be so, the answer is that in no other instance have anthropologists seriously tried to describe the whole of a complex society, basing their work on the simultaneous study and comparison of a series of selected communities.[4] Adams suggests one possible reason why such studies are rare. "Perhaps," he argues, "the problem is that higher levels of integration cannot be understood without reference to the quite asymmetrical, which is to say often downright unpleasant, relationships of political and economic power on which they ultimately depend" (1977: 271). Whatever the reasons, the fact that such studies remain uncommon has not detracted from the modified climate of opinion that now permits anthropologists to study "nonprimitive" peoples, to admit that the notion of primitivity is open to critical review, and to try to understand how complex social systems are ordered and articulated.

[3] The only seemingly analogous study was Robert Redfield's Yucatán project, which resulted in, among other works, *The Folk Culture of Yucatán* (1941). But the similarities are mostly superficial (see Mintz 1953).

[4] Readers may find of interest the papers published in a special issue of the journal *Revista Interamericana* entitled "Social Anthropology of Puerto Rico" (3, no. 1 [Spring 1978]), devoted entirely to the Steward project and *The People of Puerto Rico*.

To the extent that these various assertions ring true for anthropology, they should resonate for the anthropology of China as well. Though foreign and local anthropologists carried out fieldwork in China before the Second World War, much of it substantial, foreign scholars like Morton Fried and G. William Skinner got to China only after the War. Since 1949, the anthropology of China as practiced by foreigners has been an overseas anthropology, so to speak. Still, it is largely with the work of these foreign observers that an anthropology of China begins.

But there is an anthropological *curiosum* concealed behind this assertion. Though the study of ordinary villagers, townsmen, or non-primitive folk was anthropologically tabooed everywhere (or considered, as it often still is, *infra dignitatem*), the Western scholar who specialized on a sufficiently abstract level in some great, literate, but non-Western civilization was somehow acceptable, even if he professed to be an anthropologist. That the civilization in question had to be largely unconnected to the Greco-Roman and Judeo-Christian traditions raises an interesting question, and intellectual historians may be able to establish one day whether it was a large dose of racism that underlay the treatment of complex but non-Western civilizations as anthropologically researchable. Still, studying the exotic peoples within exotic civilizations—Karen, Lolo, Meo, whatever—was for a long time more acceptable *anthropologically* than studying the civilizations that surrounded them. (All the more credit, then, to Malinowski for having encouraged his student Fei Hsiao-tung to study a Chinese peasant village.) Thus, we have been given the established anthropology of supposedly primitive, homogeneous, non-Western, kin-based, technically rudimentary societies on the one hand, and high-level studies of large and complex but non-Western and politically prostrate civilizations on the other.

In spite of the work of Fei Hsiao-tung and others, insights arising from the anthropological study of communities within China did not form a highly appreciated segment of our discipline's literature, a literature whose center of gravity lay with the "primitive" (whatever that was). Even so distinguished a colleague as Professor Maurice Freedman was not, it seems, considered quite as "anthropological" as those of his British associates who had worked in Africa or in other less familiar parts of Asia, outside China's sphere. To some extent, at least the same biases that prevailed in the profession half a century ago are still operative—a kind of powerful minority consensus about what anthropology is, and what it should be. But the legitimation of China anthropology has come about, one supposes, both because the field at large has changed and because anthropologists of China have taken on new and innovative tasks.

In his essay on the sociology of Chinese religion (1974) and in his presidential address to the Royal Anthropological Institute (1969), Maurice Freedman raised the issue of an anthropology of China within world anthropology, though happily he wasted no time "justifying" such an anthropology. Instead, he concentrated on two issues, one methodologically significant, the other largely of a contemporary political relevance. How, Freedman asked, will anthropologists of China cope with China's vastness of scale and organization when field studies must inevitably concern matters that are microscopic by comparison? And again, in the light of contemporary affairs, how will anthropologists of China continue to study China, restricted as they are in their fieldwork to entities that lie at its borders or outside it? Though Freedman's answers to these vexing questions were neither complete nor entirely reassuring, they were at the least optimistic. The relationship between small-scale field studies and large-scale societies will get another glance further along in this commentary. But the problem of studying China from afar or by example deserves a word here, since the work under consideration in this volume was executed entirely in Taiwan, and since the light it may throw on mainland China must be, in some senses at least, indirect. In some senses, yes; but surely not in all. In his 1974 paper, cited earlier, Freedman writes at length about the substantial and important ethnography provided by field studies in Hong Kong, Singapore, Taiwan, and elsewhere. But he also refers specifically to the role of such work in furthering our understanding of China, particularly when he notes that Potter's findings in Hong Kong (1968, 1970) confirmed his own analysis of the structure of the large-scale Chinese lineage (Freedman 1969: 9). Similarly, Freedman sees research in Taiwan as opening up new possibilities of a comparative kind, particularly—his own penchant—with reference to kinship and social organization.

But Freedman's first question—about the contrast between a vast, complex society, and narrow, detailed field studies—is neither unique to the China field nor altogether answerable as yet. In his article on the sociological study of Chinese religion, Freedman refers to the difficulties, both methodological and conceptual, that face the scholar inclined to extrapolate from small-scale field studies of religious phenomena to Chinese religion on a grand scale (or vice versa). Yet Freedman insists that China manifests "a great community of religion" (1974: 39–40), and does so in terms directly apposite to the argument here: "How could China fail to constitute a community of ideas when the political center made itself responsible for disseminating its beliefs . . . when the elite were based as much in the countryside as in the towns, and when social mobility ensured a steady interchange of style between the common run of men and the high-literate?" It is precisely the relationship between center and hinterland, expressed both nationally and in the ties of town and countryside, that requires us to remember that "rural" and "urban" describe a process, not two paired compartments, polarities, or opposites. The nature of that process will come into view once more, as promised, later in this essay.

To turn briefly to a subject rather more familiar to the writer than the anthropology of Taiwan, we may take note of another latecomer to anthropological inquiry, Caribbean studies. Whereas the study of China was not authentically anthropological unless the concerns were sufficiently abstract, the study of the Caribbean was not authentically anthropological because the region was too Western and "mixed." If China was too cultured for anthropology, the Caribbean was too uncultured. Leaving aside the early anthropology of the Caribbean and the massive contributions of Afro-Americanists, modern study dates from two undertakings in particular: Steward's Puerto Rico project (1956) and Raymond Smith's pioneering book, *The Negro Family in British Guiana* (1956). Here were the students of two scholars (Kroeber was Steward's mentor, Fortes was Smith's) who could not be taken lightly by the profession. But even more importantly, of course, each work, in spite of certain flaws, made asking the questions they asked part of the discipline's normal discourse. At the risk of caricature, the English came to the Caribbean expecting to find lineages patterned after anthropologists' elegant abstractions in West Africa, whereas the North Americans came expecting to find town halls and middle classes along the lines of those in Muncie, Indiana, or those in Newburyport, Massachusetts. What is worse, they—both the English and the North Americans—succeeded; and Caribbean ethnology has only now begun to recover. Perhaps comparable, but very different, problems occur in the intellectual history of sinological studies, but this writer is unable to address them.

What the contributions in this volume reveal, among other things, is a substantial concern or involvement with the idea of community. People are clearly struggling to separate units of survey from units of study; to identify different kinds of linkages among individuals and between groups; to abstract from the endless particulars of daily life a reality concealed behind and by behavior. There is revealed as well the admirable desire to get at general processes, at regular relationships among phenomena—in ritual, in social organization, and elsewhere—in the expectation that the findings will have a relevance that transcends the local, the relativistically unique, and the particular. This raises such research above the community. You do community studies; but you also aim to understand the human animal.

In the work on ritual, for example, one infers the presence of at least three different kinds, or levels, of research objectives. One level has to do (rather simply in one sense, though not in terms of the demands it may make on the fieldworker) with understanding how a ritual or some equivalently complex event is conducted and of what it consists. Another goes further, and has to do with what such a ritual does for individuals and for a social system or subsystem, with reference to definable groups, and in terms of their ongoing social relationships. The third, seemingly far grander, has to do with what ritual means for theories of religious behavior and for theories of religion in general.

All of this is to the good. But another kind of research—reflected in the papers by Pasternak and Gates among others—promises different and additional sorts of insights. This research, perhaps only now in its beginnings, aims at treating Taiwan as a whole society or at treating some segment of that society—a class, an ethnic group, a region, perhaps an elite—in terms of the entire group of relationships that define it. Some may view such emphases as deflections. They are not—or, at any rate, they need not be. In this connection one thinks of at least three—there are doubtless many more—different angles of attack.

A first angle of attack would deal with Taiwan as a total society, concentrating on its internal organization and differentiation as these are now constituted. Burton Benedict's study of Indians in Mauritius (1961), Vincenzo Petrullo's treatment of Puerto Rico (1947), Cornelius Osgood's book on Korea (1951), and Raymond Smith's volume on British Guiana (1962) provide fitting but varying examples of such an approach. The book by Steward and his co-workers (1956) belongs here too.

A second angle of attack would look at Taiwan as an offshoot, extension, or derivation of Chinese culture. Much of the work reported here, in fact, is directly akin to this perspective, even though it may seem at first glance to be local in outlook and explanatory intent. Those studies that see their subjects as bearers of a massive and transported tradition, perhaps more common in history than in anthropology, are of this kind.

Finally, a third angle of attack would have to do with Taiwan as a whole society in its contemporary dependent relationships. It would be useful to look at Taiwan as the dependency of successive world powers: in this case, of Japan, China, and the United States. If one selects from Taiwanese history a small number of historical turnings, one can see the outlines of the sequence, however sketchily: the coming of Koxinga; the cession to Japan and the resulting economic developments in camphor, tea, rice, and sugarcane cultivation; the retrocession to China; the Nationalist migration; the land reform, which apparently signified deep structural changes in class composition and in the locus of power; and, finally, the staggering investment of foreign capital and the very rapid industrialization that accompanied it.

These are not so much events as manifestations of determinable political, economic, and social pressures. They may serve to represent different steps or stages in the integration of Taiwanese society into wider systems of social, economic, and political relationships. At each such step or stage, Taiwan was a differently constituted society, and its regions and communities were differentially integrated or affected. Thus, for instance, one would expect that camphor gathering and sugar cultivation differently affected communities in different regions during the period of Japanese rule. After the termination of that rule and the changes in those industries, the affected communities were no longer what they had been before; they stood perforce in new relationships to other communities and regions of Taiwan.

There is no rule, it seems, by which one can determine a priori the extent to which a particular community is, or is not, defined by its integration into a regional or national society. Thus, to say it briefly and superficially, agricultural communities that depend on the export of cash commodities must, in times of severe market contraction, give up what they sold and what they got for what they sold. Eric Wolf, analyzing peasant responses to changing external economic forces (1966), shows us how the peasantry may be forced to increase their productivity on the one hand, or tighten their belts on the other. Under certain conditions, of course, they may organize and resist. Under other conditions, they may end up exporting themselves rather than their products. But whatever the nature of their disengagement from a previous integration, it always involves changes in the ways in which their community is defined. Disengagement may mean that the community is more definable in terms of itself; engagement usually signifies the contrary. The point is simple enough. It is not just that we understand the organization of a community better if we also understand how it is linked to the outside, but that the precise ways in which it is linked to the outside declare what the community is. In attempting to make this point more clearly in regard to studies of markets and market systems, this writer has stated it as follows:

> An adequate conceptualization of this kind is not concerned simply with "fitting" or "linking" the community as such to wider systems; to a very substantial degree, it is the nature of that integration which actually *helps to define the community itself*. The view of communities as firmly bounded and isolated groupings, gradually losing their separateness and intactness to outside pressures, while conveying a generally accepted understanding of how change occurs, is not quite adequate, then, in dealing with the reality of larger sociocultural wholes. Surely one reason for the popularity of anthropological marketing studies in recent years has been the growing recognition that the analytical "reality" of communities is no greater than the analytic "reality" of marketing systems; when employed as heuristic devices, these abstractions may even serve in part to define each other. (1976: xii–xiii.)

The wider point is solidly anthropological. One certainly ought not to be distracted by whether a particular local response takes a primarily political, religious, economic, or other form, and therefore be led to decide that what is involved is of greater (or lesser) concern to anthropologists. Economic changes interlink with political, religious, and other changes—if these "categories" can be considered truly separable at all, other than for heuristic reasons. Economic opportunities are, in some basic anthropological sense, a coefficient of sociocultural forces and preconditions.

Of course, it is one thing to say that a community can be understood only by taking full account of the large-scale extracommunity forces that may give it characteristic shape and consistency. It is quite another to argue that anthropologists can, on a level beyond that of the so-called community, try to observe and to interpret such large-scale extracommunity forces.[5] Seeking to understand how large-scale changes that affect a whole society's history are produced may carry the implication that history is conspiratorial, or must so be interpreted. It is enough to say, perhaps, that it can be—but that it need not be altogether. The different segments that make up the controlling groups in a large, complex society usually have no unanimity in their intentions. One such group wants land for its factories; another wants labor for its urban undertakings; a third wants sugar, tea, camphor, or rice; yet another is interested in buyers, not in sellers, of labor and products. Thus, the organization of people in communities, and the composition of classes and of ethnic groups, is at least to some extent the unanticipated precipitate of the differing objectives of groups that do not have either perfect consensus on what is to be done or the absolute power to do it. They must, moreover, deal with groups possessing different histories, living in different circumstances, and displaying different varieties of local culture. Economic and political objectives do not always mesh, even among those in power. Nor does the overlapping and interlocking membership of controlling groups form an undifferentiated bloc. The results of these struggles, then, are more often expressed as new or persisting tendencies than as definitive resolutions; and at times they consist of counterposed and unresolved tensions. But to attempt to understand how differing segments of power holders affect each other, and how the results of their struggles may unequally affect those whose labor, land, or products they desire to control, is an entirely justifiable undertaking.

Whether such an undertaking is a fitting task for anthropology and anthropologists is perhaps debatable. This writer thinks, however, that it is not only fitting but necessary. It is striking how many anthropologists' ideas about the organization of behavior and about the ways of testing social theories have found their way into the work of historians, political scientists, geographers, and economists. One thinks, for example, of such things as coalitions, patron-client relationships, peasant movements, internal market systems, and

[5] Wolf 1957 and Skinner 1964 must be mentioned among the more daring and important early contributions that strove for a supracommunity perspective. Skinner's work seems especially important for sinology, representing as it does a real step upward from the community study perspective in anthropology.

heaven knows what else—concepts that anthropologists themselves might employ for precisely the same analytical objectives for which their colleagues have borrowed them. Surely if anthropologists will not use their own insights to better understand and explain the modern world, they can count on others to take their ideas and do it for them. Freedman has some interesting remarks on this matter (1969: 11–12). Adams engages it more broadly:

Clearly a bundle of closely related themes runs through our work, to which we commonly address ourselves only in their particulars—peasant studies, networks, marketing systems, urban-rural relations, situational analysis, regional approaches, levels of integration, cultural brokers, spheres of interaction, ecosystems, and the like. Those particulars are undoubtedly the kinds of limited domains in which we must generally write articles, design good research projects, and advance scholarship. But the responsibility of scholarship, and particularly of anthropological scholarship, is to be an observer as well as a participant. That involves seeking broader perspectives on the work we do, looking for patterns of congruence or the lack of it with broader fields, and giving serious, detached attention to the boundaries set by our own conventional research models and their probable consequences. It also involves occasionally taking time to consider the relationship between our premises, models, and research priorities, on the one hand, and the broader context of societal change, debate, and choice, on the other. (1977: 276.)

It seems to this writer that some of the contributions in this volume do involve a figurative raising of the eyes to wider themes and deeper implications. To say that papers by Pasternak and Gates, among many others, impress in this manner is also to say that the insights that arise in studying Taiwan can illuminate much else in anthropology. At the same time, to take seriously Adams's encouragements to all of us should mean that the rest of anthropology may also illuminate some things in Taiwan. What no anthropologists dealing with the modern world can afford to permit to happen is that their field grow up around them. Here, again, Adams's message is for all of us:

When we step back to enlarge the field of vision, we do not retreat from phenomena but better perceive their significance. We have tended to define the groups we study largely on the basis of their self-constituted structure, their aspect as independent organisms. Increasingly, however, an approach based on the web of interrelations that individuals as well as groups maintain seems at least equally valid and more consistent with the main course of development of the world we know. The aspect of groups as differentiated organs struggling to maintain themselves in wider, multilevel systems does not present us with merely their external face, but is essential even to an analysis of the core processes that provide for self-identification and continuity. (*Ibid.*: 276.)

Indeed, such a line of argument has been touched upon at many points in this volume, as it was during the conference: by Pasternak's paper, where we are told that "we do not study Taiwan simply for the sake of understanding the Taiwanese or even, for that matter, the Chinese"; by Gates's paper, which asks us to learn from those who did fieldwork in the midst of the most massive social revolution of the century, and who saw "only placid villages and traditional Chinese families"; by Fried's comment that "we know enough about the political organization of Taiwanese society to begin to play with major questions." And yet Gallin's book, Arthur Wolf tells us in his paper for this volume, "is still the only major work addressed to the problem of social change. The rest of us write as though the society under scrutiny came to dead halt about midway through our first field study. When we return to the field, we go back to our aging informants and take up where we left off. If we do not actively regret what has happened in the meantime, we at least ignore it, with the result that some of us are in danger of becoming historians without ever having taken an active interest in the subject."

In fact, all that Arthur Wolf has to say in his paper firmly rejects this way of defining history. History is not, of course, the freezing in time of an epoch or an event, but the functional analysis of events. Such events happen to be arranged ordinally, in time. Though historians have contributed substantially to this volume, a more frankly historical orientation in some of the anthropological contributions could, I believe, have added to their usefulness. By making it possible to expose the interconnection among events co-occurring, events that, in Lesser's phraseology, are not "merely coexistences," history enables us to see beneath "the contemporary surface of events" (Lesser 1935: 392). The somewhat limited emphasis on temporal sequence in these papers can be highlighted by referring to a problem perhaps so obvious as to require no further reflection. It is not entirely clear whether Taiwan may be usefully seen as divided into a mainland and a Taiwanese sector. But note the following assertion by Stavis that "the officials supervising the [land reform] program were mainlanders, not native Taiwanese. This meant that they were not related to the landlords or politically indebted to them. On the contrary, they may have seen the landlords as a rival, indigenous, independent political force. . . . The Nationalist Government had freedom of action with regard to the landlords on Taiwan which it never had while it was on the mainland." (1974: 38, 39.)

How would this writer, surely no sinologist, interpret this assertion? Well, effective land reform in Taiwan could have been a means of winning massive rural support while simultaneously disfranchising an entrenched, indigenous, landed aristocracy. This writer has no idea if that is what happened. But certainly it becomes an interesting hypothesis for social scientists and, indeed, for anyone interested in the rural sociology of Taiwanese society. If Stavis's claim is correct, what did land reform signify for the class composition of the rural communities from which today's female factory proletariat is being recruited? Perhaps more to the point, how might that reform have affected the vitality and character of the ceremonial, kinship, and other institutions in communities throughout Taiwan?

Take yet another such assertion. Gates tells us that foreign investment in Taiwan is heavily American—that about $2.5 billions have been lent or invested to date by U.S. firms. This not insignificant sum, pumped into what had been a predominantly rural society, must have had consequences of the most noticeable sort. It would surely be unwise to assume that those consequences are incommensurable with the phenomena in which we are all interested. Indeed, it would be very surprising if the effects of so massive an injection of new capital were not felt in every hearth and hamlet of a society as small, as densely populated, and as changing as Taiwan. To write off our concern with large-scale changes of this kind by labeling them "economic" is to deny the interconnectedness of the social life we claim to be our principal interest.

Here is a third such notion, this one with no substantiation at all. The Japanese apparently went in heavily for camphor harvesting, tea growing, and sugar manufacture, among other enterprises. The *Encyclopaedia Britannica* for 1905 indicates a total sugar production for Japan and Taiwan of some 93,000 tons annually, averaged over the three or four preceding years. Apparently the Japanese either failed to impose plantation production or soon abandoned it, getting their canes largely via contractual arrangements with smallholders. This, for a Caribbeanist, is a very interesting—even irritating—deviation. The early years of the twentieth century were the very years when U.S., British, and French interests were actively creating vast rural sugar proletariats in the Antilles, Fiji, Mauritius, and elsewhere. Why did the Japanese go to smallholders in defiance of what appears to have been a more common entrepreneurial practice? In the absence of a sure answer, one might guess that this happened because smallholder arrangements placed production risks upon the cultivator—a solution typical of low-capital situations, as in the postbellum U.S. South. One would like to know as an anthropologist not only why the Japanese took this approach but also what their production decisions meant in terms of the Taiwanese rural economy. One could probably find out, too.

My final point is of a different order, and it has several parts. First, one can only be moved by Kung's description of the working girl who burned her hand, and was afraid to tell anyone for fear of getting into trouble. Kung's paper thus evokes with cruel immediacy the not-too-distant past of our own and Western European society: the dreadful fear of failing; the desire not only to excel, but to be accepted; the deadening effect that assembly lines commonly have on working people in developing societies. Yet an apparent contradiction emerges in these young proletarians' very clear and articulate understanding of the cold, impersonal, exacting circumstances with which they must deal. Perhaps there has been here too little concern with the vast literature on industrialization going back to Marx, Engels, Veblen, Weber, and Sombart, as well as too much insouciance about the issue of working-class consciousness. The issue of class consciousness, like the issue of class definition itself, is a serious one. To learn of a society in which large numbers of young females are drained from the countryside to become part of a large industrial structure where their activity can be transformed into investment capital is to encounter one of the great dramas of modern times.

A second matter also concerns Kung's factory worker, too frightened to report her burns. Taiwan looks like a society with high entrepreneurial payoffs. It is not clear whether a higher percentage of the total value produced is available for skimming, or whether there is merely a run-of-the-mill percentage of an unusually high total—but in either case, the payoff looks good. Why is this so? How does it happen? And is it not interesting that women who are not formally part of the wage-earning sector are now providing part of its surplus product? There is, among other things, a very Chinese—that is, not only Taiwanese—aspect to this question. Gates quotes a *New York Times* advertisement on Taiwan's capacity to provide substantial rake-offs. Not all societies deliver in these ways, as we know well; and finding out why some *do* involves, among other things, a reflective consideration of socialization practices, viewed cross-culturally. One suspects that this rake-off is as available in the PRC as it is in Taiwan. What does this mean? And how do we approach this question?

Whatever "economic development" is, this writer is just reactionary enough to be sure that he is not always for it and that he would like to know more about it. He would also like to know when to be for it. But if industrialization, labor immigration, and all the rest that typifies contemporary Taiwanese society goes on as "economic development" is going on, then he is surely certain that he would like to see anthropologists study it.

Neither synthesis nor summation, this commentary has been intended to provide one outsider's personal view of what is really the contributors' field—and theirs, by the way, to make or break. The writer wishes to stress his strong feeling that the quality of scholarship displayed here is conspicuously, unusually high. And that it must rest on such a massive base of difficult prior learning lifts it even higher. At the same time, the relative lack of a close fit with the literature of anthropology at large is puzzling. Surely the last thing sinologists need is yet another Chinese wall, constructed around themselves.

# Reference Matter

# References Cited

*Winckler: National, Regional, and Local Politics*


Ahern, Emily M. 1973. *The Cult of the Dead in a Chinese Village*. Stanford, Calif.

——— 1978. "Chinese Ritual and Politics." Paper presented to the Columbia University Seminar on Traditional China.

Appleton, Sheldon. 1970. "Taiwanese and Mainlanders on Taiwan: A Survey of Student Attitudes." *China Quarterly* 44: 38–65.

Barclay, George W. 1954. *Colonial Development and Populations on Taiwan*. Princeton, New Jersey.

Bedeski, Robert. 1975. "The Evolution of the Modern State in China: Nationalist and Communist Continuities." *World Politics* 27: 541–68.

Caldwell, J. Alexander. 1976. "The Financial System in Taiwan: Structure, Functions, and Issues for the Future." *Asian Survey* 16, no. 8: 729–51.

Chang, Han-yu, and Ramon H. Myers. 1963. "Japanese Colonial Development Policy in Taiwan, 1895–1906: A Case of Bureaucratic Entrepreneurship." *Journal of Asian Studies* 22, no. 4: 433–49.

Chen, Ching-Chih. 1967. "The Police and the Hoko Systems in Taiwan under Japanese Administration (1895–1945)." In Albert Craig, ed., *Papers on Japan*, vol. 4. Cambridge, Mass.

——— 1973. "Japanese Sociopolitical Control in Taiwan, 1895–1945." Ph.D. dissertation, Harvard University.

Chen, Chung-Min. 1977. *Upper Camp: A Study of a Chinese Mixed-Cropping Village in Taiwan*. Taipei.

Chen, Edward I-te. 1972. "Formosan Political Movements under Japanese Colonial Rule, 1914–1937." *Journal of Asian Studies* 31, no. 3: 477–97.

Chu, Samuel. 1964. "Liu Ming-ch'uan and Modernization of Taiwan." *Journal of Asian Studies* 23, no. 1: 37–53.

Clough, Ralph N. 1978. *Island China*. Cambridge, Mass.

Cohen, Myron L. 1976. "Mei-nung: State and Community in Rural Taiwan." *Third World Review* 2, no. 1: 1–22.

Cole, Allan B. 1967. "Political Roles of Taiwanese Enterprisers." *Asian Survey* 7, no. 9: 645–54.

Crissman, Lawrence W. 1969. "Each for His Own: Taiwanese Political Response to KMT Local Administration." Paper presented to the East and Southeast Asian Studies Conference, Ste. Adèle-en-haut, Quebec.

Crozier, Ralph C. 1977. *Koxinga and Chinese Nationalism: History, Myth, and the Hero*. Cambridge, Mass.

DeGlopper, Donald R. 1973. "City on the Sands: Social Structure in a Nineteenth-Century Chinese City." Ph.D. dissertation, Cornell University.

——— 1974. "Religion and Ritual in Lukang." In Arthur P. Wolf, ed., *Religion and Ritual in Chinese Society*. Stanford, Calif.

——— 1977. "Social Structure in a Nineteenth-Century Taiwanese Port City." In G. William Skinner, ed., *The City in Late Imperial China*. Stanford, Calif.

Durdin, Tillman. 1975. "Chiang Ching-kuo and Taiwan: A Profile." *Orbis* 18, no. 4: 1023–42.

Fei, John C. H., and Gustav Ranis. 1975. "A Model of Growth and Employment in the Open Dualistic Economy: The Cases of Korea and Taiwan." *Journal of Development Studies* 11, no. 2: 32–63.

Feuchtwang, Stephan. 1974. "City Temples in Taipei under Three Regimes." In Mark Elvin and G. William Skinner, eds., *The Chinese City Between Two Worlds*. Stanford, Calif.

——— 1976. "Mountainstreet's Place in the Class System of Taiwan." Paper presented at the Conference on Anthropology in Taiwan.

——— 1977. "School-Temple and City God." In G. William Skinner, ed., *The City in Late Imperial China*. Stanford, Calif.

Gallin, Bernard. 1963. "Land Reform in Taiwan: Its Effect on Rural Social Organization and Leadership." *Human Organization* 22, no. 2: 109–12.

——— 1964. "Rural Development in Taiwan: The Role of the Government." *Rural Sociology* 29, no. 3: 313–23.

——— 1968. "Political Factionalism and its Impact on Chinese Village Social Organization in Taiwan." In Marc J. Swartz, ed., *Local-Level Politics*. Chicago.

——— and Rita S. Gallin. 1977. "Sociopolitical Power and Sworn Brother Groups in Chinese Society: A Taiwanese Case." In Raymond D. Fogelson and Richard N. Adams, eds., *The Anthropology of Power: Ethnographic Studies from Asia, Oceania, and the New World*. New York.

Ho, Samuel P. S. 1971. "The Development Policy of the Japanese Colonial Government in Taiwan, 1895–1945." In Gustav Ranis, ed., *Government and Economic Development*. New Haven, Conn.

——— 1978. *Economic Development of Taiwan, 1860–1970*. New Haven, Conn.

Hsing, Mo-huan. 1970. "Taiwan: Industrialization and Trade Policies." In Mo-huan Hsing, John H. Powers, and Gerardo P. Sicat, eds., *Taiwan and the Philippines, Industrialization and Trade Policies*. Paris.

Huang, Mab. 1976. *Intellectual Ferment for Political Reforms in Taiwan, 1971–1973*. Ann Arbor, Mich.

Jacobs, J. Bruce. 1971. "Recent Leadership and Political Trends in Taiwan." *China Quarterly* 45: 129–54.

——— 1975. "Local Politics in Rural Taiwan: A Field Study of Kuan-hsi, Face, and Faction in Matsu Township." Ph.D. dissertation, Columbia University.

Jacoby, Neil H. 1966. *U.S. Aid to Taiwan: A Study of Foreign Aid, Self-Help, and Development*. New York.

Kerr, George H. 1965. *Formosa Betrayed*. Boston.

——— 1974. *Formosa: Licensed Revolution and the Home Rule Movement, 1895–1945*. Honolulu.

Ku, Tun-jou. 1966. "Hsin-chuang Village: A Study of a Taiwanese Village in the Political Context of Lungchiang Township." *Chinese Culture* 7, no. 2: 65–106.

Kuhn, Philip A. 1975. "Local Self-Government under the Republic: Problems of Control, Autonomy, and Mobilization." In Frederic Wakeman, Jr. and Carolyn Grant, eds., *Conflict and Control in Late Imperial China*. Berkeley, Calif.

——— 1977. "Local Taxation and Finance in Republican China." Paper presented to the Columbia University Seminar on Modern China.

Lamley, Harry J. 1964. "The Taiwan Literati and Early Japanese Rule, 1895–1913." Ph.D. dissertation, University of Washington.

——— 1969. "The 1895 Taiwan Republic." *Journal of Asian Studies* 27, no. 4: 789–862.

——— 1970–71. "Assimilation Efforts in Colonial Taiwan: The Fate of the 1914 Movement." *Monumenta Serica* 29: 496–520.

——— 1977. "The Formations of Cities: Initiative and Motivation in Building Three Walled Cities in Taiwan." In G. William Skinner, ed., *The City in Late Imperial China*. Stanford, Calif.

Lerman, Arthur J. 1972. "Political, Traditional, and Modern Economic Groups and the Taiwan Provincial Assembly." Ph.D. dissertation, Princeton University.

——— 1977. "National Elite and Local Politicians in Taiwan." *American Political Science Review* 71, no. 4: 1406–22.

Lin, Ching-yuan. 1973. *Industrialization in Taiwan, 1946–72: Trade and Import-Substitution Policies for Developing Countries*. New York.

Linz, Juan. 1964. "An Authoritarian Regime: Spain." In Erik Allardt and Yrjo Littunen, eds., *Cleavages, Ideologies, and Party Systems*. Helsinki.

——— 1973. "The Future of an Authoritarian Situation and the Institutionalization of an Authoritarian Regime: The Case of Brazil." In Alfred Stepan, ed., *Authoritarian Brazil*. New Haven, Conn.

——— 1975. "Authoritarianism and Totalitarianism." In David Greenstein and Nelson W. Polsby, eds., *Handbook of Political Science*, vol. 3. Reading, Mass.

Long, Yu-hsien. 1968. "Taiwan Local Elections: An Introduction." *Chinese Journal of Administration* 10: 37–41.

——— 1969. "The Administration of Local Elections in Taipei." *Chinese Journal of Administration* 12: 20–27.

Mancall, Mark, ed. 1964. *Formosa Today*. New York.

Martin, Roberta. 1975. "The Socialization of Children in China and on Taiwan: An Analysis of Elementary School Textbooks." *China Quarterly* 62: 242–62.

Mendel, Douglas. 1970. *The Politics of Formosan Nationalism*. Berkeley, Calif.

——— 1974. "Formosan Nationalism in Crisis." In Yung-hwan Jo, ed., *Taiwan's Future*. Tempe, Arizona.

Meskill, Johanna Menzel. 1970. "The Lins of Wufeng: The Rise of a Taiwanese Gentry Family." In Leonard M. P. Gordon, ed., *Taiwan: Studies in Chinese Local History*. New York.

Myers, Ramon H. 1971. "Taiwan under Ch'ing Imperial Rule, 1684–1895: The Traditional Order." *Journal of the Institute of Chinese Studies of the Chinese University of Hong Kong* 4: 495–520.

——— 1972a. "Taiwan under Ch'ing Imperial Rule, 1684–1895: The Traditional Economy." *Journal of the Institute of Chinese Studies of the Chinese University of Hong Kong* 5: 373–409.

——— 1972b. "Taiwan under Ch'ing Imperial Rule, 1684–1895: The Traditional Society." *Journal of the Institute of Chinese Studies of the Chinese University of Hong Kong* 5: 414–51.

——— 1973. "Taiwan as an Imperial Colony of Japan: 1895–1945." *Journal of the Institute of Chinese Studies of the Chinese University of Hong Kong* 6: 425–51.

——— and Adrian Ching. 1964. "Agricultural Development in Taiwan under Japanese Rule." *Journal of Asian Studies* 23, no. 4: 555–70.

Montgomery, John D. 1962. *The Politics of Foreign Aid: American Experience in Southeast Asia*. New York.

———, Rufus B. Hughs, and Raymond H. Davis. 1964. *Rural Improvement and Development—The JCRR Model*. Washington, D.C.

O'Donnell, Guillermo A. 1973. *Modernization and Bureaucratic-Authoritarianism: Studies in South American Politics*. Berkeley, Calif.

Pasternak, Burton. 1969. "The Role of the Frontier in Chinese Lineage Development." *Journal of Asian Studies* 28, no. 3: 551–61.

——— 1972. *Kinship and Community in Two Chinese Villages*. Stanford, Calif.

Peng, Ming-min. 1971. "Political Offenses on Taiwan: Laws and Problems." *China Quarterly* 47: 471–93.

——— 1972. *A Taste of Freedom: Memoirs of a Formosan Independence Leader*. New York.

Pillsbury, Barbara K. L. 1978. "Factionalism Observed: Behind the 'Face' of a Chinese Community." *China Quarterly* 74: 241–72.

Riggs, Fred W. 1952. *Formosa under Chinese Nationalist Rule*. New York.

Rohsenow, Hill Gates. 1973. "Prosperity Settlement: The Politics of Paipai in Taipei, Taiwan." Ph.D. dissertation, University of Michigan.

Saso, Michael R. 1970. "The Taoist Tradition in Taiwan." *China Quarterly* 41: 83–102.

Schipper, Kristofer M. 1977. "Neighborhood Cult Associations in Traditional Taiwan." In G. William Skinner, ed., *The City in Late Imperial China*. Stanford, Calif.

Shieh, Milton J. T. 1970. *The Kuomintang: Selected Historical Documents, 1894–1969*. Jamaica, New York.

Silin, Robert H. 1976. *Leadership and Values: The Organization of Large-Scale Taiwanese Enterprises*. Cambridge, Mass.

Speidel, W. 1968. "Liu Ming-ch'uan in Taiwan, 1884–1891." Ph.D. dissertation, Yale University.

Stavis, Benedict. 1974. *Rural Local Governance and Agricultural Development in Taiwan*. Ithaca, New York.

Tai, Hung-chao. 1970. "The Kuomintang and Modernization in Taiwan." In Samuel Huntington and Clement Moore, eds., *Authoritarian Politics in Modern Society: The Dynamics of Established One-Party Systems*. New York.

Tien, Hung-mao. 1975. "Taiwan in Transition: Prospects for Socio-Political Change." *China Quarterly* 64: 615–44.

Tozzer, Warren. 1970. "Taiwan's 'Cultural Renaissance.'" *China Quarterly* 43: 81–99.

Tsurumi, E. Patricia. 1967. "Taiwan under Kodama Centaro and Goto Shimpei." In Albert Craig, ed., *Papers on Japan*, vol. 4. Cambridge, Mass.

——— 1977. *Japanese Colonial Education in Taiwan, 1895–1945*. Cambridge, Mass.

Uhalley, Stephen, Jr. 1967. "Taiwan's Response to the Cultural Revolution." *Asian Survey* 7, no. 11: 824–29.

Walker, Richard L. 1968. "Local Political Development in Taiwan's Frontier Land." Paper presented at the regional meeting of the Association for Asian Studies, Durham, North Carolina.

——— 1974. "Taiwan's Movement into Political Modernity, 1945–72." In Paul K. T. Sih, ed., *Taiwan in Modern Times*. New York.

Wang, Kuo-chang. 1968. "Local Government in Taiwan: An Introduction." *Chinese Journal of Administration* 10: 27–36.

Wang, Shih-ch'ing. 1974. "Religious Organization in the History of a Chinese Town." In Arthur P. Wolf, ed., *Religion and Ritual in Chinese Society*. Stanford, Calif.

Wang, Sung-hsing, and Raymond Apthorpe. 1974. *Rice Farming in Taiwan: Three Village Studies*. Taipei.

Wei, Yung. 1973. "Political Development in the Republic of China on Taiwan." In Hungdah Chiu, ed., *China and the Question of Taiwan: Documents and Analysis*. New York.

——— 1974. "Political Development in Taiwan: Reflections and Projections." In Yung-hwan Jo, ed., *Taiwan's Future*. Tempe, Arizona.

——— 1976a. "A Methodological Critique of Current Studies of Chinese Political Culture." *Journal of Politics* 38, no. 1: 114–40.

——— 1976b. "Modernization Process in Taiwan: An Allocative Analysis." *Asian Survey* 16, no. 3: 249–69.

——— n.d. "Political Culture and Socialization on Taiwan: Findings from Interviewing College Students." Unpublished research report.

Wilson, Richard W. 1970. *Learning to Be Chinese: The Political Socialization of Children in Taiwan*. Cambridge, Mass.

Winckler, Edwin A. 1974. "The Politics of Regional Development in Northern Taiwan: Case Studies and Organizational Analyses." Ph.D. dissertation, Harvard University.

Wolf, Arthur P. 1974. "Gods, Ghosts, and Ancestors." In Arthur P. Wolf, ed., *Religion and Ritual in Chinese Society*. Stanford, Calif.

Wolf, Margery. 1968. *The House of Lim: A Study of a Chinese Farm Family*. New York.

——— 1972. *Women and the Family in Rural Taiwan*. Stanford, Calif.

——— 1974. "Chinese Women: Old Skills in a New Context." In Michelle Zimbalist Rosaldo and Louise Lamphere, eds., *Woman, Culture, and Society*. Stanford, Calif.

Yang, Martin M. C. 1970. "Changes in Power Structure and Leadership in Rural Communities." In Martin M. C. Yang, ed., *Socio-Economic Results of Land Reform in Taiwan*. Honolulu.

*Chen: Government Enterprise and Village Politics*

Chen, Chung-min. 1977. *Upper Camp: A Study of a Chinese Mixed-Cropping Village in Taiwan.* Taipei.
Hsiao, Kung-chuan. 1960. *Rural China: Imperial Control in the Nineteenth Century.* Seattle.
Löffler, Reinhold. 1971. "The Representative Mediator and the New Peasant." *American Anthropologist* 73: 1077–91.
Wolf, Eric R. 1956. "Aspects of Group Relations in a Complex Society: Mexico." *American Anthropologist* 58: 1065–78.
Yang, Martin C. 1945. *A Chinese Village: Taitou, Shantung Province.* New York.

*Winckler: Roles Linking State and Society*

Appleton, Sheldon. 1970. "Taiwanese and Mainlanders on Taiwan: A Survey of Student Attitudes." *China Quarterly* 44: 38–65.
——— 1973. "Regime Support among Taiwan High School Students." *Asian Survey* 13, no. 8: 750–60.
——— 1974. "The Prospects for Student Activism on Taiwan." In Yung-hwan Jo, ed., *Taiwan's Future.* Tempe, Arizona.
Crissman, Lawrence W. 1969. "Each for His Own: Taiwanese Political Response to KMT Local Administration." Paper presented to the East and Southeast Asian Studies Conference, Ste. Adèle-en-haut, Quebec.
Huntington, Samuel P. 1968. *Political Order in Societies.* New Haven, Conn.
——— and Joan M. Nelson. 1976. *No Easy Choice: Political Participation in Developing Countries.* Cambridge, Mass.
Jacobs, J. Bruce. 1975. "Local Politics in Rural Taiwan: A Field Study of Kuan-hsi, Face, and Faction in Matsu Township." Ph.D. dissertation, Columbia University.
Karp, Walter. 1974. *Indispensable Enemies: The Politics of Misrule in America.* New York.
Key, V. O. 1950. *Southern Politics.* New York.
Lerman, Arthur J. 1977. "National Elite and Local Politicians in Taiwan." *American Political Science Review* 71, no. 4: 1406–22.
Linz, Juan J. 1964. "An Authoritarian Regime: Spain." In Erik Allardt and Yrjo Littunen, eds., *Cleavages, Ideologies, and Party Systems.* Helsinki.
——— 1973. "The Future of an Authoritarian Situation and the Institutionalization of an Authoritarian Regime: The Case of Brazil." In Alfred Stepan, ed., *Authoritarian Brazil.* New Haven, Conn.
——— 1975. "Authoritarianism and Totalitarianism." In David Greenstein and Nelson W. Polsby, eds., *Handbook of Political Science*, vol. 3. Reading, Mass.
Nelson, Joan M. 1969. *Migrants, Urban Poverty, and Instability in New Nations.* Cambridge, Mass.
Skinner, G. William, ed. 1977. *The City in Late Imperial China.* Stanford, Calif.
——— and Edwin A. Winckler. 1969. "Compliance Succession in Rural Communist China: A Cyclical Theory." In Amitai Etzioni, ed., *A Sociology Reader on Complex Organizations*, 2d ed. New York.
Tai, Hung-chao. 1970. "The Kuomintang and Modernization in Taiwan." In Samuel

Huntington and Clement Moore, eds., *Authoritarian Politics in Modern Society: The Dynamics of Established One-Party Systems*. New York.
Wei, Yung. n.d. "Political Culture and Socialization on Taiwan: Findings from Interviewing College Students." Unpublished research report.

*Crissman: The Structure of Local and Regional Systems*

Ahern, Emily M. 1973. *The Cult of the Dead in a Chinese Village*. Stanford, Calif.
Bailey, F. G. 1969. *Stratagems and Spoils*. Oxford.
Chen, Cheng-siang. 1953. *Cities and Rural Towns of Taiwan*. Taipei.
Christaller, Walter. 1966. *Central Places in Southern Germany*. Trans. Carlisle W. Baskin. Englewood Cliffs, N.J.
Cohen, Myron L. 1976. *House United, House Divided: The Chinese Family in Taiwan*. New York.
Crissman, Lawrence W. 1967. "The Segmentary Structure of Urban Overseas Chinese Communities." *Man*, n.s. 2: 185–204.
——— 1969. "Each for His Own: Taiwanese Political Response to KMT Local Administration." Paper presented at the Conference on Revolutionary and Reforming Governments, Ste. Adèle-en-haut, Quebec.
——— 1972. "Marketing on the Changhua Plain, Taiwan." In W. E. Willmott, ed., *Economic Organization in Chinese Society*. Stanford, Calif.
——— 1973. "Town and Country: Central Place Theory and Chinese Marketing Systems, with Particular Reference to Southwestern Changhua Hsien, Taiwan." Ph.D. dissertation, Cornell University.
——— 1975. "A Cognitive/Structural Approach to the Analysis of Socio-Cultural Systems." Unpublished paper.
——— 1976a. "Specific Central-Place Models for an Evolving System of Market Towns on the Changhua Plain, Taiwan." In Carol A. Smith, ed., *Regional Analysis, Vol. I (Economic Systems)*. New York.
——— 1976b. "Spatial Aspects of Marriage Patterns as Influenced by Marketing Behavior in West Central Taiwan." In Carol A. Smith, ed., *Regional Analysis, Vol. II (Social Systems)*. New York.
——— 1976c. "The Development of Local Taiwanese Factions." Paper presented at the American Anthropological Association Annual Meeting, Washington, D.C.
DeGlopper, Donald. 1969. "Accommodation and Consensus in Taiwanese Local Politics." Paper presented at the Conference on Revolutionary and Reforming Governments, Ste. Adèle-en-haut, Quebec.
——— 1973. "City on the Sands: Social Structure in a Nineteenth-Century Chinese City." Ph.D. dissertation, Cornell University.
——— n.d. "Temple Organization and Local Level Politics." Unpublished paper.
Diamond, Norma. 1969. *K'un Shen: A Taiwan Village*. New York.
Feuchtwang, Stephan D. R. 1972. "Religion and Society in Northern Taiwan." Ph.D. dissertation, London School of Economics and Political Science.
Freedman, Maurice. 1958. *Lineage Organization in Southeastern China*. London.
Gallin, Bernard. 1960. "Matrilateral and Affinal Relationships of a Taiwanese Village." *American Anthropologist* 62: 632–42.
——— 1966. *Hsin Hsing, Taiwan: A Chinese Village in Change*. Berkeley, Calif.

——— 1968. "Political Factionalism and Its Impact on Chinese Village Social Organization in Taiwan." In Marc J. Swartz, ed., *Local-Level Politics: Social and Cultural Perspectives*. Chicago.

Harrell, Stevan. 1974. "Belief and Unbelief in a Taiwan Village." Ph.D. dissertation, Stanford University.

Hsieh, Jih-chang Chester. 1978. "Structure and History of a Chinese Community in Taiwan." Ph.D. dissertation, University of Washington.

Huang, Shu-min. 1971. "Peasant Marketing Network in Taiwan." *Bulletin of the Institute of Ethnology, Academia Sinica* 32: 191–215.

——— 1977. "Agricultural Degradation: Changing Community Systems in Rural Taiwan." Ph.D. dissertation, Michigan State University.

Huang, Ta-chou. 1966. "Social Differentiation in Taiwanese Communities." M.A. thesis, Cornell University.

——— 1970. "The Process of Social Differentiation in Taiwanese Communities." *Cornell Journal of Social Relations* 5: 1–9.

Jacobs, J. Bruce. 1975. "Local Politics in Rural Taiwan: A Field Study of Kuan-Hsi, Face, and Faction in Matsu Township." Ph.D. dissertation, Columbia University.

——— 1976. "The Cultural Bases of Factional Alignment and Division in a Rural Taiwanese Township." *Journal of Asian Studies* 36: 79–97.

——— 1979. "A Preliminary Model of Particularistic Ties in Chinese Political Alliances: *Kan-Ch'ing* and *Kuan-Hsi* in a Rural Taiwanese Township." *China Quarterly* 78: 237–73.

Jordan, David K. 1972. *Gods, Ghosts, and Ancestors: Folk Religion in a Taiwanese Village*. Berkeley, Calif.

Knapp, Ronald G. 1968. "Spatial Aspects of Economic and Social Behavior in Taiwan." Ph.D. dissertation, University of Pittsburg.

——— 1971. "Marketing and Social Patterns in Rural Taiwan." *Annals of the Association of American Geographers* 61: 131–55.

——— 1976. "Chinese Frontier Settlement in Taiwan." *Annals of the Association of American Geographers* 66: 43–59.

Kuo Wen-hsiung. 1965. *Yenshui Town: A Socio-Anthropological Analysis*. Tunghai University, Department of Sociology. Taichung.

Lerman, Arthur J. 1972. "Political, Traditional, and Modern Economic Groups and the Taiwan Provincial Assembly." Ph.D. dissertation, Princeton University.

——— 1978. *Taiwan's Politics: The Provincial Assemblyman's World*. Washington, D.C.

McCreery, John L. 1973. "The Symbolism of Popular Taoist Magic." Ph.D. dissertation, Cornell University.

Pannell, Clifton W. 1970. "City and Regional Growth in Taiwan." *Journal of the China Society* 7: 1–17.

Pasternak, Burton. 1972. *Kinship and Community in Two Chinese Villages*. Stanford, Calif.

Seaman, Gary. 1974. "Temple Organization in a Chinese Village." Ph.D. dissertation, Cornell University.

Schipper, Kristofer M. 1977. "Neighborhood Cult Associations in Traditional Taiwan." In G. William Skinner, ed., *The City in Late Imperial China*. Stanford, Calif.

Skinner, G. William. 1964. "Marketing and Social Structure in Rural China, Part I." *Journal of Asian Studies* 24: 3–23.
——— 1965. "Marketing and Social Structure in Rural China, Part III." *Journal of Asian Studies* 24: 363–99.
———, ed. 1977. *The City in Late Imperial China*. Stanford, Calif.
Vander Meer, Canute. 1971. "Water Thievery in a Rice Irrigation System in Taiwan." *Annals of the Association of American Geographers* 61: 156–79.
Vander Meer, Paul. 1967. "Farm Plot Dispersal: Luliao Village, Taiwan." Ph.D. dissertation, University of Michigan.
Wolf, Arthur P. 1964. "Marriage and Adoption in a Hokkien Village." Ph.D. dissertation, Cornell University.
Wolf, Margery. 1968. *The House of Lim: A Study of a Chinese Farm Family*. New York.
——— 1972. *Women and the Family in Rural Taiwan*. Stanford, Calif.
Yuan, D. Y., with the assistance of Edward G. Stockwell. 1964. "The Rural-Urban Continuum: A Case Study of Taiwan." *Rural Sociology* 29: 247–60.

*Harrell: Social Organization in Hai-shan*

Ahern, Emily M. 1973. *The Cult of the Dead in a Chinese Village*. Stanford, Calif.
——— 1976. "Segmentation in Chinese Lineages: A View through Written Genealogies." *American Ethnologist* 3: 1–16.
Anderson, E. N. 1970. "Lineage Atrophy in Chinese Society." *American Anthropologist* 72: 363–65.
Baker, Hugh D. R. 1968. *A Chinese Lineage Village: Sheung Shui*. Stanford, Calif.
Cohen, Myron L. 1970. "Developmental Process in the Chinese Domestic Group." In Maurice Freedman, ed., *Family and Kinship in Chinese Society*. Stanford, Calif.
Diamond, Norma. 1969. *K'un Shen: A Taiwan Village*. New York.
Freedman, Maurice. 1958. *Lineage Organization in Southeastern China*. London.
Fried, Morton H. 1953. *The Fabric of Chinese Society: A Study of the Social Life of a Chinese County Seat*. New York.
Harrell, Stevan. 1974a. "Belief and Unbelief in a Taiwan Village." Ph.D. dissertation, Stanford University.
——— 1974b. "Close-Knit Households." Unpublished paper.
——— 1976. "The Ancestors at Home." In William H. Newell, ed., *Ancestors*. The Hague.
Ho. 1893. *Hsiao-shan Ch'in-i Ho-shih tsung-p'u* (The genealogy of the Ho lineage of Ch'in-i, Hsiao-shan county, Chekiang).
Liang. 1922. *Yung-shang Liang-shih chia-ch'eng* (The genealogy of the Liang lineage of Yung-shang, Ningpo, Chekiang).
Pasternak, Burton. 1972. *Kinship and Community in Two Chinese Villages*. Stanford, Calif.
Potter, Jack M. 1968. *Capitalism and the Chinese Peasant: Social and Economic Change in a Hong Kong Village*. Berkeley, Calif.
Skinner, G. William. 1964. "Marketing and Social Structure in Rural China, Part I." *Journal of Asian Studies* 24: 3–43.

——— 1965a. "Marketing and Social Structure in Rural China, Part II." *Journal of Asian Studies* 24: 195–228.

——— 1965b. "Marketing and Social Structure in Rural China, Part III." *Journal of Asian Studies* 24: 363–99.

Wang Sung-Hsing. 1971. "Pooling and Sharing in a Chinese Fishing Economy: Kuei-shan Tao." Ph.D. dissertation, Tokyo University.

Watson, James L. 1975. *Emigration and the Chinese Lineage: The Mans in Hong Kong and London*. Berkeley, Calif.

Wolf, Arthur P. 1974. "Gods, Ghosts, and Ancestors." In Arthur P. Wolf, ed., *Religion and Ritual in Chinese Society*. Stanford, Calif.

*Pasternak: Economics and Ecology*

Ahern, Emily M. 1973. *The Cult of the Dead in a Chinese Village*. Stanford, Calif.

Baker, Hugh D. R. 1968. *A Chinese Lineage Village: Sheung Shui*. Stanford, Calif.

Bessac, Francis B. 1964. "Some Social Effects of Land Reform in a Village on the Taichung Plain." *Journal of the China Society* 4: 15–28.

Chang, Han-yu and Ramon Myers. 1963. "Japanese Colonial Development Policy in Taiwan, 1895–1906: A Case of Bureaucratic Entrepreneurship." *Journal of Asian Studies* 22: 433–49.

Chow, Yung-teh. 1966. *Social Mobility in China*. New York.

Chu, Solomon S. P. 1970. *Family Structure and Extended Kinship in a Chinese Community*. (Ann Arbor: Univ. Microfilms 70-4047.)

Chuang Ying-chang. 1972. "T'ai-wan nung-ts'un chia-tsu tui hsien-tai-hua te shih-ying" (The adaptation of family to modernization in rural Taiwan). *Bulletin of the Institute of Ethnology, Academia Sinica* 34: 85–98.

——— 1973. "T'ai-wan han-jen tsung-tsu fa-chan te Jo-kan" (Temples, ancestral halls, and patterns of settlement in Chu-shan). *Bulletin of the Institute of Ethnology, Academia Sinica* 36: 113–40.

Cohen, Myron L. 1967. "Variations in Complexity among Chinese Family Groups: The Impact of Modernization." *Transactions of the New York Academy of Sciences* 2d ser., 29: 638–44.

——— 1968. "A Case Study of Chinese Family Economy and Development." *Journal of Asian and African Studies* 3: 161–80.

——— 1969. "Agnatic Kinship in South Taiwan." *Ethnology* 8: 167–82.

——— 1970. "Developmental Process in the Chinese Domestic Group." In Maurice Freedman, ed., *Family and Kinship in Chinese Society*. Stanford, Calif.

——— 1976. *House United, House Divided: The Chinese Family in Taiwan*. New York.

Crissman, Lawrence W. 1972. "Marketing on the Changhua Plain, Taiwan." In W. E. Willmott, ed., *Economic Organization in Chinese Society*. Stanford, Calif.

——— 1976. "Specific Central-Place Models for an Evolving System of Market Towns on the Changhua Plain, Taiwan." In Carol A. Smith, ed., *Regional Analysis*, vol. 1. New York.

DeGlopper, Donald R. 1972. "Doing Business in Lukang." In W. E. Willmott, ed., *Economic Organization in Chinese Society*. Stanford, Calif.

Diamond, Norma. 1969. *K'un Shen: A Taiwan Village*. New York.

——— 1975. "Women under Kuomintang Rule: Variations on the Feminine Mystique." *Modern China* 1: 3–45.
Ember, Carol R., Melvin Ember, and Burton Pasternak. 1974. "On the Development of Unilineal Descent." *Journal of Anthropological Research* 30: 69–94.
Frank, Andre G. 1969. "The Development of Underdevelopment." In Andre G. Frank, ed., *Latin America: Underdevelopment or Revolution*. New York.
Freedman, Maurice. 1958. *Lineage Organization in Southeastern China*. London.
——— 1966. *Chinese Lineage and Society: Fukien and Kwangtung*. New York.
Fried, Morton H. 1954. "Community Studies in China." *Far Eastern Quarterly* 14: 11–36.
——— 1966. "Some Political Aspects of Clanship in a Modern Chinese City." In Marc J. Swartz, Victor W. Turner, and Arthur Tuden, eds., *Political Anthropology*. Chicago.
Gallin, Bernard. 1960. "Matrilateral and Affinal Relationships of a Taiwanese Village." *American Anthropologist* 62: 632–42.
——— 1963. "Land Reform in Taiwan: Its Effect on Rural Social Organization and Leadership." *Human Organization* 22: 109–12.
——— 1966. *Hsin Hsing, Taiwan: A Chinese Village in Change*. Berkeley, Calif.
——— and Rita S. Gallin. 1974. "The Integration of Village Migrants in Taipei." In Mark Elvin and G. William Skinner, eds., *The Chinese City Between Two Worlds*. Stanford, Calif.
Griffin, Keith. 1974. *The Political Economy of Agrarian Change: An Essay on the Green Revolution*. Cambridge, Mass.
Gross, Daniel R. 1971. "The Great Sisal Scheme." *Natural History* 53: 48–55.
Havens, A. E., and W. Flinn. 1971. "Green Revolution Technology and Community Development: The Limits of Action Programs." In George Dalton, ed., *Economic Development and Social Change: The Modernization of Village Communities*. Garden City, N.Y.
Ho, Ping-ti. 1962. *The Ladder of Success in Imperial China*. New York.
Hsiao, Kung-chuan. 1960. *Rural China: Imperial Control in the Nineteenth Century*. Seattle.
Hsieh Jih-chang. 1973. "Shui-li ho she-hui wen-hua chih shih-ying" (Irrigation and sociocultural adaptations). *Bulletin of the Institute of Ethnology, Academia Sinica* 36: 57–77.
Hsu, Cho-yun. 1972. "I-lan in the First Half of the 19th Century." *Bulletin of the Institute of Ethnology, Academia Sinica* 33: 51–70.
Huang, Shu-min. 1971. "Peasant Marketing Network in Taiwan." *Bulletin of the Institute of Ethnology, Academia Sinica* 32: 191–215.
Knapp, Ronald G. 1970. "Itinerant Merchants in T'ai-wan." *Journal of Geography* 69: 344–47.
——— 1971. "Marketing and Social Patterns in Rural Taiwan." *Annals of the American Association of Geographers* 61: 131–55.
Kung, Lydia. 1978. "Factory Work, Women, and the Family in Taiwan." Ph.D. dissertation, Yale University.
Mark, Lindy Li. 1972. "Taiwanese Lineage Enterprises: A Study of Familial Entrepreneurship." Ph.D. dissertation, University of California, Berkeley.
Marsh, Robert M. 1968. "The Taiwanese of Taipei: Some Major Aspects of

their Social Structure and Attitudes." *Journal of Asian Studies* 27: 578–84.
——— and Albert R. O'Hara. 1961. "Attitudes Toward Marriage and the Family in Taiwan." *American Journal of Sociology* 67: 1–8.

Myers, Ramon H., and Adrienne Ching. 1964. "Agricultural Development in Taiwan under Japanese Rule." *Journal of Asian Studies* 23: 555–70.

Myrdal, Gunnar. 1971. "Regional Economic Inequalities." In George Dalton, ed., *Economic Development and Social Change: The Modernization of Village Communities*. Garden City, N.Y.

O'Hara, Albert R. 1962. "Changing Attitudes of University Students Toward Marriage and the Family in Taiwan." *Journal of the China Society* 2: 57–79.

——— 1967. "Comparative Values of American and Chinese University Students in Choosing a Mate." *Journal of the China Society* 5: 93–100.

Olsen, Stephen M. 1972. "The Inculcation of Economic Values in Taipei Business Families." In W. E. Willmott, ed., *Economic Organization in Chinese Society*. Stanford, Calif.

Pasternak, Burton. 1968a. "On the Social Consequences of Equalizing Irrigation Access." *Human Organization* 27: 332–43.

——— 1968b. "Some Social Consequences of Land Reform in a Taiwanese Village." *Eastern Anthropologist* 21: 135–54.

——— 1972a. *Kinship and Community in Two Chinese Villages*. Stanford, Calif.

——— 1972b. "The Sociology of Irrigation: Two Taiwanese Villages." In W. E. Willmott, ed., *Economic Organization in Chinese Society*. Stanford, Calif.

——— 1973. "Chinese Tale-Telling Tombs." *Ethnology* 12: 259–73.

——— 1976. *Introduction to Kinship and Social Organization*. Englewood Cliffs, N.J.

Potter, Jack M. 1968. *Capitalism and the Chinese Peasant: Social and Economic Change in a Hong Kong Village*. Berkeley, Calif.

——— 1970. "Land and Lineage in Traditional China." In Maurice Freedman, ed., *Family and Kinship in Chinese Society*. Stanford, Calif.

Singer, Hans. 1971. "The Distribution of Gains Between Investing and Borrowing Countries." In George Dalton, ed., *Economic Development and Social Change: The Modernization of Village Communities*. Garden City, N.Y.

Speare, Alden, Jr. 1974. "Migration and Family Change in Central Taiwan." In Mark Elvin and G. William Skinner, eds., *The Chinese City Between Two Worlds*. Stanford, Calif.

Ts'ai, Wen-hui. 1964. "Changing Attitudes Toward Marriage and the Family in Taiwan." *Thought and Word* 2: 211–19.

Vander Meer, Canute. 1971. "Water Thievery in a Rice Irrigation System in Taiwan." *Annals of the Association of American Geographers* 61: 156–79.

Wang, Sung-hsing, and Raymond Apthorpe. 1974. *Rice Farming in Taiwan: Three Village Studies*. Taipei.

Wolf, Arthur P. 1966. "Childhood Association, Sexual Attraction, and the Incest Taboo." *American Anthropologist* 68: 883–98.

——— 1968. "Adopt a Daughter-in-Law, Marry a Sister: A Chinese Solution to the Problem of the Incest Taboo." *American Anthropologist* 70: 864–74.

——— 1970. "Chinese Kinship and Mourning Dress." In Maurice Freedman, ed., *Family and Kinship in Chinese Society*. Stanford, Calif.

Wolf, Margery. 1968. *The House of Lim: A Study of a Chinese Farm Family*. New York.
——— 1970. "Child Training and the Chinese Family." In Maurice Freedman, ed., *Family and Kinship in Chinese Society*. Stanford, Calif.
——— 1972. *Women and the Family in Rural Taiwan*. Stanford, Calif.
Yang, Martin. 1945. *A Chinese Village: Taitou, Shantung Province*. New York.
——— 1962. "Changes in Family Life in Rural Taiwan." *Journal of the China Society* 2: 68–79.

*Kung: Perceptions of Work among Factory Women*

Dore, Ronald P. 1973. *British Factory—Japanese Factory: The Origins of National Diversity in Employment Relations*. Berkeley, Calif.
Fong, H. D. 1932. *Cotton Industry and Trade in China*. Tientsin.
Kung, Lydia. 1976. "Factory Work and Women in Taiwan: Changes in Self-Image and Status." *Signs, Journal of Women in Culture and Society* 2: 35–58.
——— 1978. "Factory Work, Women, and the Family in Taiwan." Ph.D. dissertation, Yale University.
Lieu, D. K. 1936. *The Growth and Industrialization of Shanghai*. Shanghai.
Liu, Keh-chung. 1974. "The Present Situation of Labor Movement and Youth Workers in the Republic of China." In the *Third International Metalworkers' Federation Asian Youth and Women Symposium Report*. Taipei.
Silin, Robert H. 1976. *Leadership and Values: The Organization of Large-Scale Taiwanese Enterprises*. Cambridge, Mass.
Tsui, Tsu-kan. 1972. "Women Workers in Taiwan." In China Council on Sino-American Cooperation in the Humanities and Social Sciences, ed., *Sino-American Conference on Manpower in Taiwan*. Taipei.
Wolf, Margery. 1972. *Women and the Family in Rural Taiwan*. Stanford, Calif.

*Wickberg: Continuities in Land Tenure, 1900–1940*

Asada Kyōji. 1968. *Nihon teikokushugi to kyū-shokuminchi jinushi-sei* (Japanese imperialism and the landlord system of the former colonies). Tokyo.
Azuma Yoshio. 1944. *Taiwan keizai-shi kenkyū* (Studies on the economic history of Taiwan). Taihoku, Taiwan.
Barclay, George. 1954. *Colonial Development and Population in Taiwan*. Princeton, N.J.
Barrows, Richard L. 1974. "African Land Reform Policies: The Case of Sierra Leone." *Land Economics* 50, no. 4: 402–10.
Buck, John Lossing. 1937. *Land Utilization in China*. Chicago.
Chang, Han-yu. 1969. "A Study of the Living Conditions of Farmers in Taiwan, 1931–1950." *Developing Economies* 7, no. 1: 35–62.
Chen, Han-seng. 1936. *Agrarian Problems in Southernmost China*. Shanghai.
Cohen, Myron. 1976. *House United, House Divided: The Chinese Family in Taiwan*. New York.
Frankel, Francine. 1971. *India's Green Revolution: Economic Gains and Political Costs*. Princeton, N.J.

Freedman, Maurice. 1958. *Lineage Organization in Southeastern China*. London.

Griffin, Keith. 1974. *The Political Economy of Agrarian Change: An Essay on the Green Revolution*. Cambridge, Mass.

Ho, Samuel P. S. 1978. *The Economic Development of Taiwan, 1860–1970*. New Haven, Conn.

Jamieson, George. 1888. "Tenure of Land in China and the Condition of the Rural Population." *Journal of the North China Branch, Royal Asiatic Society* n.s. 23: 59–174.

JCRR (Chinese-American Joint Commission on Rural Reconstruction, Rural Economics Division). 1956. *Taiwan Agricultural Statistics, 1901–1955*, Economic Digest series, no. 8. Taipei.

Jo Teruhiko. 1975. *Nihon teikokushugi-ka no Taiwan* (Taiwan under Japanese imperialism). Tokyo.

Kawada, Shiro. 1928. "The Tenant System of Formosa." *Kyoto University Economic Review* 3, no. 2: 86–109.

*Keizai (Chōsa keizai shiryō hōkoku* [Reference materials and report from an investigation of the economy]), vol. 2. 1905. Tokyo.

Knapp, Ronald. 1975. "Land Tenure in Eighteenth Century Taiwan." *China Geographer* 2: 39–48.

Kobayashi Rihei. 1905. "Tōki tetsuzuki-jō ni okeru futatsu dai-gigi" (Two major uncertainties in registration procedure). *Taiwan kanshū kiji* 5, no. 8: 12–19.

Kubota Bunji. 1967. "Shin-matsu Szechwan no dai-den-hu" (The big tenants of late-Ch'ing Szechwan). In Tōkyō kyoiku daigaku, Tōyō shigaku kenkyū shitsu, and Ajia shi kenkyū kai, eds., *Kindai Chūgoku nōson shakaishi kenkyū*. Tokyo.

Lee, Teng-hui. 1971. *Intersectoral Capital Flows in the Economic Development of Taiwan, 1895–1960*. Ithaca, N.Y.

Lin Account Books (Rent collection account books of the eldest branch of the Lin family of Pan-ch'iao). 1874–1895. Made available in 1966 by permission of Lin Hsiung-hsiang.

McAleavy, Henry. 1958. "Dien in China and Vietnam." *Journal of Asian Studies* 17: 403–15.

Myers, Ramon, and Adrienne Ching. 1964. "Agricultural Development in Taiwan under Japanese Rule." *Journal of Asian Studies* 23: 555–70.

*NKCS (Nōka keizai chōsa, dai-nihō* [Survey of farm household economy, second report]). 1923. *Nōgyo kihon chōsa sho* (Basic survey of agriculture), no. 5. Taihoku, Taiwan.

Pasternak, Burton. 1972. *Kinship and Community in Two Chinese Villages*. Stanford, Calif.

*Provincial Report (Provincial Report on Investigations of Laws and Customs in the Island of Formosa)*. 1902. Okamatsu Santarō, et al., comp. Kyoto.

Rawski, Evelyn S. 1972. *Agricultural Change and the Peasant Economy of South China*. Cambridge, Mass.

Rosen, George. 1975. *Peasant Society in a Changing Economy: Comparative Development in Southeast Asia and India*. Urbana, Ill.

Tai Yen-hui. 1963. "Ch'ing-tai T'ai-wan chih ta-hsiao-tsu yeh" (The *ta-tsu* and *hsiao-tsu* property rights in Taiwan in the Ch'ing period). *T'ai-pei wen-hsien* 4: 1–47.

*Taiwan kyūkan*. 1906. *Rinji Taiwan kyūkan chōsa kai. Dai nikai hōkoku* (Second report of the temporary commission for the study of old customs in Taiwan), vol. 1. Taihoku, Taiwan.

*Taiwan shihō* (Private law in Taiwan), vol. 1. 1910. Taihoku, Taiwan.

*TCTY* (*T'ai-wan-sheng wu-shih-i-nien-lai t'ung-chi t'i-yao* [Fifty-one year statistical summary of Taiwan province]). 1946. Taipei.

*Tochi kankō* (*Taiwan tochi kankō ippan* [An outline of land customs in Taiwan]), vol. 3. 1905. Taihoku, Taiwan.

"Tochi ni kansuru" ("Tochi ni kansuru kyūsei kyūkan torishirabe sho" [An investigation of old systems and old customs concerning land]). 1901. *Taiwan kanshū kiji* 1, no. 11: 1–16.

Vander Meer, Canute, and Paul Vander Meer. 1968. "Land Property Data on Taiwan." *Journal of Asian Studies* 28: 144–50.

Wang I-t'ao. 1964. *T'ai-wan chih t'u-ti chih-tu yü t'u-ti cheng-tse* (Land systems and land policies in Taiwan). Taipei.

Wickberg, Edgar. 1969. "The Tenancy System in Taiwan, 1900–1939." Unpublished manuscript prepared for the Columbia University Seminar on Modern East Asia.

——— 1970. "Late Nineteenth Century Land Tenure in North Taiwan." In Leonard H. D. Gordon, ed., *Taiwan: Studies in Chinese Local History*. New York.

——— 1975. "The Taiwan Peasant Movement, 1923–1932: Chinese Rural Radicalism under Japanese Development Programs." *Pacific Affairs* 48: 558–82.

Yanaihara Tadao. 1929. *Teikokushugi-ka no Taiwan* (Taiwan under Japanese imperialism). Tokyo.

*Gates: Ethnicity and Social Class*

Appleton, Sheldon L. 1972. "Taiwan: The Year It Finally Happened." *Asian Survey* 22, no. 1: 32–37.

Barth, Fredrik, ed. 1969. *Ethnic Groups and Boundaries: The Social Organization of Cultural Difference*. Boston.

*Chung-hua Min-kuo t'ung-chi t'i-yao* (Statistical abstract of the Republic of China). 1974. Taipei.

Cohen, Abner. 1974a. *Two-Dimensional Man: An Essay on the Anthropology of Power Symbolism in Complex Society*. Berkeley, Calif.

——— 1974b. *Urban Ethnicity*. London.

Cole, Allan B. 1967. "Political Roles of Taiwanese Enterprisers." *Asian Survey* 7, no. 9: 645–54.

De Vos, George. 1975. "Ethnic Pluralism: Conflict and Accommodation." In George De Vos and Lola Romanucci-Ross, eds., *Ethnic Identity: Cultural Continuities and Change*. Palo Alto, Calif.

Diamond, Norma. 1969. *K'un Shen: A Taiwan Village*. New York.

——— 1973. "The Status of Women in Taiwan: One Step Forward, Two Steps Back." In Marilyn B. Young, ed., *Women in China*. Ann Arbor, Mich.

Djilas, Milovan. 1957. *The New Class*. New York.

Domhoff, G. William. 1974. *The Bohemian Grove*. New York.

Eberhard, Wolfram. 1965. "Chinese Regional Stereotypes." *Asian Survey* 5, no. 12: 596–608.

Enloe, Cynthia H. 1973. *Ethnic Conflict and Political Development: An Analytic Study*. Boston.

Feuchtwang, Stephan D. R. 1972. "Religion and Society in Northern Taiwan." Ph.D. dissertation, London School of Economics and Political Science.

*Foreign Trade of Japan*. 1974. Japan External Trade Organization.

Gallin, Bernard, and Rita Gallin. 1974. "The Rural-to-Urban Migration of an Anthropologist in Taiwan." In George M. Foster and Robert V. Kemper, eds., *Anthropologists in Cities*. Boston.

Harris, Marvin. 1964. *Patterns of Race in the Americas*. New York.

——— 1975. *Culture, People, Nature*, 2d ed. New York.

Hsieh, Tien-chiao. 1972. *Migrant Factory Workers' Social Adaptation in Kaohsiung City, Taiwan*. Tainan.

Hsu, Chia-ming. 1976. "The Community Organization of Hakka Migrants in the Chang-hua Plain." Paper presented at the Conference on Anthropology in Taiwan, Portsmouth, N.H.

Jacoby, Neil H. 1966. *U.S. Aid to Taiwan*. New York.

Jordan, David K. 1969. "The Languages of Taiwan." *Monda Lingvo-Problemo* 1: 65–76.

Koo, Anthony Y. C. 1973. "Economic Development of Taiwan." In Paul K. T. Sih, ed., *Taiwan in Modern Times*. New York.

Lau, Joseph S. M. 1975. "'Crowded Hours' Revisited: The Evocation of the Past in *Taipei Jen*." *Journal of Asian Studies* 25, no. 1: 31–48.

Leach, Edmund. 1954. *Political Systems of Highland Burma: A Study of Kachin Social Structure*. London.

Light, Ivan H. 1973. *Ethnic Enterprise in America. Business and Welfare among Chinese, Japanese, and Blacks*. Berkeley, Calif.

Lo Hoai-un. 1975. "The Rise of Chiang Ching-kuo and the Future of Taiwan." *Independent Taiwan* 46: 6.

Magdoff, Harry, and Paul M. Sweezy. 1971. "Notes on the Multinational Corporation." In K. T. Fann and Donald C. Hodges, eds., *Readings in U.S. Imperialism*. Boston.

Mendel, Douglas. 1970. *The Politics of Formosan Nationalism*. Berkeley, Calif.

Nee, Victor G., and Barry Nee. 1973. *Longtime Californ'*. New York.

Pillsbury, Barbara L. K. 1973. "Cohesion and Cleavage in a Chinese Muslim Minority." Ph.D. dissertation, Columbia University. (Ann Arbor: Univ. Microfilms.)

Rohsenow, Hill Gates. 1973. "Prosperity Settlement: The Politics of Paipai in Taipei, Taiwan." Ph.D. dissertation, University of Michigan. (Ann Arbor: University Microfilms.)

*T'ai Fu ti-chü kung-shang yeh p'u-ch'a pao-kao* (1971 industrial and commercial censuses of Taiwan and Fukien area, Republic of China), vol. 1. 1973.

*T'ai-pei shih t'ung-chi yao-lan* (Statistical abstract of Taipei city). 1973.

*T'ai-wan kung-shang 500 jen-ming-lu* (Taiwan business who's who). 1973. Taipei.

*T'ai-wan sheng cheng-fu jen-shih t'ung-chi t'i-yao* (Statistical abstract of personnel of the provincial government of Taiwan). 1974. Taichung.

Tien, Hung-mao. 1975. "Taiwan in Transition: Prospects for Socio-Political Change." *China Quarterly* 64: 615–44.

Vogel, Ezra. 1963. *Japan's New Middle Class: The Salary Man and His Family in a Tokyo Suburb*. Berkeley, Calif.

Wagley, Charles, and Marvin Harris. 1964. *Minorities in the New World: Six Case Studies*. New York.

Willmott, W. E. 1970. *The Political Structure of the Chinese Community in Cambodia*. London.

*Lamley: Subethnic Rivalry in the Ch'ing Period*

Chang K'ai-ch'üan. 1963. *Hui-an feng-t'u chih* (Annals of the customs and manners of Hui-an county). n.p.

Chang T'an. 1970. "Ch'ing-tai ch'u-ch'i chih T'ai cheng-ts'e ti chien-t'ao" (An investigation of government strategies for ruling Taiwan in the early Ch'ing). *T'ai-wan wen-hsien* 21, no. 1: 19–44.

——— 1974. "Ch'ing-tai T'ai-wan fen-lei hsieh-tou p'in-fan chih chu-yin" (Principal causes of subethnic feuds in Ch'ing Taiwan). *T'ai-wan feng-wu* 24, no. 4: 75–85.

——— 1976. "I-lan liang-tz'u hsieh-tou shih-chien chih p'o-hsi" (An analysis of the armed feuds that twice occurred in I-lan). *T'ai-wan wen-hsien* 27, no. 2: 54–71.

Ch'en Cheng-hsiang [Chen Cheng-siang]. 1959. *T'ai-wan ti-li t'u chi* (*Geographical Atlas of Taiwan*). Taipei.

Ch'en, Chi-lu. 1972. "History of Chinese Immigration into Taiwan." *Bulletin of the Institute of Ethnology, Academia Sinica* 33: 119–33.

Ch'en Han-kuang. 1972. "Jih-chü shih-ch'i T'ai-wan Han-ts'u tsu-chi t'iao-ch'a" (An investigation of the ancestral registry of the Han Chinese of Taiwan in the Japanese period). *T'ai-wan wen-hsien* 23, no. 1: 85–104.

Ch'en Shao-hsing. 1964. *Jen-min chih; Jen-k'ou p'ien* (A record of the inhabitants; Section on population). In T'ai-wan sheng wen-hsien wei-yüan-hui, comp., *T'ai-wan sheng t'ung-chih kao*. Taipei.

Cheng Chen-t'u. 1887. "Chih hsieh-tou i" (A proposal to cure *hsieh-tou*). In Ho Ch'ang-ling, comp., *Huang-ch'ao ching-shih wen-pien, chüan* 23. Taipei; 1963 reprint.

Chou Hsi. 1832. *Chang-hua hsien chih* (Chang-hua county gazetteer). Taipei; 1962 reprint.

Chou K'ai. 1839. *Hsia-men chih* (Gazetteer of Amoy). Taipei; 1961 reprint.

Chuang Chin-te. 1964. "Ch'ing-ch'u yen-chin yen-hai jen-min t'ou-tu lai T'ai shih-mo" (History of the early Ch'ing prohibition against coastal people's illegal crossings to Taiwan). *T'ai-wan wen-hsien* 15, no. 3: 1–20; no. 4: 40–62.

——— 1973. *Ch'ing-tai T'ai-wan chiao-yü shih-liao hui-pien* (A collection of historical material on education in Taiwan in the early Ch'ing). Taichung.

Chung Jen-shou. 1973. *Liu-tui K'o-chia hsiang-tu chih* (A record of the Liu-tui Hakka districts). P'ing-tung, Taiwan.

Cohen, Abner. 1974. "Introduction: The Lesson of Ethnicity." In Abner Cohen, ed., *Urban Ethnicity*. London.

Cohen, Myron L. 1969. "Agnatic Kinship in South Taiwan." *Ethnology* 8, no. 2: 167–82.

Crissman, Lawrence W. 1972. "Marketing on the Changhua Plain, Taiwan." In

W. E. Willmott, ed., *Economic Organization in Chinese Society*. Stanford, Calif.

Enloe, Cynthia H. 1973. *Ethnic Conflict and Political Development*. Boston.

Fan Hsin-yüan. 1974. "Ch'ing-tai T'ai-wan min-chien hsieh-tou li-shih chih yen-chiu" (Research on the history of armed feuds among Taiwan's inhabitants during the Ch'ing). *T'ai-wan wen-hsien* 25, no. 4: 90–111.

Fang Hao. 1971. "Kuang-hsü chia-wu teng nien chang-lun chü hsin-kao so-chien chih T'ai-wan hang-chiao" (Drafts of Taiwan *chiao*-guild letters that appeared in the postal transmission offices during 1894 and other years of the Kuang-hsü reign). *Kuo-li Cheng-chih ta-hsüeh hsüeh-pao* 24: 21–51.

Forrest, R. A. D. 1948. *The Chinese Language*. London.

Freedman, Maurice. 1958. *Lineage Organization in Southeastern China*. London.

——— 1966. *Chinese Lineage and Society: Fukien and Kwangtung*. London.

Fu I-ling. 1948. "Ch'ing-tai ch'ien-ch'i Hsia-men yang-hang k'ao" (An investigation of the foreign trade guilds of Amoy during the Ch'ing). In Sa Shih-wu, et al., eds., *Fu-chien tui-wai mao-i shih yen-chiu*. Fukien.

Gibson, J. Campbell. 1901. *Mission Problems and Mission Methods in South China: Lectures in Evangelistic Theology*. London.

Gluckman, Max. 1956. *Custom and Conflict in Africa*. New York; 1969 reprint.

Ho, Ping-ti. 1959. *Studies on the Population of China, 1368–1953*. Cambridge, Mass.

Hsiao, Kung-chuan. 1960. *Rural China: Imperial Control in the Nineteenth Century*. Seattle, Wash.

Hsieh, Chiao-min. 1964. *Taiwan—Ilha Formosa: A Geography in Perspective*. London.

Hsieh, Kuo-ching. 1932. "Removal of Coastal Population in Early Tsing Period." *The Chinese Social and Political Science Review* 15, no. 4: 559–96.

Hsieh Tung-min. 1954. "T'ai-wan shui-li shih" (History of water control in Taiwan). In Lin Hsiung-hsiang, et. al., eds., *T'ai-wan wen-hua lun-chi*. Taipei.

Hsü Chia-ming. 1973. "Chang-hua p'ing-yüan Fu-lao-K'o ti ti-yü tsu-chih" (Territorial organization of Hoklo-ized Hakka in the Chang-hua Plain). *Bulletin of the Institute of Ethnology, Academia Sinica* 36: 165–90.

Hsu, Cho-yun. 1972. "I-lan in the First Half of the 19th Century." *Bulletin of the Institute of Ethnology, Academia Sinica* 33: 51–70.

Hsü Tuan-fu. 1970. *Hung Ch'i-sheng hsien-sheng i-shu* (Writings bequeathed by Mr. Hung Ch'i-sheng). Taipei.

Hu P'u-an. 1923. *Chung-hua ch'üan-kuo feng-su chih* (A record of the customs of the entire country of China), vol. 1. Taipei; 1968 reprint.

Huang Chao. 1899. *Shih-k'u i cheng* (A statement about Shih-k'u). Taipei; 1970 reprint.

Huang Ch'i-mu. 1953. "Fen-lei hsieh-tou yü Meng-chia" (Subethnic feuds and Meng-chia). *T'ai-pei wen-wu* 2, no. 1: 55–58.

Huang Chung-sheng. 1960. *Hsin-chu feng-wu chih* (A record of Hsin-chu customs). Hsin-chu, Taiwan.

Huang Hsiu-cheng. 1976. "Ch'ing-tai T'ai-wan fen-lei hsieh-tou shih-chien chih chien-t'ao" (An investigation of subethnic feuds in Ch'ing Taiwan). *T'ai-wan wen-hsien* 27, no. 4: 78–86.

Huang Shih-ch'iao. 1968. "Ju-nan Chou-shih Min-Yüeh ch'ien T'ai tsu-p'u k'ao"

(An investigation through genealogies of the migration of Ju-nan Chou-surname kindred from Fukien and Kwangtung to Taiwan). *T'ai-wan wen-hsien* 19, no. 2: 122–30.

——— 1969. "Huang hsing p'ai-hsi fen-chih ch'ien T'ai k'ao" (An investigation of the branches of the Huang surname line that migrated to Taiwan). *T'ai-wan wen-hsien* 20, no. 4: 92–117.

——— 1971. "T'ai-wan Wu-kung Chou-shih tsu-p'u tzu-liao hui-chi" (Collected materials from the genealogy of the Taiwan Wu-kung Chou lineage). *T'ai-wan wen-hsien* 22, no. 1: 103–22.

Huang Shu-ching. 1736. *T'ai-hai shih ch'a lu* (A record of being dispatched by raft on the Taiwan sea). Taipei; 1957 reprint.

Inō Yoshinori [Kanori]. 1928. *Taiwan bunkashi* (A record of Taiwan's culture), vol. 1. Tokyo.

Jordan, David K. 1972. *Gods, Ghosts, and Ancestors; The Folk Religion of a Taiwanese Village*. Berkeley, Calif.

Lamley, Harry J. 1964. "The Taiwan Literati and Early Japanese Rule, 1895–1915." Ph.D. dissertation, University of Washington.

——— 1970. "The 1895 Taiwan War of Resistance: Local Chinese Efforts Against a Foreign Power." In Leonard H. D. Gordon, ed., *Taiwan: Studies in Chinese Local History*. New York.

——— 1977a. "The Formation of Cities: Initiative and Motivation in Building Three Walled Cities in Taiwan." In G. William Skinner, ed., *The City in Late Imperial China*. Stanford, Calif.

——— 1977b. "*Hsieh-tou*: The Pathology of Violence in Southeastern China." *Ch'ing-shih wen-t'i* 3, no. 7: 1–39.

Li Han-ching. 1974. *Nan-an hsü chih (hou-p'ien)* (Nan-an county supplementary gazetteer, latter chapters). Taipei.

Li Ju-ho. 1970. "Ch'ing T'ai-wan pan-ping chih-tu yü t'un-t'ien mu-ping chih i" (An explanation of Taiwan's troop rotation system and military colonist recruitment during the Ch'ing). *T'ai-wan wen-hsien* 21, no. 2: 1–21.

Li Tung-ming. 1976. "T'ai-wan chü-min chi-kuan pieh hsing-shih yen-chiu" (A study of the surnames of Taiwan's inhabitants by their original place of registry). *T'ai-wan wen-hsien* 27, no. 4: 64–77.

Li Yung-ming. 1959. *Ch'ao-chou fang-yen* (Local dialects of Ch'ao-chou). Peking.

Liang Hsi-yu. 1956. "K'o-tsu t'uan-t'i ming-ch'eng yü hsing-chih" (Appellations and the disposition of Hakka group organization). In Chang Tzu-ming, comp., *K'o-tsu wen-hsien sui-chin*. Djakarta.

Lien Wen-hsi. 1971. "K'o-chia ju k'en T'ai-wan ti-ch'ü k'ao lüeh" (A general investigation of Hakka reclamation efforts in Taiwan). *T'ai-wan wen-hsien* 22, no. 3: 1–25.

——— 1972. "K'o-chia chih nan ch'ien tung i chi ch'i jen-k'ou ti liu-pu" (The southward migration and shift eastward of Hakka and their population spread). *T'ai-wan wen-hsien* 23, no. 4: 1–23.

Lin Hui-ling. 1977. "Sung-wu Pao-chung tz'u (i-min miao) hsiao k'ao" (A brief inquiry on the Sung-trust Pao-chung shrine—an *i-min* temple). *Shih-chi k'an-k'ao* no. 5: 55–61.

Lin Yün-ku. 1956. "Mei hsien wen-hua yüan-yüan" (Origins of Mei county

culture). In Chang Tzu-ming, comp., *K'o-tsu wen-hsien sui-chin.* Djakarta.
Liu Hsing-t'ang. 1936. "Fu-chien ti hsieh-tsu tsu-chih" (The organization of Fukien's lineages). *Shih-huo pan-yüeh k'an* 4, no. 8: 35–46.
Liu Kuei-nien. 1881. *Hui-chou fu chih* (Hui-chou prefectural gazetteer). Taipei; 1966 reprint.
Lo Hsiang-lin. 1971. *Chung-kuo tsu-p'u yen-chiu* (A study of Chinese genealogies). Hong Kong.
Ni Tsan-yüan. 1894. *Yün-lin hsien ts'ai-fang-ts'e* (Archival material of Yün-lin county). Taipei; 1959 reprint.
Pasternak, Burton. 1969. "The Role of the Frontier in Chinese Lineage Development." *Journal of Asian Studies* 28, no. 3: 551–61.
——— 1972. *Kinship and Community in Two Chinese Villages.* Stanford, Calif.
Shih Chen-min [See Chinben]. 1973. "Chi-ssu-ch'üan yü she-hui tsu-chih—Chang-hua p'ing-yüan chü-lo fa-chan mo-shih ti t'an-t'ao" (The religious sphere and social organization—an exploratory model for the settlement of the Chang-hua Plain). *Bulletin of the Institute of Ethnology, Academia Sinica* 36: 191–208.
Skinner, G. William. 1957. *Chinese Society in Thailand: An Analytical History.* Ithaca, New York.
——— 1971. "Chinese Peasants and the Closed Community: An Open and Shut Case." *Comparative Studies in Society and History* 13, no. 3: 270–81.
——— 1977. "Cities and the Hierarchy of Local Systems." In G. William Skinner, ed., *The City in Late Imperial China.* Stanford, Calif.
Ssu-fa hsing-cheng pu. 1969. *T'ai-wan min-shih hsi-kuan t'iao-ch'a pao-kao* (A report on an investigation of customs related to civil affairs in Taiwan). Taipei.
Tai Yen-hui. 1963a. "Ch'ing-tai T'ai-wan hsiang-chuang chih chien-li chi ch'i tsu-chih" (The establishment and organization of Taiwan's rural villages of the Ch'ing). In T'ai-wan yin-hang ching-chi yen-chiu shih, comp., *T'ai-wan ching-chi shih chiu chi.* Taipei.
——— 1963b. "Ch'ing-tai T'ai-wan hsiang-chuang chih she-hui ti k'ao-ch'a" (An examination of Taiwan's rural village society during the Ch'ing). *T'ai-wan yin-hang chi-k'an* 14, no. 4: 198–228.
Ts'ai Chen-feng. 1897. *Yüan-li chih* (Record of Yüan-li district). Taipei; 1959 reprint.
Ts'ai Mou-t'ang. 1976. "Pao-chung-t'ing i-min miao ti pai-pai" (A religious festival at the Pao-chung-t'ing *i-min* temple). *T'ai-wan feng-wu* 26, no. 1: 31–36.
Wang Shih-ch'ing. 1972. "Min-chien hsin-yang tsai pu-t'ung tsu-chi i-min ti hsiang-ts'un chih li-shih" (A history of folk religion among villages of immigrants with different ancestral registries). *T'ai-wan wen-hsien* 23, no. 3: 1–38.
Wang, Sung-hsing. 1972. "Pa Pao Chün: An 18th Century Irrigation System in Central Taiwan." *Bulletin of the Institute of Ethnology, Academia Sinica* 33: 165–76.
Wang Ta-lu. 1920. *Ch'ih-ch'i hsien chih* (Ch'ih-ch'i county gazetteer). Taipei; 1967 reprint.
Watson, James L. 1975. *Emigration and the Chinese Lineage: The Mans in Hong Kong and London.* Berkeley, Calif.
Wen Chung-ho. 1903. *Kuang-hsü Chia-ying chou chih* (The Kuang-hsü reign edition of the Chia-ying departmental gazetteer). Taipei; 1962 reprint.
Yün-lin Record. 1972. T'ai-wan sheng wen-hsien wei-yüan hui, comp., "Yün-lin

hsien shih ti min-su tso t'an-hua hui chi-lu" (Record of a meeting convened to discuss the history, geography, and folkways of Yün-lin county). *T'ai-wan wen-hsien* 23, no. 2: 119–24.

*Yin: Voluntary Associations and Rural-Urban Migration*

Banton, Michael. 1957. *West African City: A Study of Tribal Life in Freetown*. London.
Barnes, Sandra T., and Margaret Peil. 1977. "Voluntary Association Membership in Five West African Cities." *Urban Anthropology* 6, no. 1: 83–106.
Ch'en Cheng-hsiang. 1955. *P'eng-hu hsien chih* (P'eng-hu county local gazetteer). Ma-kung, P'eng-hu, Taiwan.
——— 1963. *Taiwan*. Taipei.
Ch'en Jui-t'ang. 1969. "Ho-hui" (Friendly societies). *T'ai-wan min-shih hsi-k'uan t'iao-ch'a pao-kao* 3: 519–604.
Crissman, Lawrence W. 1967. "The Segmentary Structure of Urban Overseas Chinese Communities." *Man* 2, no. 2: 185–204.
Dewey, Alice G. 1962. *Peasant Marketing in Java*. New York.
——— 1968. "Restructuring Roles as a Strategy of Urban Adaptation." In Robert Van Niel, ed., *Economic Factors in Southeast Asian Social Changes*. Honolulu.
——— 1970. "Ritual as a Mechanism for Urban Adaptation." *Man* 5, no. 3: 438–48.
Diamond, Norma. 1969. *K'un Shen: A Taiwan Village*. New York.
Doughty, Paul. 1972. "Peruvian Migrants' Identity in the Urban Milieu." In T. Weaver and D. White, eds. *The Anthropology of Urban Environments*. Lexington, Kentucky.
Fei, Hsiao-tung. 1939. *Peasant Life in China*. London.
Freedman, Maurice. 1967. "Immigrants and Associations: Chinese in Nineteenth-Century Singapore." In Lloyd A. Fallers, ed., *Immigrants and Associations*. The Hague.
Gallin, Bernard. 1966. *Hsin Hsing, Taiwan: A Chinese Village in Change*. Berkeley, Calif.
——— and Rita S. Gallin. 1974a. "The Rural-to-Urban Migration of an Anthropologist in Taiwan." In George M. Foster and Robert Kemper, eds., *Anthropologists in Cities*. Boston.
——— 1974b. "The Integration of Village Migrants in Taipei." In Mark Elvin and G. William Skinner, eds. *The Chinese City Between Two Worlds*. Stanford, Calif.
Ho Ping-ti. 1966. *Chung-kuo hui-kuan shih-lun* (Historical survey of associations of fellow countrymen among migrants in China). Taipei.
Inō Yoshinori. 1928. *The Cultural Record of Taiwan*. Tokyo.
Kao-hsiung shih wen-hsien wei-yüan-hui. 1958. *Kao-hsiung shih chih: Kaohsiung Port*. Kaohsiung.
Kerri, James N. 1977. "Studying Voluntary Associations as Adaptive Mechanisms: A Review of Anthropological Perspectives." *Current Anthropology* 17, no. 1: 23–47.
Lang, Olga. 1968. *Chinese Family and Society*, 2d ed. Hamden, Conn.
Li Yih-yuan. 1970. *An Immigrant Town*. Taipei.

Lin Hao. 1894. *P'eng-hu t'ing chih* (P'eng-hu county local gazetteer). Taipei.

Little, Kenneth. 1957. "The Role of Voluntary Associations in West-African Organizations." *American Anthropologist* 59: 579–96.

——— 1965. *West African Urbanization: A Study of Voluntary Associations in Social Change*. Cambridge, England.

——— 1973a. "Urbanization and Regional Associations: Their Paradoxical Function." In Aidan Southall, ed., *Urban Anthropology: Cross-Cultural Studies of Urbanization*. New York.

——— 1973b. *African Women in Towns*. London.

——— 1975. "Some Methodological Considerations of the Study of African Women's Urban Roles." *Urban Anthropology* 4, no. 2: 107–21.

P'eng-hu *hsien* Government. 1950, 1971. *P'eng-hu Hsien Statistical Abstract*. Annual. P'eng-hu, Taiwan.

P'eng-hu t'ing. 1936. *P'eng-hu t'ing yao-lan* (Statistical abstract of P'eng-hu county). Ma-kung, P'eng-hu, Taiwan.

Potter, Jack M. 1968. *Capitalism and the Peasant: Social and Economic Change in a Hong Kong Village*. Berkeley, Calif.

Skinner, G. William. 1958. *Leadership and Power in the Chinese Community of Thailand*. Ithaca, N.Y.

Suzuki, Hisahisyi. 1918. "Topographic Records of P'eng-hu." Unpublished article in the National Taiwan University Library.

*Taiwan Demographic Fact Book*. 1971. Taipei.

Taiwan Provincial Governor-General's Office. 1946. *Statistical Summary of the Past Fifty-One Years*. Taipei.

T'ien, Ju-k'ang. 1953. *The Chinese of Sarawak: A Study of Social Structure*. London.

Topley, Marjorie. 1967. "The Emergence and Social Function of Chinese Religious Associations in Singapore." In Lloyd A. Fallers, ed., *Immigrants and Associations*. The Hague.

Tou Chi-liang. 1943. *Studies on the Organization of T'ung-hsiang Hui*. Chungking.

Wang-an Yi Chi Hui. 1925. *Wang-an Yi Chi Hui hui-tse* (Constitution of the Wang-an Yi Chi Hui). Kaohsiung.

Watson, James L. 1975. *Emigration and the Chinese Lineage: The "Mans" in Hong Kong and London*. Berkeley, Calif.

Willmott, W. E. 1969. "Congregations and Associations: The Political Structure of the Chinese Community in Phnom-Pen, Cambodia." *Comparative Studies in Sociology and History* 11, no. 3: 282–301.

Wu, David Y. H. 1974. "To Kill Three Birds with One Stone: The Rotating Credit Associations of the Papua New Guinea Chinese." *American Ethnologist* 1, no. 3: 565–84.

Yin, Alexander Chien-chung. 1969. "P'eng-hu jen i chu T'ai-wan pen-tao ti yen-chiu" (A study of P'eng-hu–Kaohsiung migration). M.A. thesis, National Taiwan University.

——— 1975. "Migration and Voluntary Associations in Rural and Urban Taiwan: A Study of Group Adaptative Strategies in Social Change." Ph.D. dissertation, University of Hawaii.

——— 1976. "Jen-k'ou jen-lei-hsüeh" (Demographic anthropology). In *Population Problems and Studies*. Taipei.

——— 1978a. "Homogeneous Migration and Heterogeneous Migration: A General Typology of Anthropological Migration Studies." *Journal of Population Studies* 2: 1–26.

——— 1978b. "Hsüeh jen-lei-hsüeh i-hsiang kan-ch'u" (Rethinking the development of anthropology in China). *Humanity and Culture* 10: 4–5.

——— 1978c. "Jen-lei-hsüeh yen-chiu liang-hua yu piao-chun-hua wen-t'i" (Problems of quantification and standardization of anthropological research). *Journal of Humanities and Social Sciences* 3: 59–77.

*Wolf: Domestic Organization*

Ahern, Emily M. 1973. *The Cult of the Dead in a Chinese Village*. Stanford, Calif.

Barclay, George W. 1976. *Colonial Development and Population in Taiwan*. Princeton, N.J.

Cohen, Myron L. 1976. *House United, House Divided: The Chinese Family in Taiwan*. New York.

Fei, Hsiao-tung. 1939. *Peasant Life in China*. New York.

Freedman, Maurice. 1958. *Lineage Organization in Southeastern China*. London.

——— 1963. "The Chinese Domestic Family: Models." In *VIe Congrès international des sciences anthropologiques et ethnologiques*, vol. 2, part 1. Paris.

——— 1966. *Chinese Lineage and Society: Fukien and Kwangtung*. London.

——— 1967. "Ancestor Worship: Two Aspects of the Chinese Case." In Maurice Freedman, ed., *Social Organization: Essays Presented to Raymond Firth*. Chicago.

Gallin, Bernard. 1966. *Hsin Hsing, Taiwan: A Chinese Village in Change*. Berkeley, Calif.

Ikeda Toshio. 1944. *Taiwan no katei seikatsu* (Home life in Taiwan). Taipei.

Kajiwara Michiyoshi. 1941. *Taiwan nōmin seikatsu kō* (Peasant life in Taiwan). Taipei.

Okada Yuzuru. 1949. *Kiso shakai* (Elementary groups of society). Tokyo.

Olsen, Nancy J. 1973. "Family Structure and Inependence Training in a Taiwanese Village." *Journal of Marriage and the Family* 35: 512–19.

——— 1974. "Family Structure and Socialization Patterns in Taiwan." *American Journal of Sociology* 79: 1395–1417.

——— 1975. "Social Class and Rural-Urban Patterning of Socialization in Taiwan." *Journal of Asian Studies* 34, no. 3: 659–74.

Pasternak, Burton. 1972. *Kinship and Community in Two Chinese Villages*. Stanford, Calif.

Sa, Sophie. 1975. "Family and Community in Urban Taiwan: Social Status and Demographic Strategy among Taipei Households, 1885–1935." Ph.D. dissertation, Harvard University.

Sung, Lung-sheng. 1975. "Inheritance and Kinship in North Taiwan." Ph.D. dissertation, Stanford University.

Wang, Sung-hsing. 1971. "Pooling and Sharing in a Chinese Fishing Economy: Kueishan Tao." Ph.D. dissertation, Tokyo University.

Wolf, Arthur P. 1974. "Marriage and Adoption in Northern Taiwan." In Robert J. Smith, ed., *Social Organization and the Applications of Anthropology*. Ithaca, New York.

——— 1975. "The Women of Hai-shan: A Demographic Portrait." In Margery Wolf and Roxane Witke, eds., *Women in Chinese Society*. Stanford, Calif.

——— 1976. "Childhood Association, Sexual Attraction, and Fertility in Taiwan." In Ezra F. Zubrow, *Demographic Anthropology: Quantitative Approaches*. Albuquerque, New Mexico.

——— and Chieh-shan Huang. 1980. *Marriage and Adoption in China, 1845–1945*. Stanford, Calif.

Wolf, Margery. 1968. *The House of Lim: A Study of a Chinese Farm Family*. New York.

——— 1972. *Women and the Family in Rural Taiwan*. Stanford, Calif.

*Sung: Property and Family Division*

Ahern, Emily M. 1973. *The Cult of the Dead in a Chinese Village*. Stanford, Calif.

Bodman, Nicholas C. 1955. *Spoken Amoy Hokkien*. Kuala Lumpur.

Cohen, Myron L. 1970. "Developmental Process in the Chinese Domestic Group." In Maurice Freedman, ed., *Family and Kinship in Chinese Society*. Stanford, Calif.

——— 1976. *House United, House Divided: The Chinese Family in Taiwan*. New York.

Freedman, Maurice. 1958. *Lineage Organization in Southeastern China*. London.

——— 1963. "The Chinese Domestic Family: Models." In *VIe Congrès international des sciences anthropologiques et ethnologiques*, vol. 2, part 1. Paris.

——— 1966. *Chinese Lineage and Society: Fukien and Kwangtung*. London.

Hsu, Francis L. K. 1943. "The Myth of Chinese Family Size." *American Journal of Sociology* 48, no. 5: 555–62.

——— 1949. "The Family in China: The Classical Form." In Ruth Nanda Aushen, ed., *The Family: Its Function and Destiny*. New York.

Lang, Olga. 1946. *Chinese Family and Society*. New Haven, Conn.

Sung, Lung-sheng. 1975. "Inheritance and Kinship in North Taiwan." Ph.D. dissertation, Stanford University.

Wolf, Arthur P. 1973. "Line, Lineage, and Family." Unpublished paper.

*Seaman: The Sexual Politics of Karmic Retribution*

Ahern, Emily M. 1975. "The Power and the Pollution of Chinese Women." In Margery Wolf and Roxane Witke, eds., *Women in Chinese Society*. Stanford, Calif.

Bodman, Nicholas C. 1955. *Spoken Amoy Hokkien*. Kuala Lumpur.

Seaman, Gary. 1974. *Breaking the Blood Bowl* (film). Far Eastern Audio Visuals, Cedar Park, Texas.

——— 1977. *Journal to the West* (film). Far Eastern Audio Visuals, Cedar Park, Texas.

——— 1978. *Temple Organization in a Chinese Village*. Taipei.

Soothill, W. E. 1937. *A Dictionary of Chinese Buddhist Terms*. London.

Topley, Marjorie. 1974. "Cosmic Antagonisms: A Mother-Child Syndrome." In Arthur P. Wolf, ed., *Religion and Ritual in Chinese Society*. Stanford, Calif.
——— 1975. "Marriage Resistance in Rural Kwangtung." In Margery Wolf and Roxane Witke, eds., *Women in Chinese Society*. Stanford, Calif.
*Tz'u-pei hsüeh-p'en-ch'an* (Blood Bowl Sutra). 1939. Taichung.
Waley, Arthur. 1960. *Ballads and Stories from Tun-huang*. London.
Wolf, Margery. 1975. "Women and Suicide in China." In Margery Wolf and Roxane Witke, eds., *Women in Chinese Society*. Stanford, Calif.

*Ahern: The Thai Ti Kong Festival*

Ahern, Emily M. 1973. *The Cult of the Dead in a Chinese Village*. Stanford, Calif.
Bloch, Maurice. 1974. "Symbols, Song, Dance, and Features of Articulation: Is Religion an Extreme Form of Traditional Authority?" *European Journal of Sociology* 15: 55–81.
Bodman, Nicholas C. 1955. *Spoken Amoy Hokkien*. Kuala Lumpur.
Burkhardt, V. R. 1955. *Chinese Creeds and Customs*, vol. 1. Hong Kong.
Chesneaux, Jean. 1971. *Secret Societies in China in the Nineteenth and Twentieth Centuries*. Trans. Gillian Nettle. London.
*Chung Kuo Shih Pao*. 1975a. "Offerings of Thai Ti Kong Greatly Decreased." February 19.
——— 1975b. "Pig Gods." May 29.
——— 1976. "Big *Pai-pai* Held in San-hsia Yesterday: 50,000 Guests Consumed NT$10,000,000." February 6.
Cohen, Myron L. 1976. *House United, House Divided: The Chinese Family in Taiwan*. New York.
Dudbridge, Glen. 1970. *The Hsi-yu Chi: A Study of Antecedents to the Sixteenth Century Chinese Novel*. Cambridge, England.
Feuchtwang, Stephen. 1974. "Domestic and Communal Worship in Taiwan." In Arthur Wolf, ed., *Religion and Ritual in Chinese Society*. Stanford, Calif.
——— 1975. "Investigating Religion." In Maurice Bloch, ed., *Marxist Analyses and Social Anthropology*. London.
Geertz, Clifford. 1972. "Deep Play: Notes on the Balinese Cockfight." *Daedalus* 101: 1–37.
Godelier, Maurice. 1977. *Perspectives in Marxist Anthropology*. Trans. Robert Brain. Cambridge, England.
Hsiao, Kung-chuan. 1960. *Rural China: Imperial Control in the Nineteenth Century*. Seattle, Wash.
Jordan, David K. 1972. *Gods, Ghosts, and Ancestors: Folk Religion in a Taiwanese Village*. Berkeley, Calif.
Leach, Edmund. 1976. *Culture and Communication: The Logic by which Symbols Are Connected*. Cambridge, England.
*Lien He Pao*. 1974. "The Future Most Beautiful Sacred Temple in Taiwan: San-hsia's Tzu Shih Kung Temple." January 29.
——— 1976a. "An Excessively Ostentatious Show at San-hsia's Thai Ti Kong *Pai-pai*: Hsien Government Decides Temporarily to Suspend this Township's Development Subsidy." February 15.

——— 1976b. "More on San-hsia's *Pai-pai.*" February 20.
——— 1976c. "Rigorous Enforcement of Economical Pai-pai." February 20.
Rappaport, Roy A. 1971. "The Sacred in Human Evolution." *Annual Review of Ecology and Systematics* 2: 23–44.
Rohsenow, Hill Gates. 1973. "Prosperity Settlement: The Politics of Paipai in Taipei, Taiwan." Ph.D. dissertation, University of Michigan.
Saso, Michael R. 1972. *Taoism and the Rite of Cosmic Renewal.* Pullman, Wash.
Schreider, Helen, and Frank Schreider. 1969. "Taiwan: The Watchful Dragon." *National Geographic* 135, no. 1: 1–45.
Skinner, G. William. 1971. "Chinese Peasants and the Closed Community: An Open and Shut Case." *Comparative Studies in Society and History* 13: 270–81.
Tien, Hung-mao. 1975. "Taiwan in Transition: Prospects for Socio-Political Change." *China Quarterly* 64: 615–44.
Ts'ai Mao-t'ang. 1976. "Pao-chung t'ing i-min miao te pai-pai" (The *pai-pai* at Pao-chung T'ing I-min temple). *T'ai-wan feng-wu* 26: 31–36.
Wolf, Arthur. 1974. "Gods, Ghosts, and Ancestors." In Arthur Wolf, ed., *Religion and Ritual in Chinese Society.* Stanford, Calif.
Wolf, Margery. 1972. *Women and the Family in Rural Taiwan.* Stanford, Calif.
Wu Ch'eng-en. 1958. *Monkey.* Trans. Arthur Waley. New York.
Wu Ying-t'ao. 1969. *T'ai-wan min-su* (Taiwan folkways). Taipei.
——— 1975. *T'ai-wan yen-yü* (Taiwan proverbs). Taipei.

*Mintz: Afterword*

Adams, Robert M. 1977. "World Picture, Anthropological Frame." *American Anthropologist* 79, no. 2: 265–79.
Barth, Fredrik, ed. 1969. *Ethnic Groups and Boundaries.* Bergen.
Benedict, Burton. 1961. *Indians in a Plural Society: A Report on Mauritius.* London.
Cohen, Abner. 1969. *Custom and Politics in Urban Africa.* Berkeley, Calif.
——— ed. 1974. *Urban Ethnicity.* London.
Cook, F. Scott. 1966. "The Obsolete 'Anti-Market' Mentality: A Critique of the Substantivist Approach to Economic Anthropology." *American Anthropologist* 68, no. 2: 323–45.
——— 1974. "'Structural Substantivism': A Critical Review of Marshall Sahlins' *Stone Age Economics.*" *Comparative Studies in Society and History* 16, no. 3: 355–79.
Freedman, Maurice. 1969. "Why China?" *Proceedings of the Royal Anthropological Institute for 1969*: 5–13.
——— 1974. "On the Sociological Study of Chinese Religion." In Arthur P. Wolf, ed., *Religion and Ritual in Chinese Society.* Stanford, Calif.
Horton, Robin. 1967. "African Traditional Thought and Western Science." *Africa* 37, no. 1: 50–71; no. 2: 155–87.
Leach, Edmund. 1954. *Political Systems of Highland Burma: A Study of Kachin Social Structure.* London.
Lesser, Alexander. 1933. *The Pawnee Ghost Dance Hand Game.* New York.
——— 1935. "Functionalism in Social Anthropology." *American Anthropologist* 37, no. 3: 388–93.

Mead, Margaret. 1932. *The Changing Culture of an Indian Tribe*. New York.
Mintz, Sidney W. 1953. "The Folk-Urban Continuum and the Rural Proletarian Community." *American Journal of Sociology* 59, no. 2: 136–43.
——— 1976. "Preface." In Scott Cook and Martin Diskin, eds., *Markets in Oaxaca*. Austin, Texas.
——— 1978. "Afterword." In John Higham, ed., *Ethnic Leadership in the United States*. Baltimore.
Nagata, Judith. 1974. "What is a Malay? Situational Selection of Ethnic Identity in a Plural Society." *American Ethnologist* 1, no. 2: 331–50.
Osgood, Cornelius. 1951. *Koreans and Their Culture*. New York.
Petrullo, Vincenzo. 1947. *Puerto Rican Paradox*. Philadelphia.
Pospisil, Leopold. 1958. *Kapauku Papuans and Their Law*. New Haven, Conn.
Potter, Jack. 1968. *Capitalism and the Chinese Peasant: Social and Economic Change in a Hong Kong Village*. Berkeley, Calif.
——— 1970. "Land and Lineage in Traditional China." In Maurice Freedman, ed., *Family and Kinship in Chinese Society*. Stanford, Calif.
Redfield, Robert. 1930. *Tepoztlán*. Chicago.
——— 1941. *The Folk Culture of Yucatán*. Chicago.
Schildkrout, Enid. 1978. *People of the Zongo*. Cambridge, England.
Skinner, G. William. 1964. "Marketing and Social Structure in Rural China, Part I." *Journal of Asian Studies* 24, no. 1: 3–43.
Smith, Raymond T. 1956. *The Negro Family in British Guiana*. London.
——— 1962. *British Guiana*. London.
Spier, Leslie. 1929. "Problems Arising from the Cultural Position of the Havasupai." *American Anthropologist* 31, no. 2: 213–22.
Stavis, Benedict. 1974. *Local Rural Governance and Agricultural Development in Taiwan*. Ithaca, N.Y.
Steward, Julian H. 1950. *Area Research: Theory and Practice*. New York.
——— et al. 1956. *The People of Puerto Rico*. Urbana, Ill.
Vincent, Joan. 1974. "The Structuring of Ethnicity." *Human Organization* 33, no. 4: 375–79.
Wolf, Eric R. 1957. "Aspects of Group Relations in a Complex Society." *American Anthropologist* 58, no. 6: 1065–78.
——— 1966. *Peasants*. Englewood Cliffs, N.J.

# Character List

Hokkien (H) and Japanese (J) terms are labeled; all the remaining terms are Mandarin. When a term appears in two languages, characters are given for one language only; entries without characters refer to entries with characters. Personal names, names of major cities, and names of prefectures and higher-level administrative units are excluded. Only those written sources named in the text are included.

*ai-ti-yin*
碍地銀
An-ch'i
安溪
Ang Kong (H)
尪公
*be* (H)
尾
*be chut si-thau* (H)
未出勢頭
*buraku* (J)
部落
Cap-sa:-thi: (H)
十三添
*cau* (H)
灶
*ce* (H)
祭
*ce-suaq* (H)
祭煞
*chai-ti* (H)
彰化
Chang-hua
彰化

Chang-hua *hsien*
彰化縣
*Chang-hua hsien chih*
彰化縣誌
Chang Ping
張丙
*chao-keng tai-chieh*
招耕帶借
*chen*
鎮
*chen-chang*
鎮長
Chen-p'ing
鎮平
Chen Wu
真武
Ch'en-p'ai
陳派
*cheng-ch'ang-t'ien*
蒸嘗田
Ch'eng-chung
城中
Ch'eng-fu
成福

Chhiu:-chhiu Khut (H)
樟樹窟
Chi-chin
旗津
*chi-kuan*
籍貫
Chi-mei
七美
*chi-ssu kung-yeh*
祭祀公業
Ch'i-ch'ien-ts'o
溪墘厝
Ch'i-chou
溪州
Ch'i-hu
溪湖
Ch'i-nan
溪南
Ch'i-pei
溪北
*ch'i-ti yin*
磧地銀
Ch'i-tung
溪東

*chia* (family)
家
*chia* (land measure)
甲
*chia-chang*
家長
Chia-i
嘉義
Chia-nan
嘉南
Chia-ying
嘉應
*chiao* (guild)
教
*chiao* (ritual)
醮
Chiao-ling
蕉嶺
*chiao-tsu*
餃子
Chiao-tzu-t'ou
橋子頭
*chiao-wei*
醮尾
*chieh-shou*
結首
*ch'ien hui*
錢會
Chin-chiang
晉江
Chin Kuang Fu
金廣福
*ch'in-ch'i*
親戚
*ch'in-tzu*
親族
Ching-mei
景美
Ch'ing Shui Tsu Shih
清水祖師
*chiu-ti giap-san* (H)
手置業產
Ch'o-shui Ch'i
濁水溪
*chu* (pig)
猪
*chu* (settlement) (H)
厝
Chu I-kuei
朱一貴
Chu-shan
竹山
Chu-t'ang
竹塘
*chuang*
庄
Chung-chuang
中庄
Chung-i Tz'u
忠義祠
Chung-li
中壢
Chung-shan
中山
Chung-she
中社
*ch'ü kung so*
區公所
*Ch'üan ho lun*
勸和論
*ci:-iu-tia:* (H)
炙油鐤
*ciok-pik siu-kim* (H)
祝百寿金
Co Su Kong (H)
祖師公
*co-thuan giap-san* (H)
祖傳業產
Erh-lin
二林
*fa-jen*
法人
*fang*
房
*fang-tsu yin*
防租銀
Fang-yüan
芳苑
*fen-chia*
分家
*fen-hsiang*
分香
*fen-lei hsieh-tou*
分類械鬥
*fen-ling*
分靈
Feng-shan
鳳山
Fu-hsing (H)
福興
*Fu-lao*
福佬
*gai* (J)
街
*giap-po* (H)
業報
*go-ciang* (H)
五障
*gou-ci:* (H)
高錢
*gua-hia* (H)
我彼
*gun* (J)
郡

*gun-tau* (H)
阮兜
Hai-feng
海豐
Hai-shan
海山
Han
韓
Han-chiang
蚶江
Heng-ch'i
橫溪
*hi-su* (H)
喜事
*ho* (H)
戶
*ho* (J)
保
*ho hui*
合會
*hok-kim* (H)
福金
*hoko* (J), see *pao-chia*
保甲
Hsi-yü
西嶼
Hsi-yüan
西園
Hsia-men
廈門
Hsia-tan-shui
下淡水
*hsiang*
鄉
*hsiang-chang*
鄉長
*hsiang-tou*
鄉鬪
*hsiao-tsu*
小租
*hsiao-tsu hu*
小租戶
*hsieh-tou*
械鬪
*hsien*
縣
*hsien-chang*
縣長
*hsien-hsia-shih*
縣轄
*hsien-yü*
鹹雨
*hsin-ch'eng*
新城
Hsin-chu
新竹
Hsin-chuang
新莊
Hsin-hsing
新興
Hsin-kang
新港
Hsin-p'u
新埔
Hsing-fu (pseudonym)
幸福
Hsing-hua
興化
*hu*
戶
*hu-a* (H)
符仔
Hu-hsi
湖西
*hueq-phun* (H)
血盆
Hui-an
惠安
I-lan
宜蘭
*i-min*
義民
*i-min chih-min*
以民治民
*iu-png*(H)
油飯
Iu: Kong (H)
羊公
*ka* (H)
甲
K'ai Chang Sheng Wang
開漳聖王
*kan-ch'ing*
感情
Kan-yüan
柑園
*k'an-t'ien t'ien*
看天田
*kang-kut* (H)
公骨
*kang-se:* (H)
公姓
*ke* (H)
家
*ke-sieng* (H)
繼承
*k'en-hu*
墾戶
*khaq-tua* (H)
較大
Khei-ki:-chu (H)
溪墘厝
*khuan se* (H)
勸世

*khun-ti* (H)
睏猪
*kiet tng* (H)
結堂
*kin-ciou-kha* (H)
芎蕉脚
*ko* (H)
股
*ko* (J), see *chia* (family)
家
Ko-ma-lan
噶瑪蘭
*K'o-chia*
客家
Ku-shan
鼓山
Ku-t'ing
古亭
Kuan Yin
觀音
Kuan Yu
関羽
Kuang Tse Tsun Wang
廣澤尊王
Kuei-shan
龟山
*kui* (H)
鬼
*kui-khi* (H)
貴氣
*lau-pun* (H)
老李
*li*
里
*li-chang*
里長
*li min ta hui*
里民大會
*li-min-tai-piao*
里民代表
*lian ki* (H)
煉乩
*liang-min*
良民
Liang-tien
良田
*lien-chia*
联甲
*lien-chuang yüeh*
联莊約
*lieng* (H)
鑾
*lin*
鄰
*lin-chang*
鄰長
Lin-chao Kung
霖肇宮
*lin-hia* (H)
你彼
Lin-p'ai
林派
Lin Shuang-wen
林爽文
*lin-tau* (H)
你兜
*liu-mang*
流氓
*liu-min*
流民
Liu-tui
六堆
*lo-cu* (H)
爐主
Lo-tung
羅東
*lou-kuei*
陋規
Lu-kang
鹿港
Lu-k'ou-t'su
路口厝
Lu-shang
路上
*Lu-ying*
綠營
Lung-shan Ssu
龍山寺
Lung-yen
龍岩
Ma-kung
馬公
Ma Tsu
媽祖
*man-t'ou*
饅頭
Mei-nung
美濃
Meng-chia
艋舺
Miao-li
苗栗
Min
閩
Min-nan
閩南
Mu-chia
木柵
Nan-an
南安
Nan-ao
南澳
Nan-kang
南港

Nan-ling
南嶺
Nan-yang
南洋
Nan-yüan
南園
Nei-hu
內湖
*o-kau* (H)
黑狗
*o-kau-cia*: (H)
黑狗精
*o-kau-hueq* (H)
黑狗血
*o-kau-the* (H)
黑狗胎
Pa-li-fen
八里坌
*pai* (H)
拜
Pai-chi
白雞
*pai-pai* (H)
拜拜
*p'ai*
派
*p'ai-hsi*
派系
Pan-ch'iao
板橋
*pang-thau* (H)
房頭
*pao*
堡
*pao-chia*
保甲
*pao-chung*
褒忠

Pao I Ta Fu
保儀大夫
*pao-p'u*
包贌
Pao Sheng Ta Ti
保生大帝
Pei-kang
北港
Pei-tou
北投
Pei-yüan
北園
P'eng-fu
彭福
P'eng-hu
澎湖
P'eng-hu T'ing Min Hui
澎湖廳民會
*p'eng-lai*
蓬萊
*phau-hueq-phun* (H)
炮血盆
*pho-to* (H)
普渡
P'i-t'ou
埤頭
P'ing-tung
屏東
P'ing-tung *hsien*
屏東縣
P'u-li
埔里
*p'u-tu*
普渡
P'u-yen
埔鹽
*pun-ke* (H), see *fen-chia*
分家

*pun-ke-he* (H)
分家伙
Sai-te-chu (H)
三塊厝
San-hsia
三峽
San-i
三邑
San-min
三民
San Shan Kuo Wang
三山國王
*san-tao*
三刀
*she-ch'ü*
社區
*shen-ming-hui*
神明會
*sheng-fan*
生番
*sheng-yüan*
生員
*shih*
市
Shih-lin
士林
Shih-t'ou-hsi
石頭溪
*sho* (J)
庄
Shu-lin
樹林
Shu-lin *chen*
樹林鎮
*siou-gun* (H)
小銀
*siu-kim* (H)
壽金

*song-su* (H)
喪事
Ta-an
大安
Ta-ch'eng
大城
Ta-ch'i
大溪
*ta-hsing*
大姓
Ta-kuai-ch'i
大檜溪
Ta-tao-ch'eng
大稻埕
Ta-tieh
打鐵
*ta-tsu*
大租
*ta-tsu hu*
大租戶
*ta-tsu yeh*
大租業
*ta tsung-tz'u*
大宗祠
Tai Ch'ao-ch'un
戴潮春
*t'ai-mei*
太妹
*t'ai-pao*
太保
Tan-shui
淡水
T'ao-tzu-chiao
桃仔脚
T'ao-yüan
桃園
Thai Ti Kong (H)
刣猪公

*than-ciaq-lang* (H)
賺食人
*thau* (H)
頭
Thi: Kong (H)
天公
Tho-a-kha (H)
桃仔脚
Tho Te Kong (H)
土地公
Ti Kong (H)
猪公
Ti Ma (H)
猪媽
*tien*
典
Ting-p'u
頂埔
*t'ing*
廳
*tng-kut* (H)
轉骨
Tokoham (J)
大嵙崁
Tou-liu
斗六
*tsu-tou*
族鬭
*ts'un*
村
*ts'un-chang*
村長
*tsung-li*
總理
*tsung-p'u*
總贌
*tsung-tz'u*
宗祠

T'u-ch'eng *hsiang*
土城鄉
Tua Bong Kiong (H)
大墓宮
*tua pai-pai* (H)
大拜拜
*tua-thia:* (H)
大廳
Tung-kang
東港
*tung-shih*
董事
Tung-yüan
東園
T'ung-an
同安
*t'ung-chuang*
同庄
*t'ung-hsiang*
同鄉
*t'ung-hsing*
同姓
*t'ung-hsüeh*
同學
*t'ung-ti-fang*
同地方
*Tz'u-pei hsüeh-p'en-ch'an*
慈悲血盆懺
Wa-tzu
挖子
Wan-hua
萬華
Wang-an
望安
Wang-an Yi Chi Hui
望安義濟會
Wang Yeh
王爺

Wen Wu Sheng Tien
文武聖殿
Wu-hu-men
五虎門
Ya-tsu
押租
Yen-ch'eng
塩埕
*yin*
陰

Ying-ko
鶯歌
Ying-ko *chen*
鶯歌鎮
*yung*
勇
Yung-an Kung
永安宮
Yung-ch'un
永春

Yü Huang Ta Ti
玉皇大帝
*yüan-liao-wei-yüan*
原料委員
Yüan-lin
員林
Yüeh
粵
Yün-lin
雲林

# Index